CANADA'S FRANCOPHONE MINORITY COMMUNITIES

Canada's Francophone Minority Communities

Constitutional Renewal and the Winning of School Governance

MICHAEL D. BEHIELS

McGill-Queen's University Press

Montreal & Kingston · London · Ithaca

© McGill-Queen's University Press 2004
ISBN 0-7735-2586-6 (cloth)
ISBN 0-7735-2630-7 (paper)

Legal deposit first quarter 2004
Bibliothèque nationale du Québec

Printed in Canada on acid-free paper that is 100% ancient forest free (100% post-consumer recycled), processed chlorine free.

This book has been published with the help of a grant from the Canadian Federation for the Humanities and Social Sciences, through the Aid to Scholarly Publications Programme, using funds provided by the Social Sciences and Humanities Research Council of Canada.

McGill-Queen's University Press acknowledges the support of the Canada Council for the Arts for our publishing program. We also acknowledge the financial support of the Government of Canada through the Book Publishing Industry Development Program (BPIDP) for our publishing activities.

National Library of Canada Cataloguing in Publication

Behiels, Michael D. (Michael Derek), 1946–
    Canada's francophone minority communities : constitutional renewal and the winning of school governance / Michael D. Behiels.

Includes bibliographical references and index.
ISBN 0-7735-2586-6 (bnd)
ISBN 0-7735-2630-7 (pbk)

    1. Canadians, French-speaking – Civil rights.   2. Canadians, French-speaking – Education.   3. Linguistic minorities – Canada – Provinces.   4. Canada. Canadian Charter of Rights and Freedoms. I. Title.

FC139.S36B44 2003   323.1'1114   C2003–904472–6

Typeset in 10/12 Baskerville by True to Type

Contents

Abbreviations

ACFA	Association canadienne-française de l'Alberta
ACFC	Association culturelle franco-canadienne de la Saskatchewan
ACFÉO	Association canadienne-française d'éducation de l'Ontario
ACFO	Association canadienne-française de l'Ontario
ACJC	Association catholique de la jeunesse canadienne-française
AÉCFM	Association d'Éducation des Canadiens-Français du Manitoba
AEFO	Association des enseignants franco-ontariens
AFCSO	Association française des Conseils scolaires de l'Ontario
AFN	Assembly of First Nations
ATABE	Alberta Trustees Association for Bilingual Education
BÉF	Bureau de l'éducation française
CAP	Comité ad hoc de planification de la gestion scolaire au Manitoba
CCLF	Comités consultatifs de langue française (Ontario)
CCMC	Continuing Committee of Ministers on the Constitution
CEFCUT	Conseil des écoles françaises de la communauté urbaine de Toronto
CEFM	Commissaires d'écoles franco-manitobains
CÉFO	Conseil d'éducation franco-ontarienne
CELF	Conseil de l'enseignement en langue française (Ontario)
CICS	Canadian Intergovernmental Conference Secretariat
CJP	Conseil jeunesse provincial (Manitoba)
CNPF	Commission nationale des parents francophones
CPÉ	Comité provinciale de l'éducation (Alberta)
CRCCF	Centre de recherche en civilisation canadienne-française
ÉFM	Éducateurs franco-manitobaines
FCFA	Fédération des communautés francophones et acadiennes du Canada

FFHQ	Fédération des Francophones Hors Québec
FJA	Francophone jeunesse de l'Alberta
FPCP	Fédération provinciale des comités de parents (Manitoba)
FPFA	Fédération des parents francophones de l'Alberta
MAST	Manitoba Association of School Trustees
MTS	Manitoba Teachers' Society
PAA	Public Archives of Alberta
OSSTA	Ontario Separate School Trustees Association
SAANB	Société des Acadiens et Acadiennes du Nouveau Brunswick
SFM	Societé franco-manitobaine
SHSB	Société historique de Saint-Boniface
SLF	Sections de langue française
SNA	Société nationale de l'Acadie

Foreword

Professor Michael D. Behiels' examination of the history of minority linguistic rights since the enactment of the Charter of Rights in 1982 deals with a subject that has been a vital part of our history since Confederation. The recognition of minority rights has been at the core of our identity as a nation. It is what makes Canada unique. The representatives of the four colonies from which the Canada of today emerged recognized the need to guarantee the rights of the French- and English-speaking minorities. A vision of minority rights inspired our federal structure of government.

Our constitution, the fundamental law of the land, was based on the idea of a new nation that would see the coexistence of both English and French. In this new country the majority would not assimilate the minority, eventually grinding down any differences. Instead, the constitution was inspired by a more generous and more humanistic vision of the relationship among human beings. The law, in providing the foundation of our political union, enshrined the right of citizens to be different and challenged the majority to moderate its force and restrain its levelling powers.

Despite the noble ideas entrenched in laws meant to maintain and protect these basic rights, Professor Behiels reveals that our politicians have often given in to pressure from majorities and powerful interest groups. Sadly, linguistic minorities have frequently been overlooked and abandoned by politicians. But, more encouraging, Professor Behiels tells us how francophone minorities have learned to fight for themselves.

Lord Sankey, L.C. of the Judicial Committee of the Privy Council recognized the importance of the historic compromise at the heart of Confederation in a 1932 decision that is still seen as a turning point in Canadian jurisprudence:

INASMUCH as the Act (The Constitution 1867) embodies a compromise under which the original Provinces agreed to federate, it is important to keep in mind that *the preservation of the rights of minorities was a condition on which such minorities entered into the federation, and, the foundation upon which the whole structure was subsequently erected.* The process of interpretation as the years go on ought not to be allowed to dim or to whittle down the provisions of the original contract upon which the federation was founded, nor is it legitimate that any Judicial construction of the provisions of ss. 91 and 92 should impose a new and different contract upon the federating bodies.[1] (Emphasis added)

   The entire political dilemma that surrounds the rights of minority language groups is wrapped up in that one short paragraph: the ideal of recognizing, respecting, and developing the minority rights that are the cornerstone of Canada. This humanist vision of the country is entirely "Canadian" and was unique in its time. It challenged the English Protestant and French Catholic rivalries that were a substantial feature of that era and withstood the test of political realities, although it did not always succeed.

   For years, French-speaking minorities lived in the shadow of parochialism, within the boundaries of their ancestral lands. Cherishing the idea of the civilizing mission of Catholicism forcefully advocated by Canon Lionel Groulx, the French-speaking minority was content with assurances of an isolated eternal life.[2] By 1965, however, it was evident that a fundamental change was taking place. The Laurendeau-Dunton Commission concluded that this protective vision was increasingly being seen as an illusion.

   The first significant move toward change occurred in 1971 at the Victoria Conference. In the warm glow of enthusiasm and confidence generated by the 1967 Centennial and the Conference on the Confederation of Tomorrow, the provinces of Ontario, Manitoba, Nova Scotia, New Brunswick, Prince Edward Island, and Newfoundland agreed to become officially bilingual. Despite this extraordinary commitment, which would have changed the status of francophone minorities throughout Canada, Premier Bourassa later refused to sign the Victoria Charter and this historic agreement collapsed.[3] In taking this position, Quebec effectively turned its back on the glorious achievements of its explorers, discoverers, colonizers, and missionaries. Instead it promoted the idea that to develop its French heritage it did not have to concern itself with the condition of French-speaking minorities elsewhere in Canada and their heroic struggles to survive.

   Quebec's refusal to accept the Victoria Charter had serious repercussions that still reverberate. Not only was Quebec cutting itself off from the French Canadian family tree, but the other provinces were left to themselves in the treatment of their official language minorities. In 1989 the Quebec government refused to intervene in the courts of Saskatchewan and Alberta to support the education rights of the French-speaking minority communities after they had invoked section 23 of the constitution, protecting the rights to education. Its argument was that each province had to be able to captain its own ship when it came to dealing with the rights of its official language minority. In reality, this argument justified the position that each provincial government is free to discriminate at will. Quebec took this stance at a time when it was fighting to be recognized as the "champion" of the French in America, claiming full member status at the Sommet de la Francophonie – a contradiction that did not seem to embarrass its political leaders. The table was now set for a change in the essential nature of Canada.

In fact, during these years there were two opposing trends in Canada. On one hand, there were federal initiatives to confirm the equality of status of French and English in the Official Languages Act (enacted in 1969),[4] efforts to implement programs to offer the teaching of official languages, and initiatives to support the development of effective leaders within minority communities. This trend culminated in the adoption of the Charter of Rights and Freedoms, which recognized, for the first time, a role for the courts in guaranteeing respect for linguistic rights. On the other hand, there was a political will, often proclaimed in Quebec, that linguistic minorities outside Quebec were not its responsibility. Worse, an argument was made that suggested that support for the recognition and development of minorities outside Quebec would impede Quebec's initiative to adopt its own linguistic policy to protect French language.

It is at this stage of history that Professor Behiels focuses his research.

Reviewing the struggle of the various minority communities regarding the management of their schools, Professor Behiels highlights the "evolutionary" nature of the rights guaranteed in section 23 of the Charter. He points to the wisdom of the Charter's authors in adopting broad principles capable of evolving,[5] rather than a rigid text that would have been contrary to the original constitutional philosophy. As Lord Sankey noted: "The B.N.A. Act planted in Canada a living tree capable of growth and expansion within its natural limits."[6]

His research describes the tug-of-war between minorities and provincial governments; the crucial financial support provided by the federal Court Challenges Program,[7] and the generous "remedial" interpretation of section 23 of the Charter by the Supreme Court.

Were it not for the Charter rights recognized by the courts, minorities would have been crushed and their access to education reduced to a bare minimum, if not totally ignored.

Professor Behiels dissects the Meech Lake episode and the aborted attempt to redefine Canada by splitting the country in two: the English on one side and the French on the other.[8] He recalls the attempt by some provinces to eliminate section 23 of the Charter and the refusal by the two protagonists, in Quebec City and in Ottawa, to acknowledge the fate French-speaking minorities could expect in that redefined Canada. That entire chapter provides overwhelming evidence of how, without constitutional and legal protections, official language minorities could be wiped out with a stroke of the pen, given the tendency to put the political interests of the governments of the day over any other considerations.

During the Meech Lake period, the provinces witnessed the spectacular turnaround in Manitoba following the decision in *Forest*.[9] The courts, supporting minority education rights, inflamed the media in the West and heightened the pressure on the federal government to end the Court Challenges Program, the source of much of the minority-group litigiousness, which had already resulted in numerous favourable judgments. In 1992 the Mulroney government used budget cutting and program reorganization as its excuse for eliminating the program, which was fuelling the "nerve centre" of that judicial battle. But, the Chrétien government later restored it, honouring a formal promise made in the 1993 "Red Book".[10] Professor Behiels demonstrates beyond any doubt that the rule of law is the only bulwark official language minorities have against the inclinations of majorities to homogenize rules, standardize systems, and gobble up public funds.[11]

If more evidence were needed that the Canadian courts are the only real protection against political temptations (or initiatives) that disregard the constitutional status of official language minorities in Canada,[12] the detailed account Professor Behiels gives of the rise and fall of the Charlottetown Accord should resolve the doubts of any sceptics. In 2002, the federal minister responsible for official language minorities invited the communities to abandon their "legalistic" approach and put more emphasis on political lobbying and pressure. Such advice, if accepted, would leave minorities at the mercy of tenacious prejudices and the vindictiveness of public opinion.[13] The leadership for the promotion and respect of linguistic minority rights, which are at the core of our national interests, must be federal; it cannot be left to the sole initiative of various provincial governments.

It is especially disappointing that the federal government is still reluctant to recognize the full constitutional status of official language minority groups by refusing to legally enforce Part VII of the Official Languages Act,[14] "Promotion du français et de l'anglais – 'Advancement of English and French' (sections 41 to 45)". Were the government to take this formal step, it would confirm its responsibility to minorities and solidify its leadership among the provinces[15] and territories, which are far behind the federal government in supporting such initiatives.

At stake is our government's credibility, in the eyes of the country's minorities and the various provincial governments, as an institution that lives up to its responsibility to maintain the rights and principles that define us and form the foundation of Canadian society.

How can the national government not intervene (in support of Montfort in the Ontario Court of Appeal), both to forestall action by other governments that might be tempted to imitate Ontario and withdraw previous concessions, and to demonstrate to critics of the Canadian option that the federal government stands its ground when a minority is unfairly treated?[16]

Who better than the Government of Canada to defend and exemplify the generous, humanistic vision of its founders which brought together two great language communities, born of two empires that had been fierce rivals and even belligerent enemies for centuries? When the Government of Canada hesitates, evades, or tries to eliminate its responsibilities to official language minorities,[17] it imperils the values that are fundamental to its existence and identity, and that give the Charter its inspiration.

We must be grateful to Professor Behiels for his careful research. It reveals how the Canadian ideal has been carried forward not by our politicians but by ordinary citizens who are not often seen in the media and whose names are not often remembered. People who, in their everyday lives, and in their own neighbourhoods, have battled the establishment for their schools and to have their rights respected. In so doing, they preserve the noble vision of Canada, the one advocated by its founders. They contribute an essential element to the democratic way of life that all Canadians enjoy today. They, in fact, make real the assumption that recognition of the status of one kind of a minority has an effect on the advancement of the status of all others. They keep Canada true to its original ideal.

Serge Joyal, P.C., O.C.
Senator

NOTES

1 *Re The Regulation and Control of Aeronautics in Canada*, [1932] A.C. 54, 70.
2 Wilfrid Morin, *Nos Droits Minoritaires: Les minorités francaises au Canada*,
    Montréal : Fides, 1943, 56–80.
3 Canadian Constitutional Charter – 1971, Victoria, British Columbia, 14
    June 1971, Part II – Language Rights, Articles 10–19.
4 Although the federal government of the day said that the Official Lan-
    guages Act was merely *declaratory* and not enforceable in court. It took
    the judgment of Mr Justice Jules Deschênes in *Joyal v. Air Canada* in 1976
    to give the principle of equality its mandatory effect and make it enforce-
    able in the courts. Furthermore, the court declared that the principle of
    equality was applicable in the language policy in the workplace in the
    federal administration
       Following that court decision, with two other MPs, Jean Robert Gau-
    thier (Ottawa-Vanier) and Pierre de Bané (Matane), we convinced the
    government (Pierre E. Trudeau and then Joe Clark, prime minister in
    1979) to amend the Rules of the House of Commons, and the Senate, to
    establish a Standing Joint Committee of the Senate and House of
    Commons to review the implementation of the Official Languages Act
    on a permanent basis.
5 The courts' interpretation of section 15 of the Charter, "Equality rights,"
    is another example.
6 *In Re Section 24 of the B.N.A. Act (Edwards v The Attorney General of Canada*,
    [1930] A.C. 124), also known as "The Persons Case," at 106–107.
7 The Court Challenge Program was expanded in 1983, at the time I was
    Canada's secretary of State, to cover cases involving sections 16 to 23 of
    the Charter of Rights and Freedoms, and expanded again in 1985 by
    then secretary of State Benoit Bouchard to include sections 15, 27, and
    28 of the Charter.
8 "Bilingualism unites people, dualism divides them. Bilingualism means
    you can speak to the other – Duality means you can live in one language
    and the rest of Canada will live in another language and we will all be
    good friends, which is what Mr Levesque always wanted ... No wonder the
    French-speaking minorities in the rest of Canada and the English-speak-
    ing minorities in Québec do not like it, and some of them are humili-
    ated" (Pierre Elliott Trudeau in his testimony in the Committee of the
    Whole in the Senate, 30 March 1988, 2993).
9 A challenge to one little unilingual parking ticket led all the way to the
    Supreme Court and to the invalidation of all legislation enacted by the
    Manitoba Legislature since 1890. George Forest applied for financial
    support from the Secretary of State in 1983 to help pay the legal costs.
    The federal Department of Justice advised me, as secretary of State

responsible for the court challenges program, that Mr Forest could not
be right, because ultimately that would mean that all legislation enacted
in English only since 1890 would have to be declared invalid, and "that
can't be, it's too huge"; against their advise, I signed the authorization
for funds, and once the judgment was delivered I negotiated and signed
an agreement with Premier Howard Pawley to cover a large majority of
the costs of translating all legislation enacted since 1890.

10 Red Book, Liberal Party of Canada, 1993, 86. "The Conservative regime
abolished the Law Reform Commission and cancelled the Court Challenges Program, a Liberal program to fund equality-seeking groups and
individuals who seek to use the Charter to establish their legal and constitutional rights. A Liberal government will be committed to restoring the
Law Reform Commission and the Court Challenges Program." The
program was reinstated in October of 1994. In a letter dated 23 May 2003,
to Senator Jean-Robert Gauthier, the minister of Canadian Heritage confirmed her decision to extend the Court Challenge Program for a year.

11 In 1996 the Ontario Government, through its policy of budget cuts, cancelled the construction of the French School ordered in a previous court
decision. The Court of Appeal reversed the government decision and
ordered the construction of the school on the basis that education in
one of the official languages is a constitutional right, not administratively
negotiable. *Dufferin-Peel Roman Catholic Separate School Board v. Ontario
(Minister of Education and Training)*, (1996-07-08) ONCA mI8700.

12 Recently, on 6 November 2003, the Supreme Court of Canada, in *Doucet-
Boudreau v. Nova Scotia (Minister of Education)* (2003 SCC 62), expanded
judicial powers by ruling that judges can follow up court decisions in
matters of official languages' minority rights by forcing governments to
prove they are carrying out court orders.

13 "The Proper Use of the Law in the Area of the Official Languages," notes
for an address by the Honourable Stéphane Dion, keynote address to
members of the Ontario Bar Association, Toronto, 24 January 2002.

14 Sen. Jean-Robert Gauthier has submitted two private member's bills on
this subject, in 2001, S-32 (1st session, 37th Parliament), and in 2003, S-
11 (2nd session 37th Parliament), which were debated in the Senate.

15 It should be noted that New Brunswick is the exception; it agreed that its
obligations and responsibilities to its Acadian population should be fully
entrenched in the constitution in 1982 and 2001.

16 Letter of the author to the prime minister of Canada, 9 August 2000
asking that the attorney general for Canada intervene in the Ontario
Court of Appeal in support of Montfort Hospital claim to be recognized
as an essential francophone hospital.

17 Ottawa's status as the bilingual capital of Canada has yet to be confirmed
in section 16 of the Constitution Act, 1867.

Acknowledgments

This study emerged from a conjuncture of novel circumstances and serendipitous encounters with a number of Canadians – francophone, anglophone, and allophone – who have devoted a great deal of time and energy to the defence and promotion of Canada's official language minority communities. The patriation and amendment of the Constitution in 1980–82 and the reopening of constitutional negotiations in the mid-1980s by the federal and Quebec governments renewed my longstanding interest in Canada's constitutional development. Along with other Constitution watchers, I witnessed how the Constitution Act, 1982, with its various amending procedures and the Charter, dramatically altered the dynamic of Canada's traditionally elitist and deferential political culture of constitutional renewal. Official language minority communities, aboriginal peoples, women's organizations, ethnocultural communities, and civil libertarians quickly came to the defence of "their" Charter. Canada's constitutional evolution was no longer the prerogative of white males in suits making deals behind closed doors. Canadians, far less deferential than in the past and eager to exercise their new-found constitutional sovereignty, insisted on having their say on when, how, and even whether their Constitution required amending.

When the political turmoil subsided somewhat following the referendum of 1992, I was encouraged by Senator Roméo LeBlanc – former journalist, long-time minister in the Trudeau government, and soon-to-be Governor General of Canada – to investigate Canada's Acadian and francophone minority communities and their campaigns for school governance under s. 23 of the Charter. Ann Marie Kelly, another dedicated and wise Canadian and New Brunswick native, sharpened my political/constitutional instincts while suggesting innumerable questions and avenues for my investigations. Having been raised in a bilingual community in northern Alberta, and having received my secondary and some post-secondary education at Collège St-Jean in Edmonton and the University of Ottawa, I considered that it would be well worth studying both the substance and the process of constitutional renewal from the ground up rather than from the top down.

Encouraged by sympathetic and helpful colleagues, especially Pierre Savard, Marcel Martel, and Joseph Magnet, I set to work researching and analysing the role played by Canada's francophone minority communities in the achievement and implementation of s. 23 rights. I wish to thank those graduate students of mine who have shown a keen interest in these communities. In particular, I am indebted to two of them. First, Derek McNeil, a New Brunswick Acadian, for assisting me with some of the laborious archival research for this project. Second, Matthew Hayday, for his excellent PhD dissertation on Canada's Official Languages in Education Program of 1970–84, which gave me crucial insights into the linguistic and educational context underlying my analysis of education rights for Canada's official language minority following the arrival of the Charter.

Undertaking research in various archives and in the offices of Canada's francophone minority community organizations was an exceptionally pleasant and rewarding experience. I wish to thank the efficient and supportive staff at the Centre de recherche en civilisation canadienne-française at the University of Ottawa, especially Lucie Pagé, Head Archivist, and Bernadette Legault Routhier, Reference Archivist. Hélène Laporte of the University of Ottawa Faculty of Law's Canadian Centre for Linguistic Rights was helpful in locating legal documentation. Alfred Fortier and Angèle Chaput of the Société Historique de Saint-Boniface and the staff of the Société franco-manitobaine made my research experience in Winnipeg most memorable. The staffs of the Association canadienne-française de l'Alberta and the Provincial Archives of Alberta were also of considerable assistance.

The University of Ottawa Faculty of Arts Research and Publications Committee provided funding for a much-needed computer as well as a research trip to Manitoba and Alberta. I benefited greatly from a full sabbatical in 2001–02 devoted to complete revisions of the manuscript. I am especially grateful to Georges Arès, Denis Tardif, Raymond Hébert, Raymond Théberge, Rhéal Teffaine, and Rolande Faucher for reading drafts of various chapters, a tremendous service that helped me avoid some egregious errors in both fact and interpretation. I also wish to express heartfelt gratitude to the anonymous reviewers of McGill-Queen's University Press and the SSHRC's Aid to Scholarly

Publications program. Their constructive reports helped me further clarify and substantiate the over-arching thesis that binds this story together. Finally, I wish to acknowledge the inspired work of my hands-on editor, Olga Domján, with whom it was a pleasure to work. Of course, any remaining flaws are those of the author.

Most importantly, I was able to persevere through the many years of research and innumerable drafts thanks largely to my wife Linda's irrepressible optimism, marvelous sense of humour, and eagerness to join me in learning the challenging game of golf as a way of escaping the confining spaces of our office environments. As usual, our two sons, Marc and Justin, while chiding their father for spending too much time cloistered in his office, were supportive if somewhat puzzled by the fact that there is so much to this unknown story.

This study is dedicated to Canada's francophone minority communities, organizations, and leaders for their dedication and their determination to survive as modern, thriving collectivities in the face of inordinate obstacles. Given the political context over the past four decades, they are to be commended for their steadfast dedication to their vision of a pan-Canadian linguistic dualism and cultural pluralism.

Introduction

This study is a descriptive analysis of Canada's francophone minority communities' quest for renewal and regeneration through constitutional reform and the winning of school governance. Their remarkable achievements on both counts took place in interconnected phases over four tumultuous decades, beginning in the 1960s.

The first phase entailed the arduous but ultimately successful rebuilding of Canada's francophone minority communities at the provincial and national levels. It was subsequent to the collapse of French Canada – as a symbol and as a nationally integrated institutional network – following the rise of Québécois neo-nationalism and secessionism during Quebec's Quiet and Not-So-Quiet Revolutions of the 1960s and 1970s. Occurring over nearly two decades, this first phase enabled francophone organizations to participate in the next, which involved them in the hurly-burly of mega-constitutional politics – that is, in the formal renewal of the British North America Act, 1867 following the Trudeau government's defeat of the Parti Québécois' secessionist option in the May 1980 referendum. During the controversial but productive second phase, francophone organizations campaigned for constitutional recognition of education rights for Canada's official language minority communities. Despite their deep-seated internal cleavages over religion, education and schooling policies, and urban-rural competition, the revitalized and determined provincial and national francophone minority community organizations obtained constitutional recognition in the Constitution Act, 1982. The Act's innovative Canadian Charter of Rights and Freedoms entrenched official bilingualism and protected and promoted the individual rights of all Canadians, as well as the collective rights of specific minority communities.

The most innovative component of the Charter, section 23, which mandated education rights for Canada's official language minorities, constituted a watershed, given that time and again since Confederation provincial rights trumped the language rights of Canada's francophone minority communities. The section handed these communities the constitutional empowerment they required to pursue the third phase in their regeneration: the protracted, difficult, often divisive, but ultimately fruitful political and judicial campaigns of Ontario, Alberta, and Manitoba francophone minority organizations, leaders, and parents for full school governance. Their separate but coordinated campaigns for segmental autonomy in the field of education forced them to master the arcane skills of informal microconstitutional politics, which entailed pursuing the enforcement of their education rights through political lobbying and the courts. It was with the backing of both their national organization and the Canadian government that francophones in these three provinces attained their goal of school governance. In so doing they played a significant role in the metamorphosis of what had been the extraordinary phenomenon known as Catholic French Canada into a national network of modern, secular francophone minority communities.

While pursuing their micro-constitutional campaigns, the francophone organizations were drawn into the fourth phase of this story. They felt compelled to participate in two new rounds of unsuccessful mega-constitutional political negotiations: the Meech Lake Accord, 1987–90, and the Charlottetown Consensus Report, 1990–92. They were driven by the need to protect – and, they hoped, to enhance – the constitutional gains of 1982, particularly the rights under s. 23. Instead, they found themselves caught up in a heated and destabilizing struggle to defend and promote their conception of a pan-Canadian linguistic and cultural dualism against attempts by Prime Minister Brian Mulroney and Premier Robert Bourassa – with the support of most but not all premiers – to entrench a territorial Quebec/Canada dualist conception in a revised Canadian Constitution. Thanks to the support of Charter federalists and Canadians in every region, the Constitution Act, 1982 and the Charter withstood both challenges. Meanwhile, s. 23 rights were given a liberal and expansive interpretation by the Supreme Court of Canada.

During the cantankerous and strenuous 1990s, Canadians became conscious of a remarkable and historically significant phenomenon: the three-decade-long renaissance of Canada's francophone and Acadian minorities, in the course of which parents in these communities achieved French language education for their children in every province. In many provinces, they obtained limited or full governance

over their homogeneous French language schools, an achievement
that a generation earlier was only a forlorn utopian dream.[1]

The winning of school governance by Canada's francophone minority communities is a truly extraordinary achievement. It is especially
so when viewed in the context of French Canada's numerous bitter,
protracted, and largely unsuccessful political and judicial battles for
language rights, especially instruction in the French language, since
Confederation. Time and time again, a dominant ideology of cultural
and linguistic homogeneity in conjunction with sacrosanct provincial
autonomy trumped francophone minority linguistic and education
rights. These humiliating defeats were perplexing and demoralizing
experiences for many French Canadians, undoubtedly contributing to
their growing belief that their fate was integration and eventual assimilation into the surrounding English-speaking majority. Fortunately,
most French Canadians and their religious and lay leaders used these
setbacks to harden their resolve and find creative ways to preserve
their language, culture, and Catholic religion.[2]

Achieving school governance was even more remarkable given the
comprehensive demographic, socioeconomic, cultural, linguistic, educational, and political transformation experienced by Canada's francophone and Acadian minority communities following World War II.[3]
French Canada, a pan-Canadian community of functioning French
and Catholic communities largely but not exclusively emerging from
and nurtured by Quebec's majority francophone society, was laboriously and successfully imagined, defended, and promoted for well
over a century by determined French Canadians. Indeed, a French
Canada stretching from coast to coast survived and expanded thanks
to the dedication and hard work of French Canadians working
through an elaborate network of religious, socioeconomic, cultural,
educational, health, and recreational institutions administered and
funded by the Catholic Church. Their idealistic, yet realistic, goal was
to create a French and Catholic stateless nation dispersed throughout
Canada and certain regions of the United States. Until the Great
Depression of the 1930s and the global war that followed, their drive
and determination to create a dynamic French Canada succeeded in
varying degrees in specific regions of North America.[4]

Paradoxically, just as the goal of creating both the imagined and the
real French Canada was reached, the demographic, socioeconomic,
ideological, political, and institutional foundations of that community
began to crumble under various pressures, some internal, some origi-
nating in the wholesale centralization and expansion of the provincial
and Canadian governments after 1945. A final factor was the bitter,
public rupture with the majority French Canadian community of

Quebec during the 1960s and 1970s. In the words of two sociologists, "En effet, la transformation des rapports sociaux ethniques au Canada et le renforcement concomitant de la gestion étatique de ces rapports a engendré la structuration de nouveaux espaces ethniques caractérisés par un changement au niveau des élites, de l'identité et des représentations collectives, des projets politiques et des discours scientifiques."[5] The fascinating, multifarious process of renewal and re-identification was fluid and dynamic. It occurred at different times, in distinct ways, and at varying speeds from one francophone minority community to the next. The highly destabilizing changes transformed the symbolic and political space known as French Canada into separate francophone and Acadian minority communities structured within provincial boundaries, institutions, and political cultures. The final outcome was the collapse of French Canada.[6]

The prelude was the ideological transformation that took place in Quebec. After World War II, a new generation of the urban middle class redefined their traditional French Canadian clerical nationalism into a secular state-centred Québécois neo-nationalism. A modern interventionist state – not the moribund Catholic Church – would henceforth be the central institution in the struggle for the preservation of the Québécois nation. This revolution of mentalities and ideologies precipitated Quebec's Quiet Revolution of state-building, which was ushered in by the election of Jean Lesage's Liberal government in June 1960.[7]

Within a few years, neo-nationalists inside and outside the government were seeking special constitutional status for Quebec within a bi-national Canadian federation. A small but vocal minority of secessionists launched a campaign to transform their dynamic secular state into an independent Québécois nation-state. The radicalized constitutional debate seriously threatened Canada's political and territorial integrity when various right- and left-wing secessionist movements coalesced in 1968 into René Lévesque's Parti Québécois. Its first objective was to establish an independent Quebec republic in North America for the Québécois people. Neo-nationalists and secessionists alike, drawn largely from the burgeoning ranks of the new francophone middle class of professionals, business people, and state technocrats, categorically rejected French Canada and the nomenclature "French Canadian", re-identifying themselves as Québécois and referring to the continued survival of French Canada as a myth.[8] One secessionist described Confederation as "the graveyard of the minorities" because the assimilation rate of francophones living in Canada's western provinces had reached nearly 50 per cent by the 1950s. René Lévesque cavalierly and sardonically characterized members of the French Canadian minority communities as "dead ducks."[9]

Symptomatic of the imminent collapse of French Canada was the demise in the mid-60s of the Ordre de Jacques-Cartier, a secret society founded in 1926, and of the Conseil de la vie française en Amérique, founded in 1937 at the apex of French Canada. Both organizations had worked tirelessly and effectively to promote its interests; both were supported by the Catholic Church and by nationalist institutions such as the Sociétés Saint-Jean-Baptiste and the Mouvement Desjardins, located largely but not exclusively in Quebec. All these organizations preached a traditional French Canadian nationalism based on the two founding peoples conception of Canada. Québécois neo-nationalists and secessionists rejected what they viewed as Henri Bourassa and Lionel Groulx's outmoded and unrealistic conception of a cultural and linguistic dualism. In its place, they aggressively promoted a territorial dualism comprising two nation-states, Canada and Quebec, united in a decentralized, binational federation.[10]

The final act in the rupture between Canada's francophone and Acadian minority community leaders and the Québécois neo-nationalists and secessionists took place during the Estates General of French Canada, a vast assembly convened on several occasions between 1967 and 1969. In the words of Yvon Thériault, "Les États généraux du Canada français furent donc, dans la mémoire collective de ma génération, une grande messe consacrant la mort du Canada français."[11] Even before the highly symbolic break it was clear that the politicians and mandarins of the new Quebec state were not interested in supporting or working with the traditional institutional network created to sustain French Canada. Instead they had created their own state-run institutions – the Service du Canada français d'outre-frontières and the Maisons du Québec located in the provincial capitals – through which they planned to exercise a form of Québécois cultural imperialism. Henceforth, it was Quebec, not the Catholic Church, the Société Saint-Jean-Baptiste, or the Conseil de vie française en Amérique, that would act as the national state of Canada's francophones and Acadians. French Canadians throughout the diaspora were encouraged to abandon their utopian dream of a strong pan-Canadian French Canada in favour of joining the Québécois in their struggle for an independent Quebec.[12]

So it is that the 1950s and 1960s were challenging times for Canada's francophone minority communities and their beleaguered network of Catholic and lay institutions and organizations.[13] Serious challenges included these factors:[14]

- the relentless decline of most rural parishes, as French Canadians headed to the cities in pursuit of increased education and better job opportunities
- post-war immigration transforming the cities into multicultural, multilingual environments
- the rapid erosion of the Catholic Church's ability to sustain, via its dwindling personnel and financial resources, the institutional network it had constructed so laboriously for over a century
- the expanded roles of centralized and bureaucratized provincial and federal states after World War II to meet the social, economic, and educational needs of Canadians
- the secularization of French Canadians' mores, norms, and values
- the omnipresence of English-language electronic media, compelling French Canadians living outside Quebec to become functionally bilingual if they wished to participate fully in and benefit from the modernization of Canadian society

The growing secularized and better-educated French Canadian élites felt tremendous pressure to form new institutions capable of continuing the historical struggle for survival and equality. Canada's beleaguered but still largely intact francophone and Acadian minority communities, led by a new generation of dedicated leaders and backed by a supportive Canadian government, set out to rebuild their shattered institutions and identities. They were determined not to become marginalized peoples or even to be perceived as being among Canada's increasingly numerous urban-based ethnocultural communities. They set out to reconstitute themselves as modern national entities interconnected by a pan-Canadian francophone community. Working against enormous odds they largely succeeded. "Bref, les communautés minoritaires francophones du Canada," comments Yvon Thériault, "qui regroupent encore à ce jour près d'un million d'individus, demeurent une caractéristique constitutive du Canada. Ces communautés continuent toujours à nommer et à occuper le pays, à faire l'histoire, à intervenir politiquement, à créer des liens sociaux, bref à produire et à reproduire une culture autour du français comme langue de communications."[15]

This study adopts a descriptive and critical approach based on the extensive archival documents, private and public, generated by the various provincial and national francophone organizations and the governments with which they negotiated for over four decades. Canada's francophone minority communities achieved their renaissance through their struggle for school governance. Rather than approaching the history of Canada's recent constitutional renewal from the top down, this book analyses the process from the bottom up. In so doing, it highlights the remarkable ongoing democratization of Canada's constitutional development and traditionally deferential political culture. The phenomenon resulted in part from social and political changes brought about by post-war prosperity, urbanization, mass immigration, and secularization. But it was equally the by-product of active communities, such as those of the francophone minority, determined to empower themselves and exercise agency over their future. The democratic fervour was accelerated by Prime Minister Pierre Elliott Trudeau's political philosophy of participatory democracy, which permeated his government and the federal bureaucracy for nearly two decades. There were and remain important limits on this process of democratization, as francophone community leaders discovered. Under the amending formulae spelled out in the Constitution Act, 1982, the prime minister, the premiers, and their respective legislatures retained the final decision-making authority over constitutional renewal. What political leaders could no longer control after the Charter became law was the Supreme Court of Canada as the ultimate arbiter of the full range of mandated individual and minority rights. This development, too, ensured that Canada's political culture would function henceforth in a more democratic manner, because the Charter empowered minorities.

How did Canada's francophone minority communities respond to the internal challenges to their continued survival? How did they overcome the demise of French Canada and the loss of their traditional French Canadian identity? How did they react to the rise of the Québécois secessionist movement after 1968 and its rejection of their continued presence in Canada? This study provides revealing and interesting answers to these important questions. Its central theme is the renaissance of three provincial francophone minority communities via a three-stage process of renewal and self-empowerment.[16] In the course of their four decades of struggle to rebuild their communities, obtain the inclusion of s. 23 in the Charter, and achieve school governance while defending their s. 23 rights, these communities learned to master the complex processes of mega- and micro-constitutional politics.

Interwoven with this central theme are several related sub-themes, many of them integral to Canadians' historical experience but played out in original ways:

- competing visions of dualism: pan-Canadian versus Quebec/Canada
- competing priorities and interests of the Québécois majority and the francophone diaspora

- competing conceptions of Canadian federalism: centralist or decentralist
- majority rights expressed via provincial autonomy versus minority rights of francophones backed by the Canadian government
- conflicting interests in francophone minority communities over Catholic versus public French language education
- differing approaches within francophone communities respecting micro- and mega-constitutional politics

Chapter 1 explores the first phase of the process of renewal: the takeover of provincial francophone organizations by a new generation of leaders during the late 1960s and 1970s. This secular, forward-looking leadership redefined its policy objectives and the means of achieving them. It also became wary of the threat posed by the neo-nationalist and secessionist movements in Quebec to the survival of French Canada; in response, it created a national umbrella organization, the Fédération des communautés francophones et acadiennes du Canada. Capitalizing on Trudeau's vision of a bilingual Canada and his efforts at constitutional renewal, the Fédération and its affiliates pursued their own constitutional vision, one considerably more expansive and ambitious than what most premiers, especially in Quebec, were prepared to endorse.

Chapter 2 examines the second phase; it analyses the highly successful role played by francophone organizations in the Trudeau government's revision of the Canadian constitution following its victory over the Parti Québécois in the May 1980 referendum on sovereignty-association. With the full backing of the Trudeau government, francophone minority community leaders obtained the constitutional entrenchment of official bilingualism in the Charter at the federal level, with an opting-in clause for the provinces, as well as the all-important s. 23 on official language minority education rights. Despite intense lobbying of the Ontario, Manitoba, and New Brunswick governments by francophone minority organizations, only the latter agreed to become officially bilingual. Initially, the leaders had serious reservations about the Charter's education rights clause. But in learning to play the game of mega-constitutional politics, they gave new hope to their communities. It was incumbent upon them to pursue their goal of full school governance via political lobbying and strategic judicial challenges.

Chapters 3 to 5 tell of the third phase of renewal. Chapter 3 looks at the ultimately successful campaign whereby several organizations, led by the Association canadienne-française de l'Ontario and the Association française des Conseils scolaires de l'Ontario, convinced the

Ontario government to implement section 23 education rights for Franco-Ontarian families. Having learned the right combination of political and judicial pressures, they were able to induce a reluctant provincial government to change the Education Act so that it complied with s. 23 rights as interpreted by the courts, first in Ontario, then at the Supreme Court level.

Chapter 4 focuses on the interesting political/judicial dynamic in Alberta, with its small but increasingly radicalized francophone minority community in Edmonton and its more conservative Catholic rural francophone communities dispersed throughout the north and northeast of the province. As soon as Royal Assent was given to the Constitution Act, 1982, a group of Franco-Albertan parents created the Association Bugnet to campaign for homogeneous French-language minority schools and public school board, under s. 23. Initially the conservative and politically cautious Association canadienne-française d'Alberta was reluctant to back the Association Bugnet's aggressive campaign. Its leaders felt that most Franco-Albertan parents supported the existing system of bilingual and French immersion schools, which were open to all Alberta children, but reversed their position once they were convinced that these schools accelerated rather than stemmed assimilation of Franco-Albertan students. The Association Bugnet, backed by the ACFA and the Fédération, was the first francophone parents' group to take its case all the way to the Supreme Court of Canada, where it won a ground-breaking favourable ruling on s. 23 in 1990. The decision in the *Mahé* case set the stage for five years of political negotiations with successive Alberta Conservative governments, culminating in a province-wide system of French language regional school boards and coordinating councils.

Chapter 5 reveals that the struggle for school governance in Manitoba was somewhat more complicated. The Franco-Manitoban community and its leaders in the Société franco-manitobaine were involved in a divisive political and constitutional struggle for the restoration of official bilingualism, s. 23 of the Manitoba Act, 1870, which had been abolished in 1890. The climate for negotiating school governance was not very auspicious. Manitoba's Conservative and New Democratic governments were torn among the opposition of the majority, the constitutionally mandated religious rights of Franco-Manitoban Catholics, and the mandated language education rights of all Franco-Manitobans – divisions that they exploited. The campaign for school governance culminated in the Supreme Court, which rendered a favourable decision on s. 23 education rights in the 1993 Manitoba reference case. Following exhaustive political nego-tiations, Franco-Manitobans eventually obtained a single

province-wide school board in charge of all urban and rural French
language schools.

Chapters 6 and 7 recount the fourth phase: the protracted political
challenges to s. 23 rights and the francophone minority conception of
Canadian dualism. When the Meech Lake Accord surfaced in April
1987, francophone minority community organizations felt constrained to participate in the complexities of mega-constitutional politics. Premier Robert Bourassa and Prime Minister Brian Mulroney
attempted to redefine the longstanding cultural dualism of French-
speaking and English-speaking Canadians into a Canada/Quebec conception of the federation. If Quebec obtained exclusive jurisdiction
over language rights – including those of its official language minority
– via the Accord, the premiers were determined to lay claim to the
same powers in the hope of undermining their respective francophone communities' campaigns for school governance. Chapter 6
examines the ambiguous and divisive role played by provincial and
national francophone organizations in the ideological and political
struggles surrounding the rise and eventual demise of the Meech Lake
Accord between April 1987 and June 1990. Chapter 7 analyses the
Canada Round initiated by Mulroney in 1990 and brought to a startling halt by Canadians' rejection of the Charlottetown Accord in the
October 1992 referendum.

Chapter 8 concludes the book with a look at the debate within the
francophone minority communities over how best to use their hard-
won systems of school governance to guarantee their survival and
enhance their development over the coming decades.

Their success in achieving school governance has led many francophone leaders to take the position that their community's transformation into a national entity should precipitate a renewed solidarity with
their alienated francophone compatriots of Quebec. Their goal was
attained against enormous odds and contrary to most predictions. To
have achieved segmental autonomy over education in every province
and territory is an exceptional accomplishment, given how rare it is
when a linguistic and cultural minority is widely dispersed throughout a state, and especially when that state is a federation
in which the sub-units – the provinces – have exclusive control over
education.[17]

CANADA'S FRANCOPHONE MINORITY COMMUNITIES

1

The Renaissance of Canada's Francophone Minority Communities

In the 1960s and 1970s, Canada's francophone minority communities had come to a significant crossroads. To astute observers they appeared exhausted, beleaguered, anachronisms in the world swirling around them. Had they laboured so long and hard to survive only to see themselves swept into the dustbin of history? Meanwhile, Premier Jean Lesage's neo-nationalist Liberal government, with its "équipe de tonnèrre," had transformed Quebec into a powerful secular state. The Quiet Revolution entered a not-so-quiet phase with the rise of right- and left-wing separatist movements and the surprise victory of Daniel Johnson's Union Nationale over Lesage's Liberals in 1966. Johnson, backed by the neo-nationalists and secessionists, demanded "égalité ou indépendence": the creation of a Canada/Quebec federation or Quebec's secession from the federation. Those were heady times not only for Canadians generally but for French Canadians and Acadians who felt they had much to lose if Quebec seceded from Canada.

Francophone minority community leaders, elated yet concerned at the emergence of an assertive Québécois state, faced two options. They could stand by and watch their tradition-bound communities slowly dissolve into their sociocultural and linguistic surroundings. Or, as on many occasions, they could embark on a long-term plan of regeneration. Fortunately for them, as well as for Canadians, they opted for renewal: to undertake a series of protracted struggles, the most important among them the timely and heroic battle for full school governance. Francophone minority community parents and leaders firmly believed that designing and managing their children's education was one of the best ways of ensuring their continued existence. Their political and legal battles over linguistic rights, especially in the context of education, provided excellent opportunities for reconstructing their symbolic and political spaces following the collapse of French Canada as their institutional framework.[1]

The francophone leaders were shocked into action by a combination of significant developments: the Quiet Revolution, the Royal Commission on Bilingualism and Biculturalism (1963–68), the election of Pierre Trudeau as prime minister and the subsequent passage of the Official Languages Act, 1969, and the disruptive Estates General of French Canada (1967–69). However, when the Quebec government of Daniel Johnson, with the support of Ontario's Premier John Robarts, pressured the government of Prime Minister Lester Pearson to open negotiations on the British North America Act in 1968, they were ill-equipped to play any significant role in the constitutional talks. Three years later, when Trudeau's first attempt at mega-constitutional negotiations, the Victoria Charter of 1971, failed, the francophone leaders were disappointed – but they were also determined never to be left on the sidelines again.

The Victoria Charter's demise jolted the revitalized provincial francophone associations into realizing that they needed a national federation of organizations. In 1975, following considerable debate, the Fédération des Francophones Hors Québec came into being as their official voice in Ottawa. In 1991, the FFHQ was renamed the Fédération des communautés francophones et acadiennes du Canada (hereafter, the Fédération), to reflect the importance of these communities' identities. The hope was that a national organization would help the francophone minority communities develop solidarity and reconstruct their national identity in the absence of French Canada. Further, it would monitor the implementation of the programs associated with the Official Languages Act, 1969 while lobbying for their expansion. Even more importantly, such an organization would ensure that the aspirations of the francophone minority would not be overlooked during the next round of constitutional negotiations.

Between 1975 and 1979, the Fédération developed a highly critical analysis of the Canadian government's official language policies and programs, then lobbied for fundamental changes to them. When the Trudeau government attempted to restart constitutional negotiations following the election of the separatist Parti Québécois government in November 1976, the national organization and its affiliates hammered out their approach to the renewal of Canada's constitution. During this period, the provincial francophone organizations and their leaders, who determined the Fédération's policies, came to realize that lobbying at the national level was a time-consuming and difficult business. To be successful, it required exhaustive preparation combined with astute professionalism. Fortunately, these leaders were quick learners.

THE "QUIET REVOLUTIONS" OF CANADA'S FRANCOPHONE MINORITY COMMUNITIES, 1960–1975

During the post-war era of expansion and prosperity, nearly a million French Canadians and Acadians from Nova Scotia to British Columbia faced pressure to integrate with and eventually be assimilated into the surrounding English-speaking communities. The war had already enticed many of their young men into industry and the Armed Forces, where they acquired new trades, language skills, and mobility. Once peace returned, most of the workers remained in the cities, while returning soldiers found employment outside their native communities.[2] Thus, the demographic and socioeconomic transformation of Canada's francophone minority communities was well advanced by the 1960s. Their traditional clerical and lay leaders were ill-prepared to appreciate the full scope of what was happening to their communities, much less to respond effectively.[3]

The emergence of the Canadian social service state and the need for higher levels of education were two of the central factors accelerating the transformation of the francophone communities. The interventionist state demanded by Canadians during and after the war was largely designed and partially funded by nationalistic Liberal and Conservative governments; its components were firmly in place by the mid-60s.[4] Moreover, the post-war baby boom necessitated the expansion and modernization of the provincial primary, secondary, and post-secondary educational systems by the 1960s.[5] Spurred by federal funding, expansive provincial governments and bureaucracies intensified their centralizing and homogenizing control over hospitals, social welfare agencies, educational institutions, and municipalities. The networks health, educational, and cultural institutions run by the Catholic Church came under intense pressure in all provinces. In due course, provincial intervention in all these areas well-nigh eradicated the local autonomy of the religious and lay leaders of francophone minority communities. Francophones seeking provincial or municipal government services increasingly found themselves facing unsympathetic, even hostile, English-speaking public and para-public civil servants. Urbanized francophone families found their children thrust unprepared into English language schools, more often than not public rather than Catholic. Furthermore, a great many francophone workers found themselves surrounded by English-speaking employers and fellow employees; their very occupation diminished their ability to retain their language and culture and pass them on to their children.[6]

Given the challenges, it is little wonder that the traditional franco-phone and Acadian leadership was in disarray. When the new genera-tion of secular leaders emerged, they seized the opportunity to lobby the Royal Commission on Bilingualism and Biculturalism co-chaired by André Laurendeau and Davidson Dunton. Recounting the deterio-rating socioeconomic conditions of francophone and Acadian families as their traditional way of life vanished, they pleaded for a range of government policies and programs that would ensure their communi-ties' survival as integral components of Canada's increasingly pluralis-tic nation-state. To stave off assimilation, it was essential for all franco-phone parents to obtain the right to have their children educated in publicly funded French language primary and secondary schools under their own governance.[7] The Commission listened carefully and responded favourably, acknowledging the crisis facing the franco-phone minority communities. Quebec's English-speaking urban pop-ulation – whether Catholic, Protestant, or immigrant – had had access to English language instruction in both the Catholic and Protestant school systems of the province since Confederation. "The failure of the BNA Act to protect English and French as languages of instruction in Canada," the Commission declared, "has resulted in a great dispar-ity in the use of these languages in our school systems and grave inequalities in the opportunities for the French-speaking minorities to have an education in their mother tongue."[8] Further, it recommended "that the right of Canadian parents to have their children educated in the official language of their choice be recognized in the educational systems, the degree of implementation to depend on the concentra-tion of the minority population."[9]

The Commission's detailed examination of education described how the objective of creating education systems for the linguistic minority communities in all ten Canadian provinces could be achieved. The process would start with three officially bilingual provinces: Ontario, Quebec, and New Brunswick. Other provinces would have a system of bilingual districts where minority language schools would be established, together with comprehensive urban school boards offering maternal language education when warranted by sufficient numbers of students.[10]

Franco-Ontarians Take the Lead

Francophone minority community leaders across the country looked to Ontario for guidance and support. Franco-Ontarians constituted the largest of these communities and already had a long history of political struggles. By 1971 there were 733,000 Ontarians of French origin, almost double the number in 1941. Of these, some 482,000 claimed French as their maternal language. Franco-Ontarians were dispersed throughout four very socioeconomically different regions of the province: nearly one-third in the northwest, along the Sudbury to Hearst corridor; just over one-third in the east, between Hawksbury and Ottawa; approximately one-quarter in the central region, primarily in greater Toronto; and the remainder in the south, around Windsor. These were highly mobile and heterogeneous communities that were urbanizing and industrializing at a fast pace. As Franco-Ontarians moved toward and then into the metropolitan regions of Toronto, Ottawa, and Sudbury, they encountered predominantly English-speaking social and work environments. As a result of the high level of mobility and occupational change, the traditional institutional network of social agencies, hospitals, parishes, schools, and cultural outlets no longer met the needs of most Franco-Ontarians.[11]

The Association canadienne-française de l'Ontario, founded in 1910 as the Association canadienne-française d'éducation de l'Ontario, was the largest and most experienced of the provincial organizations. ACFÉO had engaged in prolonged political and judicial struggles between 1912 and 1927 for the reinstatement of French language education in those Catholic schools where Franco-Ontarian children predominated. In 1912, the Ontario government's Regulation XVII effectively abolished French language instruction beyond the second grade in the long-established and -accepted bilingual Catholic separate schools. School boards were required to hire only teachers certified in Ontario and fully fluent in English, while school inspectors responsible for what remained of the bilingual schools were to be monitored by three special supervisors. The school boards responsible for the existing bilingual schools therefore had to require their French-Canadian lay and religious teachers – the large majority from Quebec – to obtain Ontario teaching certificates and learn English. If they refused, they had no choice but to stop teaching in all provincially funded schools. In this concerted attack on the bilingual separate schools Ontario's English Protestant majority was fully supported by the Irish Catholic community and its self-appointed leader, Bishop Fallon of London, who championed the elimination of all French language instruction in Ontario's Catholic separate schools.[12]

The ACFÉO took on this *cause célèbre*, which helped forge its constituents into an identifiable Franco-Ontarian community. Supported by Franco-Ontarian parents, teachers, and clerical and lay elites, Premier Lomer Gouin's Quebec government, Wilfrid Laurier's federal Liberals, Henri Bourassa's small but influential nationalist movement, and the newspaper *Le Devoir*, the ACFÉO and the Conseil des écoles séparées d'Ottawa systematically defied the Ministry of Education's regulation as well as the judicial rulings. During World War I, Franco-Ontarian parents in the Ottawa region created a system of private French language Catholic schools. The battle over minority language and education rights was fuelled by the high-octane politics generated by the 1917 conscription crisis. Ultimately, it drove a deep wedge between French and British Canadians and between the Franco-Ontarian and Irish Catholic communities. The politics of race and religion at their worst made it difficult for Franco-Ontarians to feel that the province was their home.

Following the end of the Great War, it took the muzzling of Bishop Francis Michael Fallon by the papacy, a change of heart by several prominent Irish Catholic leaders, the creation of the Unity League by British Canadian Protestant intellectuals, two sympathetic Ontario governments, as well as a more pragmatic leadership at the helm of the ACFÉO, to resolve the conflict. In October 1925, Conservative Premier Howard Ferguson established another Commission of Inquiry into Ontario's bilingual schools. The Merchant Report which resulted formed the basis of changes to Regulation XVII on 1 November 1927. French acquired legal status in all Ontario primary schools, and a certain amount of French language instruction was allowed, even encouraged, in all Catholic and public secondary schools. But no officially sanctioned bilingual schools were established, and Regulation XVII remained on the books until 1944.[13]

The ACFÉO's victory was modest. Yet the shift in policy would prove the beginning of a rebuilding process that would gain momentum in the late 1950s and really take off in the 1960s. A feisty new generation of Franco-Ontarians took advantage of a favourable conjunction of political, social, demographic, and economic circumstances to modernize the educational opportunities and facilities available to Franco-Ontarian children across the province. They gained control of the ACFÉO and used its contacts in the Conservative governments of John Robarts and Bill Davis and in the provincial bureaucracy to replace Catholic Church officials as Franco-Ontarians' natural leaders in education.

The opportunity came in the early 1960s when a serious financial and structural crisis beset the private Franco-Ontarian Catholic secondary schools. By 1967, the ACFÉO's predominantly urban and secular leaders had negotiated the integration of these schools into the Ontario public secondary system rather than into the predominantly English language Catholic secondary system, contrary to the wishes of Church leaders. This momentous shift in the relationship between the Franco-Ontarian leadership and the Ontario government was well described by one perceptive author as "la revanche des cerveaux," as distinct from the clerical nationalist strategy of "la revanche des berceaux."

That solution was also not the preference of most Franco-Ontarian parents and both lay and religious leaders in the industrializing and urbanizing, but still largely rural, northwestern part of Ontario. It was favoured by politicians and bureaucrats at Queen's Park because it coincided with their conception of an increasingly secular and highly educated Ontario society. The government wanted to improve the educational level and therefore the job opportunities of Franco-Ontarians while enhancing the community's culture by making French language education available throughout the entire educational system, public and separate.[14] For its part, the ACFÉO considered it crucial to sever the longstanding identification of the French language and culture with the Catholic Church. The new leadership was especially determined to wrest control of education from the Church, in the belief that Franco-Ontarians would thereby be enabled to gain access to the range of modern, diverse, fully funded educational institutions. The survival and expansion of the Franco-Ontarian community was dependent on it.

With significant improvements to French language education attained throughout the system by 1969, the ACFÉO's leaders decided it was time to broaden their mandate beyond the field of education. The revamped organization would be responsible for promoting all important aspects of Franco-Ontarians' collective life, including access to public services, notably judicial services, in their own language. Since 1960, the ACFÉO had made a number of structural changes in order to reach Franco-Ontarians of all social classes and occupations and in every region, urban and rural. Twenty-four regional presidents were added to the Administrative Council in 1963, and annual general meetings began to be held. In 1965, the affiliation of other Franco-Ontarian organizations was encouraged.[15] Finally, in early 1969, the leadership announced that the 18th annual general meeting would be devoted to restructuring and strongly urged changing the organization's name to the Association canadienne-française de l'Ontario to symbolize a new stage in its development. The ACFO would function as a federation representing Franco-Ontarians via six regional councils and several affiliated organizations.[16] Its leaders were determined to renew and expand Franco-Ontarian cultural institutions by operating as a powerful lobby group vis-à-vis the provincial and federal governments. They wanted to gain access to radio and television in order to communicate with their constituents and to enable Franco-Ontarians to display their talents in all fields of individual and collective cultural, social, economic, and political endeavour. They believed that Franco-Ontarians would thereby be encouraged to use their language and live their culture daily. It was an ambitious strategy to stem the tide of assimilation.[17]

The Young Turks used the highly critical and revealing 1969 *Report of the Comité franco-ontarien d'enquête culturelle,* headed by Roger Saint-Denis and sponsored by the Ontario Committee on Confederation, to broaden the mandate of the provincial organization. Thanks to generous financial support from the Secretary of State in Ottawa, ($314,356 in 1969–70 and $724,000 by 1975–76), the ACFO and other Franco-Ontarian organizations were able to carry out a wide range of programs throughout their communities. While the provincial government was unwilling to grant Franco-Ontarians special status by creating a Conseil franco-ontarien d'orientation culturel, as proposed by the Saint-Denis Report, it did make sure that approximately five per cent of all funding was directed to their cultural programs and organizations.[18]

With funding from Ottawa, beginning in the late 1970s and continuing throughout the 80s, the ACFO devoted vast energy and resources to pressuring the Ontario government to declare the province officially bilingual. Its leaders believed that official status would help Franco-Ontarians achieve governance over French language schools and school boards and also provide them with a full complement of government services in their own language without having to resort to costly, time consuming political and judicial campaigns. While no government was willing to take this step, the Liberals under Premier David Peterson adopted Bill 8 in 1986. Fully implemented some three years later, the bill provided for a limited range of French language services in justice, health care, social services, and community programs in regions of the province where they were warranted by sufficient numbers of Franco-Ontarians.[19]

By the 1980s, the ACFO had become a sophisticated and successful political lobby group serving the wide-ranging needs of Franco-Ontarian communities throughout the province. The struggle between the urban-based modernists and rural-based traditionalists did not cease entirely, but over time urbanization and changing values favoured the secular middle-class leadership and its approaches to forwarding the interests of Franco-Ontarians.

Franco-Manitobans on the March

Western Canada's francophone minority communities faced quite different conditions than Franco-Ontarians. The economies of all three

prairie provinces remained predominantly agricultural until the
1960s. The ethnocultural and religious mix of their populations was
considerably more diverse than in Ontario. The only cities of any size
were Winnipeg, Regina, and Edmonton. Most western French Canadian communities were rural, centred around village parishes, private
social and health services, small businesses, and schools.[20]

It was not until the rapid urbanization and industrialization of the
1960s and 70s that Franco-Manitobans experienced the sort of dramatic upheaval that forced them and their leaders to analyse their
prospects for survival as an integrated and prosperous community.
In 1961, there were nearly 84,000 Manitobans, comprising 9 per
cent of the population, whose ethnic origin was French Canadian.
Only 61,000, 6.6 per cent of the population, registered French as
their maternal language. The latter proportion was the same as in
1941 but would begin to decline in the 1980s, following two
decades of urbanization.[21] The 150th anniversary of the founding of
Saint-Boniface in 1968 turned out to be more than merely symbolic
of the historic contribution of that community's French Canadian
settlers; it was also a turning point marking the revival of the Franco-
Manitoban community.

Franco-Manitobans, especially those belonging to the Métis nation,
had a difficult time almost from the moment that the province
entered Confederation in 1870.[22] At the insistence of Georges-
Etienne Cartier and Louis Riel, section 23 of the Manitoba Act, 1870
made the Legislative Assembly and the courts officially bilingual. Yet
with the rapid influx of British Canadian settlers into the province, s.
23 was abolished in 1890, when the government passed the controversial Manitoba Languages Act. Two lower court decisions, in 1892
and in 1909, ruled the latter law invalid, but they were ignored by
the province. The matter was allowed to drop because Catholic
Church leaders considered the struggle for the reinstatement of
Catholic separate schools more important. Franco-Manitobans
would wait a century before s. 23 was restored by the Supreme Court
of Canada.

Catholic and Franco-Manitoban leaders were far more concerned
over the passage of the Manitoba Schools Act, 1890. This highly controversial law, which contributed to the defeat of Prime Minister
Charles Tupper's Conservative government in 1896, replaced the publicly funded denominational schools – Protestant and Catholic – mandated by the Constitution with a system of English language public
schools. Against the wishes of their clerical leaders, a majority of
Franco-Manitobans lobbied successfully to obtain a political compromise known as the Laurier-Greenway Agreement of 1898. The deal

permitted teaching in maternal languages other than English on the basis of the number of students enrolled in a school, and also allowed for religious instruction at the end of the school day.[23]

The Laurier-Greenway Agreement held until the middle of the Great War, when Premier T.C. Norris's Liberal government, pressured by British Canadian nationalists, abolished it and compelled all teachers to provide instruction in English only, using English textbooks. At this point, Franco-Manitobans, with the support and funding of the Catholic Church, created the Association d'Éducation des Canadiens-Français du Manitoba to fight for the restoration of French language education. For decades, the AÉCFM, backed by the newspaper *La Liberté*, CKSB-Radio Saint-Boniface, established in 1946, and the Collège de Saint-Boniface, which trained many Franco-Manitoban teachers, worked diligently behind the scenes to guarantee the survival of French language Catholic education and the French language and culture throughout rural Manitoba and in the urban community of Saint-Boniface, a francophone village within the city of Winnipeg.

In the late 1950s, rural Franco-Manitobans faced the prospect of losing control over their local school districts as a result of the government's plan to create large regional school divisions. The AÉCFM was also concerned about the rate of assimilation, which seemed to be on the increase, especially among urban Franco-Manitobans. Its leaders argued that homogeneous French language education and school governance were the keys to stemming the tide. As a way of enticing Franco-Manitobans into accepting the consolidation of rural school districts into regional divisions, Premier Duff Roblin's Conservative government introduced Bill 59 in March 1967. The bill amended the Manitoba Schools Act to allow French language instruction for up to 50 per cent of the school day for all Manitoba children. Discussions to this effect had been underway within the Ministry of Education since 1962. But the Minister of Education had moved cautiously, making sure along the way that he had the support of the AÉCFM, the Manitoba Teachers' Society, and the Manitoba Association of School Trustees, together with that of a good portion of Manitobans who were increasingly supportive of a bilingual education for their children.[24]

Changing circumstances demanded a different approach. Quebec's Quiet Revolution was in full swing and the social and educational policies of the Lesage Liberal government provided young Manitobans with a vision of what could be achieved in an activist state. The Parti Québécois, founded by the feisty René Lévesque in 1968, was an even more dramatic example of Québécois neo-nationalism in action for frustrated Franco-Manitobans, a few of whom even chose to join the PQ while others encouraged it from afar. Trudeau's election as prime minister, also in 1968, followed by the election of the New Democratic Party government of Edward Schreyer in Manitoba in1969, fuelled the rising expectations of many Franco-Manitobans, encouraging them to believe that positive developments would be forthcoming if they worked together.

By the mid-1960s increasing numbers of urbanized middle-class Franco-Manitobans were dissatisfied with the lack of French language schools for their children and the overly cautious approach of the traditional Catholic elites of the province, who dominated the AÉCFM. These leaders were concerned with maintaining a good rapport with Manitoba's dominant English-speaking community and with preserving and expanding their hard-won Catholic educational system – shared by Catholics of various ethnic origins and languages – rather than promoting the development of a new, largely public, French language system.[25] The long period of their organized yet largely passive resistance was over; the ideology of clerical nationalism – centred on the fusion of culture and religion – which had forced the Franco-Manitoban community to turn inward was no longer effective. The new generation of well-educated, secular-minded leaders insisted on formulating a more comprehensive set of socioeconomic, linguistic, educational, political, and constitutional policy objectives, which had to be pursued using a far more determined style of political lobbying if wholesale assimilation of Franco-Manitobans was to be avoided. The transition to a fresh organization and new goals would prove difficult, laying bare the longstanding cleavages in Franco-Manitoban society.[26]

By 1965 the annual conferences of the AÉCFM had become tension-ridden affairs, with the "old guard" defending traditional values and the "young malcontents" demanding change. Members of the latter group – spurred on by a young Québécois separatist in exile working for Radio-Canada – founded the Association Québec-Manitoba and published scathing critiques of the traditionalists in a new bilingual weekly, the Saint-Boniface *Courier*. Beginning in June 1967, a full-time social animator paid by the federal government organized a seminar for a group of "representative" Franco-Manitobans who quickly agreed upon the need for a comprehensive social animation program for the entire community. To achieve their goal, they believed they needed a modern, secular provincial organization with a new leadership. Supported by the AÉCFM, which provided funding and helped secure government grants, they established a commission in early December 1967 to organize a process of reflection and open discussions that would convince Franco-Manitobans that it was time for change. The commission decided to sponsor the Rallye du Manitoba français, which was held 7–9 June 1968 in Winnipeg and attended by some 300 Franco-Manitobans.[27]

To the chagrin of the inexperienced militants, who wrongly assumed that the majority of the delegates would see things their way, the traditionalist took control of the process by making sure that the committee that was established to create a new organization would be expanded from ten to fifteen members, five of whom were on the AÉCFM executive and ten of whom would be chosen at large. The militants who had organized the Rallye were frozen out of the process.[28] In December, at a Congrès-Rallye attended by twice as many Franco-Manitobans as the first, the Société franco-manitobaine was formed. Its executive represented all sectors and regions of the Franco-Manitoban community. Once again, it was not the full "revolution" desired by the young generation, because five members of the executive, including the president, had belonged to the earlier organization. Nevertheless, the SFM did mark a departure, since its president, Maurice Gauthier, understood all too well the urgent need to broaden the scope and increase the pace of political lobbying efforts.[29]

In fact, renewal was already underway before the SFM was formally established. In October 1968, shortly after Trudeau was elected, AÉCFM leaders presented him with a lengthy and provocative brief depicting the intolerable situation of their community. They demanded immediate action by the Canadian government to help ameliorate the injustices and sociolinguistic damage being inflicted by an intolerant majority society bent on assimilating Franco-Manitobans. The brief declared:

Pour les Franco-manitobains, l'unité national se traduit dans les faits par l'existence d'îlots francophones reconnus avec un "modus-vivendi", non pas un "modus moriendi"; avec ses écoles publiques où la langue française est la langue d'enseignement; avec ses tribunaux sans interprête; avec ses conseils municipaux et ses commissions scolaires où le droit d'employer la langue française comme langue de travail est reconnu; avec tous les outils culturels essentieles à sa vie et avec les mêmes droits pour les minorités de langue anglaise. Et tout cela garantit par la participation fédérale et par ses octrois.[30]

The brief concluded with a series of concrete proposals that, if implemented with the help of the federal government, would allow Franco-Manitobans to participate as equals in the Just Society promised by Trudeau during the election. Six full-time social animators were needed, along with a permanent secretariat for gathering information, doing research, and preparing documentation. It was urgent that

Franco-Manitobans obtain a provincial cultural centre so that cultural festivals and plays, either home grown or from Quebec, could be presented regularly. Radio-Canada television and radio had to make room for more French Canadian programming, preferably with some production undertaken in Manitoba. Federal funds for the newspaper *La Liberté* were essential if it was to survive, since the Oblate Order could no longer afford to fund it. Student exchanges with Franco-Quebecers were necessary to help re-establish links between the two communities. The Collège de Saint-Boniface required federal funding to enable it to develop into an autonomous post-secondary institution capable of educating the fully bilingual Canadians so necessary to the Canadian government. Finally, the AÉCFM supported the entrenchment of a Charter of Rights and Freedoms in the Constitution.[31] The ambitious program reflected the remarkable re-awakening and determination of the younger generation of Franco-Manitobans.

Secretary of State Gérard Pelletier addressed the December Congrès-Rallye and assured Franco-Manitobans that the Canadian government was sympathetic to their cause and would do whatever was necessary within reason to help remedy their problems. "Nous sommes venus," he declared, "pour vous dire que nous admirons votre détermination à demeurer francophones, qu'en cela vous avez aidé le Canada tout entier et que celui-ci aujourd'hui vous retourne son aide en vous donnant les moyens de ne plus penser à survivre mais a vous épanouir dans les cadres francophones et canadiens. Car c'est de vous, en dernière analyze, que dépend l'issue de cette entreprise commune." The nascent SFM received funds from the Secretary of State to pursue social animation or – as it came to be called – community development. However, a considerable number of Franco-Manitobans – rural, Catholic and conservative – did not respond favourably to the intervention of what they considered to be urban agitators, anti-clericals, and separatists. Under pressure, Ottawa cut the program in 1971. The SFM managed nonetheless to attract considerable attention in media and government circles, to advance the cause of French language education through its contacts with the NDP provincial government, and eventually to gain the respect of the community on whose behalf its leaders and administrators were lobbying.[32]

Franco-Albertans: The Invisible Community

The Franco-Albertan community is neither as old nor as established as the Franco-Manitoban, since most French Canadians and French-speaking settlers from France, Belgium, Germany, Britain, and Switzerland arrived after 1880. The majority settled in farming communities northeast and northwest of Edmonton and, later, in the Peace River region.[33] Despite attempts by Henri Bourassa and western Catholic Church leaders, Alberta Catholics did not obtain the constitutional right to publicly funded separate schools when the province was created in 1905. Francophone Catholics were compelled to send their children to public schools or to pay for Catholic parish schools and colleges. Certain concessions were made for the teaching of French and limited Catholic instruction after hours, but the schools were administered by English language school boards under the supervision of the Minister of Education.

Franco-Albertans fared reasonably well until the Great Depression, which put tremendous strains on the farming families. In 1936, they lost their parish-based schools – which relied on the Catholic Church's diminishing financial and personnel resources – when the government created regional school units. The influx of immigrants from Europe and the decline in the number of French-Canadian settlers from Quebec after World War II created new challenges. Franco-Albertans came to be perceived as being among the many ethnocultural minorities that needed to be assimilated into the English-speaking society of Alberta.[34] By the early 1960s, Franco-Albertans were experiencing a greater degree of assimilation than their compatriots in Manitoba. In 1961 Alberta was home to nearly 83,000 citizens of French ethnic origin – compared to just 56,000 in 1951 – accounting for 6.3 per cent of the population – 6 per cent in 1951. But only 42,000 of them, 3.2 percent of the population, claimed French as their maternal language in 1961, down from 3.6 per cent in 1951.[35]

In 1925, a conference of some 400 delegates from French Canadian parishes across the province met in Edmonton to discuss ways of preserving a united, strong Catholic and French national entity in Alberta. The Association canadienne-française de l'Alberta was founded the following year. Its primary goal was to obtain French language education for Franco-Albertan children. It also undertook campaigns to establish a francophone newspaper and radio station and to improve the standard of living of Franco-Albertans by promoting economic, cultural, and community development. In 1928, assisted by the Oblate Order, the ACFA founded the newspaper *La Survivance*, which kept the dispersed rural communities informed of events, local to national, affecting their lives. But the ACFA had to use English language radio stations to air French programs until 1949, when – after a long political struggle – a French language radio station, CHFA, came into being. The ACFA also encouraged the development of *caisses populaires*, savings banks, and agricultural cooperatives throughout the rural communities.[36]

The ACFA's administrative centre in Edmonton was the jumping-off point to the Franco-Albertan communities northeast and northwest of the city. In 1965, the organization changed its constitution, creating a more centralized structure based on regional offices rather than parish locals. The revised constitution established a general council and an executive committee, but many Franco-Albertans still considered the ACFA too elitist and unresponsive to their needs. In response to the criticism, the leadership decided to hold the annual convention in rotation in different communities to better inform their constituents and mobilize support for their initiatives.

The ACFA's most important responsibility was to monitor all educational developments in schools, school boards, and the ministry of education. It sent visitors into the schools to evaluate the quality of French language teaching and teachers and provided assistance to the Association des éducateurs bilingues de l'Alberta, which fostered improvements in teaching qualifications and administered annual French language testing. It also undertook endless lobbying of Alberta politicians and bureaucrats to obtain enhanced education in French for Franco-Albertan children.[37]

During the mid-1960s, the ACFA membership passed resolutions at the annual conferences on a range of improvements to the teaching of French, including more qualified teachers and courses on French literature. The resolutions passed in 1965 and 1967 called on the leadership to lobby hard for an amendment to the Education Act that would allow the use of French as a language of instruction for subjects other than French and religion. In 1968, the ACFA was successful in getting the government to pass an amendment permitting French language instruction during 50 per cent of the school day. The growing number of bilingual schools open to all Alberta children seemed to satisfy most rural Franco-Albertan parents; however, it merely served to raise the expectations of urban, middle-class Franco-Albertans. By the mid 1970s, the latter were urging the ACFA to push for homogenous French language schools, on the grounds that the bilingual schools hastened assimilation. The ACFA responded with a degree of ambivalence: it actively assisted in the expansion of the bilingual school system while lobbying for an increase in the percentage of teaching in French to include all subjects except English. In 1976, the province responded by passing an amendment to the Education Act that permitted an increase in teaching in French to 80 per cent of all subjects, except English. This development was celebrated during the fiftieth

anniversary conference held by the ACFA the same year. The conference's theme was education, and its mandate was to create a three-year
plan of action on education for Franco-Albertans. The delegates
passed resolutions calling for the recognition in law of the right to
French language education in Alberta, and defined bilingual schools
as those in which all subjects, except English and English literature,
were taught in French.[38] Yet by this time a vocal group, some of them
recent arrivals from Quebec, had started to criticize the bilingual and
immersion programs and to campaign for homogeneous French language schools and school boards.

New Brunswick's Acadians: A Model of Renewal

New Brunswick's Acadian community served as a model for the revitalization of Canada's francophone minority communities. Its rebirth
was sparked by the 200th anniversary of the *Grand dérangement* of 1755
and accelerated by the Quiet Revolution.[39] Unlike the marginalized
Acadian communities of the other Maritime provinces, New
Brunswick's Acadians were able to respond to the challenges associated with the urbanization and industrialization that followed the
Great Depression from a strong demographic and institutional base.
By 1961, New Brunswick's 232,000 Acadians constituted almost 40 per
cent of the provincial population, a substantial increase from 164,000
– about 36 percent – in 1941. The rate of assimilation, as calculated by
French mother tongue – 157,862 in 1941 and 210,530 in 1961 – had
increased slightly, but not at the alarming rates experienced by francophone minority communities in Ontario and the western provinces.[40]

Because New Brunswick's Acadians constituted large minorities and,
in some cases, majorities in many counties of three of the province's
four main regions, they were able to elect an Acadian Liberal, Louis
Robichaud, as premier in 1960. His government ushered in an
"Acadian Quiet Revolution" by helping Acadian communities achieve
a certain level of secular local governance through more centralized
system of publicly funded regional school boards, hospital boards,
social service agencies, and reorganized municipalities. Highly significant was its creation of more homogeneous French language schools,
including École Vanier, a secondary school in Moncton. These crucial
reforms were intended to improve educational and occupational
opportunities for all New Brunswick citizens, but the greatly disadvantaged Acadians had the most to gain. Further impetus for the modernization of their communities came from the creation of the state-
funded Université de Moncton in 1963 out of the amalgamation of
several regional religious institutions. Its faculties and professional

schools were soon graduating secular, middle-class, urban Acadians qualified in a wide range of professions and determined to make their mark. Following its re-election in 1967, Robichaud's government passed the Loi sur les langues officielles du Nouveau-Brunswick in 1969, which made English and French the two official languages of the province, guaranteed bilingualism in the Legislative Assembly, and called upon the government to institute bilingualism throughout the province, beginning with education, the public service, and the justice system. Many English-speaking New Brunswickers opposed this limited conception of individual bilingualism and worked with the Conservative Party of Richard Hatfield to bring about the defeat of Robichaud's Liberals in 1970.[41]

Throughout the 1960s and 1970s, as increasing numbers of undereducated Acadians migrated from their isolated towns and villages into Moncton, Saint John, and Fredericton, their assimilation rate rose dramatically. The Société Nationale de l'Assomption, founded in 1881 and renamed the Société Nationale des Acadiens in 1957, had been created to defend the interests of Acadians in all three Maritime provinces. For nearly a century it had advanced their cause, yet it seemed impervious to the grim realities facing Acadians left behind in their resource-based communities in the northeast and northwest regions of New Brunswick and the myriad problems confronting undereducated urbanized Acadians. By the mid-1960s, the SNA's effectiveness was being questioned by younger New Brunswick Acadians with heightened expectations. They considered the SNA elitist, unrepresentative, and overly conservative in its methods and goals, and argued that it was imperative to give themselves a strong provincial organization. It took several meetings, but in 1972 the Société des Acadiens et Acadiennes du Nouveau Brunswick was established to advance their interests and define new approaches to the socioeconomic, linguistic, and cultural problems facing their diverse and dispersed communities.[42]

Initially, Hatfield gained the support of some of the Acadian leadership in the late 1960s because the Conservatives were committed to official bilingualism. These leaders believed that their backing would encourage the Hatfield government to expand on the gains of the Robichaud era. While only three Acadian MLAs were elected in the 1970s, all three were named to the Cabinet. Furthermore, Hatfield – going against the wishes of a great many English-speaking Conservatives – sent a strong signal to Acadians by refusing to rescind Robichaud's controversial Loi sur les langues officielles. The SAANB and its leaders campaigned vigorously for regional economic development, lobbying hard to convince the Conservatives to extend bilingual services to all departments and agencies of government and to have the booming unilingual municipality of Moncton, which was attracting large numbers of Acadians, declare itself officially bilingual. In response to their call for a francophone board of education, the ministry of education established a homogeneous French language school board in Moncton. Following its re-election in 1974, the Hatfield government created two autonomous language divisions in the ministry of education and appointed a new minister favourable to educational duality and committed to transforming all schools and boards from bilingual to homogeneous French language entities. New Brunswick's Acadians did not have to wait for s. 23 of the Charter to win full school governance, including a separate department of education within the ministry.[43]

Thanks to the intensive political activism of the Acadian community as expressed through the SAANB, the militant Parti acadien founded in 1972, and increased participation in the Conservative Party and government, New Brunswick's Acadians also achieved legislative recognition for their collective rights. The New Brunswick Legislative Assembly passed Bill 88, An Act Recognizing the Equality of the Two Official Linguistic Communities in New Brunswick, in a unanimous vote on 17 July 1981.[44] The Acadian community's demographic weight gave it greater political influence than that of other francophone minority groups. As a result, the implementation of s. 23 rights was achieved without the need for prolonged political and judicial battles. The SAANB and its victories on the linguistic and education fronts served as models and incentives for Canada's other francophone minority communities and organizations, especially the ACFO, ACFA, and SFM. Its experienced leaders were instrumental in establishing a national federation of provincial associations in the mid-1970s, serving as prominent and outspoken members of its general council and executive and helping it and other provincial organizations formulate approaches on school governance and related constitutional matters.[45] The Acadian community faced a higher order of challenges than francophone minority communities elsewhere in Canada, yet its successes played an important symbolic role in the renewal of French Canada.

THE VICTORIA CHARTER, 1971

The selection of Pierre Trudeau as leader of the Liberal Party and his subsequent election victory raised the hopes of francophone minority communities and catapulted their leaders into action. Despite some harsh exchanges over fundamental policy differences, francophones were well served by and remained loyal to Trudeau's government, largely because they appreciated his visceral commitment to helping them overcome the discrimination and hardships they had experienced since Confederation. Trudeau had entered federal politics to work against the rising tide of separatism in Quebec. He understood and was wary of the emotional and intellectual attraction of nationalism and an independent nation-state for ambitious young educated middle-class Quebec francophones. In the belief that it constituted the most serious threat to Canada since its inception in 1867, he responded by creating a more liberal, more just, and more democratic nation-state. Trudeau's Canada was going to be an unabashedly bilingual, multicultural, and pluralistic federation in which all French Canadians and Acadians would feel completely at home and could pursue both individual self-fulfilment and collective survival and renewal.[46]

Trudeau responded positively to many of the recommendations of the Royal Commission on Bilingualism and Biculturalism, especially those dealing with education rights for Canada's two linguistic minorities. The Canadian government, acting quickly to remedy matters within its own jurisdiction, passed the Official Languages Act,1969, a significant milestone in language policy. The Act proclaimed English and French "the official languages of Canada for all purposes of the Parliament and Government of Canada" and granted members of both linguistic communities the right to communicate with and receive services from every federal department, agency, judicial and quasi-judicial body, and Crown corporation in their maternal language. It also created a Commissioner of Official Languages, to ensure the "recognition of the status of each of the official languages" and monitor compliance with the legislation in all branches of the national government and Parliament.[47]

Early in 1968, pressured by the premiers of Quebec and Ontario, who wanted more powers, Prime Minister Lester Pearson had reluctantly set in motion Canada's first mega-constitutional renewal process, one dominated by bureaucrats, ministers, and, in the final stage, by the premiers and the newly elected Prime Minister Trudeau. In the lead-up to the Federal-Provincial Conference on the Constitution in February 1968, the Pearson government issued a policy statement, *Federalism for the Future*, which focused not on Quebec's demands for special status but rather on how to develop a broader and deeper sense of Canadian community.[48] Observant Canadians already realized Trudeau's imprint on the federal response to Quebec's constitutional demands. Once the negotiations got underway, Trudeau attempted to put education rights for the official language minorities on the agenda. In his 1969 white paper *The Constitution and the People of Canada*, Trudeau explained that his government proposed to expand language guarantees already found in s. 133 of the British North America Act and have them entrenched in a Charter of Rights and Freedoms:

The linguistic rights proposed for the charter of human rights would extend to varying degrees into all branches of the Government of Canada, into all provincial legislatures and into the executive and judicial branches of provincial governments in provinces where there are substantial numbers of persons of the official language minority or where the province so decides. A very important innovation is the guarantee of the right to choose in which official language children are to be educated, in areas where sufficient numbers choose a particular language to justify the provision of the necessary facilities. These proposed linguistic rights are designed to implement, as far as is possible in a charter of individual rights, the recommendations in Book I of the *Report of the Royal Commission on Bilingualism and Biculturalism.*[49]

Following the guidelines set out in the government's 1968 policy paper *A Canadian Charter of Human Rights*, Trudeau spelled out the elements of a comprehensive charter of fundamental rights. On the matter of language guarantees, the proposed sections 4 (a), (b), (c), and (d) would entrench official bilingualism in both Houses of Parliament and the legislatures of all the provinces; the records, journals, and enactments of the Parliament of Canada; the legislatures of New Brunswick, Ontario, and Quebec; and the legislatures of any province whose official minority exceeded 10 per cent of the population or that declared itself officially bilingual. The same provisions would apply to judicial and quasi-judicial bodies, superior courts, and the head office of every department and agency of all the governments just mentioned. Trudeau noted that "the Royal Commission recommended that bilingual services also be provided by local governments in bilingual districts. It seemed preferable to leave this matter for legislative action in each province."[50] The same approach would be adopted in dealing with education rights for the official language minorities:

4 (e) the right of the individual to have English or French as his main language of instruction in publicly supported schools in areas where the language of instruction of his choice is the language of instruction of choice of a sufficient number of persons to justify the provision of the necessary facilities.[51]

During the federal-provincial conferences of June 1969 and September 1970, most provinces, including Quebec, expressed a strong reluctance to support Trudeau's proposed Charter unconditionally. Premier Robert Bourassa, backed by Premier John Robarts of Ontario, considered the redistribution of powers far more urgent.[52] At the third working session of the Constitutional Conference of 8–9 February 1971, Quebec "lodged a general reservation" about the clause on educational rights for members of linguistic minorities and tied its approval for the amending formula to greater jurisdictional control via legislative paramountcy over social policy.

Stymied, the Trudeau government, eager to achieve some level of progress, proposed a modest constitutional reform package comprising patriation, an amending formula, and a bare bones charter that included an opting-in clause for provinces under s. 133 but did not cover education rights for Canada's official language minorities. Education was an exclusive provincial responsibility, and Trudeau felt that federal-provincial tensions would be heightened at a time when his government was working hard to reach an agreement. After bargaining in Victoria on 14–16 June 1971, Ottawa and the provinces agreed to place before their legislatures a Canadian Constitutional Charter for approval or rejection prior to 28 June 1971. The Victoria Charter, the product of three years of protracted and difficult negotiations, contained a very limited Charter of Rights and Freedoms, but also a remarkable extension of the official language concept to seven legislatures and to the statutes and courts of Quebec, New Brunswick, and Newfoundland. Finally, there was an amending formula based on four regions: Atlantic Canada, Quebec, Ontario, and the western provinces.

But Canadians and their provincial governments were not yet prepared to accept a comprehensive charter; Trudeau would have to wait until the majority were behind him. Another reason for which the Victoria Charter was never ratified was that Bourassa refused to do so for fear of alienating the increasingly strident nationalist movement, which was well entrenched both within and outside of his Liberal caucus and party, and even more inside the senior echelon of the rapidly expanding bureaucracy.[53] Indeed, it was revealed many years later that Bourassa's influential Minister of Social Affairs, Claude Castonguay, had threatened to resign if Quebec proceeded with ratification.[54]

After the demise of the Victoria Charter, the Trudeau government set up a Special Joint Committee of the Senate and the House of Commons to formulate recommendations for comprehensive constitutional reform. It was the first committee to open the process of constitutional renewal to input from individuals and organizations. The response was overwhelming. The three western francophone organizations took the opportunity to express their concerns about their

continued survival as viable communities and to offer numerous recommendations.[55] On the matter of language rights, the report of the
Molgat-MacGuigan Committee wholeheartedly endorsed Article 10 of
the Victoria Charter, which had called for the entrenchment of
English and French as the official languages of Canada.

In response to the desperate situation confronting the francophone
minority communities, the report went considerably further than the
Victoria Charter. Indeed, the committee members recommended
replacing s. 133 with "an expanded guarantee of the two languages,
which would involve all the provinces and thus render moot the question of how many provinces would have to consent to amend the
present section 133." They reasoned that the Official Languages Act,
1969 had "psychologically prepared the country for a constitutional
recognition of English and French as the two official languages of
Canada." Furthermore, they believed that if the concept of two official
languages was going to be more than "an empty symbol ... it must in
some way touch Provincial as well as Federal institutions." Yet the
intense debate surrounding the Victoria Charter made it clear to the
committee members that the three westernmost provinces could not
accept such a proposal.[56] Consequently, the Molgat-MacGuigan Committee's report recommended entrenching French and English as the
two official languages of Canada, with these rights to be extended to
the legislatures and territorial councils, judicial and quasi-judicial
federal bodies and provincial courts, federal departments and agencies, and provincial department and agency head offices only in New
Brunswick, Ontario, Quebec, Yukon, and the Northwest Territories.
Nevertheless, the door was kept ajar for the western provinces to come
on side at the opportune time. All these official language provisions
would come into effect in any province "where each language is the
mother tongue of ten per cent of the population," or whenever a legislature declared English and French the official languages of the
province.[57]

Many of the submissions to the committee from anglophone organizations in Quebec and francophone organizations in the remaining
provinces focused on the question of language of instruction. The
committee, regretting "the absence of any statement in the Charter
with respect to the language of education," endorsed the principle of
freedom of choice spelled out at the Constitutional Conference of
February 1971. Its members were fully aware of the theoretical and
practical problems that the principle of freedom of choice posed for
the Quebec government of Robert Bourassa and stated that they
favoured the "general objective of making French the working language in Quebec." Nevertheless, the Molgat-McGuigan Committee

concluded that "the right of parents to choose their children's education is a basic human right which no government can encroach upon."[58] For the first time, a joint committee of Parliament recommended that "the Constitution should recognize parents' rights to have English or French provided as their child's main language of instruction in publicly supported schools in areas where the language of their choice is chosen by a sufficient number of persons to justify the provision of the necessary facilities."[59] The demarcation lines for the linguistic and education battles of the 1970s and 1980s were being drawn. The polarization would have enormous influence on the renewed mega-constitutional negotiations that got underway in the late 1970s.

Early in that decade, the language of instruction for Canada's official linguistic minority communities once again become a hot political issue. In the aftermath of the Saint Leonard crisis in Montreal North, in 1969 Premier J.J. Bertrand's government had passed Bill 63, which guaranteed freedom of choice in the language of schooling for Quebec children. Irate Québécois nationalists and separatists demanded the abolition of Bill 63 and its replacement by coercive language legislation compelling all immigrant parents to enroll their children in French language schools, making French the working language in the public and para-public sectors, and creating a whole range of policy measures that would expand the use of French in the private sector. To appease his vociferous critics and buy some time, Bertrand created the Commission d'enquête sur la situation de la langue française et sur les droits linguistiques, presided over by Jean-Denis Gendron, with the mandate to study the thorny issue of French as the working language of Quebec.[60]

The Gendron Commission produced a two-volume report in 1972. Premier Bourassa relied upon its analysis, if not its recommendations, in implementing highly controversial language legislation in 1974. Bill 22 recognized French as the only official language of Quebec and set out language policy in five sectors: public administration, corporations and the professions, the work world, the business community, and education. It instituted a complicated system of bureaucratic language tests for determining which immigrant children had to attend French language schools. Moreover, while recognizing French as the official language of Quebec, in most sectors the bill allowed "la possibilité d'un bilinguisme de facto capable d'occulter le caractère officiel ou prioritaire du français."[61] Nationalists and separatists were even more infuriated than in 1969; they asserted that the legislation was fatally flawed and had to be made more coercive. Bill 22 quickly alienated not only francophones but also anglophones and allophones, bringing about the defeat of Robert Bourassa's crisis-ridden Liberal government in November 1976 at the hands of René Lévesque's separatist Parti Québécois. Lévesque's promise to put off the controversial matter of secession to a referendum enabled a majority of disenchanted Quebec francophones to switch to the Parti Québécois. This unforeseen development precipitated a dramatic shift in the planning and actions of the Trudeau government intended to preserve the political integrity of the federation. Francophone minority community leaders, close observers of all these events, responded by building a national organization that could help them participate more directly in the defence of their constituents' interests.

THE FÉDÉRATION: CONSTRUCTING A PAN-CANADIAN FRANCOPHONE MINORITY ORGANIZATION AND IDENTITY

The revitalization of the provincial francophone organizations in the 1960s and early 1970s combined with the developments just discussed, the federal government's rejection of biculturalism with its endorsement of multiculturalism in 1971, and its decision to rationalize funding for the official language minority communities by 1973 to make provincial francophone minority leaders keenly aware that events well beyond their borders could have a significant effect on their communities' future. It was time to get engaged at the national level, to create a network of pan-Canadian organizations to replace the traditional one based on the Catholic Church in Quebec. Francophone minority organizations, provincial and national, would increasingly look to the Canadian government for moral, political, and financial support.[62] Still, discussions among the nine provincial organizations proved considerably more arduous and protracted than many had anticipated. Finally, agreement was reached in 1975 as to the structure and mandate of the Fédération des Francophones Hors Québec. The Fédération held its founding convention the following year. In June 1991, the Fédération was renamed the Fédération des communautés francophones et acadiennes du Canada, to better reflect its activities and to recognize the divergence in identity between Franco-Québécois and other francophone Canadians.[63] By this time, it consisted of nine provincial and two territorial organizations as well as four national associations representing francophone youth, women, media, and legal groups.

The Fédération's annual General Assembly determined the principles, priorities, orientation, and statutes of the organization. But it was the Conseil national des présidents et présidentes, in conjunction with a five-person elected executive, that oversaw its daily operations. The Fédération's mandate was primarily political lobbying on behalf of the rights and interests of francophone minority communities. It considered its actions to be legitimized by the Official Languages Act and the Charter of Rights and Freedoms, and was determined to see that Charter rights were implemented fully and fairly. It also saw its role as helping its provincial affiliates acquire the social, cultural, economic, and educational infrastructure essential to the healthy development of francophone minority communities.[64]

During the first two decades of its existence the Fédération played a very active role in both national and provincial affairs. On behalf of the provincial organizations, it lobbied aggressively during the late 1970s and throughout the 1980s for improvements in the application of the Official Languages Act and for its extension to all Crown corporations and agencies and federal government-sponsored activities such as national sports teams and competitions. It supported Franco-Ontarians and New Brunswick's Acadians in their struggle to have their provinces declared officially bilingual. It worked successfully for the entrenchment of education rights for linguistic minority communities in the Constitution Act, 1982, then assisted each of its provincial affiliates in their prolonged struggles for the implementation of those rights. The Fédération also made strenuous efforts to negotiate a comprehensive strategic plan for the cultural, social, and economic development of francophone minority communities with the Secretary of State. It worked with federal politicians, bureaucrats, Radio-Canada, and the Caplan-Sauvageau Committee to improve French language radio and television programming by and for those communities. Finally, after considerable hesitation, it lobbied vigorously for the ill-fated Meech Lake Accord, then helped refine the far more comprehensive but no more successful Charlottetown Accord of August 1992. Throughout this period, its representatives participated in the various summits held under the auspices of the expanding commonwealth of francophone nations. The Fédération's limited financial and human resources were always spread too thin, but these constraints were offset by the dedication and determination of its provincial, territorial, and national organizations.

The Fédération and the Official Languages Act

By the mid-1970s, innumerable problems with the implementation of the Official Languages Act were prompting criticism from many quarters. Some English-speaking Canadians claimed that the Trudeau government was imposing universal bilingualism on the country by forcing Canadians to read French on their cereal boxes. On a more serious level, many quite rightly worried about a loss of employment opportunities in the federal bureaucracy. Nationalists and separatists denounced official bilingualism as a plot to convince francophone Quebecers that Ottawa – rather than a powerful interventionist provincial government or an independent Quebec – could best guarantee their rights and promote their survival as a collectivity. More importantly, francophone minority community organizations, for whose constituents the policy was intended, began to recognize the limitations of the Official Languages Act and its various programs.

The central target of these organizations was Ottawa's Bilingualism in Education Programme, implemented in Ontario in 1970 and subsequently extended to other provinces. Ottawa hoped to soften the growing criticism of the Official Languages Act by providing financial assistance to provincial governments that agreed to establish or expand French language education for francophone minority communities. The Quebec government availed itself of this financial aid to fund the teaching of second languages: English to francophones and French to anglophones and allophones. Between 1970 and 1977, Ottawa contributed nearly $500 million to promote second language education at all three levels of schooling in the provinces: $275 million to Quebec and $178 million to the nine other provinces. Several special projects under the aegis of the Programme were funded under cost-sharing agreements with the provinces. From 1973 to 1977, Ottawa disbursed $7 million to English language provinces for special projects in support of minority French language education. It gave Quebec $5.5 million, of which $765,000 was for French language special projects in English language communities, while the bulk went to funding English language special projects in French language schools.[65] The core Bilingualism in Education Programme, funded through the Secretary of State and administered by the provinces, encountered considerable opposition – if not downright hostility – from local and regional school boards and municipal governments. In some cases, while provincial governments were only too eager to accept federal funding for the various programs, school boards and municipalities refused to implement them.[66] Some provinces, including Quebec, absorbed the hundreds of millions of dollars into their consolidated revenues, using the rationale that these funds compensated for their spending on their expensive French language, or in Quebec's case English language, systems of education.[67]

Pushing the Trudeau government to rethink the core Bilingualism in Education Programme were the provincial francophone organizations and the newly created Fédération. Eager to establish its credibility as an effective lobbying agency, the Fédération focused much of its time and resources on demonstrating the limitations of both the Official Languages Act and the Programme.[68] Its president, Donatien Gaudet, concerned about the backlash against francophone minority communities resulting from the implementation of institutional bilingualism in the federal bureaucracy and in education, asked the prime minister to involve the francophone organizations in the government's re-evaluation of language policies and programs. Disillusioned with the lack of cooperation from the outgoing Secretary of State, in September 1976 Gaudet pleaded for a meeting with Trudeau.[69] But the Fédération was encouraged instead to open a dialogue with the new Secretary of State, John Roberts.

Rebuffed, yet inspired by the election of the Parti Québécois in November 1976, the Fédération and its affiliates decided to attract the Trudeau government's attention by publishing the results of their comprehensive evaluation of the demographic, socioeconomic, cultural, and political situation of the francophone minority communities across Canada. The extensive 1977 report, entitled *Les héritiers de Lord Durham*, constituted a damning indictment of past and present federal and provincial government policies and programs, respecting the rapidly advancing assimilation of those communities. The introductory Manifesto stated, in part:

Nous avons de formidables défis à relever. Aujourd'hui nous nous retrouvons devant des droits illusoires. Les écoles sont des foyers d'assimilation. Les communications nous échappent. Notre âme collective nous glisse entre les doigts. Enfin, nous devons pénétrer dans la sphère économique pour quitter l'univers morne d'un folklore désuet ... Les communautés francophones hors Québec doivent bien reconnaître qu'elles sont victimes d'un mirage juridique.[70]

In many respects, the report adopted the methodology used so effectively by the Royal Commission on Bilingualism and Biculturalism in its analysis of the socioeconomic and political plight of Quebec's francophone majority vis-à-vis the province's powerful Anglo-Canadian minority.

In fact, the Official Languages Act had not induced a single province to adopt French as an official language of its legislature or its courts. While New Brunswick was making valiant efforts in this direction, the only thing preventing the Quebec government from abolishing official bilingualism in the National Assembly and the courts was s. 133 of the British North America Act. The lack of official recognition of the French language at the provincial level meant that, despite their contribution to their respective provinces, the francophone minority communities perceived themselves as marginalized groups requiring the intervention of the federal government in areas of provincial jurisdiction.[71]

This was especially the case in the field of education, where francophones certainly did not enjoy equality of opportunity with their English-speaking neighbours. Only three provinces – Manitoba, Ontario, and New Brunswick – granted the right to instruction in the French language, under certain conditions and with very limited administrative structures. Meanwhile, in Alberta, Saskatchewan, Prince Edward Island, and Nova Scotia, the ministers of education had discretionary powers to allow instruction in the French language. Two provinces, British Columbia and Newfoundland, made no provisions for instruction in French. In fact, the existing systems of bilingual, mixed, and immersion schools in the various provinces "demeurent souvent le foyer privilégié de l'assimilation. Souvent la langue d'administration de l'école est l'anglais, les élèves anglophones et francophones se côtoient ou partagent la même classe, les matières enseignées en français s'appuient sur des manuels anglais, le personnel enseignant francophone s'adresse parfois aux enfants en anglais, etc."[72] Most frustrating for francophone parents was the fact that they did not possess governance over school boards, which was imperative if they hoped to transform assimilationist schools into true instruments of cultural survival and development.[73]

At the heart of *Les héritiers de Lord Durham* was a scathing critique of the manner in which the Official Languages Act was being implemented. The Fédération contended, with some justification, that the economic and political consequences of the federal government's implementation of institutional bilingualism were detrimental to the future of the francophone communities for whom the Act was in large measure intended.[74] Federal rejection of a policy of official biculturalism in favour of multiculturalism meant that substantial time, energy, and monies were being wasted on ineffective second language training directed at anglophone civil servants. Furthermore, most of the funds dispersed under the Bilingualism in Education Programme were being absorbed by rapidly expanding core French and French immersion programs for English-speaking children. In the period 1970–77, a phenomenal $1.4 billion was spent on official languages, 40 per cent on institutional bilingualism and 50 per cent by the Secretary of State for the expansion of minority and second language education programs. Well over half of the latter expenditures went to the province of Quebec. Since these funds were transferred directly to the provinces, then to the school boards, the francophone minority communities had no input into how they were spent.

Fédération president Donatien Gaudet sent the prime minister a copy of *Les héritiers de Lord Durham* on 13 April 1977. Once again he asked Trudeau for a meeting, this time to discuss the report's analysis and recommendations. When no response was forthcoming, the Fédération held a press conference on 25 April and issued an open letter to the prime minister and all MPs denouncing their silence. Intensive lobbying by francophone MPs and in the media finally produced the desired result: Trudeau invited the Fédération's executive to meet with him and some of his ministers on 31 May.[75]

Determined to make the most of this opportunity, Gaudet evaluated options and developed a strategy. He was convinced that the meeting had become a reality only because the Fédération had at long last adopted a clear and forceful message capable of attracting public support. Given the election of the Parti Québécois with its projected referendum on Quebec's place within Confederation and Trudeau's decision to re-open constitutional negotiations, the timing of the Fédération's non-partisan but aggressive strategy was considered excellent. By letting Ottawa know that it was prepared to meet and negotiate with Premier René Lévesque, the Fédération was making it clear that it was not merely Ottawa's pawn in the larger political/constitutional struggle. The Fédération was openly critical of the constitutional status quo, especially of the Secretary of State's misguided language programs, which provided only meagre assistance to the threatened francophone minority communities. In stating that these communities were no longer "des fédéralistes sans conditions," the Fédération was giving notice that it would no longer countenance Ottawa's evasive answers or excuses for inaction. It was imperative that Trudeau back up his "act of faith" in the francophone minority communities by transferring a meaningful percentage of the funds allocated to institutional bilingualism to underwrite their moral, social, economic, and cultural development.[76]

In anticipation of the meeting, Director General Hubert Gauthier informed Trudeau of the Fédération's two main objectives. The first was a comprehensive political Quiet Revolution by and for the francophone minority communities. The second was a commitment by the federal government to a "politique globale, précise, cohérente, et définitive de développement des communautés de langue et de culture françaises." The five basic elements of this global policy were

• control of the minority communities over their educational institutions

- the power to develop their own economic, social, and cultural institutions
- the extension of official bilingualism to all provinces
- the overhaul of Ottawa's system of expensive and inefficient institutional bilingualism
- the constitutional entrenchment of individual and collective rights of the official language minorities

To ensure that this long-overdue "Quiet Revolution" became a reality, the Fédération proposed the creation – with its full cooperation – of a new "mécanisme d'acceuil" within the Federal-Provincial Relations Directorate of the Privy Council rather than the despised Secretary of State.[77]

Despite its high expectations and lengthy preparations, the Fédération was quite disillusioned with the outcome of the meeting. Contrary to their request for an informal meeting with a few ministers, its leaders encountered dozens of media people, officials from the Privy Council, assistants from the PMO, and several ministers and MPs. Gauthier and Fédération president Paul Comeau expressed the view that the organization had been outmanoeuvred once again by the prime minister and his advisors. It was clear that the Fédération was not taken seriously as the representative of the francophone minority communities. Moreover, it had failed to obtain a firm commitment on its two central recommendations.[78] Following the photo opportunity, Trudeau insisted that his government had a longstanding policy for the official minorities – the Official Languages Act. He protected his Secretary of State, John Roberts, from any direct criticism. In return for the federal government's continued support, Trudeau expected all the francophone organizations to lobby their respective provincial governments for improvements and do their part in the national unity struggle. Marc Lalonde, well aware that the Fédération and some of its affiliates were flirting with the Québécois secessionists, chided its leaders for playing into René Lévesque's hands on the national unity question. At the press conference after the meeting, Trudeau also announced his government's decision – taken without consulting the Fédération – to set up an interministerial committee to report to Cabinet on *Les héritiers de Lord Durham.*[79] Despite all this, the meeting did produce two positive outcomes. John Roberts announced that the government finally realized the need for a global language and cultural policy involving all the important federal ministries and agencies. Second, the interministerial committee announced by Trudeau was formed.[80]

The Trudeau government had announced in the October 1976

Throne Speech that it would shift the emphasis of its language policy from bilingualism in the federal public service to programs serving the language needs of all Canadians, especially the young generation. To help achieve this objective, in 1977 the government prepared a statement on official languages policy entitled *A National Understanding. The Official Languages of Canada.* It provided a comprehensive overview of the nature, principles, and import of the policy and its effect on individuals and the provincial and federal governments. The prime minister stressed in the preface that language rights

have a profound effect on all aspects of the lives of Canadians: freedom of expression, the education of the young and of adults, public administration, courts of justice, parliamentary debates, the media, business relationships, communications at work, social services, cultural activities.

It is also apparent that these rights are at least as strongly affected by provincial legislation and policies as they are by federal legislation and policies, and that responsibility for dealing with them rests on all levels of government ...

In drawing attention to the role of the provinces, the government is conscious that this involves matters of provincial jurisdiction and that, moreover, practical situations vary from province to province. *I believe, however, that the government of Canada would be shirking its political and moral responsibilities if it did not, at this time, express its views as to what should be the basic language rights of all Canadians.*[81]

The statement outlined eight principles underlying the official languages policy of Canada, three of which applied to individual Canadians: that every citizen had the right to speak any language, that English and French were the official languages of Canada and had equality of status, and that voluntary bilingualism was both a personal and a national asset. Two other principles flowed from and expanded the scope of the Official Languages Act: the Act would be extended to cover all federal institutions, including Crown corporations, and the powers of the Commissioner of Official Languages would be expanded.[82]

Clearly though, the most innovative aspects of the policy statement were the three principles that impinged on provincial jurisdiction. Experience had demonstrated to the federal government that successful implementation of the official languages legislation required the active support of the provinces, which controlled crucial areas such as education, the courts, social and health services, and culture, matters that greatly influenced the lives of individuals belonging to the official minorities. The federal government could and did create programs to encourage the provinces to take initiatives in these areas. But as

Trudeau wrote in the preface to *A National Understanding*, "Strong, independent initiatives by the provincial governments are crucial, particularly if these minority groups are to be given the means to preserve and strengthen their identities."[83]

Ottawa hoped the provincial governments would be willing, in the first instance, to "recognize that the English and French languages are the official languages of Canada and have equality of status in the country."[84] Having done so, it would be relatively easy for them to accept the second principle, full education rights for children of parents belonging to linguistic minorities "wherever numbers warrant" and "subject to circumstances which may make a deferment of application necessary." The federal government, committed to the freedom of choice in education for all English- and French-speaking Canadians, was eager to discuss with the provinces "new constitutional provisions designed to enable the federal government to assume a direct constitutional responsibility, if that seems to be desirable."[85]

Finally, Ottawa hoped that the third principle, having to do with knowledge by speakers of one official language of the other one, which applied primarily to individuals, would meet with provincial approval. It looked to the provinces – spurred on by federal funding incentives – to create opportunities at all educational levels for the learning of the other official language by all students, including francophones in Quebec who wished to learn English.[86]

The official languages policy statement was clearly aimed at taking the debate beyond the limited provisions to which seven of the ten provinces had agreed at the Victoria Conference in 1971. In the view of the Trudeau government, Canada's two official languages set in a sea of diverse cultures were "both the condition and the safeguard of our continuing freedom and our unity as a country."[87] To sum up, diversity and tolerance were the hallmarks of Canadian identity.

With the government's language policy now made public, the Fédération was more determined than ever to have a say in framing any legislation or constitutional proposals that might flow from it. The organization hoped for a good working relationship with Undersecretary of Cabinet Paul Tellier, whom Trudeau had delegated to set up the interministerial committee. In a meeting with Tellier and Louis Tousignant on 8 June, Gauthier was handed a confidential document outlining the mandate and terms of reference of the new committee. Gaudet was furious with Tellier's unilateral proposal and requested that it be withdrawn immediately and reworked with the full cooperation of the Fédération. The contentious document failed to address two recommendations accepted by the prime minister: a comprehensive policy for the development of the francophone minority communities and "un nouveau mécanisme d'acceuil au sein du Conseil Privé," with formal representation from the Fédération to oversee the implementation and eventual evaluation of a mutually agreed-upon set of institutions and programs.[88]

Tellier responded by arguing that his proposed committee was action oriented and would produce a full report in less than four months. On the prime minister's instructions, its mandate was to review all existing policies within a wide range of ministries in order to update the Official Languages Act, taking into account the evolution in the conditions of the francophone minority communities as outlined in *Les héritiers de Lord Durham*. While the Fédération would not have formal representation on the committee, which was a government body, Tellier promised that the chairman, Louis Tousignant of the Privy Council Office, would be in constant communication with its representatives.[89] Tellier's letter was discussed at the Fédération's annual general meeting. The delegates responded rather naïvely by instructing Director General Gauthier to inform Tellier that the Fédération would cooperate with the interministerial committee only on the condition that the report be submitted to a Permanent Commission of the Privy Council. Further, this new body, which should include a Fédération representative, had to be fully mandated to implement the report's recommendations.[90] Following a meeting with Gauthier, Tellier indicated that he was pleased that the Fédération had agreed to cooperate with the committee, and – quite rightly – went on to note that it was impossible for the government to create the permanent commission demanded because such a mechanism would not be compatible with the assigned functions of the Privy Council. Once the committee's report was submitted to Cabinet, it would be up to the government to decide on the recommendations to accept and the most appropriate implementation procedures.[91]

Gaudet tried unsuccessfully to persuade the prime minister and members of Cabinet to accept the proposal for a permanent commission. Trudeau reminded him that the government's commitment to redressing the deplorable situation of the francophone minority communities was made very clear in his speech to the House on 5 July, in his government's recent official languages policy statement, and in the creation of the interministerial committee.[92] Following a special meeting of the administrative council of the Fédération, held in Regina in late July, Gaudet wrote to Trudeau outlining his interpretation of their meeting on 31 May, rejecting the all-too-bureaucratic interministerial committee proposal, and pleading for another meeting to put an end to the imbroglio. He reminded the prime minister that his vision of a bilingual country required not the mere

survival but rather the healthy expansion of the francophone communities. Gauthier then told Tellier that the Fédération would not be
cooperating with the interministerial committee until the matter of
the permanent commission had been settled.[93] Tellier regretted the
decision, and left the door open in case the Fédération's leaders had
a change of heart. He further assured Gauthier that the committee
would take all their demands seriously – including the permanent
commission – while Cabinet would make the final decisions and communicate the results to them.[94]

Despite a second letter in mid-August, Trudeau did not respond
until early October, when the interministerial committee's report was
about to go before Cabinet for deliberation. He indicated that he was
truly perplexed at the interpretation given by the Fédération to the
creation of the committee:

La création du comité ne constitue donc pas la réponse du Gouvernement à
vos demandes, car cette réponse est à venir. Elle viendra non pas du comité,
ni de l'un ou de l'autre des fonctionnaires de l'administration; elle viendra
du Conseil des ministres qui aura été saisi du rapport du comité. Peut-être
comprendrez-vous, dans ces circonstances, que j'aie peine à m'expliquer
pourquoi la FFHQ a refusé de participer aux travaux du comité en question et
d'y apporter la contribution unique qu'elle était en mesure de fournir.[95]

The request for an interview would be considered only after Cabinet
had formulated a new policy for the official language minority communities. Overly ambitious in its demand for a special committee
within the Privy Council, the Fédération had effectively been frozen
out of the policy-making process by senior bureaucrats and influential
ministers such as the Secretary of State.

Nevertheless, it did achieve much of what it sought. A Privy Council
document prepared for Cabinet, dated 17 October 1977, which outlined the federal government's comprehensive fifteen-point policy on
the official language minorities and provided a declaration of principles pertaining to the official languages, directly addressed all the concerns raised by the Fédération. It proposed creating a separate bureaucratic structure within the Secretary of State devoted exclusively to the
official language minorities outside the federal government. It recommended making the interministerial committee a permanent body,
with a broad mandate to oversee the application of all the programs
related to the policy statement, to maintain contact with official language minority organizations, and to prepare reports for the Secretary
of State and special memoranda for consideration by Cabinet. Surprisingly, the document also recommended either the creation of a

joint committee comprised of ministers and representatives from the minority organizations or the use of the committee of Cabinet responsible for culture and aboriginals to evaluate the work of the interministerial committee. As well, it called on all federal ministries and agencies to inform Canadians more fully on the range of official language services and programs available and to evaluate their quality and cost.[96]

Unaware of the Cabinet document, in late October the Fédération invited Gordon Robertson of the Federal-Provincial Relations Secretariat to discuss the crisis facing the francophone minority communities. Robertson replied that such a meeting was not appropriate and suggested that Gauthier contact John Roberts for a meeting instead.[97] Roberts announced in the House of Commons that he would soon table the government's new policy. A frustrated Fédération reminded the prime minister, ministers, and MPs that it had not been consulted on that policy and pleaded for public support for its two central demands: a global policy and the structures required to oversee its implementation. Trudeau's office acknowledged receipt of its letter but did not respond further.[98] On 20 December 1977, Roberts announced the comprehensive policy for the official language minorities, which formalized the creation of the interministerial committee but did not call for the creation of the joint committee outlined in the Privy Council document to Cabinet. The newly appointed Associate Under-Secretary of State for Citizenship and the Expansion of Bilingualism, Denise Moncion, informed the Fédération on 1 February 1978 of the composition of the interministerial committee and requested a meeting to discuss its priorities vis-à-vis the federal government as well as the best means of opening a dialogue.[99]

In the interim, the Fédération had acquired a copy of the Cabinet document with its recommendation for a "comité mixte" and was furious over being omitted from the new policy. The Alberta, Saskatchewan, and Manitoba francophone organizations sent a brief to Marc Lalonde, Roméo LeBlanc, Jean-Jacques Blais, and John Roberts on 11 March reminding them of the galloping rate of assimilation among the 125,000 francophones of those provinces. Western francophones, fed up with being "un folklore de spectacle," were determined to change the course of history by obtaining their own political, cultural, social, and economic institutions. A comprehensive strategy of renewal and development, they maintained, could be achieved only with the full cooperation of the federal government via a permanent "commission ou comité mixte."[100] Upping the pressure, Gaudet again wrote to Trudeau, demanding an explanation of why the recommended "comité mixte" had been dropped from the policy and renewing his request for a meeting.[101]

Trudeau was astonished at the Fédération's critical view of his government's newly elaborated global policy for the linguistic minorities. He made it clear that he was responsible for rejecting the recommendation for a "comité mixte," and urged the Fédération to cooperate with the interministerial committee.[102] Gaudet – backed by a resolution from his organization's General Assembly that characterized the measures adopted by the government as "comme décevantes" and "partielles" – pleaded for a meeting to discuss a permanent mechanism of consultation between the government and the Fédération.[103] Trudeau again turned him down. However, he kept the lines of communication open with the Fédération's new president, Paul Comeau, congratulating him on his appointment while reminding him that under his tutelage the group "sera aussi appelée à franchir le cap difficile d'une organisation qui atteint sa taille adulte."[104]

Trudeau evidently felt that the Fédération needed to mature before the federal government would take it seriously. He had responded in great detail to the Fédération's lengthy questionnaire on his government's commitment to the official language minorities. He reminded the organization of his government's extensive programs and funding for them and chided its leaders for their misguided behaviour over the interministerial committee imbroglio of 1977. In reply to their allegations, he declared that his government "*n'a pas refusé* de s'occuper des préoccupations des minorités francophones, *qu'il n'a pas négligé* d'établir des politiques à cet égard et *qu'il a bel et bien* établi des mécanismes de participation."[105] While recognizing through funding that the Fédération "constitue certainement un porte-parole important des aspirations et des préoccupations des minorités francophones," Trudeau reminded its leaders that governments are elected to represent all citizens. He reiterated that francophones and their organizations should work primarily through their elected members of Parliament.[106]

The Fédération was impervious to Trudeau's arguments. As soon as the Conservative government of Joe Clark took power in 1979, its leaders initiated a lobbying effort to hold the government to the extensive promises it had made during the election. They called upon William Jarvis, Minister of State for Federal-Provincial Relations, as well as Minister of Justice Jacques Flynn, to support the creation of a tripartite commission of bureaucrats, politicians, and Fédération representatives to oversee the implementation of government policies and programs for francophone minorities.[107] The Clark government self-destructed before any progress could be made on this matter. When Trudeau returned in February 1980, the Fédération reminded him of his election promise to create a joint commission comprised of government and Fédération representatives. It hoped that he would respond immediately and allow the joint commission to get on with crucial work on the constitutional issues concerning the francophone minority communities.[108] But the Fédération, much to its dismay, would soon discover that it was facing a far more aggressive Liberal government, one determined to settle the constitutional battle with Quebec and the other provinces on its own terms without too much interference from non-governmental organizations, at least in the initial stages of the process.

TRUDEAU'S CONSTITUTIONAL CONUNDRUM

Developments on the constitutional front had been in abeyance until after the election of the Parti Québécois in November 1976 and the subsequent passing into law of Bill 101, the Charter of the French Language. Bill 101 confirmed French as the official language of Quebec, streamed all children of immigrant and Canadian families from outside Quebec into French language schools, and introduced a myriad of regulations to enforce French as the language of work in the public and para-public sectors and encourage its use in the private sector.[109] Many of Bill 101's elements drove a stake into the heart of the Trudeau government's language policy, especially the principle of freedom of choice, which had also been advocated by both the Royal Commission on Bilingualism and Biculturalism and the Molgat-MacGuigan Special Joint Committee. One aspect of Bill 101 that particularly upset the Trudeau government and Canadians from coast to coast was the "Quebec clause," which compelled parents of English-speaking Canadians moving to Quebec from any part of Canada to send their children to French language schools.

In response to this reaction, in a letter of 21 July 1977 Premier René Lévesque attempted to bring the other premiers on side by inviting them to negotiate bilateral agreements with his government on education rights for the official language minorities. The matter was then placed on the agenda of the annual premiers' meeting at St Andrews, New Brunswick, held 18–19 August 1977. In a statement to his fellow premiers on "Reciprocity and Education," Lévesque explained the rationale behind Bill 101 as an attempt to prevent the further minoritization and eventual assimilation of Quebec's francophones. Positing that Quebec resembled "a colonized country" because the majority francophones did not control their economy and 90 per cent of immigrants integrated into the anglophone community as a result of sending their children to English language schools, Lévesque concluded that "the francophones risk becoming a minority in Montreal within a generation." In short, his government had no choice but to act quickly on language policy and remove freedom of choice for francophone and immigrant parents in the matter of schooling for their children.

Freedom of choice for children of English-speaking parents from the rest of Canada moving to Quebec, Lévesque reiterated, was open to negotiation. He suggested that such intergovernmental agreements were quite common among the provinces, and said his government was very eager to negotiate "extending access to English schools to the anglophones of other provinces on a reciprocal basis according to the modalities applicable to the anglophones of Quebec."[110] On behalf of his government, Lévesque submitted a lengthy document outlining all education agreements between Quebec and the other provinces, which showed that its Direction des Affaires éducatives et culturelles had expended $177,500 in 1976–77 on education and cultural matters in the English-speaking provinces. The budget for 1977–78 was set at $181,300.[111] Indeed, Lévesque was so confident of his strategy that he presented the premiers with a draft proposal of an agreement on education rights for linguistic minorities.[112] Underlying the offer was the concept that Canada was a compact of provinces and that the premiers alone were therefore responsible for protecting their exclusive jurisdiction over education and language policy.

Lévesque's proposal for reciprocal agreements proved far too controversial for most of the premiers. In fact, Allan Blakeney of Saskatchewan issued a news release on the first day of the conference in which he stated: "The Quebec government proposes that the children of English-speaking Canadians moving from Saskatchewan to Quebec should have rights different from the children of non-English-speaking Canadians moving from Saskatchewan to Quebec. This is incompatible with the idea of Canadianism shared by the great majority of the people of Saskatchewan."[113] Also warned off by an indignant Pierre Trudeau,[114] the premiers issued a general statement on language to the effect that "Recognizing our concern for the maintenance and, where indicated, development of minority language rights in Canada; and recognizing that education is the foundation on which language and culture rest: The premiers agree that they will make their best efforts to provide instruction in education in English and French wherever numbers warrant."[115] Further, they instructed the Council of Education Ministers to review and report on the state of minority language education in all provinces within six months. Each province would then develop and act on its own language policy and program.[116] The Quebec government did not subscribe to the premiers' noncommittal statement, but it nevertheless agreed to participate in the review process.

The Council of Education Ministers, chaired by Jacques-Yvan Morin, met in September 1977 and reaffirmed the following principles as the basis for its report: "That each province has exclusive jurisdiction in education and a responsibility to its cultural minorities, and ... that education is the foundation on which language and culture rest."[117] The report, released in January 1978 and entitled *The State of Minority Language Education in Canada,* gave a summary of the state of education in the minority languages, followed by a description of the situation in each province. While not making evaluations or recommendations, it pointed out that provisions for minority language education "concerning legislation governing the language of instruction, accessibility to existing educational services, and the nature and scope of minority language programs offered" varied widely from province to province.[118]

The premiers met at a special conference held in Montreal on 23 February 1978 to ratify the Council's report. After their deliberations, they issued a statement that, according to Pierre Foucher, recognized for the first time the principle of "collective rights of provincial minorities rather than individuals."[119] The premiers resolved that "Each child of the French-speaking or English-speaking minority is entitled to an education in his or her language in the primary or the secondary schools in each province wherever numbers warrant." This resolution was deemed an important breakthrough by the leaders of the francophone minority communities. Yet it came at some cost, since another resolution stated that "It is understood, due to exclusive jurisdiction of provincial governments in the field of education, and due also to wide cultural and demographic differences, that the implementation of the foregoing principle would be as defined by each province."[120]

The exclusivist approach adopted by the provinces on language matters eventually found strong political support in a most unusual quarter. To the surprise and chagrin of both Trudeau and francophone leaders, the Task Force on Canadian Unity set up by the Liberal government in July 1977 took a highly controversial position on language policy, especially in the realm of education. The Task Force was co-chaired by Jean-Luc Pépin, a former Cabinet minister in the Trudeau government, and John P. Robarts, a former Ontario premier. Adopting the concepts of regionalism and a territorial Quebec/Canada dualism as its two guiding principles, it recommended that Quebec be recognized as a unilingual francophone province. That is, s. 133 of the British North America Act should be repealed to allow

section III of Bill 101, which stipulated French as Quebec's official language of the National Assembly and the courts, to stand. The Task
Force's report also made the following recommendations:

2. Each provincial legislature should have the right to determine an official
   language or official languages for that province, within its sphere of jurisdiction.
3. Linguistic rights should be expressed in provincial statutes, which could
   include:

   i. the entitlement recognized in the statement of the provincial first ministers at Montreal in February 1978: "Each child of the French-speaking
   or English-speaking minority is entitled to an education in his or her language in the primary or the secondary schools in each province, wherever
   numbers warrant." This right should also be accorded to children of
   either minority who change their province of residence ...
   iv. Should all provinces agree on these or any other linguistic rights, these
   rights should then be entrenched in the constitution.[121]

Not surprisingly, the Trudeau government was deeply concerned
about Quebec's attempts to strike bilateral deals with the provinces.
Moreover, the prime minister was annoyed with his former Liberal
colleague and Cabinet minister, Jean-Luc Pépin, for the decentralist
and pro-Quebec nationalist thrust of the report of the Task Force on
Canadian Unity. The government had a very different vision of
national unity and the role played by language equality in the pursuit
of that vision. Building on its 1977 statement on official languages
policy, *A National Understanding*, the following year the Trudeau government issued a comprehensive constitutional position paper entitled *A Time for Action. Toward the Renewal of the Canadian Federation.*
Stressing the urgency of reform, the paper outlined several fundamental deficiencies of the British North America Act. A major one
was the lack of a Charter of Rights and Freedoms, which among much
else could address "the inadequacy of the language rights guaranteed
by the Constitution, which has jeopardized the progress of the French-
speaking people of Canada, led them to withdraw in spirit into
Quebec and added strength to the separatist movement in that
province."[122] Language equality must be one of the shared values
"enshrined in our national consensus." For Trudeau this meant that
"the establishment of language equality within federal institutions
must be completed and that, wherever numbers justify, provincial services must be administered to minorities in their official language."
This goal was to be achieved through a comprehensive Charter of

Rights and Freedoms that would bind the federal and provincial governments equally.[123]

Bill C-60, introduced in the House of Commons on 20 June 1978 for first reading, attempted to make concrete the principles outlined in *A Time for Action*. To the surprise of most Constitution watchers, the government proposed to extend official bilingualism to "the debates or other proceedings of the legislative assembly of any province" under a new s. 14(2). It also proposed, under new ss. 15(2) and 16(2), to extend the official bilingualism provisions of s. 133, applicable to Quebec, to the statutes and records of legislatures and to court proceedings in Ontario and New Brunswick. Bill C-60 addressed the matter of education rights for linguistic minorities in s. 21, which defined the province as the geographic region for the purpose of determining whether sufficient numbers existed to warrant minority language schools. S. 21 provided for access to minority language schools for children of parents whose first language was the minority language and who resided in the province. While the bill called for access "to facilities that are provided in that area out of public funds," it did not grant the linguistic minority communities the right to manage those facilities. Furthermore, s. 21 required that parents send a notice of intent to their local school board indicating a desire for minority language education and also protected the right of provincial legislatures to provide for reasonable methods of determining numbers.[124] In short, the provincial majority would retain control over most aspects of school policy, including administration, curriculum, and financing.

The Trudeau government had hoped to advance the cause of the linguistic minority communities without raising a red flag in the face of several recalcitrant provinces. Accordingly, it proposed to proceed with constitutional reform in two phases. The first, to be dealt with before 1 July 1979, would cover all those matters on which Parliament could legislate on its own authority. This certainly did not include education rights for the linguistic minorities! The second phase would presumably be undertaken after the national election to be held sometime in 1979, and be completed by 1 July 1981.[125] The federal government set the process in motion by convening a First Ministers Conference on the Constitution for the end of October 1978.

When the premiers met in Regina between 9 and 12 August 1978 for their 19th annual conference, the Trudeau government's constitutional proposals dominated much of their discussion. In a lengthy communiqué dated 10 August 1978, they emphasized both the process and the substance of constitutional renewal. They rejected any threat of unilateral action by Ottawa and, in conformity with the provincial compact theory of Confederation, argued that "significant constitutional reform should have the concurrence of all governments, recognizing the equality of status of all the provinces in the process." The constitutional agenda should be based on the October 1976 consensus reached by the ten provinces, the report of the Task Force on Canadian Unity, and Bill C-60. Furthermore, the premiers, reiterating their 1976 position, maintained that "the division of powers is the key issue in constitutional reform, and should be addressed in conjunction with other issues."[126]

The provincial consensus contained a confirmation of language rights as outlined in the Victoria Charter of 1971 and did not include education rights for the linguistic minorities. The Regina communiqué demonstrated agreement on enhancing provincial powers in many areas, but gave no indication that the provinces were willing to follow up on their commitments with regard to language outlined at the Montreal conference a few months earlier. In fact, some premiers, in reference to Bill C-60's proposed language guarantees, objected that they went "substantially beyond earlier proposals, and that practical difficulties may be encountered in their provinces, particularly in respect of provincial government services and courts."[127] No consensus was possible, since two premiers, William Davis of Ontario and Richard Hatfield of New Brunswick, shared a very different view of the language question. Davis supported the position, recommended in the *First Report of the Ontario Advisory Committee on Confederation, April 1978*, that official bilingualism should be entrenched in the Constitution and "language guarantees should explicitly provide for the right to minority language education." Hatfield also backed the entrenchment in the Charter of the official languages provisions – including education rights for linguistic minorities – as outlined in Bill C-60.[128]

As expected, the Trudeau government's constitutional proposals – both their substance and the process – came under heavy attack from René Lévesque as well as the western premiers at the Federal-Provincial Conference of October 1978. Indeed, in return for their agreement to participate, Trudeau had to agree to add the complex and controversial matter of the distribution of powers to the constitutional agenda for the first phase. The provincial counterstrategy had been laid out in 1976 and was meant to ensure that the provinces could barter additional powers for themselves in return for patriation and a national Charter of Rights and Freedoms.[129]

When the prime minister and the premiers reconvened in February 1979 for a working constitutional summit, it was immediately apparent that profound differences divided Ottawa and the provinces on all fundamental matters: the division of powers, the Senate, the Charter (especially language rights), the amending formula, and the process to be adopted (i.e. unilateral action versus unanimity). The timing for successful constitutional negotiations was not propitious. The federal government's mandate was quickly running out and the polls indicated that Joe Clark's Conservative party might just be able to defeat the Liberals. Many of the Conservative premiers, taking the lead from Alberta's Peter Lougheed, preferred to wait and negotiate with a federal government more amenable to provincial rights. René Lévesque was not about to help Trudeau get re-elected, thereby undermining his government's chances of winning a referendum on sovereignty-association.[130] The parameters of the forthcoming political clash over competing constitutional visions were starkly delineated and would determine the nature of the constitutional debate for two decades.

"POUR NE PLUS ÊTRE ... SANS PAYS": A NEW CONSTITUTIONAL VISION

Comme il a été dit maintes fois, les francophones hors Québec refusent violemment de se voir condamnés à la seule survivance folklorique que leur promet un statu quo érigé sur des décennies de mensonge, de trahison et d'injustice. Par le passé, on les a obligés à réclamer subventions, privilèges et permissions; composantes dérisoires d'une existence précaire. Voilà qu'aujourd'hui ils ne veulent plus rien réclamer du tout si ce n'est que l'essentiel: un pays.[131]

Paradoxically, in the emerging political struggle over Canada's constitutional future, the Fédération placed itself and its provincial affiliates on the side of the premiers, including the secessionist premier of Quebec. At its June 1978 annual general meeting the delegates established a political committee to prepare a report on constitutional reform in Canada. Chosen to preside over the committee was Michel Bastarache, an influential law professor at the University of Moncton, former president of the Société Nationale des Acadiens and secretary-general of the Société des Acadiens et Acadiennes du Nouveau-Brunswick. He was joined by Pierre Poulin, a regional economic development specialist and first president of the SAANB; Clinton Archibald, professor of political science at the University of Ottawa; and two Franco-Manitobans, Hubert Gauthier, the Fédération's first president and then director general, and Rhéal Teffaine, a well-known Saint-Boniface constitutional lawyer and member of the

Manitoba government delegation to the federal-provincial conferences on the constitution.

It was an impressive committee, one dominated by the presence of
two New Brunswick Acadians and two Franco-Manitobans. The Société
franco-manitobaine was in a feisty mood, determined to win the political battle over the restoration of s. 23 of the Manitoba Act, while the
SAANB's leaders felt pressured to become more assertive by the rise of
the secessionist Parti Acadien. The presence of René Lévesque's Parti
Québécois government, with its pending referendum on independence, added to the volatile political and ideological context in which
the committee functioned. No doubt these factors account for its
innovative and controversial 1979 report, *Pour ne plus être ... sans pays.
Une nouvelle association pour les deux peuples fondateurs.* The highly
charged document was characterized by Fédération president Paul
Comeau as "un pas de plus dans une démarche de dignité." If
members of the francophone minority communities did not feel that
Canada belonged to them, "c'est qu'ils ont été trop longtemps condamnés à l'exil psychologique par l'étroitesse d'esprit et le racisme
voilé d'une majorité dominante."[132]

Well aware that their radical constitutional proposals would upset
the political and economic power brokers, the committee's members
maintained that the recommendations were realistic and represented
the minimum required to ensure that francophones could aspire to
something more than mere "folkloric survival." Indeed, Canada had
only two options. The first entailed an imaginative and generous
acceptance of full equality between its two founding peoples and the
creation of institutions to reflect that equality. The second involved
the recognition that Quebec was the only province capable of guaranteeing the development of the francophone community in North
America, albeit without the minorities. While the Québécois had a
right to national self-determination, the committee believed that they
would chose to remain within Confederation if a true partnership
between equals was achieved.[133] The Fédération hoped to capitalize
on the threat of Quebec's secession to convince the Canadian government to entrench both the traditional pan-Canadian conception of
cultural and linguistic duality and the neo-nationalists' and secessionists' version, a bi-national state in which a quasi-independent Quebec
exercised considerably more powers than the other provinces.[134]

Underlying the committee's thirty-five constitutional recommendations were several of the principles at the heart of the Pépin-Robarts
Task Force on National Unity. The new Constitution should be
founded on the dual compact theories of Confederation: Canada is a
compact of provinces whose politicians made and can remake the

Constitution as well as a compact of two founding nations, French and British Canadian. Moreover, it should recognize the right of peoples to self-determination. The Constitution should be patriated, and Canada should proclaim itself a parliamentary federal republic, with Ottawa stripped of its powers of reservation and disallowance. The new Canadian republic would be committed to respecting fundamental freedoms, linguistic rights, and democratic freedoms, to the principle of redistribution of national wealth, the affirmation of its two founding peoples at the heart of Canadian institutions, and the recognition of the responsibility of governments to foster the development of the official language minority communities and the protection of the cultural values of aboriginals.[135]

The committee was pleased with the Trudeau government's proposed Charter, but believed that it needed to be enhanced in several ways. First, it was imperative that the Charter guarantee collective rights as well as fundamental individual rights. The expansion of the state, especially at the provincial level, had seriously eroded the traditional autonomy of the francophone minority communities over health, social welfare, and educational services. A measure of collective rights would empower them to initiate a whole range of crucial affirmative action programs and institutions, funded largely by the provincial and federal governments, but administered exclusively by the communities themselves. The francophone communities could begin by calling on a Bi-national Cultural Commission to oversee a referendum in the municipality or region making the request. In a reflection of the political aspirations of the increasingly neo-nationalistic SAANB, it was recommended that this process could be extended to the demand – based on a petition bearing 5000 signatures – for the creation of a new province![136]

The issue of linguistic rights was also central to the committee's constitutional vision, especially in the crucial fields of public administration, justice, and education. The committee was not interested in symbolic rights, but rather in the extension of practical and effective measures touching the lives of ordinary francophones. Official bilingualism should be extended to all the legislatures, while only Manitoba, Ontario, Quebec, and New Brunswick should provide translation of all laws and proceedings. Canadians should have the right to a trial in either French or English in these four provinces. The children of Canadian citizens should have the right to education in their maternal language in homogeneous schools controlled by members of the official language minority communities. To make sure that these rights were fully and fairly implemented, the committee – not convinced of the impartiality of the existing judicial structure –

recommended the creation of a special tribunal to adjudicate all linguistic disputes.[137]

It was in the area of federal institutions that the committee made its most radical suggestions, ones guaranteed to elicit a frosty reception from the Trudeau Liberal government once it was returned to office in February 1980. The committee believed that all vestiges of Canada's links with the United Kingdom had to be abolished in order to maintain the allegiance of francophones in Quebec. It called for the election for a fixed term of a head of the Canadian parliamentary republic – a francophone and an anglophone in alternation – by the House of Commons. The positions of the lieutenant-governors and the president of the Privy Council should be terminated to ensure that Ottawa had no authority over the provincial executives or legislatures.[138]

Following the lead of the Pépin-Robarts Task Force, the committee posited that drastic changes to the Senate were essential for avoiding the secession of Quebec. It recommended that the Senate be replaced by a bi-national House of the Federation comprised of 106 members, half francophones and half anglophones, elected for a seven-year term. Of the francophones, Quebec would have thirty-five, Ontario nine, the west four, and the Atlantic region five. Of the fifty-three anglophones, Ontario would have only twenty-two, the west sixteen, the Atlantic region eight, and Quebec six. Little consideration was given to the fact that both Ontario's population and its growth rate were greater than Quebec's. The House of the Federation "doit être le lieu privilégié où se retrouvent sur une base paritaire les deux peuples fondateurs du Canada ... Le gouvernement central ne peut refléter la réalité des deux peuples fondateurs s'il n'a pas à composer avec eux régulièrement et à assurer que ses projets respectent les valeurs et les priorités de chacun."[139]

Representing an intrastate model of federalism, the powers of the House of the Federation would be more extensive than those of the existing Senate. This reform, the committee argued, was required to counterbalance anglophone majority dominance over the House of Commons and the executive and to address the growing sense of alienation in the hinterland provinces. The second House would exercise a ninety-day suspensive veto over all House of Commons legislation; name justices to the Supreme Court and commissioners to the proposed Bi-national Cultural Commission; and ratify all senior-level government appointments, treaties with foreign countries, shared-cost programs between Ottawa and the provinces, and declarations that a matter was in the general interest of Canada or that a state of war or insurrection, real or apprehended, existed.[140] Paradoxically, the report also recommended reinforcing inter-state federalism by proposing the institutionalization of provincial and federal-provincial conferences to ensure provincial input into the formulation of national policies. These advocates of bi-national federalism were fully confident, despite the lack of analysis, that the proposed reforms would neither undermine the system of responsible government nor further erode the powers of the national government.

The House of the Federation would name ten commissioners, half anglophones, half francophones, to the Bi-national Cultural Commission; they would then choose a president, the eleventh member. This quasi-judicial body, replacing the Office of the Commissioner of Official Languages, would have the mandate to resolve all disputes pertaining to both the Charter of Fundamental Freedoms and the Charter of Linguistic Rights, to inquire into all linguistic matters, and to oversee the application of special features pertaining to collective language rights. The committee's rationale for this reform was that the existing judicial system was ill-suited to dealing with sensitive, complex, and far-reaching linguistic matters; moreover, it lacked any credibility among francophones. The restructuring of the judicial branch of government also reflected the Fédération's bi-national, decentralist vision of Confederation. A constitutionalized Supreme Court would have a "Chambre de jurisdiction générale" with nine judges: three from each of Quebec and Ontario, two from the west, and one from the Atlantic region. It would also have a "Chambre constitutionnelle" with five judges: two from Quebec and one each from Ontario, the west, and the Atlantic region. All these appointments would be made by the House of the Federation.[141]

Surprisingly, the committee's recommendations in the area of distribution of powers within the federation were rather limited. No doubt its members feared that wholesale decentralization would work against the interests of the francophone minorities; it was imperative for Ottawa to retain its taxing powers and to enhance its control over the economy in order to provide cultural equalization grants for the minority communities. Indeed, the committee believed that the existing distribution of powers served Canadians' interests reasonable well and would continue to do so as long as "la flexibilité acquise par l'interprétation judiciaire depuis dix ans puisse être encore élargie." It did not, however, support the expansion of concurrent powers, and wanted paramountcy established for the existing areas – immigration, communications, pensions, family allowances, and taxation – in order to avoid disputes. All residual powers should be distributed according to whether they pertained to federal or provincial matters, and have-not provinces should have the option of delegating powers to Ottawa if they could not provide an appropriate level of services to their citizens. Provinces should also be granted the right to withdraw – with full financial compensation – from shared-cost programs in areas of their jurisdiction. The Maritime provinces should be granted proprietary rights over the resources on the continental shelves.[142]

On the controversial matter of the amending formula, the committee was considerably less than radical. It naturally favoured the conservative regionally-based formula outlined in the Victoria Charter of 1971. In its slightly revised version, *all* amendments would require ratification by a two-thirds majority in both Houses of Parliament and each of the four regions of Canada: Ontario, Quebec, and at least two of the western and Atlantic provinces comprising at least 50 per cent of their regional populations. On the basis that Canada was a federation of ten provinces and two founding peoples, the committee flatly rejected the democratic idea advanced by former Minister of Justice Otto Lang that Ottawa be able to hold a referendum to override a negative decision by one or more of the regions. This end-run around the formula would create a constitutional crisis and constituted "une remise en question à peine voilée de la légitimité du gouvernement actuel du Québec."[143] Yet when it came to the matter of provincial boundaries and the regrouping of existing provinces, the committee was keen on protecting the acquired rights or political clout of an official minority community, such as the Acadians of New Brunswick. This community, comprising 35 per cent of the provincial population, should have the right, following a referendum carried out by the Binational Cultural Commission, to veto a union of the Maritime provinces or to opt either for a new Acadian province or for amalgamation of its territory with Quebec.[144]

CONCLUSION

A range of evolving internal and external circumstances during the middle decades of the twentieth century obliged Canada's francophone minority communities to take stock of their precarious existence and to take action – to fashion new ideas, policies, strategies, and organizations – if they wished to survive and develop into the next century. A strange mix of optimism and urgency, incarnated in an emerging secular, well-educated, urban middle-class leadership, ensured the revitalization of existing provincial organizations and the creation of several new ones. Once in place, these groups saw the need to create a national Fédération to coordinate and strengthen their lobbying efforts at the federal government level. With the demise of the Catholic Church as their central institution, they realized that henceforth the francophone minority communities would have to rely upon the Canadian government for political, legislative, constitutional, and financial support. But the dependence of those communities on Ottawa posed certain perceptual and political problems, since their survival and growth were also contingent on the cooperation of their respective provincial governments, which controlled most aspects of their lives. It was a serious conundrum that only a highly decentralized federal system of government could produce and a more activist Ottawa could resolve.

Spurred on by its western and eastern provincial affiliates, the Fédération carried out a systematic analysis of the demographic, economic, cultural, and political conditions of the francophone communities from coast to coast. In *Les héritiers de Lord Durham* it proposed an ambitious "Quiet Revolution" for those communities, comprised of a set of comprehensive reforms to be carried out in conjunction with Ottawa through a permanent commission. The Fédération and its affiliates would have control over designing all the reforms and supervising their implementation. This scheme was far too ambitious and quite unrealistic, given the complex nature of Canadian federalism with regard to both politics and the bureaucracy: neither the senior politicians nor the bureaucrats would grant representatives of the francophone minority communities unrestrained internal access to carry out their wholesale restructuring of the federal system to meet their particular needs. Indeed, such a process would have been demonstrably undemocratic and would have opened the floodgates to a form of corporatist governance ruled by the interests of well-organized collective entities. The federal perspective was demonstrated clearly in the Fédération's failed attempt to establish a joint committee within the Privy Council when the Trudeau government rightly rejected the proposal and instead pushed ahead with its revamping of the official languages policies and programs and its constitutional agenda.

When Trudeau attempted to kick-start mega-constitutional negotiations following the election of the Parti Québécois in October 1976, the Fédération – pushed once again by its western and Maritime affiliates – shifted gears. A political committee was set up to hammer out a comprehensive set of constitutional proposals addressing the needs and concerns of the francophone minority communities. To begin, the Fédération wanted to make certain that constitutional reforms, no matter where they might originate, would not be counterproductive for its constituents. Believing that the best defence was an imaginative and solid offence, under the shrewd direction of Michel Bastarache the committee published a report that set out its radical proposals.

The conception of a new Canada delineated in *Pour de plus être ... sans pays* lay somewhere between the Parti Québécois vision of sovereignty-association between Canada and Quebec and the centralist federalism of Pierre Trudeau. The Fédération's so-called "third option" had its origins in the Pépin-Robarts Task Force on National Unity.

The committee's controversial and contradictory constitutional proposals were intended to shock the prime minister and the premiers, as well as Canadians generally, into paying attention to the predicament of the francophone communities. However, the Fédération's leaders gambled that they would catapult the organization into an important role in the coming round of mega-constitutional negotiations. The gamble backfired. By early 1979, it was painfully evident to all concerned that the Fédération had overplayed its hand by flirting with the secessionist Parti Québécois government. It was no longer perceived as a reliable ally for Ottawa in its political and constitutional battles with the Quebec separatists and its struggle to preserve national unity.

2

The Battle for Constitutional Recognition and Empowerment

Francophone organizations faced a new challenge in 1980: the Quebec referendum on sovereignty-association. Premier René Lévesque hoped to obtain a mandate to negotiate Quebec's political independence yet retain ongoing economic ties with Canada. Logically, one would have expected the Fédération and its provincial affiliates to support the pan-Canadian conception of cultural and linguistic duality, which the Trudeau government was defending and promoting. Paradoxically, this is not what transpired.

The Fédération and its member organizations feared – with good reason – being left on the sidelines during the referendum and the ensuing constitutional negotiations. Furthermore, the francophone leaders dreaded being caught in the crossfire between Ottawa and Quebec, of being perceived as mere pawns of the protagonists. A radicalized Fédération, pushed by the western provincial associations, saw the referendum as a major political opportunity. Many francophone and Acadian leaders believed that a strong minority YES vote in Quebec would enhance their bargaining powers vis-à-vis both the federal government and the recalcitrant provincial governments. Perhaps if they were taught a lesson, federal and provincial political leaders would at long last address some of the longstanding grievances and demands of Canada's francophones.[1] This strategy would prove risky, counterproductive, and divisive, both within the francophone and Acadian minority communities and between them and government. Moreover, while it made the francophone communities less clandestine, the misguided approach did not produce the extensive reforms being sought. Yet, once galvanized into action, the chastened francophone leaders felt compelled to learn the ropes of mega-constitutional politics. In so doing, they would achieve far more constitutional empowerment than what they had hoped to obtain by supporting the YES side in the referendum.

The Trudeau government, disenchanted with the Fédération and downright angry with the behaviour of some of the provincial organizations during the referendum, pushed forward with its package of constitutional reforms without paying much attention to the increasingly extreme proposals coming from the francophone leadership. This attitude created considerable animosity, particularly when Ottawa capitalized on the radicalism of the demands to entrench its own conception of official language and education rights. In this context, it is easier to understand why the Fédération and its affiliates failed to convince their natural ally, Ottawa, to accept important amendments to the Constitution Act, 1982 before it was ratified by Parliament and sent off to receive formal sanction at Westminster. Despite its ground-breaking provisions entrenching official bilingualism and education rights for the official language minorities, the francophone organizations remained convinced that the new Constitution fell far short of what they needed to guarantee the survival and renewal of their communities.

On 17 April 1982, when Queen Elizabeth II arrived to formally proclaim the Constitution Act, 1982, few francophone leaders were in the mood to celebrate. Rather, they were gearing up to launch yet another lobbying effort to convince Ottawa to convene a federal-provincial conference dedicated to the official language minorities. Trudeau deftly deflected the pressure by urging them to convince the premiers to attend. If the premiers agreed, he would consider the francophone leaders' request. When it became apparent that the provinces had no desire to undertake further constitutional discussions, francophones were forced to devote their time and energies to turning the new Constitution to their advantage.

THE 1980 REFERENDUM

The Quebec referendum of May 1980 posed a serious challenge for the francophone and Acadian communities because it required them to make a common response, something that was not possible given their divergent histories and contexts. Within six months of the Parti Québécois' gaining office, Minister of Intergovernmental Affairs Claude Morin made a valiant effort to neutralize the francophone leaders by reassuring them that a politically independent Quebec would not jettison its moral responsibility toward the minorities, for historical, demographic, juridical, and cultural reasons. The francophone minority communities, Morin warned his Société franco-manitobaine audience, must not become Ottawa's hostages in the constitutional battle; a powerful Quebec state, inside or outside Confederation, was their best guarantee for survival. Morin reminded them that the Parti Québécois was proposing "non pas une séparation brutale et indésirable, mais une solution réaliste et raisonable fondée, d'une part, sur la souveraineté politique et d'autre part, sur l'établissement d'une association économique mutuellement avantageuse entre le Québec et le Canada."[2]

Morin's intervention had the desired effect. The Société franco-manitobaine's planning and research officer, Ronald Bisson, accepted his analysis and recommendations – but for different reasons. While Bisson was well aware that Premier Lévesque considered the francophone communities "dead ducks," he recommended that they and their leaders adopt a position of neutrality in the referendum while at the same time pressuring Ottawa and the provinces to proceed with constitutional reforms. "Si on s'implique alors dans ce débat référendaire," Bisson warned, "nous serons au pire un bâton dans les roues du Québec, au mieux, un pion dans les mains des forces fédéralistes qui désirent l'unité Canadienne." He was convinced that a massive YES was highly unlikely, and that even if it did occur it would not automatically bring about the secession of Quebec. On the other hand, a massive NO would end any chance of constitutional renewal, a clear setback for the struggling francophone communities. The best scenario, a 60/40 split either way, would force Ottawa and the provinces to the bargaining table. A strong but indecisive YES would give francophone organizations the political leverage to influence the negotiations to their benefit. The SFM, with the support of the Fédération, had to develop a clear constitutional vision, sell it aggressively to all Canadians, and push for representation at the constitutional bargaining table.[3]

Following discussions with its provincial affiliates and input from its political committee, the Fédération decided to adopt a strategy of non-involvement in the referendum. It refused to formally support the NO forces while providing informal endorsement of the Parti Québécois' campaign by allowing its western affiliates and the SAANB to campaign openly for the YES side. One of the political committee members from Manitoba, Rhéal Teffaine, offered a quite sophisticated analysis that influenced the Fédération's strategy. Teffaine saw the Fédération's role in the referendum as crucial. While recognizing the right of self-determination for Quebec, the francophone minority communities should manifest a profound disquiet about the lack of attention paid them in the Parti Québécois' White Book: "En fait, le livre blanc ne fait que confirmer la théorie de 'Dead Ducks'." Moreover, its pious wishes and reiteration of an undefined moral responsibility merely tried to buy the silence of the francophone diaspora. Teffaine suggested that the Fédération negotiate with Claude Ryan, the leader of the NO forces in

Quebec, to ensure that the constitutional proposals outlined in *Pour ne plus être ... sans pays* be given serious consideration before the Quebec Liberal Party produced its own document for the referendum.[4]

The Fédération maintained its policy of formal non-intervention even when two of its western affiliates insisted that it should formally support the YES side as a form of protest. On 14 February 1980 the Association culturelle franco-canadienne de la Saskatchewan urged the Fédération in a press release to take this controversial step because it was the only way to generate the political crisis that would force Ottawa and the provinces to the constitutional bargaining table. A NO vote would reinforce the status quo, which was leading "rapidement et sûrement à la disparition des francophones."[5] Its neighbour association the SFM urged the Fédération to become far more active in the referendum in order to promote its constitutional recommendations.

In late March, the SFM executive passed a motion of support for the YES side in the Quebec referendum.[6] During a press conference held on 1 April, Gilberte Proteau, the newly elected president, offered explanations for this controversial decision. By supporting the NO side, she contended, Franco-Manitobans would be giving consent to the abolition in 1890 of their linguistic and education rights while ignoring both the double taxation required to maintain their separate schools and an assimilation rate that had reached the 50 per cent level. Support for the YES side would send a clear message that the existing Constitution no longer served the cultural and linguistic needs of either Franco-Manitobans or Québécois. What was required was a renegotiated Constitution "fondée sur le principe de l'égalité des peuples" that would enable Franco-Manitobans to obtain a degree of institutional autonomy and completeness wherein they would feel at home. The SFM also insisted that the francophone minority communities be represented at the bargaining table by the Fédération.[7]

The SFM's decision was prompted by the legalistic response of the Manitoba government to the Supreme Court's judgment in the Georges Forest case, which favoured the restoration of bilingualism in Manitoba's courts and legislature. Conservative Premier Sterling Lyon and his Attorney General, Gerry Mercer, decided to abide by the letter of the judgment by undertaking an expensive and unnecessary translation of all of Manitoba's statutes. The SFM maintained that this approach was not in Franco-Manitobans' interest and offered instead to negotiate a minimal level of French language public services in cetain important areas, such as health and social welfare.[8] The SFM's promotion of a YES vote was intended to encourage both the province and the federal government to take the concerns of Franco-Manitobans seriously.

The SFM's controversial move raised a hue and cry not only from provincial and federal politicians and opinion leaders in the English-speaking community but more importantly from many prominent Franco-Manitobans. One member of the SFM complained in an open letter to *La Liberté* that the executive had gone against the motion passed by the organization's General Assembly to study the implications of either a YES or a NO but not to commit Franco-Manitobans to any specific option. He opined that the SFM's receipt of nearly a half million dollars of public funds to defend the interests and rights of Franco-Manitobans did not give it the right to blatantly ignore the wishes of its constituents.[9] A counter-group, the Société Pro-Canadienne, quickly took shape and gathered signatures on a petition denouncing separatism and promoting a united bilingual Canada. The community was left divided and dispirited over the nasty imbroglio.[10] President Proteau was forced to send a letter to all SFM members explaining once again the rationale behind the decision and reiterating that "un OUI de la S.F.M. n'est pas un OUI à la séparation du Québec" but rather "un OUI à la renégotiation de la constitution canadienne."[11] Her rationalization did little to mend the divisions within the Franco-Manitoban community or to diminish the tension with anglophones.

The Association canadienne-française de l'Alberta, in announcing its decision of non-involvement in the referendum, stated that Franco-Albertans respected the right of the Québécois to determine their own future. The ACFA used the occasion to press the provincial and federal governments once again for constitutional guarantees for francophones, especially as regards education.[12] Paradoxically, its strategy of non-intervention caused the ACFA as many problems as the SFM encountered. It attempted to obtain a meeting with Premier Peter Lougheed to discuss constitutional matters, but no response was forthcoming. Instead, the executive was invited to meet with Minister of Federal and Intergovernmental Affairs Dick Johnston on 5 May and asked to clarify why the group was refusing to support the federalist NO position. President Roger Lalonde replied that the ACFA was a staunch supporter of national unity, but could not in good conscience "encourager les Québécois de voter 'non' puisque les francophones de l'Alberta ne jouissent pas de droits linguistiques en éducation, dans les lois en cours." It would be wrong-headed and dishonest to lead the Québécois to believe that everything was fine in Alberta when in fact the situation was desperate. Johnston replied that his government stood firmly by the position adopted by all the provinces at the St Andrews conference in August 1977 to the effect that education was a provincial prerogative. Alberta, he reiterated, would never accept the entrenchment of either official bilingualism or education rights for its francophone minority, even in return for greater autonomy over natural resources. He concluded by saying that his government might consider setting up a tripartite commission on education, but only if the ACFA agreed to allow other ethnic groups to be included.

The minister's performance could be characterized as the equivalent of waving a red flag at an already irritated bull. The ACFA executive found his behaviour truculent and his intransigence on policy deplorable and unacceptable.[13] Lalonde issued a public statement outlining the nature of the discussions with Johnston and concluding that, if his attitude represented provincial policy, "then Canada no longer exists and the Quebec Referendum is nothing but the closing of the coffin's lid on the corpse of Canadian unity."[14] Johnston was furious with Lalonde's remarks and sent him a sharp rebuke, especially concerning the reference to his personal allegiance to Canada, which he found unwarranted and disturbing. He reminded Lalonde that the meeting had been held at the ACFA's request, and that under his government's "best efforts" approach ever-increasing numbers of Alberta children were receiving their education in French. He wondered why the ACFA, which supported the government's policy, did not want to communicate this significant improvement to all Quebecers by supporting the NO campaign.[15]

Smarting at the reprimand, Lalonde considered the minister's response to the ACFA's proposals "at best condescending" and noted that no-one in the Alberta government had denounced or retracted his questionable position and misguided statements on Franco-Albertans and their linguistic and educational rights. Lalonde made it clear that the ACFA had never endorsed the province's rather limited "best efforts" approach on educational matters. At no time did the ACFA's recommendation for a "'Joint Commission' to oversee all aspects of the development and protection of the French language community in Alberta" involve representation from interested ethnic communities. He stressed that the Alberta government should understand that the constitutional recognition and implementation of the rights of Franco-Albertans did not preclude the adoption of a coherent policy for the ethno-cultural communities, and hoped that the ACFA and the province would maintain an open and frank dialogue in the pursuit of mutually acceptable solutions.[16]

After the referendum, the Fédération held a post-mortem in which the Ontario, Manitoba, Saskatchewan, and Alberta organizations assessed the results of their various strategies. They concluded that the fallout was not as negative as was being made out in the media. The SFM argued that its support for the YES side created shock waves that brought some criticism but also greater awareness of its position, a few new members, more credibility, and increased solidarity among all Franco-Manitoban associations. Saskatchewan's ACFC admitted that its YES position was not well received by its constituents but did open the door to the Minister of Intergovernmental Affairs. The ACFA noted that the expected backlash had not materialized, while the Franco-Ontarian association claimed that its participation in the Canadian unity debate at Queen's Park was taken seriously by the media. Yet a more critical note emerged in their concluding remarks. While their YES in the referendum had reverberated loud and clear, the YES to constitutional negotiations with their full participation had reached neither political leaders nor the francophone communities. To solidify its political base in preparation for the constitutional negotiations, the Fédération announced a vast consultation among all francophone communities to explain its proposals and receive feedback.[17]

The Fédération's decision to refrain from participating actively in the referendum on the NO side while informally supporting the YES side created considerable tension between it and the Trudeau government. Hoping to keep the lines of communication open for the post-referendum developments, President Paul Comeau explained to the prime minister that "en refusant d'appuyer les partisans du "NON", la F.F.H.Q. a voulu indiquer clairement que le statu quo constitutionnel actuel était totalement inacceptable, car il alimente le processus d'assimilation et mène à la disparition des francophones hors Québec." Responses from several premiers during the referendum debate had revealed very little, if any, political will to act in favour of their francophone minority communities. It was now incumbent on the Canadian government to undertake action that would guarantee those communities linguistic and cultural rights comparable to those of the anglophone minority of Quebec.[18]

No reply was forthcoming. Little did the Fédération and its affiliates realize that they had lost enormous credibility with the Trudeau government thanks to their ambiguous and questionable behaviour during the referendum. On the other hand, Quebec Premier René Lévesque responded gracefully to Paul Comeau's "chaleureux message de confiance et d'amitié" following the defeat of the YES side in the referendum and thanked the Fédération for its encouragement and support.[19] The Fédération, much to its chagrin, had not been able to avoid being caught in the crossfire between the Québécois separatists and the federalists. Though the francophone organizations had raised their public profile considerably, it was at the price of alienating their most important ally, the federal government. They had also badly damaged their pan-Canadian approach of cultural and linguistic duality by giving credence to the Parti Québécois conception of territorial duality. They would need tremendous political skill, determination, and luck to repair the political damage and regain the confidence of the prime minister and his francophone Cabinet and caucus members.

TOWARDS THE CONSTITUTION ACT, 1982

Constitutional reform returned to the national agenda following the re-election of the Liberals in February 1980 and the Quebec referendum in May 1980. Encouraged by his Cabinet colleagues, close advisors, and a few academics, Trudeau was determined to settle the constitutional question that had been on the agenda ever since the 1960s. He was not amused at being characterized in an unofficial biography by George Radwanski as an "unfulfilled" prime minister. Upon his return to office, he was more determined than ever to leave his imprint on the Constitution, which had intrigued him ever since his short stint in the Privy Council Office in the early 1950s.[20] Trudeau faced a daunting, perhaps even impossible, challenge, because of the conviction, shared by a majority of Canada's political leaders and constitutional lawyers, that the entrenchment and promotion of fundamental rights – including minority language rights – was incompatible with both the ideology of the legal system and the watertight separation of powers between the central and provincial governments.[21]

Trudeau and his government had played crucial roles in the Quebec referendum. Addressing the House of Commons on 15 April 1980, Trudeau warned that neither Ottawa nor the provinces would negotiate Premier René Lévesque's sovereignty-association option. He then ventured into Quebec and in three speeches, on 2, 7, and 14 May, managed to turn the tide and put the Parti Québécois on the defensive. It was thanks largely to his intervention that on 20 May the NO forces won out over the YES side by a wide margin of 60 to 40 per cent. Noting the referendum result in the House the following day, Trudeau declared: "It signals, we strongly hope and believe, the end of the long period of uncertainty, of doubt, of strained relations between Quebec and the other provinces of Canada, between French- and English-speaking Canadians. It marks a new beginning, it heralds a period of freedom and rebuilding. By voting for Canada, the people of Quebec recognize that their fellow Canadians are prepared to listen to them, to understand them and meet their legitimate aspirations."[22]

During the federal-provincial conference on 9 June 1980, Ottawa and the provinces agreed to a twelve-point agenda incorporating a "people's package" – patriation, an amending formula, and a charter of rights – and a "government package" dealing with the distribution of powers. Trudeau was adamant that basic human rights would not be bartered away in the fight over the distribution of powers. Working under the threat of unilateral action by Ottawa, the Continuing Committee of Ministers on the Constitution failed in July and August to reach agreement on any of the agenda items – an outcome that did not bode well for the federal-provincial conference on the Constitution slated for 8–13 September in Ottawa. Faced with an ever-expanding list of demands from the provinces, the Trudeau government adopted a hard line by adding new elements to the agenda, including additional powers over the economy for the federal government. The result was, not surprisingly, a foregone conclusion: the conference failed miserably. This development allowed the government to proceed with the option outlined in a secret memo of 30 August 1980 from Michael Kirby, head of the Federal-Provincial Relations Office, which recommended unilateral action on the people's package. The charter of rights in the package included mobility rights and minority language education rights and was binding on both Ottawa and the provinces. It also contained provisions on equalization.[23]

Confident that he had the full support of his Cabinet and caucus, the vast majority of Canadians, as well as premiers William Davis of Ontario and Richard Hatfield of New Brunswick, Trudeau issued a statement on 2 October 1980 explaining his government's decision to proceed unilaterally with a Proposed Resolution Respecting the Constitution of Canada. Reflecting his strongly-held belief that Canada was far greater than the sum of its provinces, the prime minister declared, "In this complex and turbulent world, Canadians can no longer afford to have fundamental aspects concerning the nature of our country left unresolved and uncertain, to feed confrontation, division and disunity. We are summoned to a great act of national will: we must take unto ourselves and for our children, the ultimate responsibility for the preservation of our country."[24] All previous efforts to patriate the British North America Act with an amending formula had failed because the unfounded convention of unanimity had given "each First Minister a veto: and that veto was increasingly used to seek the particular good of a particular region or province." The Proposed Resolution, Trudeau reassured Canadians, would break the constitutional log-jam by thwarting "a radically new concept of Canada, one in which the national good was merely the sum of provincial demands."[25]

Minister of Justice Jean Chrétien laid the resolution before the House of Commons on 6 October 1980, where it faced a filibuster organized by Joe Clark, with the full support of his Conservative MPs.[26] The government had to resort to closure on 24 October in order to refer it to the Special Joint Committee for detailed examination. This marked the first time in Canadian history that a parliamentary committee opened its hearings to the public via television. The hearings thus became an effective forum for galvanizing public support for the Charter.[27] The resolution included all the items in the people's package. In his explanation of the package, Chrétien stressed his government's desire to strengthen the Canadian vision of citizenship based on the principles of sharing, freedom, tolerance, pluralism, and opportunity. These values would be entrenched in a Charter of Rights and Freedoms reflecting Canada's adherence to the International Covenant on Civil and Political Rights. The Charter would be uniquely Canadian because it would entrench the concepts of mobility rights, language rights for the official minorities, and greater equality of opportunity for all Canadians via the principle of equalization. The "made in Canada" amending formula in the package would free Canadians from the last humiliating colonial tie to Great Britain.[28]

The concept of Canadian citizenship would be based, in part, on mobility rights, which would enhance the language and education rights of the official language minorities. According to the Minister of Justice, it was the right of every Canadian "to take up residence and to pursue a livelihood anywhere in Canada without discrimination based on the previous province of residence." Chrétien then made the crucial link with education rights for linguistic minorities; the Charter would give Canadians the right

to send their children to school in their own official language where there are sufficient numbers of the minority language group to justify a school. ...

When minority language rights are taken away, the right to take up a job in any part of Canada is seriously impaired. English-speaking Canadians, if they move to Quebec, want to have the right to send their children to school in their own language. Similarly French-speaking Canadians do not want to move to other parts of Canada unless they can send their children to school in their own language. ... In effect, without a guarantee of minority language rights, there can be no full mobility rights.[29]

A key element of a Canadian citizenship characterized by sharing and opportunity was the concept of equalization, unconditional transfers of federal revenues to "enable every province to provide a reasonable level of public services, without having to impose an unreasonable tax burden on its residents."[30] What Chrétien did not mention was that members of linguistic minorities – particularly French-speaking Canadians, who were most often at the bottom of the socioeconomic scale – stood to benefit greatly from a constitutionally entrenched program of equalization payments to have-not provinces. Provincial governments would no longer be able to continue to justify discriminatory treatment of their linguistic minorities on the basis of financial exigency.

On the crucial question of education rights for Canada's official linguistic minorities, the government proposed the following formula:

23. (1) Citizens of Canada whose first language learned and still understood is that of the English or French linguistic minority population of the province in which they reside have the rights to have their children receive their primary and secondary school instruction in that minority language if they reside in an area of the province in which the number of children of such citizens is sufficient to warrant the provision out of public funds of minority language educational facilities in that area.

(2) Where a citizen of Canada changes residence from one province to another and, prior to the change, any child of that citizen has been receiving his or her primary or secondary school instruction in either English of French, that citizen has the right to have any or all of his or her children receive their primary and secondary school instruction in that same language if the number of children of citizens resident in the area of the province to which the citizen has moved, who have a right recognized by this section, is sufficient to warrant the provision out of public funds of minority language educational facilities in that area.[31]

The justice minister appealed to the Fédération to pressure Lévesque "to drop his opposition to a measure which goes further than anything in our history to protect the rights of French language minorities everywhere in Canada."[32]

The other central component of the Trudeau government's vision of Canada was laid out in sections 16 to 22 of the Charter. These sections, which pertained to the official languages of Canada, entrenched sections 2, 9, and 10 of the Official Languages Act with respect to the recognition of "the equality of status and use of both English and French in all institutions of the Parliament and government of Canada." They also extended the language rights in section 133 of the British North America Act to all proceedings of Parliament and confirmed the use of both languages in all courts established by Parliament.[33] Chrétien called upon the people of Quebec to urge the Parti Québécois government "not to oppose a measure which implements the dreams and aspirations of generations of French Canadians who, believing that all of Canada is their country, have wanted to see their rights enshrined in the Constitution of Canada."[34]

Trudeau's constitutional package, with the Charter at its core, was deliberately designed to appeal to Canadians from all regions of the country directly over the heads of the recalcitrant premiers who had vetoed constitutional renewal since Jean Lesage's rejection of the Fulton-Favreau amending formula in 1965. The Charter was at the heart of Trudeau's liberal conception of citizenship in an increasingly multilingual and multicultural world.

THE STRUGGLE FOR COLLECTIVE RIGHTS

With the return of Trudeau to office in 1980, the Fédération and its affiliates were determined to have their constitutional vision for the francophone minority communities incorporated into Ottawa's constitutional reform proposals. Its 1979 constitutional report *Pour ne plus être ... sans pays* had demonstrated that entrenchment of the principle of collective rights for the francophone minority communities was essential:

Il ne faut pas que la défense des droits fondamentaux souvent très généreux masque l'oppression discrète de collectivités défavorisées ... Le comité politique propose d'inclure dans la constitution ... une série de *droits collectifs* qui permettront aux minorités officielles d'atteindre sur le plan social et culturel un statu égal à celui de la majorité. Les *droits collectifs* se traduisent par un devoir des autorités gouvernementales d'agir suite à l'exercice d'une initiative d'une communauté minoritaire officielle en vue d'assurer à celle-ci l'octroi de pouvoir et de services sans lesquels aucune justice sociale ne sera possible. L'obligation constitutionnelle à laquelle donnent lieu les droits collectifs est double; elle comprend la reconnaissance de la collectivité officielle en situation d'infériorité et la mise en oeuvre de mesures spéciales devant pallier à cette situation de fait.[35]

Most assuredly, achieving this goal was not going to be easy. Francophone leaders decided that it was imperative to have representatives of their communities at the constitutional bargaining table to make their vision of their role in a renewed Canada a reality.

The Fédération lobbied Trudeau and the francophone members of his caucus and Cabinet in hopes of opening a dialogue on the group's constitutional proposals, as promised by one of its most vocal supporters, Jean-Robert Gauthier, the Liberal member for Ottawa-Vanier.[36] The only reply was a frosty letter from the new Secretary of State, Francis Fox, complaining that the federal government's many initiatives and programs for the francophone communities had not always received the credit they deserved. He confirmed that the Fédération's federal grant for 1980–81 had been set at $286,000. Receipt of the grant would follow the signing of an agreement outlining two obligations on the part of the Fédération: that none of the funds would be spent for partisan political purposes, and that appropriate documentation would be furnished to substantiate all expenditures.[37] Ottawa wanted to make sure that the group would not use the funds to lobby against Ottawa's constitutional package.

The Fédération did not overreact to the new funding conditions. Instead, it stepped up its requests to the prime minister for a formal role in constitutional renewal. Given that many of the premiers had gone on record as opposing the entrenchment of linguistic rights and the recognition of Canada's two founding peoples in a new Constitution, they could not represent the interests of the francophone communities. "Il en découle donc," Paul Comeau wrote, "qu'une participation directe des francophones hors Québec lors des prochaines négociations constitutionnelles s'avère essentielle." He wanted a meeting with Trudeau to work out the modalities of this participation.[38] His letter was followed by several telegrams and further letters throughout May and June 1980 as the Minister of Justice began his whirlwind tour of the provinces to sound out the premiers on Ottawa's constitutional agenda. The Fédération's new president, Jeannine Séguin, proposed the creation of a constitutional committee made up of Fédération representatives and all francophone MPs not from Quebec. Ottawa flatly rejected the proposal.[39]

The western associations were not impressed with the Fédération's ineffectiveness. In early June 1980, the Société franco-manitobaine insisted in a letter to Premier Sterling Lyon that the constitutional renewal process could not be taken seriously unless his government acted on "les revendications de la collectivité franco-manitobaine." President Gilberte Proteau requested a meeting to discuss the need for an Official Languages Act for Manitoba, a central office providing French language services, and revision of the Education Act to allow the creation of homogeneous French language schools governed by the francophone communities.[40] No reply was never received.

Responding quickly to its own difficulty in reaching the Manitoba government, the SFM assessed existing linguistic and education rights and evaluated the Fédération's linguistic recommendations in light of Franco-Manitobans' needs. Ronald Bisson considered those recommendations, outlined in *Pour ne plus être ... sans pays*, incomplete and inadequate. In his view, the political committee had a profound bias towards exclusive provincial rights, especially with regard to language and education. Why should official bilingualism be limited to four provinces? The Fédération's recommendation on the right to education in the French language was too abstract and did not take into account Ottawa's historical incapacity to enforce its constitutional obligations or the inability of the Supreme Court to impose a coercive decision on a province. Moreover, the recommendation for an administrative tribunal was not a fail-safe mechanism for obliging a recalcitrant province "à mettre sur pied un système scolaire pour répondre aux besoins essentiels de sa minorité francophone."

Simple entrenchment of vague principles would be no more effective than s. 23 of the Manitoba Act, 1870. Bisson preferred the Quebec government's proposal of reciprocal agreements with other provinces under s. 86 of Bill 101 to guarantee education rights for the linguistic minorities. He recommended that the Fédération and its affiliates contact all provincial governments requesting that they define linguistic rights and, if they favoured entrenchment, indicate what it would entail in concrete terms. Those opposed to entrenchment should explain what alternatives they would offer to guarantee respect for the fundamental rights of their francophone communities. In short, it was time the Fédération and its member groups considered alternatives to entrenchment and informed all francophones of the importance of the debate for their future prospects.[41] This approach was certainly not calculated to endear the western francophone organizations to the Trudeau government.

The political agents of the four western provinces' francophone organizations met in Calgary on 30 June to discuss their constitutional strategies and policies. All four agreed with Bisson's critical evaluation of the Fédération. They urged the national organization to become more aggressive with the premiers by developing economic and social arguments to buttress its case and to seek out allies and create partnerships with such organizations as the Canada West Foundation.[42] The Fédération's director general, Donald Cyr, responded to the pressure by firing off a letter to all the premiers in which he posed the questions outlined in Bisson's document.[43] Annoyed that it had not had an opportunity to vet the letter to Premier Lyon, the sfm's president, Gilberte Proteau, sent him a much more toughly worded missive just prior to the 21st Annual Premiers Conference, held in Winnipeg on 21–22 August 1980. Since the Manitoba government opposed entrenchment of the Charter, she requested Lyon to indicate how he proposed to protect fundamental rights, including the collective rights of Franco-Manitobans. Did Lyon recognize the two founding peoples concept of Canada and, if so, how did he propose to deal with the reality? Manitoba, she argued, had lost an excellent opportunity to reinforce national unity by recognizing the principle of French language schools in a revised Education Act.[44]

None of these lobbying efforts had any impact on the premiers. In their press release, they reiterated their support for the provincial compact theory of Confederation and stated that their priority in constitutional reform was a new distribution of powers between

Ottawa and the provinces. Their statement made only a vague reference to protecting basic human and democratic rights.[45] Responding to Proteau's letter over a month later, Lyon restated his opposition to both entrenchment of fundamental rights and the "two nations" concept. While Manitoba's Education Act did not recognize French schools in principle, because doing so would be divisive, his government was committed to creating such schools while respecting local autonomy.[46]

Once the work of the Continuing Committee of Ministers on the Constitution got underway in July, it became clear to the Fédération that the Trudeau government had no intention of going beyond general principles in its constitutional reform proposals pertaining to educational rights for the official language minorities. President Jeannine Séguin asked Trudeau what, if anything, the entrenchment of vague principles was going to accomplish for the francophone minorities. "Si l'enchâssement des droits linguistiques dans une nouvelle constitution n'implique pas des engagements politiques et financiers des gouvernements visant à permettre aux communautés francophones hors Québec de se donner et de gérer les institutions nécessaires à leur développement collectif, cela nous indiquera qu'il est temps de remettre en question l'utilité même de l'inclusion de droits linguistiques dans la constitution."[47]

It is not known what Trudeau thought of this line of reasoning, since he chose not to respond to any of the letters he received from the Fédération over the summer of 1980. Indeed, the only return communications came from the Federal-Provincial Relations Office and the Privy Council Office, which notified the Fédération by telephone during the week of 14–18 July that the prime minister had rejected its request for direct participation in the constitutional negotiations. Following the failed federal-provincial conference in September, an advisor in the Federal-Provincial Relations Office, James Hurley, responding to Donald Cyr's request to formally close the file, wrote to him explaining what had happened and providing a transcript of Trudeau's decision.[48]

Having failed to gain a place at the central constitutional bargaining table and spurred on by its western affiliates, the Fédération decided that it was urgent to change strategies. All the premiers, including the most ecalcitrant, had to be lobbied intensively with the active support of well-informed francophone communities. Premiers Hatfield and Lévesque – who the Fédération for some reason believed better understood the needs of those communities – would be singled out for special attention. Where possible and potentially productive, the provincial associations should provoke crises over certain outstanding issues in order to gain media attention. The Fédération could assist them in their lobbying by reminding the premiers of their referendum commitment to support constitutional reform. It could also renew its efforts to create a joint committee with all francophone MPs, with the mandate to convince Trudeau and his Cabinet colleagues to entrench not only the principle of linguistic rights but also the mechanisms necessary for their effective implementation.[49] By the end of September it was clear that Canada's francophone organizations had failed to gain a special role in the constitutional renewal process. Like all other interest groups, they would have to convince the government by the force of their arguments and the activism of their constituents, rather than their special relationship with the Constitution and their century of political battles for survival and equality.

THE BATTLE OVER SECTION 23 OF THE CHARTER

The Fédération and its affiliates monitored Jean Chrétien's performance before the Special Joint Committee on 7 and 12 November and were none too pleased with his remarks pertaining to linguistic and education rights for the official language minority communities. NDP member Lorne Nystrom, Liberal member Jean-C. Lapierre, and Conservative member David Crombie asked Chrétien why the government had backed away from its initial proposal to extend s. 133 of the British North America Act – official bilingualism in the legislatures and the courts of Quebec and Manitoba – to New Brunswick and Ontario, the two provinces with the largest francophone communities. His response was that it never been his government's intention to impose s. 133 on any province. Chrétien also denied Nystrom's charge that a political deal had been struck with Premier William Davis of Ontario in order to obtain his support for the Proposed Resolution Respecting the Constitution of Canada.

Chrétien informed the committee that, if it recommended extending s. 133 to all provinces, he would give the proposal serious consideration. He sensed that support for such an extension of the section had dwindled considerably since the Victoria Charter of 1971. He expressed his disappointment that Ontario was not ready to opt in, but indicated that New Brunswick's Richard Hatfield would take advantage of s. 43 of the Proposed Resolution to proclaim his province officially bilingual.[50] In fact, the resolution called for Manitoba, Ontario, and New Brunswick to be bound by the provisions of s. 133. Initially, it appeared that Davis might accept the proposal; however, fearing a backlash, he backed off and chose to forge ahead with a pragmatic legislative approach to bilingualism. Meanwhile, Hatfield indicated that New Brunswick would opt into s. 133.[51]

Rather than coerce the provinces into accepting official bilingualism, Ottawa decided to guarantee education rights for the linguistic minorities through s. 23 of the Charter. Chrétien declared:

In looking for the root of the problem, we felt very strongly that the most acute problem is always education. When you cannot send your kids to your mother language schools, official language schools, it is very difficult, especially today with TV and so on, for French-speaking families outside Quebec to keep the language in the family. So personally I felt education was extremely important, and a lot of the problems we have today exist because it was not guaranteed in the constitution for all of Canada in the past. Of course, when there is no French there is no problem ... or virtually no problem.[52]

However, New Brunswick MP Eymard Corbin argued vigorously that s. 23 was incomplete and had serious flaws, primarily because the government had failed to designate bilingual districts, thereby leaving the courts to define what was meant by "sufficient numbers." Chrétien replied that "where numbers warrant" was the term used by the premiers in the 1977 St Andrews and 1978 Montreal agreements, and went on to say:

De toute façon c'est un critère qui aurait été retenu par les cours parce que ça ne peut pas être absolu, c'est-à-dire que les tribunaux auraient voulu y appliquer le critère de raisonabilité pour une raison bien simple, c'est qu'on ne peut certainement pas exiger, pour une seule famille à une école, si c'est à des coûts absolument prohibitifs. Avec le mécanisme que nous avons développé, monsieur Corbin, c'est que les tribunaux pourront interpréter la situation au Canada anglais en fonction de la situation au Québec, et plus le Québec sera généreux pour la minorité anglophone, plus les cours pourront se servir du précédent québécois pour imposer des critères pour la minorité francophone hors Québec.[53]

Testifying before the committee on 26 November, Jeannine Séguin outlined what she considered to be the egregious flaws of the resolution. The Fédération submitted an extensive brief, to which it appended the highly critical legal opinions of Michel Bastarache, dean of the law school at the University of Moncton; R. Dale Gibson, a law professor at the University of Manitoba; and Daniel Proulx, a law professor at the University of Ottawa.[54] Séguin reiterated the Fédération's commitment to its traditional "two nations" concept of Canada and its long-held conviction that any acceptable constitutional reform had to recognize fully "l'égalité fondamentale des peuples de langues et de cultures française et anglaise." The federal government had to assume full responsibility for protecting and promoting French language and culture throughout Canada. Yet Ottawa must never "porter atteinte au dynamisme et aux pouvoirs dont dispose déjà le Québec pour assurer son développement en tant que principal foyer de la langue et de la culture française sur ce continent."[55] Since its inception, the Fédération – along with most of its affiliates – had supported the constitutional objectives of the nationalists, believing that an increasingly powerful province of Quebec, controlled by its francophone majority, would enhance the viability and bargaining rights of the francophone minority communities.

While recognizing the urgency of entrenching linguistic rights in the Constitution in order to counteract the longstanding indifference of the provinces, the Fédération denounced the status quo nature of the government's proposals and expressed its outrage at "the detestable handling of the language rights clauses since the Constitutional Conference in September." Séguin asked why institutional bilingualism was not extended to all provinces, beginning immediately with Ontario and New Brunswick. Picking up where Lorne Nystrom had left off, she answered her own rhetorical question by charging that Trudeau had made a political deal with William Davis not to impose s. 133 on Ontario, in return for Davis's support for the resolution. Official bilingualism, she insisted, had to be extended to all provincial governments and their judicial and administrative tribunals.[56] When Senator Arthur Tremblay tried to get Séguin to agree that s. 133 should apply to all provinces or to none, thereby giving each province freedom of choice, she responded curtly that she refused to be drawn into a partisan trap.[57] In an interesting development, the Association canadienne-française de l'Ontario and the Conseil des minorités du Québec submitted a joint brief to the committee declaring that it was most urgent for Ontario and New Brunswick to become recognized as officially bilingual under s. 133. The latter organization felt that Ontario's adoption of official bilingualism would allow French-speaking Quebecers to feel more secure and therefore less likely to undermine the rights of their English-speaking minorities.[58]

Following the comprehensive advice of its legal counsellors (Bastarache, Gibson, and Proulx), the Fédération opined that the proposed s. 23 was all but useless, in need of fundamental amendments before it would be of some concrete advantage to the francophone minorities:

L'article 23(1) se présente davantage comme un objectif que se fixe le législateur que la consécration effective du droit à l'instruction française pour les francophones hors Québec. Car, l'exercice concret d'un droit comme le droit à l'éducation, nécessite l'existence d'institutions précises et la volonté des gouvernements d'assurer l'encadrement et d'affecter les ressources humaines et financières pour en assurer la réalisation. Selon nous, l'article 23(1) ne peut obliger un gouvernement provincial à ouvrir, par exemple, une école française.[59]

The Fédération's brief called for the elimination of vague and troublesome terms, such as "where the number is sufficient to warrant," "educational facilities," "public funds," "regions," and "primary and secondary school instruction." The revised s. 23 must "assurer la reconnaissance pour les Francophones hors Québec du droit à l'éducation dans leur langue du pré-scolaire au post-secondaire inclusivement et du droit à des écoles et des conseils scolaires homogènes de même qu'à la gestion de leurs institutions d'enseignement." Anything less would merely perpetuate the status quo and was unacceptable to the francophone minority communities. Séguin stressed that entrenchment of abstract linguistic and education rights would be meaningless unless the Constitution included a mechanism "which had the mandate and extensive powers required to resolve the conflicts resulting from the implementation of the Charter of Language Rights."[60]

The Fédération had the full support of its provincial affiliates on all matters concerning language policy, especially education rights. The joint brief of the Association canadienne-française de l'Ontario and the Conseil des minorités du Québec stressed the need for members of both official language minority communities to be guaranteed post-secondary education in their maternal languages and the full right to administer their own schools unencumbered by the "where numbers warrant" condition.[61] The Association culturelle franco-canadienne de la Saskatchewan reminded the committee of its longstanding court battles with the Ministry of Education and local school boards in Saskatchewan, which made it sceptical of the government's ambiguous formulation of s. 23. In its view, the section would remain a dead letter and therefore doubly humiliating for the Fransaskois.[62]

Advised by University of Ottawa constitutional law professor Joseph Magnet, the Société franco-manitobaine adopted an even more aggressive stance before the Special Joint Committee, taking direct aim at s. 1 of the Charter, which contained the "reasonable limits" clause. The section reasserted parliamentary supremacy over the Charter, a situation that the Charter was designed specifically to attenuate because s. 1 allowed the majority to ride roughshod over the inherent rights of individuals and minorites. The sFM backed the Canadian Jewish Congress in recommending its deletion. Concerned with problems in the implementation of the Official Languages Act,

Magnet urged that official bilingualism be extended to the "quasi-judicial and administrative sides of government."

On the crucial question of minority education rights, Magnet had this to say:

Minority educational rights are critical to the development of the Franco-Manitoban community. This is the key. We must tell you frankly that we are unconvinced our needs are the same as the needs of the anglophone community in Quebec. We want to impress upon you the needs of the Franco-Manitoban community which are distinct. Our need is for schools, for freedom of choice in schools. That is the long and short of it. That has been our primary need since 1870 and it is still the crucial, essential foundation upon which a healthy Franco-Manitoban community must be built. So we have suggested that with respect to Manitoba, freedom of choice prevail; that public funds support minority language education; that the administration of French language schools be confided to the minority community. ... We would extend this right to immigrants to Manitoba. ... So we propose that the constitution recognize the right to official language immersion education.[63]

Senator Arthur Tremblay picked up on the SFM's provincialist approach and asked whether it was something the committee should seriously consider. Magnet responded that s. 23, as written, addressed the situation of the anglophone minority in Quebec, where Bill 101 streamed all immigrants into the majority's French language schools. On the other hand, freedom of choice in Manitoba would allow immigrants to opt for French schools and therefore help offset the drastic demographic decline of the Franco-Manitoban community. Bryce Mackasey objected to the SFM's willingness to leave English-speaking minority and newly arrived immigrants at the mercy of the French-speaking majority. Magnet replied that the 54.3 per cent assimilation rate experienced by Franco-Manitobans required a different approach to minority language education than the one adopted by the Quebec government in Bill 101, a policy that he understood but did not advocate.[64]

The Association des juristes d'expression française de l'Ontario, presided over by Robert Paris, in its brief to the Special Joint Committee condemned the resolution as "un luerre" and the Charter as "un miroir aux alouettes." It warned that s. 23 would allow Franco-Ontarian taxpayers to transfer their support from the existing system of Catholic separate schools managed by francophone Catholics to a weak French language public system largely in the hands of anglophone bureaucrats. The brief concluded: "Nous croyons ... il serait suicidaire pour la minorité francophone de l'Ontario de consentir au rapatriement de la Constitution canadienne assorti d'une Charte des droits et libertés dont elle serait exclue."[65] The Franco-Ontarian lawyers represented by the Association feared conflicts between Franco-Ontarian parents wanting to expand the French language Catholic separate school system under s. 133 and those wishing to create a new non-denominational francophone system.

In its toughly worded brief, the Association canadienne-française de l'Alberta provided a political analysis of the language and education proposals that reflected the unique context of Alberta, with its expanding system of French immersion schools and its influx of Quebec francophones in search of employment opportunities. The ACFA made the point that the term "founding people" in reference to Alberta's francophone community was meaningless when its members were continuously denied their linguistic and educational rights by an intransigent provincial government. In the ACFA's view, s. 23 was drafted almost entirely to please the anglophone minority of Quebec, which feared that its linguistic and education rights would be abolished under Bill 101, while the Quebec government would be allowed to continue to stream immigrant children into French language schools. The "where numbers warrant" provision was included in s. 23 to please the English-speaking provinces, especially Ontario, whose support for the constitutional package was essential.[66]

In tandem with the SFM, the ACFA pointed out that s. 23 did not allow parents of the majority – French or English – to send their children to schools of the linguistic minority. Since many English-speaking parents in Alberta enrolled their children in French immersion schools, the ACFA saw no reason why some of those children could not be enrolled in French schools under s. 23 if school boards could not afford to support immersion schools for financial reasons. "L'article 23(1), tel qu'il se trouve dans le projet de résolution," declared the ACFA in its brief "rehaussera la langue française à peine au statut de langue seconde et aura tout simplement enchâssé dans la Constitution l'inégalité actuelle entre les deux communautés linguisitiques principales et aura privé les autres Canadiens du libre choix de l'une ou de l'autre langue officielle. Aura-t-on pour des raisons purement politiques enchâssé des injustices?" It wanted s. 23 to provide all Canadians with the right to an education in either of Canada's two official languages.[67]

This approach was not endorsed by either the Fédération or the ACFO. Both organizations' leaders strongly opposed open access to French schools for two reasons. First, a high number of anglophone students would transform many French language schools into "mixed schools," which studies had revealed operated as centres of assimilation for francophone students. Second, the costs of running such schools were likely to be considerably greater, jeopardizing entrenched education rights for the francophone minority communities.[68]

The Fédération garnered support for its critique of the Charter from the Commissioner of Official Languages, Max Yalden, who indicated his unqualified support for the entrenchment of language guarantees to ensure that official language minorities would no longer be left "at the mercy of shifting political and administrative winds." Yalden truly believed that, by reinforcing national cohesiveness, this symbolic act would renew the Confederation bargain. Nevertheless, he regretted that "so far as official bilingualism at the provincial level is concerned," the resolution merely perpetuated the status quo. In his view, s. 133 needed to encompass the provinces of Ontario and New Brunswick, home to over 90 per cent of francophones outside Quebec. The commissioner also regretted s. 20 of the resolution, dealing with the Official Languages Act's provisions giving the public the right to communicate with and receive services from federal institutions in English or French. His view was that the section was far too limited and vague.[69]

Yalden was delighted with the government's proposal to entrench education rights for the official language minorities. Nevertheless, he had three serious reservations respecting s. 23: the qualification of citizenship, the criterion of sufficient numbers, and the lack of a "guarantee to the minorities regarding the administrative control of their own educational institutions." While favouring parental freedom of choice in education, the commissioner felt that the mother tongue limitation should apply to all Canadians, citizens and landed immigrants alike. If the citizenship criterion remained, it would create all sorts of anomalies for immigrant families that obtained citizenship after three years. Some children would be streamed into majority language schools, while their younger brothers and sisters would have access to minority language schools. Yalden further considered that the subclause dealing with sufficient numbers was too ambiguous and wordy, and gave the impression that "minority-language education may sometimes cost more than our society can or wishes to pay." In fact, in reply to a question from Manitoba Progressive Conservative MP Jake Epp, he opined that it was unnecessary and only created "an air of grudging, ungenerous, attitude toward the minority." He called on the committee to redraft the language provisions to "create the conditions in which languages and the cultures they express can flourish in dignity and without fear of assimilation."[70]

In a follow-up letter to the committee's co-chairs, Yalden re-emphasized all these points, especially recognizing the right of official language minorities to administer their own educational institutions.

He also indicated that he shared the concern about the possible implications of s. 43 of the resolution, which granted the provinces and Ottawa bilateral opting-in or opting-out of the language provisions in s. 133 of the British North America Act and s. 23 of the Manitoba Act, 1870. Moreover, he was concerned that s. 1 of the Charter could be used to limit the effect of s. 23 substantially, if the words "where numbers warrant" were retained.[71]

The Fédération and its affiliates hoped that their arguments before the Special Joint Committee, based as they were on extensive legal advice, would bear fruit in the form of significant amendments to both the linguistic and education rights clauses. They sent the prime minister a copy of their brief asking that he support the Fédération's amendments. In his reply, Trudeau indicated that he was well aware that the Fédération did not feel that the government's constitutional proposals went far enough, and gave assurance that both the committee and the government would give serious consideration to its suggestions before drafting the final version of the resolution.[72] Having raised the Fédération's expectations, the Trudeau government then proceeded with a series of amendments that enraged francophone leaders and prompted them to increase their lobbying efforts on Ottawa and the premiers. Trudeau had shrewdly used the francophone organizations' radical proposals to convince the premiers and the public that his government's constitutional package, with the very popular Charter, was far more reasonable.

THE CONSTITUTION ACT, 1982:
SHATTERED EXPECTATIONS

In mid-January 1981, Jean Chrétien tabled a series of amendments to the resolution under study by the Special Joint Committee. Responding to concerns raised by the Canadian Civil Liberties Association, the Canadian Bar Association, as well as the Fédération and the Société franco-manitobaine, he agreed to narrow the scope of s. 1 of the Charter "to such reasonable limits prescribed by law as can be demonstrably justified in a free and democratic society."[73]

On the question of language rights, Chrétien did not significantly alter the resolution's ss. 16–20, entrenching official bilingualism, except to incorporate Premier Richard Hatfield's desire that New Brunswick be recognized as officially bilingual. "It has never been the policy of the government," Chrétien reiterated in referring to the campaign to include Ontario under these sections, "to impose institutional bilingualism on any province."[74] On the crucial matter of educational rights for linguistic minorities, the Minister of Justice proposed only minor changes to s. 23 in order to protect acquired rights. The term "educational facilities" would be replaced with "provision out of public funds of minority language instruction." One amendment to the French language version, however, would in due course provide a monumental gain for the official language minorities. Initially, the English word "facilities" was translated as "installations," but in the final text a more accurate and much broader term, "établissements," was used instead. "Établissements" incorporated a certain notion of management that the term "installations" lacked.[75] Still, Trudeau and his Cabinet refused to accept the thrust of the numerous criticisms from both the francophone organizations and the Commissioner of Official Languages pertaining to the recognition of collective rights and to the right of the linguistic communities to fully manage their own schools on the basis of that recognition. Indeed, the wording of s. 23 was general enough that the issue of whether or not the rights under the section were to be enjoyed individually or collectively was quite intentionally left for the courts to decide.

The francophone organizations reacted to Chrétien's proposed amendments to the resolution with disappointment and anger. They felt deeply betrayed by the Trudeau government, which – as they reminded everyone – had promised so much yet delivered so little. The SFM lobbied Robert Bockstael, the MP for Saint-Boniface, Chrétien, Trudeau, and several other MPs, expressing profound dissatisfaction with three elements of the government's amended resolution. First, s. 23 as it stood would be virtually impossible to implement effectively in Manitoba and therefore needed to be rewritten. Second, under the proposed s. 34, it was possible for the government of Manitoba and the Parliament of Canada to abolish s. 23 of the Manitoba Act, 1870, which pertained to official bilingualism in the legislature and the courts. The SFM demanded that any amendment to s. 23 of the Manitoba Act must require the approval of all the provinces and Parliament. Third, s. 133 must be applied to the province of Ontario, as was being requested by the ACFO and the vast majority of Franco-Ontarians. Without these changes, it was impossible for the SFM to support the Constitution Act, 1982, since its Charter provisions did not meet Franco-Manitobans' aspirations. Indeed, some of the community's leaders construed the Charter as a setback.[76]

The Fédération and its affiliates launched a new campaign, spending hundreds of hours and enormous energy lobbying the provincial and the federal governments to get s. 133 of the British North America Act extended to Ontario at the very least. Furthermore, the francophone leaders sincerely believed that s. 23 had to be framed on the basis of collective rights or it would be useless in the ongoing struggle for French language education and schools.[77] Delegates at the Fédération's General Assembly in Montreal on 14–15 February 1981 passed a motion by the SFM's president that denounced the weakness of the linguistic sections of the Charter and called on the Fédération to keep up the struggle until the Canadian Constitution recognized francophones as first-class citizens with collective rights. A second motion called on it to organize a delegation to lobby the Trudeau government to improve the linguistic provisions of the Charter.[78]

The Association des juristes d'expression française de l'Ontario was outraged at the government's intransigence. Its members were convinced that it was suicidal for Franco-Ontarians to consent to the patriation of the Constitution with a Charter from which they were excluded; it was better not to have any Charter than one that was deeply flawed and would require unanimity for any amendments. "De plus," declared the lawyers, "quel effet aurait une charte dans l'interprétation des garanties douteuses qui lui concède la Constitution canadienne? La minorité francophone ne fait pas le poids. Elle ne vaut guère mieux qu'une ressource naturelle en voie d'épuisement, non renouvelable et non négotiable. Elle pourrait, tout au plus, tenter sa chance en tant 'qu'inégalité régionale' possible de péréquation. Elle souffre du mal français."[79]

In late February 1981, a delegation of francophones from across the country marched on Parliament Hill to protest while the Fédération issued a manifesto pleading for the politicians to grant the francophone minority communities "une vraie égalité dans la Constitution et dans les faits au Canada"; anything short of this would fail to prevent the ravages of assimilation.[80] But the Fédération and its affiliates achieved neither of their two main objectives pertaining to s. 133 of the British North America Act and s. 23 of the proposed Charter. Florent Bilodeau, the Fédération's vice-president, tried to explain the failure by means of some of the political analysis of the Alberta association: the Trudeau government's primary motive for proceeding with its constitutional package was not to remedy the longstanding plight of the francophone minorities but rather to protect the "privileged" anglophone minority of Quebec against the worst features of Bill 101. Bilodeau regarded this approach as tragic, considering the duration of the hardships endured by the francophone communities in comparison with those of the anglophone community of Quebec. He welcomed ss. 16 – 23 of the Charter, but felt they remained "trop peu et nettement insuffisant pour notre développement en tant que composante de l'un des deux peuples fondateurs de ce pays."[81]

Ottawa was all too aware of the disappointment of the francophone organizations. Shortly before the constitutional conference of 2 October

1981, during which a final agreement was hammered out with all provinces except Quebec, the Fédération's president made a final plea to Trudeau and the premiers to adopt the recommendations outlined in its brief to the Special Joint Committee pertaining to s. 133 of the British North America Act and s. 23 of the Charter.[82] Unfortunately for the Fédération, its vision of Canada was not acceptable to the majority of the premiers, while Trudeau was determined to be guided by his political principles in achieving his goal of renewing and Canadianizing the Constitution. Ottawa adopted minor amendments to the proposed resolution on the basis of the two fundamental principles of individual rights and equality of opportunity for all Canadian citizens. The penultimate version omitted from s. 23(2) the ambiguous clause, "Where a citizen of Canada changes residence from one province to another," replacing it with a more affirmative phrasing pertaining to official language of instruction and mobility rights. To the maternal language criteria was added one pertaining to the primary language of instruction of the parents. Thirdly, a numerical threshold for the right to "educational facilities" was deleted, but reserved for the right to "instruction."[83]

In the final form of the Constitution Act, 1982, s. 23 was again amended. The phrase "in an area of the province" was replaced with "applies wherever in the province," followed by an indeterminate criterion for numbers, "is sufficient to warrant," in s. 23(3)(a), dealing with the right to minority language instruction. In s. 23(3)(b), regarding the right to minority language education facilities, the phrase "where the number of those children so warrants" was reinstated. As a result of these amendments, the final version of s. 23 read as follows:

Minority Language Educational Rights
23.(1) Citizens of Canada
   (a) whose first language learned and still understood is that of the English or French linguistic minority population of the province in which they reside, or
   (b) who have received their primary school instruction in Canada in English or French and reside in a province where the language in which they received that instruction is the language of the English or French linguistic minority population of the province,
have the right to have their children receive primary and secondary school instruction in that language in that province.

(2) Citizens of Canada of whom any child has received or is receiving primary or secondary school instruction in English or French in Canada, have the right to have all their children receive primary and secondary school instruction in the same language.

(3) The rights of citizens of Canada under subsections (1) and (2) to have their children receive primary and secondary school instruction in the language of the English or French linguistic minority population of a province

(a) applies wherever in the province the number of children of citizens who have such a right is sufficient to warrant the provision to them out of public funds of minority language instruction; and

(b) includes, where the number of those children so warrants, the right to have them receive that instruction in minority language educational facilities provided out of public funds.[84]

There was a very important discrepancy between the English and French versions of s. 23(3)(b). The former refers to "instruction in minority language education facilities" whereas the latter provides some semblance of a collective right in the form of the wording "de les faire instruire dans des établissements d'enseignement de la minorité linguistique."[85] This variance in language would prove useful during the 1980s when francophone parents, with the backing of their provincial associations, sought implementation of s. 23 through the courts.

At the heart of the Trudeau government's constitutional package were three elements: patriation of the British North America Act, pan-Canadian language protection for the English- and French-speaking minorities, and a Charter of Rights and Freedoms. During the winter of 1981, it began to appear obvious to many in the government that its unilateral approach to Westminster was not politically possible. A question emerged in the minds of some Cabinet ministers and constitutional advisors: On which elements of the package was Cabinet prepared to compromise, and which elements were essential to its vision of Canada? Following the Report of the Special Joint Committee, the Supreme Court ruled that Ottawa's unilateral approach was legal technically but unconstitutional in a conventional sense. The Trudeau government had to abandon unilateralism and decide what its priorities were in order to reach an agreement with a sufficient number of provinces. The Charter, with its uniquely Canadian entrenchment of language and education rights for the two official minority communities, was clearly the cornerstone of the Liberal vision of Canada. To accomplish its central constitutional objective, the Trudeau government relinquished its region-based amending formula, a version of the one in the Victoria Charter, and adopted the Vancouver amending formula of seven provinces and 50 per cent of the population favoured by the eight premiers who opposed patriation. To the dismay of many – including himself – Trudeau even compromised s. 2 and ss. 7–15 of the Charter with the unpopular s. 33, the "notwithstanding clause". But he refused categorically to allow s. 33 to apply to the official language sections, 16–23. After all, they were one of the main reasons for amending and patriating the Constitution.[86]

The Liberal vision of Canada explains why the government did take to heart the criticisms pertaining to enforcement of Charter rights. On this important question, the final version of the Charter contained an important provision not found in the original. Section 24(1) gave individuals whose rights or freedoms under the Charter had been infringed or denied the right "to apply to a court of competent jurisdiction to obtain such remedy as the court considers appropriate and just in the circumstances."[87] The government took its responsibilities in this regard quite seriously and even voted considerable funds, dispersed through the Court Challenges Program, to help individuals and organizations take test cases all the way to the Supreme Court.

Furthermore, there were two indications that the language rights in ss. 16–23, especially minority language education rights, were the central component of the Liberal government's vision of nationhood and national unity. In fact, the University of Toronto political scientist Donald Smiley ruefully referred to the "initiative of 1980–81 ... as our Third National Policy."[88] First, language and education rights were made immune to s. 33, the notwithstanding clause, which allows Parliament or the provincial legislatures to override other fundamental Charter provisions for periods up to five years. Second, all the language rights in ss. 16–23 were made subject to the amendment formula in s. 41, which required unanimity.[89]

It is evident in the Constitution Act, 1982 that the prime minister and the premiers did not want to unduly antagonize the government of Quebec on the matter of education rights for linguistic minorities. The Trudeau government sought to redress some of the harshest features of Bill 101 by creating a common definition of citizenship. Despite the plea of Commissioner of Official Languages Max Yalden, s. 23 maintained the criterion of citizenship, thereby allowing the province of Quebec to continue to have full control over non-English and non-French access to educational institutions as spelled out in Bill 101. Furthermore, s. 59 of the Constitution, ratified *after* the federal-provincial agreement of 5 November 1981, exempted Quebec from s. 23(1)(a) until authorized otherwise by the Legislative Assembly or government of Quebec.[90] This provision actually creates two classes of immigrants who eventually choose to become citizens. "Under the existing rules," writes Eric Apps, "a French-speaking immigrant to Ontario subsequently becoming a citizen has a preferential position to that of an anglophone immigrant in Quebec. ... Thus the true test of whether Quebeckers have confidence in the spirit of s. 23 may well be whether they agree to proclaim s. 23(1)(a)."[91]

The Trudeau government's primary intent was to enhance a sense of pan-Canadian citizenship based upon a shared set of clearly defined values outlined in the Charter. It aimed to redress the long-standing historical grievances of the beleaguered French-speaking minorities by granting them access to French language education in their own schools. It was hoped that, if Canada's francophones could feel secure and thrive in all parts of Canada, Franco-Quebecers would identify less with the Quebec state and the pressure for secession would subside. The government's second, but equally important, objective was to guarantee English-speaking citizens residing or wishing to take up residence in Quebec their historical right to send their children to English language schools. It was hoped that this guarantee would encourage English-speaking Quebecers to remain in that province, thereby contributing to its growing sociological and political pluralism.

CONCLUSION

The Fédération and its affiliates fought a determined political battle throughout the entire process of mega-constitutional renewal beginning with the Quebec referendum. Their respective decisions to adopt a position of either neutrality or outright support for the Parti Québécois did not endear them to members of their respective communities; nor did it please their long-time ally, the federal government. The strategy had the effect of raising the profile of the francophone organizations by giving them opportunities to explain their particular constitutional vision of Canada, which was quite different from that of the Parti Québécois. But it undoubtedly also undermined their efforts to influence constitutional reform.

The francophone leaders learned much about the role of non-governmental lobby organizations in the process of constitutional renewal. The first lesson – and it was a difficult one to swallow – was that, apart from the SAANB, the francophone organizations had virtually no direct political power because their constituents controlled very few provincial or federal seats; they could not threaten incumbent governments with voting for their opponents. If for some reason a government decided to ignore them completely there was very little they could do to alter its behaviour. Furthermore, because there was no convention requiring a referendum on constitutional amendments, it was impossible for the francophone organizations to appeal to public opinion in order to influence the Trudeau government.

But, all was not doom and gloom. Working wisely and diplomatically, the francophone organizations exercised considerable influence over both the negotiating process and the final contents of the constitutional package. Their strongest weapons were the force and intelligence of their arguments in demonstrating that their concept of Canada coincided with the bilingual and multicultural vision offered Canadians by the Trudeau government. For instance, the Société franco-manitobaine concluded that many of its recommendations to the Special Joint Committee had found their way, in whole or in part, into the new Constitution. The scope of s. 1 of the Charter had been narrowed considerably, limiting the power of politicians to diminish hard-won constitutional rights. While Manitoba was not officially proclaimed a bilingual province, it could choose to opt into this status at any time. Importantly, s. 20 of the Charter, pertaining to government bilingual services, was broadened to include services offered outside central and regional offices. A remedy clause, s. 24, was added to the Charter, enabling the courts to enforce their decisions more effectively if they chose to impose a remedy on an offending government. The recommendation to protect s. 23 of the Manitoba Act from a bilateral amendment was not followed, but any changes to the section henceforth would require the approval of the Manitoba legislature, not just the government. All laws in conflict with the Charter, even if passed prior to its adoption, would have to be abolished or amended. The SFM felt it had been least successful with respect to its recommendations pertaining to education rights. S. 23 did not grant freedom of choice to all Canadians in the area of the language of education, nor did it entrench the right to second language immersion schools for members of the majority communities. What s. 23 did do, according to the SFM, was to accept that the language of school administration should be the same as the language of instruction in the school: "Lorsque le nombre le justifie, les francophones ont droit à des installations d'enseignement, ce qui semble signifier des écoles dont la langue d'enseignement et d'administration est le français, et peut-être des conseils scolaires francophones."[92]

As the following chapters will demonstrate, the SFM's optimism in this regard was going to be severely tested over the next decade, as the various provincial francophone associations endeavoured to get their respective governments to interpret s. 23 of the Charter liberally and to implement its provisions with the full generosity and magnanimity they deserved.

3

The Struggle for School Governance:
Franco-Ontarian Organizations
Take the Lead

Section 23 ... represents a linchpin in this nation's commitment to the values of bilingualism and biculturalism. (Supreme Court of Canada)[1]

Since the passage of the Constitution Act, 1982, Canadians have witnessed the ongoing struggle by francophone parents and their provincial and national organizations to obtain full implementation of s. 23 of the Charter of Rights and Freedoms, which deals with minority language education rights. While the battle would spread to every province and territory by the 1990s, it was Franco-Ontarian parents and their organizations that spearheaded the contemporary movement for school governance. The Franco-Ontarian community's quest for control over its own schools and school boards formed a large part of its comprehensive campaign of socioeconomic, cultural, and linguistic regeneration.[2] The community found itself challenged by a series of crises: demographic decline; rapid loss of traditional occupations in agriculture, forestry, mining, and construction; demands for more and better education and new occupational skills; rapid urbanization; secularization of its values, norms, and customs; and, not least, incessant pressure to work, live, and play in English.[3] Franco-Ontarians responded by rebuilding their shattered Church-based institutional network and reformulating their sense of identity.

The fight for school governance commenced in the early twentieth century. Seven decades of political lobbying had failed to secure access to a comprehensive system of French language primary and secondary schools and school boards. The Charter infused the community with renewed energy and purpose. The struggle appeared to flounder at times, as a result of persistent provincial intransigence; government officials and ministers continually exploited the growing rural/urban cleavage within the Franco-Ontarian community. The division was most evident in the clash between secularized Franco-Ontarians and those seeking to preserve an integral Catholic education for their children. Franco-Ontarian Catholics and their Church leaders feared that the implementation of s. 23 language rights in the form of homogeneous Franco-Ontarian schools and school boards would undermine the Catholic separate schools. Backed by English-speaking Catholic organizations, Franco-Ontarian Catholics were determined to preserve their historic s. 93 right to Catholic schools and school boards and to achieve equal funding for the separate system. Secular Franco-Ontarians advocated the creation of a publicly funded system of homogeneous French language schools and school boards to function as the cultural and social centre of their community.

When the significant gains in French language education since 1982 are compared with the lack of success of the previous seven decades, it is obvious that s. 23 of the Charter constitutes a significant watershed in Franco-Ontarians' struggle for school governance. But it was not the only factor. Another was a shrewd combination of enhanced provincial organizations and concerted political lobbying by dedicated, determined, and well-organized leaders. Moreover, these efforts were assisted by several important judicial decisions, beginning with the 1984 Ontario reference case and culminating in the Supreme Court case of *Mahé v. Alberta* (1990) and the 1993 Manitoba reference case. Indeed, Franco-Ontarians obtained education rights to a degree deemed impossible by their leaders at the proclamation of the Constitution Act, 1982. To date, most of the analysis of this significant achievement has focused on the nature and import of the legal process, that is, on the legal principles and declaratory measures encompassed in the several court decisions pertaining to s. 23. Little attention has been paid to the role played by francophone organizations in attaining – in different ways and to varying degrees – the implementation of s. 23 education rights.

Rather than recognizing the positive effects of the Charter, two "Charterphobic" groups of academics, one from the left and another from the right, have emerged to denounce interest groups such as the francophone organizations for seeking their constitutional rights. In the words of Richard Sigurdson, "both left- and right-wing Charterphobes assail the Charter in the way best calculated to evoke shock and horror in a society like ours – that is, they accuse it of generating antidemocratic political consequences."[4] On the left, the Critical Legal Studies Movement perceives the Charter as a liberal document and therefore limited conceptually, socially, legally, and politically because it fails to address inequalities of condition in a social democratic manner. A leading member of this group, Osgoode Hall Law School professor Michael Mandel, has denounced the document and the values it espouses for undermining political democracy and parliamentary responsibility by institutionalizing the legalization of politics. He has characterized this development as fundamentally dishonest, authoritarian, and anti-democratic because powerful interests have used the legal profession and the judiciary to reinforce the status quo and legitimize "the expansion of official repression."[5] Mandel interprets s. 23 as a conspiratorial, undemocratic, legalized political attack on Quebec's highly popular and democratically constituted Bill 101. In his view, the Trudeau government came to the rescue of Quebec's dominant anglophone minority by allowing it to use the courts to challenge and undermine the threat posed by the "dominated" francophone majority's use of the Quebec state to overcome its longstanding oppression. He ridicules Chief Justice Jules Deschênes for the politically motivated, convoluted logic he used to deny the Quebec government's recourse to s. 1 of the Charter to justify the "Quebec clause" of Bill 101 in the case *Quebec Protestant School Boards, 1982.* [6] In 1984, the Supreme Court confirmed the decisions of the Quebec Superior Court and Court of Appeals in this case. In so doing, the justices refused to address the merits of Bill 101 and defined s. 23 as a political compromise rather than a fundamental right that could not be overridden by the "reasonable limits" clause. For Mandel, this confirmed the legalized political nature of the process and the Charter itself.[7] The Supreme Court had turned the conflict between the interests of the dominated francophone majority and the socially dominant anglophone minority into "a contest of *individual* rights, that is, the rights of abstract, equivalent, free-willing subjects."[8] On the matter of the education rights of the francophone minorities, Mandel argues that the abstract individual rights they received were not equivalent to the social power that was reaffirmed for English Canadian interests, majority and minority. "The ability to go to school and to the post office in French," he concludes, "will not preserve a cultural community that must go to work in English."[9] As this study will demonstrate, this interpretation is itself politically motivated and quite premature, given the important developments emanating from s. 23 since the appearance of Mandel's study. Furthermore, Mandel fails to take into account the complex process of micro-constitutional democratic politics learned and practised by the provincial and national francophone organizations, which invoked the intervention of the judicial system usually as a last resort but with considerable effect.

In his 1993 book on the Charter, McGill University political scientist Christopher P. Manfredi also examines in great depth the relationship between judicial power and liberal constitutionalism, but does so from a different philosophical vantage point than Mandel. A staunch defender of Canadian parliamentary democracy, Manfredi takes critical aim at "the use of judicial power to review and nullify or modify the policies enacted by democratically accountable decision-makers." He concludes that "left unchecked, judicial power poses the same threat to liberal democracy as do other forms and uses of political power."[10] In a further analysis of the subject, Manfredi demonstrates how s. 23 set in motion a highly complex process of "micro-constitutional politics." He uses the term to distinguish this process from the comprehensive process of "macro-constitutional politics," which Canadians have come to know all too well over the past three decades and about which Peter Russell has written so eloquently in his study *Constitutional Odyssey. Can Canadians be a Sovereign People?*[11] (Russell uses the term "mega-constitutional politics" for the process.) "In contrast to the formal amendments produced by macro-constitutional politics," Manfredi explains, "micro-constitutional politics involves institutional design through litigation."[12] According to Manfredi, francophone organizations and their communities, together with the federal government, have been able to effect considerable changes to the education laws and institutions of several provinces through an undemocratic constitutionalized judicial process funded by Ottawa. In the view of the Charter's critics, then and now, jurocracy is threatening Canadian democracy.

Both Mandel and Manfredi fail to recognize the crucial function of s. 23 in helping the francophone minority communities overcome a century of provincial opposition to granting them school governance. Nor do they appreciate the catalyzing role played by francophone parents, their provincial organizations, and the Fédération in micro-constitutional democratic politics. Indeed, the Charter has served to reinforce the effectiveness of the francophone minority communities' numerous political campaigns directed at convincing their respective provincial governments to comply – to varying degrees – with s. 23 rights as interpreted by all levels of courts. Furthermore, the pro-active role they have chosen to play in the entire process of micro-constitutional politics accounts for the rather broad and liberal inter-pretation of s. 23 granted by the courts, an interpretation that incorporates a reasonably defined collective dimension to minority language education rights. Since the mid-1980s, but especially since the 1990 and 1993 Supreme Court decisions in the *Mahé* and Mani-toba reference cases, the education statutes of every province and ter-ritory have been amended to meet the test of s. 23 of the Charter.

FROM MEGA- TO MICRO-CONSTITUTIONAL POLITICS

Once the Constitution Act, 1982 received Royal Assent on 17 April 1982, the Fédération and its provincial affiliates were forced again to rethink their political strategies and tactics. They had to move beyond the highly symbolic and confrontational process of mega-constitutional politics surrounding the drafting, amending, and ratification of the Constitution. The transition was not easy. Believing they had not achieved their objectives, the leaders of the Fédération and the Association canadienne-française de l'Ontario criticized the new Constitution and called on the Trudeau government to re-open negotiations, especially on the crucial matter of education rights set out in s. 23. At the same time, the ACFO, frustrated with the stalling tactics of the Davis government in education reform, was eager to use s. 23 to challenge the province both politically and judicially.

Despite the Fédération's disappointment, it reluctantly decided to support the Constitution Act, 1982 once it was the law of the land.[13] Encouraged by its president, Jeannine Séguin, to perceive the constitutional glass as half-full rather than half-empty, the Fédération remained determined to work towards a liberal and productive interpretation of the language measures of the new Charter. This was especially true for s. 23, which Séguin now characterized as "l'acquisition la plus importante pour les francophones hors Québec puisqu'il leur donne le droit tant recherché d'un enseignement dans leur langue et même, dans certain cas, le droit à des établissements d'enseignements."[14] Indeed, challenged by a warm and generous letter of encouragement from the prime minister, Séguin declared the Fédération's intention to do everything in its power to turn s. 23 to the full benefit of all francophone minority communities. Trudeau regretted that Ontario had not opted to become officially bilingual and expressed his sincere belief that "les dispositions de la nouvelle Constitution touchant les droits linguistiques seront plus avantageuses pour les francophones hors Québec que toute autre proposition qu'ont adoptée les gouvernements depuis la Confédération." This was especially the case, he reassured her, with the guarantee of minority language rights, a goal for which francophones had been struggling since the 1870s. His Liberal government was firmly committed to extending the rights of Canada's linguistic minorities. Trudeau urged all francophone associations to prove to their respective provincial governments that minority rights "sont essentiels non seulement à la sauvegarde et à l'épanouissement de votre langue et de votre culture, mais aussi à votre bien-être."[15]

In making the important transition from mega- to micro-constitutional politics, the Fédération and its affiliates were quick to set into motion parallel political and judicial pressure campaigns. First, the national organization continued to lobby the federal government, especially the Secretary of State, as well as the provincial ministers of education. The francophone leaders wanted the Secretary of State to undertake a fundamental restructuring of the program of subsidies for bilingual education. More than two-thirds of the nearly one billion dollars spent on bilingual education between 1970–71 and 1978–79 had gone to the development of French immersion programs for English-speaking Canadians; less than one-third had been dedicated to the development of comprehensive education programs for children of francophone minority families.[16]

Having failed to gain an audience before the Council of Ministers of Education to air its grievances, the Fédération submitted a detailed brief to the Council outlining its complaints against the Secretary of State's criteria for the allocation of funds for bilingual education and the unwillingness of the English-speaking provincial governments to act more quickly on developing comprehensive educational programs for their francophone communities. The Fédération recommended the creation of a separate education program for the francophone minority communities so that the funds intended for them did not get allocated to programs for French as a second language. It also urged that the federal government use its spending powers to entice recalcitrant provinces to implement French language education programs that would be managed and controlled by francophone parents, teachers, and administrators.[17]

At its annual General Assembly of 12–13 June 1982, the Fédération launched a concerted political campaign to prompt the provinces to implement full education rights for their francophone communities, including the right of school governance. It announced that it would also coordinate the efforts of its provincial affiliates in bringing significant legal cases before the courts to effect the speedy and comprehensive application of s. 23 rights, calling on them to proceed without delay in identifying specific cases of Charter violations.[18] The Fédération did not have to wait very long; by early December 1982, the ACFO gave notice that it intended to bring a court challenge based on s. 23. Its objective was to obtain the right for Franco-Ontarian parents to manage their own schools via duly constituted francophone school boards.[19]

Fearful that legal battles would be costly and time-consuming, the Fédération wanted to see whether Ottawa and the provinces would clarify the intent and meaning of s. 23. As it had in November 1981, in late October 1982 the Fédération, with the support of Jean-Robert Gauthier, Liberal MP for Ottawa-Vanier, urged the Trudeau government to convene a federal-provincial conference to address the implementation of the Charter's language rights clauses. It hoped that representatives of all provincial francophone organizations would be invited, and that Ottawa could be pressured into providing financial incentives for those provinces willing to implement ss. 16–23 of the

Charter. Trudeau's response was sympathetic but diplomatic: he would meet with representatives of the francophone organizations, though it was up to them to convince the premiers to attend a conference on linguistic matters.[20]

The provinces refused to be drawn into a discussion of language rights; their energies were focused on the aboriginal rights conference of 15–16 March 1983 required by the Constitution. Trying to put a positive spin on the rejection, President Séguin claimed that the aboriginal rights conference served as an excellent precedent for a future conference on language rights. A year later, however, the Fédération was still complaining that the premiers were continuing to undermine national unity by refusing to recognize the rights of their francophone communities and provide basic linguistic services for them.[21] Despite having signed the Constitution Act, 1982, most premiers were uncooperative while a few were downright obstructionist. Western premiers were especially angry at having been coerced into accepting s. 23 rights and were determined to restrict their scope and application.

The Fédération had no choice but to encourage the provincial organizations to undertake their own comprehensive political and judicial campaigns. It realized that, if the judicial option was to succeed, it had to educate its provincial associations as well as francophone community leaders and parents about their Charter rights, which the Fédération believed included the management and control of their own schools. Between September 1982 and 30 June 1983, it carried out a national information program to this end. Funded by the Secretary of State, the program was renewed in September 1983 for several more months.[22]

The Fédération's first concern was to make sure that sufficient federal funding was available to take challenges under s. 23 all the way to the Supreme Court if necessary. The unflinching support of the Trudeau government was imperative if the judicial approach was to succeed. One of the strongest supporters of Canada's official language minorities and an outspoken advocate of a bilingual Ontario, Serge Joyal, was named Secretary of State in the fall of 1982. In this capacity he was responsible for minority and second language programs. Joyal stated publicly that his ministry was willing to support francophone community organizations, the ACFO, and the Fédération in their joint efforts to achieve full implementation of s. 23. But Joyal did not see s. 23 as including the right of francophones to manage and control their own schools. He was quick to point out that this right had been requested by all the francophone organizations but had not been written into the final resolution by the Special Joint Committee or the government for fear of alienating the provinces.[23] His view of the matter would not deter the ACFO and other Franco-Ontario organizations determined to obtain full school governance.

THE PROTRACTED PRE-CHARTER STRUGGLE

The ACFO did not need much prompting to take the lead in the microconstitutional battle for the implementation of s. 23 rights. Indeed, it had been fighting for homogeneous francophone classes, schools, and school boards since the mid-1960s. In due course, it obtained assistance from various parent and teacher organizations, the most powerful and dynamic of which was the Association française des Conseils scolaires de l'Ontario. Formed in 1944 as an organization comprising Franco-Ontarian Catholic trustees overseeing the bilingual Catholic separate schools, the AFCSO was reluctantly drawn into the battle for homogeneous francophone schools and boards in the late 1970s. Its objective was to preserve the Catholic separate school system by turning existing bilingual Catholic schools into French language schools and bringing public secondary francophone schools under its control. Driving the AFCSO was a militant group of parents in the Ottawa-Carleton region. In 1979, under the guidance of Lucien Bradet, Aurèle Lalonde, Odile Gérin, and several others, a phantom francophone school board, the Conseil francophone de planification scolaire d'Ottawa-Carleton, came into being. For a decade the Conseil's outspoken members lobbied successfully for a homogeneous regional school board encompassing all the francophone children enrolled in the area's four boards.[24]

Upon the arrival of the Charter, the AFCSO had no choice but to join forces with the Conseil to help make sure that any new language-based educational structure would not jeopardize the francophone Catholic separate schools. The two organizations would butt heads on more than one occasion and, for a short time, would be forced to compromise their respective goals. The AFCSO's goal was complicated by educational reforms dating to the late 1960s. In some ways, these early reforms served as a catalyst for the militant Franco-Ontarian nationalists in the Conseil, who had come to see language and culture rather than Catholicism as the central instruments for guaranteeing the survival and renewal of the Franco-Ontarian community.[25]

In 1968, the Ontario government under Premier John Robarts was convinced that greater equality of educational opportunity for Franco-Ontarians was needed, especially at the secondary level. Via Bills 140 and 141, it amended the Education Act, the Schools Administration Act, and the Secondary Schools and Boards Act to recognize the right of Franco-Ontarian children to an education in their own language; to authorize the Ministry of Education to create French language and bilingual primary and secondary classes and schools within the public system; and to establish consultative bodies, the Comités consultatifs de langue française, comprising four Franco-Ontarian members elected by their communities.[26] Robarts wanted to increase the participation rate of Franco-Ontarian children in secondary education and to see to it that, by the time they graduated, they were fluently bilingual and able to compete effectively with their English-speaking compatriots in the labour market.[27]

An increasingly secularized and urbanized ACFO leadership, supported by some of the other francophone educational organizations, accepted the government's rationale. The ACFO sold francophone public secondary education to its constituency by stressing modern education as the best means of preserving their language and culture. There were deep divisions and turmoil between the Franco-Ontarian communities and the Catholic Church over several issues: guaranteed religious instruction, bilingualism versus uniligualism, and the thorny question of school governance for francophone trustees elected to majority anglophone boards. In 1968–69, the financially troubled system of private Catholic Franco-Ontarian secondary schools was incorporated into the Ontario public secondary school system by the government. Thereafter, most Franco-Ontarian children had access to public secondary schooling all the way to grade 13 without their parents having to endure double taxation, as Franco-Ontarian parents did who sent their children to English or bilingual Catholic separate schools, which had funding only to grade 10.[28] In this remarkable and unexpected development lay the seeds of the subsequent campaign for full school governance by Franco-Ontarian parents. The ACFO, which had been instrumental in these developments, established the Comité d'orientation et de recherche en éducation to monitor the results. Backed by its committee, the ACFO joined a number of other francophone organizations in pursuing a course of action that nearly twenty years later would lead to Franco-Ontarians gaining full governance over a comprehensive system of French language schools.[29]

These important but cautious reforms – the culmination of years of debate – were accomplished just in time to accommodate a dramatic increase in Franco-Ontarian enrolment in secondary schools: from 16,984 students in 1968–69 to 30,250 students by 1978–79.[30] Nevertheless, serious problems emerged immediately. First, most school boards used their discretionary powers under Bill 141 to veto the creation of French language classes and schools. Nor were they obliged to set up the committees known as Comités consultatifs de langue française. Furthermore, if and when a school board did sanction the creation of such a committee it was not required to follow its advice. The result was a number of community protests, beginning in 1969–70 with *L'affaire Champlain*, which erupted when parents objected to the Ottawa School Board's creation of a French language high school in the city's west end. This was followed by an outcry in Sturgeon Falls when the Nipissing School Board refused a request for a francophone secondary school. Pressured by the ACFO, the government appointed Tom Symons, the president of Trent University, to investigate the situation. He met with the Conseil provisoire des CCLF as well as the ACFO and made seventy-six recommendations for improving the system of French education.[31] Bills 180 and 181, passed in 1973, made only modest changes, however: the number of members on a committee was increased to six, the president could attend school board and permanent committee meetings, and a school board was obliged to put its reasons in writing when it refused a committee's recommendation for French language classes or schools. The government also established the Commission des langues d'enseignement de l'Ontario as another consultative body to hear appeals from the CCLF. The Commission could make non-binding recommendations to the school boards and the Minister of Education.[32]

These modest reforms did not make school boards any more responsive to the needs of Franco-Ontarian parents and their children. In its battle for a French school, which started in the early 1970s, for example, the community of Penetanguishene witnessed numerous public protests both for and against. In 1973, a mixed school was opened, but it proved unsatisfactory. The CCLF recommended a francophone school in 1978 but the Simcoe Board of Education refused to budge. Despite a 1979 province-wide protest in favour and a positive recommendation from a mediator appointed by the Ministry of Education, the Davis government refused to grant the request of the francophone parents of Penetanguishene. Completely frustrated, they set about establishing an illegal homogeneous francophone high school in September 1979. L'École secondaire de la Huronie's first principal was none other than Jeannine Séguin, president of the ACFO – a fact that made national headlines and attracted support for the Franco-Ontarian cause from all three federal party leaders, including Prime Minister Pierre Trudeau. Yet Premier Davis and his Minister of Education, Bette Stephenson, still refused to provide the school so desperately needed to stem the assimilation rate among Franco-Ontarian children. In April 1980, after further protests and prolonged negotiations, Stephenson agreed to the construction of a new francophone school on the same site as Penetang Secondary School. It took two years and more protests – one on Parliament Hill – before the new school was opened to students on 24 April 1982, just as Canadians received their new Charter with its education rights for minority communities.[33] No doubt this *cause célèbre* contributed to Trudeau's determination to entrench minority education rights in the Charter.

During the 1970s, the quest for school governance centred on two regions. The main battle took place in the Ottawa-Carleton area, historically home to the largest proportion of the Franco-Ontarian population.[34] The second, in Metropolitan Toronto, which was attracting an influx of francophones from all parts of the province, the rest of Canada, and the world, would soon begin to attract the attention of Franco-Ontarian elites. In Ottawa-Carleton, the banner was taken up in 1974 by members of the CCLF and a number of Franco-Ontarian trustees in all four local boards. They were inspired by Gérard Lévesque, outspoken and dynamic member of the Ottawa board's committee, ACFO activist, member of the AFCSO, and Catholic board trustee. With the help of a team, in 1977 he published a pamphlet calling for the creation of a single French language school board for Ottawa-Carleton.[35]

In the interim, Lévesque and his colleagues capitalized on the Ontario government's Mayo Commission, established in July 1974 to study the administrative restructuring of the rapidly expanding Ottawa-Carleton region. While school governance had not been specified as part of the Commission's mandate, the Union de parents et de contribuables francophones of the Carleton region presented an impressive brief before the commissioner, Henry Mayo. They convinced him of the urgent need of the area's Franco-Ontarians to govern their own French language public and Catholic school systems.[36] In its 1976 report, the Mayo Commission recommended that Ottawa-Carleton's Franco-Ontarians be granted their own Catholic school board – later to include a public sector – since schools were quickly replacing parishes as the social and cultural centres of the community.[37] Premier Davis was not pleased, to put it mildly. The recommendation also prompted strong opposition from both the Ottawa and Carleton separate school boards and no doubt aroused the ire of the Catholic teachers' organizations. As he often did, Davis procrastinated by soliciting responses to the Mayo Report in March 1977.

The decision prompted several Franco-Ontarian parent, teacher, and trustee organizations in Ottawa-Carleton, under the leadership of the ACFO's regional office, to form a so-called Common Front. Meetings were held in April and May 1977, and the tense discussions between supporters of a Catholic board and those favouring a language-based board prompted the regional office to expand its Comité pour le conseil scolaire to include representatives from all interested parties. The resolutions emerging from the 9 April meeting called for the creation of a homogeneous and autonomous francophone school board offering credit courses in religion and obligatory French courses. They prompted heated debate in the Franco-Ontarian community and reached a national audience when the proceedings of the 30 May meeting, confirming the earlier resolutions for a language-based rather than religion-based school board, were broadcast by Radio Canada.

Fearful of losing the support of Franco-Ontarian Catholics and the Ottawa and Carleton separate school boards, the regional ACFO convinced Mgr Joseph-Aurèle Plourde, Archbishop of Ottawa, to join its Comité du conseil scolaire and the Common Front. Plourde announced his support for the Mayo Commission's recommendation for a francophone Catholic board that would at some point incorporate a public sector. In October 1977 Plourde even undertook to refute publicly the constitutional objections to the recommendation raised by the Ontario Separate School Trustees Association. The Ottawa-Carleton Common Front, together with other provincial francophone organizations, had to adjust tactics and strategy accordingly. On 30 August 1977 the Comité du Conseil scolaire homogène de langue française de l'ACFO régionale had convened all the interested parties, which agreed to lobby the government for a homogeneous francophone school board that respected religious rights.[38] Separate school parents, teachers, and trustees were clearly going to be the major obstacle to the restructuring of Ontario's school system along linguistic lines. They had their own political agenda, which entailed obtaining full funding for the separate school system, and would steadfastly resist every compromise on any fundamental language-based restructuring of the educational system until their goal had been achieved.

Delegates at the ACFO's annual general meeting on 26–27 August 1977 broadened the campaign by passing two resolutions. The first asked the Davis government to create a provincial system of homogeneous French language school boards protecting the religious rights of Franco-Ontarians. The second called on it to proceed immediately with the establishment of a French language board for the Ottawa-Carleton region. The ACFO regional council presented a brief outlining these points, which were supported by all four school boards in the region, to the government in September 1977.[39]

It was a delicate matter, since many Franco-Ontarian Catholics, especially outside Ottawa-Carleton, feared that the precedent of a public francophone board would jeopardize their constitutional right to separate schools. It was important to keep the Franco-Ontarian community united behind the common goal of francophone school governance, Catholic and public. So controversial was the issue that in the early stages of the Ottawa-Carleton struggle the AFCSO refused to get involved on the grounds that a French language board was not part of its mandate.[40] Yet when events appeared to pass it by and Archbishop Plourde joined the ranks of the movement, the AFCSO's members decided it was time to get involved. On 17 March 1978, they passed a resolution at their annual convention supporting the Ottawa-Carleton campaign for a French language elementary and secondary school board on condition that it respect the acquired constitutional rights of francophone Catholics.[41] The AFCSO presented its views on the matter to the Ministry of Education in early February 1979 in a brief dealing with services in French in the ministry.[42] Franco-Ontarian organizations and leaders had achieved a consensus that they hoped would influence the provincial government.

They were badly disappointed. In February 1979, the Ministry of Education issued a Declaration, known as the Green Book, in which it categorically rejected the Mayo Commission's recommendation for a homogeneous francophone Catholic school board in the Ottawa-Carleton region that would include the French language schools under its jurisdiction. The Davis government had no intention of creating a precedent by establishing a third system of school boards based on language. Instead, it proposed a series of models whereby francophone trustees on public boards would be given greater decision-making powers over all aspects of education related to French language and culture. Under three of the five proposed models, Franco-Ontarian parents would obtain French language sections in some public boards and guaranteed representation by elected francophone trustees mandated to administer these sections.[43]

The ACFO and all the Franco-Ontarian educational organizations in Ottawa-Carleton were angered by the rejection. At its annual general meeting on 26 May 1979, the ACFO's members flatly rejected the Green Book's five options on the basis that all failed to address the demographic and administrative problems of the Ottawa-Carleton region and none gave Franco-Ontarians effective control over their own schools. Two of the models, one granting additional authority to the CCLF and another setting up francophone and anglophone sections within existing public boards, were considered inadequate responses to the school governance issue. The ACFO urged the Minister of Education to grant full school governance for Franco-Ontarians in the Ottawa-Carleton region, where the concept had the support of the four existing boards and the community at large.[44]

In its 6 July 1979 response to the Green Book, the AFCSO revealed its own disappointment over the rejection. In fact, the Green Book did not even make reference to the Ottawa and Carleton Catholic boards, where the majority of francophone elementary school children were enrolled. Yet the AFCSO remained cautious, since its mandate was not to campaign on behalf of any one region of the province. Unlike the ACFO, it had not rejected the five proposed models outright. In fact, CCLF members of the Ottawa and Carleton boards, while renewing their demand for a francophone board, preferred an amended version of the option whereby their amalgamated boards would create a well-defined French language section controlled by elected franco-phone trustees. Following their lead, the AFCSO was ready to accept the idea of two groups of trustees within existing boards as long as the new system respected the principles of confessionality, guaranteed repre-sentation, and decision-making power over administrative, financial, and granting matters. It reminded Bette Stephenson that its priority, like that of the Ottawa and Carleton CCLF, remained the creation of a homogeneous francophone Catholic board.45

Frustrated by the lack of progress but determined to press on thanks to the Trudeau government's renewed efforts to entrench edu-cation rights for minority communities in the Constitution, members of the Common Front created a new organization on 16 November 1979. The Conseil francophone de planification scolaire d'Ottawa-Carleton brought together all thirty-two elected francophone trustees of the region. This parallel Conseil gave itself the tasks of preparing for the transition to a unified francophone board and acting as a lobby group before provincial and local authorities on behalf of this goal as well as the overall improvement of educational services for Franco-Ontarians.46 It did not have the formal support of the four local school boards or the cooperation of the AFCSO, which consid-ered it an interloper.

On 28 December 1979, after receiving input from all the community organizations and learning of the decision of the Ottawa Board of Edu-cation to open a francophone elementary school in September, Minis-ter of Education Bette Stephenson reiterated that the government would not accept the recommendation for a French language Catholic school board for Ottawa-Carleton. Instead, her ministry would proceed with the creation of English and French sections within each of the Ottawa and Carleton public boards, as outlined in the Green Book.47 The ACFO, the Conseil francophone de planification, and all four school boards in the region denounced the decision and asked to meet with Stephenson. At their meeting in April 1980, she acknowledged their objections and indicated that an official from the Ministry of Edu-cation would study the matter further before taking any action.

In April 1980, the AFCSO's administrative council decided to make lobbying the Ontario government its top priority in order to obtain homogeneous French language school boards respecting religious rights for all Franco-Ontarian communities choosing to have a board. Premier Davis, speaking to the Montreal Board of Trade three weeks before the Quebec referendum of 20 May and to the legislature on 6 May, made it abundantly clear once again that his government had no intention of creating a French language school board in Ottawa-Carleton because it would result in a province-wide demand for a third school system, and further fragmentation would raise education costs without improving the quality of programs and services for students. Pressure had been put on Davis by the ACFO and the Conseil franco-phone de planification, whose members appeared at his Montreal press conference to demand justice for Franco-Ontarians.[48] In late 1980, these two organizations and the AFCSO appeared before the Special Joint Committee demanding the constitutional entrenchment of school governance for the official language minority communities throughout Canada.[49]

On 13 July 1981, during its annual seminar, the AFCSO held a mini-conference devoted to the question of school governance. A debate ensued between the trustees from Prescott-Russell and Ottawa-Carleton over the latter's demand for a francophone school board without regard for the rights of Franco-Ontarians in the rest of the province. The delegates passed a series of resolutions reiterating the principles of guaranteed representation and exclusive decision-making powers for francophone trustees over all financial and admin-istrative matters. The AFCSO would consider any government proposal that respected these principles once the government had formally rejected the concept of homogeneous francophone school boards. The Conseil d'éducation franco-ontarienne fully endorsed the AFCSO resolutions and made recommendations on this basis to the Minister of Education.[50] The Conseil francophone de planification was not pleased with the lack of results on school governance for Franco-Ontarians; its president, Lucien Bradet, wrote to the AFCSO in late Sep-tember to this effect. AFCSO president Albert Morin took umbrage at the criticism and noted that his constituency did not like the Conseil negotiating with the government behind their backs, especially when Bradet was willing to accept a minimalist proposal that would endan-ger the ultimate goal of full school governance. It was incumbent upon everyone involved in the struggle to stand united and prepare such a thoroughly convincing case that the government would have no choice but to proceed with the appropriate restructuring of Ontario's educational system.[51]

AFTER THE CHARTER

The Davis government came under even more intense pressure once Parliament adopted the Charter on 2 December 1981. Later the same month, the AFCSO published a document entitled *La Gestion scolaire pour les francophones par les francophones* that was endorsed by the ACFO, the Fédération des associations de parents et instituteurs, the Conseil francophone de planification, the Conseil d'éducation franco-ontarienne, and the Association des surintendants franco-ontariens. It reiterated their request for "Conseils scolaires homogènes de langue française garantissant les droits religieux catholiques acquis." If the government was not ready to accept this proposal at this time, the Franco-Ontarian educational organizations were willing to consider any other proposal that guaranteed francophone trustees representation within anglophone majority school boards along with exclusive decision-making powers over finances and administration.[52] Copies were sent to Premier Davis and Minister of Education Bette Stephenson.

The premier responded by convening a meeting of himself, Stephenson, and all the Franco-Ontarian organizations on 9 February 1982. He listened to the brief presented by the AFCSO on behalf of the groups but once more rejected their plea. Instead, he agreed to set up a Joint Committee comprising three government officials, two representatives from the AFCSO, and one each from the Conseil des écoles séparées catholique d'Ottawa and the CÉFO to review all developments and make appropriate recommendations for another model.[53] The co-presidents were Associate Deputy Minister of Education Berchmans Kipp and Director General of the AFCSO Gisèle Lalonde.[54] The Conseil francophone de planification was not represented, much to the chagrin of Lucien Bradet, its president – no doubt because the Conseil rejected the principles and solution proposed by the other educational organizations. The government was trying to do an end-run around the Ottawa-Carleton militants. In a meeting with the Joint Committee as well as in an angry letter to Gisèle Lalonde in her capacity as co-president, Bradet argued that forced amalgamation of the public and separate boards in the Ottawa-Carleton region would merely anger anglophones and seriously jeopardize the school governance project for francophones. He called on the Joint Committee to add to its recommendations "une structure régionale consultative francophone" comprised of all the elected francophone trustees of the region to guarantee continuity for francophone children from kindergarten to grade 13 and to serve as a transition to a homogeneous francophone regional school board.[55]

Lalonde and Kipp submitted the *Report of the Joint Committee on the Governance of French Language Elementary and Secondary Schools* to Premier Davis on 8 April 1982.[56] It made a series of recommendations:

- "the right of every francophone citizen to education in his/her mother tongue from junior kindergarten to the end of secondary school"
- proportional and guaranteed francophone representation on both separate and public boards of education using sliding-scale criteria, with francophone trustees having exclusive authority over programming, teaching staff, and per capita funding
- the amalgamation of the Ottawa and Carleton public and separate boards into two new boards of education in order to facilitate this francophone representation
- the granting of increased powers to the Languages of Instruction Commission of Ontario

Despite the request of the ACFO and the Conseil francophone de planification, the report did not recommend the creation of a homogeneous francophone school board. To assuage the militants, francophone representatives issued a minority report in which they reiterated the community's preference for French language homogeneous school boards respecting religious rights and the extension of the Catholic separate school system to Grade 13.[57]

Fearful that the government would sit on the report, the AFCSO organized an extensive public campaign to pressure the government to release it. The premier received hundreds of letters from Franco-Ontarian parents and organizations urging him to act quickly on its recommendations.[58] The government made the report public on 14 May during the annual conference of the Ontario Public School Boards and released it in the legislature four days later. The AFCSO was very pleased that the report endorsed its four principles: guaranteed proportional representation of francophone trustees on school boards, some exclusive decision-making powers for those trustees, certain defined financial powers, and specified administrative powers. Nevertheless, aware of strong criticism from the ACFO, the Association des enseignants franco-ontariens, and the Conseil francophone de planification, the AFCSO convened the educational organizations to hammer out a consensus so that the government would not have a reason to shelve the report.[59] The AFCSO, the ACFO, the Conseil, and three other organizations gave the Minister of Education their official response to the report on 16 June. They did not consider the recommendations on the special projects for the Ottawa-Carleton and

Metropolitan Toronto regions to be a priority, and feared that too much attention to these specific cases would delay the implementation of the report's main principles. Further, they wanted the base figure for francophone trustee representation to be 300 rather than 500 students and insisted that both majority and minority trustees have a veto over the selection of the director of education. They also argued that the recommendations on financial matters, especially on capital expenditures, would be a disaster for Franco-Ontarian minority communities and their trustees unless they gained the right to set their own tax rates.[60]

The fragile consensus among the Franco-Ontarian educational organizations was not enough to move the government into action in time for the fall school elections. The AFCSO was very disappointed. Its president, Jean-François Aubé, wondered out loud "whether a war of attrition is being waged against francophones." He reminded Premier Davis that the Joint Committee was his creation, that its members had worked feverishly to meet his April deadline, and that its recommendations were in line with the compromise imposed on the Joint Committee by government policy. The ball was now in the government's court. Franco-Ontarians deserved and expected action.[61] Once again, facing strong opposition from a number of quarters, especially the OSSTA and the Loyal Orange Association in Ontario, the Davis government temporized.[62]

During a meeting on 2 September between the premier, the Minister of Education, the Minister of Intergovernmental Affairs, political advisors and officials, and the representatives of several Franco-Ontarian educational organizations led by the AFCSO, Davis informed everyone present that he had made a mistake in not naming some English-speaking members to the Joint Committee. He indicated that the government needed more time to consult the school boards and teachers' organizations as well as legal experts before deciding on any amendments to the Education Act, 1974. Franco-Ontarian Catholics were concerned about the loss of their right to separate schools under a new system of school governance based on language. The OSSTA objected to the prospect of francophone trustees being elected to school boards. The premier promised to have a bill based on the report's recommendations ready for the spring of 1983 and passed in time for school trustee elections in 1985.[63] Losing patience, the AFCSO chided the province for its continued procrastination. It urged the premier to accelerate the legal decision on the Ottawa-Carleton and Metropolitan Toronto special projects as well as to submit the government's amendments to the Education Act to the legislature in March and limit discussions to two months. Jean-François Aubé promised to provide a list of suggested amendments within a few weeks and requested a meeting with Davis in November. The premier indicated that the Minister of Education would handle the matter of the legal opinion and suggested a meeting with AFCSO representatives at the end of January 1983.[64]

Not all the Franco-Ontarian educational organizations were ready to continue to cooperate with the government. The ACFO, the AEFO, and the Conseil francophone de planification decided to disassociate themselves from the process and initiate a court challenge to the Education Act under s. 23 of the Charter.[65] The ACFO reactivated its Comité d'éducation to sensitize Franco-Ontarians about their education rights and the need for a court reference. It also asked community activist Rolande Soucie to assess the problems facing Franco-Ontarian communities in their quest for control over their schools. She concluded that "la Loi de 1974 sur l'éducation n'est pas adéquate pour répondre aux droits scolaires des Franco-Ontariens tels qu'ils sont énoncés à l'article 23, alinéa 3 a) et b) de la Charte canadienne des droits et libertés."[66]

On 13 December the AFCSO gave Bette Stephenson its list of amendments to the Education Act. This action prompted a meeting on 16 February 1983 among the premier, the Minister of Education, the Minister of Intergovernmental Affairs, and various Franco-Ontarian educational organizations. The latter were told that the government would have its response to the Joint Committee's report ready by the end of March and that Premier Davis wanted them all to assure him that they would be supportive. On 23 March Davis convened a meeting of his colleagues, senior bureaucrats, and representatives of all the Franco-Ontarian educational organizations to present the government's response in the form of a White Paper to the Joint Committee's report on school governance. The government gave formal approval to all the recommendations, except those dealing with the amalgamation of the Ottawa and Carleton Catholic separate and public boards of education. It decided to delay the application of any amendments to the Catholic separate school boards until they indicated their desire to be included through the OSSTA, and only when it was clear that rights under s. 93 of the British North America Act (now the Constitution Act, 1867) were not being violated.[67] Pressured by the government and assisted by the president of the CÉFO, Onésisme Tremblay, the AFCSO and the OSSTA set up a joint committee. By late December 1983 representatives from both sides hammered out a lengthy, convoluted, tentative agreement on the governance of minority language schools within Ontario's system of Catholic separate schools. While the OSSTA was pleased, the AFCSO gave the deal only lukewarm approval at its meeting in April 1984. The agreement would be rendered obsolete by the 1984 Ontario reference case decision, which gave the AFCSO a convenient way out.[68]

In the interim, the ACFO was the first to respond to the province's most recent proposal with a categorical rejection. Given that it was pursuing the government in court, it had little choice but to reiterate this hard line. It reminded the government that despite all the education-related improvements for Franco-Ontarians since 1968, including s. 23 of the Charter, the number of conflicts within English language majority school boards kept growing year by year. It rejected the creation of French language sections within existing school boards and called on the Ontario government "d'emboîter le pas et de reconnaître à sa minorité linguistique ... le droit de gérer ses propres institutions scolaires par l'établissement d'un réseau complet de conseils scolaire homogènes de langue française." The ACFO maintained that the proposal was awkward, confusing, and ultimately unworkable; furthermore, since it did not incorporate the Catholic separate school system, it did absolutely nothing for over two-thirds of Franco-Ontarian elementary school children.[69]

The AFCSO set up a committee to study the government's White Paper and prepare a response by late September. While acknowledging the improvements to education since 1968, the group let Minister of Education Bette Stephenson know of its growing impatience with the government's constant stonewalling on the issue of school governance for Franco-Ontarians by offering "plutôt des palliatifs ou solutions de rechange qui ne sont pas de nature à guérir le problème à sa source, mais risquent de l'accroître par des débats interminables." As noted earlier, the AFCSO's goal was a system of complete school governance for Franco-Ontarians that respected acquired religious rights. It was willing to accept an interim solution as long as it gave elected Franco-Ontarian trustees all the authority required to make the administrative and financial decisions pertaining to any and all matters involving francophone schools. While it urged the government to act quickly on behalf of Franco-Ontarians in Metropolitan Toronto, the AFCSO reiterated that it was only willing to support the Conseil francophone de planification's campaign for a homogeneous school board if it respected religious rights. It then listed a series of modest changes to the government's proposed amendments to the Education Act.[70]

Feeling the political heat from school boards across the province, Premier Davis decided in December 1983 to assemble a study group, the Minority Language Governance Study Committee. It included representatives from the Ministry of Education and from among the twenty school boards affected by the White Paper, and was chaired by a trustee, Marilyn Sullivan. Its mandate was to examine various models of school governance, to establish school board procedures for selecting and implementing one specific model, and to propose a monitoring procedure to ensure that the model operated effectively in a specific school region. The Sullivan Report, released in February 1984, rejected outright the homogeneous minority language school board model, per the premier's instructions, and concentrated on two others. The first called for the creation of six-member Minority Language Education Councils elected by minority language electors, two of whom would be appointed to sit on the full school board. These councils would have the same areas of exclusive jurisdiction as those proposed in the government's White Paper. The Sullivan Report recommended significant changes to the model set out in the White Paper, which removed the upper limit on the number of minority language trustees under the proportional representation formula while reducing the overall number of guaranteed representatives. Though it retained the same areas of exclusive jurisdiction proposed in the White Paper, the Sullivan Report considerably expanded the responsibilities falling within the common jurisdiction of the board as a whole, thereby diminishing the authority of the minority language section.[71] The Sullivan Report, another government attempt to appease the existing educational elites and retain intact the existing educational structure, was rendered obsolete by the decision of the Ontario Court of Appeal in the education reference case.

Unhappy with the Sullivan Report, the AFCSO lobbied to no avail for immediate action on the school governance issue, since further delay would impede making reforms in time for the 1985 school elections; indeed, any resolution of the matter would be deferred for another three years.[72] Intensive political lobbying by the AFCSO and other Franco-Ontarian educational organizations had failed miserably in achieving even modest changes to the Education Act, not to mention in attaining their dream of genuine school governance. It was high time to take the Ontario government to court and challenge the constitutional validity of the Education Act. The ACFO had been preparing to do just that for some time.

Interpreting Section 23

A fruitless fifteen-year political struggle explains why the Fédération had little difficulty in convincing the ACFO to launch a concerted legal challenge to the Education Act. In the fall of 1982, the ACFO consulted the Secretary of State and the Ministry of Justice in order to begin the process of coordinating a community plan of action leading to one or more court cases concerning the management of schools in Ontario. Its president, André Cloutier, submitted a request to the Secretary of State in mid-October 1982 for a substantial grant under the Court Challenges Program. He estimated that the process would require a total budget of $104,600, of which the ACFO could afford only $19,400. He concluded his request by saying that the role of the Ministry of Justice in the judicial process pertaining to educational rights for Ontario's francophone community was being negotiated and "tout augure bien." The ACFO was successful in its request for funds, and the Fédération's president thanked the Secretary of State for Ottawa's generous support.[73] In early December 1982, the ACFO submitted a brief to its legal firm instructing its counsel to begin a court challenge to the constitutionality of Ontario's Education Act based on s. 23 of the Charter.[74] As we shall see in the next section, this challenge was preempted by the 1984 Ontario reference case.

By the fall of 1983, the requests for support under the Court Challenges Program had become so numerous that Ottawa felt compelled to hold a meeting on 1 November to review the terms of the program as well as the state of the cases under the Charter being funded by it: four of them completed, and five pertaining to minority language and education issues still before the courts.[75] The increase in the number of judicial proceedings prompted the Fédération's administrative council to debate criteria for its intervention in them. The Court Challenges Program did not allow funding for intervenors, especially when the Attorney General of Canada was an intervenor in a case. An ad hoc committee of the Fédération met to make some important decisions: along with its provincial affiliates, it had to create a joint legal fund; it had to intervene when a provincial organization did not; if an affiliate intervened at the appellate stage, the Fédération could join as a co-intervenor with the agreement of both parties; and finally, it would agreed to establish a judicial committee under the direction of a lawyer hired on contract to oversee its role in s. 23 cases.[76]

The Fédération had to work out a policy clearly defining its role in these challenges. Was its role merely one of catalyst and coordinator? Was it going to be the plaintiff, a co-plaintiff, or an intervenor? Should it advocate a strategy of swamping the courts with cases in order to force Ottawa to undertake a reference case on s. 23 at the Supreme Court? Pierre Foucher, professor of constitutional law at the University of Moncton, was invited by the Fédération to address these issues at a March 1985 meeting of provincial executive directors. Foucher gave them a shrewd analysis of the complicated interplay between political pressure tactics and judicial proceedings, which he viewed as micropolitics by other means. He proposed a five-stage strategy: community education and awareness; a political pressure campaign on provincial governments by francophone parent organizations; the preparation of court cases; the presentation of those cases and the decisions; and, as the final step, further negotiations leading to legislative changes. He contended that, as more language-based cases were heard and decisions rendered, the amount of time and energy spent on subsequent challenges would be diminished and the process of political negotiations would be accelerated.

While recourse to the courts was almost inevitable, Foucher cautioned with great prescience that individual francophone communities had to be fully aware of the stakes involved because "sans le désir d'écoles homogènes gérées séparément, la lutte n'en vaut pas la peine." He stressed that it was imperative for judicial proceedings to originate with parents and their local organizations, since they were the holders of rights under s. 23 and the courts would hear their grievances with greater sympathy. The national and provincial associations should take on the role of co-plaintiffs or intervenors, depending on the importance they wanted to place on their participation in specific cases. Foucher cautioned against swamping the courts with cases as some in the Fédération were proposing, because the idea "a l'inconvénient de ne pas produire l'impact décisif requis puisque le jugement est alors perçu comme une intervention fédérale dans un champs de compétence provinciale."[77]

The potential of an out-and-out confrontation with the provinces had already been made clear by Joseph Magnet in 1982 when he pointed out the unprecedented nature of s. 23 rights. Their implementation required the expenditure of public funds for new schools, equipment, transportation, and even the redrawing of school board boundaries. Such decisions required the government to exercise cautious judgment if it wished to avoid placing itself in "an adversarial position to large segments of the population." Indeed, Magnet encouraged provincial governments to avoid the political uncertainty of litigation by anticipating and identifying "intelligent strategies of implementation" that incorporated participation from minority language communities and their organizations. Failure to act expeditiously and courageously, Magnet warned, could result in the courts eventually imposing remedial measures that the provinces would be bound to implement against their will.[78]

Perhaps Foucher's most pertinent point was that francophone organizations and parents should not believe that the courts could settle all their linguistic and educational grievances. He reminded his listeners that negotiations would be required after every court decision, and advised them to prepare in advance so that concrete proposals could be presented to provincial authorities soon after a decision had been rendered. Foucher concluded on an optimistic note: the adoption of the Charter had not yet budged the provincial politicians, "mais les opinions du plus haut tribunal du pays pèseront leur poids dans la balance des négotiations."[79] In fact, a shrewd combination of timely micro-political pressure campaigns and judicial challenges would characterize the battle over s. 23 leading up to the landmark Supreme Court decision in the *Mahé* case.

Both strategy and tactics were important in the practice of micro-constitutional politics. It was also imperative for francophone plaintiffs and their lawyers, as well as francophone organizations acting as co-plaintiffs and intervenors, to have at their disposal scholarly analyses of s. 23 that would enable them to present solid arguments and corroborating evidence to convince the courts that their interpretation of the section was the appropriate one. It did not take long for a small number of constitutional lawyers and political scientists to show an interest in Charter issues, particularly minority language educational rights, and to develop a range of arguments that were drawn upon by francophone plaintiffs and the intervenors pleading their causes. Some of their arguments ultimately found their way into court decisions.

Joseph Magnet was one of the first to address certain problems associated with the interpretation of s. 23. He saw the three central concepts at work in the section as linguistic equality, the section's remedial nature, and its historical context, which, for him, required a broad and liberal interpretation of both its intent and its objectives.[80] If a comprehensive remedial approach was to prevail in the advancement of education rights for francophone minority communities, it was imperative that the courts infuse s. 23 with a "large, liberal, and robust interpretation, sufficient to lay to rest all residual hostility harboured by official language minorities against Canadian governments."[81] Failure to do so would render the section worthless to the francophone communities.

According to Magnet, "minority language educational facilities," as specified in s. 23(3)(b), would pose problems of interpretation if the courts adopted a too narrow and literal approach. "Educational facilities" implied aspects of school administration and operations, in his view. It remained questionable whether or not this right extended all the way to francophones' long-cherished desire to "control the administration of francophone schools." It was well known that the SFM, the ACFO, and the Fédération had pleaded with the Special Joint Committee to give francophones the right to manage their own school systems.

Magnet recalled Jean Chrétien's statement before that committee to the effect that the aim of s. 23 was "to provide francophones outside Quebec with approximately the same rights as the anglophones in Quebec enjoy, or once enjoyed," and argued that, since Quebec's English language minority controlled its own school system, it was only appropriate that francophone minority communities obtain the same right.[82]

Magnet also pointed out that s. 23 was "entirely silent as to when numbers are sufficient to warrant minority language education rights." He believed, nonetheless, that neither the legislators nor the bureaucrats had the discretionary power to determine what constituted sufficient numbers, and argued that, since s. 24 granted recourse to the courts for a remedy to a violation of s. 23 rights, it was clear that only the courts could render "an authoritative interpretation of the numbers test." Magnet demonstrated that the courts could turn to the history of educational conflicts for legal precedents as well as to existing provincial legislation in establishing the number of students necessary to compel the provinces to provide minority language instruction, then minority language educational facilities. He noted that there would be a debate over whether the numerical requirement would be based on "experienced demand" or on the percentage of the francophone population in a given region.[83]

Magnet maintained that the raison d'être of s. 23 was to give Canada's official minorities a comprehensive remedial mechanism for fostering greater racial harmony. "To the extent that courts choose to respect the spirit of duality and linguistic equality that is radiated by section 23, the 'educational facilities' concept may well require establishment of minority-language school boards, or other means of self-government, where minority numbers are especially concentrated."[84] Initially his argument received only cautious endorsement from Pierre Foucher, who was considerably more circumspect about reading into s. 23 an explicit right to francophone school governance. Foucher recalled that s. 93 of the Constitution Act, 1867 did not grant Catholics and their school boards "un droit complet à la gestion scolaire," but hoped that the Supreme Court would be more generous in its interpretation of s. 23 rights "de façon à accorder aux minorités linguistiques le droit à une structure scolaire autonome et distincte."[85]

One important dimension of this legal debate had to do with whether s. 23 rights were classical legal rights founded on principles, or second-order social rights founded on political compromise. Justice Jean Beetz, in the 1986 Supreme Court case *Société des Acadiens du Nouveau Brunswick v. The Association of Parents for Fairness in Education,* argued forcefully that the courts had to address rights based on political compromise, such as those in s. 23, with considerable caution; that they must not be turned into agents of change in the area of linguistic rights.[86] In his 1987 analysis of the Supreme Court's interpretation of linguistic rights, Pierre Foucher remarked upon the justices' distinction between fundamental rights and s. 23 rights, which they maintained were of a political remedial nature. He also noted the restrictive approach of the Supreme Court to cases involving disputes over official bilingualism under ss. 16–20 of the Charter. He concluded that, overall, the Charter was "un coup d'épée dans l'eau" and hoped that the Supreme Court's approach to s. 23 rights would become less restrictive.[87] By 1989, Foucher had changed his point of view and argued that the courts had rendered creative decisions on many sections of the Constitution Act, 1867 that entailed political compromises. The distinction between classical legal rights and rights emerging from political compromise was spurious and untenable; linguistic rights, while based on political compromise, were fundamental rights and had to be treated as such by the courts. The political compromises incorporated in the linguistic rights under s. 23 were between a territorial versus a personal approach; between an individual versus a collective approach; between their political nature and their fundamental nature. The rights applied to specified territories and provinces and to specified groups of persons: those whose maternal language was French and those who had received their elementary education in French in Canada. While they were granted to individuals, the origin, the objectives, the criteria of application, and the area of intervention – education – clearly predicated that any successful implementation of s. 23 had to take into account the concept of collective rights.[88]

Perhaps the most original point made by Foucher was that s. 23 was an audacious political compromise because it involved a social right as opposed to a legal right. While the latter was immediately executory, the former required the intervention of the state. In his view, "l'article 23 pose pour la première fois au Canada la relation directe entre le pouvoir législatif et le pouvoir juridiciaire dans le domaine des droits sociaux."[89] How were social rights to be put into effect? There were only two options, according to Foucher. First, the provincial legislatures could pass legislation putting into effect the principles outlined in s. 23. Second, the courts could impose ordinances on provincial governments or school boards requiring them to fulfill certain obligations, such as building a new school for francophone children. Foucher noted that the courts felt uneasy about their new role with respect to social rights, while the linguistic minorities found the legal approach time-consuming, costly, and problematic when evidence to buttress their case was difficult to find. He urged jurists and legal experts to articulate a theory that would allow a new definition of the relationship between the judiciary and the executive, "entre la mise en oeuvre statutaire et la mise en oeuvre judiciaire d'un droit social." Since most provincial legislation pertaining to schools was silent on the question of minority language rights, it was far from easy to articulate a case to take before the courts. Until the Supreme Court ruled that s. 23 created a "duty to legislate" in conformity with its principles, concerted pressure on the political elites to take action would be required; otherwise, s. 23 would become both a political and a judicial failure.[90]

Charter scholars had, early on, laid out many of the legal arguments that would find their way into the court cases pertaining to s. 23 in the decade following its passage. Many of these would be used by francophone provincial organizations and parents to support their claim to full school governance. Ironically, one or more of the same arguments would be adduced by various provincial governments in their valiant but ultimately fruitless attempts to limit the nature and extent of the education rights granted under s. 23 of the Charter. The first judicial testing ground was the province of Ontario, where the Conservative government of Premier Bill Davis agreed to refer its Education Act, 1974 to the Ontario Court of Appeal for a ruling.

The ACFO's Court Challenge and the Ontario Reference Case

After the adoption of the Charter, one of the activities of the ACFO was to direct its regional presidents and the Association française des Conseils scolaires de l'Ontario to monitor the elections of the Comités consultatifs d'éducation for irregularities. The regional committee, in turn, called on the ACFO to renew its support for Franco-Ontarian parents of the Cochrane-Iroquois Falls region, who were demanding a French language entity within their school. The parent organization gave the regional office $1000 to help advance this cause and urged all the francophone educational groups to undertake a province-wide publicity campaign explaining to Franco-Ontarian parents the advantages of French language schools and school boards.[91]

Encouraged by these and other developments, the ACFO believed it was time to undertake a court challenge to the province's Education Act under s. 23 of the Charter. With the permission of his board, president André Cloutier instructed the ACFO's solicitor, Brian Crane, of the Ottawa firm of Gowling and Henderson, to prepare the case on behalf of Franco-Ontarian parents in Cochrane-Iroquois Falls. He reminded Crane of the perennial battles over school rights in several

communities and the unsympathetic attitude of Premier Davis and
Minister of Education Bette Stephenson to the educational needs of
Franco-Ontarians. Cloutier indicated that the ACFO wanted "faire
reconnaître par les tribunaux que la seule façon pour la minorité linguistique francophone en Ontario d'exercer les droits que leur reconnaît la Charte canadienne des droits et libertés est de posséder la
gestion des ses écoles par le biais des conseils scolaires de langue
française."[92]

Intent on educating a wide spectrum of Franco-Ontarians about
their s. 23 rights, thereby garnering broad community support for its
legal action as suggested by Pierre Foucher, the ACFO organized a
"recontre de concertation" to discuss the education-related problems
confronting francophone parents across the province. The meeting,
held in North Bay on 5 February 1983, involved representatives from
the ACFO and its regional councils, the Fédération, the Association des
enseignants franco-ontariens, the community-based Comités de coordination de langue française, and bureaucrats from the Ministry of
Education. After a frank discussion of the obstacles faced by Franco-
Ontarian parents trying to obtain access to French education from
recalcitrant local school boards, the delegates decided that concerted
political action was required to bolster the legal challenge. The delegates unanimously supported the ACFO's decision to take the government to court, but also called for a meeting between the Franco-
Ontarian organizations, francophone parents, and the Minister of
Education and her deputy minister to determine whether a negotiated
settlement might be possible.[93]

Confident of the political support of its constituency, the ACFO,
through its solicitor Brian Crane, sent the Attorney General of
Ontario a draft statement of claim seeking declaratory orders and
naming the Attorney General as defendant.[94] Director of Constitutional Law John Cavarzan indicated by phone that the government
would cooperate in expediting the action and stated that officials in
the Ministry of Education "were of the view that the present Education Act was constitutionally valid as were the new proposals." When
asked by Crane whether the government was considering a constitutional reference, Cavarzan replied that it was being contemplated as
a future option but the government had not reached that stage in its
deliberations.[95]

The attempts at a negotiated settlement came to naught. Hearing
nothing further from the Attorney General or the Minister of Education, the ACFO, the AEFO, and four Franco-Ontarian parents filed a
statement of claim before the Supreme Court of Ontario in Sudbury
on 25 May 1983. Their press release summarized their case as follows:

The plaintiffs question the discretionary power granted to school boards in the Education Act of Ontario with respect to the establishment and management of the French language community's educational institutions. It is deemed necessary to obtain a court decision regarding these questions since many school boards consistently fail to meet the needs of the French-speaking community. If the right of Francophones to manage and control their education institutions were recognized, the problems which affect many regions would disappear quickly. ... the education needs of the Franco-Ontarian community would be met better by their own Francophone school boards and it is imperative that this right be recognized in law.[96]

In forwarding the statement of claim to Bette Stephenson, the ACFO's president remarked that a successful outcome would have positive results for all of Canada's francophone communities and "rehaussera considérablement auprès d'elles l'impact de la Charte comme instrument de protection des droits et pourra inciter ceux qui s'y opposaient à reconnaître sa valeur au regard de la collectivité francophone canadienne."[97]

Still hoping to avoid a costly and risky court battle, the ACFO and its supporters continued to lobby the Davis government for a political settlement. Fortuitously, they avoided the expense when Davis and his Cabinet decided to take the lead in the matter. Convinced that its proposed amendments to the Education Act met the test of s. 23, the government decided to undertake a reference to the Ontario Court of Appeal. In early August 1983 Attorney General Roy McMurtry, through an Order-in-Council, referred four questions respecting the Education Act and s. 23 of the Charter to the Court of Appeal under the Constitutional Questions Act. Given that three of the four questions were based on their statement of claim, the ACFO and AEFO instructed their solicitor not to proceed with their case, on condition that they be made parties to the reference.[98] Chief Justice W.G.C. Howland convened counsel for all interested parties on 31 August 1983 and set out the timetable for the case, with the hearing slated for 16 January 1984.[99]

The ACFO informed all organizations planning to intervene on behalf of Franco-Ontarians' educational rights that the arguments of certain opposing intervenors would hinder "la reconnaissance tant espérée, et enfin obtenable, des droits de notre communauté à contrôler et à gérer ses propres établissements d'enseignements." It also warned them not to say or do anything that might jeopardize the principles put forward in the statement of claim or the viability of a system "qui assurerait la gestion et le contrôle pleins et entiers, par des francophones, des établissements d'enseignement de ceux-ci." Finally, it urged them to continue to support, "avec leur rigueur et lucidité habituelles," the plaintiffs in the reference case.[100]

The plaintiffs, backed by the Fédération and several other intervenors, submitted a lengthy factum outlining their arguments on the four questions referred to the Court of Appeal by the province. They emphasized the demographic, socioeconomic, political, and administrative obstacles to full education rights for Franco-Ontarians. They also appealed to the court not to rely too heavily on the statements of politicians and civil servants in establishing the true intent of s. 23; it was more important to understand the political and social environment prevailing at the time the Charter was drafted.[101]

In the factum, the ACFO and AEFO applauded such developments as the creation of the Comités consultatifs de langue française in 1968, the Commission des langues d'enseignements de l'Ontario in 1974, and the Ottawa-Carleton Review Commission's 1976 recommendation for a French language board in the region. Yet the fact remained that the Ontario government steadfastly refused to grant Franco-Ontarians the right to manage their own school boards. They reminded the court that the April 1982 report of the Joint Committee on the Governance of French Language Elementary and Secondary Schools had recommended French language sectors in each of the Ottawa and Carleton public and separate boards with exclusive jurisdiction over all matters relating to instruction in French. In its March 1983 White Paper proposals on changes to the Education Act, the province had accepted the Joint Committee's recommendations. The ACFO and the AEFO contended that s. 23 had moved the goal posts; that it granted francophone minority communities the right to manage and control their own schools.[102] The section was the result of recognition of this right by a wide variety of royal commissions, task force reports, independent studies, and federal and provincial government committee reports. Furthermore, numerous federal/provincial conferences, including one that produced the Victoria Charter, the premiers' conference at St Andrews, New Brunswick in August 1977, together with the Trudeau government's constitutional proposals in Bill C-60, acknowledged that the francophone communities faced enormous pressures for assimilation that could only be countered successfully by giving them the right to school governance. The factum quoted Minister of Justice Jean Chrétien at the introduction of the Canada Bill in October 1980: "We are seeking to protect, once and for all, the education rights of francophones outside Quebec. The aim of this initiative is to provide francophones outside Quebec with approximately the same rights as the anglophones in Quebec enjoy, or once enjoyed."[103] Given that the primary intent of s. 23 was remedial, the

ACFO and AEFO argued that it was imperative for the court to give it "une interprétation large et libérale qui reflète ce rôle réparateur."[104]

The first question submitted by the province asked, "Are sections 258 and 261 of the Education Act inconsistent with the Canadian Charter of Rights and Freedoms and, if so, in what particular or particulars and to what extent?" In their response the plaintiffs argued that the two sections were unconstitutional in several respects. First, they provided a very narrow definition of who was eligible to instruction in the minority language because, under s. 23, it was not only francophone students choosing to receive education in French but rather all children of eligible francophone parents who had to be taken into account when determining whether the numbers justified the granting of educational services. Secondly, these sections granted school boards total discretion in deciding whether or not to offer French language instruction or schools to the children of eligible francophone parents, as defined under s. 23. In the view of the ACFO and the AEFO, s. 23 was mandatory, and French language instruction and schools had to be provided whenever sufficient numbers of students warranted. Finally, the sections set out arbitrary and unjustified numbers – twenty-five for primary school and twenty for secondary school – and determined them on the basis of existing school board boundaries rather than provincial boundaries, as set out in s. 23(3)(a) of the Charter.[105]

The third question put to the court was, "Do minority language educational rights in the Canadian Charter of Rights and Freedoms apply with equal force and effect to minority language instruction and educational facilities provided for denominational education under parts IV and V of the Education Act and to minority language instruction and education facilities provided for public education under the Education Act?" The ACFO and the AEFO responded to it in the affirmative; as long as Catholics continued to manage their own educational system, there would be no incompatibility between s. 23 of the Charter and s. 93 of the Constitution Act, 1867.[106]

The fourth question dealt with the proposed White Paper amendments delineating the form and extent of francophone representation on Catholic separate school boards. The two organizations supported the argument that the Legislative Assembly of Ontario had the authority to amend the Education Act, as proposed in its White Paper, to provide for the election of minority language trustees to these boards to exercise certain exclusive responsibilities pertaining to minority language education. This limited form of shared governance, they argued, did not infringe on the constitutional right of Catholics to administer their separate schools but merely implied "une modification du système aux termes duquel l'enseignement confessionale est administré."[107] If they won this point, the ACFO and AEFO opened the possibility that francophone parents could send their children to either French Catholic schools or French public schools and thereby obtain some degree of governance in either system. It was therefore strategically wise for the plaintiffs to support the government's proposal to amend the Education Act.

On the all-important second question, the ACFO and the AEFO argued that the Education Act was inconsistent with the Charter because it did not grant Franco-Ontarian parents the right to control their own French language instruction and educational facilities. They agreed with the Attorney General that this right was not explicitly enunciated in the Charter, but contended that it was implicit because, if it was not, then the right of Franco-Ontarians to French language education would have no substance. Francophones were in the minority in the vast majority of Ontario's public and separate school boards. Executory decisions about the nature and extent of French language instruction were made by elected representatives of the anglophone majority, most often against the recommendations of the Comités consultatifs de langue française. Over and above its remedial intent, the goal of granting educational rights to linguistic minorities was to ensure the promotion of their linguistic and cultural heritage, thereby allowing their members to live their respective cultures in their own languages.

Invoking the principle of equality inherent in the Charter, the ACFO and AEFO argued that linguistic minority taxpayers had the right to enjoy the same level of management and control over their classes and school establishments as majority language taxpayers. Inasmuch as the Education Act did not guarantee this right to the linguistic minorities, it was inconsistent with the Charter – a fact that the court was obliged to note. They also pointed out that the French version of s. 23(3)(b) was couched in broad and institutional terms, indicating that its drafters wanted to grant the linguistic minorities an effective role in the control and management of "*leurs établissements d'enseignements* (établissements de la minorité)." The ACFO and AEFO were willing to leave the exact form and extent of such control and management open to negotiations between representatives of the francophone communities and the Ministry of Education. They pointed to the fact that both New Brunswick and Quebec had already established linguistically homogeneous school boards.[108]

The ACFO and AEFO had formulated well-documented arguments that would be difficult for the Ontario Court of Appeal to ignore. Paradoxically, what worried them more than the Ontario government's position on the four questions was how the federal government would approach the thorny issue of school governance. Ottawa's ambivalent attitude was revealed early in the process, in the fall of 1983, when the Fédération requested intervenor status before the Court of Appeal in support of the francophone plaintiffs. Since the Ontario decision would have repercussions for francophones in other provinces, it was imperative for the Fédération to represent their interests. It wanted to make sure that the Court of Appeal would give the Charter a "large and liberal interpretation" so that it could be applied "generously and uniformly across the country." The Fédération applied to the Court Challenges Program for funding to underwrite its role as intervenor. Much to its dismay, it was turned down on the grounds that the Secretary of State was already funding the ACFO and that the Attorney General of Canada had decided to be an intervenor in the case. The Fédération's president wondered what Ottawa had up its sleeve.[109] Although refused funding, the organization was granted intervenor status.

The Fédération supported the ACFO and AEFO on the first two questions respecting the constitutional validity of Ontario's Education Act but for strategic reasons chose not to comment on the other two. Its main role was to serve as a catalyst in coordinating support for the plaintiffs from a wide variety of sources. The individuals and organizations intervening on behalf of the ACFO's and AEFO's arguments on some or all of the four questions included the Attorney General of Canada, the Association française des Conseils scolaires de l'Ontario, the Association canadienne d'éducation de langue française, the Ottawa Board of Education, the Conseil francophone de planification scolaire d'Ottawa-Carleton, the Ontario Association of Alternative and Independent Schools, the Coalition for Language Rights in Ontario, the Liberal and New Democratic parties of Ontario, the Commissioner of Official Languages, the Quebec Association of Protestant School Boards, and Alliance Québec. On the other side of the debate, the Attorney General of Ontario found support on some or all of the four questions from the educational establishment, including the Ontario Public School Trustees' Association, the Metropolitan Toronto School Board, the Ontario Secondary School Teachers' Association, the Ontario English Catholic Teachers' Association, the Ontario Separate School Trustees' Association, and the Metropolitan Separate School Board.[110]

It came as a shock to the Fédération and the plaintiffs that the Attorney General of Canada was not willing to provide unqualified support for an interpretation of s. 23 that included the right of the linguistic minority communities to manage and control their own educational establishments. The Fédération got involved in the issue after the ACFO issued a press release on 19 January 1984 denouncing the Minister of Justice and was subsequently upbraided by Jean-Robert Gauthier, MP for Ottawa-Vanier, who advised the provincial organization to target the real villain, the Ontario government. Gauthier also expressed his disappointment that the ACFO had refused to support his efforts to convince the Minister of Justice to submit additional notes of clarification to the Court of Appeal.[111] Fédération President Léo Letourneau wrote to Minister of Justice Mark MacGuigan expressing his indignation at the comments of the Attorney General of Canada's representative, Brad Smith, before the court in the reference case. Smith had contradicted MacGuigan's factum when he proclaimed that s. 23 did not guarantee Franco-Ontarians the right to manage and control their own educational institutions.[112] Letourneau wondered whether the Minister of Justice should intervene in any future language rights cases if "ses représentants continuent à défendre de telles positions et à présenter une vision aussi limitative de l'esprit et de la lettre de la Chartre des droits et libertés."[113] The Fédération demanded and expected unqualified support from the Trudeau government.

When no response was forthcoming from the MacGuigan, Letourneau sent a telegram to the prime minister complaining about Smith's offending remarks. He asked Trudeau to call upon his Minister of Justice to clarify the government's position on s. 23, especially the crucial matter of school governance. In short, was Ottawa in favour of a broad and liberal interpretation of the Charter allowing for expanded recognition of francophone minority communities' rights across Canada? Once again, there was no reply. Letourneau then wrote to Trudeau asking him to use his influence to encourage the Minister of Justice to submit additional notes of clarification to the Ontario Court of Appeal, as was being suggested by both Secretary of State Serge Joyal and Jean-Robert Gauthier, MP for Ottawa-Vanier.[114] On an incongruous note: The ACFO's appeal was being made possible by the generous funding of the Secretary of State while the Minister of Justice's ambivalent intervention was threatening its claim to full school governance.

In the interim, the ACFO called on the leader of the New Democratic Party, Ed Broadbent, to inquire into the positions of both the Secretary of State and the Minister of Justice on the matter of school governance. Broadbent was reassuring on Joyal's strong financial support for the cause of Franco-Ontarians and his repeated criticism of the Ontario government's policy of "petit pas."[115] However, Broadbent could not tell the ACFO that the Trudeau government unconditionally supported the right to school governance.

Nevertheless, the Fédération's aggressive political campaign began to produce some results. The ACFO and the Fédération were invited on several occasions to meet with Deputy Attorney General Roger Tassé to clarify issues. In late April 1984, after several months of intense negotiations, Minister of Justice Mark MacGuigan informed the Fédération that he had applied to the Court of Appeal for permission to submit additional notes of clarification, and indeed had already submitted them on 30 March.[116] This action brought considerable relief to the ACFO and the Fédération. The submissions called on the court to interpret s. 23 in a most liberal manner, because the right accorded "(a) relates to the fundamental bilingual character and duality of Canada, (b) represents a qualification on the provincial power in relation to education, (c) seeks to provide education to the minority on a basis of equality with the majority, and (d) is remedial in nature." Clarifying this position further, the Attorney General argued that to guarantee the creation of educational establishments that could be considered objectively as belonging to the minority "il faut que la minorité soit investie du pouvoir de direction et de l'autorité décisionnelle appropriés sur ces établissements." Finally, the degree of management and control should be the same for the minority linguistic community as for the majority.[117]

Once the matter was settled, Trudeau wrote to the Fédération indicating that he hoped that the undertaking of his Minister of Justice had rectified the misunderstanding as to his government's position on the rights of the official language minorities.[118] Even more importantly, Trudeau – approaching the end of his tenure as prime minister – sent Premier Davis a remarkably candid letter outlining all the reasons why his government should declare the province officially bilingual. Trudeau applauded Ontario for its progress in making French language facilities and services available in many areas of provincial responsibility. But, he believed, it was time for Ontario "to move beyond the statutory and administrative dimension of linguistic equality and to embrace broader constitutional recognition for the French language." Such a gesture would lift the Canadian spirit and strengthen the bonds of nationhood against the threat of separatism in Quebec.[119] Davis welcomed the opportunity to explain to Trudeau, in some detail, his government's "gradualist" and "pragmatic" approach to the implementation of language rights for Franco-Ontarians, an approach that respected Ontario's "political traditions of steady maturation and dynamism." He intimated that a symbolic step of entrenchment might satisfy many in Quebec but would create rancour and disruption in Ontario, destroying the consensus required for further progress.[120] These developments, arising from their lobbying efforts, demonstrated the degree to which the Fédération and the ACFO had mastered the art of micro-constitutional politics.

In the interim, all the francophone organizations anxiously awaited the decision of the Ontario Court of Appeal. When it came, on 26 June 1984, it marked a watershed in the development of education rights for Canada's francophone minorities. The justices understood perfectly well that they were moving into new constitutional territory. Acknowledging that historical arguments do not engage the law, they nevertheless chose to abandon a "narrow and strict constructionalism" in favour of "a broader approach, which would include a consideration of the historical developments, particularly in the field of education." They felt that following this path was necessary in order to ascertain the intent of the constitutional amendments pertaining to minority language education.[121] Accepting uncritically the historical analysis provided by the plaintiffs, the justices were convinced that Franco-Ontarians faced strong assimilation pressures. They noted that federal and provincial leaders had shown increasing concern for minority language education rights since the Victoria Conference of 1971. They agreed with the Fédération and the ACFO that the primary intent of s. 23 was remedial, given the discrimination historically suffered by Franco-Ontarians. They further believed that remedial action was the clear intent of Minister of Justice Jean Chrétien in his statement to the Special Joint Committee in 1981.[122]

On the first question, the justices agreed with the ACFO and AEFO that ss. 258 and 261 of the Education Act were inconsistent with the Charter because they (a) placed restrictions on the beneficiaries of s. 23 rights, (b) gave too much discretion to the school boards, (c) stipulated numbers for the provision of educational services that were too rigid, and (d) restricted the provision of educational services to existing territorial boundaries of school boards.[123] On the third question, the justices maintained that there was no constitutional conflict between linguistic and denominational rights. Consequently, in their view, s. 23 applied "with equal force and effect" to both the public and the denominational school systems in Ontario.[124] On the fourth question, the justices replied in the affirmative; the proposed amendment to the Education Act did not contravene s. 93(1) of the Constitution Act, 1867. The Ontario government had the authority to make changes to the structure, management, and financing of separate schools as long as they did not prejudicially affect the denominational character of the separate school system.[125]

On the central matter of management and control rights in question two, the Court of Appeal ruled that s. 23 limited the exclusive power of the Ontario legislature to make laws in relation to minority language education. Under s. 23 it was mandatory for the legislature "to provide for educational facilities which, viewed objectively, can be said to be or appertain to the linguistic minority in that they can be regarded as part and parcel of the minority's social and cultural fabric. The quality of education to be provided to the minority is to be a basis of equality with the majority." Yet, much to the dismay of Franco-Ontarian leaders, the justices then stated that the degree of participation and control outlined in the White Paper, which did not call for a homogeneous francophone board in the Ottawa-Carleton region, appeared to meet the requirements of the Charter.[126] In a warning not to abuse the courts, they reminded all interested parties that the judiciary was not the sole guardian of constitutional rights. In conclusion, they advised that "minority linguistic rights should be established by general legislation assuring equal and just treatment to all rather than by litigation."[127] The Court of Appeal was encouraging the parties in the dispute to make a further attempt to resolve the matter through political negotiations.

IMPLEMENTING LIMITED SCHOOL GOVERNANCE

The Fédération and its Ontario affiliates were relatively satisfied with the decision of the Court of Appeal. They agreed to set up a working group to study it and to prepare an implementation proposal for the Ontario government in time for the fall session of the legislature.[128] The province indicated that it was eager to implement the recommendations in its White Paper. Within days of the decision, Minister of Education Bette Stephenson introduced Bill 119, the Education Amendment Act 1984, which proposed reforms based on some aspects of that document. At long last, it appeared that the Davis government was ready to move: Bill 119 held out much promise.[129]

The AFCSO responded by setting up a Comité provisoire de la gestion scolaire to review and propose amendments to the bill, as well as to prepare a brief to the government's proposed Commission de planification et de mise en oeuvre and to monitor its implementation procedures. The AFCSO'smembers believed they had entered the final stage of their difficult and protracted struggle.[130] Their excessive optimism can be understood, in part, on the basis that Davis had announced just two weeks before the reference case decision that his government was prepared to extend Catholic separate schooling to grade 13 with full public funding. The AFCSO hoped that resolution of this longstanding grievance would encourage most English language Catholic boards to accept some level of school governance for their Franco-Ontarian students and parents. Perhaps Davis also believed this would happen. But both the premier and the AFCSO were to be quickly disabused of their optimism. Public and Catholic school board trustees alike jealously guarded the autonomy and power of their respective institutions; they did not want their prerogatives and resources diluted by the intrusion of a third system based on the French language.

When the AFCSO and the members of its Comité provisoire received a draft of Bill 119, they were most unhappy. Rodrique Landriault, the AFCSO's president, met with members of the Social Development Committee of the Ontario legislature to express his organization's gratitude that the government was, at long last, formally recognizing minority education rights by guaranteeing every Franco-Ontarian student the right to elementary and secondary education in his/her own language. But his tone soon changed: "The AFCSO notes and deplores the absence of any provision by Bill 119 to give the citizens of the French linguistic minority in Ontario the right to manage and control their own French language classes of instruction or autonomous French language educational units established for the education of their children." The province was not even willing to proceed with the limited form of school governance outlined in its White Paper. Given the decision in the Ontario reference case, Bill 119 was baffling and inadequate, to say the least. Its proposal for French-Language Advisory Committees in school boards offering instruction in French to francophone students was unacceptable because it "is devoid of power and, as such, does not represent a suit-able alternative, nor an interim solution, to the management of French-language educational units for Francophones, by Franco-phones." The AFCSO asked the Davis government to reconsider Bill 119 and replace it with legislation that established "French-language homogeneous school boards respecting acquired religious rights," as demanded by Franco-Ontarians for the previous fifteen years.[131]

Bill 119 passed into law on 14 December, the day after the Minister of Education introduced Bill 160, which authorized partial and condi-tional school governance for francophone trustees within school boards where there were 500 Franco-Ontarian students or where they comprised 10 per cent of the total enrolment. Franco-Ontarian educa-tional organizations were trapped in a Catch-22. The Court of Appeal had confirmed Franco-Ontarians' right to some form of meaningful school governance wherever they lived in the province. Bill 160 promised, for the very first time, a modest degree of school governance for public and separate school francophone trustees in some – but not all – Ontario boards and districts. The ACFO was left to decide whether or not Franco-Ontarians should accept the modest but meaningful gains outlined in Bill 160, or reject them outright in the hope that improved legislation would abide completely by the court's ruling. Denouncing the bill as too complex, confusing, unworkable, and, most importantly, unconstitutional, the ACFO proposed significant amendments that, it argued, would bring Bill 160 into line with its interpretation of the reference case decision.[132]

The AFCSO adopted a different tack. Well aware of the limitations of Bill 160, it nevertheless saw the legislation as an important step forward. Bill 160 recognized a francophone electorate and the election of trustees based on language, and furthermore gave the latter exclusive powers over all matters pertaining to the French language sections. The AFCSO argued that practical solutions could be found to some of the foreseeable problems and omissions in the legislation that would undoubtedly emerge during its implementation. It was time for Franco-Ontarian trustees to roll up their sleeves and "tordre, d'extraire et de tirer tout ce qu'il y a de possible et de quasi-impossible pour les francophones avec les outils qui nous ont été donnés." If the problems proved insurmountable, the AFCSO advised its members and the government that it would demand appropriate and significant amendments to Bill 160.[133]

It was at this juncture that a transformation of Ontario's political scene played an important role in the struggle for school governance. In early October 1984, Premier William Davis announced his decision to retire. He left office on 26 January 1985, once Frank Miller was chosen as the new leader of the Conservative Party and sworn in as premier. The shift opened up the possibility that a party other than the Conservatives might form the next government after the elections on 2 May 1985. This is exactly what transpired. Losing twenty seats, the Conservative Party was reduced to a minority government, which was defeated in the legislature on 18 June, shortly after introducing Bill 28, a revised version of Bill 160. Assured of the support of the NDP, Liberal Party leader David Peterson was called on to form a government on June 26. The Liberal government and its NDP supporters were committed to extending Catholic separate schooling to grade 13 with full and equitable funding, as well as to some level of school governance for Franco-Ontarians. The Liberals promised to introduce legislation on both matters following full consultation with all interested parties.

Reacting quickly, the ACFO's president denounced Bill 28 on precisely the same basis as its predecessor, Bill 160, hoping to encourage the Peterson government to begin afresh. The new Minister of Education, Sean Conway, did just that on 12 July 1985.[134] By the end of the month Conway had created two commissions. The first, chaired by H.

Ian MacDonald, was to deal with the funding of primary and secondary education; the second, chaired by William Newham, was charged with making recommendations on the planning and implementation of a Catholic school system.[135]

The startling defeat of the Conservative government spread undue fear among some Franco-Ontarian educational organizations while raising unrealistic expectations among others. In anticipation of a meeting on 26 July with the Minister of Education, they set aside their differences during a series of meetings throughout the month to hammer out a common set of principles and a coherent political strategy. They hoped to pressure the minority Liberal government of David Peterson, which depended on support from the NDP, to introduce an entirely new bill that incorporated a more effective system of school governance for Franco-Ontarians. Any acceptable legislation would have to respect the decision of the Ontario Court of Appeal to the effect that Franco-Ontarians had the right to manage their own school system. It would also have to incorporate a parallel francophone structure within the Ministry of Education to oversee the new system. The francophone organizations maintained that two bills – one for the public system, another for the Catholic system – would provide the flexibility required to avoid confusion and further delays. Moreover, the number of francophone trustees would have to be based strictly on the number of francophone students, and would range from a minimum of three for between one and 899 students to a maximum of seven for over 7000 students. In effect, all the CCLF would be replaced with elected francophone trustees. The exclusive powers of the francophone sections in Catholic boards would have to include religious instruction and exercises; a double majority for determining shared responsibilities, with all non-specified residual authority belonging to the linguistic minority sections; and the inclusion of a conflict resolution mechanism.[136]

Bill 30, which provided for the expansion of a fully-funded Catholic separate school system, was the Liberals' response. It caused political problems for Franco-Ontarian Catholics and the AFCSO because they believed it would end the support of the OSSTA for some measure of francophone school governance within English-majority Catholic school boards. The result would be that the public school system would expand its elementary and secondary French language schools; Franco-Ontarian Catholics would then enrol their children in these schools because the public boards would offer some measure of school governance and would have better facilities and a wider range of programs. In his brief on Bill 30, AFCSO President Rodrique Landriault strongly urged the government to grant school governance to Franco-

Ontarians before or at the same time as it expanded the Catholic separate school system. He also recommended that the expanded Catholic system be given the same level of financial resources per student as the public school system, particularly in cases where large numbers of Catholic francophone secondary students were expected to transfer from the public system.[137]

Sensing that it was losing momentum, the Eastern Ontario office of the AFCSO, under the presidency of Jeannine Séguin, used a $15,000 grant from the Secretary of State to hire the constitutional lawyer Pierre Foucher to design model legislation for a homogeneous francophone school board that met the test of both s. 23 of the Charter and s. 93 of the Constitution Act, 1867 with respect to religious rights. The hope was that it could be implemented in the three regions of Ottawa-Carleton, Prescott-Russell, and Stormont, Dundas, and Glengarry. The detailed model was a variant of the one long advocated by the Conseil francophone de planification scolaire d'Ottawa-Carleton. Foucher made the point that the boundaries of the bicameral – public and Catholic – Conseil scolaire de langue française would be those of the District scolaire de langue française and would not correspond to any of the existing boards, in order to ensure the maximum encapsulation of Franco-Ontarian students. The Catholic and public sectors would negotiate at their first meeting following school elections those matters which they desired to administer in common and those which would remain exclusive to each. Each sector would exercise a veto, have its own financial resources, and set its own tax rate; disputes would be resolved by an independent administrative tribunal. The Conseil scolaire would be granted access to revenues from commercial and industrial taxes for common purposes, while special provincial and federal grants for French language education would be disbursed to each sector on a per capita basis.[138]

Foucher's model was discussed within the AFCSO and ACFO, then analysed by educational and constitutional experts, including Michel Bastarache. At a colloquium in early October 1985 it was debated, amended, and approved by francophone trustees from Eastern Ontario. A legislative proposal based on the amended model was then sent to the Minister of Education. Encouraged by Jean Comtois, director of the eastern region in the Ministry of Education, the Conseil francophone de planification scolaire asked Maurice Lapointe, coordinator of French language teaching at the University of Ottawa's Faculty of Education, to prepare a more detailed proposal entitled *Un conseil à suivre*. The document specified just how governance legislation could be implemented in the three regions previously named. Published on 1 March 1986, the pamphlet was forwarded to the

Minister of Education and widely distributed throughout Ottawa-Carleton and Eastern Ontario.[139]

All the intensive lobbying, including the efforts of a work group from the Ministry of Education comprising ministry officials and representatives from educational organizations, finally paid off. With former York University president H. Ian MacDonald's *Report of the Commission on Financing of Elementary and Secondary Education in Ontario* in hand, Minister of Education Sean Conway introduced Bill 75 on 12 December 1985. The bill outlined a model of limited school governance for French and English language minorities within Ontario's existing school boards and also created a public French language school board for Metropolitan Toronto. Conway further promised that the province would introduce legislation for the creation of a homogeneous French language school board for Ottawa-Carleton in December 1988; his ministry would set up a study group comprising all stakeholders in the region to prepare the groundwork.[140] Under Bill 75 every school board that operated French language instructional units would get a Conseil de l'enseignement en langue française as of 1 December 1986; these would be transformed into Sections de langue française on 1 December 1987. Each CELF/SLF would have a minimum of three and a maximum of eight trustees elected no later than 30 October 1986 by public and separate francophone ratepayers. By the school elections of fall 1988, all francophone trustees would be elected as representatives of Franco-Ontarian ratepayers. Franco-Ontarian trustees as members of the CELFs/SLFs were granted exclusive authority over admission committees; the recruitment and assignment of teachers and support and supervisory staff; the planning, creation, administration, and closing of French instructional units; the planning and implementation of all programs and courses; and the negotiation of agreements with other boards for space and services.[141]

The Franco-Ontarian educational organizations were pleased that the province was moving ahead on all fronts; the AFCSO even issued a press release congratulating Sean Conway and the government. Its president, Rodrique Landriault, was confident that Conway would be open to suggestions for improvements to Bill 75 and hoped that it would pass through the legislative stages quickly.[142] The francophone groups met on 20 January 1986 to develop a consensus about amendments to the bill. One decision was to leave the question of what constituted a linguistic minority in Ontario up to the constitutional experts. The educational organizations also wanted the Minister of Education to undertake a study on how to regroup widely dispersed Franco-Ontarians in order to make a French language education council or section available to them in the school board of their choice. They were concerned that the proposed allocation of financial resources to very small French language sections was not adequate to meet their needs and wanted special provision to be made in the bill to address the problem in the same manner as for existing small boards.[143]

Michel Bastarache was far less sanguine about Bill 75 than the Franco-Ontarian organizations. He made them aware of its shortcomings in his address to francophone school trustees on 27 January; the scathing critique threw a bucket of cold water on the entire scheme.

Le projet de loi ne rencontre pas les objectifs fondamentaux poursuivis au plan pédagogique. Il offre cependant, par le mécanisme de gestion, et de façon tout à faite implicite, la possibilité de créer des écoles homogènes et, de ce fait, d'éliminer les établissements mixtes. Au seul plan de la gestion, il propose un mécanisme très insatisfaisant parce qu'il confirme le statut minoritaire des francophones et leur interdit tout affranchissement, et parce qu'il les enferme dans une formule de financement potentiellement inéquitable. Les modalités relatives au regroupement des élèves francophones sont très imparfaites – les frontières scolaires sont statiques et les possibilités de coopération laissées à la discrétion des administrations. Rien n'est dit d'Ottawa/Carleton ni des conseils exclus par la définition de l'article 1.[144]

As a result of Bastarache's analysis, in their briefs to and testimony before the Standing Committee on Government Affairs both the ACFO and the AFCSO lauded Bill 75 as an important step forward but then denounced its fundamental flaw. The ACFO's president, Serge Plouffe, declared that it granted Franco-Ontarians "tout au mieux, un droit de gestion tronqué qui ne saurait être pleinement satisfaisant ... Leur champs de compétence est limité, leur pouvoir de taxation est inexistant et, plus grave encore, il ne contrôle pas la répartition budgétaire."[145] AFCSO President Rodrique Landriault, with the full backing of the president of the Eastern Ontario region, was just as blunt. Bill 75 as it stood was unacceptable. It preserved the CCLF, which had no decision-making powers, where there were fewer than 300 students. The French language sectors granted very limited management rights to Franco-Ontarian trustees and, most importantly, denied them any control over their financial resources and budgets. Landriault concluded with a strong recommendation that the Ontario government create, without delay, a commission to plan and implement francophone school boards throughout Ontario.[146] But Bill 75 was enacted on 10 July 1986 without the substantive amendments sought by the ACFO, the AFCSO, and the other francophone educational organizations. The long battle for school governance now entered its final stage.

STRIVING FOR FULL SCHOOL GOVERNANCE

We have seen that, when it introduced Bill 75, the Peterson government promised to create a system of French language Catholic and
public schools in the Ottawa-Carleton region in late 1988. This
remained a highly divisive matter. Ontario's Catholic bishops, in a
March 1986 meeting with Catholic trustees, declared their preference
for a single Catholic school board for the Ottawa-Carleton region that
would incorporate a public French language section. They feared that
an autonomous public French board would undermine the integrity
of the separate school system.[147] Franco-Ontarians once again felt torn
between their religious and cultural identities. Little wonder that the
Peterson government was reluctant to move quickly. Hoping to
smooth the way for the implementation of French language education
in Ottawa-Carleton, on 23 January 1986 Minister of Education Sean
Conway created a Comité d'étude pour l'éducation en langue
française d'Ottawa-Carleton chaired by Albert Roy, former MLA for
Ottawa-East. In the interim, the Ottawa and Carleton public school
boards replaced their CCLF with CELFs overseen by three elected
francophone trustees. The Ottawa separate school board had eight
trustees on its CELF, while the Carleton separate board had seven.

The Roy Committee's broad mandate was to propose a structure
that would respect both the religious and language rights of Franco-
Ontarians. It also had to address the financing of the new school
board, the range of its programs and services, and its impact on the
four existing boards. The committee was guided by six principles:
local control, equitable financing, preservation of language and
culture, excellence in education, equality of opportunity, and respect
for constitutional rights.[148] Its five members consulted widely during
April and May and discovered that most, but not all, Franco-Ontarian
organizations and individuals supported in principle the governance
model proposed by Pierre Foucher and Maurice Lapointe. In its
report, made public in January 1987, the Roy Committee recommended the establishment of a French language school board with
two sectors, Catholic and public. The number of trustees for each
sector – elected by ward – would be determined by the number of
voters. The respective responsibilities of the board and each sector
should be left up to the trustees to define, but they had to respect the
constitutional rights of both Catholic and public voters. A constitutional specialist, Professor Gérald Beaudoin of the University of
Ottawa, assured the committee members that this could be done. On
the crucial matter of financing, the committee recommended that the
new French language school board – especially the public sector – be
given a proportional amount, based on student registration, of the

pooled industrial and commercial taxes.[149]

Once the Minister of Education had the report in his hands, it was up to the government to act. Unfortunately, it was having great difficulties in creating an electoral list that distinguished all categories of voters, especially Franco-Ontarian Catholic and public sector voters. The law considered all taxpayers to be supporters of English language public schools unless they stated otherwise. Pushed by its eastern regional division, the AFCSO proposed that all voters in the province be mailed a bilingual questionnaire asking them to identify themselves as supporters of English or French language schools, Catholic or public. There would be a follow-up to make sure that every voter returned the questionnaire. In May 1988 the Ontario government adopted this approach for the school board elections later in the year. It even agreed to fund a vast campaign by the educational organizations to ensure that all Franco-Ontarian voters understood what was at stake and to encourage them to register on the proper list.[150]

On 28 January 1988, in anticipation of pending legislation, the government created two committees by Order in Council: the Comité de planification de l'enseignement en langue française dans Ottawa-Carleton, comprising the twenty-one local francophone trustees, and the Ottawa-Carleton Joint Education Impact Committee, comprising one trustee and one CELF member from each board. Their sheer size and the divergence of the interests represented created considerable tension and divisions that quickly erupted into public squabbling via the media. On 11 April 1988 the Minister of Education, Chris Ward, introduced Bill 109, which created the Conseil scolaire de langue française d'Ottawa-Carleton, a single French language board with Catholic and public sectors for the Ottawa-Carleton region. The bill was scrutinized by the Social Affairs Committee of the legislature during April, prompting amendments to protect the Catholic schools; the government was intent on heading off a constitutional challenge by Ontario's Catholics. Bill 109 passed into law on 29 June. Contrary to the recommendation of the Roy Committee's report, the new legislation defined quite precisely the extensive exclusive powers, functions, and rights of the public and Catholic sectors and the rather limited powers of the full board. Some exclusive jurisdictions assigned to each sector required approval by the majority of its members. At the beginning of a new mandate, these could be transferred to the full board if the sectors agreed, but they could also be repatriated from the full board, together with all the resources allocated to them.[151] Indeed, once in operation it would become clear that the French language board of Ottawa-Carleton was in reality two highly segregated boards, Catholic and public, operating under one roof.

The new Comité de planification faced the enormous job of bringing together all the existing French language resources – human, financial, and physical – from the four existing Catholic and public boards. It had to make sure that the region's francophones received their fair share of all the existing educational assets, so that their new board would be able to carry out its educational, linguistic, and cultural mandates effectively. To sort out the redistribution of the various resources and debts, the Comité used the guidelines set out in Bill 30 for full funding for Catholic separate schools. Inevitably, there were a great many disagreements, some of which had to be resolved through mediation or court action. The gargantuan task was complicated by the fact that there were three new employers – the central board, the public sector, and the Catholic sector – to which employees had to be assigned.[152]

Following the November 1988 school elections, the Conseil scolaire de langue française d'Ottawa-Carleton, with 600 supporters in attendance, held its inaugural meeting at Vanier City Hall on 5 December. Twenty-two trustees – fourteen for the Catholic and eight for the public sector – elected their respective presidents and vice-presidents, then the officers of the general board. Given the tremendous animosity that had built up between the advocates of Catholic French language education and the militants in favour of public French education, it is not surprising that the hybrid Conseil scolaire barely survived five years. After a long political struggle, full funding for Catholic secondary schools had been achieved; Catholic trustees wanted to exercise their new powers. But along came Franco-Ontarians who demanded and received a system of primary and secondary public French language schools. Prior to the restructuring, the secondary schools had enjoyed access to the lucrative industrial and commercial tax base of the region. Yet the new French language school board never received the necessary government funding – including compensation for losing a share of industrial and commercial taxes – to carry out a comprehensive restructuring of a French language educational system, public and Catholic, that met the standard prevalent in the English schools of the region. Its trustees and administrators waited over fifteen months for the government to decide how it was going to fund the new board, which by that time was deeply in debt.

Adding to both the costs and the tensions was the fact that the trustees for the Catholic and public sectors had agreed to a very limited number of shared jurisdictions, preferring to run what essentially became two autonomous and segregated boards within the larger board, which was perceived as expensive and redundant. Moreover, the public sector never accepted its minority representation on the French language board. To raise its profile and assert its autonomy, its trustees decided in April 1989 to rename their sector the Conseil de l'éducation publique d'Ottawa-Carleton, a clear violation of Bill 109. Its president even envisaged agreements with the English language public boards of Ottawa and Carleton in lieu of cooperation with the Catholic sector of its own board. Determined to maintain the same level of services to students as existed prior to the restructuring, the public sector saw its deficit reach $18M by the time it was placed in receivership by the province in September 1991. Having lost its autonomy, the public board was administered thereafter by a receiver, Rosaire Léger, who slashed the staff and budget of the general board, which also affected the Catholic sector. Despite a 60 per cent cut in administrative expenses and a 30 per cent cut in the number of schools, the deficit remained at $5M in 1993. The following year, the government quietly allowed the trustees of the public sector to resume their authority while it settled lawsuits brought by both the public and Catholic sectors out of court. Everyone realized – though no-one admitted publicly – that the French language school board had been drastically underfunded since its inception. The province agreed to new financial deals with both the public and Catholic sectors, with retroactive funding to wipe out part of their deficits. Resolution of the financial crisis did not improve relations between the two sectors, however; both demanded the right to become autonomous school boards. The government agreed and on 1 July 1994 created two new boards, the Conseil des écoles catholiques de langue française d'Ottawa-Carleton and the Conseil des écoles publiques d'Ottawa-Carleton.[153]

The establishment of the Conseil des écoles françaises de la communauté urbaine de Toronto on 1 December 1988 proved far less acrimonious than had been the case in Ottawa-Carleton. By 1987 the school boards of Toronto, North York, and Scarborough and their CCLF administered French language classes and schools for nearly 1,700 students. In January 1987 Minister of Education Sean Conway set up a broad-based working committee to plan the implementation of the CEFCUT. In February 1988 the committee submitted its unanimous final report to the new francophone public board, which comprised nine trustees elected at the same time and in the same manner as the English language trustees. The CEFCUT was granted the same powers as all the other boards of the greater Toronto region. Equally important, it shared property taxes and industrial and commercial taxes on the same per capita basis as the other public boards. Consequently, it did not experience a revenue shortfall and was able to offer its students a very high level of educational programs and services.[154] By 1990, the Toronto and Ottawa-Carleton French language boards oversaw the education of 20,000 Franco-Ontarian students in fifty-seven schools.[155]

The situation in Prescott-Russell in eastern Ontario was somewhat more complicated and not as easy to resolve. The area's Franco-Ontarian parents had been seeking an integrated Catholic French language board to replace the existing Conseil des écoles séparées de Prescott-Russell, which administered elementary schools, and Conseil d'éducation de Prescott-Russell, which administered secondary schools. The majority of students in both boards were Franco-Ontarian Catholics. The implementation of full funding for Catholic separate schools made this goal more realistic. The parents put pressure on Conway, who agreed to form a Comité d'étude des conseils scolaires de Prescott-Russell in January 1987. Its report, made public in September, proposed the creation of a hybrid French language board to oversee the public and Catholic sectors, together with two English boards, one Catholic and one public. Given the problems emanating from the Conseil scolaire de langue française d'Ottawa-Carleton, Conway decided to postpone any decision.

As the 1980s drew to a close, the situation of 75,000 francophone students in 300 schools governed by sixty-five mixed school boards with English and French trustees became increasingly unacceptable to Franco-Ontarian leaders. During the prolonged implementation of Bill 75 many serious problems emerged, and Franco-Ontarian educational organizations, led by the AFCSO, were forced to lobby aggressively for amendments. The AFCSO especially monitored the Ministry of Education's attempts to implement the provisions of Bill 75 requiring the creation of French language sections in the public and separate systems. Still, the Franco-Ontarian trustees attempted to carry out their duties as they interpreted them.[156]

On 7 February 1989, Minister of Education Chris Ward responded to the situation by striking a ministerial working committee that included representatives from the Franco-Ontarian organizations. The committee held six meetings between March and July 1989 to suggest additional amendments to Bill 75. However, it never met to finalize its recommendations in late August because its work was terminated when Ward was replaced by Sean Conway.[157] The educational organizations were livid that the committee's suggested amendments had been aside without explanation. After pleading unsuccessfully for a meeting with Conway, they decided that it was time to go public with their comprehensive criticism of Bill 75.[158] At a well-attended press conference at Queen's Park on 10 January 1990, francophone leaders questioned the commitment of Premier David Peterson's Liberals to the education rights of Franco-Ontarians. They wondered whether the government had altered its stated policy on the matter, noting that Bill 75 was manifestly unjust and unconstitutional because it denied Franco-Ontarian parents their right to control and manage their own schools. The limit of three francophone trustees was unrealistic and unworkable. The allegedly autonomous French language sections did not have the power to adopt budgets related to their needs. While they had the power to hire teachers and administrative staff, only the entire school board had the authority to fire these individuals, whether or not the French language section agreed. They also had the authority to open and close schools but could not decide on the construction, renovation, or placement of schools and modules. Only the full school board could appoint or fire the executive director, the key person in the interpretation and application of Bill 75. Finally, the French language sections had no legal status to conclude contracts or to exercise their functions effectively. Moreover, the bill's definition of who was a francophone for the purposes of education excluded a great many francophones. Just as importantly, Franco-Ontarians in most regions of the province still did not have access to the very limited school governance provisions of the bill. Several Franco-Ontarian organizations put the government on notice that they intended to contest Bill 75 in the courts using s. 23 of the Charter.[159]

SCHOOL GOVERNANCE AFTER THE *MAHÉ* DECISION

Finding the right model for implementing full school governance province-wide would take several more years. The catalyst was the landmark Supreme Court decision in *Mahé* v. *Alberta*. On 15 March 1990 the justices ruled, "Where numbers warrant, s. 23 confers upon minority language parents a right to management and control over the education facilities in which their children are taught. Such management and control is vital to ensure that their language and culture flourish ... The measure of management and control required by s. 23 may, in some circumstances and depending on the number of students to be served, warrant an independent school board."[160] The political and constitutional implications of the decision were enormous and far-reaching, inasmuch as it indicated a clear right to school governance – a right that every premier had denied since 1982.

The unexpected ruling altered the political dynamic between Franco-Ontarians and their government. In April Premier Peterson finally replied to the AFCSO that his government remained committed to school governance for Franco-Ontarians. He insisted, however, that his Minister of Education needed more time to study the *Mahé* decision and consult with the francophone educational organizations before proceeding with amendments to the Education Act.[161] On 10 July 1990 Sean Conway announced the creation of Le Groupe de travail sur la gestion de l'éducation en langue française, but its work was delayed for several months. To the surprise of most political observers, Peterson's Liberals were defeated in the August election by the NDP, led by Bob Rae. Marion Boyd, Minister of Education in the new government, set up the French Language Education Governance Advisory Group on 14 November 1990 with a mandate to consult widely and recommend criteria for establishing French language school boards, propose other models of school governance, and outline procedures for implementing them.[162] The Advisory Group's president, Tréva Cousineau, strongly encouraged the AFCSO and all other Franco-Ontarian organizations interested in education to participate in its proceedings.[163]

Speaking before the Advisory Group, AFCSO President Lorraine Gandolfo called for the greatest possible flexibility in addressing the school governance requirements of Franco-Ontarian parents, whose educational choices for their children should be respected. Making constant reference to the *Mahé* decision, she argued that it was imperative that both official language communities in Ontario have the same quality of education and services. It was also essential for Franco-Ontarian children who remained under the aegis of an amended Bill 75 to be granted the highest level of financial, pedagogical, and administrative autonomy within existing school boards. Since there was now a legally recognized remedial dimension to s. 23 of the Charter, it was essential that the Ontario government provide French language sections and school boards with additional funds to enable Franco-Ontarians to achieve the same literacy and educational participation levels as English-speaking Ontarians. Franco-Ontarian schools, she declared, were at the heart of the struggle for the survival and renewal of the Franco-Ontarian collectivity and its distinctive culture. Governance over completely restructured local or regional school boards, based on more realistic and flexible boundaries encompassing the greatest number of Franco-Ontarians, was not sufficient; it was necessary to restructure the Ministry of Education to give them greater control over all government decisions affecting the education of their children. Implementation of s. 23 rights, Gandolfo readily admitted, required courage, determination, and some imagination on the part of the NDP government. It was time to bring an end to a century of linguistic and educational crises. If, on the other hand, the government chose to procrastinate, Gandolfo reminded the Advisory Group that s. 24 of the Charter allowed Franco-Ontarians to seek reparations for any violation of their constitutional rights. She hoped the AFCSO would not have to go down that road.[164]

The Advisory Group issued its comprehensive report in September 1991.[165] Drawing heavily upon the *Mahé* decision, its members adopted the philosophy and principles of the AFCSO and several other Franco-Ontarian educational organizations. The report strongly asserted that any governance structures of French language education had to respect not only s. 23 rights but also s. 93 of the Constitution Act, 1867.[166] It laid out the legal and constitutional bases for school governance by Franco-Ontarians, reviewed the historical background and current situation of French language education governance, and described the models used in other provinces and in Ontario. It also reviewed various governance structures, their financing, and the key criteria for putting in place fully functioning French language school boards. Coming to the heart its mandate, the Advisory Group made fifty-seven recommendations. Among much else, it proposed that the government establish two French language boards, public and Catholic, in each of the six school regions of Ontario; a series of francophone district boards; and French school boards wherever requested by local Franco-Ontarian ratepayers. All remaining consultative committees were to be disbanded and replaced by French language sections, which would have one or two additional trustees. It also recommended the formation of impact study committees to oversee this restructuring, implementation committees, and mediation and arbitration mechanisms. The Advisory Group considered it imperative that the government guarantee full financing, as well as additional catch-up funds, in advance for every new board. This goal could be accomplished easily if all industrial and commercial taxes were pooled and redistributed to the boards on a per capita student basis. The Advisory Group also strongly recommended that the province provide at least four regional French language cooperative educational service centres and, with the help of the federal government, establish comprehensive community education centres.[167]

Taking up Marion Boyd's invitation to respond, the AFCSO gave her a detailed analysis of the report, along with further recommendations. It applauded the Advisory Group for its vision and many of its proposals. But the AFCSO was not happy with the rather vague description of the various school boards – regional, district, and local – proposed for the diverse and dispersed Franco-Ontarian communities. The suggested methods of financing these boards did not fulfill the conditions set out by the courts. The criteria proposed for the three new governance structures – 1,500 students; the same boundaries as existing boards, kindergarten to grade 12; an approved implementation committee – would not guarantee viable school boards and would violate the principles established in *Mahé*. The AFCSO remained wedded to the Ottawa-Carleton hybrid model for the six proposed regional boards, to ensure the largest units possible. Going beyond the Advisory Group's report, it called for the abolition of all French language sections because they did not meet the conditions of s. 23. It also argued that the report's recommendations on financing were too vague and timid and ignored the remedial dimension of the section; they had to be strengthened by a more structured conflict resolution mechanism. Finally, the AFCSO's president reminded the Minister of Education that it was almost ten years since the adoption of the Charter and that "un droit ignoré pendant 10 ans est un droit violé."[168]

The NDP government remained committed to school governance for Franco-Ontarians, but was reluctant to move on the report's major recommendations before considering the broader political and financial implications. It made a few minor amendments to Bill 75 to increase the autonomy of the French language sections of school boards. In July 1991, the province signed an agreement with the French and English language sectors of the Conseil des écoles catholiques de Prescott-Russell to create two Catholic boards, one French and one English. Both were ensured adequate financing to avoid the crisis that then prevailed in Ottawa-Carleton. Ten years of political lobbying and planning, accelerated by the *Mahé* decision, were beginning to pay dividends.[169]

Lacking a consensus among the Franco-Ontarian organizations and facing serious financial constraints, the government decided to buy some time. On 5 May 1993 it created a Royal Commission on Education to advise it on a long-term vision and plan of action for primary and secondary education in Ontario. The co-chairs were Gerry Caplan, professor at the University of Toronto's OISE and long-time political advisor to the Ontario NDP, and Monique Bégin, Dean of the Faculty of Health Sciences at the University of Ottawa. The Royal Commission submitted its comprehensive and quite radical report, comprising 167 recommendations, in December 1994, and the government made it public at the end of the following month.

Somewhat contradictory, the report unconditionally supported full school governance for all Franco-Ontarians and encouraged the government to move quickly on its implementation. It also recommended that the government provide the funds required to promote the wholesale cultural renewal of Franco-Ontarian communities using their school system.[170] Unfortunately, it then went on to recommend that the pedagogical and financial powers of all school boards be reduced at the expense of the Ministry of Education, the teachers, and the school principals. Just as Franco-Ontarians had obtained legal recognition of school governance, the Royal Commission proposed that the Ontario government remove the financial powers of all school boards to guarantee funding equity for all students in all regions of the province. The government intended to transfer revenues from wealthy urban boards, namely those of Toronto and Ottawa, to other regions. Not fully understanding the implications of the report's contradictory recommendations, the AFCSO and other Franco-Ontarian educational organizations applauded the commissioners for their work. The NDP proceeded quickly with the recommendations pertaining to the centralization of programming and the creation of school committees. It then set up yet another study group, chaired by former Liberal Minister of Social Services John Sweeney, to examine how it might dramatically reduce the number of school boards and trustees throughout Ontario. It wanted more than seventy French language boards, sections, and consultative committees to be reduced to fifteen boards.

Before the Sweeney study group could submit a report, the NDP government was defeated in the election of June 1995. Premier Mike Harris's "Common Sense Revolution" Conservative Party took office. Harris allowed the study group to complete its report, which it did by February 1996. The report recommended the creation of fifteen very large French school boards, ten Catholic and five public. Before proceeding, the government should reform the system of funding education to guarantee adequate financing for the new system.[171] Many Franco-Ontarians and their organizations were concerned that such large boards, especially those covering most of northern and southwestern Ontario, might not be viable. Harris, determined to reduce expenditures on education, health, and social welfare in order to cut taxes, established a new committee on "Who Does What?" with David Crombie, former minister in the Mulroney Conservative government, at its head. Crombie formed a sub-committee on financing education, which recommended that school boards focus on education and contract out their management functions. It also suggested that the province should settle the issue of school governance for the French language schools of Ontario by adopting the Sweeney study group's proposal of fifteen boards, ten Catholic and five public. Finally, it proposed that the government centralize the funding of education by establishing a province-wide commercial and industrial property tax, the returns of which would be redistributed on a per capita student basis to all school boards.

The Harris government moved quickly. On 23 April 1997, Minister

of Education John Snobelen passed Bill 104, which mandated a drastic
reduction in the number of Ontario's 167 school boards. On the
French language side, the four existing boards, fifty-nine sections, and
eight consultative committees would be replaced by twelve boards,
eight Catholic and four public.[172] Bill 104 also called for the creation
of an implementation commission to see the process through to an
orderly completion. The commission created a francophone sub-
committee to oversee the setting up of the twelve boards and to make
recommendations on the best way to finance their operations and the
sharing of resources with the French language community colleges.[173]
In 1998 the new system was put in place, thanks to a financial agreement between Minister of Canadian Heritage Sheila Copps and
Ontario's Minister of Education, David Johnson. Ottawa granted the
Ontario government $90 million over a five-year period to establish a
French language school governance system that conformed to s. 23 of
the Charter.[174] The Franco-Ontarian educational organizations and
media were delighted that the bitter struggle for school governance
had, at long last, come to a successful conclusion. ACFO President
André Lalonde triumphantly declared, "We are being given everything
we have been requesting for over a hundred years."[175]

But the celebrations were somewhat premature. Just as the system
was being implemented, the Harris government drastically cut education funding and curtailed the financial and pedagogical autonomy of
all school boards. Ironically, the new French and English language
school boards, public and Catholic, would have far less authority than
what the smaller community-based school boards had exercised since
the 1840s. Commissioner of Official Languages Victor Goldbloom felt
obliged to remind the Ontario government that it was not sufficient to
simply create a new system of French language school boards; full
compliance with s. 23 required that they have decision-making powers
over budgets and programming that enabled them to reflect the
values of the communities they served.[176] The battle to retain effective
control over the education of their children and their school governance system would present Franco-Ontarians and their organizations
with renewed challenges calling for a new generation of leaders and
ideas. As in the past, the community would provide both, and the
struggle for survival and renewal would continue unabated.

CONCLUSION

The Franco-Ontarian community, the largest in Canada, and its
myriad established educational institutions plunged into the battle
for school governance with high expectations, despite their belief

that s. 23, as written, did not mandate school governance. Their concerted political campaign since the mid-1960s had produced some remarkable results. The Conservative governments of premiers John Robarts and Bill Davis had been quite determined to improve the educational opportunities of Franco-Ontarian children. Indeed, Davis was an early supporter of education rights for Canada's official language minority communities under s. 23, and he never wavered on the issue despite strong opposition from most other premiers. He was also very supportive of Franco-Ontarians' historic demand for full funding for Catholic secondary schools. His government would eventually implement the necessary legislation – at considerable political cost, since the Conservative Party lost power in 1985. Moreover, Davis was quite sympathetic to urbanized Franco-Ontarians' later demand for a system of public French language schools and boards. Nevertheless, his concern about a political backlash from Ontario's expansive post-war Catholic community prevented his government from responding favourably to the latter request despite a strong plea from a departing Prime Minister Trudeau.[177] In short, the growing divisions between the traditionalists and the modernists in the Franco-Ontarian community threatened to erupt into a political battle between the religious rights of Ontario's Catholics and the language rights of Franco-Ontarians.

Nearly two decades of hard experience, including intensive negotiations after 1982, proved that political negotiations alone would not produce the desired outcome: full school governance. The ACFO, AEFO, AFCSO, and francophone parents in Ottawa-Carleton and other regions were determined to test the constitutional limits of s. 23 in the courts as soon as possible. Threatened with a series of court challenges to Ontario's Education Act, Premier Davis referred the legislation to the Court of Appeal in the belief that its provisions complied with s. 23. As we have seen, the court ruled that, in principle, s. 23 accorded the official language minorities the right to educational facilities equal to those of the majority. However, the Ontario government's proposed plan for limited school governance for Franco-Ontarians in the Ottawa-Carleton region did meet the requirements of the Charter.

The Franco-Ontarian educational organizations pursued the implementation of limited school governance under Bill 75, as well as the controversial hybrid model of French public and Catholic school governance in Ottawa-Carleton. Cooperation was not forthcoming from most Ontario school boards, and Bill 75 created a litany of complaints. The hybrid model exacerbated deep-seated divisions within the Franco-Ontarian community of the capital region, while the severe funding shortfall put the public section of the new French language school board into receivership. The Peterson and Rae governments created numerous education committees and received several reports while awaiting the outcome of the Supreme Court's deliberations on s. 23 rights. Its liberal and expansive interpretation of those rights in the 1990 *Mahé* case forced the Rae and Harris governments into action. They had no choice but to revamp Ontario's Education Act to provide full school governance for Franco-Ontarians wherever they resided in the province. It was a historic moment for Franco-Ontarians, who had fought for over a century for this prize. Paradoxically, their well-deserved victory was undermined when the Harris government dramatically reduced funding for education and curtailed the financial and pedagogical powers of every school board in Ontario. In continuing their struggle for effective school governance, Franco-Ontarians would be advancing the renewal and redefinition of their culture. Their failures helped other provincial organizations avoid the provincial government's procrastination tactics. Their victories, partial as they might seem, acted as catalysts encouraging their compatriots in other provinces to persevere and be rewarded with even greater victories.

4

Franco-Albertans, the Charter, and School Governance

Mais que voulions-nous? Que veulent les parents dans toutes leurs revendications? Une école française de qualité. Seulement et entièrement.[1]

After the passage of the Charter, the Association canadienne-française de l'Alberta, the Association Georges-et-Julia Bugnet, and the Fédération des parents francophones de l'Alberta worked for over a decade to achieve full school governance. Franco-Albertans had to overcome a deep-seated fear of disturbing the equilibrium they had worked so hard to achieve in their relationship with Alberta's majority English-speaking community and its established leaders. Initially, the ACFA moved with caution on s. 23 rights because of the vocal opposition of many Albertans to the Official Languages Act and the Charter. Thanks to the perseverance, hard work, and convincing arguments of the Association Bugnet, sceptical parents and an overly cautious ACFA were emboldened to pursue full implementation of their rights under s. 23. Franco-Albertans and their leaders soon recognized that school governance was not an end in itself, but rather an important instrument – one of many – helping them carve out new symbolic and political spaces within the province. Winning school governance would solidify their identity as Franco-Albertans and make them an important element of the redefined national network of francophone minority communities.

Once convinced that full school governance was both necessary and attainable, increasing numbers of urban and then rural Franco-Albertan parents joined the crusade. Responding to pressure, the ACFA leadership had no choice but to learn the complex skills of micro- and mega-constitutional political bargaining in a hostile sociocultural and political environment. The Constitution Act, 1982, especially the controversial Charter, was not welcomed by Alberta's political and social elites. Premier Peter Lougheed's Conservative government was determined to limit the Charter's impact on Alberta's populist, conservative political culture, which was characterized by deference and virtually single-party rule. In the course of protracted negotiations over s. 23 minority language education rights, Lougheed was convinced by Prime Minister Pierre Trudeau that the section would not undermine the province's exclusive jurisdiction over education. He grudgingly signed on, but both he and his successor, Don Getty, made every effort to see to it that provincial autonomy prevailed over official language minority rights. When the Association Bugnet, the ACFA, and Franco-Albertan parents took their struggle all the way to the Supreme Court, Lougheed and Getty did everything in their power to convince the justices that the framers of s. 23 never intended it to include full school governance.

Unsure of where the majority of Franco-Albertans stood on the issue, unwilling to disturb the ethnocultural status quo, and fearful of wading into the turbulent political waters stirred by the backlash against official bilingualism and the Charter, the ACFA procrastinated. Its leaders were convinced that, given time, they could draw upon their contacts in government to fashion a political settlement – a "made-in-Alberta solution," as the government referred to it – on the sensitive matter of minority language education rights. Given Lougheed's repeated assertion that his government would never grant full school governance, they concluded that the best approach was to seek a compromise falling just short of unfettered governance. Within a couple of years, however, it became painfully obvious to the ACFA's leaders that they had virtually no political clout with the Lougheed Conservatives. Its board therefore agreed, albeit reluctantly, to support the Association Bugnet's decision to seek a judicial remedy, first in the Court of Queen's Bench, then at the Alberta Court of Appeal. Obtaining ambivalent and unsatisfactory legal decisions on s. 23 rights, the Association Bugnet decided to take its case to the Supreme Court.

By 1986, the Association Bugnet, the ACFA, and the FPFA were determined to obtain the full complement of education rights provided in s. 23, from French language classrooms in predominantly English language Catholic schools to French language public and separate schools and school boards with trustees elected by francophone parents. At first, this goal seemed utopian. As a second round of political negotiations proceeded – reinforced by two judicial rulings in the province – it became apparent that their interpretation of s. 23 rights was gaining grudging support from some of Alberta's political and educational leaders, beginning with the Minister of Education and his senior bureaucrats. But the overall climate within the province remained hostile and a political resolution remained as elusive as ever. The ACFA and FPFA renewed their lobbying when the

Supreme Court of Canada ruled partly in favour of the Association Bugnet in the 1990 *Mahé* case. Some three years later, their efforts bore fruit in the form of Bill 8. Passed by Premier Ralph Klein's government, the bill revised Alberta's noncompliant School Act, providing full school governance for Franco-Albertans in all regions of the province. Their successful struggle transformed Alberta's French Canadians into Franco-Albertans enjoying a small but significant degree of segmental autonomy in the field of education.

FULL RIGHTS UNDER THE CHARTER VERSUS A "MADE-IN-ALBERTA" POLITICAL COMPROMISE

Franco-Albertan parents had considerably more limited educational options for their children than Franco-Ontarian parents. Though they did have access to publicly funded Catholic separate schools, the Alberta government refused to transform some of these into homogeneous French language public schools managed by Franco-Albertans. Indeed, using French as the language of instruction was forbidden in Alberta's school system as late as 1968. By the 1970s, thanks to the Official Languages Act and the funding for Ottawa's Bilingualism in Education program, the separatist movement in Quebec, and the vocal demands of an expanding urban middle class, the province offered a range of French language programs in both public and Catholic schools. These programs – including the very limited core French, the bilingual program, and the increasingly popular French immersion – were available to all Alberta children. Franco-Albertan parents wanting something more than core French for their children had to send them to ethnically and religiously mixed bilingual or French language immersion schools. The elaborate system was plagued from the outset by two major problems: the bilingual and French immersion programs were swamped by non-francophone children, and Franco-Albertan parents had absolutely no governance rights over these schools.[2]

Well-off Franco-Albertan parents opted for these programs because the traditional private school alternatives were no longer available. Collège St-Jean and l'Académie Assomption had terminated their intermediate and high school programs; eventually, the latter shut its doors altogether. The majority of Franco-Albertan families could not have afforded private schools in any case. These parents paid local school taxes and seemed satisfied that their children were at long last receiving half or all of their education in French, even if the school environment remained largely non-francophone. By the late 1970s, this system of French language education programs had become well entrenched. It appeared to meet the educational needs of most Franco-Albertan parents, especially those living outside Edmonton and Calgary. The ACFA campaigned for more bilingual and immersion schools and for the transportation to get Franco-Albertan children to them.[3] The urbanization of Franco-Albertans increased dramatically throughout the 1970s – swelled in part by thousands of migrants from Quebec – as they sought better education and employment in the booming economies of Edmonton and Calgary. It was only a matter of time before the educational status quo would come under serious scrutiny.[4]

A small but vocal group of francophone academics and parents in Edmonton, many of them recent arrivals from Quebec, started pressuring the ACFA and the Ministry of Education to consider the educational needs of their children. Some had campaigned for the inclusion of s. 23 rights in the Charter, and once the Charter was the law of the land, they were ready to use it to obtain full school governance for Franco-Albertans. Furthermore, they considered the existing bilingual and immersion schools to be instruments of assimilation, and the emerging social science literature agreed that these programs accelerated the assimilation of minority language children.[5]

Among this group of Edmonton parents were Jean-Claude Mahé and Angéline Martel. In early November 1981, they met with the ACFA's Comité d'éducation to ask it to hire a full-time employee to take charge of creating a research institute to analyse Alberta's French language education programs. They believed the results would show the advancing assimilation of Franco-Albertan children in immersion schools, which would help convince both parents and the ACFA to pursue the goal of school governance. The Comité d'éducation agreed to consider their request, and on 11 December the ACFA executive decided to convene a special meeting of Franco-Albertans concerned with education.[6] At the meeting, held on 1 February 1982, it was decided to refer Mahé's and Martel's request to an Ad Hoc Committee. Having concluded that the ACFA should not undertake the formation of a research institute, the committee sent Mahé a letter on 29 June 1982 recommending instead that he form a parental organization to set one up. Discouraged by the ACFA's procrastination, by its defence of the status quo, and by its outright rejection of their request, Mahé and Martel decided to form an association of Franco-Albertan parents to fight for homogeneous French language schools and school boards across the province.

Thus was born the Association Georges-et-Julia Bugnet. It had a broad mandate: to undertake further research on educational matters, to educate Franco-Albertans about their education-related rights under the Charter, to lobby the Minister of Education and Edmonton's Catholic and public boards, to seek financing for all these ventures, and, if need be, to pursue the implementation of their s. 23 rights through the courts.[7] Its primary goal was to pressure both the recalcitrant ACFA and the hostile Alberta government into fully implementing s. 23 rights.[8] The Association Bugnet was particularly concerned about the social and educational problems facing Franco-Albertan children; its own studies as well as those of other specialists on the effect of French immersion confirmed that it was accelerating their assimilation.[9] What did the Association want? Mahé asked rhetorically many years later, when he became the honoured recipient of the Ordre de la fidélité française from the Conseil de la vie française. Quite simply, they wanted the assimilation of their children enrolled in immersion schools to cease – something that would be achieved only when Franco-Albertans controlled their own French language schools."[10]

These were highly ambitious goals for an organization with very few members and limited financial resources. Yet within eight years of its founding the Association Bugnet had obtained a remarkably favourable landmark decision on s. 23 rights at the Supreme Court. Throughout 1982, it continued to pressure the ACFA indirectly and directly to take action on Franco-Albertans' education rights. The following year, it polled parents on the educational needs of their children and began to educate them about their rights. Against the wishes of the ACFA, it also lobbied Minister of Education David King to pressure the Edmonton Catholic school district no. 7 and the Edmonton public school board to open negotiations on establishing Franco-Albertan schools and granting parents management rights over them. Refusing to get involved, King handed off the task to the Association Bugnet. The Catholic school district and the public board responded by saying that Alberta's School Act did not allow for the delegation of management rights to parents. Moreover, the former rejected the Association's proposal that the teaching of religion should be made optional, while the latter rejected any teaching of religion. The Association then sought and received funding from the Court Challenges Program to pursue a legal challenge of the School Act. It also sought – but was refused – financial support from the Fonds Saint-Jean, which was administered by the ACFA. Finally, it gained the support of Canadian Parents for French, whose president, Carole Anderson, was convinced that Alberta's School Act contravened s. 23 rights.[11]

The Association Bugnet gained momentum mainly because the ACFA was reluctant to take charge of the school governance issue in the early stages of the struggle. Indeed, its commissioned 1982 annual report, the *Rapport Perron*, declared that its policy was to proceed cautiously. Mahé later recalled: "Parce que les leaderships francophone et anglophone de l'Alberta ne croyaient pas aux écoles françaises et encore moins à l'importance de leur gestion, un large débat a été enclenché, débat qui a duré jusqu'à ce que la Cour du banc de la Reine vienne légitimer notre position et nos revendications en juillet 1985."[12] Why was the ACFA so hesistant? According to the *Rapport Perron*, a majority of Franco-Albertan parents favoured bilingual or immersion schools, primarily because they feared that homogeneous schools would prevent their children from learning English and marginalize their communities. The ACFA's initial policy response was to support both homogeneous and immersion schools, leaving the choice up to its regional associations or to parents groups.[13] The Franco-Albertan community was divided, and the ACFA, whose leaders and members were drawn from the established elites, reflected that political reality in its approach to s. 23 rights.

At the ACFA's annual general meeting on 5 March 1983, Paul Dubé, speaking on behalf of the Association Bugnet, denounced it for doing nothing to further the cause of homogeneous French language schools and boards. He wondered why the ACFA was so concerned about the future of the established system of immersion and bilingual schools – supported and well funded by both the provincial and federal governments – when there was no francophone minority community system. He reminded his listeners that Carole Anderson of Canadian Parents for French was more critical of the Alberta government for not living up to its obligations under s. 23 than the ACFA was. The proper function of the ACFA, in Dubé's view, was not to take polls and support the existing educational system; instead, it should "concentrer ses efforts à faire un lobbying honnête et intelligent au niveau provincial afin d'établir des conseils scolaires francophones." It should begin by educating Franco-Albertan parents about their education rights under the Charter. The ACFA was not pleased with the forceful criticism, to say the least, but it did try to reassure the delegates that the education issue would receive careful attention.[14]

This assurance was not enough for the Association Bugnet, which decided to campaign for school governance independently of the ACFA. With the support of the ACFA's Comité d'éducation and its regional association for the Edmonton region, the Association Bugnet lobbied the Minister of Education and the Edmonton Catholic and public school boards to establish francophone schools in compliance with s. 23. When it was rebuffed at all levels, it decided to open a private francophone elementary school – the École Georges-et-Julia-

Bugnet – in September 1983, in response to the demand from parents in Edmonton, home to over 17,000 Franco-Albertans. Despite the enrolment of nearly 130 students, the school was forced to close before the end of the 1983–84 school year as a result of serious financial constraints and the lack of community support, including the ACFA's opposition to the project because it did not take the existing educational structures into account.[15] When the Association Bugnet blamed the Edmonton Catholic school district for its school's failure, ACFA president Guy Goyette was quick to point out that the decision not to reopen the school for the 1984–85 school year had been made by the Association and not the school district. He reminded Franco-Albertans that there were two homogeneous francophone elementary schools, one in Edmonton with 250 children and a second in Calgary with 120 children, which would provide a solid base for further expansion once the ACFA obtained the amendments needed to make the School Act compliant with s. 23.[16] Goyette's critique was more than a little disingenuous, since it was primarily the Association Bugnet's initiative that had prompted the Edmonton Catholic school district to transform one of its immersion schools into a school for Franco-Albertan children.[17]

It was clear that Edmonton's Catholic and public school boards jealously guarded their autonomy and did not relish having to compete with a third school system for students and funding. The ACFA was torn between Catholic Franco-Albertan parents who wanted to maintain the existing system of separate schools with their range of French language programs and secular, middle-class parents who were determined to get a public Franco-Albertan system. Hoping to undermine the growing strength of the Association Bugnet and stall its drive for a public francophone system, the ACFA continued to lobby the Minister of Education for a made in Alberta solution.[18] In May 1983 it convened a special meeting having to do with the need for a Catholic French school. In short order, Edmonton's Catholic Franco-Albertan parents organized the Société des parents francophones pour les écoles francophones à Edmonton, which managed to convince the Edmonton Catholic school board to open an elementary school, the École Maurice Lavallée, in September 1984. A second one opened in 1988. However, the board would not grant the parents and their trustees any authority to manage these schools. It also steadfastly refused to create a francophone high school until 1989, on the grounds that there were insufficient students and the province would not pay the capital costs.[19] The persistent barriers to obtaining compliance with s. 23 merely reinforced the Association Bugnet's early decision to take its campaign for full school governance to the courts.

Taking the political approach pioneered by the ACFO, the ACFA finally set out in the fall of 1983 to attempt to negotiate a mutually acceptable implementation of s. 23 rights with the government. For three years it expended a great deal of its limited time, energy, and financial resources on convincing Premier Peter Lougheed and his Conservatives to live up to his signature on the Constitution Act, 1982. The prolonged search for a made in Alberta solution would prove frustrating and ultimately elusive. Nevertheless, the experience matured the ACFA and enabled it to see more clearly how it could achieve its objective.

The ACFA spelled out its policy on s. 23 rights at its General Council meeting in May 1983. From its perspective, the new Constitution granted Franco-Albertans the right to the establishment of French language schools wherever the need existed throughout the province. It defined a French school as follows: "Conçue pour des Franco-albertains, l'école française est une institution qui vit en français, dont l'ambiance est française, dont le personnel est d'expression et de culture françaises et au sein de laquelle toutes les communications se font en français. Ainsi l'école française est une institution qui véhicule la culture canadienne-française et plus précisément la culture franco-albertaine." Such schools would be open to all French-speaking children and could be under the jurisdiction of existing school boards until separate French boards were established. The ACFA noted that it would study all judicial avenues to make sure Franco-Albertan parents obtained responsibility over French education for their children.[20]

In the fall of 1983, the ACFA set up a rather elaborate Comité provincial de l'éducation with a dual mandate. First, the CPÉ was to act as a consultative body for the ACFA executive on education policy in general, as well as on specific issues such as developing the criteria for admission to schools established under s. 23, proposing school governance models, and outlining the role of parents in these schools. Second, it was to use the ACFA's regional offices and other francophone organizations to educate Franco-Albertan parents about their s. 23 rights. Because of the pressure from the Association Bugnet, the executive opted to include a representative from the CPÉ in meetings with the Minister of Education and his senior bureaucrats. The ACFA wanted to reassure concerned Franco-Albertans that it was not about to make a deal behind closed doors; indeed, it hoped that strong parental support would strengthen its hand in bargaining with the government.[21]

In preparation for meeting with Minister of Education David King on revisions to the School Act, the ACFA issued a declaration of

principles. The new School Act should recognize the right of francophone parents to educate their children in their own language at
public expense in French classrooms, at a minimum; in French
schools, whenever feasible. If neither a French classroom nor school
was available, the government should provide alternative arrangements at public expense for all children wishing an education in
French. Franco-Albertan parents should be able to exercise effective
control over French classrooms and schools, beginning with input on
who was eligible to attend them. The province should create "classes
d'acceuil" for francophone students lacking the French language skills
necessary for full integration into these classes or schools. The ACFA
also asked King to allow francophone parents in regions where alternatives were not available to continue to send their children to French-
as-a-second-language (immersion schools). The last measure was an
attempt to appease francophone parents who preferred this option for
ideological or practical reasons.[22]

King met with a large ACFA delegation on 7 March 1983, assuring
them that the proposed education policy statement would reflect the
group's declaration of principles. He indicated that all services provided under the education policy for Franco-Albertans would be conditioned by the number of students wishing to pursue their education
in French.[23] It was not long before the ACFA learned a hard lesson
about who decided what in Alberta. The delegation returned to meet
with the minister on 14 June, to be told that the premier and Cabinet
had decided that the current School Act complied with the minority
education rights section of the Charter. King explained that the real
reason for putting off revisions to the School Act was the government's
fear of a political backlash from the legal action being planned by the
Association Bugnet. Hoping to drive a wedge between the ACFA and
the Association Bugnet, King took another line of attack. In lieu of a
revised School Act, he promised he would pressure all school boards
to respect s. 23 rights by setting out for them "une grille de critères et
de recommandations à employer en ce qui a trait à l'établissement et
à l'administration de programmes et d'écoles francophones" before
September 1984.

The ACFA indicated in a press release that it was deeply disappointed with the government's refusal to respect Franco-Albertans'
education rights. The province was clearly trying to put pressure on
the ACFA to get the Association Bugnet to back away from its legal
challenge. The ACFA decided it had nothing to lose by cooperating
with King in pressuring school boards to comply with s. 23, because
this just might advance its cause; however, given the uncertainty of
entrenching s. 23 rights in a revised School Act, it quite wisely

decided to explore its own legal options.[24] The decision to pursue both political and judicial options simultaneously was prompted by two developments. First, the ACFA's contact in the government, Adrien Bussière, had gotten hold of the proposed directives that David King would be encouraged to send to the school boards, and they appeared promising. On the legal front, there was the encouraging outcome of the Ontario Court of Appeal's decision in the reference case, which could be expected to have some impact on the Alberta judiciary in any future court action.[25]

The Minister of Education gave the ACFA a copy of his proposed directive for the school boards during a meeting on 3 October 1984. Subsequently, ACFA President Guy Goyette, while thanking King for the opportunity to respond, indicated that the draft was fine except for the reference to three distinct groups of students for whom French minority language education was intended, which failed to reflect the understanding reached during their meeting. The ACFA and King had "agreed that students who do not meet the test of s. 23, who are already fluent in French and whose parents want to avail themselves of French minority language education opportunities, are likely to be the exception rather than the rule in Alberta." The letter to the school boards had to spell out clearly the "primary intent of s. 23 and the steps you [King] intend to take to meet the needs of students who meet the test of the Charter." Whatever the government intended to do for students fluent in French who did not meet the test of the Charter should be clarified in a separate document to avoid any ambiguity.[26]

At the 3 October meeting, the ACFA had also received a draft of the proposed policy statement, guidelines, and procedures concerning French language educational services, as well as suggested amendments to ss. 158 and 159 of the School Act. Its executive studied all the documents carefully and authorized Goyette to send King a lengthy and critical confidential evaluation. The ACFA felt that the definition of "where numbers warrant" as one student was very enlightened, as was the concern to provide education in French for students not eligible under the Charter. But there was little else in the proposals that the ACFA found acceptable. Notably, it objected to "the absence of a definition of the educational program that would implement the requirements of the Charter and the advisory nature of the parents' influence over this program." The government seemed to be trying to assimilate a French-as-a-first-language program with the existing French-as-a-second-language, that is, the popular immersion program. Goyette suggested the following definition: "A French language minority program is one designed to meet the educational needs of French-speaking Albertans; it pursues and promotes French Canadian culture; it is characterized by the predominance of French language usage within the school and within the home." Further, he indicated that a purely advisory role for parents "may not meet the intent of the Charter" and was therefore not the "most appropriate management framework." The ACFA would cooperate in the interim with an advisory management framework on condition that the proposed "French Education Council [would have] exclusive authority to make recommendations in the areas indicated as part of its mandate." Both the school board and the French Education Council would have to agree before any recommendation was implemented.[27]

As for the amendments to the School Act, the ACFA wanted the legislation to entrench s. 23 of the Charter by incorporating "a clause requiring Boards to provide French minority language education" and by spelling out in detail that "'where numbers warrant' means one student; a definition of the French minority language program; the equitable treatment to be provided to the French minority language program; and the power and rights of Charter parents with regard to management."[28] Legislation would provide greater assurance and stability for Franco-Albertans than regulations, guidelines, and procedures, which could be changed by Cabinet and senior bureaucrats. If the School Act did not define a French minority language program, then it was crucial for the guidelines to do so. Furthermore, it was inappropriate for Guideline no. 3 to refer to immersion and restrict the meaning of the Charter phrase "minority language educational facility" to only a district school building, something quite contrary to the meaning outlined in the Ontario reference case. Any reference to immersion classes or programs, Goyette argued, should be removed and "Guideline no. 3 should simply state that 'a minority language educational program and its related services are normally housed in a distinct school building'."

Finally, the ACFA suggested amendments to the procedures pertaining to the election of members to the French Education Council that reflected the concerns discussed above.[29] Its critique of the proposals demonstrated that it had a clear vision of how education rights should be defined and implemented throughout the province. Subsequent developments would demonstrate that this vision was not shared by the Minister of Education or his colleagues in Cabinet and the caucus. At a meeting of the Alberta Trustees Association for Bilingual Education held on 4 November 1984, King announced that amendments to the School Act would not be introduced during the fall session. Goyette wrote him a few days later expressing the ACFA's concern that negotiations over French minority language education appeared to have been derailed. He requested an explanation in person, prior to the General Council meeting on 1 December, as to why the letter to the school boards had not gone out and why the government was not proceeding with amendments to the School Act. He reminded King that this was the third time that a time table for implementation had been set aside. The fifteen months spent by the ACFA on negotiating a made in Alberta solution was seriously compromising its credibility with its constituents. "The Charter has been in effect since 1982 ... Nothing concrete appears to result from our negotiations, except further delays. We feel we have reached the point where we must ask ourselves whether the truism 'rights delayed are rights denied' applies."[30]

Without responding to the ACFA's concerns, King sent a letter on 19 November to all school board chairs declaring the government's support for s. 23 and its intention "to ensure, through co-operation with local school boards, the development, the implementation and the assessment of French language educational programs which are appropriate to the needs of students." He indicated that the government's policy would address the needs of all three groups of students seeking an education in French.[31] Damning the letter with faint praise as "un tout petit pas dans la bonne direction," Goyette reminded Franco-Albertans that not a single one of the ACFA's recommendations had been accepted. He called on the government to exercise effective leadership if it hoped to arrive at a made-in-Alberta solution with the ACFA.[32]

Feeling the pressure, King met with Goyette on 20 November, then arranged for a further meeting with the Education Committee of the ACFA for the 28th. In anticipation of this meeting, the minister finally responded to all of Goyette's letters. He denied the allegation that the ACFA was being kept in the dark when it suited the Ministry of Education, and explained that his plans for legislation had been altered by the untimely death of the leader of the Alberta New Democratic Party, Grant Notley, which curtailed the fall session. He reiterated that it was the government's intention to convey to the school boards that French minority language education was designed to encompass all students, both those covered by the Charter and those who were not, although he believed the numbers of the latter to be so small as not to distort the overall policy. He asserted that all three forms of French language education – bilingual, immersion, and minority – could coexist in Alberta without the latter being perceived as "an elite form of immersion." Furthermore, it was not appropriate to provide a rigid definition of French language education because doing so would go beyond the requirements of the Charter and the province's "Goals of Basic Education" statement. King assured Goyette that the province was not "attempting to assimilate French language education into an immersion program and to destroy by assimilation the Franco-Canadian culture." He categorically denied having promised that amendments to the School Act would find their way through the legislature during the fall session, followed by order-in council regulations and a published policy, guidelines, and procedures statement on French language education. While he agreed that the proposed French Education Council should have full information, it could not be granted final authority over the selection of key administrative personnel. Other matters raised by Goyette remained open for further discussion.[33]

After the meetings with King, the ACFA evaluated the all-too-meagre results of its lengthy efforts to negotiate a made in Alberta solution.[34] The delegation proposed a series of recommendations to help the executive prepare for the General Council meeting on 1 December. The ACFA and its regional committees should step up their lobbying efforts by sending letters to Premier Peter Lougheed, Prime Minister Brian Mulroney via the Secretary of State, Senator Arthur Tremblay, and all MLAs and MPs. The French language media should be given better information about the ACFA's position and the state of negotiations. The ACFA should also set up a legal aid fund to seek donations from Franco-Albertans. Following advice from constitutional experts, it should indicate its moral and financial support for Franco-Albertans willing to challenge the Alberta government's failure to implement s. 23 education rights.[35] All the recommendations were accepted, but a preamble was added directing the executive to inform David King of the ACFA's intention to step up its lobbying efforts while preparing for a legal challenge.[36] It appears that moderates within the group hoped that forewarning of this more aggressive plan of action would be enough to convince the province to bargain in good faith.

It was becoming increasingly clear that the government's definition of a made in Alberta solution was quite different from that envisaged by the ACFA and many Franco-Albertan parents. A prominent Franco-Albertan lawyer, Louis A. Desrochers, urged Premier Lougheed in late October 1984 to amend ss. 158 and 159 of the School Act to bring them into conformity with s. 23 – something the premier had agreed to do in 1981. Section 158 stated that all students in Alberta should be taught in the English language, while s. 159(1) permitted a school board to authorize the use of French as a language of instruction if it so chose. The problem was that most boards categorically refused to invoke s. 159. Lougheed's reply of 22 January 1985 confirmed his government's intention of doing so. "I can assure you that Alberta will take the necessary steps to ensure that opportunities for students to be instructed in French are provided not only for those students who qualify under Article 23 of the Charter of Rights and Freedoms, but also for other Alberta students who either speak French or wish to learn the language."[37] The goal was separating language and culture and formulating a comprehensive French language education policy that would address the desire of all Albertans wanting an education in French for their children, rather than focusing exclusively on the obligation to fulfill s. 23 rights.

The ACFA participated in a lengthy meeting with the Minister of Education on 21 February 1985 where both parties discussed the statistics on French language enrolments for 1984–85, the School Act review document, and the ACFA's action plan. The group contested the Ministry's statistics, which showed 1,300 children receiving French minority education and 17,600 children registered in the immersion program. According to the ACFA, the criteria used to identify minority language students were unrealistic, since many Franco-Albertan parents had no choice but to enroll their children in French immersion. Both parties agreed to disagree on the proposed amendments to the School Act when King could not convince the delegation to envisage the changes to French language education in the context of the revision of the School Act. As regards the ACFA's decision to embark on an aggressive public campaign of lobbying federal and provincial politicians, King supported the decision to go public but urged the group not to adopt an adversarial approach to the government because it would be counterproductive. He reiterated that he did not want further fragmentation of school boards, nor was it his intention to coerce them into complying with s. 23 rights. He suggested that a persuasive approach acknowledging the progress made so far would "broaden the zone of tolerance of the Alberta community and succeed in changing the School Act." The government was facing considerable opposition from school boards, teachers' associations, and members of its own caucus. King pleaded with the ACFA to meet with all these organizations to convince them to support the proposed amendments. He even offered to set up meetings with the executive committee of caucus and the Policy Advisory Committee for the School Act review.[38]

The ACFA proceeded with the full implementation of its political action plan. However, it also decided to inform King of its executive's decision of 1 March 1985, approved at the annual general meeting the following day, to seek intervenor status in the legal proceedings undertaken by the Association Bugnet. Its new president, Myriam Laberge, admitted that a judicial decision was not likely to produce a made in Alberta solution to the minority education rights issue. But the ACFA had reached the conclusion that "it is necessary to intervene in order to attempt to ascertain that there be solid underpinnings to the application of Section 23 of the Charter in Alberta." Laberge hoped that, contrary to rumours, the province would not oppose the court's granting the group intervenor status. In the interim, the ACFA would proceed with all facets of its action plan, as King was told during a meeting on 21 February.[39]

When the ACFA met with the Policy Advisory Committee for the School Act review on 10 June 1985, verbal fireworks ensued. The chair of the committee indicated that draft legislation of the revised School Act would be introduced only in the spring session of 1986. When the ACFA's president objected that Franco-Albertan children should not be forced to wait any longer, the chair stated that the matter was outside the mandate of the committee and had to be taken up with the Minister of Education. President Laberge complained to King that further delays in the implementation of s. 23 could "only be seen as foot-dragging and buck-passing." If his government was serious about its desire to achieve a political solution there was absolutely no reason to use the Association Bugnet's court challenge as an excuse for once again delaying amendments to ss. 158 and 159 of the School Act. She assured the minister that the school boards were looking for leadership from his office and awaited the promised framework for local decision-making. Further procrastination would undermine socially harmonious implementation of s. 23.[40] In actual fact, the protracted search for a negotiated political settlement with the Alberta government was over for the moment.

THE ASSOCIATION BUGNET
TAKES THE ALBERTA GOVERNMENT TO COURT

Having failed to get the backing of the ACFA or a majority of Franco-Albertan parents, the Association Bugnet decided that its only option was to take the province to court. Despite the ACFA's opposition and hostility from the government and the media, its leaders, Jean-Claude Mahé, Angéline Martel, and Paul Dubé, launched proceedings in the Court of Queen's Bench of Alberta in October 1983 to obtain recognition of the right of Franco-Albertan parents to French language education for their children and school governance. When the Secretary of State announced the reintroduction of the Court Challenges Program, the Association Bugnet obtained crucial financial support for its lengthy battle, which would go all the way to the Supreme Court.[41] Without this backing from the Canadian government, it is highly unlikely that the group would have launched its legal challenge, since its attempts to obtain the necessary funding from other sources proved unsuccessful.[42]

It took almost two years for the case to be heard in the Court of Queen's Bench of Alberta on 15–19 April 1985. The ACFA got its wish and was accepted as *amicus curiae* by Judge S.S. Purvis, being represented by constitutional lawyers Michel Bastarache and L. Carr. Judge Purvis based much of his decision, brought down on 24 July 1985, on the Ontario reference case. He argued that the Charter, as a constitutional document, must be the subject of large and liberal interpretation, and agreed with the argument in the Ontario case that since "the Charter of Rights and Freedoms is clearly remedial" it should be construed liberally.[43] On the basis of these principles, he accepted some but not all of the claims made by the three plaintiffs and the Association Bugnet, concluding that, in principle, "the Alberta School Act should award to the citizens of Canada who qualify under s. 23(1) and (2) of the Charter, the right to exercise a degree of control over French minority language of instruction for their children in Alberta. This right should apply where the numbers of those children are sufficient to warrant the provision to them, out of public funds, of minority language of instruction in minority language educational facilities."[44] While Judge Purvis found that there were sufficient numbers of students in the Edmonton metropolitan area to justify the application of ss. 23(1) and (2), the numbers were not sufficient to warrant the creation of a separate French school board under s. 23(3). He believed that, as per the Ontario reference case, "the necessary degree of control and management might be accomplished if *minority representation was guaranteed* on local boards or authorities," and if the minority representatives had exclusive control over all important matters pertaining to minority language instruction.[45] Finally, he ruled that ss. 158, 159, and 27 of the School Act – the last of which gave a local advisory board the right to request instruction in the French language and obliged it to institute such instruction when practical – should be altered to comply with s. 23 of the Charter, while Regulation 490/82, requiring 15 to 20 per cent English language instruction, was justified under s. 1 of the Charter "as a reasonable and desirable limitation which can be demonstrably justified in a free and democratic society."[46]

The ruling was an astute acknowledgment of the complex realities of educational politics in the province. Judge Purvis gave credit to the government and the Edmonton Catholic school board for the positive steps that both had undertaken in the matter of minority education rights. At the same time, he also gave notice that the court would not tolerate further procrastination on amending the School Act. Of course, the Association Bugnet, far from being satisfied with his ruling, was determined to take its case to the Supreme Court if need be, beginning with an application to the Alberta Court of Appeal. For its part, the ACFA hoped to use the decision to apply renewed political pressure on the Minister of Education to move forward with the revision of the School Act. President Myriam Laberge, in a letter to King on the day of the judgment, urged an immediate renewal of negotiations on not only the amendments but also the draft policy statement and guidelines.[47] Ignoring the importance of the Ontario reference case, King contended that Judge Purvis's decision "recognized that the Alberta situation is unique and that we are not bound by what happens in other provinces." He emphasized the judge's endorsement of the government's actions, as well as the latitude that his ruling granted it to fashion a made in Alberta solution. He promised quick action on the amendments and said he would instruct his officials to consult with the ACFA and the Alberta School Trustees' Association on the matter.[48]

Responding in early September to Laberge's letter of 24 June, King restated what he had said earlier and promised to restart discussions very soon on the government's proposed policy for French minority language education.[49] The ACFA met with the minister and his officials on 16 October to be apprised of his plan of action, in particular his decision to circulate for discussion and comment a working paper entitled *French Language Education in Alberta*. Unfortunately, the political situation prevented any progress, since the premier-elect, Don Getty, seemed to be unsure of the direction his government would take on this sensitive issue. Both parties concurred that, under the circumstances, there was "an absence of political will on the part of the Government and the Caucus to establish the major parameters of a delivery system which meets the intent of Section 23 of the Charter of Rights and Freedoms."[50] Once again, the search for the made in Alberta solution was proving to be a chimera, profoundly disillusioning to all Franco-Albertans, especially their leadership.

Supported by seven intervenors, including the ACFA and the Fédération, the Association Bugnet appealed the Court of Queen's Bench decision in August 1985. The Alberta Court of Appeal heard the case on 23–25 September 1986 and Judge J.A. Kerans rendered his decision on 26 August 1987.[51] The appellants, Mahé, Martel, Dubé, and the Association Bugnet, based their appeal of Judge Purvis's ruling on three grounds and proposed several measures of relief. To begin, the trial judge erred in "declining to find that the French Linguistic Minority Population in Alberta is entitled to equal powers of management and control over minority language instruction and educational facilities" to those enjoyed by the English majority population under the Alberta School Act, as well as in finding that the Charter's s. 15 (equality rights) did not apply to the case. The purpose of s. 23 was to guarantee the preservation of the minority culture, English or French, "*through the provision of publicly funded minority language instruction and facilities* (where numbers warrant)." The term "minority language educational facilities" implied that the framers of s. 23 intended the linguistic minorities to have control over their own schools. Second, Judge Purvis had erred in not ruling that certain sections of the School Act and Regulation 490/82 violated ss. 15 and 23 of the Charter. S. 13 of the School Act, which empowered the Minister of Education to create new school jurisdictions, was entirely discretionary, thereby violating s. 15 and s. 23, which rendered mandatory a French minority language school jurisdiction and board whenever numbers warranted. Regulation 490/82 was not supported by evidence, nor could it be justified under s. 1 of the Charter as a reasonable limit.

Third, when Judge Purvis ruled that there were sufficient numbers of francophone children to warrant instruction in the French language, he erred by concluding that the École Maurice Lavallée, established under the Edmonton Roman Catholic Separate School Board's authority, satisfied all the requirements of s. 23 of the Charter. The school was not a homogeneous French minority language school, but rather a "mixed" elementary school where Franco-Albertan children shared facilities with English language students enrolled in a French-as-a-second-language program. The school existed entirely at the discretion of the Ministry of Education and the Edmonton Roman Catholic Separate School Board; it was controlled by trustees elected by a constituency the majority of which was English-speaking and Catholic. The Parent Advisory Committee of the Ecole Lavallée, set up under s. 27 of the School Act, had no say over the management and control of the school and therefore did not satisfy s. 23.

The appellants asked the Court of Appeal to set aside the offending parts of the trial judge's decision and make a declaration to the effect that Franco-Albertans were "entitled to powers of management and control of French Linguistic Minority school instruction and educational facilities by virtue of s. 23 of the Charter equal to those presently enjoyed by the English Linguistic Majority under the School Act." They wanted the relevant portions of the School Act and regulations to be declared of no force and effect, and the Minister of Education to create a school jurisdiction in the Edmonton area controlled and managed by and for the Franco-Albertan parents of the region.[52]

Alberta's Attorney General disputed the statement of facts presented by the Association Bugnet about the state of French language education in Edmonton. The province agreed with Judge Purvis's rulings on the non-applicability of s. 15 of the Charter, the compliance of s. 13 of the School Act and Regulation 490/82 with the Charter, and with the full compliance of the existing minority language education programs with s. 23. On the crucial issue of school governance by the linguistic minority, the Alberta government was emphatic that s. 23 did not provide such a right, contrary to the decision in the Ontario reference case. It saw as both erroneous and *obiter dicta* the Ontario ruling that "parents qualifying under s. 23 of the Charter have the right to exercise a degree of control over the education of their children in those circumstances where the numbers of parents are more than those required for language instruction and are sufficient to warrant the provision of instruction in minority language facilities." Since the linguistic minority was not entitled to management and control over education equal to that of the majority, there was no right to separate school jurisdictions, and s. 13 of the School Act complied with the Charter while Regulation 490/82 could be justified under s. 1. To sum up: All evidence indicated that the École Maurice Lavallée and the École J.H. Picard provided French language education from kindergarten to grade 12, thereby fulfilling the requirements of s. 23. Counsel for Alberta maintained that the Association Bugnet and the intervenors should not be allowed to turn their case into a reference on s. 23 of the Charter.[53]

Judge Kerans, writing for the Alberta Court of Appeal, ruled that, on the evidence presented, parents in the Edmonton area who wanted education in French for their children had not been deprived of that right and suffered no discrimination. On the other hand, he rejected the government's argument that the case should not become a reference on s. 23: "With respect the answer is not so simple as that. One cannot say that a person has been, or has not been, deprived of a constitutional right without first defining the right." He then proceeded to give a thorough analysis of what rights he believed to be available under s. 23. Having defined them, he concluded that the appeal must be dismissed because the evidence presented did not correspond to his reading of those rights; therefore, the situation did not warrant the "untimely or drastic remedies" requested by the appellants and the intervenors.[54]

Judge Kerans differed from Judge Purvis in his general observations on the Charter. Following the argument laid out by Justice J. Beetz in the 1986 *Société des Acadiens du Nouveau Brunswick* case, he distinguished between fundamental legal rights, which were rooted in principle, and language rights, which while entrenched in ss. 16–23 were based on political compromise. Each of these two categories of rights required a different judicial approach. Reaffirming the paramountcy of provincial rights, Judge Kerans wrote:

In my view, the words under review were chosen for their very imprecision. The compromise expressed in s. 23 is between those, both anglophone and francophone, who say that matters of education policy are best handled at the provincial level, and those who say that some language rights must be entrenched. As result, the Charter does not embrace any particular modality of education. It leaves all that to the province in exercise of its constitutional mandate, which is a compromise reflecting one side of a political question ... The conclusion I draw is that the widest possible discretion is left to the province in terms of institutional arrangements.

At the same time, interpretation must also reflect the *other* side of the political question. An historical viewpoint commands that one recognize that the first purpose of the section is to prevent assimilation of one language group or the other in any part of Canada, and at least in that limited way enhance a society in which the two languages acknowledged by s. 16 of the Charter to have pre-eminent status shall continue to be used ...

I conclude that the two ideas reflected in s. 23 are to offer strong rights to the s. 23 group to prevent assimilation and foster the growth of both official languages everywhere in Canada and, at the same time, interfere as little as possible with provincial legislative jurisdiction over educational facilities. To the extent that these ideas are in conflict, s. 23 is a compromise.[55]

Given Judge Kerans's interpretation of language rights as a political compromise, it is not difficult to understand his rulings on the specific issues in dispute. To the question "Do the words 'minority language education facilities' in s. 23(3)(b) mean 'a school system exclusively managed and controlled by the minority language group'?" he gave an answer in the affirmative. But having established the political right of linguistic minorities to run schools, he then rejected the approach proposed by Judge Purvis of a sliding scale of rights. Instead, he argued that no specific form of governance was entrenched in s. 23; the essence of the political compromise was that the section incorporated two options, the first of which excluded governance while the second offered the full benefits of governance when numbers warranted. At all times, the province retained the unimpeded right to determine the institutional form and the implementation of the right to governance, if and when it was granted by the province. All of this, of course, was subject to the right of the linguistic minority to appeal to the courts if it felt aggrieved. The right to governance was also conditioned by the cost involved, which was subject to s. 1 of the Charter, as well as by the need to respect s. 93 of the Constitution Act, 1867, which pertained to denominational, separate, or dissentient schools.[56]

On the question of whether the numbers warranted a "facility" under s. 23(3)(b) in the Edmonton metropolitan region, Judge Kerans ruled that the Association Bugnet and the intervenors had not presented evidence to prove their case "that numbers in Edmonton could provide, at reasonable cost, a new system equal to that offered now." It followed from his argument of exclusive provincial jurisdiction over institutional arrangements for the implementation of rights under s. 23(3)(a) and (b) that he would rule that the School Act did "not yet acknowledge s. 23, but nothing about it explicitly contradicts the rights in that section." Judge Kerans also dismissed the extensive arguments of the plaintiffs against the School Act based on the equality section of the Charter. He challenged the assumption "that the public school system in Alberta is somehow 'English' so that s. 15 commands that, in the name of equality, there be an identical system in place that is 'French'." Respect for cultural minorities flowed from the Charter, but "for the purposes of this case, it cannot be translated into a right to a school system organized like the public school system."[57] Since there was no breach of Charter rights, Judge Kerans ruled that no relief was warranted. However, he did conclude with a warning: "Now that the law is explained, Alberta can act."[58]

The two Alberta court cases demonstrated the complexity of the issues involved in interpreting what appeared to many observers as a straightforward issue of minority language education rights entrenched in the Charter. Where Judge Purvis perceived a mandatory sliding scale approach to school governance by the Franco-Albertan minority leaving the Alberta government no discretionary power, Judge Kerans posited a theory of no governance versus complete governance, with the province having the power to decide when each would apply and the nature of its institutional form. Two schools of jurisprudence had emerged pertaining to s. 23; it would be up to the Supreme Court to choose which would prevail.

The Association Bugnet and the ACFA were furious with Judge Kerans's dismissal of the appeal, because his argumentation and reasons were potentially much more damaging than those provided by Judge Purvis in the trial court. In the interim, both the Fédération des parents francophone de l'Alberta and the ACFA had made attempts to expedite the proceedings in order to curtail the enormous legal costs they foresaw in having to pursue the matter on their own. In December 1985 and January 1986, the ACFA made overtures to the Mulroney government through Senator Arthur Tremblay to undertake a reference case on s. 23. With the advice of Michel Bastarache, Myriam Laberge provided a long list of reasons why Ottawa should do so, starting with the argument that s. 23 was ambiguous and vague and left far too many loopholes for provincial governments wanting to avoid having to amend their education legislation to make sure it was proactive rather than just non-discriminatory. Clarification of s. 23 by the Supreme Court was of national interest because it was the federal government, through the Secretary of State, that in large measure financed the implementation of rights under the section.[59]

The Mulroney government made it clear that it was not interested in undertaking a reference case, mostly out of fear of disturbing the negotiations leading to the Meech Lake Constitutional Accord. Shortly after the 26 August 1987 ruling of the Alberta Court of Appeal, the Association Bugnet made application to the Supreme Court for leave to appeal the judgment. On 7 December 1987 the application was accepted; hearings opened in June 1989, and the landmark decision in the *Mahé* case was handed down in March 1990, as we shall soon see.[60]

GALVANIZING SUPPORT
FOR SCHOOL GOVERNANCE

Following the July 1985 Queen's Bench ruling, the ACFA set out to prepare systematically for the eventual acquisition of school governance by Franco-Albertan parents. The dispute between it and the Association Bugnet had created tensions and divisions within the francophone community, making it necessary to mend fences and map out a common plan of action. It became increasingly clear to the ACFA's leaders that they had to mobilize Franco-Albertans at all levels of society and in all regions in a renewed (and ultimately successful) effort to pressure the provincial government to legislate school governance. At the same time, they had to show the government that the ACFA had widespread support among Franco-Albertans and that its various constituents were not working at cross purposes.

At the General Council in September 1985, the ACFA decided it was time to create the Fédération de comités de parents francophones en Alberta. In late January 1986, Yvon Mahé, director of the ACFA's Bureau d'éducation, organized a symposium for all the associations, committees, and parent groups interested in French minority education. The result was an Ad Hoc Committee comprised of representatives of these organizations: Georges Arès, president of the Société des parents pour les écoles francophones d'Edmonton and Alberta's representative on the Commission national des parents francophones; Hélène Gignac, president of Parents de l'école francophone Sainte-Anne de Calgary; and François Picard, representing francophone parents from the Saint-Paul region. The Ad Hoc Committee, working under the aegis of the Bureau d'éducation, was mandated to prepare a report on the situation in Alberta and to make appropriate recommendations to the ACFA on what line of action to adopt.[61] It also served as a conduit through which Yvon Mahé could keep the membership well informed of the ACFA's lobbying efforts with the new Minister of Education, Neil Webber, and Premier Don Getty. The committee in turn kept its member organizations up to date on all developments and coordinated their efforts so they learned to work together effectively for the cause of French minority education. Having written a draft constitution, it prepared to transform itself into the Fédération des parents francophones d'Alberta by late September 1986.[62] The formal launching of the new organization took place during the Congrès de la francophonie in late October 1986. In May 1987, after several months of negotiations, the ACFA and the FPFA arrived at an agreement on the transfer of responsibilities having to do with education and the sharing of other activities. The ACFA's main responsibility was coordinating all the francophone groups involved in lobbying at the provincial and federal levels. It agreed that its public statements on education – especially those concerning school governance – would reflect the views of all interested parties, including teachers, students, and school trustees. While the ACFA and the FPFA shared responsibility for school governance, legal challenges, and studies and polls related to these matters, it was up to the ACFA to take the initiative. All other issues of primary and secondary education were eventually to be transferred to an autonomous FPFA, allowing the ACFA to dissolve its Bureau d'éducation. The agreement was signed by Hélène Gignac, the first president of the newly formed FPFA, and Georges Arès, the new president of the ACFA.[63] Two deeply concerned and determined Franco-Albertan parents and community leaders had gained control over the institutions dealing with the politically sensitive issue of education rights for their children.

The two groups realized that they required a comprehensive analysis of the legal situation of Franco-Albertans, as well as up-to-date information about francophones in all regions of Alberta so they could begin to conceptualize different models of school governance. With these items in hand, they could approach the government for discussions and, they hoped, reach a deal. If the province refused, they could submit their chosen governance plan along with a detailed estimate of the costs to the courts, requesting a ruling that would force the government to grant the Franco-Albertan community the public funds required to administer its own education system. On the recommendation of Jean-Claude Le Blanc, a senior bureaucrat in the Office of the Commissioner of Official Languages, the ACFA hired Professor Lionel Desjarlais, former Dean of the Faculty of Education at the University of Ottawa, to carry out the study.[64]

Working closely with the ACFA and FPFA and receiving feedback from Jean-Claude Le Blanc, in 1989 Desjarlais produced a lengthy report that was distilled into a fifty-page pamphlet published in both official languages and entitled *C'est maintenant, l'heure de l'école franco-albertaine.* Desjarlais synthesized all the legal arguments developed by the Association Bugnet and the ACFA in demonstrating why it was imperative for the proper legal and regulatory framework to be established in Alberta, to reflect both the spirit and the letter of s. 23 of the Charter. In his view, the January 1988 amendments to the Alberta School Act, effective one year later, did not provide the necessary framework. Section 5(1) of the Act merely affirmed, "If an individual has rights under section 23 of the Canadian Charter of Rights and Freedoms to have his children receive school instruction in French, his children are entitled to receive that instruction in accordance with those rights wherever in the Province those rights apply." Desjarlais also reminded his readers that the determination of "where numbers warranted" could not be made in the context of existing school board boundaries, nor could the question of potential costs be used to deny s. 23 rights once it was determined that a sufficient number of students existed to warrant French minority language education.[65]

Using two different methods of calculation, Desjarlais posited that there was a pool of over 13,000 potential francophone students spread throughout fifteen of the 1981 census divisions of Alberta. There were 13,820 Canadian citizens in the Calgary division and nearly 25,000 in the Edmonton division who registered French as their maternal language. Indeed, a confidential 1985 study for the Ministry of Education had stated that there were eight regions in Alberta where the numbers could justify the creation of school programs for Franco-Albertan children. Furthermore, a 1986 province-wide poll and a 1988 poll in the Smoky/Peace River region for the ministry confirmed that a significant percentage of Franco-Albertan parents would choose French schools for their children if they were available. "La conclusion est simple," declared Desjarlais; "les nombres sont là. C'est à chaque communauté francophone de les identifier et des les récupérer."[66] Finally,

Desjarlais laid out in eloquent fashion the numerous arguments against French immersion programs, together with those in favour of the "école franco-albertaine" constituted as "une communauté linguistiquement homogène où à travers le curriculum et les événements journaliers on approfondit le sens de son appartenance."[67]

On the crucial issue of school governance, Desjarlais reiterated that it was imperative for Franco-Albertan parents to protest loudly in order to gain full control over their educational system, if they wanted to stem the high rate of assimilation sweeping through their communities. He outlined four governance models in general terms: (a) the existing system of public and Catholic school boards in each school district; (b) the New Brunswick system of minority language school boards within the same jurisdiction as majority language school boards; (c) the creation of a provincial school board to serve the needs of francophone parents, as proposed in Saskatchewan and Manitoba; and (d) the Ontario system of guaranteed proportional representation of the francophone minority community within the existing public or Catholic boards. In Desjarlais' view, the most appropriate model for Franco-Albertans was based on the creation of several regional school boards covering the territory of several existing boards. For the cities of Edmonton and Calgary, he advocated the Ontario model of guaranteed proportional representation within an existing Catholic school board.[68]

The ACFA trumpeted the Desjarlais report in a press release, because it demonstrated, according to Georges Arès, that Franco-Albertans were second-class citizens when it came to educational rights for their children. However, in a private memorandum to Jean-Claude Giguère, the ACFA's education bureau director, Yvon Mahé was highly critical of it for not being audacious enough at a crucial period in the evolution of Franco-Albertan history. Desjarlais had failed to spell out in closer financial, administrative, pedagogical, and demographic detail the various school governance models proposed. Mahé was particularly incensed at the suggestion that Franco-Albertan parents in the Edmonton region should drop their demand for an autonomous French school board. He suggested that the report not be made public until another, more detailed, study on the implications of the governance models was well underway. The ACFA accepted Mahé's suggestions and delayed the formal publication of the report until October 1989, when it was ready to announce the striking of two more committees to build on the Desjarlais report in order to make sure Franco-Albertans obtained full school governance as soon as possible.[69]

Throughout the summer and fall of 1989 the ACFA, the FPFA, and the Francophonie Jeunesse de l'Alberta were embroiled in a dispute between the Société des parents pour l'éducation francophone (St-Paul et région) and the St Paul Public School District No. 2228 and the County of St Paul #19 Board of Education. Many Franco-Albertan parents throughout the St Paul region wanted both boards to cooperate in setting up a French minority elementary school as a replacement for the existing bilingual schools, which they argued contributed to their children's assimilation. Many others, however, were opposed, and lobbied the County of St Paul board not to go along with the proposal.[70] The ACFA and FPFA recognized that the problem had two dimensions. First, more time and effort had to be spent on educating Franco-Albertan parents about the benefits of homogeneous French language schools. Second, Minister of Education Jim Dinning had to be convinced that it was his responsibility to exercise leadership by putting pressure on school boards to cooperate in the implementation of s. 23 rights and the development of a clear language policy for education, as promised.

In September 1989, the ACFA decided to hire two consultants, Denis Tardif and Phillip Lamoureux, to undertake an extensive process of educating and debating with Franco-Albertans in several regions of the province before providing a comprehensive report to the ACFA and FPFA on the principles, management models, and plan of action for implementing school governance. The consultants were to outline several models of school governance, explain the workings of each model to the Franco-Albertan communities, and receive and evaluate the feedback from parents.[71] They were to be assisted and supervised by the Comité consultatif sur la gestion des écoles franco-albertaines, which was comprised of representatives from various associations appointed by the ACFA and FPFA. Yvon Mahé was named to the new committee, while Annette Labelle of Calgary and Jacques Moquin of Saint-Isidore were the co-presidents.

The committee's mandate was to educate Franco-Albertan parents and teachers about their education rights, consult with them about the best way to obtain and implement those rights in their respective communities, and establish principles that had to be incorporated into any school governance model. It was also to establish contact with the various associations of school trustees, school superintendents, and teachers throughout Alberta in order to inform them of its work and sound out their views on school governance by Franco-Albertans. The consultants and the committee were to report to the ACFA and FPFA before 30 April 1989 on the implementation of one or more models of governance.[72]

While these two organizations were preparing for school governance, the Association Bugnet was granted leave to appeal the decision of the Alberta Court of Appeal to the Supreme Court. The case was guaranteed to attract national attention because it came right in the middle of the heated political debate over the controversial and ill-fated Meech Lake Accord.

VICTORY IN THE SUPREME COURT:
MAHÉ V. *ALBERTA* [1990]

The return to mega-constitutional politics in 1986–87 represented both an opportunity and a challenge for the ACFA's leadership. At the Mont-Gabriel Conference on 9 May 1986, Quebec's Minister of Inter-governmental Affairs, Gil Rémillard, outlined his government's five conditions for reopening constitutional negotiations. In his conclud-ing remarks, Rémillard indicated his strong support for the franco-phone minorities and declared that "the rights of the non-Quebec francophones would be improved considerably if it were specified in Section 23 that the expression 'minority language educational facili-ties' signifies the right to administer these institutions."[73] In private discussions with the ACFA in August 1986, he revealed that improve-ments to s. 23 constituted Quebec's sixth condition in the upcoming constitutional negotiations.[74] The Fédération was prompted by these developments to set up a Comité des affaires juridiques/constitution-nelles in May 1986 in order to monitor both the micro- and mega-constitutional processes and be ready to intervene aggressively at the appropriate moment.[75]

When the Meech Lake Accord emerged from the marathon ses-sions at Meech Lake on 30 April 1987, Rémillard's sixth condition was not part of the deal. The ACFA's leaders met with Premier Robert Bourassa and Rémillard in mid-June at the "bunker" in Quebec City for an explanation, only to be told that nine premiers had rejected any strengthening of s. 23. Subsequent events would show that Quebec had never really intended to push for it.[76] Nonetheless, because of Rémillard's promise, the francophone organizations, espe-cially the ACFA, were incensed and demoralized. Both the ACFA and the Fédération undertook an intense lobbying campaign to convince the premiers to amend the Meech Lake Accord to allow the federal government to promote as well as preserve and defend the linguistic minority communities.[77]

It was in the midst of this campaign that the Association Bugnet, with the backing of the ACFA, proceeded with its appeal to the Supreme Court. Wanting to guarantee strong local input and avoid a fight with the constitutional committee of the Fédération, Georges Arès asked the national organization to support the ACFA's request to be named as an intervenor in the hearing. In return for a commitment from the Fédération not to request intervenor status, Arès promised that the ACFA would submit its factum to the national group for its comments so they could reach a consensus on approach and substance. Fédération Director General Aurèle Thériault agreed and indicated that his organization had no intention of requesting intervenor status in the Association Bugnet's challenge.[78]

While the various parties prepared their factums, the Fédération's constitutional committee monitored the proceedings. It was especially concerned about what Quebec would say in its submission to the Supreme Court. Fédération President Guy Matte wrote to Minister of Education Claude Ryan in early March 1989, requesting discussions with members of the Quebec government before its factum was submitted. Ryan replied that his government had given serious thought to the implications of its position for the francophone minorities but made it amply clear that Quebec's legitimate interests had to prevail. While it was too late to change Quebec's factum, Ryan agreed to instruct his deputy minister, Thomas Boudreau, to meet with representatives of the Fédération to see whether further discussions would be useful.[79] Guy Matte and Michel Bastarache, the ACFA's lawyer and a member of the constitutional committee, met with Ryan on 20 March 1989, then with Quebec government officials the following day. Aurèle Thériault assured Georges Arès that he was confident Quebec would support the ACFA's position before the Supreme Court.[80]

Meanwhile, Bastarache feared the worst. On the crucial issue of the right of the linguistic minorities to control and manage their own schools, it was clear to him that "Québec est d'accord pour dire qu'il y a un droit implicite de participation, mais a des réserves quant à la nature du contrôle que doit exercer la minorité sur ses établissements." In his view, Quebec was trying to justify its Bill 107, in which it proposed to create two language-based school systems wherein parental or school committees, not school boards, would guarantee the minimum degree of participation required by the Constitution. Bastarache advised the Fédération that, contrary to Quebec's proposed legislation, it was crucial for the linguistic minorities to obtain a ruling that management rights were established in constitutional law as well as in fact. Finally, he opined that the parental or school committees were not management instruments but merely consultative organizations.[81]

Following up on their March discussions, on 5 May Bastarache asked Jean-K. Samson, the associate deputy minister of justice, to send the Fédération a copy of Quebec's factum before it was submitted to the

Supreme Court. "La Fédération souhaite donc voir l'occasion de signaler les problèmes qu'elle pourrait déceler dans le mémoire du Québec et ainsi éviter, si possible, une confrontation publique."[82] When Bastarache received the document, he found it even more devastating than expected, since it revealed that the Quebec government categorically rejected the Ontario Court of Appeal's ruling in the reference case. Quebec was siding with Alberta, Manitoba, and Saskatchewan in opposing a liberal and remedial interpretation of s. 23, one that would convey the right to control and management. In a memorandum to Thériault, Bastarache characterized the Quebec position as very "political." He was confident that the factum would not be well received by the Supreme Court and that Samson would be called upon to provide "des explications beaucoup plus claires dans son exposé oral."[83]

Refusing to rely on the good sense of the Supreme Court justices and pushed by the ACFA, the Fédération launched a letter-writing campaign and invited all its affiliates to do likewise. Its correspondence of 11 May 1989 to Premier Robert Bourassa, Gil Rémillard, and Claude Ryan expressed deep dismay with the position adopted by the Quebec government. It implored Quebec to revise its approach in its final submission to the court, to state clearly a commitment to the principle "selon lequel toute minorité a droit à un traitement généreux au niveau de ses droits scolaires." The Fédération warned that it reserved the right to publicly denounce, at the appropriate moment, the Quebec government's position on the matter.[84]

Taking its lobbying to a new level, in a press release on 1 June 1989 the group expressed its strong opposition to Quebec's position. In the belief that it was still not too late, Guy Matte invited Bourassa to open a dialogue with the francophone minorities as soon as possible. If he failed to do so, Quebec would remain allied with provinces whose governments were trying to restrict the constitutional rights of their minorities.[85] Working behind the scenes, Bastarache, Matte, and Marie-Hélène Bergeron, the Fédération's representative in Quebec City, met on 2 June 1989 with four government officials to see whether they could alter the province's position in any meaningful way. The meeting was not very productive; Samson stated that Quebec would not alter its factum in form or substance. However, during its oral presentation before the Supreme Court, it would give clarification on three of the four points raised by the Fédération and ACFA. The province agreed on the importance of the cultural as well as linguistic homogeneity of the schools under s. 23, and also "ajouter au droit d'accessibilité à un système d'éducation de 'qualité égale' pour la minorité." Further, it would raise the matter of the responsibility of the provinces to introduce legislation on education rights for their linguistic minorities. But it would not agree to rescind its request for the Supreme Court to overturn the Ontario reference case decision.[86]

Far from pleased, the Fédération once again urged its affiliates to write to Bourassa, Rémillard, and Ryan.[87] Still, it should not have been surprised, having been warned a few months earlier by the ACFA that the Quebec government would not be supportive. Prepared to step into the breach, Georges Arès and several ACFA representatives flew to Quebec City to meet with Claude Ryan and his legal advisors at the National Assembly on 7 June. Ryan agreed to make some changes to the government's oral presentation and to try to do the same in its written submission.[88] Arès was not convinced, however, that Ryan could sway Rémillard.

Given that the ACFA's constituents had the most to lose from Quebec's refusal to alter its position, Arès launched a dramatic media campaign in early June 1989 – just before the Supreme Court hearings were to begin. One element of it was a press release denouncing Bourassa and his two ministers, Rémillard and Ryan, for their lack of understanding, compassion, and justice in siding with the Alberta government against the Charter rights of the Franco-Albertan community. The ACFA asked rhetorically whether Premier Bourassa wanted the disappearance of the Franco-Albertans.[89] Arès also led an ACFA delegation into Quebec to meet with representatives of the print and electronic media, government officials, and Cabinet ministers, in an effort to make Franco-Albertans' case directly to the Quebec people.[90] Hoping to broaden the discussion and raise a few eyebrows, he charged Bourassa with having sold out Franco-Albertans in return for Alberta's support for the Meech Lake Accord.[91] The response of the Quebec media, English and French, was quite positive. It was not the time to create a new cleavage between Quebec and the franco-phone minorities, warned Le Devoir. Both Lise Bissonnette and Marcel Adam pointed out the absurdities and contradictions in the province's rigid position and opined that the least the government could do to limit the damage was to withdraw from the case. Adam reminded the Quebec government that the Conseil de la vie française en Amérique had denounced its actions in this crucial but sensitive matter.[92]

The provincial government found some solace in the fact that the media blitz was denounced by one of the appellants in the case. Paul Dubé, president of the Association Bugnet, chastised Arès and the ACFA for being latecomers in the controversial and difficult battle for Franco-Albertan school governance. His letter to Arès was leaked to

Le Devoir in an attempt to take some wind out of the ACFA's sails, but the revelation only managed to reveal the deep cleavages among Franco-Albertans. While Dubé's critique was an accurate assessment of the initial stage of the struggle, it could not fairly be applied to the subsequent stages. Arès had been a witness for the Association Bugnet before Judge Purvis; the ACFA was present at that trial in the capacity of *amicus curiae*, and later was an intervenor before the Alberta Court of Appeal. What really irked Dubé and the Association Bugnet was the ACFA's denunciation of Bourassa and his government for siding with Alberta. In Dubé's view, Franco-Albertans and the ACFA had only one real opponent: their provincial government. But his perspective was only partially accurate. The ACFA was an outspoken critic of the Alberta government but also understood the grave political and constitutional implications of the Alberta/Quebec axis.[93] Underlying the ongoing tension between the two organizations was a fundamental disagreement about competing constitutional conceptions of duality: the pan-Canadian cultural and linguistic approach promoted by the ACFA versus the Canada/Quebec territorial duality promoted by the Bourassa government and its supporters inside and outside Quebec. The imbroglio between the Quebec government – intent on defending what it considered to be its constitutional interests – and the ACFA – struggling to advance the interests of Franco-Albertans at the Supreme Court – revealed that the process of judicial interpretation of s. 23 had become unduly politicized by its association with the mega-constitutional politics of the Meech Lake Accord. This politically charged context would characterize the court's deliberations as well as the responses to its decision.

Starting with the Ontario reference case, the duration of the battle over the educational rights of Franco-Albertans was an indication of the fundamental nature of the issues at stake. On the one hand, Franco-Albertan leaders and parents were determined to infuse s. 23 with real power. On the other hand, the Alberta government – with the support of other provinces, including Quebec – was just as determined to prevent all attempts by Franco-Albertans to use s. 23 to diminish its exclusive jurisdiction over education. The Supreme Court justices, in their decision in *Mahé*, went a great distance towards resolving the historical conflict between minority rights and provincial rights. Their astute and learned ruling provided an equitable and pragmatic compromise between the new Charter-based federalism of individual and group rights and the long-established federalism of provincial and national government powers and prerogatives.

The appellants, Jean-Claude Mahé, Angéline Martel, Paul Dubé, and the Association Bugnet, were supported by several intervenors.[94] One was the ACFA, which was mandated by the Fédération to represent the interests of all francophone minority communities.[95] The appellants put four questions to the Supreme Court. The first and third focused on the specific situations pertaining to metropolitan Edmonton schools and the Alberta School Act and asked whether or not an infringement or contravention of s. 23 rights existed. The second asked whether s. 23(3)(a) and (b) included management and control by the minority of instruction and educational facilities; if so, what was the nature and extent of such management and control? The final question asked how the rights guaranteed under s. 23 were affected by s. 93 of the Constitution Act, 1867, s. 29 of the Charter, and s. 17 of the Alberta Act.

The appellants placed a great deal of emphasis on the historical background of Franco-Albertans' struggle for cultural survival. They outlined the longstanding restrictive regulations against French language instruction in Alberta, which, they maintained, had contributed immensely to the high assimilation rates prevalent by the 1980s. Furthermore, the enrolment of Franco-Albertan children in French bilingual and immersion classes and schools in the 1970s had not stemmed the rates of assimilation; these educational models were being abandoned by Franco-Albertan parents.[96] The appellants and the ACFA stressed repeatedly that the intent of s. 23 was remedial. According to the ACFA, "L'article 23 est nouveau. Il doit s'interpréter dans le contexte des années 1980, comme créant une norme nationale qui n'est pas sujette à dérogation et qui vise à créer un équilibre entre les droits de la minorité au Québec et ceux des autres minorités provinciales."[97] Most importantly, the remedial intent of the section created a duty for the provinces to legislate in order to guarantee the linguistic minorities equality before the law. Since language and culture were intimately related, it was not only desirable but essential that any effective educational legislation grant them – "where numbers warranted" – access first to homogeneous classes, then to homogeneous schools wherein reigned an ambiance reflecting the cultural values of the minority. Mixed or bilingual schools were therefore unacceptable under s. 23.[98]

Given the principles enshrined in the section, the appellants and the ACFA had little difficulty demonstrating that the Alberta Court of Appeal had erred in concluding that there were insufficient numbers of students in metropolitan Edmonton to warrant the establishment of minority language educational facilities as well as a school jurisdiction pursuant to s. 23(3)(b). The Minister of Education had refused to create a French language education program and minority language facilities, despite the fact that there were 3750 children between the ages of five and nineteen whose parents qualified under the maternal language provision of s. 23. By using the actual rather than the eligible numbers of students and by referring to the prospect of higher costs for minority language schools, the Alberta Court of Appeal was resorting to a very restrictive and constructionist interpretation of s. 23, which violated the liberal and remedial intent of the section's framers. In fact, Alberta's Minister of Education had accepted the existence of many low-enrolment majority language school boards throughout Alberta yet was unwilling to treat the minority language community in Edmonton in the same equitable manner.[99]

The Alberta government challenged the appellants' statement of facts by putting forth evidence that it claimed demonstrated it had complied fully with s. 23 rights. The Edmonton Catholic Separate School District No. 7 operated a homogeneous francophone school in Edmonton, École Maurice Lavallée, with a duly constituted Parents' Advisory Committee. Despite extensive advertisement of the school facility – capable of accommodating 720 students – only 242 students were enrolled in kindergarten to grade 6. Furthermore, two of the seven members of the Edmonton Catholic school board were francophones and the Ministry of Education had created a Language Services Branch staffed by francophones to plan and implement French language programs throughout the province. The government did not dispute that there were 2,948 parents with 3,750 children in the metropolitan Edmonton region who qualified under s. 23, but pointed out that the vast majority of them were separate school supporters.[100] In fact, according to the province, the Edmonton Catholic school board had gone beyond the legal requirement of s. 23 by providing a minority language educational facility – i.e., a school building – when in the estimation of the trial judge and the Court of Appeal the actual enrolment numbers did not warrant it under s. 23(3)(b).[101]

The second question concerned the minority's governance of its own instruction and educational facilities. On this crucial matter the appellants drew sustenance from the Ontario reference case, which had linked the achievement of the remedial objective of s. 23 with a variety of forms and degrees of management and control. They argued persuasively that "the words 'minority language facilities/ établissements d'enseignement de la minorité linguistique' confer upon the linguistic minority the right to exclusive management and control of its educational programs within homogeneous institutional settings established under the central authority of the province." To further buttress their case on this issue, both the appellants and the ACFA adduced s. 15 of the Charter (equality under the law and equal benefit of the law) in arguing that the province had the duty to legislate an educational regime pursuant to s. 23 that was "equal in quality to that offered to the majority linguistic group." If systemic discrimination was to be overcome, it was necessary to grant Franco-Albertans the right to manage French language education via their own school boards, as the majority language community did.[102]

The Alberta government categorically rejected all these arguments, maintaining that "such an interpretation is contrary to the wording of s. 23 and contrary to the intention of the framers of the section, and encroaches upon provincial jurisdiction over education." Describing s. 23 language rights as based on a political compromise, the province contended that they were "not to be interpreted with the same liberal construction as fundamental rights." Consequently, the terms "minority language educational facilities/établissements d'enseignment de la minorité linguistique," could reasonably bear no other meaning than "school buildings" – not autonomous school systems as alleged in error by the appellants and the Ontario Court of Appeal. Referring to the statements of Minister of Justice Jean Chrétien before the Special Joint Committee in January 1981, the respondent attempted to demonstrate that the "framers of the Charter never intended to include in s. 23 a right of the minority to manage and control educational facilities." Indeed, Alberta argued, Chrétien's various statements made it very clear that Ottawa did not intend s. 23 to allow – in the minister's own words – "'meddling in the administration of education which is and which should remain the responsibility of the provincial government'." Any attempt to read into s. 23 a right of the minority to manage and control educational facilities would be, in Alberta's view, an encroachment upon provincial jurisdiction over education under s. 93 of the Constitution Act, 1867.[103]

The third question asked, first, whether Alberta's School Act and its regulations were incompatible with or contrary to s. 23 and second, if so, could that situation be justified under s. 1 of the Charter? S.13 of the School Act was deemed unconstitutional by the appellants because it empowered, but did not require, the Minister of Education to create new school jurisdictions in compliance with s. 23 even when there were sufficient numbers to warrant minority language instruction and facilities. Ss. 158 and 159 of the School Act were also regarded as unconstitutional because they granted school boards absolute discretion over the use of languages of instruction other than English. This discretionary power was reflected in Regulation 490/82, which required a minimum of 15 to 20 per cent of English language instruction in all schools, including minority language schools. The appellants considered the requirement "entirely arbitrary" and unjustified by any outstanding evidence. Finally, the Alberta government could not justify with the appropriate evidentiary foundation any of these contraventions of s. 23 under s. 1 of the Charter; in any event, s. 1 applied only to statutes, not regulations.[104]

The province, for its part, argued that its revised School Act, 1988 rendered moot the consideration of the question on the unconstitutionality of ss. 158 and 159 of the old Act and requested the Supreme Court not undertake any related review. It also maintained that Regulation 490/82 complied with s. 23; if the court found it did not, Alberta argued that it could be maintained under s. 1 of the Charter as a reasonable limit demonstrably justifiable in a free and democratic society, since "all Albertans require a knowledge of English."[105]

The appellants argued, with respect to the fourth question, that there were no limitations placed on minority educational rights under s. 23 by the right to religious instruction guaranteed under s. 93 of the Constitution Act, 1867 or, as amended, under s. 17 of the Alberta Act. In fact, they maintained – contrary to the ruling of the Alberta Court of Appeal – that s. 23 added a third category, "the minority linguistic system," which "impacts upon *both* the public and separate school systems equally, and therefore discriminates against neither." [106] In short, the Alberta government had to create a harmonious educational regime that met the s. 23 rights of the minority linguistic group while respecting those of the denominational group.

Frustrated at Alberta's persistent refusal to implement s. 23, the appellants called on the Supreme Court to use its authority under s. 24 of the Charter to grant such remedies as may be appropriate when s. 23 rights were infringed on or denied. They requested not only relief in the form of declarations stating that their positions on the four questions were valid but also two orders. The first of these would confirm that there were sufficient numbers of persons qualified under s. 23 in the metropolitan Edmonton area to warrant minority language instruction and facilities out of public funds. The second order would direct Alberta's Minister of Education to create a minority language school board to manage and control said instruction and facilities, pending the amendment of the School Act.[107]

The province's rejoinder was that Franco-Albertans were not entitled to the extensive management and control rights over education they were claiming. Such matters were exclusively within provincial jurisdiction over education, while some of the rights sought encroached upon "the rights of separate schools as set out in s. 93 of the Constitution Act, 1867, s. 17 of the Alberta Act, and s. 29 of the Charter." Claiming that it had satisfactorily refuted the appellants' arguments on all four questions, the Alberta government submitted "that this appeal be dismissed with costs."[108]

The Supreme Court handed down its unanimous decision on 15 March 1990. Cutting through all the confusion and verbiage, Chief Justice C.J. Dickson indicated that there were two basic questions at stake in the appeal: "(1) Do the rights which s. 23 mandates, depending upon the numbers of students, include a right to management and control; and (2) if so, is the number of students in Edmonton sufficient to invoke this right?"[109] In short, the court had to determine the principles underlying s. 23, then apply them to the specifics of the Edmonton situation with respect to Franco-Albertans. Rejecting the narrow constructionist approach advanced by the Alberta government and its supporters in favour of the liberal, remedial, and equitable interpretation advocated by the Association Bugnet, the ACFA, and the Fédération, Chief Justice Dickson argued that it was crucial to consider the underlying purpose of s. 23. Linking language and culture, as per the *Report of the Royal Commission on Bilingualism and Biculturalism*, he declared that the general purpose of the section was "to preserve and promote the two official languages of Canada, and their respective cultures ... by granting minority language educational rights to minority language parents throughout Canada." While s. 23 was the product of a political compromise, the specific purpose of that compromise was clearly to remedy the defects of Canada's educational regimes vis-à-vis the linguistic minorities. No doubt, the courts had to be cautious since s. 23 "confers upon a group a right which places positive obligations on government to alter or develop major institutional structures." Nevertheless, caution must not impede the courts from breathing life into the expressed purpose of s. 23 by having an open mind to innovative solutions.[110]

The second principle invoked by Chief Justice Dickson was a sliding scale of rights under s. 23, ranging from a minimum applicable under the term "instruction" in s. 23(3)(a) to an upper level under "minority language educational facilities" in s. 23(3)(b). This approach was preferable to the "separate rights" approach advocated by the respondents, he contended, because it was in line with both the text and the purpose of s. 23 and guaranteed the minority group the full protection its numbers warranted by avoiding categorical "either/or" solutions that could well be harmful in some specific cases.[111]

The Chief Justice's analysis of the issue of management and control under s. 23(3)(b) was succinct and masterful. He quickly disposed of the appellants' argument that ss. 15 and 27 of the Charter could be useful in interpreting s. 23, while reminding the Alberta government that the Supreme Court had consistently taken the view that evidence from the legislative debates "contributes little to the task of interpreting s. 23, and, accordingly, I place no weight upon it." Concurring with the reasoning of the Ontario Court of Appeal in the reference case, Chief Justice Dickson concluded that "s. 23 mandates, where the numbers warrant, a measure of management and control." It was self-evident that the right to instruction under s. 23(3)(a) implied the right to school facilities. Consequently, the term "minority language educational facilities" in s. 23(3)(b), if it was to be meaningful in helping to achieve the general and specific remedial intentions of s. 23, must of necessity refer to something more than just school facilities. Indeed, keeping in mind the concept of a sliding scale of rights, s. 23(3)(b) must be viewed "as setting out an upper level of management and control."[112]

At the heart of the Supreme Court's ruling was Chief Justice Dickson's careful delineation of the meaning of "management and control." It was crucial to find the delicate balance between s. 23 rights mandated by the Charter and the provincial prerogative to education under s. 93 of the Constitution Act, 1867. The court's role was to outline the general requirements mandated by s. 23 while leaving it up to the provinces to develop and implement the "specific modalities" best suited to their individual circumstances. Contrary to the claim made by the appellants and their supporters, the right to management and control did not automatically entail the right to autonomous francophone school boards having the right to tax in all circumstances. Indeed, in cases where the numbers of students were not sufficiently large to meet the test of s. 23, the creation of small independent school boards with limited resources could work to the educational disadvantage of the minority language group. In such cases, it was both necessary and sufficient for the minority to achieve control over the linguistic and cultural aspects of education by being guaranteed proportional representation on existing majority language separate and public school boards. The minority language representatives, Chief Justice Dickson maintained, should have exclusive authority over all matters relating to minority language instruction and facilities. Under this demarcated degree of management and control, it was imperative for the quality of education available to the minority to be, in principle, on a basis of equality with that afforded the majority – but this did not imply identical treatment in terms of facilities, institutional structures, or funding. Finally, the Chief Justice

tried to allay the fears of provincial ministers of education by stipu-
lating that "the management and control accorded to s. 23 parents
does not preclude provincial regulation" in determining "the contents and qualitative standards of educational programmes" if such
did "not interfere with the linguistic and cultural concerns of the
minority."[113]

Before addressing the specific situation in Edmonton, the Chief
Justice had to resolve two theoretical issues. He quickly disposed of the
Alberta government's argument that conferring powers of management and control under s. 23 on minority language parents constituted an infringement of the powers granted to separate schools
under s. 17 of the Alberta Act. He ruled that "the transfer of the
powers in respect of management and control thus amounts to the *regulation* of a non-denominational aspect of education, namely, the language of instruction, a form of regulation which the courts have long
held to be valid."[114] In short, linguistic rights did not interfere with
denominational rights but complemented them; both kinds of rights
could be administered concurrently by boards of education comprising representatives from both communities.

Second, in interpreting the "where numbers warrant" provision, the
Chief Justice reminded everyone that s. 23 did not create an absolute
right; the determination should be made neither on the actual
demand nor on an estimated potential demand but rather on a
number somewhere in between, to be established in practice once the
right had been in effect for some period. Two factors – one based on
the appropriate level of services required for a given number of students, the second based on the cost of those services – had to be considered in determining requirements under s. 23. Nevertheless, the
remedial nature of the section made the maintenance of the status
quo unacceptable. Therefore, in Chief Justice Dickson's view, "pedagogical considerations will have more weight than financial requirements in determining whether numbers warrant." A flexible approach
differentiating between urban and rural areas and making calculations
of the relevant numbers on a basis other than existing school boundaries was essential to achieving the remedial objective of s. 23.[115]

Having laid out the general interpretative principles of the section,
the Chief Justice then turned his mind to the situation in Edmonton.
He needed to evaluate whether francophone parents had a right to a
degree of management and control over the existing École Maurice
Lavallée, with its 242 students in kindergarten to grade 6.[116] Referring
to the overall structure of some 147 educational jurisdictions in
Alberta wherein larger boards were the norm, he concluded: "I am
not satisfied on the basis of the present evidence that it has been

established that the number of students likely to attend francophone schools in Edmonton is sufficient to mandate under s. 23 the establishment of an independent francophone school board." On the other hand, what s. 23 did require, given the then-current numbers of francophones in Edmonton, was a guarantee "of minority language representation on school boards administering minority language schools in the manner and with the authority above described. The province must enact legislation (and regulations, if necessary) that are in all respects consistent with the provisions of s. 23 of the Charter."[117]

Chief Justice Dickson did not find that ss. 13, 158, and 159 of the Alberta School Act contravened s. 23 rights or were a positive barrier to their implementation, as the appellants argued. Rather, they were permissive measures well within the prerogatives of the provincial government. The real problem resided in the continued failure of the Alberta legislature to discharge its clearly mandated obligation under the Charter to enact a precise legislative scheme "providing for minority language education instruction and educational facilities where numbers warrant."

Finally, the Chief Justice ruled that Regulation 490/82 – which required a full 300 minutes of English instruction per week in all of Alberta's schools – be struck down as an impediment to attaining the purpose of s. 23. Furthermore, while agreeing with the Alberta courts that it was important for francophones to receive a certain amount of instruction in English, the Chief Justice maintained that the province had not adequately proven the necessity for the full extent of this infringement. Consequently, the existing regulation could not be saved under s. 1 of the Charter. Given that the appellants had succeeded on most points in their appeal, the Chief Justice granted them costs for all three court cases since 1985.[118]

IMPLEMENTING SCHOOL GOVERNANCE
IN ALBERTA

Considering the distance travelled by the Supreme Court, it was surprising to many observers that the ACFA, the Fédération, and the Commission nationale des parents francophones were quick to declare their disappointment with its decision. The ACFA considered the ruling a step in the right direction but was upset that the justices had not ordered Alberta to enact legislation within a specified time frame. The group also viewed it as passive, allowing the province to stonewall indefinitely and force further expensive court action. It left too many questions unanswered and placed far too much discretionary power in the hands of the government with regard to designing and implementing the institutional structures required to make school governance a reality.[119] For his part, Fédération President Guy Matte declared that the decision constituted only a partial gain for the francophone minority communities. The Supreme Court had recognized the principle of management and control; unfortunately, however, the gain was not complete since the right was made subject to "where numbers warrant." The problem resided not with the Supreme Court but with the constraints imposed by s. 23. It was urgent, Matte argued, for the Fédération to campaign for amendments to the section to remove all impediments to full management and control.[120] The president of the CNPF, Raymond Poirier, expressed concern that the Supreme Court's notion of a sliding scale of rights would open the door to a more restrictive interpretation by politicians and other courts called upon to render decisions based on "where numbers warrant." He wondered whether the first ministers should not explore the possibility of amending s. 23 to prevent the need for francophones to undertake expensive and time-consuming court challenges.[121]

The decision in *Mahé* prompted two conferences, one sponsored by the CNPF in Montreal on 29 April 1990 and another organized by the Faculty of Law at the University of Ottawa on 11–12 May 1990. The lawyer for the Fédération, François Dumaine, in his preliminary assessment for delegates attending one or both of the conferences, carefully outlined the strengths and shortcomings of the ruling. He was pleased with the Supreme Court's broad and liberal approach to and confirmation of the remedial purpose of s. 23. He believed that its adoption of a sliding scale would lay to rest the protracted debate over management and control. While the Fédération was not pleased that the court had ruled against the right to a francophone school board in Edmonton, the directive to the province to implement a legislative scheme for minority language instruction and educational facilities "without delay" was most encouraging. The overall concern was that the Supreme Court's systematic reliance on "where numbers warrant" favoured the larger, more established francophone communities and would necessitate further expensive court actions on behalf of the smaller, more fragile communities.[122] Guy Matte reiterated all these points to the delegates attending the University of Ottawa conference. He reminded them that the Fédération had always maintained that "la condition du nombre portait gravement atteinte au caractère 'réparateur' de l'article 23," and he concluded that the ruling was perhaps "un bon jugement pour un article manifestement incomplet." S.23 as written and interpreted by the Supreme Court left the smallest, assimilation-ravaged communities with fewer rights than the larger, more self-supporting communities. Without saying so directly, Matte left the unmistakable message that it was time to rethink s. 23.[123]

The Association Bugnet, by contrast, put a very positive spin on *Mahé*, declaring in a press release that the Supreme Court had largely confirmed its own expansive and liberal interpretation of s. 23 rights. The justices had affirmed that the section had three main objectives: the maintenance and expansion of the language and culture of the official language minorities; the treatment of Canada's two major linguistic groups as "equal partners"; and the requirement imposed by its remedial nature that governments put measures in place to stem assimilation. Underlying them were the propositions that culture and language were inseparable and that education in one's maternal language played a crucial role in the maintenance and expansion of the official language minorities. The judgment gave the Franco-Albertan community and the Alberta government four important guiding principles with which to construct an education system that complied with s. 23 rights. First, the quality of education given to the minority should be equal but not necessarily identical to that provided for the majority. Second, public funding should be adequate; if necessary, supplemental funds could be justified. Third, the calculation of numbers was not to be limited to the existing school districts, and numbers could be estimated on the basis of two criteria: the demand relative to service and the total of holders of s. 23 rights. Finally, it was justifiable to consider that the expression "établissements d'enseignement de la minorité linguistique" set a higher level of management and control, the ideal being an independent school board.[124]

Paul Dubé criticized the ruling's detractors, especially those who argued that the "where numbers warrant" provision made the implementation of s. 23 rights almost impossible in certain cases and that it was therefore imperative to have it rescinded. According to Dubé, this point of view was based on the notion – contrary to the relativism of "where numbers warrant" – that s. 23 should confer absolute rights free of all restrictions, including those under s. 1 of the Charter. Such an approach was utopian and impractical. Moreover, it failed to recognize the full significance of the Supreme Court ruling, which clearly stated that the global objective of s. 23 was to "preserve and promote" the language and culture of the linguistic minorities everywhere in Canada.[125] The problem, Dubé correctly concluded, did not reside with the decision in *Mahé* but rather with the provincial government, which would continue to stonewall the Franco-Albertan community. Why? … Because a majority of Franco-Albertans and leaders remained unconvinced of the urgent need for a francophone system of school governance. It was the lack of community consensus and unimaginative leadership that allowed the government to impose its agenda. It was up to Franco-Albertan parents to unite and insist that their leaders take advantage of the powerful bargaining tools handed to them by Canada's Supreme Court.[126]

The ACFA's leadership, which had the responsibility for negotiating with the province, was neither sanguine nor optimistic. Its president believed – quite correctly, as events would prove – that Alberta would do the very minimum under the Supreme Court's broad interpretation. Yet when representatives of the ACFA and FPFA met with Minister of Education Jim Dinning and Deputy Minister Reno Bossetti on 27 March 1990 to discuss the decision that had just been handed down, they left feeling reasonably assured that a political deal was close at hand. The minister indicated that the ruling had clarified many outstanding questions about the School Act and Regulation 490/82. It was incumbent upon the government to find a way to legislate a French language education system, and he personally wanted "to do it quickly and do it right," during the current session of the legislature if at all possible. When asked to be more specific, Dinning would say only that the province would evaluate all the existing models of school governance and come up with a solution that was right for Alberta. He mentioned that the caucus had welcomed the Supreme Court decision and that he believed the political climate was ripe in Alberta for the government to resolve the education question.[127]

Denis Tardif and Phillip Lamoureux, the consultants hired by the ACFA in September 1989, had completed their meetings in a dozen locations across Alberta by February 1990 and submitted a preliminary report to the Comité consultatif at the end of March for evaluation and comment.[128] Bearing in mind the *Mahé* decision, the committee discussed and revised the sixteen principles on which a French language minority education program and school governance should be established in Alberta.[129] By mid-April, the consultants prepared a second report; they then proceeded to hold a second round of discussions on these principles with francophone representatives in a dozen communities. Tardif and Lamoureux confirmed that Franco-Albertans were divided over the need to create homogeneous French minority schools and school boards. The majority were Catholics, and they feared that non-denominational French language education would further fragment their communities and create unnecessary tensions with their English-speaking neighbours. The consultants' goal was to demonstrate to the divided Franco-Albertan community that the sixteen principles were in conformity with the judgment in *Mahé.* They tried to reassure Franco-Albertans that what their leaders were doing was simply asking the Alberta government for a French minority educational system, which was the constitutional right of all Franco-Albertans – that it was their intention to strengthen, not weaken, the beleaguered francophone communities by stemming the tide of assimilation through new and creative educational and cultural institutions under the control of Franco-Albertans.[130]

In June 1990 the consultants produced a comprehensive final report entitled *An Educational System for Franco-Albertans.*[131] It outlined and evaluated the principles bearing on the management of French language instruction, discussed the existing delivery of education in the province, and defined the nature and components of an educational system for Franco-Albertans, from classes to school boards. It concluded with an analysis of a system of regional francophone school boards – the model preferred by Franco-Albertan parents – and a plan of action for their implementation. The sixteen principles flowed from three tenets: the equality of Canada's official language groups, as set out in the Charter; the democratic right of parents to make decisions respecting the education of their children; and the right of parents under s. 23 to "a certain type of educational system which provides the appropriate services to their children and the necessary powers of management and control over programs and facilities."[132]

All these principles, the final report maintained, could be incorporated into a flexible system of regional French school boards capable of encompassing the sufficient numbers of francophone students presently served by existing boards throughout the major urban centres and many rural counties of the province. These regional boards would have the same powers as the majority boards – excepting those related to taxation – with trustees elected at large from all eligible and interested Franco-Albertan voters. They would be supported by a francophone division in the Ministry of Education under an assistant deputy minister; a consortium of professional and remedial services would implement cultural animation strategies reaching beyond the schools to the communities to effect linguistic recovery and halt assimilation. In time, provincial associations of francophone teachers, administrators, and trustees would emerge to buttress and influence the development of French language education in the province.[133] The report warned, however, that while consensus was readily achieved on the matter of principles, much more work had to be done within the francophone communities on the best methods for achieving their application, in order to alleviate the widespread fears about change. Since it was "at the local level that the francophone community will be most successful in advancing the educational opportunities for their children," it was imperative that the ACFA and FPFA provide the encouragement, information, and concrete assistance required by Franco-Albertans to exercise their rights under s. 23 in a meaningful fashion.[134]

With the consultants' preliminary report and the Supreme Court decision in hand, the newly-elected ACFA president, France Levasseur-Ouimet, wrote to Premier Don Getty in late March 1990 requesting a meeting to discuss the government's plans for implementing s. 23 rights. The premier assured Levasseur-Ouimet that his government would "respect and abide by the Court decision" and advised the ACFA to continue to work with the Minister of Education and his officials on this important matter.[135] Yet it was clear by early June that Jim Dinning was not ready – as he had hoped to be – to introduce legislation amending the School Act during the current session of the Legislative Assembly. As a compromise, he instructed the St Paul School District #2228 and the County of St Paul #19 School Board to cooperate fully in establishing a French minority language school for francophone children.[136]

Determined to spur the Minister of Education into quicker action, the ACFA's president sent him an advance copy of *An Educational System for Franco-Albertans*. The minister thanked Levasseur-Ouimet for the report, which, he remarked, reflected the efforts and vision of the ACFA. He assured her that its recommendations would be taken into consideration in his ministry's discussion paper on "alternatives to meet the requirements of Section 23 of the Charter and the Supreme Court decision in the Mahé case."[137] The government was not about to formally endorse the consultants' report by being associated with its release to the public. When the FPFA and ACFA managed to get hold of a copy of the discussion paper, they were none too pleased – though not surprised – at its ungenerous, minimalist approach to the ruling. They asked University of Moncton constitutional expert Pierre Foucher to evaluate it. Foucher's scathing critique, confirming the government's minimalist solution, concluded that "malgré les déclarations de principe du début, on sent l'extrême réticence des auteurs du document à se conformer à l'esprit du jugement." The working paper lacked a plan of action for the establishment of classes, schools, and transportation, the purchase of services, and the reorganization of francophone children into distinct school districts or regions. Given the positive nature of the Supreme Court decision, he strongly recommended that Franco-Albertan parents and their organizations abandon their defensive posture. Instead, they should prepare – in much greater detail than what was outlined in the Lamoureux-Tardif report – for intensive negotiations to achieve a comprehensive agreement for the creation of regional school boards. Foucher also advised all Franco-Albertan associations, including parent groups, to coordinate their efforts in order to prevent the government from practising the time-honoured strategy of "divide and rule."[138]

Forewarned, the ACFA and FPFA lobbied Jim Dinning to open up the policy- and decision-making process. Having won the unconditional support of the Alberta Teachers' Association and the Alberta School Trustees Association for the concept of autonomous francophone regional school boards, they formally launched the Lamoureux-Tardif report in early September.[139] Both groups stated that they fully supported its recommendations, while deploring the procrastination of the Minister of Education. They demanded that he establish "a special task force to study the situation and make recommendations that will guide the Government as it prepares its forthcoming legislation in compliance with the Supreme Court decision in the Mahé case."[140] When no answer was forthcoming, ACFA President France Levasseur-Ouimet wrote to Dinning in mid-October asking when the government's discussion paper would be publicly released. She also urged him to consider seriously the ACFA's request for a special task force, to make sure that acceptable amendments to the School Act could be passed into law no later than the spring 1991 session of the legislature. Dinning replied somewhat curtly that he would consult with the ACFA before tabling legislative amendments to the Act.[141]

Throughout the summer and fall of 1990, work continued on the discussion paper. Finally, in November, Alberta Education released its final version, *Management and Control of French Education in Alberta*. Michel Bastarache, asked to evaluate the document for the Commission nationale des parents francophones and the FPFA, indicated that the Minister of Education's approach was based on many highly questionable premises and some blatant errors of fact. In contravention of the *Mahé* decision, the document argued that existing school boards had the authority to apply s. 23 within their boundaries; that only one francophone school trustee was required in Edmonton to satisfy the court's concept of a sliding scale of management and control rights; that no region in Alberta had sufficient numbers to warrant a francophone school board; and that, if a regional board was ever created, it could manage both Catholic and public schools. Bastarache advised the CNPF and FPFA to see the publication as the Alberta government's opening bid in the bargaining process and to push for a forum in which meaningful negotiations could take place.[142] Similarly critical opinions were provided to the ACFA by Edgar Gallant, a consultant overseeing French language working groups in Manitoba and British Columbia, and François Dumaine, legal counsel for the Fédération in Ottawa.[143]

Pressured by the ACFA and FPFA with support from the Alberta School Trustees Association and the Alberta Teachers' Association, the Minister of Education finally decided on 11 January 1991 to open up the consultative process. He established the French Language Working Group, whose ten members represented the government, the public, school boards, superintendents, teachers, the ACFA, and the FPFA. Its mandate was to review *Management and Control of French Education in Alberta*, consult with appropriate individuals in communities where significant numbers of francophones resided, and make recommendations to the minister on options for the management and control of francophone programs and schools, all by the end of March.[144] At long last, the ACFA and FPFA had obtained the government sanctioned forum in which they could advance their case for school governance by Franco-Albertans.

To guarantee that concerned parents presented a common front to the French Language Working Group, the ACFA reminded its regional offices that they should support the recommendations laid out in the Lamoureux-Tardif report: the creation of francophone regional school boards, a provincial consortium of professional services, and a francophone section within the Ministry of Education. All the offices received the assessments of *Management and Control ...* prepared by Bastarache, Gallant, and the Fédération.[145] In fact, when appearing before the Working Group, regional presidents did inform the chair that their organizations fully endorsed the consultants' proposals.[146] The ACFA's president also wrote to Secretary of State Gerry Weiner to encourage him not to sign an agreement with the government of Alberta for a transfer of funds until it had promulgated a revised School Act acceptable to the Franco-Albertan community.[147]

Of the Working Group's ten members, four were Franco-Albertans: France Levasseur-Ouimet, president of the ACFA; Claudette Roy, president of the FPFA; Louis Desrochers, lawyer and past president of the ACFA; and Gérard Bissonnette, from the Ministry of Education. John Brosseau of the Edmonton Catholic school board was not part of the francophone community. The four Franco-Albertans were assured of the support of Charles Hyman, representing the Alberta Teachers' Association. They felt they could convince the chair of the Working Group, Walter Paszkowski, MLA for Smoky River, to support their approach to implementing s. 23 rights. They hoped to develop a consensus by having the Working Group devise an acceptable model for a francophone regional school board comprising Smoky River, Spirit

River, and Peace River, where the Minister of Education faced a hostile and uncooperative Falher school district. This model, with an appropriate transition mechanism, could then be applied to other regions of the province whenever a sufficient number of Franco-Albertan parents made a request to the minister.[148]

During March 1991 the Working Group analysed two models. Assistant Deputy Minister of Education Steve Cymbol proposed a model for a francophone regional board for the Peace River region on the basis of input received from all stakeholders during meetings throughout the winter of 1990–91. The second model, proposed by the Alberta Teachers' Association, consisted of two levels of school governance triggered by a numbers formula. In Type I, a francophone regional school board would be established; in Type II, a francophone board would be empowered to negotiate a contract with any existing board for the provision of services to francophone students.[149]

The ACFA and FPFA were favourably disposed towards the first of these models, which had been considerably improved since its introduction in December. They would nevertheless propose several improvements to allay the fears of Franco-Albertan parents in the region, who feared the disappearance of Catholic schools for their children. Denis Tardif was very critical of the second model because "ce modèle pourrait être vite vu comme inconstitutionelle parce qu'il est basée sur un choix de nombre arbitraire pour déclencher l'établissement de conseil scolaire du Type I."[150] The major concern was to make certain that any new francophone regional school boards would be guaranteed adequate financing under the revised School Act and its implementation guidelines and regulations. Since these boards would not have the power to impose local taxes, there had to be a mechanism to see to it that all the existing school boards transferred the appropriate per capita funds to them. Furthermore, the province and Ottawa had to make additional funds available for not only remedial programs but also capital start-up costs and somewhat higher operating costs over the short term.[151]

During its meetings of 22 and 27 March and 12 April 1991, the French Language Working Group hammered out a unanimous report incorporating the essentials of both the model for the Peace River Region and that involving two types of governance.[152] Minister of Education Jim Dinning tabled it in the legislature on 24 June 1991. The report proposed dividing Alberta into six regions. Two of them, greater Edmonton and area and Smoky River/Peace River, would be granted full-fledged francophone regional school boards. Four regions – the northeast, St. Paul/Bonnyville, central Alberta, and Bow Area South – would be granted "co-ordinating Councils which would act as brokers or agents for francophone parents." When sufficient numbers of parents requested a full regional school board the minister would comply with the request. Initially the Ministry of Education would appoint the members of the regional boards and coordinating councils; later, candidates meeting the qualifications for any school board election would be voted on by parents of school-aged children who opted for French language education. The government would guarantee all the funds required, including special grants and 100 per cent capital costs.[153]

The ACFA and FPFA were very pleased with the general thrust of the report and were anxious to have Dinning put forward a bill revising the School Act on the basis of its recommendations. They were shocked when he informed them that the government had no intention of introducing legislation until it had had sufficient time to evaluate the report and receive feedback from various constituencies. The ACFA, the FPFA, the Alberta Teachers' Association, and Louis Desrochers all wrote Premier Getty expressing their disappointment and frustration with the delaying tactics and highlighting the serious damage to Canadian unity that was being inflicted by Alberta's bad-faith bargaining and downright intransigence in the matter of francophone education rights.[154] The ACFA publicly requested the province to reconsider its decision, and pointed out that the best way for it to contribute to national unity was to respect the constitutional rights of its francophone community in the same way that Quebec had respected those of its anglophone community since Confederation.[155]

The Association Bugnet, with the support of the ACFA, indicated that it was prepared to take the Alberta government to court once again if it did not move quickly in complying with the ruling in *Mahé*. The ACFA contemplated, then delayed for a period, its president's proposal to take its cause to the Human Rights Committee of the United Nations.[156] It did appeal to Prime Minister Brian Mulroney to refer the School Act to the Supreme Court, so a deadline could be imposed on the province for its compliance. Two ACFA presidents pleaded at different times with Joe Clark, the federal Minister of Intergovernmental Affairs, to use his influence with certain members of the Alberta Cabinet to convince the premier to change his mind, but to no avail.[157] The province would not be budged – a position that was made amply clear in the Minister of Education's responses to the ACFA, the FPFA, and Louis Desrochers.[158]

Refusing to give up, the ACFA decided to make contact with Premier Robert Bourassa through his senior advisor Jean Claude Rivet, to see whether he would use his influence with Premier Getty to encourage him to proceed expeditiously with legislation on school governance. The approaches began in December 1991 and continued through the next two months. Getty gave Bourassa a timely opportunity to make contact with him when he made some rather derogatory remarks about bilingualism to the media in January. Bourassa's intervention, of which the ACFA became aware in May, proved very helpful to Franco-Albertan parents seeking school governance.[159]

Much to their surprise, the ACFA's leaders were invited to meet with Getty in March 1992. They anticipated hearing excuses for continued non-action. Instead, Getty gave them every assurance that his government would pass a bill on francophone school management in the fall session. In the spring and early summer of 1992, as the provinces and Ottawa edged their way towards final negotiations on an expanded version of the failed Meech Lake Accord, Alberta finally decided to introduce Bill 41, the School Amendment Act, 1992, which adopted the regional and coordinating council model recommended by the French Language Working Group. Bill 41 proposed the creation of six francophone school boards and one coordinating council. Following second reading in June, Assistant Deputy Minister of Education Steve Cymbol invited the ACFA, the FPFA, the Alberta Teachers' Association, and the Alberta School Boards Association to join a committee of the Ministry of Education mandated to study the bill, propose improvements where necessary, and develop a strategy for implementation once it became law. The ACFA appointed its new president Denis Tardif and Phillip Lamoureux to the committee.[160] When asked for his advice, Michel Bastarache responded that the bill appeared to comply with the Supreme Court's interpretation of s. 23; however, he wanted to see the implementing regulations before rendering a final evaluation. Still, he had some questions: Why did the Minister of Education rather than Cabinet have the authority to determine the boundaries of the regional boards? Why was the electoral list so narrowly defined, and why were non-francophones eligible to be candidates for election? Finally, he wondered why the bill did not address the issue of confessionality, since all the francophone schools in Alberta were Catholic and Catholic schools had no constitutional obligation to enrol non-Catholic francophones.[161]

Unfortunately, Franco-Albertans were to be disappointed yet again. The intense political wrangling surrounding the Charlottetown Accord throughout the summer and fall virtually destroyed any prospect of Bill 41 receiving approval in the Alberta legislature. At the outset of the Charlottetown negotiations, Premier Don Getty indicated his intention to resign by the end of the year, thereby transforming himself into a political lame duck. Contrary to his promise to the ACFA, he refused to reconvene the legislature to deal with Bill 41, despite the pleas of that group, the FPFA, and their many supporters, including Prime Minister Brian Mulroney and some premiers.[162] Mega-constitutional politics had once again scuttled the strenuous efforts of the francophone organizations to extract a deal from a reluctant and nervous Alberta government.

Ralph Klein replaced Getty as the leader of the Conservative Party and premier in December. During a bitterly fought leadership campaign, Klein indicated that he had some serious reservations about Bill 41.[163] These statements worried Denis Tardif, who wrote to Klein on 14 December congratulating him on his new post and reminding him of the previous premier's promise to pass the bill before the end of 1992. The adoption of Bill 41, Tardif argued, would considerably advance the cause of national unity as well as re-establish social harmony in many Alberta communities, where Franco-Albertan parents had been battling for their educational rights for nearly a decade. Premier Klein, replying a month and half later, indicated that it was his government's intention to pass Bill 41 and encouraged the ACFA to work closely with the new Minister of Education, Halvar Jonson.[164] The minister re-established the Francophone Implementation Committee under the chairmanship of Steve Cymbol, but its hard work came to an abrupt halt when in May 1993 Klein prorogued the legislature for a provincial election in which his government was returned to office.[165]

In the interim, Franco-Albertan parents and their organizations intensified their lobbying for homogeneous French language schools – public and/or Catholic – in Edmonton, Lethbridge, Legal, Saint-Paul, Medley, Plamondon, and Fort McMurray. The process was made more tense by a simultaneous struggle – heated, divisive, and ultimately unsuccessful – over official bilingualism in Alberta's legislature and courts.[166] Nevertheless, the ACFA's and FPFA's persistence and their organizational and lobbying skills had paid off. Mastering the complex game of micro-constitutional politics meant that by 1992 Alberta had twelve French language schools with 2062 students, compared to two schools with 367 students in 1984.[167]

Outraged by the setback, the ACFA renewed its threat to take the case of Franco-Albertans before the United Nations, thereby giving the province a black eye in the international community. If Quebec's anglophone community could receive a favourable response to its complaints of discrimination on the issue of signage at the UN, it was not hard to imagine what the Human Rights Committee would make of the Alberta government's persistent violation of s. 23 of the Charter. In 1991, the ACFA's legal counsel, Michel Bastarache, had indicated that a UN committee might rule in favour of Franco-Albertans, but the legal costs would be prohibitive and a large budget would be needed to obtain the media coverage that would effectively embarrass the Alberta government into action.[168]

Georges Arès sought legal advice on behalf of the ACFA from Daniel Turp, a University of Montreal professor of international law and constitutional advisor to the Parti Québécois. Turp advised him that individual Franco-Albertans had a 60 per cent chance of winning an appeal to the Human Rights Committee based on Article 27 of the International Agreement on Civil and Political Rights, which concerned the right of minorities to engage in a cultural life with members of their own community. The agreement had been ratified by the Canadian and provincial governments in August 1976. Turp argued that since the committee had already dealt with an appeal from Quebec's anglophones it would feel bound to address one from Franco-Albertans. For his part, Arès was convinced that the threat of an appeal would force the province to defend itself, thereby providing Franco-Albertan organizations with plenty of political fodder. The proceedings would also compel the federal government to side with either the Alberta government or the francophone minority.[169]

The ACFA asked the FPFA to participate in the appeal to the United Nations. Both organizations made plans to raise the funds for the expected legal costs as well as the necessary media campaign. The appeal was almost abandoned when one of the ACFA's vice-presidents, Marc Arnal, argued that it should be terminated for political reasons, raising the spectre of what would happen if Franco-Albertans completely alienated the Klein government and the people of Alberta. Nonetheless, Turp was instructed by the ACFA and FPFA to proceed with the final preparation of the written submission to the UN. At a reception on 14 July 1993 given by the Bureau du Québec in celebration of Bastille Day, Sandra Cameron, principal lawyer for Alberta Education, asked Arès how the submission to the UN was progressing. Arès informed her that Turp had been instructed to proceed with it and that the ACFA had every intention of approaching the UN as soon as possible. The final submission was ready when the Alberta government, fully aware of the public relations fiasco it would face, decided to proceed with the education bill. As Sandra Cameron later admitted to Arès, the pressure tactic had worked beautifully.[170] It had cost the ACFA and the FPFA $23,000 in legal fees, but the political payoff would be enormous.[171]

At the same time, the ACFA had kept up the pressure on Premier Ralph Klein. Denis Tardif conversed with him during the St-Jean-

Baptiste celebrations at Quebec House in Edmonton and left reasonably reassured that Bill 41 would be re-introduced into the legislature in September and passed quickly. He hoped the premier would announce the adoption of francophone school governance during the ACFA's annual general meeting in late October. However, while Klein reiterated his government's commitment to the legislation, he would not promise its passage in time for the AGM.[172] The legislature was to reconvene in September 1993; the ACFA organized a small demonstration outside the building on 30 August. It also undertook a media blitz to encourage the premier to keep his word.[173]

Another figure that it was crucial to convince was Minister of Education Halvar Jonson. Encouraged and financed by the ACFA and FPFA, the Coalition pour l'éducation française (Rivière-la-paix), which comprised some half-dozen organizations in the region, prepared an excellent brief for Jonson. It recounted the prolonged and bitter battle between Franco-Albertan parents in the region, who had set up the only homogeneous francophone school, the École Héritage in Jean Côté, and the trustees of the Falher Consolidated School District No. 69. "Disharmony and a general malaise transpired though the whole of our francophone community as the conflict intensified and remained unresolved." Since 1988, the Falher Consolidated trustees had refused to transfer tuition fees for resident students attending the École Héritage. Indeed, they defied a ministerial order of 18 March 1992, then took the Minister of Education to court to have it quashed. On 13 March 1993 the Alberta Court of Appeal ordered the Falher Consolidated School District No. 69 to abide by the ministerial order and to pay the legal costs of the four Falher parents who had been granted intervenor status. But the trustees continued to flout the law, refusing to comply with the ruling. Meanwhile, Halvar Jonson failed to "demonstrate leadership through clear and decisive action" by enforcing the School Act in the rebellious district. All the francophone organizations of the Peace River region pleaded with him to pass and implement Bill 41 in order to guarantee that Franco-Albertan parents received their rights and to "calm this violent storm, ease this rage of tremors and prevent the volcano from erupting."[174]

After nearly ten years, Alberta finally decided to fulfill its constitutional obligation by passing Bill 8, the School Amendment Act, 1993 on 10 November 1993. In so doing, the Klein government sanctioned school governance for Franco-Albertans with the precise regional structure of school boards and coordinating councils to which all the parties involved in drafting Bill 41 had agreed over a year earlier. At long last, Franco-Albertan parents and organizations were duly rewarded for their tremendous patience, determination, and hard work. The ACFA applauded the premier and promised, "We intend to point out to our Quebec cousins at every possible opportunity the progress which is being made in Alberta to ensure the viability and legitimacy of the Franco-Albertan community."[175]

The Ministry of Education set September 1994 as its target date for having francophone school governance in place. Assistant Deputy Minister Steve Cymbol set out a timetable for the decisions, ministerial orders, and regulations necessary to achieving this deadline.[176] An implementation committee comprising representatives from the ACFA, the FPFA, and various local parent organizations was set up to oversee the process of selecting candidates for the three regional school boards – Edmonton, St Paul, and Peace River – and the four coordinating councils – Fort McMurray, Red Deer, Calgary, and Lethbridge – that would oversee the education of just over 2,100 students out of a total of nearly 22,000 eligible Franco-Albertan children, many of whom unfortunately lacked maternal language skills.[177] Considerable organizational work was done in preparation for school elections in October 1995 by Franco-Albertan parents who had children enrolled in francophone schools.[178] The process was accelerated by the preparedness of the Franco-Albertan educational organizations to move once Bill 8 was law. The FPFA published a special edition of its bulletin, Le Chaînon, celebrating the achievement of school governance and explaining the significant social, cultural, and educational benefits that would flow from it. FPFA President Dolorèse Nolette urged all Franco-Albertans to cooperate fully in its implementation, in order to make the school environment a culturally enriching experience for their children.[179] At the same time, however, the process was complicated by the government's termination in 1994 of the power of all school boards to levy taxes, which comprised about 42 per cent of their revenues. Instead the province gave each board $4,200 per student. In 1994–95, the French language boards and coordinating councils received an additional $332 per elementary student and $406 per secondary student to help defray the extra costs associated with French language education.[181]

The political skids for the passage of Bill 8 and its subsequent rapid implementation had been greased by the promise of long-awaited special agreements between Alberta and Ottawa. Under the terms of one, signed in October 1993, Ottawa gave the province a grant of $16.3 million for the establishment of the new French language school system: $4.5 million for school construction and $5.4 million for management costs. Under another agreement, Alberta was given $6 million for renovations to Faculté Saint-Jean in Edmonton, where many French language teachers were educated.[182] A separate Canada-

Community development agreement, signed on 17 September 1994, provided funding of $12 million over five years from the Ministry of Canadian Heritage. While these funds did not directly benefit schools and educational programs, they did enhance cultural and social opportunities for all Franco-Albertans.[182] The ACFA was instrumental in these successes; it had maintained strong continuous pressure on the federal government since 1988, encouraging the Secretary of State to use his spending powers and political influence to entice the Alberta government into granting Franco-Albertans their constitutional rights.[183]

CONCLUSION

In 1983, only a handful of Franco-Albertan parents in the Association Bugnet believed that Franco-Albertans should, could, and would win full school governance less than a decade thence. The vast majority, taking the lead from the ACFA and other organizations, were convinced that Premier Peter Lougheed's highly popular Conservative government, which remained staunchly opposed to the Official Languages Act and repeatedly denounced the Charter, would never grant them this right. For a long while, it appeared that Alberta would succeed in having its rather limited conception of francophone minority education rights accepted. Indeed, the ACFA's leadership, believing that the government's approach was precisely what a majority of Franco-Albertan parents wanted, tried very hard to negotiate a settlement along those lines. Alberta's politicians, bureaucrats, and educational leaders insisted that Albertans had to find their own made in Alberta solution rather than having one shoved down their throats by what was regarded as Trudeau's Charter. Aware of the volatile political climate and sensitive to the concerns of Catholic small-town Franco-Albertans, the ACFA attempted to negotiate with the government.

Meanwhile, it kept open the far more controversial option of homogeneous Franco-Albertan schools and school boards. The Association Bugnet made sure that it did so by arguing convincingly that any made in Alberta political solution would fall far short of what Franco-Albertans required for their survival, and would, in any case, be a violation of their constitutional rights under s. 23 of the Charter. It wanted nothing less than complete school governance, that is, a comprehensive network of French language schools and boards. Responding to constant pressure from the Association Bugnet and to the realization that negotiations with the Alberta government were going nowhere, the ACFA reluctantly decided to support its legal challenge to Alberta's School Act. The case took Jean-Claude Mahé and the other appellants all the way to the Supreme Court, where they won a favourable landmark decision in 1990. The remarkable ruling gave the ACFA and FPFA the political clout they needed to force the Alberta government back to the bargaining table.

The province realized, too late in the game, that it had been drawn into political and judicial battles that it had less and less ability to control and could not win. Premiers Lougheed and Getty adopted a strategy of political procrastination and legal stonewalling to buy time. All the while, they exerted themselves to obtain a constitutional amendment that would confirm the Alberta government's minimalist interpretation of s. 23 rights. The demise of the Meech Lake Accord in June 1990, followed by the defeat of the Charlottetown Consensus Report in October 1992, made it painfully clear to Premier Klein that no constitutional miracle was going to salvage his government's approach. Despite strong opposition from his caucus, Klein recognized that Alberta had no choice but to comply with the Supreme Court's ruling in *Mahé*. In 1993, his government passed Bill 8, which contained the long-sought amendments to Alberta's School Act that brought it into compliance with the Charter and made school governance a reality for Franco-Albertans.

Giving credit where credit is due, the Klein government's amendments to the School Act went further than what was strictly required by the Supreme Court decision. The province could have insisted on proportional representation for francophone trustees within existing majority English language boards but chose full school governance for Franco-Albertans as the wisest course of action. Furthermore, once the decision was made to move forward, Alberta Education's cooperation in the implementation of school governance was excellent.

Franco-Albertan parents, the ACFA, and the FPFA acquired the legal clout essential to winning school governance thanks to the foresight and determination of the Association Bugnet and its small band of true believers. The ACFA made an important contribution to the cause by learning and applying the skills of mega-constitutional politics, thereby preventing any weakening of s. 23 rights. Along with the FPFA, it also learned the skills of micro-constitutional politics necessary for taking advantage of the *Mahé* decision. The Charter truly empowered Franco-Albertan parents – working through the Association Bugnet, the ACFA, the FPFA, and the Fédération, all funded by the visionary Court Challenges Program – in reaching what most considered a utopian goal in the early 1980s. In attaining their dream, Franco-Albertans and their leaders did not distort the democratic rights of the majority, as many Charterphobes would have us believe. It is also evident that the Supreme Court exercised great prudence and creativity in addressing the demands of both the appellants and the respondents in *Mahé*. The justices, in their wisdom, charted a course of action that respected provincial jurisdiction while guaranteeing that s. 23 rights would be fully and fairly implemented. In fact, they untied the Gordian Knot of provincial versus minority education rights, an issue plaguing Canadian politics since 1867.

5

Franco-Manitobans and the Charter's Section 23

The number of potential French-language students warrants the establishment of an independent French-language school board in Manitoba under
the exclusive management and control of the French-language minority.[1]

Beginning in the late 1970s, Franco-Manitobans became embroiled in
two quite different yet related constitutional battles involving s. 23.
The first focused on making Manitoba officially bilingual once again
by restoring s. 23 of the Manitoba Act, 1870, which had been abolished in 1890. The second entailed intertwined political and juridical
campaigns to achieve implementation of official language minority
education rights under s. 23 of the Charter. Given the continuing
opposition of Manitoba's English-speaking majority to any formal
recognition of the Franco-Manitoban community, both struggles
proved extremely arduous. Nonetheless, through hard work and perseverance, Franco-Manitoban leaders, backed by their community,
acquired the micro- and mega-constitutional political skills necessary
to winning victory in both s. 23 conflicts. In the process, the numerous
cleavages – religion versus language, urban versus rural, tradition
versus modernity, pan-Canadian cultural duality versus territorial
Quebec/Canada duality – that characterized Franco-Manitoban
society were revealed and exacerbated. In a classic "divide and rule"
strategy, Manitoba's dominant political and social elites exploited
them in order to limit the scope of s. 23 of the Charter. Thanks to the
rulings of the Supreme Court in *Mahé*, then in the 1993 Manitoba reference case, the strategy collapsed.
   Both s. 23 struggles were the outcome of a remarkable revival of the
Franco-Manitoban community in the mid-1960s paralleling that of
francophones in other provinces. The resulting well-deserved constitutional victories enabled Franco-Manitobans to carve out new symbolic and political spaces within not only the province but also the
revitalized minority community across the country.

Between 1981 and 1985 the battle over s. 23 of the Manitoba Act, 1870 monopolized the energies of Franco-Manitobans and their organizations. Following the expansion of an urban, secular Franco-Manitoban middle class in the 1970s, two lawyers, Georges Forest and Roger Bilodeau, backed reluctantly and belatedly by the Société franco-manitobaine and the community at large, pursued a series of court challenges leading to the restoration of that section of the Act, which made Manitoba's legislature and courts officially bilingual once again.[2]

The Manitoba Act was the federal statute that established the province following the Red River colony's resistance, led by Louis Riel and his fellow Métis. Modelled on the official language and confessional school provisions of the province of Quebec, it was imposed on the colony in an atmosphere of bitter religious, cultural, and linguistic conflict. In 1890, the Manitoba government abolished official bilingualism together with the denominational schools. This controversial political decision was triggered by a precipitous decline in the Catholic French Canadian and Métis nations' proportion of Manitoba's population and occurred in the context of an emerging belligerent British-Canadian nationalist movement. For over three-quarters of a century, most Franco-Manitobans, preoccupied with retaining Catholic and French language education for their children, deliberately ignored the abolition of s. 23 of the Manitoba Act.[3] The eventual restoration of rights under the section involved an epic series of court challenges, culminating in victories in the Supreme Court in 1979 and 1985.[4]

During this very turbulent period, the SFM and several lobbying organizations concerned with education – particularly the Fédération provinciale des comités de parents, created in 1976 – were negotiating full school governance for Franco-Manitobans. Their first task was to hammer out an internal consensus to avoid the provincial government's longstanding strategy of "divide and rule." The prevailing complex system of rural and urban, public and separate, French language, French immersion, and bilingual schools appeared to meet the immediate needs of most Franco-Manitoban parents and their children. As in Ontario and Alberta, the francophone organizations had to educate Franco-Manitobans about why the existing system, while adequate in some ways, was incapable of stemming assimilation. Moreover, since these schools were centrally administered, Franco-Manitobans exercised no effective authority over the education of their children.

Following the Ontario Court of Appeal's decision in the reference case in 1984 and the Supreme Court ruling in *Mahé* in 1990, Franco-Manitobans sought a made in Manitoba political solution to the thorny issue of school governance. Unsuccessful in reaching either community consensus or an acceptable agreement with the province, the SFM and FPCP were forced to resort, in their turn, to the Supreme Court. The ruling in the 1993 Manitoba reference case compelled all parties to negotiate an acceptable political resolution leading to the implementation of school governance.

THE RESTORATION OF
FRENCH LANGUAGE EDUCATION

The situation of francophones in Manitoba was significantly different than in Alberta. Beginning in the mid-1960s, a wide range of French language education options was made available to Franco-Manitoban parents and their children in both urban and rural areas. In the spirit of Canadian unity and growing acceptance of bilingualism by urban middle-class Manitobans, successive governments attempted to redress the injustices inflicted on Franco-Manitobans since the infamous Manitoba Schools Question of the 1890s.

In March 1890, the Liberal government of Premier Thomas Greenway decided to abolish the existing system of denominational schools mandated by s. 22 of the Manitoba Act and, at the same time, to terminate the use of French in the provincial legislature and courts. A new system of public education under a Minister of Education was established along the lines of that in New Brunswick. The continued influx of English-speaking Ontarians – especially after the completion of the Canadian Pacific Railway in 1885 – was dramatically altering the sociopolitical and demographic profile of the province in favour of English-speaking Protestants. All Manitoba Catholics were incensed at the abolition of denominational schools, but it was the Franco-Manitoban Catholic community that reacted collectively, because the disappearance of publicly funded Catholic separate schools and the creation of an English language Ministry of Education threatened to undermine and eventually terminate instruction in French. Franco-Manitobans, like all French Canadians at the time, saw their language as the guardian of their Catholic faith, and vice versa.

Catholic leaders from various ethnic and linguistic communities participated in a vigorous political and legal campaign led by Church officials to have the offending legislation declared *ultra vires* – that is, unconstitutional – in the Judicial Committee of the Privy Council in London. In January 1896, the Judicial Committee ruled that the education laws of 1890 were constitutional but that the constitutional rights of the Catholic minority had been abrogated, and authorized the Canadian government to remedy the situation. When the Conservative government of Prime Minister Charles Tupper failed either to obtain cooperation from the Greenway government or to pass the necessary legislation prior to its electoral defeat in 1896, it became all too evident that denominational public schools would never be re-established in the province. Indeed, the victorious Liberal Party, under its first French Canadian Catholic leader, Sir Wilfrid Laurier, was eager to protect exclusive provincial control over education and refused to impose remedial legislation on Manitoba.

Since, unlike in Alberta, there was no formal legislative sanction against teaching in French, all the rural public school boards controlled by Franco-Manitobans continued to teach the curriculum in that language while providing religious instruction after formal school hours. Indeed, many of the teachers were French Canadian nuns and priests sent west by their religious orders. Much to the chagrin of Bishop Adélard Langevin, who remained determined to have the denominational system fully restored, this political accommodation – satisfactory to the majority of Franco-Manitoban parents – was formalized in the Laurier-Greenway Agreement of November 1896. The agreement remained in force until the middle of the Great War, when the British-Canadian nationalist sentiment expressed daily in the pages of the *Winnipeg Free Press* led an increasingly vocal majority of Manitobans to pressure the newly elected Liberal government of T.C. Norris into abolishing it. However, Norris had promised Franco-Manitobans that he would not touch the Laurier-Greenway Agreement and that, if possible, he would work to restore Catholic schools. Under the agreement a whole range of bilingual schools in which the Catholic religion was taught after school hours flourished as the province filled up with immigrants from all parts of Europe.

Bitter resentment towards enemy aliens, including Germans and other ethnic groups from all parts of the Austro-Hungarian Empire, together with hostility against French Canadians for refusing to enlist voluntarily, fuelled the clarion call of the well-established nationalist movement for one language – English – one culture – British-Canadian – and the necessity of conscription to win the war against the detested Kaiser. On 10 March 1916, s. 258 of the Public Schools Act was repealed, thereby making English the sole language of instruction in all Manitoba schools. Education was made compulsory for all children, while religious instruction was still allowed after school hours. Although the large numbers of Catholic voters guaranteed some protection for the Church, the declining Franco-Manitoban population could do little to salvage education in its own language.

The six Franco-Manitoban members of the legislature, four Conservatives and two Liberals, protested loudly – but to no avail. In the years that followed, Franco-Manitoban leaders came to realize that the failure to successfully contest the abolition of s. 23 of the Manitoba Act, first in the Saint-Boniface County Court in 1892 and again in 1909, was an enormous blow to the healthy development of their community.[5] Successive Manitoba governments simply ignored the court rulings. By 1916, the majority of British-Canadian Manitobans, migrants from Ontario who brought along their Orange Lodge ideology, considered French just one more foreign language, rather than one of the two official languages of the province. In their view, if Canada was to develop into a powerful, autonomous nation-state within the British Empire, it was imperative for English to become dominant in public and private life alike. This would transpire only if the public schools used English to transform all students, regardless of ethnic, linguistic, or religious background, into solid, loyal English-speaking citizens of Canada and the Empire.

Lacking the political clout to alter the decision to outlaw French language instruction in the public schools, Franco-Manitoban leaders launched the Association d'Éducation des Canadiens-Français du Manitoba with the support of cautious, prudent Catholic Church leaders. By defending Manitoba's French Canadian community and the French language, the latter hoped to guarantee the survival of a threatened Catholicism.[6] The mandate of the new organization was to promote the rights of all Franco-Manitobans, primarily in the field of education, which was considered crucial to the survival of the isolated francophone Catholic communities of rural Manitoba. Between 1916 and 1968, the AÉCFM effectively functioned as an informal and clandestine parallel Ministry of Education for the francophone communities. The school boards controlled by Franco-Manitobans hired only qualified bilingual francophone Catholic teachers and provided them with a complete primary school curriculum and books imported from Quebec. Schools where Franco-Manitoban children predominated operated as efficient bilingual schools to which inspectors and the government turned a blind eye. The establishment of a French language radio station, CKSB, in Saint-Boniface in 1946 helped Franco-Manitoban communities address isolation and depopulation by making it possible for their lay and religious leaders to communicate more effectively and provide rural families with a constant source of French language news and information as well as a wide assortment of cultural and leisure programming.

With the arrival of Duff Roblin as leader of the Conservative Party and premier of the province in 1958, Franco-Manitobans found a bilingual ally in their struggle for the restoration of French language instruction. By 1961, the Franco-Manitoban population numbered nearly 84,000, just over 9 per cent of the province, but a great many had lost the ability to speak their maternal language. As their representatives struggled, with some success, to make sure that the small francophone-dominated school boards were not swallowed up in the controversial process of school board restructuring, the Roblin government promised in 1962 that the use of French would be reintroduced into all Manitoba elementary schools. After lengthy negotiations, Bill 59 amending the Public Schools Act became law in 1967. The legislation authorized – at the discretion of the Minister of Education – instruction in French for a period not exceeding 50 per cent of the school day. In short order, a division was created within the Ministry of Education to develop and administer the French language program. The result was the development of a number of mixed or bilingual schools. Soon thereafter, Premier Roblin resigned his office to seek – unsuccessfully – the leadership of the national Progressive Conservative Party.

When the New Democratic Party under the leadership of Edward Schreyer took office in 1969, a more progressive phase of Manitoba's education history got underway. The previous year, Trudeau and his Liberals had been elected to office. His newly appointed Secretary of State, Gérard Pelletier, congratulated Franco-Manitobans in Saint-Boniface in early December 1968 for their skill and determination in remaining francophones in the face of myriad adversities and setbacks. "En cela," he concluded, " vous avez aidé le Canada tout entier et que celui-ci aujourd'hui vous retourne son aide en vous donnant les moyens de ne plus penser à survivre mais a vous épanouir dans les cadres francophones et canadiens. Car c'est de vous, en dernière analyse, que dépend l'issue de cette entreprise commune."[7] The political changes raised expectations and served to galvanize a new generation of Franco-Manitoban leaders into action.

Many Franco-Manitobans were dissatisfied with the mixed or bilingual schools, seeing them as institutions of assimilation because their administrative and cultural environment remained predominantly English. Acting on a 1969 study by Roger Frechette, which indicated that a third of Franco-Manitoban students no longer understood or spoke French, in 1970 the NDP government passed Bill 113 modifying the Public Schools Act. It was now permissible to use French for up to 100 per cent of the school day from kindergarten through grade 3 and up to 75 per cent from grade 4 through grade 12. Over the next decade, ten homogeneous French language schools for Franco-Manitoban students were set up. The Minister of Education also established the French and English Language Advisory Committees and the Bureau de l'éducation française in 1974, to develop education policies and curriculum for a series of proposed new French schools to replace the existing immersion schools attended by Franco-Manitoban students in most rural areas. At the time, only two all-French schools existed in the entire province, and one, École Taché, was being threatened with closure by the Saint-Boniface School Division in 1974. To help advance their cause, the BÉF published a comprehensive blueprint entitled "Pour un réseau d'écoles françaises," which, to the chagrin of the SFM, was never formally adopted by the Ministry of Education.

The SFM worked constantly on two fronts. First, it had to persuade many Franco-Manitoban parents to shift their children from the immersion, mixed/bilingual, and English language schools to the proposed system of new French language schools. A great many parents feared that their children would not learn proper English, thereby being disadvantaged in the job market. The SFM had to convince them that, given the dominance of television, learning English was no hardship for young Franco-Manitobans, while learning proper French was definitely a major problem. Accomplishing this goal required substantial financial resources, as well as social animators capable of carrying out effective grassroots recruiting programs without creating a backlash from parents and children and thereby dividing the communities. The SFM's second front was political: it lobbied the Schreyer government for clarifications to Bill 113 and for detailed regulations that would help Franco-Manitoban parents deal with recalcitrant school boards refusing to comply with its provisions.[8]

By 1976, when the number of local conflicts in schools had begun to accumulate, the SFM and Franco-Manitoban parents decided to form a lobby organization separate from the overburdened existing group to deal with educational matters. The FPCP was mandated to coordinate the efforts of all local parent committees in convincing the recalcitrant boards to provide French language education. The hope was that a well-run FPCP, located in Winnipeg and working closely with the BÉF, would provide some relief to the overworked SFM, which could direct its energies and resources to the time-consuming task of lobbying the premier, the Minister of Education, and other provincial and federal politicians for more and better French language schools. This division of bureaucratic and political lobbying tasks, SFM leaders believed at the time, would result in a more productive campaign for school governance.[9] When conflict eventually erupted over the sharing of the lobbying function, the SFM insisted on regaining control and having the FPCP focus its efforts at the community level.

In the election of 1977, the NDP was replaced by the Conservative administration of Premier Sterling Lyon. His pro-business government, based on an established south Winnipeg/southwest Manitoba

electoral alliance, was intent on cutting back on services, including the
rising cost of education. Despite Lyon's sympathetic remarks on edu-
cation to delegates attending the SFM's annual general meeting in
March 1978, the Conservatives' proposed amendments to the Public
Schools Act ignored all the demands of that group and the FPCP.
Indeed, in June 1979 SFM President René Piché condemned the pro-
posed amendments as "a definite step backward for the status of
French education in this province."[10]

In October 1979, the SFM and FPCP, in their respective submissions
to the Intercessional Committee of the Legislative Assembly, reiterated
their support for Bills 59 and 113, which made "the French language
element of Public Education available, at least in principle, to all who
desire it, including, but not restricted to, Manitobans whose mother
tongue was French." French immersion schools were welcomed
because they broadened the demographic base of those who appreciated and supported the survival of the Franco-Manitoban communities. Nevertheless, the two organizations pointed out that several years
of attempting to implement Bill 113 had proved that it was too permissive, that it granted far too much discretionary authority to school
boards, superintendents, and the Minister of Education. When
parents asked for its provisions to be applied in their community they
encountered determined opposition from school boards and so-called
"concerned parents" wanting to preserve the status quo. Any change
required constant lobbying – including public demonstrations – of
board members as well as the minister. The SFM and FPCP recommended that the Public Schools Act be amended to make French language official minority and immersion public school education for all
Manitoba children a statutory right rather than a privilege granted at
the discretion of local school boards or the Minister of Education.
Both also suggested the striking of a quasi-judicial tribunal, the Languages of Instruction Board, empowered to settle disputes through
binding arbitration between parents and their school boards or the
Ministry of Education. In this way, the SFM and FPCP hoped to depoliti-
cize the potentially explosive matter of French language education.[11]

The Lyon government was not very responsive to these proposals.
They ran counter to the premier's opposition to entrenching official
bilingualism in a renewed Canadian Constitution, which was based on
his government's rejection of French language education as a right. In
September 1981 representatives of the SFM and FPCP, French language
teachers, and French school trustees were granted a meeting with
Lyon to discuss the complex and somewhat confusing relationship
between official French minority and immersion programs and
schools. They also wanted to clarify the role of the BÉF in the future

orientation of French education.[12] At the meeting the francophone organizations argued that federal funding for French language education, minority and immersion, should be divided into two separate programs so that Franco-Manitobans could be assured that their education needs were being addressed. They also stressed that the role of the BÉF needed to be expanded to include transportation policies, construction of school facilities, education financing, as well as overall education policy development and planning for French education. The BÉF would receive assistance from a French language advisory committee.[13] Indeed, the SFM had found itself proposing at an executive meeting in April 1980 that all the Franco-Manitoban organizations concerned with education should study other, more drastic, options such as the creation of "une seule division scolaire homogène de langue française au Manitoba."[14] The concept of a single board had been proposed initially in 1976 by parents to Raymond Hébert, the BÉF's first Assistant Deputy Minister.[15] It would take over a decade before the conditions were ripe for it to take hold within the Franco-Manitoban leadership and educational organizations.

Once it had sunk in that the Constitution Act, 1982 and the Charter of Rights and Freedoms were the law of the land, the SFM and FPCP began to alter their approach. Soon after the election in 1981 of an NDP government led by Howard Pawley, the SFM lobbied the new premier to support the holding of a federal-provincial conference on the linguistic and education rights of francophone minority communities.[16] Unhappy with the wording of s. 23 of the Charter, the Franco-Manitoban organizations hoped that the premiers and the prime minister would agree to one or two important amendments. Still bruised by the mega-constitutional political slugfest, not a single premier was interested in the proposal. The SFM and FPCP would have to pursue the implementation of minority education rights as they were defined in s. 23 of the Charter.

FRANCO-MANITOBAN ORGANIZATIONS FORGE A CONSENSUS

Throughout the turmoil over the restoration of official bilingualism – s. 23 of the Manitoba Act – the SFM and FPCP encountered some difficulty in defining their respective roles in the "other section 23" campaign. At its AGM in early 1983, the FPCP passed resolutions to the effect that it was going to take charge of the campaign to achieve school governance for Franco-Manitoban parents. It would begin by taking the necessary steps to ensure that the provincial government clearly defined French language schools and immersion schools, then established admission criteria for children wishing to attend French minority schools. In addition, given that the FPCP represented a considerable number of Franco-Manitoban parents and that political leadership in the field of French education remained somewhat ambiguous, it was resolved that the organization "tout en continuant son rôle de sensibilisation auprès des parents, assume ce leadership politique." That is, the FPCP would define the major components of the campaign for school restructuring and assume responsibility for the campaign vis-à-vis both parents and the provincial government.[17]

At its own AGM in March of the same year, the SFM's delegates passed a resolution giving their executive a mandate for assuming responsibility for the school governance campaign and allotting the human and financial resources needed by the FPCP and other educational organizations to attain that objective. A second resolution called on the SFM to accept the FPCP's leadership in this matter and to support "toute démarche de la FPCP ayant pour but d'obtenir un maximum de contrôle sur nos institutions scolaires." When it became apparent that their respective mandates overlapped, the boards of directors of the two organizations met on 26 April 1983 to talk over the situation. They agreed to create a joint committee, the Comité directeur du dossier structures scolaires, to handle the question of school governance. Its first task was to send an application to the Secretary of State for funding for its work. The next one was to ask parent groups to give it information so it could document all the problems stemming from the lack of school governance.

In the spring of 1984, when it was apparent that the FPCP's work was not progressing very well, delegates at the SFM's AGM passed two further resolutions. The first called on all the francophone educational organizations to cooperate in drawing up a dynamic and aggressive plan of action capable of achieving governance. Given that education remained a priority for the group, the delegates also passed a resolution directing its leaders to lobby the government to create a study commission involving all these organizations, with the mandate to recommend "des modèles de *structures scolaires qui répondraient aux besoins des Franco-manitobaines.*"[18] The awkward attempt to differentiate the mandates of the two organizations failed to resolve the tension between them.

In early November, Michèle Lagimodière-Gagnon, the president of the FPCP, sent a letter to Gilberte Proteau, president of the SFM, suggesting that their boards of directors meet on 13 November to resolve their debate over principles and "ré-affirmer conjointement la position de la francophonie face à l'école française en vue d'obtenir la gérance."[19] The meeting was necessary because, at a meeting of the Comité directeur on 23 October, Proteau had made a personal proposal that was not approved by the SFM board.[20] She had urged that the Comité directeur abandon "la poursuite d'une structure scolaire homogène autonome pour et par les francophones et s'allier avec l'immersion pour ainsi créer une commission ou des commissions scolaires francophones (pour immersion et français)." As long as this contradiction persisted between the views of the SFM and its president, stated the FPCP's president, she would refuse to sign the letter of the francophone organizations destined for the Minister of Education.[21]

Gilberte Proteau complained that her comments had been either misunderstood or misinterpreted. She attempted to smooth things over by saying in a letter to Lagimodière-Gagnon that she was simply suggesting various models for school governance, but clarified that the joint governance model involving immersion and French schools was not the official policy of the SFM. The immersion system, she reminded the FPCP, was the fastest-growing sector in the province; English language parents who supported it should not be ignored. She hoped their two organizations would continue to cooperate in the work of the Comité directeur in order to achieve the best model of school governance for Franco-Manitobans.[22] Hoping to quell the conflict, the SFM's Administrative Council adopted a proposal at its meeting of 12 November 1985 stating that English language students could only be admitted to Franco-Manitoban schools on three conditions. First, they must pass written and oral exams in French for the grade they wanted to enroll in. Their parents had to accept all the principles of the Franco-Manitoban school. Finally, if their children failed to meet the criteria of the school, parents had to consent to their transfer to another, more suitable school.[23]

Throughout the winter of 1985, the members of the Comité directeur, with the Ontario reference case decision in hand, worked hard to specify the objective of French minority schools and create a set of guiding principles for the model of school governance for Franco-Manitobans. The SFM adopted both the objective and the principles at its AGM on 2 March 1985. The delegates also voted to broaden the base of the Comité directeur by including representatives from the Éducatrices et éducateurs francophones du Manitoba, the Conseil jeunesse provincial, and the Commissaires d'écoles franco-manitobains.[24] These principles, not surprisingly, formed the basis of the Comité directeur's lucid brief, "Vers l'accès, l'égalité et la gestion," presented to Minister of Education Maureen Hemphill on 21 March 1985. It argued that the restructuring of the French schools must have as its primary objective the "épanouissement culturel et linguistique des francophones du Manitoba."[25] This laudable goal could only be achieved once certain conditions had been met:

- Franco-Manitobans had acquired full school governance.
- All their children, regardless of their place of residence, had access to a French language school at no additional cost.
- The entire curriculum, except English, was taught in French.
- French was the language of communication and of the schools.
- The French schools had acquired the same level of services as all other schools.
- All teachers were fully qualified to teach in French.
- The criteria of admission gave priority to children whose home language was French.
- The French schools functioned as cultural and social centres for their respective communities.

Given that the Ontario Court of Appeal had ruled in the reference case that s. 23 of the Charter was remedial in nature and sanctioned the principle of school governance for the linguistic minorities, the Comité directeur strongly recommended that the minister amend the Public Schools Act to bring it into conformity with the section. Moreover, in the wake of the Supreme Court's ruling in *Attorney General of Quebec v. Quebec Association of Protestant Schools Boards,* which gave precedence to s. 23(1)(b) of the Charter – the Canada clause – over ss. 71 and 72 of Bill 101 – the Quebec clauses – and reaffirmed the remedial intent of s. 23, it was imperative for Franco-Manitoban parents to be directly involved in formulating these amendments.[26] The Comité directeur's members thanked Hemphill for the meeting but noted that they were disappointed in not having received definitive answers from her on these issues. They hoped that her government would cooperate in the search for a political solution.[27]

The francophone organizations were not overly surprised to discover that the NDP government's idea of cooperation was based on a different reading not only of its education legislation but also of the political climate of the province. It was mid-October before Hemphill replied to the Comité directeur's March brief. On the crucial matter of school governance she had this to say:

En ce qui concerne le droit à l'éducation, une étude récente portant sur la loi scolaire du Manitoba et sur la Charte canadienne des droits et libertés, démontre que le Manitoba aurait déjà prévu certain dispositifs dans la loi scolaire qui font que celle-ci s'aligne sur la Charte. Plus précisément, la loi scolaire reconnaît le droit et garantit l'accès à l'éducation française pour sa population francophone. Pour ce qui est de la question de la gestion scolaire, j'ai le plaisir de vous annoncer que le Conseil des ministres a endossé une revue de la correspondance de la Loi des écoles publiques du Manitoba avec la Charte des droits et libertés du Canada.[28]

Lucille Blanchette, first vice-president of the SFM, replied on behalf of the Comité directeur. She thanked Hemphill for agreeing to endorse fully the curriculum policy document that had been developed for the officially designated Franco-Manitoban schools. However, she noted that, while Regulation 64/85 of the Public Schools Act guaranteed access to French education, certain regional or divisional school boards refused to comply with it; if the minister did not remedy the situation, the SFM would be forced to take steps to make sure that they met their constitutional responsibilities. The Cabinet's decision to endorse a Ministry of Education study on the relationship between the Public Schools Act and the Charter represented "une reconnaissance du principe de la gestion scolaire par la minorité. Il reste donc à s'entendre sur la question des structures." Blanchette reminded Hemphill that the Comité directeur had studied school governance in considerable depth; she hoped the study was not just another delaying tactic. The SFM wanted to know the time-frame for the study and requested that the five organizations belonging to the Comité directeur be allowed to participate in order to accelerate the process.[29]

When Hemphill indicated that she needed additional time to respond, SFM President Réal Sabourin replied that the Franco-Manitoban community had serious reservations about the Ministry of Education's initiatives in a number of areas, particularly in school governance. The SFM would not countenance any further delays.[30] Hemphill's response in late November clarified, in part, a few of the outstanding issues, such as French language services, special grants for Franco-Manitoban schools, curriculum policy, and access. However, her answer on school governance was pure evasion: the study of the issue by Assistant Deputy Ministers Guy Roy and Glenn Nicholls was making progress but their mandate had not been fully clarified. Frustrated, Sabourin demanded a meeting with Hemphill as soon as possible.[31]

In preparation for an election in 1986 or 1987, Premier Pawley juggled his Cabinet, promoting Jerry Storie to the post of Minister of Education. As the SFM's leaders attempted throughout May and June of 1986 to convince the new minister to negotiate a political settlement on school governance, it became increasingly apparent that the government had absolutely no intention of granting Franco-Manitoban parents any system of French minority school boards. At the end of June, Storie stated that he had not promised that the Roy-Nicholls Commission would issue its report on the governance issue within the next few months. He reminded the SFM that all he had promised was that Cabinet would decide by the end of August whether the matter would be settled politically or by the courts. Before arriving at a decision Cabinet wanted to consult all the school divisions that managed Franco-Manitoban schools.[32] It was clearly time for the SFM and the

FPCP to give the judicial option serious consideration if they were going to achieve their goal.

PONDERING THE RISKS OF THE JUDICIAL OPTION

In reality, it had already become obvious in 1985 that the judicial approach would have to be added to the political. It was decided that the political lobby campaign would remain primarily the SFM's responsibility; the FPCP, representing the parents, would focus on the legal option, that is, on preparing the documentation for a court case to contest the constitutional validity of Manitoba's Public Schools Act.[33] This attempt to allocate interrelated aspects of the struggle to the two organizations would prove virtually impossible. At the SFM's annual meeting on 2 March 1985 the delegates voted to grant the Comité directeur the mandate to pursue a court challenge on the school governance issue if necessary.[34] The Comité directeur began almost immediately to seek legal advice from several quarters. At an educational seminar held at the AGM, Pierre Foucher had informed the Comité directeur that it was not necessary to have a definition of French language schools entrenched in the Public Schools Act. This piece of advice was later confirmed by another lawyer, L.J. Roy of the Winnipeg firm of Monk, Goodwin.[35]

In late June 1985 the Comité directeur approached Michel Bastarache, who advised it not to expect a reference case and to attempt instead to find "un *cas type* qui présente des possibilités intéressantes de soulever les *questions* de principe fondamentales dans le contexte manitobaine." He also informed the Comité directeur that there were some glaring constitutional errors in its March submission to Minister of Education Maureen Hemphill. He then laid out six precise steps that the Comité directeur should use in identifying its test case and preparing the background documentation and evidence to achieve the desired results: access to French language schools equivalent to those of the English-speaking majority, as well as their governance by Franco-Manitoban parents.[36] The SFM's political analyst, Charles Gagné, advised the Comité directeur in October that, given the animosity over the campaign for the restoration of official bilingualism, it was crucial to obtain the full support of the Franco-Manitoban community for a court challenge and to be sure that funds could be obtained from the Court Challenges Program.[37] In December, the Comité directeur got advice from Bastarache on putting together its funding request.[38] Later the same month, SFM President Réal Sabourin addressed an open letter to all member organizations of the Comité directeur, local parents' groups, and school principals bringing them up to speed on the school governance issue. He asked parents whether they were interested in obtaining full control over their French minority schools by means of a regrouping, as recommended by the Comité directeur. The letter enclosed the most recent issue of the FPCP's *Entre parenthèses*, which contained the correspondence between the Comité directeur and Minister of Education Maureen Hemphill. The intent was to galvanize the community into supporting both the political and the judicial campaigns.[39]

In June 1986 the Comité directeur issued a working paper on school governance in which it explained its decision to recommend the creation of one or more homogeneous Franco-Manitoban school divisions as per s. 23 of the Charter; the hope was that parents' groups would choose to opt in at the appropriate time. The Comité directeur encouraged two or more of these groups to apply for the amalgamation of their French schools under the provisions of the existing Public Schools Act. According to s. 5 of the Act, the Minister of Education would then have to ask the Reference Board to decide whether or not to hold a vote of all the parents involved; its refusal would constitute the basis for legal action.[40] This avenue was closed when, on 5 September, Jerry Storie announced that the government had no intention of amending the Public Schools Act since it believed the legislation complied with s. 23 of the Charter. Four days later the FPCP held a press conference during which s. 23 rights were characterized as unalterable and non-negotiable. The group then announced the launching of a challenge in the Manitoba Court of Queen's Bench to test the constitutional validity of the Public Schools Act. Two years of concerted political pressure had failed to produce any results; in fact, the FPCP reminded Manitobans, no provincial government had voluntarily amended its education legislation to make it conform to the Charter. Court decisions in Ontario and Alberta had confirmed that s. 23 rights comprised the right to school governance by parents of the linguistic minority. The community was assured that the Comité directeur's request for funds from the Court Challenges Program would be successful. It was time to stem the assimilation of Franco-Manitobans with the aid of school governance.[41]

Deciding on the nature and timing of the legal challenge proved far more difficult than the Comité directeur and its affiliates had anticipated. A dispute erupted between the FPCP and the SFM over a whole range of issues related to the preparation and submission of the case on 26 September 1986. Uneasy about not only the lack of progress in the case but also the two-month delay the court had granted the province, SFM President Réal Sabourin sought advice from two constitutional lawyers at a Montreal conference organized by the Commission nationale des parents francophones in late November. One of them, Michel Bastarache, evaluated the FPCP's court submission and found its approach seriously flawed because, by trying to fight too many battles in one case, the group would make it impossible for the court to exercise its discretionary powers in a way that would guarantee victory for Franco-Manitobans. In Bastarache's view, a successful ruling under s. 23 could be obtained in two ways. The first would be a broad approach based on the principles of s. 23 that sought to obtain a general declaration on the unconstitutionality of certain sections of the Education Act and/or its regulations, which might lead to a political settlement. Used in the Ontario reference case, this method produced only limited results. The second approach would be to focus on a specific case in which a group of Franco-Manitoban parents could demonstrate a violation of their s. 23 rights with very extensive evidence in hand, and to request a mandatory court ordinance against their school board and the Attorney General. Bastarache considered it imperative that the FPCP and SFM adopt a specific approach, because it would produce more immediate, tangible results. "Il faut établir," he concluded, "qu'en dépit de l'inconstitutionnalité de la loi scolaire, il existe un devoir pour la cour d'assurer le respect de la constitution et de la mise en oeuvre de l'article 23; de là l'utilité d'un recours direct contre un conseil scolaire pour le forcer à prendre des measures d'application immédiates."[42]

Armed with this legal opinion, on 2 December Sabourin informed the FPCP of his organization's deep concerns. He charged it with having broken the agreement among all member organizations of the Comité directeur whereby a Franco-Manitoban lawyer would be hired to present the case once either Michel Bastarache or Pierre Foucher had been fully consulted before a submission was made to the court. This condition was a *sine qua non* for all the francophone organizations, including the SFM, to support the application for funds from the Court Challenges Program. As of December, the FPCP had not gathered all the evidence required for the case; this failure threatened to delay the legal process considerably. Sabourin revealed that both Bastarache and Pierre Foucher had advised the SFM that it was not too late to revise the four questions before the Court of Queen's Bench in order to make sure that any positive ruling would force the government to act expeditiously. He called for a meeting of both boards of directors and other member associations as soon as possible to clarify these matters.[43]

FPCP President Gilbert Savard was outraged at both the substance and the aggressive tone of Sabourin's comments. He asked whether Sabourin had consulted the SFM's Administrative Council or the other members of the Comité directeur before charging the FPCP with a lack of sincerity bordering on dishonesty. Savard denied that there had ever existed a *sine qua non* condition that the Comité directeur's counsel, Laurent Roy, must consult specific lawyers before presenting the submission. He did, however, concur that not all the evidence required for the case had been gathered; the FPCP was waiting to hear from the province as to whether it would agree to a reference of the matter to the Manitoba Court of Appeal and was unwilling to spend its limited funds on lawyers and specialists until it was imperative to do so. Savard was furious that Sabourin had consulted Bastarache and Foucher while attending the conference of the Commission nationale des parents francophones. Moreover, he questioned Bastarache's argument that revising the FPCP's submission to focus on a specific case in order to guarantee that the ruling went beyond the general principles established in the Ontario reference case would force the Manitoba legislature to act more quickly in the event of a positive result. Savard believed that Sabourin had over-reacted to the questionable advice proffered by the two constitutional lawyers and asked him to stop making accusations, in the broader interests of the Franco-Manitoban community.[44]

Cooler heads prevailed: the SFM and the FPCP arrived at a mutual understanding in order to allow the court case to go forward with the full cooperation of all parties. The Comité directeur resumed its meetings in early January 1987.[45] Furthermore, the SFM received additional legal advice from Michel Bastarache, who communicated his concern that the FPCP's lawyer, Laurent Roy, did not appear to be giving his or Pierre Foucher's suggestions the attention they deserved. He reiterated with greater precision his former critique of the FPCP's submission to the Court of Queen's Bench. In his learned opinion, it failed to ask directly whether specific sections of the Public School Act were unconstitutional and, if so, in what respects. If the group was taking the general approach it was imperative to ask this pointed question. The submission was flawed because it did not compel the court to rule that the province had a duty to assure Franco-Manitoban parents local representation on school boards, central administration, or, most importantly, the exercise of full school governance. In addressing the important issue of educational services of equal quality the submission had to link it to the concept of a homogeneous French school whose program was distinct from that of an immersion school serving the majority. Finally, the submission failed to raise two crucial issues: the problem of the geographic boundaries of the existing school divisions, which prevented regrouping; and the need to guarantee transportation for Franco-Manitoban students under the Public Schools Act.[46] These were not mere petty legal wrangles but important questions of procedure and argument that could make or break the FPCP's and SFM's case for school governance.

Fearful of the financial costs and other risks inherent in pursuing a court challenge, the FPCP and SFM lobbied the Pawley government vigorously throughout 1986 to undertake a reference case in the Manitoba Court of Appeal. In December, the premier announced that his government intended to do so and the Attorney General called on the interested parties to make suggestions as to the number and form of the questions that should come before the court.[47] The ensuing process was arduous and highly frustrating. SFM President Lucille Blanchette, writing on behalf of the Comité directeur, complained to the premier in September 1987 that the "legal beagles" in the Attorney General's office appeared to be imposing unwarranted and unacceptable delays. Furthermore, they were framing questions "contraire aux engagements originaux du Ministre de l'Éducation ainsi qu'à la direction qu'a voulu donner la Fédération provinciale des comités de parents francophones à son projet ce contestation de septembre 1986." She called on the premier to convene a meeting of all the parties to the promised reference case to prevent further delays.[48] Her letter finally brought the desired result; by Order in Council no. 74, dated 20 January 1988, the province initiated a reference on certain aspects of its Public Schools Act. Franco-Manitoban organizations and parents expected a decision at least as favourable as those in Ontario and Alberta.

The court battles placed enormous strain on the FPCP, which always lacked sufficient funds even for its day-to-day operations. A financial crisis in 1986 almost closed down the operations of the Comité directeur, until the Secretary of State came to the rescue by giving the FPCP more funds.[49] Gaining access to funding under the Court Challenges Program also proved more difficult than the FPCP's board of directors had anticipated. Through the Commission nationale des parents francophones, the FPCP pleaded with the Secretary of State to earmark 2 per cent of the budget of the Official Languages in Education Program for parents' groups, so they could play an effective role as intervenors in the work for s. 23 rights. FPCP President André Frechette asked the SFM to support this reallocation of funds.[50] The latter's board of directors took the opportunity to spell out the terms of the working relationship between the SFM and the FPCP on the issue of school governance. As long as the FPCP respected "le mandat officiel de la SFM de faire les démarches politiques en éducation auprès des instances gouvernementales," the SFM was willing to support an increase in the grant to the FPCP from the Official Languages in Education Program.[51]

Determined to act as a privileged intervenor in the reference case, the SFM applied in its turn to the Court Challenges Program in early May 1988. With Michel Bastarache's assistance, it received a grant of $18,000, then a second grant of $11,000. Ordinarily intervenors were not eligible for grants. But, since this was a reference case, the Canadian Council on Social Development, which administered the Court Challenges Program, decided to provide funding to the FPCP as principal intervenor. It would have been politically impossible for the CCSD to then deny the request of the SFM. Furthermore, the CCSD recognized that Michel Bastarache, the SFM's lawyer, was one of the leading experts in the field of linguistic litigation under the Charter; his contribution to the court proceedings would be invaluable.[52] The funding allowed both the FPCP and the SFM to put the best possible case before the Manitoba Court of Appeal.

PARTIAL VICTORY
IN THE MANITOBA COURT OF APPEAL

A detailed look at the reasoning of the justices in the Manitoba reference case provides insights into the complexity of the issues before the court. It also reveals the enormous ideological and political hurdles that had to be passed before any degree of judicial consensus could be achieved; the justices were too closely bound to their historical, social, and political context to render a truly objective decision on such a sensitive matter as school governance.

The questions placed before the Manitoba Court of Appeal were as follows:

(a)(i) Does the combined effect of section 79(3) and 79(4) and 79(7) of The Public Schools Act meet Manitoba's Constitutional obligations pursuant to section 23 of the Canadian Charter of Rights and Freedoms, insofar as the number of students entitled to instruction in the minority language is concerned?

(ii) If the combined effect of those subsections does not meet these obligations,

(aa) may the legislature specify any number as either a minimum number or guideline for the provision of French language instruction? or

(bb) may the legislature delegate the determination of a minimum number or whether numbers warrant the provision of instruction, to a school board, minister or other body?

(b) What does the right to have one's children receive instruction "in minority language educational facilities" guaranteed by section 23(3)(b) of the Charter mean? In particular, does it include the right to have one's children receive instruction in a distinct physical setting?

(c)(i) Do section 23 and section 15 of the Charter grant any right of management or control in connection with section 23's guarantees of French language instruction and facilities?

(ii) If so, do the provisions in Part I, II, and III of The Public Schools Act concerning the formation of school divisions and districts, the election of school boards, and the powers and duties of school boards meet Manitoba's constitutional obligations with reference to such a right of management or control? If not, in what essential elements do the provisions fail to do so?[53]

Chief Justice Michel A. Monnin wrote the central decision, while Justices Gordon C. Hall, Joseph F. O'Sullivan, and A. Kerr Twaddle, with Alan R. Philp concurring, wrote separate dissenting decisions on some of the questions. In theory, the justices of the Manitoba Court of Appeal, like those of Ontario, opted for a generous and liberal, rather than legalistic, interpretation of the Charter. To them, the Constitution "is necessarily capable of growth and there exists a need for a broad perspective of approach: the 'living tree' doctrine. The meaning of a right or freedom is to be ascertained by an analysis of the purpose of that guarantee."[54] The Chief Justice addressed head-on the argument of Justice Jean Beetz in *Société des Acadiens du N.B. Inc. v. Assn. of Parents for Fairness in Education, Grand Falls Dist. Branch 50 (1986)* to the effect that language rights, unlike legal rights, were the result of a political compromise and therefore had to be approached with considerable restraint. "I have no difficulty," he retorted, "with the notion that legal and language rights are conceptually different, but I balk at the suggestion that they would not carry the same weight and I am of the view that they ought to be treated with the same respect and with the same generosity and liberalism as other rights." Chief Justice Monnin was confident that Justice Beetz's call for judicial restraint should not be applied to minority language education rights. S. 23 did not warrant that "extra caution or overabundance of caution must be used in interpreting it or that such interpretation must be very narrow in order not to disturb the political compromise."[55] The purpose of s. 23 of the Charter was to "advance the prime element of Canadian nationhood by fostering the greater use of the English and French languages by official minority groups across the entire breadth of Canada." Accordingly, it was open to the courts "'to breathe life into a (political) compromise that is clearly expressed'."[56] Chief Justice Monnin's views were eminently sensible, yet they failed to produce a consensus among the judges, especially on the central issue of governance.

On all aspects of question (a) the Manitoba Court of Appeal ruled by and large in favour of the francophone organizations. With Justice Hall dissenting, the court decided that s. 79 of the Public Schools Act

violated s. 23 rights in at least three ways. First, it stipulated that specific numbers of students – twenty-eight at the elementary level and
twenty-three at the secondary level – were required before Franco-
Manitoban parents could obtain French language education for their
children following a formal petition. Second, s. 79 called for the delivery of all instruction within the boundaries of the existing school districts or divisions. Third, the section required a petition from Franco-
Manitoban parents before their rights under s. 23 could be initiated.
The court also ruled, with Chief Justice Monnin dissenting, that the
legislature could neither specify any number for the provision of
French language education nor delegate that task "to a school board,
minister or other body." The legislature could, however, determine
"whether numbers warrant," subject to a review of its decision by the
courts. It was therefore imperative for the Manitoba Legislative Assembly to positively legislate s. 23 rights rather than continually defer its
obligations to the Minister of Education and the bureaucracy.[57]

On question (b), all the judges with the exception of Justice Hall
responded in the affirmative. Considering that the Attorney General
of Manitoba had argued in great detail in his factum that the existing
Franco-Manitoban schools constituted a network of "minority language educational facilities" within the meaning of the Charter, it was
logical to conclude that "facilities" meant "a totally distinct and separate physical setting or building, not one shared with any other
group."[58] The FPCP and SFM were especially pleased with this part of
the ruling, but the Manitoba government, insisting that the justices
had misconstrued both the facts and the argument in its factum,
would later refer question (b) to the Supreme Court.

School governance, addressed in question (c), proved to be the
most controversial and complex matter confronting the court. After
reviewing carefully the extensive evidence and arguments presented
by the Attorney General, the FPCP, and all the intervenors as to the
origin and eventual formulation of s. 23 of the Charter, the Manitoba
Court of Appeal concluded that the section contained neither an
explicit nor an implicit right of governance. The justices were convinced that Minister of Justice Jean Chrétien and the members of the
Special Joint Committee had grappled at length with the issue during
the 1980–81 hearings on the constitutional resolution, only to conclude that the provinces had exclusive control over education, including the crucial responsibility of determining the governance of
schools. In fact, francophone organizations had pleaded with Chrétien
and the Special Joint Committee to amend the resolution to make the
right to governance explicit, to no avail. "Regrettably," wrote Justice
Monnin, "the framers of s. 23 did not go so far as granting governance;

in point of fact they could not since the final say in matters of education remains by virtue of our Constitution in the hands of each of the
respective provinces."[59] The Manitoba justices felt it was their duty to
defend provincial autonomy against any intrusions that might evolve
from a misconstruction of the Charter.

Justice O'Sullivan made a particularly valiant effort to undermine
what he considered to be the two fundamental assumptions underlying the FPCP's and other intervenors' claims to school governance.
Quoting Pierre Trudeau, he rejected the argument that s. 23 conferred collective rights on the linguistic minorities; instead, rights
under the section pertained to individuals, not collectivities. Furthermore, according to O'Sullivan, s. 27 of the Charter, which enshrined
multiculturalism, belied the notion that the Constitution entrenched
the principle of official biculturalism, French Canadian and English
Canadian. "In accordance with the liberal tradition in Canada," he
opined, "governments are not concerned about official cultural
values." Furthermore, he regarded it as important to guarantee that
the constitutional right of Franco-Manitoban Roman Catholics to publicly funded denominational schools was not undermined by such
organizations as the FPCP and the SFM, which wanted governance over
a new system of French language secular schools.[60]

Justice Twaddle, with the concurrence of Justice Philp, offered
lengthy arguments that appeared inferentially to support the French
language education policy proposal being offered by the province to
Franco-Manitobans. He favoured a parallel system of French education for Franco-Manitoban students equal to that available to English-
speaking Manitobans. But, as he emphasized time and time again, this
goal must not be accomplished by undermining the complete autonomy of each province in the field of education. While acknowledging
that s. 23 "undoubtedly limits provincial autonomy in the field of education," Justice Twaddle contended that the recognition of an implicit
right of governance entailed a transfer of provincial control to a
minority. It was his learned opinion that "a transfer of the right of governance from the province as a whole to those of its linguistic minority would constitute a massive intrusion into provincial autonomy in
the field of education. So massive would that intrusion be that I would
expect to find it made by a constitutional amendment expressed in
much clearer language than found in s. 23."[61] For Twaddle, as for all
his colleagues, provincial autonomy was sacrosanct.

Chief Justice Monnin found these arguments on governance highly
persuasive and very difficult to counter. Nevertheless, hoping to
salvage the situation for Franco-Manitoban parents, he propounded
that the right could be justified more directly under s. 15 than under

s. 23. To him it was patently clear that the basic equality rights of Franco-Manitobans – "a discrete and insular minority" – had been violated repeatedly over several decades. It was the duty of the Manitoba legislature or the Cabinet to rectify this longstanding pattern of discrimination by granting Franco-Manitobans one or more school divisions or districts with an unfettered right of governance. This historically based line of argument was not very convincing. Justice Twaddle was quick to dismiss it on the grounds that the "particularized bases on which discrimination is banned do not include language."[62] The equality rights clause, s. 15, was of no assistance.

No doubt the outcry of the FPCP and the SFM against the decision of the Manitoba Court of Appeal would have been much louder had the Supreme Court not come to their rescue in March 1990 with the favourable ruling in *Mahé* that approved the principle of school governance on the basis of a vague sliding scale formula necessitated by the "where numbers warrant" clause. Furthermore, while the reference case was before the Manitoba Court of Appeal, the FPCP and SFM were working diligently to extract a political settlement from the Manitoba government. The process proved considerably more difficult than Franco-Manitoban leaders had imagined because the province's NDP and Conservative governments became embroiled in the Meech Lake Accord. In fact, it was in the Manitoba Legislative Assembly that the Accord ultimately foundered in late June 1990, when an aboriginal MLA, Elijah Harper, refused to grant permission to alter the rules in order to enable his colleagues to ratify the deal.

PREPARING FOR SCHOOL GOVERNANCE

A series of educational developments at the community level throughout the 1970s and 80s provided the infrastructure that would serve as both catalyst and vehicle in the grassroots struggle for school governance for Franco-Manitobans. In a political twist, the cause was given renewed momentum in 1988 with the defeat of the NDP by a Conservative government led by Gary Filmon. Unlike his predecessor Stirling Lyon, Filmon was sympathetic towards Franco-Manitobans and wanted to consolidate his party's political support among them.

In March 1987 the Comité directeur had established the Comité ad hoc de planification de la gestion scolaire au Manitoba – CAP, as it was known – to outline the details of a school governance model for Franco-Manitobans. The CAP's six educational experts and administrators issued its report, *La gestion des écoles: un modèle à suivre*, in January 1988. According to the 1981 census, the constituency in the governance issue comprised 31,000 Franco-Manitobans who claimed

French as their maternal language – an alarming decline of some 30,000 since the 1961 census. The CAP estimated that the assimilation rate reached a peak of 34 per cent in the 1970s, stabilizing at around 20 per cent in the 1980s. By 1987–88 there were 5,678 Franco-Manitoban children enrolled in French schools, a sharp decline from 9,523 in 1974–75. The alarming trend demonstrated all too vividly the urgency of achieving school governance.

Assimilation statistics had sparked the creation of the FPCP in 1976. By 1988 it had twenty-four school committees and thirty-four kindergarten committees under its jurisdiction, to the end of drawing more Franco-Manitoban children into a French language education experience. In contrast, the French immersion schools had nearly 15,000 students registered in 1987–88, up dramatically from a mere 652 in 1974–75. A study undertaken by the Commission nationale des parents francophones calculated that nearly 70 per cent of eligible Franco-Manitoban students were enrolled in English language or immersion schools. It seemed clear that, once the mixed French/English schools were closed, many Franco-Manitoban parents opted for English or French immersion schools, thereby creating tensions within certain communities.[63]

The driving force behind the movement to expand French language education came from the thousand teachers employed in the growing number of French minority and immersion schools. The Éducatrices et éducateurs francophones du Manitoba formed a sub-group within the Manitoba Teachers' Society. Its members were highly conscious of their leadership role in the struggle against assimilation and for ultimate school governance. They had the support of over thirty Commissaires d'écoles franco-manitobaines in a dozen school boards or districts. These elected officials belonged to the Manitoba Association of School Trustees but were eager to have their own boards or districts to administer all the French schools, as well as their own trustees' association where they could do their work in French.[64] The Collège de Saint-Boniface offered French language post-secondary education to Franco-Manitoban high school graduates. It had a Faculty of Arts and Sciences as well as a Faculty of Education, which trained teachers for the province's French and immersion schools. The college educated the Franco-Manitoban elites and served as a social and cultural centre for many of the community's major events and celebrations.[65]

By the 1980s, Franco-Manitoban professional educational organizations had established a solid presence within the provincial bureaucracy. Within a few years of the introduction of a comprehensive French curriculum in 1970, the Ministry of Education created the Bureau de l'éducation française to oversee all French language education programs throughout the province. The BÉF offered a French library service and prepared pedagogical material in that language for the ministry and teachers. It administered supplementary grants amounting to $1.4 million to school divisions providing French language education: $200 per student. Cost-shared by the Secretary of State in Ottawa, the grants allowed the school boards to provide a degree of equity in services offered to children in all three school systems – French, immersion, and English. According to the French education policy developed by the BÉF and endorsed by the ministry in 1985, the primary role of the French schools was to reinforce and promote the cultural dimensions of the Franco-Manitoban community, which were integrated with the entire curriculum and teaching methodologies. This policy was not always possible to apply because the Ministry of Education did not provide funds to enable much interaction among students located in the geographically dispersed French language schools.[66]

While great strides had been made in French language education since 1967, and especially since 1974, the CAP contended that the primary problem facing its further development was the absence of school governance by Franco-Manitobans. The English-speaking majority's control over the province's school boards and districts meant that francophone parent committees continually had to convince trustees of the legitimacy of their children's different needs. Furthermore, Franco-Manitoban students, teachers, and administrators were isolated from one another and forced to function in English once they left the classroom. In fact, a 1987 Ministry of Education study, the FRAME Report, revealed that – notwithstanding the supplemental grants – it cost on average $200 per student *less* to educate students in French schools than in English schools. It was becoming apparent that the integrated system worked to the economic disadvantage of Franco-Manitobans. "Le contrôle politique par les Francophones," concluded the CAP, "signifierait la fin du cercle vicieux de la tutelle politique où la minorité doit s'appliquer sans cesse à convaincre des intermédiaires qui n'ont d'oreilles, en dernière analyse, que pour la majorité des électeurs."[67]

The CAP then asked what sort of school governance model would meet the needs of Franco-Manitobans while complying with all the education rights spelled out in s. 23 and the equality rights in s. 15. All Franco-Manitoban parents had the right to choose French language classes for their children, regardless of numbers. Second, when there were sufficient numbers to constitute several classes, as in many communities, the parents had the right to obtain minority language education facilities separate from majority language facilities. Third, when one or more francophone schools existed, Franco-Manitoban parents had the right to obtain partial or complete governance over them by electing some of the school trustees to the majority board or all of the trustees to a French minority board. Given that the intent of s. 23 was remedial, additional funding should be granted not only to redress the damage done by neglect but also to make sure that the level of education offered in minority language schools was of the same quality as in the majority language schools. Finally, the CAP argued that an effective model would allow Franco-Manitoban parents to transform their schools into the active social, cultural, and linguistic community centres so essential to the health of their communities.[68]

The CAP recommended that Manitoba's Public Schools Act, 1987 be made to comply with s. 23 of the Charter. At the heart of the proposed amendments was the right of Franco-Manitoban parents to a single province-wide francophone school board. Eleven trustees would be responsible for administering all Franco-Manitoban schools in conjunction with four regional councils made up of representatives from their respective local school committees. Under the CAP's proposed model, each of the three rural regional councils would elect two trustees, while the urban council would elect five trustees to the francophone board. This system would engender equitable funding for all regions and all schools while giving Franco-Manitoban parents the challenge and rewards of governing – in the broadest sense of the term – the future of their children's education.[69] It was a bold and imaginative approach that would galvanize the attention of the community, its leaders, and the government over the ensuing years, as everyone concerned awaited the decisions, first of the Manitoba Court of Appeal, then of the Supreme Court in both the *Mahé* case and the appeal of the Manitoba reference case.

As we have seen, the ruling of the Manitoba Court of Appeal was distressing to the FPCP and the SFM because it rejected the concept of the right of Franco-Manitobans to any degree of school governance. Fortunately, the judicial setback proved temporary when the Supreme Court decision in the *Mahé* case was handed down the following month. FPCP President Jacques Gagnon wrote to Premier Gary Filmon to request a meeting of representatives of the SFM, the FPCP, the Comité directeur, three prominent members of the Franco-Manitoban community, the premier, the Minister of Education, and the Attorney General to discuss what steps the government was contemplating in light of the decision. Gagnon hoped that the parties might agree on a plan of action to design and implement a school governance system for Franco-Manitobans.[70] Filmon agreed to meet with the delegation; one of its members, Guy Jourdain, a well-known Franco-Manitoban lawyer in the firm Pitblado & Hoskins, prepared a brief for the encounter. It called on the premier to give his government's consent to "une ordonnance de la Cour suprême du Canada qui infirmerait, pour ce qui est du principe de la gestion, la décision rendue par la Cour d'appel du Manitoba concernant le renvoi sur la validité de la Loi sur le écoles publiques." A time frame should be stipulated for amending the offending aspects of the Public Schools Act, 1987 during which existing legislation would remain valid. The brief also recommended that the province set up a working group mandated to formulate the required amendments to the Act and to develop a detailed plan for the implementation of school governance. The working group would include representatives from all six Franco-Manitoban educational organizations as well as specialists in the financial, administrative, and pedagogical aspects of school governance.[71]

The Filmon government accepted the proposal to form a working group but flatly rejected the rest. On 2 August 1990 Minister of Education and Training Len Derkach announced the creation of the Manitoba Task Force on Francophone Schools Governance. He noted that the government had selected Edgar Gallant, former secretary to the Economic Council of Canada and to the Federal/Provincial Constitutional Conference and former chair of the Public Service Commission and the National Capital Commission, to head up the Task Force. Gallant had chaired similar task forces on French education in British Columbia and Saskatchewan and was fully conversant with the complex issues of implementing school governance.[72]

The Task Force was not fully operational until 5 November 1990, when Derkach announced its complete slate of members and its mandate, which was to "examine all issues surrounding the governance of Franco-Manitoban schools and to advise the government on all matters related to the establishment of a school governance system for Franco-Manitobans, who have the right of management and control of schools according to a Supreme Court of Canada ruling in March 1990." In addition to Edgar Gallant as chair, the Task Force included two representatives from the Ministry of Education and Training; two representatives from the Manitoba Teachers' Society, one anglophone and one francophone; and one representative from each of the Manitoba Association of School Business Officials, the Manitoba Association of School Trustees, the Manitoba Association of School Superintendents, the Franco-Manitoban School Trustees, the SFM, and the FPCP. The minister asked the Task Force to submit its report by 31 May 1991.[73]

Edgar Gallant was very keen to take on the challenge of finding a solution to the issue at hand. He quickly met with the various groups that had requested representation on the Task Force and was impressed by their positive outlook and eagerness. Gallant saw his role as facilitator for a team of well-informed educational specialists who would work hard to reach a consensus on the school governance model best suited for Franco-Manitobans and on the most effective way to implement it. As a firm supporter of the Charter, in his view the entrenchment of two official languages and s. 23 education rights were revitalizing the noble vision of linguistic duality. He told delegates at a conference in late October 1990: "That is the Canada I wish to see for my children and my grandchildren and their children! That is the Canada I believe we all have a responsibility to promote if we want our country to survive."[74] In order to keep all the member organizations of the Comité directeur informed of the Task Force's progress, the FPCP announced that the work of the former would be suspended for several months. In the interim, its functions would be undertaken by the Conseil des présidents et des présidentes, with the aim of maximizing the effectiveness of their respective representatives on the Task Force.[75]

The Task Force in large measure adopted the basic principles that had been put forward by the six organizations forming the Comité directeur. A Franco-Manitoban system of school governance must promote full accessibility for all students covered by s. 23 of the Charter; preserve and promote the French language and culture; offer a quality of education on par with that available to majority language students; have a guaranteed source of funding; be flexible and adaptable to the needs of the students, teachers, staff, and community, especially during the transition years; encourage the full participation of Franco-Manitoban parents at every level of governance; operate within the framework of the provincial public school system; and function in French.[76]

The Task Force also evaluated various school governance models in use throughout Canada. Ontario's "proportional and guaranteed" model maintained the existing school divisions and boards; Franco-Ontarians elected their own members to a board on the basis of the proportion of francophone students enrolled. The "dual map" system – found in New Brunswick, Prince Edward Island, and the Ottawa-Carleton region of Ontario – involved the creation of distinct school divisions and boards for each official language, though the boundaries often overlapped. The "small local councils and provincial council" model, under discussion for Saskatchewan, resembled the dual map model but did not grant local councils taxing powers. The Frontier School Division, which served students throughout Manitoba's vast northland, had features that could be applied to a Franco-Manitoban model. Following some indirect consultation with rural communities, the Task Force opted for a variant of the dual map model. One school board for the entire province was recommended, because it would be less costly and more efficient to administer; it would also lead to a more consistent approach to Franco-Manitoban education and more effective negotiations with the government. This "made in Manitoba" solution entailed elected local school committees as advisory bodies to the school principals, the regional councils, and the school board. The francophone school division would have four regional councils: one comprising metropolitan Winnipeg; one for the eastern region, incorporating the Seine River division; one for the central region, comprising the Red River division; and one for the western region, taking in French schools in the Mountain, Turtle River, and Birdtail divisions. The needs of Franco-Manitoban students outside the geographical limits of these divisions would have to be addressed on an individual basis. The regional councils would serve as two-way conduits between the boards and their respective schools on curriculum, budgets, special student services, transportation, and coordination of cultural activities.

After much discussion, the Task Force proposed that "the regional councils should be the directly elected level, with representation from each community or group of communities encompassing a school." They would then select trustees from among their members, two each for the three rural regional councils and five for Winnipeg, for a total board membership of eleven. The francophone division and board would have the same powers and responsibilities as all the others, except the power to levy property taxes. In addition, because of the special needs and goals pertaining to minority language education and the unique governance structure, the francophone board should have a statutory obligation to consult regularly with the regional councils about all program and budgetary matters and hear all delegations from local schools and communities. Because of the remedial intent of s. 23, it "should have enhanced responsibilities and capacity to promote cultural activity throughout the division." These should include coordinating the pre-school program with the regular school program in order to capture a greater percentage of the potential French language school population and operating an outreach and information service for Franco-Manitobans outside the division.[77]

Also recommended was that all the "partial French program schools" be integrated within the new system and phased out over five years. An advisory admissions committee should be created to evaluate the linguistic abilities of certain students eligible under s. 23 and stream the non-French speakers into remedial classes before allowing them into the mainstream. Hoping to broaden the support base for the francophone school division, the Task Force posited that "the right to participate in governance should extend to anyone who would qualify under Section 23 if they had school age children." The sole proviso was that every regional councillor or trustee required an active knowledge of French, since that was to be the only language of internal operations. The Task Force also made some pertinent and sensible recommendations to effect a smooth transition for approximately 380 teachers and 145 support, technical, and administrative personnel from the existing division employers to the francophone employer.[78]

At the heart of the autonomy and power of the new francophone division were the financial arrangements. It "must be guaranteed, by legislation, full support annually for legitimate expenditures for preservation and promotion of minority language and culture within Section 23 of the Charter." It should receive the basic provincial grants and, in addition – since it would not have a right to either local property taxation or special levy – it should get the appropriate grants for each Franco-Manitoban student residing within the various anglophone school divisions who opted for French language education. The Task Force envisaged additional costs associated with economies of scale, general administration over a dispersed geographic area, transportation, higher-cost French textbooks and teaching aids, and a wide range of remedial measures. It urged the provincial government to legislate additional funding while attempting to recover some of these costs through an agreement with Ottawa.[79]

The Task Force was particularly concerned with establishing an implementation process that would involve all concerned Franco-Manitobans and with setting a timetable for school governance that would meet community expectations without compromising other important objectives. It suggested that the government take several steps:

- announcing its intention to proceed immediately with the recommended system
- setting up an Implementation Support Team comprised of all the appropriate representatives
- enacting amendments to the required legislation
- consulting with all schools to determine which would opt into the new division
- undertaking the election of regional councils and school board trustees
- preparing a detailed plan of transfer of personnel and assets, the location of the new school board, and budget preparations

While many Franco-Manitobans wanted school governance in place by September 1992, the Task Force's report noted that it might be more realistic to set September 1993 as the target date.[80]

Hoping to influence the Task Force's recommendations and prepare for the government's response, the FPCP undertook a province-wide consultation of fifty pre-school and school committees and other community groups comprising more than 1200 parents in order to educate them about all aspects of the school governance question and explain the principles in *Mahé*. It then gathered feedback on various school governance models and aspects of the implementation process. Its hope was to mobilize Franco-Manitobans' opinion against the recalcitrant provincial government once the Task Force published its report. At the FPCP's Annual Assembly of 6 April 1991, delegates passed forty recommendations on all aspects of school governance based on its consultations; these were later submitted to the Task Force. The vast majority of Franco-Manitoban parents wanted the province to stick to its promise of school governance by September 1992. The FPCP stated that it was imperative for the government to strike a working group, including representatives of parents' groups, to assist the provisional francophone school board and the Ministry of Education with implementing the Task Force's recommendations.[81] The strategy worked beautifully; the Task Force's report mirrored nearly all the recommendations adopted by the FPCP at its annual meeting. As always, it would prove considerably more difficult to influence the provincial government.

Minister of Education Len Derkach made the report public on 27 June 1991. He noted the unanimous nature of the Task Force's endorsement of a single francophone school division and board, as well as the fact that the immersion schools would not be part of the new structure. Derkach said that the government would carefully analyse the Gallant Report (as it was now called) before presenting legislative measures to implement school governance.[82] The FPCP, with the support of the Conseil des présidents et des présidentes, issued a press release announcing its overall satisfaction with the Gallant Report, especially the call for a single francophone school division and board. The FPCP challenged the Filmon government to set up an implementation committee immediately so it could meet its promised deadline of September 1992, and gave assurance that it would remain "doublement vigilants afin d'empêcher qu'un manque de volonté d'agir ne s'installe et retarde encore plus longuement l'obtention de la gestion scolaire si longtemps recherchée par les Franco-Manitobains."[83]

The SFM was very pleased with the report. Its president, Raymond Bisson, thanked Edgar Gallant for his effective chairship. The only thing that remained was for the province to follow the Task Force's recommendations.[84] But thanks to a July 1991 letter from feisty Liberal leader Sharon Carstairs fully endorsing the report, the SFM became aware that that the Filmon government, facing strong opposition from many of its backbenchers, would most likely procrastinate.[85] During a meeting with Len Derkach on 8 October, the FPCP was told that an internal committee had been struck to study the report and the minister could not discuss the issue until he received its assessment sometime in January 1992. In a speech at the SFM's annual meeting on 1 November, the premier also promised that he would reveal his government's response early in the new year.[86]

True to form, however, the Filmon government took nine months to review the Gallant Report. On 20 March 1992 the premier met with the Conseil des présidents et des présidentes to make known the province's decision to act on school governance. Details of the long-awaited policy were made public by a new Minister of Education, Rosemary Vodrey, on 26 March 1992. In her provocative press release the minister announced that "Based on the Gallant report the government plan will provide for one administrative jurisdiction to govern the francophone schools in those communities that choose to participate. The new francophone school board will be composed of trustees from the elected regional councils and will have the same basic powers and responsibilities as other school divisions in Manitoba. Local school committees will be established in each community to serve in an advisory capacity." Vodrey noted that the unique feature of the model was that it gave francophone communities the choice of joining the new francophone school board or remaining within their current school division, which would be allowed to continue offering existing French language programs to s. 23 students as well as to others. She also introduced the Implementation Support Team, which comprised all the stakeholders that would help her ministry set up the new system by September 1994.[87]

Immediately following Vodrey's statement, the FPCP, speaking on behalf of the Conseil des présidents et des présidentes and backed by the Fédération in Ottawa, issued a press release denouncing the plan as unconstitutional and illegal. "En acceptant de permettre à des divisions scolaires autres que la commission scolaire francophone de dispenser un enseignement en français langue première, le gouvernement du Manitoba va à l'encontre de la Charte canadienne des droits et libertés."[88] If the Manitoba model was to comply with s. 23, it had to guarantee that only the francophone school board would have the right to manage French minority education. Schools refusing to join the new board could no longer be called French minority language schools. The FPCP viewed this part of the proposal as a devious way of undermining the much-needed solidarity within the Franco-Manitoban community:

Cette façon de procéder vise à diluer la gestion scolaire qui serait remise aux Franco-manitobains. On veut rendre plus facile pour la collectivité de ne pas choisir son droit pour ensuite imposer à l'ensemble de la collectivité d'être soumise à une programmation scolaire en français dans un système géré par la majorité. Donc, on cherche à camoufler le statu quo sous un habit inconstitutionnel. Cette approche n'est pas conforme au jugement Mahé qui a reconnu un degré de gestion appartenant à chaque ayant droit. De plus, c'est une approche qui veut fragmenter la communauté et au bout de ligne faire en sorte que les francophones soient en moins bonne position pour répondre à leurs besoins plutôt que de créer des regroupements homogènes viables pour assurer l'épanouissement linguistique et culturel et freiner l'assimilation.[89]

This alone was enough to elicit non-cooperation from the Conseil des présidents et des présidentes, which also deemed three further elements of the plan unacceptable. First, it was outrageous that all the "intervenants de la communauté soient demandés de se prononcer sur la nécessité ou non d'adhérer à la nouvelle commission scolaire francophone." It was the government's responsibility to put the francophone school board in place, and then only Franco-Manitobans covered by s. 23 could choose whether or not they wanted their children to attend a French minority school operated by the new board. Second, a further two-year delay – until September 1994 – was unconscionable; the government must abide by the deadline of September 1992 proposed by the Task Force. Third, it was inappropriate that the Implementation Support Team was not composed entirely of representatives from francophone organizations. Given that the Supreme Court had ruled that Franco-Manitobans had the right to govern their own schools, they should also have the right to manage the implementation of their own school governance.[90]

After issuing the press release, the FPCP reiterated its demand that the premier and the Minister of Education meet immediately with the Conseil des présidents et des présidentes. When Vodrey asked for the name of the FPCP's representative on the proposed Implementation Support Team, its president, Gilbert Savard, informed her that his organization would decide on its participation only after the requested meeting with her and the premier.[91] At the meeting, held on 5 May 1992, members of the Conseil itemized all their reasons for rejecting the government's proposed school governance model, which were based on the legal opinion that it was in some respects unconstitutional. First, all French minority schools must be under the governance of Franco-Manitoban trustees. Second, admission criteria under s. 23 must be respected. Third, the program of instruction must conform to the Supreme Court judgment laid out in *Mahé*.

The Conseil proposed a political compromise. All the existing designated French minority schools would be incorporated immediately into the new francophone board without further consultation, while the implementation process announced by Vodrey would apply only to those French language schools that were not designated as homogeneous French minority schools. The Conseil let Filmon know that, if the compromise was acceptable, then the other outstanding matters could be sorted out relatively easily. If, on the other hand, it was not, then the Franco-Manitoban organizations would have no choice but to refuse to cooperate with the Implementation Support Team and to seek further guidance from their lawyers and their constituency.[92]

Filmon replied that he would seriously consider the proposed compromise, and agreed that Franco-Manitobans should constitute a majority of the team, while the other members should be fluently bilingual so it could function in French. A further meeting would be held as soon as possible to work out the details of both the Conseil's proposal and the Minister of Education's consultation process.[93] When, however, he refused to meet with the Conseil within the stipulated month, Savard informed him that the parents' groups at thirteen designated French minority schools had adopted resolutions in favour of implementing the francophone school board for September 1993. Four others had passed resolutions urging Rosemary Vodrey to begin consultations in their communities so their schools could join the established francophone board in September 1994. Savard assured Filmon that there was no disagreement among Franco-Manitobans on this crucial issue because they all understood that they had a right to school governance and had been waiting a very long time "qu'on leur fasse justice." The Conseil had offered an equitable compromise in good faith and was eagerly awaiting the promised second meeting to get things underway.[94]

That meeting never transpired; without informing the Conseil, the province decided that the compromise was unacceptable. The members learned later that Cabinet had adopted it, only to have it rejected by the caucus.[95] A meeting with the Minister of Education on 4 August produced no positive results, leaving the FPCP and SFM to wonder what the government's motives were in creating an Implementation Support Team with representatives from the anglophone educational organizations having a mandate to undertake referendums in

Franco-Manitoban communities. They concluded that the implementation group was clearly "un mécanisme d'obstruction à la mise sur pied d'un système de gestion scolaire répondant aux besoins des Franco-manitobains, nettement moindre à ce que propose le rapport Gallant et certainement pas conforme à ce que propose le jugement de la Cour suprême dans le cas Mahé."[96]

On 3 September 1992 the Conseil met to decide whether it would select from its member organizations representatives to sit on the Implementation Support Team. The francophone leaders agreed not to do so until Vodrey had outlined its mandate in greater detail, so they could assess whether it would function in the spirit of s. 23 of the Charter. As it stood, her plan was patently unconstitutional.[97] On 23 June 1992 Judge Charles Doherty Gonthier of the Supreme Court ruled that he would grant the FPCP leave to appeal the decision of the Manitoba Court of Appeal in the reference case. Hearings would begin on 3 December 1992. The Conseil became concerned that if it participated in the proposed team, which it considered unconstitutional, its appeal to the Supreme Court would be undermined.[98]

On 22 September, Vodrey announced her decision to appoint former Chief Justice Michel Alfred Monnin as chair of the Implementation Support Team, as per her plan. The team's primary mandate was "to design, facilitate and implement an enumeration process and a registration process and administer a balloting process within the approved guidelines to ascertain the will of Section 23 parents to join the model in a timely fashion." It was also to recommend a process for the election of regional councils in those communities that voted to join the new francophone school division.[99] The same day, Assistant Deputy Minister of Education John Carlyle wrote to the SFM and the FPCP asking them, for the second time, to name their representatives to the team.[100]

The Conseil was not pleased with the minister's decision to forge ahead with her unrevised implementation plan. Under it, the team would not play an interim role in school governance until the election of the new board, as recommended by the Task Force. Furthermore, it would not participate in the discussions about amending the offending clauses of the Public Schools Act to bring it in line with s. 23. Inasmuch as the Manitoba Court of Appeal had ruled in 1990 that certain clauses of the Act violated that section, it was incumbent on the government to undertake interim administrative measures to redress the situation while preparing the required amendments as quickly as possible.[101] The Conseil's member organizations were incensed that the province was refusing to proceed with the amendments before the consultations with Franco-Manitoban communities were completed and that parents with children in French minority schools were going to have to vote on whether they wanted their schools to join the new francophone division or remain under the anglophone boards. Having to make a choice was contrary to the recommendation of the Gallant Report and a clear violation of the ruling in *Mahé*.

The FPCP and SFM also warned that the province should not use its power to replace a representative from the Bureau de l'éducation française on the team with political appointees to exert control over the work. The fact that the majority would consist of four representatives from anglophone organizations and three government appointees forced the francophone groups to question the government's good faith: "La vérité c'est qu'il n'y a pas d'engagement politique de la part du gouvernement et on tente de gagner du temps en mettant sur pied un comité 'appui' encastrant les membres dans un mandat qui est inconstitutionnel, qui doit être à chaque étape sanctionné par la ministre, qui fait miroiter la domination du système majoritaire sur les francophones et qui doit aboutir au statu quo."[102] They further charged that the government's procedures threatened to create tensions and divisions within the Franco-Manitoban communities, undermining the consensus that had been achieved though their hard work and determination.

Following the advice of their lawyers, the FPCP and SFM urged the Franco-Manitoban organizations not to participate in the Implementation Support Team. "Le gouvernement nous a construit un échafaud en nous imposant ce comité de facilitation et maintenant, on nous invite à y monter en apportant notre propre corde. Nous ne devons pas devenir complice de ce qui est inconstitutionnel à notre égard."[103] They convened a meeting of the administrative boards of all the members of the Conseil on 7 October 1992 to discuss the deadlock over governance. It was also an opportunity to explain their decision to boycott the team. Edgar Gallant attended in his capacity as former chair of the Task Force. Michel Bastarache and Laurent Roy analysed the legal aspects of the government's chosen approach to school governance and explained the status of the FPCP's appeal to the Supreme Court. Those in attendance supported two decisions: the Franco-Manitoban organizations would not send representatives to the Implementation Support Team, and they would pursue the appeal of the Manitoba reference case in the Supreme Court.[104] Both were communicated to Rosemary Vodrey two days after the meeting.[105] Once again, francophone groups would have to resort to the Supreme Court before a provincial government would proceed with an acceptable approach to school governance.

THE SUPREME COURT:
SPRINGBOARD TO SCHOOL GOVERNANCE

In the hope of achieving a made in Manitoba political agreement, the FPCP and SFM had put off the appeal for two years. As in Alberta, the strategy had failed. Still, the ruling in the Manitoba reference case had forced the reluctant province to commit itself to amending the offending aspects of the Public Schools Act, and the decision in *Mahé* had induced it to proceed with designing and eventually implementing a francophone school governance model. But Franco-Manitoban parents and leaders flatly rejected the province's proposal. Faced with a legal deadline, the FPCP and SFM were obliged to pursue their appeal on the basis of the questions framed in 1987 and accepted by Judge Gonthier in June 1992, rather than on ones that directly addressed the flawed governance plan. The FPCP's arguments were supported – in whole or in part – by the Commission nationale des parents francophones, the Fédération des communautés francophones et acadiennes du Canada, the Conseil jeunesse provinciale, the Commissioner of Official Languages, and the Attorney General of Canada.

Given this barrage of opposition, it was not surprising that the first line of attack of the Attorney General of Manitoba was to argue that the appeal was moot and should not be entertained by the Supreme Court. The assertion was that, on the basis of the *Mahé* decision, Manitoba fully accepted the right of Franco-Manitoban parents to school governance. The province was proceeding as rapidly as possible with implementing a model reflecting the social, cultural, demographic, and political features of Manitoba society in general and its francophone communities in particular. Moreover, it was adhering to the principles set out in *Mahé*. The Attorney General saw no need for the Supreme Court to elaborate on them, since the questions before it were not specific to the school governance scheme proposed for Manitoba.

The questions in the appeal were the three that had received a negative response from the judges of the Manitoba Court of Appeal, (b) and both parts of (c). (Refer to pages 213–14.) The FPCP adopted an aggressive approach in its factum; it asked the Supreme Court to elaborate on the arguments and principles it had set out in *Mahé*. It also called on the justices to address, even indirectly, what they regarded as the fundamental flaws of Manitoba's proposed model. This was the FPCP's innovative way of attempting to spare Franco-Manitobans further delays, perhaps even the need to return to the Supreme Court for further guidance in the event that an unacceptable governance model became law.[106] Michel Bastarache, who prepared the factum for the Commission nationale des parents francophones, argued at some length that the appeal was most certainly not moot, nor was it an attempt to open a new reference case within the existing one. Rather, it was clear – in Justice John Sopinka's words – that a "live controversy" over conflicting principles of school governance prevailed in Manitoba and that the principles developed in *Mahé* needed to be clarified and expanded in order to address the specifics of the Manitoba context. In short, how should the sliding scale concept be applied in the province? What was the link between the offer of educational services to the minority and the duty to propose a school governance regime meeting the larger goal of s. 23? Finally, what recourse was available to the appellant in case the Manitoba legislature refused to act? In was imperative and urgent that the Supreme Court address the substance of the appeal.[107]

On the basis of the court-established remedial intent of s. 23, the FPCP drew upon the expansive sociocultural arguments of constitutional expert Pierre Foucher to answer question (b) in the affirmative. A minority language educational facility was a homogeneous French language school offering a curriculum designed to fit the needs of the minority community. "Ce 'centre scolaire communautaire' constitue un milieu linguistique et culturel reflétant la langue et les valeurs de la minorité et, de ce fait, elle suppose la disponibilité de lieux physiques distincts pour et de la minorité." According to the FPCP, these publicly-funded "educational community centres" were essential to the continued survival of the francophone communities; without them, assimilation would continue unabated and s. 23 rights would remain a dead letter.[108] Michel Bastarache made the point that the right to distinct physical facilities flowed from the obligation of the province to guarantee the full rights of the linguistic minority by doing everything possible in each case "pour rencontrer l'objet plus large de l'article 23, soit de fournir a cette minorité les meilleurs moyens éducatifs disponibles, compte tenu des nombres, de façon à promouvoire l'épanouissement de sa culture et la préservation de sa langue."[109]

Shifting his ground from the original reference case, the Attorney General of Manitoba rejected outright the FPCP's argument for homogeneous Franco-Manitoban schools – educational community centres – located in distinct physical settings. Instead, he adopted what he believed was the Supreme Court's approach to the question of "educational facilities" outlined in the *Mahé* decision, whereby "s. 23(3)(b) is intended to indicate the upper range of possible institutional requirements which may be mandated by s. 23. 'Facilities' is not to be interpreted as a reference to physical structures. Rather, the entire term 'minority language educational facilities' is to be viewed as setting out an upper level of management and control." Contrary to the argument of the appellant, the right to "a distinct physical setting" was not absolute but derived from the sliding scale concept of management and control within s. 23 as a whole and, in particular, within s. 23(3)(a). The Attorney General called on the court simply to reiterate the principles established in *Mahé* and to avoid venturing into the specifics of the Manitoba situation, since those issues were not before it.[110]

On question (c)(i), school governance, the FPCP and SFM took it for granted that there were sufficient numbers of Franco-Manitobans to warrant the establishment of an autonomous francophone school board. Indeed, this point was not being contested by the government of Manitoba. What remained in dispute was the precise nature of that board, the character and scope of its governance, and the process for implementing governance. Both old and new arguments were advanced to buttress the case that no remedial measures could be entirely effective within an educational system that remained under the control – even partially – of the linguistic majority. The two groups contended that s. 23 necessitated a wholesale reorganization of the existing system. Franco-Manitoban parents had a right to exclusive and comprehensive control over all the educational facilities of the linguistic minority. It was not acceptable for the school boards of the English-speaking majority to maintain a competing right to manage the minority's schools. Maintaining a competing, parallel system of French language school governance controlled by the majority would diminish the s. 23 rights of the minority and ultimately lead to their negation. The francophone organizations believed that this was precisely what Manitoba was proposing to do with its amendments to the Public Schools Act and its use of the province's regulatory authority to hold divisive referendums in every Franco-Manitoban community.[111]

On this central issue the Attorney General of Manitoba submitted to the Supreme Court that "for the reasons given in *Mahé* v. *Alberta*, s. 23 clearly encompasses a right of management and control over those aspects of minority language education which pertain to or have an effect upon minority language and culture. The measure of management and control required by s. 23 of the Charter depends on the number of students to be served."[112] He went on to posit that the argument that the minority must have an exclusive right of control over all French language instruction and facilities was inconsistent with the sliding scale principle set out in *Mahé*. Furthermore, the francophone groups' attempt to get the Supreme Court to rule inferentially on this principle of exclusivity was tantamount to asking it to intervene in the ongoing political dispute over the controversial issue of choice for

Franco-Manitoban parents. The Attorney General reminded the justices that the Minister of Education's 26 March 1992 policy statement on school governance was not before the court and therefore should not be addressed directly or indirectly by them.[113]

Question (c)(ii), on the constitutionality of ss. 79(3), (4), and (7) of the Public Schools Act, gave the FPCP and SFM an opportunity to apprise the Supreme Court of all the existing legislative and institutional impediments to the full exercise of Franco-Manitobans' rights under s. 23. S. 79 was not in conformity with the Charter section, and the province had not amended it following the *Mahé* decision. In emphasizing classes rather than facilities, it failed to take into account the linguistic antecedents of families; it did not require French language instruction to take place in distinct physical facilities; and, finally, it did not grant Franco-Manitobans exclusive control over their educational facilities. S. 79(3) made no mention of s. 23's admissibility criteria for distinguishing immersion students from students under s. 23. It also prescribed a minimum of twenty-three students in a given school division or district before instruction in French would be provided. Both these provisions violated s. 23, which neither specified the number of students nor restricted the boundaries of French language schools or boards to the existing ones. S. 79(4), in giving the Minister of Education discretionary power to reduce this threshold, also violated s. 23 rights. The existing institutional arrangements for minority education were such that only eight of fifty-five divisions or districts offered a French language program. The absence of vocational or special education schools for Franco-Manitobans forced many parents to incur additional costs. Funding for French language educational programs was inadequate. The attitude of the Manitoba government toward its francophone minority since the adoption of the Charter in 1982 seldom surpassed the threshold of benign neglect; indeed, it was often one of indifference and laissez-faire.[114]

The FPCP and SFM demanded bold action, arguing that, given the urgency of reversing the trend of assimilation of Franco-Manitobans, it was manifestly intolerable for the province to continue refusing to fulfill its constitutional obligations under s. 23 by denying rights that had been deliberately excluded from the "notwithstanding clause" of the Charter because they were deemed so fundamental and imperative. The appellant asked the Supreme Court to force the hand of the provincial government by declaring the entire Public Schools Act invalid by virtue of s. 52 of the Constitution Act, 1982, which established the primacy of the Constitution. Franco-Manitoban community leaders would then participate in drafting a constitutionally valid Public Schools Act; the existing one would remain in force until the end of an agreed-upon period.[115] In the words of the SFM's lawyer Michel Bastarache, "il importe que les directives concernant l'obligation de légéférer soient assez précises pour établir que le droit de gestion maximum est justifié au Manitoba et que celui-ci comporte le droit de contrôler de façon exclusive la prestation de l'instruction en français langue première."[116] While Bastarache agreed that a reference did not permit the Supreme Court to issue mandatory decrees, it was crucial for it to become more interventionist. The Commission nationale des parents francophones, for its part, urged the justices to grant the appellant "remedial directives" by setting a minimum period of delay and imposing a range of sanctions – from an injunction to financial compensation – if the deadline was not respected.[117]

The Attorney General concurred with the FPCP's and SFM's contention that the provisions of the Public Schools Act did not meet Manitoba's constitutional obligations. Given the presence of a requisite number of Franco-Manitoban students, it did not provide for school governance "over those aspects of minority language education which pertain to or have an effect upon minority language and culture."[118] He then asked the justices whether a collateral attack on the Manitoba government's policy announcement for school governance was permissible. He went on to argue forcefully that it should not be, since a "reference initiated in 1988 cannot be construed as a request for a judicial opinion on a policy announcement taken by a subsequent government after these appeal proceedings were initiated." Furthermore, the francophone organizations' adherence to the exclusivity model of school governance constituted "a fundamental misunderstanding of Charter s. 23," which neither required provinces to compel all minority parents to adhere to a single form of school governance nor prevented some minority parents from choosing to remain under the governance of majority school boards. Finally, the *Mahé* decision recognized the "plenary jurisdiction of the Legislature and the wide scope it enjoys in the choice of institutional means to implement the right of governance."[119]

The Attorney General submitted that the Supreme Court did not have jurisdiction to issue the sweeping declarations called for by the appellant; precedent clearly indicated that it could not venture beyond the three questions under consideration. The appellant's request for the Public Schools Act to be declared invalid in its entirety was inadmissible because the vast majority of its provisions were not before the court. Moreover, question (c)(ii) did not raise the validity of parts of the Act but merely asked whether they met the test of governance. Finally, even in *Mahé* the Supreme Court had refused to declare public school legislation invalid.[120] The Manitoba government considered itself bound by the principles of school governance set out in *Mahé* and informed the court that it was proceeding as quickly as possible with implementing a system of school governance for Franco-Manitobans based upon them. Only when the system was completely in place would it be both possible and appropriate for Franco-Manitobans to contest the legality of one or more of its provisions. Under these circumstances, the Attorney General reiterated, there was "no necessity or justification for this Court to raise the spectre of such draconian remedies to the Legislature or Government of Manitoba."[121]

On 4 March 1993 the justices of the Supreme Court – Chief Justice Antonio Lamer, Gérard Vincent La Forest, Claire L'Heureux-Dubé, Charles Doherty Gonthier, Peter Cory, Beverley McLachlin, and Frank Iacobucci – issued what one legal commentator appropriately dubbed "a judgment for all seasons."[122] Their clearly reasoned, zen-like unanimous decision avoided the rigid arguments and remedies advanced by both the appellant and the respondent. They took the opportunity to reiterate and expand on their approach to s. 23 rights laid out in *Mahé*. In addition to addressing the three questions before the court, they had to grapple with the new issues of "choice" and "exclusivity" raised by Manitoba's school governance policy. Asked either to affirm the principle of choice for Franco-Manitoban parents promoted by the Attorney General or to sanction the concept of exclusivity advanced by the appellant and its supporters, the justices cleverly avoiding being drawn into a conflict of principles. Instead, they decided that it was more important – and, it was hoped, more effective – to send an unambiguous message to the Manitoba government: it must promptly design and implement a system of school governance incorporating s. 23 rights and reflecting the wishes and needs of the Franco-Manitoban community.[123]

On the important matter of whether the appeal was moot, the justices were not convinced by the rather thin arguments of the Attorney General of Manitoba. "The constitutional questions as stated," they ruled with an air of disdain, "remain within the scope of the original reference, and, further, the decision of the Manitoba Court of Appeal in this case, handed down before *Mahé*, remains in conflict with this Court's decision in that case."[124] Reiterating that the courts must adopt a purposive and remedial approach to s. 23 rights and responding favourably to the Attorney General's reference to Judge Jean Beetz's reasoning in *Société des Acadiens du Nouveau-Brunswick Inc. v. Association of Parents for Fairness in Education*, the justices reintroduced the idea that language rights were founded on political compromise and were therefore of a fundamentally different nature than the other rights protected by the Charter. In short, the Supreme Court needed to be cautious and prudent before deciding to act as an agent of institutional change in the field of language rights. Finally, the justices reminded everyone that the court had determined in *Mahé* that "there is no right to a particular legislative scheme flowing from the Charter, but rather a right to a type of educational scheme."[125] Having set the parameters for their deliberations, they then addressed the questions before them.

On question (b), what was meant by instruction "in minority language education facilities," the justices reminded the nation that "the term 'facilities' should not be interpreted as a reference to physical structures alone." The right to facilities was a subsidiary matter flowing from the degree of school governance, which was determined, at the outset, by the sliding scale approach to s. 23 rights. Once the threshold of school governance was reached, the only way minority language educational facilities could belong to parents eligible under s. 23 was for them to have control over a space with defined limits, that is, a distinct physical setting. Rejecting the claim of the Manitoba government and accepting the arguments of the FPCP and SFM by extending the logic of *Mahé*, the justices declared that, if minority schools were to play a valuable role as "cultural centres" as well as educational institutions, it seemed "reasonable to infer that some distinctiveness in the physical setting is required to successfully fulfil this role." Endorsing a general right to distinct physical settings, they nevertheless considered it unwise to determine what such facilities might entail in the case of Manitoba, since the court did not have before it a specific factual or geographic setting. The kind of facilities deemed appropriate, in accordance with the standards set out in *Mahé*, might well be significantly different for Franco-Manitoban children in Winnipeg than for those in Manitoba's remote or rural areas.[126] While the FPCP and SFM stood to gain by the court's expansion of the principles established in *Mahé*, the province managed to dissuade the court from ruling directly on the specifics of the Manitoba situation.

Since the Manitoba government had agreed to accept and abide by the decision in *Mahé* pertaining to school governance, what remained in dispute was "how precise the Court should be in setting out the parameters of the management and control of language and educational facilities required under s. 23 and the Charter." The degree of governance required, the justices reiterated, was determined "by reference to both actual and potential numbers," which in Manitoba's case ranged from 5,617 – the number submitted by the province – to 18,975 – the figure claimed by the FPCP. According to the court, even the lower number fell on the high end of the sliding scale, warranting – at the least in some regions of the province – the creation of a separate francophone school board. Indeed, the justices noted that

Manitoba had already agreed to a single francophone board to oversee French education, on condition that Franco-Manitoban parents have the right to choose to keep their children in existing French minority schools. Chief Justice Antonio Lamer chastised the province for – by its own admission – not living up to its constitutional obligations since 1990: "There is a positive obligation on the province to discharge that obligation, and it must, if it is to comply with its duties under the Charter, deliver the system without delay."[127]

Since Manitoba had already conceded the matter, the court ruled emphatically on question (c)(ii) that the Public Schools Act did not meet constitutional obligations under s. 23 with regard to governance. To the great relief of the province, however, the justices – abiding by the principles set out in *Mahé* – refused to rule either on the constitutionality of its school governance plan, which offered parents a choice, or conversely on the FPCP's and SFM's claim for exclusive control by Franco-Manitobans. Nonetheless, having established the principle of non-intervention with respect to implementing specific "modalities," they did set out some lucid guidelines to assist the province with framing legislation that would meet the test of s. 23, hoping thereby to avoid further litigation.

First, the implementation of any scheme of minority language education would require the participation of Franco-Manitoban parents or their representatives in assessing educational needs and creating facilities and services. Second, inferentially addressing the referendum issue, the justices reminded the parties that s. 23 rights were granted to minority language parents and their entitlement was determined by the "where numbers warrant" provision, not by any majority among the minority. Third, in order to give Franco-Manitoban parents a meaningful choice, the province was obliged to offer their children well-advertised and accessible educational services on par with but not necessarily identical to those available to the majority. Finally, the justices inferentially ruled that the new board could not have exclusive control over francophone minority education, though at the same time they cautioned the province not to be mischievous or devious by granting Franco-Manitoban parents the right of opting out or by deliberately carving out school districts which would hamper the growth of that board. "Arrangements and structures which are prejudicial, hamper, or simply are not responsive to the needs of the minority are to be avoided and measures which encourage the development and use of minority language facilities should be considered and implemented."[128]

The Supreme Court flatly rejected the FPCP's and SFM's request to have Manitoba's unconstitutional Public Schools Act declared invalid, on the grounds that in a reference case it had only the jurisdiction to answer the questions referred to it, not the authority to apply s. 52(1) of the Constitution Act, 1982. As in *Mahé*, the court walked the fine line "between the remedial aspect of s. 23 and the need to avoid interfering in legislative discretion or implementation." Being prudent and politically sensitive, the justices chose a path midway between Manitoba's request that the court impose on it no constitutionally required course of action and the far-reaching, dramatic remedies proposed by the FPCP and the SFM for the invalidation and rewriting of provincial legislation. They thereby reinforced the ground-breaking approach adopted in *Mahé*, which married their deepseated commitment to respect for provincial rights with the longstanding need to safeguard minority education rights. In so doing, the justices displayed the wisdom of Solomon.

Michel Bastarache provided a succinct and incisive assessment of the ruling. He started by reminding the FPCP and the SFM and other intervenors of their three main objectives. The first was to confirm the impact of the *Mahé* decision on Manitoba: did it guarantee a homogeneous francophone school board for the Winnipeg metropolitan region at the very least, and did it reaffirm the general right to homogeneous French language schools wherever numbers warranted? Their second objective was to resolve the conflict over principles – choice versus exclusivity – by forming an indissoluble link between the right to a school and the right to manage it, and by demonstrating that it was unconstitutional to ask francophone parents to renounce their right to school governance. The third goal was to clarify the obligation of the Manitoba government to act, and to seek sanctions in case it refused to do so with dispatch.[129]

How successful had the Franco-Manitoban organizations been in achieving their three objectives? Bastarache was of the opinion that the Supreme Court decision, if read with an open mind and a modicum of good faith, was highly positive for Franco-Manitobans. In fact, the justices had effectively dealt with nearly all the central issues. He had only two caveats. There remained room for further controversy because the court, first, had reaffirmed the province's prerogative in formulating a system of school governance for its linguistic minority and, second, had left open the possibility of parallel and competing French language school systems. Nevertheless, Bastarache believed that Manitoba's discretionary powers had been significantly curtailed by the Supreme Court's affirmation of its responsibilities in the exercise of its discretionary authority. The justices had clarified and even expanded upon the nature of the rights flowing from s. 23; reaffirming the purposive and remedial intent of the section, they had argued that the most effective means of meeting that goal was to institute homogeneous French schools which served as cultural centres for the minority community. They had also reiterated that the "where numbers warrant" trigger mechanism was to be activated by potential, not actual, enrolments. In applying these principles to Manitoba, the Supreme Court had ruled that "distinct physical settings" were necessary to make sure that the schools belonged to the minority community and operated as cultural centres. This ruling would force the Manitoba government to review its plan for school governance.[130]

Bastarache concluded that the judgment constituted a clear condemnation of the educational status quo in Manitoba, "une affirmation bien claire que le régime actuel, que le gouvernement veut maintenir en parallèle, ne répond pas aux besoins de la minorité linguistique." While the justices did not want to comment directly on the province's governance plan, they did discuss it indirectly by clarifying Manitoba's constitutional obligations in the exercise of its discretionary authority over educational matters. Any system of school governance had to preserve the Franco-Manitoban culture while repairing the damage caused by the existing system. The province could meet these responsibilities only if it fully understood the needs of its linguistic minority, something it could do only by guaranteeing Franco-Manitoban parents a role in determining their children's educational needs and creating the facilities and services best able to meet those needs. According to Bastarache, this requirement clearly undermined the government's proposal for a parallel system of French language schools administered by some of the majority boards. Furthermore, the court's confirmation that s. 23 rights belonged to individuals and were not linked to the will of the minority group to which they belonged meant that the province could not proceed with its regional referenda asking Franco-Manitoban parents to relinquish their right to school governance.

In Bastarache's view, the province's obligation to guarantee the minority an education system on par with that of the majority constituted a critique of the partial French schools and the immersion schools. It compelled the government to undertake the greatest possible regrouping of francophone children to bring about an effective, efficient system of homogeneous schools with the widest possible range of programs. Finally, the onus on the province to avoid all measures and structures that would undermine or prevent the fulfilment of the minority's educational needs was a gift. "Ce sont là des mots empruntés directement à notre plaidoirie," wrote Bastarache, "et qui devraient servir à déclarer indirectement le projet gouvernemental inconstitutionnel." He was convinced that the Supreme Court had thereby deliberately given

Franco-Manitoban parents a victory on the substance of their dispute with the province without having had to rule directly on the government's plan. While the justices had not invalidated Manitoba's Public Schools Act, they had made it abundantly clear that if the plan did not meet the needs of Franco-Manitobans they could return to the courts better armed to win their case for redress.[131]

The province moved swiftly to amend its proposed plan to bring it in line with the Gallant Report's recommendations and the Supreme Court's directives. Minister of Education Rosemary Vodrey introduced Bill 34, the Public Schools Amendment (Francophone Schools Governance) Act, in the legislature in the spring session of 1993; it was proclaimed on 27 July 1993. Her ministry prepared the necessary regulations, which were registered on 3 December 1993 with the proviso that the new Division scolaire franco-manitobaine n° 49 had to be fully operational by September 1994. The new system of governance largely corresponded with the model proposed by the Task Force chaired by Edgar Gallant. The Division scolaire, established on 20 January 1994, was made responsible for administering four regions with ten elected members for the urban region, eleven for the eastern region, six for the southern region, and six for the western region. The four regional committees in turn elected a total of eleven trustees – seven for the rural areas and four for the metropolitan Winnipeg area – to the Franco-Manitoban division. They also consulted regularly with all the school committees in their respective regions and advised and made recommendations to the division.[132]

The Implementation Support Team played its part by consulting with the Franco-Manitoban communities in hopes of persuading as many as possible to join the francophone school division. Over 90 per cent of parents in the thirteen designated French schools voted to join, while seven out of the fifteen other schools consulted opted into the new system. Under the amended Public Schools Act, beginning in grade 4 at least 75 per cent of classroom instruction had to be in French; English as a second language was mandatory.[133] Franco-Manitobans whose children were still in partial French or immersion programs after September 1996 could follow the detailed procedures laid out in the Public Schools Act to petition the Minister of Education to have their entire school, part of it, or just the "dissident" entitled persons, transferred into the Division scolaire. Once the opting-in process had been completed there was no provision for opting out.[134] The procedure was a variation of the one recommended in the Gallant Report.

On Canada Day 1994, when the Division scolaire franco-manitobaine n° 49 became operational, its first president, Louis Tétrault, stated that "from 1916 to 1994 there were dark days, but today marks the beginning of a new era" because the Franco-Manitoban community had officially received "the keys to the house the parents wanted so much." Premier Gary Filmon, Prime Minister Jean Chrétien, and Commissioner of Official Languages Victor Goldbloom congratulated Franco-Manitobans and their leaders for having achieved their long-sought goal and wished the francophone division every success in its efforts at governing twenty schools enrolling 4,200 children.[135] On 5 November 1994, Canada and Manitoba signed an agreement whereby the province would receive $15 million over five years to help defray the costs of implementing school governance for Franco-Manitobans.[136] In June 1995 Louis Tétrault was able to congratulate the 249 students who were the first to complete their high school diploma under the new system. He reminded the fully bilingual students that "vous pouvez frapper à deux fois plus de portes qu'un jeune unilingue." On the same occasion the Division scolaire's first director general, Raymond Bisson (who was also past-president of the Fédération in Ottawa), thanked all the Franco-Manitoban parents and teachers who had braved the twenty-five-year struggle for French classes, then French minority schools, and finally francophone school governance.[137]

That October Franco-Manitoban parents for the first time elected thirty-three representatives to the four regional councils, which in turn elected eleven members to the new francophone board. The over-representation of the rural regions in comparison to the Winnipeg region soon became a source of friction within the Division scolaire that would take a concerted effort to overcome. [138] Despite a reduction in its expenses, during its initial years the Division scolaire struggled with a deficit that was kept at a reasonable level thanks to funds derived from the Canada-Community agreement. According to the FPCP, the Public Schools Act imposed too many financial and administrative constraints on the Division scolaire. Considering these limitations detrimental to a fair and reasonable application of Franco-Manitobans' rights under s. 23, the FPCP once again challenged the constitutionality of the Act. Their action prompted lengthy negotiations with the provincial government in the hope that additional funding would be made available via a renewed Canada-Community agreement.[139] In the long run, the financial stability of the Division scolaire will be attainable only if Franco-Manitoban leaders are able to convince a great majority of the parents of the 10,000 eligible children to enroll them in their own school system.

CONCLUSION

The 1960s and 1970s witnessed the rejuvenation of the Franco-Manitoban community and its social, economic, and political leadership. By the 1980s, the SFM and its numerous affiliates operated a fairly sophisticated apparatus for practising the art of micro-constitutional politics. It enabled Franco-Manitobans to restore s. 23 of the Manitoba Act, 1870, then to go on to win the battle for the implementation of s. 23 of the Charter. Working from the restoration of a limited degree of French language education under the Roblin and Schreyer governments, the SFM and its offshoot the FPCP pressured successive governments to negotiate a made in Manitoba system of minority language educational institutions, from classes to school boards. Franco-Manitoban community leaders and educators managed over time to convince a majority of francophone parents that the partial French, bilingual, and immersion classes and schools contributed to, rather than prevented, the assimilation of their children. Like their counterparts in Alberta and Ontario, they came to regard homogeneous francophone schools under the control of Franco-Manitoban parents as the only educational system capable of renewing their language and culture.

Following a period of trial and error, SFM and FPCP leaders developed a consensus about the nature of rights under s. 23 of the Charter and the best way to actualize them. They also learned how to coordinate their respective mandates and their activities, both within the varied Franco-Manitoban rural and urban communities and vis-à-vis the politicians and bureaucrats in the Ministry of Education. The FPCP developed its skills at community action through the creation of local parent committees whose activities helped alleviate the fear of losing existing Catholic schools. It also disseminated information on the struggles between Franco-Manitoban parents and their English language school boards. The SFM maintained its contacts with successive premiers, Ministers of Education, and leaders of the opposition parties in order to obtain a negotiated implementation of s. 23 rights. By late 1985, when it became clear that a negotiated settlement was not forthcoming, the francophone organizations investigated legal options. After some internal wrangling over the nature of the risks and how best to present their case, the SFM and FPCP decided to proceed with the latter's challenge to Manitoba's Public Schools Act in the Court of Queen's Bench. However, wishing to avoid the legal costs, they instead went along with the provincial Attorney General's decision to undertake a reference case on s. 23 at the Manitoba Court of Appeal. This approach allowed the government to frame the questions placed before the court, thereby avoiding any mandatory declarations from it, which is what the SFM and FPCP were seeking. The strategy paid off: the Court of Appeal ruled that s. 23 did not entail a right to school governance but merely called for appropriate changes to the Public Schools Act. Fortunately for the francophone organizations, a month later the Supreme Court came to their rescue with its ground-breaking *Mahé* decision. Using that ruling as a bargaining tool, the SFM undertook another well-organized attempt at reaching a negotiated settlement with the province as to the precise nature and extent of school governance for Franco-Manitobans.

Negotiations once again reached an impasse when the government refused to abide by the recommendations of the Gallant Report, which urged the creation of a province-wide francophone school board and the phasing out of French language education within the majority boards. The province's school governance plan tried to restrict the application of the recommendations by giving Franco-Manitoban parents the option of retaining French education within the existing English boards. Rejecting the government's attempt to divide and rule, the FPCP and SFM decided to appeal the Manitoba reference case to the Supreme Court. Their position was that the francophone board must have exclusive jurisdiction over all French minority education and facilities. Elaborating upon the principles set out in *Mahé*, the justices ruled that Franco-Manitobans had the right to school governance, but confirmed that it was the province's prerogative to establish its precise form and extent. Fortunately for Franco-Manitobans, they outlined in some detail the parameters of provincial authority given its equally binding constitutional obligations under s. 23 of the Charter.

The 1993 Supreme Court decision made it relatively easy for the FPCP and SFM to come to an understanding with the Manitoba government over the appropriate amendments to the Public Schools Act and the related regulations. By September 1994, the Division scolaire franco-manitobaine was fully operational. The Franco-Manitoban community had reached a new milestone in its development. Crucial to its success were s. 23 of the Charter, a group of liberal-minded and forward-looking Supreme Court justices, a supportive national government, and a provincial government that finally understood the importance for national unity of fulfilling its constitutional obligations in a spirit of generosity and cooperation.

6

Competing Conceptions of Dualism: Confronting the Meech Lake Accord

Toute défaillance au sein des avant-postes francophones en Amérique affaiblit le Québec, sa culture et même son économie. À l'inverse, tout renforcement de nos communautés contribue à la solidité du Québec.[1]

From 1987 to 1990 the Fédération and its affiliates found themselves drawn into a new round of mega-constitutional negotiations around the Meech Lake Constitutional Accord. The Accord was an attempt by the premiers, led by Quebec's Robert Bourassa, to curtail what they – and many constitutional experts – claimed was the deliberate centralization fostered by the Canadian Charter of Rights and Freedoms.[2]

After the deal was cobbled together by Prime Minister Brian Mulroney and the premiers on 30 April 1987, it was taken back to Parliament and the provincial legislatures for ratification. The francophone organizations were both pleased and disappointed with the Accord. They were angry that Bourassa had not gained improvements to s. 23 as promised, but gratified that the two founding nations, French Canada and English Canada, were to be recognized in the Constitution as a "fundamental characteristic" of the country. However, much of their support would evaporate when they saw the final legal text of the Accord, which contained changes based on strong criticism from former prime minister Pierre Trudeau and other prominent Canadians. In the "fundamental characteristics" clause, the recognition of two founding nations was replaced by a reference to French-speaking and English-speaking Canadians. A limited individual-based linguistic duality had replaced the collective duality of two founding nations, one French, one English.

This crucial change in definition and the absence of any mention of government promotion of francophone minority communities engendered a divisive three-year debate that exacerbated existing faultlines within those communities and their organizations. Their paltry financial and human resources were already stretched to the limit pursuing the implementation of school governance under s. 23 of the Charter.

Nevertheless, some provincial organizations felt they had no choice but to get involved. Their leaders argued, quite convincingly at first, that Canada's francophone minority communities should take this opportunity to remedy some of the flaws of s. 23. Appropriate amendments to the section would allow them to avoid further protracted and expensive micro-constitutional political and judicial battles. Further, they urged their constituencies to campaign for formal recognition of their communities as national collectivities. Initially, the Fédération was trapped in playing the role of mediator between feuding provincial organizations: those supporting an unamended Meech Lake Accord and those advocating significant amendments before its ratification. Pressured by the Mulroney/Bourassa alliance and the pro-Meech francophone organizations, the Fédération's leaders worked hard to convince its provincial affiliates and francophone militants to lobby for the ratification of an unamended Meech Lake Accord. This approach almost destroyed the Fédération.

Why did the francophone organizations get involved in this first round of mega-constitutional politics, the so-called "Quebec Round"? There were two compelling reasons. First, the Meech Lake Accord would transfer increased powers to the provinces over national institutions such as the Senate and the Supreme Court. At the heart of its decentralizing thrust was a territorially-based Canada/Quebec conception of duality to trump the pan-Canadian linguistic and cultural vision. The Fédération and its affiliates had no option but to oppose the constitutional entrenchment of the former. Second, francophone leaders had to come to the defence of s. 23 rights. What they had not anticipated was an all-out attack on those rights by western premiers, backed by the premier of Quebec. It forced the Fédération, prodded by its western affiliates, to undertake a concerted yet highly divisive political battle to save s. 23 rights and, if possible, clarify them. The Fédération was compelled to flip-flop several times on its initial support for the Meech Lake Accord, since the western organizations, led by the ACFA, advocated a hard-line rejection of the deal, while the ACFO and SAANB supported its ratification without amendments. Both the Fédération and its affiliates had learned important political skills since the 1980–82 mega-constitutional round; however, they were often not used effectively.

Depending on their demographic and political clout, the provincial organizations developed three different strategies to deal with the Meech Lake Accord. The most cohesive, politicized organization, the SAANB, was initially opposed to it. This encouraged New Brunswick's incoming Liberal premier, Frank McKenna, to demand amendments before his government would ratify it. Ironically, pressured by the

Quebec government and Acadian neo-nationalists, the SAANB later became an unconditional supporter of the Accord. In the interim, it denounced the rejection of French Canada and English Canada as two autonomous founding national collectivities. Its leaders used the opportunity to advance their own constitutional objective, the entrenchment of the collective rights of the Acadian community of New Brunswick by means of the bilateral amending procedure provided by the Constitution Act, 1982.[3]

For some time, the ACFO, representing Canada's largest francophone minority community, encouraged the Fédération and other provincial organizations to reject the Accord until amendments pertaining to minority language and education rights had been made. In June 1988, under a new president, it abandoned this approach and began to lobby all francophone organizations for their unconditional support. Most would give it by February 1989.

The western affiliates, especially those of Alberta and Manitoba, which represented smaller and more vulnerable francophone communities and had to cope with recalcitrant premiers, refused until February 1990 to support the Meech Lake Accord. Their leaders insisted on amendments that would ameliorate the precarious situation of their communities, especially the federal government's obligation to promote their economic, social, and cultural development with new programs and increased funding.

Initially, the Fédération opposed the Accord but intense pressure from francophone militants in Ontario and New Brunswick, Québécois neo-nationalists, and the Mulroney and Bourassa governments forced it to change tack. By mid-1988, it was campaigning alongside the ACFO and SAANB to convince other organizations and their constituents to endorse the deal. In the final three months before the ratification deadline of 23 June 1990, the Fédération and all but one of its affiliates, the ACFA, reached a fragile consensus. It was all in vain. As we shall see, however, the Meech Lake Accord ultimately met its fate at the hands of Elijah Harper, a Cree member of the Manitoba legislature who blocked its ratification on the grounds that it failed to address the constitutional rights of Canada's aboriginal peoples.

While injurious to the francophone organizations' solidarity, the constitutional debate also paradoxically advanced their cause, solidifying their conception of themselves as a pan-Canadian national community made up of provincial communities. This vision was not easy to attain, given that the Meech Lake Accord had forced all Canadians to attempt to reconcile two conceptions of the nation: a pan-Canadian cultural and linguistic duality and Bourassa's Canada/Quebec duality. In the process, francophone leaders educated their communities and the public about the fundamental principles at stake, thereby contributing to the development of a culture of democratic deliberation that had previously been absent from constitutional renewal.

Unfortunately, neither the Fédération and its affiliates nor other Canadians had a formal role in the amending process. The power to amend the Constitution resided squarely in the hands of federal and provincial leaders and their respective legislatures. In the arena of mega-constitutional politics, the francophone organizations discovered that they were never on the same playing field as the prime minister and the premiers, who controlled not only the amending procedures but also the political agenda. Ironically, it was these very executive-driven procedures that allowed one isolated aboriginal Manitoba MLA to derail the controversial and divisive Meech Lake Accord.

THE ROAD TO MEECH LAKE
VIA MONT GABRIEL

The renewal of mega-constitutional politics in the mid-1980s involved a complicated web of characters and a special set of unpredictable circumstances. The catalysts for yet another round of divisive constitutional wrangling were both personal and political. The debate originated with the departure of Pierre Trudeau and the arrival of a very different Liberal leader, John Turner, who understood little about the national unity issue. These developments gave a revitalized Conservative Party humiliated by the defeat of its minority government in 1980 a second chance to bring about the political realignment that Joe Clark had been seeking so desperately since 1976. In the interim, Premier René Lévesque's decision not to sign the Constitution Act, 1982 and to apply s. 33, the notwithstanding clause, of the Charter to all of Quebec's legislation had only minor political impact until a national political party emerged to exploit the situation. The opportunity emerged more quickly than most observers had anticipated when Joe Clark was defeated in a leadership race by Brian Mulroney in the fall of 1983. On 4 September 1984 Mulroney was elected prime minister in a relatively easy victory over the ill-prepared John Turner.[4]

Mulroney, the "boy from Baie Comeau" on Quebec's North Shore, seized the leadership of the Conservative Party from Clark with the help of delegates with Union Nationale, Liberal, and Parti Québécois backgrounds. He was determined to destroy the almost century-old stranglehold of the federal Liberal Party in Quebec; indeed, he was confident that he could exploit the volatile political situation to bring about a long-sought-after political realignment.[5] In the lead-up to the 1984 election, Mulroney and his legal and business colleagues put

together a political machine in Quebec comprising fundraisers, orga-
nizers, candidates, and militants drawn from all three provincial
parties. With this "adopted" political coalition in place, his spin
doctors, aided by francophone journalists, portrayed the Quebec-born
Conservative Mulroney as the only national leader willing and able to
preserve and promote the national aspirations of Quebec's French-
speaking majority. Eager to attract disgruntled nationalist Québécois
voters, Mulroney, persuaded by his friend Lucien Bouchard, made a
vague but crucial political promise on 6 August 1984. While campaigning at Sept-Iles, he promised to do whatever was necessary to get
the Quebec government's "signature on our constitution, with honour
and enthusiasm."[6]

The well-timed yet fateful promise paid off in spades. As the Tories
won the expected sixty-seven seats in Ontario, the Quebec coalition
delivered a stunning blow to the seemingly impenetrable Liberal
bastion of Quebec, winning fifty-eight of the seventy-five ridings. The
federal Liberal Party was reduced to a rump of seventeen constituencies, most of them in predominantly English-speaking metropolitan
Montreal. Nationally, the Conservative Party won 211 of 282 seats with
50 per cent of the vote.[7] The impressive – potentially watershed –
victory, built on Mulroney's drive, determination, and unbridled ambi-
tion, was the opening stage in his plan to bring about the first major
political realignment in Canada since Laurier's election in 1896. Consolidating a political hold over his first, then second, administrations
would prove a far greater challenge whose success depended on his
ability to deliver on his promise to Quebec's francophone voters while
not alienating the increasingly right-of-centre western elements of the
Conservative Party.[8]

Sensing that the Parti Québécois was in disarray and preferring to
negotiate with his political ally Robert Bourassa, Mulroney waited
for the results of the provincial election held on 2 December 1985.
In the interim, the Quebec Liberal Party, under the guidance of its
constitutional expert Gil Rémillard, outlined in a preliminary
fashion some of Quebec's conditions for signing on to the Constitution Act, 1982.[9] Bourassa's Liberals won a resounding victory, garnering ninety-nine seats with 56 per cent of the vote, while the Parti
Québécois held on to only twenty-two seats with 40 per cent of the
vote. Following a meeting in late January 1986, Mulroney and
Bourassa announced that they would be giving Quebec's constitutional aspirations top priority. In March 1986 Quebec's Minister of
Intergovernmental Affairs, Gil Rémillard, announced in what was
considered a goodwill gesture that the Charter of Rights and Freedoms would be given precedence over the Quebec Charter. The

Quebec government would no longer automatically invoke the notwithstanding clause when ratifying legislation.

Rémillard kick-started the mega-constitutional political process using the Quebec Liberals' February 1985 platform, "Mastering Our Future," as the basis of negotiations. The document outlined Quebec's five conditions for formally consenting to the Constitution. Rémillard explained the logic of these conditions to the hand-picked delegates attending the Mont-Gabriel conference "Rebuilding the Relationship: Quebec and its Confederation Partners," held 9–11 May 1986. The conference was organized by the Institute of Intergovernmental Relations at Queen's University – which became responsible for galvanizing academic support behind the Meech Lake Accord – with the assistance of Montreal's nationalist/secessionist daily *Le Devoir* and the École nationale d'administration publique.[10] "If the Canadian Charter poses few problems for Quebec, the same is not true for other aspects of the Constitution Act of 1982 which negates Quebec's historic rights." Rémillard went on to present the five conditions:

- explicit recognition of Quebec as a distinct society
- guarantee of increased powers in matters of immigration
- limitation of the federal spending power
- recognition of a right of veto over amendments to national institutions: the House of Commons, the Senate, and the Supreme Court
- participation in appointing judges to the Supreme Court[11]

Rémillard also stated that his government would push hard to improve the constitutional situation of the francophone communities throughout Canada, though this aim was not among Quebec's conditions. He believed he could convince the premiers to agree to amend s. 23 of the Charter, making explicit the francophone minority communities' right to school governance and removing the "where numbers warrant" condition.[12] But this commitment conflicted with the new conception of constitutionally entrenched territorial duality sought by Québécois nationalists of all political stripes. While sincere about their support for the francophone minority communities, Bourassa and Rémillard had as their primary goal a new Canada comprising two territorially-based nations: one English-speaking, consisting of Ottawa and nine provincial governments; the other French-speaking, consisting of Quebec. They regarded constitutional recognition of Quebec as a distinct society as the key to consolidating, then advancing, this Quebec/Canada duality in which Quebec would have exclusive control over all social, cultural, and linguistic matters, including the education of its anglophone minority.[13]

Mulroney and Bourassa, eager to get the constitutional issue behind them, met on 4 June 1986 to discuss Quebec's conditions and agree on a winning strategy. Much was at stake: Mulroney's Secretary of State, Benoît Bouchard, along with several other speakers, had warned the Mont-Gabriel conference delegates that the negotiations must succeed at all costs or Quebec's sense of exclusion from the federation would be enhanced and the moribund secessionist movement would regain its lost strength.[14] On 4 July 1986 Mulroney announced his decision to launch the "Quebec Round," a constitutional blitzkrieg headed up by his long-time friend Senator Lowell Murray. Appointed as Minister of Federal-Provincial Relations to work with Rémillard, Murray's role was to convince all nine premiers to get on board the constitutional train. Leaving nothing to chance, Mulroney, in a confidential letter dated 21 July, urged the premiers to set aside their own constitutional agendas for the moment and to look favourably on Quebec's five conditions during their annual conference, to be held in Edmonton in August. Initially, this strategy proved successful. The premiers issued a terse communiqué, the "Edmonton Declaration," in which they agreed to participate in constitutional discussions based on Quebec's five conditions in order to facilitate "Quebec's full and active participation in the Canadian federation." The Mulroney/Bourassa alliance was cemented; no challenge – and there were several – managed to break their personal and political alliance over the next six years.[15]

There followed several months of secretive and inconclusive meetings between Rémillard and his provincial counterparts and their respective officials under the watchful eye of Senator Murray. On 17 March 1987, Mulroney decided – on the advice of Murray, who was responsible for keeping the process on track – to convene the premiers at Willson House, Meech Lake, on 30 April 1987 to review their progress. To the surprise of most of the premiers, the informal gathering, at which no officials were present, was quickly transformed by the prime minister into a hard-nosed all-day bargaining session. The result was the Meech Lake Constitutional Accord. A fragile consensus was achieved around Quebec's five conditions because four of them – immigration, the Supreme Court, the veto, and spending power – were extended to all the provinces. In short, the "Quebec Round" was transformed into the "Provincial Round" by applying of the concept of the equality of the provinces, with Mulroney playing his cherished role of mediator. Furthermore, the premiers managed to extract from him a commitment to convene annual constitutional conferences to address their respective shopping lists of issues, from Senate reform to fisheries. The politicians and their officials departed Meech Lake late that evening in a celebratory, even giddy, mood, believing that they had accomplished the impossible: a unanimous agreement on constitutional reform, something which, as Mulroney informed the media, had eluded Pierre Trudeau.[16]

Over the next month, the principles agreed upon at Meech Lake were forged into a draft constitutional document for the prime minister and premiers to peruse, amend if necessary, and sign during their meeting in Ottawa at the Langevin Block on 2 June. That meeting continued all day and throughout the night as the exhausted and frustrated politicians and officials haggled over the implications of the clauses on Quebec as a distinct society and Ottawa's spending power. The concerns raised by former prime minister Trudeau and other critics about these two matters had forced some of the premiers, led by Ontario's David Peterson and Manitoba's Howard Pawley, to request further clarifications and, if necessary, additional guarantees to protect the integrity of the Charter and Canada's national social security and health systems. Given Mulroney's unwillingness to defend Canada's national interests – "Who Speaks for Canada?" Trudeau boldly asked – it was left up to Peterson and Pawley to articulate the public's fears, which had emerged with the publication of the Meech Lake Accord. Mulroney and Bourassa stood firm, allowing the pressure to build. They relied on their officials and other premiers to convince first Pawley, then Peterson, that it was the Meech Lake Accord as negotiated or nothing. The tactic worked: the two reluctantly agreed to take the deal back to their provinces for public hearings and, ultimately, ratification by their legislatures within the constitutionally mandated three-year time frame. Once again, Mulroney had rolled the political dice and come up a winner. Premier Robert Bourassa had attained all five of his province's demands, including the much-vaunted interpretative distinct society clause applying to the entire Constitution.[17]

The initial response of journalists and the public was great relief that the constitutional wrangling with Quebec was over. Most Canadians wanted their political leaders to get on with practical issues such as job creation and shoring up health, education, and social service programs. Few, if any, of the framers of the Meech Lake Accord or the journalists who had recounted its development in considerable detail envisaged the three years of political turmoil that would follow its signing. Canada's francophone leaders played a central role in the constitutional debacle.

CONFLICTING NATIONAL VISIONS:
PAN-CANADIAN VERSUS QUEBEC/CANADA

As the prime minister, the premiers, and their respective ministers and officials were negotiating the terms of the Meech Lake Accord, the

Fédération was reaffirming itself as the primary lobbying force of the francophone minority communities – some one million Canadian citizens. On the constitutional issue, the Fédération saw its role as presenting "en tout temps une position claire et documentée concernant la place des communautés de langues officielles en situation minoritaires dans les institutions publiques canadiennes et ce, dans un contexte d'égalité." Its stated objective was to reinforce all constitutional and legal mechanisms that would guarantee the collective rights of the francophone communities, including the opportunity for their members to participate, individually and collectively, in the political decisions affecting their future.[18] Trudeau's departure from the national stage had dramatically altered the political climate and the relationship between Ottawa and provinces, thereby allowing conflicting visions of the country – Québécois and western Canadian – to come to the fore.

Defeated in the referendum and unwilling to accept the Constitution Act, 1982 with its Charter, Premier René Lévesque had adopted a new political strategy, dubbed the "beau risque" because it entailed considerable risks for himself, his government, and his party. Abandoning the Parti Québécois's primary goal – sovereignty-association – he instead sought a constitutional deal with Prime Minister Brian Mulroney based on a lengthy list of twenty-two conditions. Preferring to negotiate with a Liberal government, Mulroney had watched while the Parti Québécois self-destructed throughout the spring and early summer of 1985. PQ hardliners led by Jacques Parizeau abandoned the party, forcing Lévesque, a tired and broken man, to resign on 20 June. Robert Bourassa's Liberal Party, which proposed a minimum list of five conditions for signing on to the Constitution Act, easily won the election on 2 December. Few Canadians were aware that another destabilizing stage in Quebec's political evolution was underway, one that would test the very fabric of the Canadian nation-state.[19]

Always vigilant in safeguarding the interests of its affiliates and their constituents, in the spring of 1985 the Fédération sought advice from constitutional expert Michel Bastarache about the "beau risque" strategy of the Parti Québécois government as well as the more limited constitutional objectives of Bourassa's Liberals. Bastarache reminded the Fédération's leaders that the Liberals, like the former PQ, would settle for nothing less than constitutional recognition of the specificity of the "nation québécoise." For Quebec's political class this entailed the creation of a territorially-based federation comprising a francophone Quebec and an anglophone Canada. Opposing this conception was the pan-Canadian vision of duality based on the idea of two founding nations and recognized through institutional bilingualism. Driving the Bourassa government's constitutional grievances on mobility rights, education rights for its official language minority, the veto question, and the legitimacy of the Charter of the French Language was its commitment to building its own more moderate version of a Quebec/Canada bi-national federation. Aware that Mulroney and Bourassa were negotiating, Bastarache advised the Fédération that it must decide to what extent, and on which issues, these two competing visions were compatible. It was imperative for it to lobby to make certain that both were equally recognized in a renewed Constitution. Whenever the two clashed, the Fédération had to decide how to promote the interests of the francophone communities. It was time for it to make its presence felt in the ongoing constitutional debate.[20]

Concerned that matters would proceed quickly following the election of the Liberals in December 1985, the Fédération's president met with Gil Rémillard on 31 January 1986 to learn what direction Quebec intended to take on the constitutional front. He was assured that it would adopt a position that would assist the francophone minority communities, especially on s. 23 and school governance.[21] In February the Fédération established a Constitutional Affairs Committee, chaired by its president, Yvon Fontaine, and including Michel Bastarache, Pierre Foucher, the Franco-Manitoban constitutional lawyer Guy Jourdain, as well as representatives from the group and its affiliates. Edgar Gallant and Clinton Archibald, a professor in the University of Ottawa Faculty of Administration, would join at a later date. The committee's mandate was to advise the Fédération on the upcoming constitutional negotiations between Quebec and Ottawa and on all the court cases involving language and education issues.[22] Foucher attended the Mont-Gabriel conference as an observer and wrote up a critical report for the Fédération. He warned that, unlike in 1980–82, an alliance between Ottawa and Quebec was emerging, negotiations were taking place behind closed doors, and developments would be swift. It was crucial for the Fédération to involve itself in all aspects of the constitutional debate in order to defend francophone interests.[23]

In July Réal Sabourin, president of the SFM, wrote to Gil Rémillard to congratulate him for the commitment to the francophone minority communities that he had expressed at Mont-Gabriel and for his promise to push for an amendment to s. 23 recognizing an explicit right to school governance. On the advice of Pierre Foucher, the SFM lobbied Rémillard to see to it that Quebec's constitutional demands would not be fulfilled at the expense of those communities.[24] The ACFA took the same approach and congratulated Rémillard for wanting to relieve the plight of the francophone minorities. Initially, it was inclined to support the Quebec government's five conditions because they would lead to "un Québec fort" that was confident and capable and therefore willing to come to the assistance of the minority communities. In a brief to Rémillard, the ACFA argued that it was important that the Quebec government "affirme sans ambage que le Canada a un idéal national qui veut que les francophones puissent vivre en tant que francophones partout au pays et que cet idéal doit se traduire et ne pas se limiter à des déclarations de droits sans lendemains."[25] Following up on the brief, a delegation met with Rémillard prior to the premiers' meeting in Edmonton in late August 1986 to make him aware of the critical nature of Franco-Albertans' demographic and political situation and to suggest how Quebec might help improve and even reinforce their constitutional rights, starting with those under s. 23. Rémillard promised the ACFA that his government would attempt to clarify the section to make sure that school governance for francophones was specified ... that this would indeed be Quebec's "sixth condition." Nonetheless, the ACFA was not so sanguine as to mistake the promise for a *fait accompli*, and would not be so easily convinced to get on board the Meech train. Indeed, it would become one of the Accord's fiercest critics.[26]

For its part, the Fédération was determined to take advantage of the renewal of constitutional talks to improve the language and education provisions of the Charter and to see to it that any amendments would not have negative effects on the francophone minority communities.[27] At its November 1986 meeting in Montreal, its Conseil national des présidents made a preliminary assessment of the Bourassa government's five conditions, then passed a resolution committing it to preparing a white paper outlining a common constitutional policy and a strategy for implementing it.[28] In March 1987, its Constitutional Affairs Committee issued a highly critical analysis of Quebec's conditions and the language clauses of the Charter. The policy documents were approved by all the presidents at their meeting the same month and served as the Fédération's points of reference throughout the disputation over the Accord. The chief point of contention was the condition that Quebec be recognized as a "distinct society." While the Fédération and its affiliates were all sympathetic to the constitutional recognition of Quebec as a distinct society, they wanted to make sure that the entrenchment of a Quebec/Canada duality was not achieved at the expense of the francophone communities. They urged Quebec to recognize the original, broader conception of linguistic and cultural duality entrenched in s. 133 of the Constitution Act, 1867, s. 23 of the Manitoba Act, 1870, and the laws of New Brunswick: "La reconnaissance des besoins précis du

Québec en Amérique du Nord est incontestable, toutefois, elle ne doit en aucun cas s'opposer à la proclamation de l'égalité des communautés de langue officielle partout au Canada. Il faut en effet reconnaître le caractère spécial du Canada comme territoire que se partagent deux grandes collectivités linguistiques. Cette reconnaissance est pour nous aussi fondamentale qu'est la reconnaissance de la spécificité pour le Québec."[29]

The committee pointed out that since 1967 various premiers had used the concept of Quebec as a distinct society to justify a range of constitutional demands, from special status to sovereignty-association. All constructed a Quebec/Canada duality by seeking additional powers and new institutions for the province. The distinct society clause, as written, was inherently contradictory and potentially injurious to the francophone communities. If the constitutional specificity of Quebec extended beyond the Civil Code and matters of language and culture – something Bourassa and Rémillard argued it most assuredly did – then it would severely undermine the recognition of the equality of Canada's two linguistic communities. Quebec governments would henceforth use the clause to construct, step by step, politically and judicially, a Quebec/Canada duality. "Dans les réformes des institutions fédérales, dans l'interprétation judiciaire du partage des compétences législatives ou des droits linguistiques reconnus par la Constitution, les instances politiques et judiciaires devront désormais tenir compte de la spécificité du Québec. Tout doute devra donc mener à des interprétations et des développements favorables aux intérêts historiques et vitaux du Québec." The Fédération had no objection to Quebec wielding all the powers it needed to protect its French language and culture, as long as their exercise was never to the detriment or the exclusion of the national mandate of Parliament and the government of Canada to foster the French language and francophone culture throughout the country. The two concepts of dualism had to be mutually reinforcing rather than at loggerheads.[30]

The Fédération fully supported Quebec's aspirations to increased control over immigration and a guarantee of three Quebec civil court judges in the Supreme Court. Indeed, it wanted all the provinces, not just Quebec, to participate in nominating judges to the highest court.[31] On the crucial matter of an expanded veto applying to all national institutions, it accepted in principle that Quebec should exercise this right over constitutional change, since having it would guarantee a voice for all francophones at the national level. Such a veto could be obtained by means of Bourassa's proposal to replace the amending formula based on the seven provinces with 50 per cent of the population, known as the 7/50 formula, with a 7/75 formula, or by returning to an amending process based on four regions, as outlined in the Victoria Charter of 1971. With regard to language, the Fédération proposed that s. 43(b) of the amending formula, which involved Parliament and one or more provinces, be used to entrench an increase in language rights, while s. 43(c), which called for unanimity, be required for any reduction in linguistic rights.[32] Finally, with respect to Quebec's power to limit Ottawa's spending in areas of provincial jurisdiction, the Fédération made it amply clear that it would not accept any such limitation without a formal guarantee that the government of Canada could continue to guarantee the maintenance and development of the francophone minority communities through appropriate funding mechanisms, including shared-cost programs.[33]

The Fédération also gave notice that it intended to bargain hard to obtain amendments to ss. 16 to 20 of the Charter, on official language rights, to make sure that linguistic equality was not simply "a principle of progression," as ruled by the Supreme Court, but rather "un concept assurant un traitement égal des collectivités devant la justice."[34] While language rights might be defined by some as political rather than fundamental rights, this view should not lead the courts to interpret them in a restrictive manner. The best way of achieving effective equality before the courts was to include in the preamble to the Charter – preferably as an interpretative clause applying to the entire Constitution in the same manner as the distinct society clause – some reference to the equality of Canada's francophone and anglophone communities.[35]

The Constitutional Affairs Committee devised a lucid and forceful statement of constitutional objectives for the Fédération and its affiliates. Unfortunately, they were prone to disregarding excellent legal advice obtained at considerable cost. According to ACFA President Georges Arès – a lawyer by profession – francophone leaders were always far too eager to rely on their contacts with the appropriate politicians, rather than basing their policies and strategies on solid legal arguments.[36] As events surrounding the Meech Lake Accord would demonstrate, this approach was not very productive. It turned out that the greatest challenge confronting all francophone leaders was to bring some influence to bear on the secret negotiations that, to everyone's surprise, culminated in the Accord at the end of April 1987.

FRANCOPHONE ORGANIZATIONS' REACTIONS
TO THE MEECH LAKE ACCORD

During a press conference on 26 May 1987, the Fédération expressed its support in principle for the Meech Lake Accord. It made only one recommendation: that Parliament and the provincial legislatures be made responsible for promoting as well as preserving linguistic duality.

The 30 April draft statement of principles pertaining to Quebec as a distinct society stated that "the Constitution of Canada shall be interpreted in a manner consistent with a) the recognition that the existence of French-speaking Canada, centred in but not limited to Quebec, and English-speaking Canada, concentrated outside Quebec but also present in Quebec, constitutes a fundamental characteristic of Canada; and b) the recognition that Quebec constitutes within Canada a distinct society."[37] Not surprisingly, then, the Fédération was less than pleased with the legal text of the Accord issued after the meeting at the Langevin Block on 2 June, because it altered the definition of the "fundamental characteristic" clause and did not include an obligation to promote.[38] The version of the clause adopted at that meeting referred to "French-speaking Canadians" and "English-speaking Canadians."[39] Remarkably, Fédération President Yvon Fontaine had met with some of the main participants in the June 2 meeting the previous day, and had never been informed that there would be a shift from collective to individual rights. For the clause to be of any assistance to the francophone communities, according to Fontaine, it had to recognize a duality based, not on two official languages, but rather on "the existence of two major cultural communities whose permanence constitutes an essential condition for Confederation."[40] Only then could francophones living outside Quebec obtain the right to their own institutions, their own social life, and their own self-governing communities. "What we want out of provisions 16 to 20," declared Fontaine, "is for those linguistic rights to give us the rights to institutions that will facilitate our development." At the heart of this drive for institutional completeness was the acquisition of homogenous francophone schools and the right to govern them.[41]

As mentioned earlier, this fundamental alteration to the Accord resulted from the criticisms of certain prominent Canadians, including Pierre Trudeau. On 27 May, Trudeau had made a scathing attack on the deal in the *Toronto Daily Star*. "Those who have never wanted a bilingual Canada – Quebec separatists and western separatists – get their wish right in the first paragraphs of the accord, with recognition of 'the existence of French-speaking Canada ... and English-speaking Canada.' ... Those Canadians who fought for a single Canada, bilingual and multicultural, can say goodbye to their dream."[42] The comments hit home with some premiers, who urged changes to the draft of the Accord. Brian Mulroney, fearing that Trudeau's denunciation would dissolve the fragile unanimity of the premiers, devoted most of his opening remarks at the Langevin Block meeting to a personal attack on him. He then pointedly reminded everyone present that he, not Trudeau, governed the country.[43]

At its annual general meeting in June, the Fédération passed a formal resolution against the Meech Lake Accord. It was prepared to support s. 2(1)(b), the distinct society clause, as well as clause 2(3), which confirmed the role of the legislature and government of Quebec in preserving and promoting the distinct society. In turn, Ottawa and the provinces had to recognize a francophone presence outside Quebec, as well as the need to promote it. The Fédération maintained that the competing conceptions of duality could be made compatible, but only if Canadians embraced an asymmetrical federalist approach to language and cultural rights. Preservation entailed the continuation of the status quo, which involved accelerating rates of assimilation.

In mid-June, Bourassa and Rémillard summoned Fédération representatives Yvon Fontaine, Michel Doucet, Serge Plouffe, and Georges Arès to Quebec City to explain the Accord, with an eye to softening their opposition. Rémillard argued that there were many good things in it for the francophone minority communities. The legal opinions demonstrating these benefits could not be made public, for fear that the "Anglos" would then use them as a basis for opposing the deal. Bourassa took a more pragmatic approach: Quebec's improved economy allowed him to promise increased financial support for the francophone communities. When asked what had happened to the promotion clause and the clarification of s. 23 as regards school governance, he replied that he had tried hard but faced a solid wall of opposition from the other premiers. The Fédération representatives were not impressed with either the arguments or the promise of financial assistance. They concluded that Rémillard was taking them for fools when he claimed he had legal opinions showing benefits for francophones.[44]

Yvon Fontaine appeared before the Special Joint Committee of the Senate and the House of Commons on 5 August 1987 to give testimony on the Meech Lake Accord:

The importance of entrenching the obligation to promote minority language development is underscored by the inclusion in the Accord of subsection 2(4), which was absent from the Agreement of April 30. This passage in fact confirms that subsection 2(2) creates no additional substantive right(s) in the area of language rights that would be opposable to the provincial legislatures and Parliament. The powers of the provinces and Parliament remain intact. What remains of the interpretive clause in this case? What can it be applied to? At best it will serve to interpret the language rights entrenched in the Constitution. Yet, these rights are limited to three provinces, Manitoba, New Brunswick and Quebec.[45]

When asked by a member of the committee whether the Fédération would support the Accord if it was not amended as the group wished, Fontaine replied that the collective rights and promotion amendments would not undermine Quebec's recognition as a distinct society. The Fédération could not "accept the idea of waiting for a second round to round out and improve the rights of francophones outside Quebec," because, despite aggressive lobbying, the matter was excluded from the future constitutional agenda to which Brian Mulroney and the premiers had agreed.[46]

The Special Joint Committee issued its report on 9 September 1987. The Conservative government and the NDP members of the committee recommended to Parliament that the Constitutional Accord should be adopted without amendment. However, they also called for a second round of negotiations to address a wide range of important constitutional issues raised during the hearings. The Liberal members of the committee abstained and issued a minority report detailing a series of amendments they believed were necessary to improve the Accord.[47] On the question of whether the recognition of Canada's linguistic duality and Quebec's distinct society would disadvantage French-speaking Canadians outside Quebec, the committee concluded that it would not, and indeed, that the Accord's "explicit and unanimous acknowledgment of Canada's 'linguistic duality' across the country ... [was] a major achievement." It also concurred with most observers "that the earlier language of the Meech Lake Accord could have been misinterpreted as approval of 'two Canadas' and the change in language was generally considered to be an important improvement."[48] The committee refused to accept the argument that the distinct society clause laid the constitutional foundation for the future consolidation and expansion, not of pan-Canadian linguistic dualism, but rather of an increasingly French language Quebec and English language rest of Canada.

The Fédération Attempts to Flip-flop

The Fédération was not positive about the report. Nevertheless, Yvon Fontaine and Director General Aurèle Thériault, both Acadians, made public statements following a meeting with Premier Bourassa in October in New Brunswick to the effect that it was time for the Fédération to back the Accord, to set aside objections and proposed amendments until the second round of negotiations. Their pronouncements set off a firestorm of opposition within the organization, as no consultation had taken place with the provincial presidents. Some of them saw Fontaine and Thériault as attempting to set the organization's stance on the Accord to suit their personal views, rather than taking the position adopted at the June AGM. A growing perception that the Acadians, overly influenced by the SAANB, were in charge of the Fédération and were using it to advance their own cause created considerable hostility, especially from the smaller, more vulnerable associations in western Canada.[49]

Michel Doucet, president of the SAANB and a close colleague of both Fontaine and Thériault, became a supporter of the Accord despite his and his group's initial opposition. His pro-Meech arguments were based on the SAANB's campaign to have New Brunswick's Bill 88, An Act Recognizing the Equality of the Two Official Linguistic Communities in New Brunswick, entrenched via s. 43 of the Constitution Act, 1982. The strategy of a parallel amendment on Bill 88, which avoided the reopening of negotiations on the fragile but necessary Meech Lake Accord, influenced the thinking of both Fontaine and Thériault. Coupled with a second round of negotiations, it would eventually become the official position of New Brunswick's Liberal government, which failed to consult with or give any credit to the SAANB's leadership. Little wonder that Doucet resigned over the matter. He and his colleagues considered, quite rightly, that the SAANB's discourse had been confiscated by Premier Frank McKenna for his own political ends![50] Nevertheless, while this constitutional policy admirably suited the political context and objectives of New Brunswick's Acadian leaders, it accomplished little or nothing for francophones in other provinces, who were more dependent on the federal government's willingness to promote their language and educational rights. The divergent conditions, needs, and aspirations of the various francophone minority communities created serious tensions with the Fédération.

In an unauthorized letter dated 2 October 1987, Yvon Fontaine informed Prime Minister Mulroney of the Fédération's acceptance of the Meech Lake Accord. In his belated reply of mid-January 1988 Mulroney indicated that the federal government had wished to go further on promotion but could not budge the reluctant, even hostile, premiers and added that serious consideration was being given to placing the issue on the agenda of the next round.[51] Meanwhile, influenced by developments in New Brunswick, where Frank McKenna's new Liberal government was demanding changes to improve the rights of the Acadian community, the Fédération issued a joint press release with the SAANB outlining why it would be dangerous for the francophone communities to reject the Meech Lake Accord if the changes they wanted were not made. The two organizations agreed to lobby Ottawa not only to entrench New Brunswick's Bill 88 but also to pressure all the provinces to implement s. 23 of the Charter.[52]

The Fédération's western associations, especially the ACFA under Georges Arès, continued to reject the Accord and were outraged by Fontaine's and Thériault's quiet acquiescence, which was contrary to the Fédération's official position. At a critical and rather boisterous Conseil national des présidents meeting in Edmonton in late November, Arès led a successful campaign to induce the Fédération to stand by its June rejection of the Accord. Playing political hardball, he threatened to withdraw the ACFA from the national organization if the latter failed to defend the needs of all the francophone minority communities.[53] Arès saw the obligation of the federal government to promote the development of the linguistic minorities as crucial to their survival. It therefore had to be entrenched in any amended Constitution. Moreover, he was concerned that the Meech Lake Accord would take precedence over the Charter. Since Frank McKenna had similar reservations, Arès wanted the Fédération to develop a strategy that would take advantage of the premier's viewpoint to push for the amendments it had outlined before the Special Joint Committee. After heated discussion, the presidents agreed to create a sub-committee of four provincial presidents and Yvon Fontaine to clarify the Fédération's position vis-à-vis the Accord.[54] The sub-committee reached a consensus at its 16 January 1988 meeting and presented its report to the Conseil national des présidents on 2 February. The presidents approved the report, as well as a motion by Arès calling on the Fédération to communicate its "clarified" original position to the prime minister and the premiers: that its opposition was to remain in effect until satisfactory changes to the Accord had been achieved. The presidents also created another sub-committee of three – Arès, Fontaine, and Doucet – to work out a new political strategy.[55]

Arès took the initiative by presenting a brief to the Senate Submissions Group on the Meech Lake Accord on 29 February 1988. He began on a less than conciliatory note: "How can we dare to accept the Meech Lake Accord with no changes when it contains serious basic flaws that absolutely must be corrected before the Accord is proclaimed? The signatories to the Accord have all contributed to these flaws, but not a single one is prepared to acknowledge them."[56] He then outlined the plight of Franco-Albertans, who were facing ever-increasing assimilation and a hostile provincial government looking for a way out of its responsibilities under the Charter. Arès blamed Mulroney and Bourassa for sacrificing the interests of the francophone minorities on the altar of political expediency. He pleaded with the senators to reject the Meech Lake Accord because "once Quebec obtains its distinct society clause without having to accept the federal government's promotional role, the Quebec government will refuse to make this change once and for all."[57] Michel Bastarche, in his statement to the Senate Submissions Group on 18 March, drove home many of the same points raised by Arès.[58]

On 2 March 1988, a somewhat chastened Yvon Fontaine once again wrote to Brian Mulroney to express the Fédération's displeasure with the Meech Lake Accord, referring to clauses pertaining to the francophone minority communities as "incomplete and unacceptable." On the advice of several constitutional experts, the Conseil national des présidents pleaded with the prime minister through Fontaine to revisit the Accord in order to entrench additional guarantees for Canada's official language minorities. The amendments requested included the recognition of the collective dimension of linguistic duality; the obligation for Parliament, the provincial legislatures, and their respective governments to promote as well as preserve Canada's linguistic and cultural duality; and the elimination of the non-derogatory clause 2(4), which had been put in to prevent any expansion of state powers or prerogatives pertaining to language matters. Fontaine reminded the prime minister that the Special Joint Committee had recognized the legitimacy of these amendments in its final report. While acknowledging that the Accord was necessary to get Quebec's signature to the Constitution Act, 1982, Fontaine reiterated that, as it stood, it was unacceptable to the francophone minority communities.[59]

Responding at the end of March, Mulroney expressed regret that the Fédération had changed its position on the Accord. Like most outside observers, he continued to believe, erroneously, that the group had done an about-face when, in fact, its president had taken an unauthorized position. The prime minister reiterated that the Accord, which represented the central element in his government's plan of national reconciliation and unity, could not be revisited: there was no guarantee that the unanimity required to achieve ratification would be forthcoming. He also warned that the Fédération's denunciation of the deal would allow others to use the francophone minorities as a basis for arguing that it should be rejected, an eventuality that Yvon Fontaine had declared in November his organization wished to avoid.[60]

At their meeting in Quebec City in late March, the presidents struggled over which of two constitutional strategies to adopt. One involved obtaining an unconditional formal guarantee from all the provinces before accepting the Accord that recognized the federal government's obligation to promote Canadian dualism. The second involved obtaining a declaration from the federal government on its commitment to promotion, along with a guarantee that all outstanding issues would be placed on the agenda of the next constitutional conference. Representatives of the Quebec government present at the meeting reaffirmed their moral commitment to the survival of the francophone minority communities. This assurance helped convince the presidents, even a skeptical Georges Arès, to favour an elaborate variation on the second option. After heated negotiations, they approved a confidential report prepared by the Ad Hoc Committee on Strategy outlining a lengthy list of constitutional, legislative, administrative, and financial demands that had to be addressed by Ottawa and the provinces before the Fédération would consent to the ratification of an unamended Meech Lake Accord. The unrealistic shopping list read like a record of outstanding grievances. Heading it up was the Fédération's insistence on being present at the second-round negotiating table when promotion was being discussed. The group no longer trusted the federal government and Quebec to defend francophone interests.[61]

Proof that Georges Arès's skepticism and distrust were well-founded came soon enough when controversy erupted over the issue of official bilingualism in Alberta's legislature. In 1987, a Franco-Albertan MLA, Léo Piquette, had asked in both French and English why the government was denying Franco-Albertans their right to school governance. The Speaker of the Legislative Assembly insisted that Piquette use only English or lose his right to speak. The matter was referred to the Standing Committee on Privileges and Elections, which ruled in favour of the Speaker, reaffirmed English as the official language, but recommended a more liberal policy on the use of other languages in the legislature.[62] A heated public debate over bilingualism ensued, fueled by developments in the Supreme Court. In *Mercure* v. *A.G. Saskatchewan* [1988] the justices ruled that s. 110 of the North-West Territories Act, 1875 still bound Alberta and Saskatchewan to official bilingualism but that the section could be amended unilaterally by the provincial legislatures. The ACFA and other francophone organizations hoped that a generous and open-minded Alberta government would reaffirm official bilingualism. Despite intense pressure from the ACFA and Franco-Albertans, however, the province quickly introduced Bill 60, the Languages Act, 1988, abolishing s. 110 of the North-West Territories Act while allowing the use of other languages in the legislature under certain conditions. The ACFA even pleaded with Premier Bourassa to intervene but to no avail, since he regarded language issues as a provincial prerogative. According to Arès, his comments on Bill 60 demonstrated that Franco-Albertans had to be content with the minimum definition of language rights that their government was willing to offer them. Disgusted and dejected, he announced that the meeting with Bourassa scheduled for 12 April 1988 was cancelled.[63] When Premier Grant Devine of Saskatchewan introduced an identical Languages Act, 1988, Arès wrote to Prime Minister Mulroney stating that the Meech Lake Accord had failed its first real test. Francophones were learning that, for Saskatchewan's anglophones and for Quebec's francophone majority, protecting Canada's fundamental characteristic – its cultural and linguistic duality – "se traduit par la diminution des droits des francophones hors Québec et probablement par la diminution des droits des anglophones au Québec. Les Franco-Albertains savent maintenant à quoi s'attendre de leur gouvernement provincial." Arès pleaded with Mulroney to use the federal power of disallowance, as well as spending power, to prevent the governments of Saskatchewan and Alberta from abolishing official bilingualism.[64]

Other associations, including the ACFO, waded into the fray. The prime minister refused its request to intervene in a coercive manner, offering to use Ottawa's spending power to entice both Alberta and Saskatchewan into adopting a progressive and generous policy toward their francophone communities. In addition, he advised the ACFO's president to get in touch with Secretary of State Lucien Bouchard to put the ACFA's case.[65] The ACFO was not amused. When Alberta Premier Don Getty proceeded with the adoption of Bill 60 on 30 June, its director general, Fernand Gilbert, informed Mulroney that the flagrant injustice had forced his organization to rethink its support for the Meech Lake Accord. If two signatories to the Accord could behave in such a refractory manner, "nous refusons de croire en la bonne volonté des leaders politiques et exigeons que des garanties précises soient enchassées dans la Constitution."[66]

Georges Arès reacted to the adoption of Bill 60 by demanding that the prime minister abandon his failed policy of cooperation with Getty over the abolition of the fundamental rights of Franco-Albertans. Disallowance was the only remaining option if official bilingualism was to be restored in Alberta.[67] Arès also told Frank McKenna that the passage of the bill proved the Meech Lake Accord needed amendment and expressed a hope of meeting with him to discuss how they might cooperate in achieving this shared objective.[68] Fearful that matters might escalate out of control, Mulroney dispatched Lucien Bouchard to meet with ACFA representatives on 23 August 1988. Arès reminded Bouchard of his organization's demand for disallowance and financial penalties and named a series of stringent conditions that had to be fulfilled before the ACFA would accept the Accord, as well as an Alberta/Ottawa/ACFA agreement on the extension of French services in Alberta.[69] Senator Lowell Murray, Minister of State for Federal-

Provincial Relations, who was also present at the meeting, tried to pressure the ACFA into agreeing to put the question of minority language rights over to a second round. Arès was willing to accede, on condition that Murray obtain from Bourassa a written statement to the effect that he (Bourassa) and the Quebec government would support enshrining the obligation of the federal and provincial governments to promote the official language minorities at the future conference. Murray, knowing all too well that Bourassa would never agree – before or after the Meech Lake Accord was ratified – was furious at Arès's challenge.[70]

Ottawa's steadfast refusal to intervene reinforced the ACFA's already militant opposition to the Accord. Arès asked rhetorically whether the francophone minority communities had to turn to premiers McKenna and Filmon for support since they had been abandoned by Mulroney and Bourassa. The federal government was ceding important powers and revenues to the provinces without obtaining guarantees for the equitable treatment of the francophone minorities. In short, political and constitutional reconciliation with Quebec was being achieved at the expense of the federal policy on official languages and to the detriment of francophones.[71] It was several months before the prime minister answered Arès's letter of 11 October pleading with him to intervene. Mulroney revealed that he had tried to negotiate with Getty prior to the adoption of Bill 60 and reminded Arès that he had publicly expressed his displeasure over Alberta's decision to proceed. He went on to outline his government's many supportive measures for the francophone minority communities and reaffirmed his commitment to their future development. It was clear that the prime minister would do nothing more to change the mind of the Alberta government on official bilingualism; if he pushed too hard, Getty would drop his support for the Meech Lake Accord.[72]

Thanks to a parallel course of developments internal to Manitoba, the SFM became increasingly critical of the Accord throughout 1988. It sought legal counsel from Michel Bastarache on the effects of the deal on the official linguistic minorities. Bastarache's trenchant analysis highlighted both the strengths and the weaknesses of the Accord. While the Fédération believed it could live with specific flaws, Bastarache warned the SFM to pay attention to the comprehensive ideological thrust of the Accord, which undermined not only the rights of the linguistic minorities but the very foundations of the federation, inasmuch as it incorporated a narrow definition of linguistic duality and represented the entrenchment of a territorial duality to the detriment of pan-Canadian cultural and linguistic duality.

Le text comprend une affirmation du principe de dualité, mais la formule uti-lisée propose, à première vue, une interprétation individualiste plutôt que collective. Ceci risque de renforcer le penchant de la Cour suprême pour une interprétation minimaliste des droits linguistiques, comme dans le cas des droits judiciaires où l'on a trouvé que le droit d'utiliser le français ne comporte pas le droit d'être compris par la Cour. L'accord comprend aussi une clause de sauvegarde qui semble réduire la valeur juridique de la dualité et confirmer la vision de la dualité que proposait la Commission Pépin-Robarts, c'est-à-dire la dualité Québec français/Canada multiculturel.[73]

The SFM invited Bastarache to present his conclusions to its membership on 13 December 1988. Its objective was to educate all Franco-Manitobans on the complex issues and prepare them for any change in position that the SFM might want to adopt in the controversial debate over the Accord's ratification by the province. Bastarache concluded his remarks by stating that he considered it unjust that the minorities directly affected by the Accord were being forced to state their objections to it in the absence of an opportunity to propose amendments that would clarify the text without jeopardizing Quebec's support.[74] The SFM issued a bulletin explaining that it shared all of Bastarache's concerns and hoped that further discussions would help guide its approach to the controversial issue.[75]

In March 1989 the SFM faced a crisis when the new Secretary of State, Gerry Weiner, tied funding for the Franco-Manitoban community to its support for the Meech Lake Accord. Ottawa denied the attempt at coercion, but Weiner's notes for a meeting with the SFM were picked up by some journalists. SFM President Denis Clement denied that his organization was selling out for funds. However, Raymond Hébert, a political science professor at the Collège Universitaire de Saint-Boniface and a staunch opponent of the Accord, revealed that after the meeting with Weiner the SFM dropped plans for a conference of 4 April on the Accord at which he was invited to speak.[76] The president of the Conseil jeunesse provincial, Aline Taillefer, expressed outrage and demanded that the Franco-Manitoban community be kept fully informed about developments involving the SFM and the Accord. One SFM member, a priest, warned that the organization lacked credibility in the community and encouraged its president to be as honest as possible in all of its dealings on constitutional issues.[77]

The dispute had a salutary effect on the SFM's leaders. In their comprehensive brief to the Committee of the Manitoba Legislative Assembly in April 1989, they explained why certain crucial amendments reflecting the arguments of the group's legal counsel, Michel Bastarache, were necessary if the Meech Lake Accord was to become acceptable to Franco-Manitobans. The rights of francophone minority communities would be taken seriously by the courts and the provinces only if they were fully recognized in the Constitution and could be implemented without the judicial and political battles associated with rights under s. 23. The SFM recommended that the Manitoba government should make every conceivable effort to obtain its proposed amendments before ratifying the Accord. If this strategy was unsuccessful, the province should support the parallel proposal of New Brunswick Premier Frank McKenna.[78]

The Fédération Champions the Accord

While these events were transpiring in western Canada, the lengthy list of demands of the Conseil national des présidents was placing the Fédération, especially its president, in a difficult situation. At a meeting of the Conseil on 24 June 1988, Yvon Fontaine reported very limited success in securing those demands. He had managed to convince the prime minister to write to Saskatchewan Premier Grant Devine of expressing Ottawa's displeasure at the decision to rescind s. 110 of the North-West Territories Act. In the same letter Mulroney had informed Devine that his government intended to address "the issue of minority rights in their broadest context" during the second round of constitutional negotiations.[79] Considering the meagre results, Fontaine was forced to tell Lucien Bouchard that the Fédération remained opposed to the ratification of an unamended Accord. Also at the 24 June meeting, Georges Arès reported on the progress of the Alberta government's Bill 60 abolishing French as an official language of the province and reiterated his association's vehement opposition to an unamended Accord.[80]

The Fédération came under tremendous pressure from both the Mulroney and Bourassa governments to support ratification of the Accord as it stood. At the same time, it was also being pressured by the ACFO, which had started to shift its position on the deal. In June 1988, Rolande Soucie was elected as the new president of the ACFO. She was personally convinced that her organization, the other provincial francophone organizations, and the Fédération should all support an unamended Meech Lake Accord "afin de permettre au Québec de réintégrer dans l'honneur le giron confédératif." Soucie used her position to lobby the other presidents to get behind ratification.[81] No doubt one of the main reasons for Yvon Fontaine's decision to step down as Fédération president in December 1988 was that he no longer felt comfortable with the hard-line policy of the Conseil national des présidents on the constitutional question. In his last report, Fontaine argued that the only enlightened policy was for the

Fédération to accept an unamended Accord because it would lead to stronger support from Quebec for the francophone minority communities.[82] A second, more effective, flip-flop was well underway. The Fédération and its leaders were looking increasingly amateurish and, to the western affiliates, quite unreliable.

Sensing that the Fédération was about to alter its policy once again, Georges Arès proposed at the December 1988 meeting of the Conseil national des presidents that the organization undertake negotiations with the Mulroney and Bourassa governments with the intention of signing a tripartite agreement, approved *a priori* by all the member associations, "pour assurer la *promotion* et la *garantie* des droits des francophones hors Québec ... avant de donner notre appui à l'entente du Lac Meech." This resolution was defeated, as was second one by Arès calling on the Fédération to begin a massive publicity campaign to educate Canadians about francophones' concerns. Instead, the presidents passed a resolution stating that the Fédération would lend its support to the Meech Lake Accord on three conditions: that the entrenchment of francophone minority community rights would be placed on the agenda of the next constitutional round; that a federal/provincial conference would be held on s. 23 of the Charter to the end of achieving school governance; and that the federal government would complete the negotiations for the Canada-Community agreements, especially with Alberta, without further delay.[83]

The hard-line associations, led by Georges Arès, had lost their battle within the Fédération. Yet the ACFA's president was not deterred from continuing to speak out against the Accord. The Fédération was now content to defer its constitutional demands while pushing Ottawa and a number of provinces for some non-constitutional concessions. Michel Doucet, the Fédération's first vice-president, and two members of the organization's staff met with Secretary of State Lucien Bouchard and a couple of senior bureaucrats in an attempt to extract a formal commitment from the government on the three conditions.[84] Discouraged by Bouchard's tepid response, Doucet wrote Senator Lowell Murray on 27 January 1989 outlining the Fédération's new position and asking for a written guarantee from the Mulroney government on the first two conditions. Murray replied within three days expressing his pleasure that the Fédération now supported the reintegration of Quebec into the Canadian constitutional family. He also reminded Doucet of the commitment made by Brian Mulroney to Yvon Fontaine on 12 January 1988, which was repeated in his 8 April 1988 letter to Grant Devine. Both conditions would be on the agenda at the second round of constitutional negotiations.[85]

The presidents learned of the Fédération's minimal progress on its constitutional demands at a meeting in Toronto in March 1989. Arès reminded everyone that the three conditions of the December resolution had not been met and that, in his view, Senator Lowell Murray's letter was not satisfactory. Furthermore, he was furious that Quebec had decided to weigh in on the side of the Alberta government in the *Mahé* case, which was going before the Supreme Court. He was convinced that more political pressure had to be put on Mulroney and Bourassa if any amendments were to be achieved.[86]

The delegates attending the Fédération's AGM on 23–25 June 1989 appeared to agree with Arès; they passed a resolution calling on their leadership to put forward constitutional proposals that would "Èlargir, revendiquer et faire respecter nos droits collectifs sur une base d'égalité en proposant un nouvel arrangement constitutionnel."[87] The response was a set of proposals reflecting the Fédération's systematic pursuit of the constitutional recognition of the collective rights of Canada's francophone minority communities. During the round of negotiations following ratification of the Accord, the Fédération should seek several changes. First, the fundamental characteristics clause must state that all interpretations of Canada's Constitution should concur with the recognition of two collectivities equal in status, rights, and privileges – one English-speaking, the other French-speaking. Second, Parliament and the provincial legislatures must be responsible for preserving this duality. Third, both Parliament and the government of Canada must actively promote this duality. (Bourassa rejected any reference to Quebec's promoting linguistic and cultural duality.) Fourth, the legislature and government of New Brunswick should actively promote both of its official language communities. Finally, s. 23(3)(b) of the Charter should be amended to specify that francophone minority parents had the right to manage their homogeneous French language schools.[88] Yvon Fontaine, when asked for his professional advice on the document, recommended that the term "collectivity" replace the term "community" on the basis that Quebec could never accept the Fédération's proposed amendment to the fundamental characteristics clause recognizing the equality of two pan-Canadian communities, one anglophone and one francophone, since it would virtually negate any recognition of Quebec as a distinct society. In Fontaine's opinion, it would be foolish to expect that Ottawa, the provinces, and Quebec would agree to such an amendment in a second round. It would be better for the Fédération to support the ratification of the Accord, then to develop other constitutional means of achieving the objective of collective recognition of Canada's francophone minority communities and their rights.[89]

The Fédération tried to maintain the pressure on the Mulroney-Bourassa alliance and the premiers as the June 1990 deadline for ratification approached. In November 1989 the presidents reaffirmed their commitment to their resolution of December 1988 outlining the three conditions required for the Fédération's backing for the Accord.[90] Before adopting a final position in February, the Fédération had an interview with Bourassa on 22 January 1990 to attempt to persuade him to support the conditions. Its new president, Guy Matte, reminded Bourassa once again that his organization was one of Quebec's strongest allies. It fully supported Bourassa's five constitutional demands, as well as his decision, taken after the Supreme Court ruling on commercial signage, to legislate in favour of external French signage with internal bilingual signage. Moreover, it gave its support despite the considerable political cost in many parts of Canada. Matte also reminded the premier that Gil Rémillard had promised in a letter to the Fédération dated 5 April 1988 that during a second round of constitutional negotiations Quebec would see to it that the constitutional rights of Canada's francophone minority communities would be clarified and enhanced. He asked Bourassa for a guarantee that the group's constitutional requirements would either be part of any parallel accord that was being drawn up behind closed doors or be included on the second-round agenda. Given the delay in the implementation of their education rights and the promise made by Gil Rémillard at Mont-Gabriel, Matte also asked Bourassa to place discussion of s. 23 rights before the ministers of education, then consider the matter at the next First Ministers' conference. The Fédération and its provincial associations were very conscious that "le Québec est depuis toujours le château fort du fait français au Canada et en Amérique"; it was equally important that francophone Quebecers and their political and intellectual leaders understand that all francophones must make common cause. "Toute défaillance au sein des avant-postes francophones en Amérique affaiblit le Québec, sa culture et même son économie. À l'inverse, tout renforcement de nos communautés contribue à la solidité du Québec."[91]

The western francophone organizations, too, continued to struggle with what they regarded as a seriously flawed Accord. The SFM again considered its options on 13 January 1990 in the light of the fact that the report of the Manitoba Task Force on the Accord had rejected its recommendations, even proposed to weaken the existing protection clause. Its Comité des revendications politiques urged the Administrative Council to recommend ratification despite the deal's flaws, contingent on a process to entrench expanded constitutional guarantees for the protection and promotion of official language minorities

before the end of 1993. It saw a possible solution in the proposals of
the New Brunswick Legislative Assembly's Select Committee on the
1987 Constitutional Accord.[92]

The SFM found itself caught between a rock and a hard place. After
heated deliberations on 12 February 1990, the Administrative Council
decided that it would neither support nor oppose the Accord, given
the even balance between its strengths and weaknesses. The SFM challenged political leaders in Ottawa, Quebec, and Manitoba to assume
fully their respective responsibilities in the protection of national
unity. "Mieux sauver l'unité du pays que de vouloir à tout prix sauver
un document imparfait," was its warning to Ottawa. Manitoba should
develop a more open and pro-active attitude toward the Franco-
Manitoban communities, while Quebec needed to remind itself of
the importance of solidarity in the Franco-Canadian family and stop
taking political and legislative positions bearing negative consequences for francophone minority communities. In short, the SFM saw
the Accord as badly flawed; everyone concerned had to modify it to
prevent further fragmentation and divisions within Canada.[93] It would
be very difficult, if not impossible, to maintain this position of neutrality as the 23 June deadline loomed.

Forging a Fragile Consensus

Guy Matte reported to the presidents at their mid-February meeting in
Winnipeg that the January meeting with Premier Bourassa had gone
very well. Apparently, Bourassa gave the Fédération verbal assurances
for the two central conditions it was seeking. Matte also indicated that
discussions with Premier McKenna about a parallel accord addressing
the concerns of the francophone communities had met with success.
In addition, overtures had been made to Senator Lowell Murray and
his senior staff, and the appropriate guarantees pertaining to a possible parallel accord and a second constitutional round had been
received on 15 February 1990.[94] Brian Mulroney let it be known that
he was contemplating a parliamentary committee that would consider
McKenna's proposal for a parallel deal before the ratification of the
Meech Lake Accord.[95] These developments allowed Guy Matte – with
ACFO President Rolande Soucie taking the lead role[96] – to convince the
presidents to support the ratification of an unamended Accord. After
hours of discussion, the presidents passed a resolution – proposed by
Raymond Bisson of Manitoba – recognizing the Fédération's duty to
support the Accord, on condition that a range of important issues
should be addressed in a parallel accord: the federal government's
right to promote, not just preserve, linguistic equality; additional

guarantees for gender equality; aboriginal self-government; the creation of new provinces; and Senate reform.[97]

The prime minister was undoubtedly pleased with the Fédération's newfound support. With that problem out of the way, he turned his attention to the recalcitrant premiers. In a deft political manoeuvre, when McKenna introduced his Companion Resolution – his own proposed parallel accord – into the New Brunswick legislature on 21 March, Mulroney responded the very next day by striking a Special Committee chaired by Conservative Jean Charest to hold hearings and call witnesses on the resolution. Close observers of the Meech debacle were well aware that Senator Lowell Murray had played a leading role in the formulation of the resolution. He had the support of Jean Chrétien, who was campaigning for the leadership of the Liberal Party. For different reasons, both desperately wanted to get Frank McKenna out of the corner into which he had painted himself over the previous three years. Murray managed to change the dynamic of McKenna's resolution by having it characterized as a companion rather than a parallel process. A parallel resolution would demand closure at the same time as the Meech Lake Accord, something that was unacceptable to Bourassa. According to one perceptive journalist, Mulroney was merely trying to legitimize the Meech Lake process with pseudo-public hearings while deliberately letting the clock run out to prevent any time being spent on the formal amendments to the Accord demanded by the two holdouts, Manitoba's Gary Filmon and Newfoundland's Clyde Wells.[98]

Subsequent developments confirmed that this was indeed Mulroney's cynical strategy. Yet even if the Fédération and some of its affiliates realized what was going on at this early stage, they were not dissuaded from playing along with the prime minister. The francophone organizations were reeling under the backlash against their constituents. By this time, strong public opposition to the Meech Lake Accord was being expressed daily in all the media. It was accentuated by Bourassa's inopportune Bill 178, a coercive law that imposed external French language commercial signage using the notwithstanding clause, because unilingual commercial signage violated the Supreme Court's decision. The Fédération, the SAANB, the SFM, and the ACFO were among the hundreds of organizations and individuals to give testimony before Charest's committee beginning on 3 April. Conspicuous by their absence were the ACFA's leaders, who steadfastly opposed the Accord as long as its proposed amendments were not written into the document. Its new president, France Levasseur-Ouimet, was a strong believer in francophone solidarity and had voted in favour of the February resolution supporting the Accord despite finding it highly objectionable. The struggle over Meech Lake had polarized Canadians along the historic linguistic and cultural divide; the ACFA naturally rallied in a crunch to the francophone side but still could not bring itself to formally endorse the Accord.[99]

In their testimony before the Special Committee, the Fédération and several provincial affiliates reiterated their February decision to accept ratification unconditionally. They all supported the Companion Resolution because it did not affect the integrity of the Accord but opened avenues for further amendments. In a brief entitled *Ouvrons-nous les yeux: le sort du Canada est en jeu*, the Fédération stressed the importance of having Quebec formally recognize the Constitution Act, 1982 so the process of constitutional renewal could move forward. Guy Matte and the other presidents firmly believed that this magnanimous gesture would help dissolve the linguistic and political tensions that were producing a nasty backlash against all French-speaking Canadians. Few English-speaking Canadians had rallied to the Fédérations's position that the federal and provincial governments should promote the French language and culture.[100]

The only discordant note before the Special Committee came when SFM President Raymond Bisson outlined his organization's dilemma. It wanted to see "Quebec back within the Canadian constitutional fold" but had serious reservations about the imperfections of the Accord as regards the rights of francophones outside that province. While the SFM supported the Companion Resolution, Bisson pointed out that the "project does not go so far as to confer upon the governments and provincial legislatures the role of promoting Canada's linguistic duality." He urged that a mechanism for second-round constitutional discussions be agreed upon before ratification, since he remained doubtful that it would be possible for Ottawa and the provinces to agree on minority language rights once the Accord was ratified.[101]

The Fédération's primary goal for the second round was seeing to it that Ottawa took on the constitutional responsibility of promoting Canada's fundamental characteristic: the presence of two linguistic communities. Guy Matte countered the testimony given by political scientist Peter Russell and a former senior federal bureaucrat, Gordon Robertson, to the effect that a promotion clause was both unnecessary and political unwise. He reminded the Special Committee's members that its legal experts, including Yvon Fontaine, had proven that a promotion clause was a perfectly legitimate legal instrument and would not affect the distinct society clause. He also pointed out that both Robert Bourassa and Gil Rémillard favoured such a clause; opposition came from the anglophone provinces, not Quebec. He claimed – without supporting documentation – that the Fédération had obtained further assurances from Bourassa that his government, along with those of Ottawa, Ontario, and New Brunswick, would support a promotion clause during the second round.[102]

The SAANB, which opposed the linguistic duality clause because it failed to recognize collectivities, decided that it would not push for a promotion clause because it would weaken the legal situation of the Acadian community under Bill 88. Instead, the group advocated an Acadian solution entailing the entrenchment of Bill 88 in the Constitution via the bilateral amending formula of s. 43. The beauty of this arrangement was that it did not require any amendment to the Meech Lake Accord and was compatible with the distinct society clause, which also recognized the collective rights of Quebec's francophone majority community.[103] Under the presidency of Rolande Soucie, the ACFO had put its considerable influence to good use in convincing first the SAANB, then the Fédération, that the Accord should be ratified unamended. Indeed, a promotion clause was no longer perceived as necessary since the ACFO had gained access to certain French language services wherever numbers warranted through Bill 8. The absence of the clause should therefore no longer be used to prevent ratification. Besides, the ACFO believed that effective promotion of the Franco-Ontarian community could be achieved only under a formal and comprehensive federal-provincial agreement achieved at the province's initiative. Once such an agreement was in place, Soucie believed that it could be entrenched in the Constitution as per the bilateral amending formula proposed by the SAANB.[104] Once again, the larger and stronger eastern francophone organizations had abandoned their compatriots in western Canada.

In early May 1990, Soucie made a trip to Quebec to encourage Bourassa to accept McKenna's Companion Resolution. She also met with Gil Rémillard to convince him that the Quebec government should support a promotion clause in the second round of negotiations. Rémillard made it clear that Quebec could never endorse such a clause but might allow Ottawa to play a role in the defence of linguistic rights if its efforts did not affect Quebec's jurisdiction.[105] Bourassa came under tremendous pressure from Rémillard, who was backed by militant Québécois nationalists within and outside the government, to make sure that any promotion clause would not apply to Quebec. Contrary to its earlier position, the Fédération was no longer advocating that all the provinces be obliged to promote linguistic duality, because this approach was unacceptable to many of them. Furthermore, as Bourassa repeatedly reminded everyone, such a clause was perceived by most Québécois nationalists as undermining the distinct society clause. Convinced by Bourassa, the Fédération adopted an asymmetrical approach to promotion because the francophone communities, including Quebec's, faced the everyday threat of assimilation while the English-speaking minority of Quebec did not. The Bourassa government had insisted on the non-derogatory clause 2(4) because it guaranteed that Ottawa's responsibility to preserve and possibly promote Quebec's English language minority was strictly limited to areas in its own jurisdiction. When asked by André Ouellet, Liberal MP for Papineau-Saint-Michel, why the Fédération had shifted its position, Guy Matte and Aurèle Thériault answered that the provinces must not be coerced but rather enticed over time into backing the promotion clause. This new viewpoint ran counter to the Féderation's long-standing belief that only "coercion" by the Supreme Court would force most provincial governments to grant school governance to their francophone communities. Yet, ever aware of the growing concern for the future of Quebec's linguistic minority, especially after the passage of Bill 178 on signage, the Fédération opined that "we must be ready to agree to the preservation and promotion of a minimum number of institutions for all linguistic minorities in Canada."[106] In short, there should be promotion if necessary but not necessarily promotion, so that both conceptions of duality, pan-Canadian and Quebec/Canada, could co-exist in an asymmetrical federation.

The Special Committee on the Companion Resolution tabled its unanimous report on 18 May 1990. It recommended adoption, with some minor amendments and several additions responding to demands from Manitoba and Newfoundland. In a bow to the francophone organizations, the report stated that "minority language rights require continuing deliberation and should be included on the Agenda of the Annual First Ministers Conference on the Constitution."[107] It also gave notice that the 23 June 1990 deadline was a "political reality" and that any and all deliberations about extending it were purely hypothetical and would not help resolve the crisis. On the crucial issue of "certainty" – a guarantee for his Companion Resolution – raised by Premier Frank McKenna, it concluded that "timing and process leading to additional amendments to the Constitution of Canada can only be negotiated by First Ministers."[108] In fact, by agreeing to a companion rather than a parallel resolution, McKenna had abandoned his attempt to obtain amendments before ratification. With no guarantee for any amendment before ratification, it appeared for the moment that Mulroney and Bourassa had won their mega-constitutional political gambit.

THE MEECH LAKE ACCORD'S INEVITABLE DEMISE

A twist of fate would undo all their manoeuvring. By the winter of 1990, the Meech Lake Accord had fallen out of favour with the

Canadian public. To most Meech-watchers and to critics, who gained inspiration from the polls, it appeared doomed. A Gallup Poll taken on 8 March showed less than a quarter of the population supporting the deal, substantially down from 56 per cent in August 1987. A formidable array of diverse anti-Meech Lake forces had coalesced around numerous national and provincial aboriginal, women's, and civil liberties organizations. At the same time, an informal but highly effective national network of constitutional specialists working under an umbrella organization called the Canadian Coalition on the Constitution, with ready access to the media, were educating the public about what they perceived as the Accord's egregious flaws. Indeed, the turnaround was so dramatic that a coterie of pro-Meechers – including academics Charles Taylor and Jeremy Webber of McGill University, former mandarins Gordon Robertson and Jake Warren, and retired politicians such as Robert Stanfield, Jack Pickersgill, Richard Hatfield, and Brian Peckford – formed the Friends of Meech Lake, then Canadians for a Unifying Constitution in a desperate attempt to reverse the precipitous slide in public opinion.[109]

Despite incessant demands for public input into the process of constitutional renewal, the final outcome of the three years of wrangling over the life or death of the Meech Lake Accord remained squarely in the hands of the prime minister and the premiers. Two recalcitrant premiers were especially instrumental. Gary Filmon, who would have signed the Accord were it not for a groundswell of public opposition galvanized by Manitoba's Liberal opposition leader Sharon Carstairs, backed off. Clyde Wells objected on principle to what he considered a grievously flawed deal. On 6 April, just as the Special Committee began its review of the Companion Resolution and the Quebec National Assembly passed a motion stating that it would not accept a single alteration to the Accord, Newfoundland's Liberal government rescinded the previous government's ratification of the deal.[110]

Paradoxically, a near-fatal blow was delivered by Lucien Bouchard, Brian Mulroney's highly influential but politically volatile Environment Minister. He announced his resignation, using the Special Committee's report as his long-sought opportunity for bailing out. The ambitious and mercurial Bouchard saw the Meech Lake Accord as the bare minimum acceptable to the nationalistic Québécois political class. The report recommended a federal role in the promotion of linguistic duality as well as the recognition of aboriginal peoples as the first founding nations of Canada. It also asserted, without any supporting evidence, that the distinct society clause could influence but not override the Charter. Bouchard strongly believed that this interpretation, when combined with the proposed additions, seriously diminished the limited and fragile gains for Quebec in the original Accord. An angry Bouchard predicted, quite prophetically, that the demise of the Accord would result in irreparable damage to relations between Quebec and Ottawa. He also mused that it would open the door to Quebec's eventual secession from the federation.[111]

Bouchard's resignation seriously constrained the manoeuvring room that Mulroney and Bourassa could have used in resolving the impasse with Wells and Filmon. Bouchard, who was being urged to form the secessionist Bloc Québécois, put the prime minister and his ally on notice that if the Accord was diluted or defeated, they would face him as a powerful foe in the political arena. Waiting till the very last moment, as he had planned even before the Special Committee's report, Mulroney "rolled the dice" as he later boasted to two *Globe & Mail* reporters: he summoned the premiers to a dinner to be held on 3 June 1990 at the Canadian Museum of Civilization in Hull. Doggedly determined to obtain ratification of an unamended Meech Lake Accord, he agreed to negotiate a considerably expanded list of agenda items at the next round of constitutional talks. The dinner turned into a week-long high-stakes drama in the Government Conference Centre located in Ottawa's restored railway station across from the Chateau Laurier Hotel. In mixed awe and consternation, Canadians watched the morning and evening scrums as well as the incessant and often asinine commentary of journalists, political spin-doctors, senior bureaucrats, and constitutional experts. For six tension-ridden, tumultuous days, the prime minister and eight premiers harangued, cajoled, and threatened the principled and stubborn Wells and the bewildered Filmon, first into exhaustion and eventually into submission.[112]

The backroom constitutional slugfest culminated in a highly fragile deal based on a concoction of elements drawn from the Companion Resolution and the resulting report. It committed Wells, Filmon, and McKenna to submitting the Meech Lake Accord "for appropriate legislative or public consideration and to [using] every possible effort to achieve decision prior to" the 23 June deadline.[113] Wells's signature was conditional; arriving back in Newfoundland, he immediately regretted having compromised his principles of individual and provincial equality. In return for their acquiescence, he and Filmon had received formal and informal commitments from the prime minister and the other premiers, including Bourassa, regarding a comprehensive agenda of future constitutional changes. These included a national commission to study the "Triple E Senate" – elected, equal, and effective – sought by himself and the western premiers, aboriginal rights conferences every three years, improvements to women's and linguistic minority rights, and a parliamentary committee to study the expanded Canada clause proposed by Manitoba. Finally, a somewhat suspect legal opinion on the distinct society clause, which stated that it did not infringe on the Charter, was appended to the agreement. The despondent Wells, who in his final speech pleaded with the people of Quebec to put Canada first and Quebec second, made it clear that his signature meant only that he was agreeing to take an unsatisfactory and unacceptable agreement back to his Cabinet and caucus for a decision on whether to hold a free vote or a referendum on the Accord. Only after its ratification or rejection would he accept or repudiate the questionable companion agreement of June 1990.[114]

Prior to the meeting at the Government Conference Centre, the Fédération's leaders were despondent at the prospect of the Accord's demise. The francophone organizations had consumed so much time, energy, and funds in achieving a fragile consensus, which now appeared shattered. An internal report outlined several political and ideological factors that the Fédération considered to be responsible for the groundswell of opposition to the Accord. Like the Mulroney government, it placed most of the blame on the media, which in its view had failed to educate the public about the nature and importance of the deal. Instead, seeking their own self-aggrandizement, most of the media had chosen to polarize the debate, portraying two distinct, increasingly hard-line, camps while deliberately ignoring organizations such as the Fédération that tried to advance a nuanced position of conditional support. From this perspective, the Meech Lake Accord came to symbolize Canada's socioeconomic, cultural, linguistic, and political faultlines.[115]

After the agreement of June 9, which ostensibly drew the recalcitrant premiers on side, the Fédération was somewhat more optimistic. Three days later, Director General Aurèle Thériault presented a brief to the Constitutional Committee of the Quebec Liberal Party in which he outlined an ambitious post-Meech constitutional agenda. First and foremost, the competing visions of duality had to be reconciled. He urged Quebec to form a new partnership with all the francophone and Acadian communities represented by the Fédération, to bring about further constitutional gains for all of Canada's French-speaking citizens. In fact, all francophones, including those in the multilingual and multi-ethnic region of greater Montreal, faced the same challenge: fending off assimilation. Thériault pointed out that "plus le français est utilisé et utilisable dans le reste du Canada, plus il s'enracinera au Québec," and concluded that "la victoire de l'un est aussi celle de l'autre; les préoccupations de l'autre sont aussi celles du premier. En arriver à une autre conclusion, c'est se mentir à soi-même."[116]

The SFM was drawn into the final debacle over the Meech Lake Accord because Premier Gary Filmon had to hold public hearings before the Manitoba Legislative Assembly could vote to ratify it in time to meet the deadline. The SFM convened representatives from eighteen Franco-Manitoban organizations for a meeting on 13 June 1990 to encourage them to lobby their respective MLAs to support ratification.[117] The Association des juristes d'expression française du Manitoba presented a brief to the Legislative Committee urging the government and the opposition to ratify the Accord despite its imperfections regarding the linguistic minorities; its demise would terminate the process of constitutional renewal, "ce qui de toute évidence va à l'encontre de l'intérêt supérieur des minorités francophones hors-Québec."[118] In its own brief, the SFM congratulated Premier Filmon and both opposition leaders, Sharon Carstairs and Gary Doer, on the courageous decision to support an agreement that would allow ratification without prior amendment. While the francophone communities had not obtained the constitutional guarantees they were seeking, the SFM was putting its trust in the formal commitment of the prime minister and the premiers to place the rights of the linguistic minorities on the second-round agenda. Ratification before the deadline was essential to reaching that next stage.[119] On 21 June, SFM President Raymond Bisson wrote to Filmon and the opposition leaders, as well as to Clyde Wells and the members of the Newfoundland House of Assembly, pleading with them to ratify the Accord without further delay.[120]

The ACFO was delighted at the outcome of the meeting between the prime minister and the premiers during the week of 3–9 June. President Rolande Soucie congratulated Premier David Peterson on his undaunted support for the distinct society clause, which would allow Quebec to be reintegrated into the constitutional family "dans la paix et dans l'honneur." She applauded his generosity on the question of Senate reform in agreeing to give up some of Ontario's Senate seats to obtain a deal. Soucie assured Peterson that the ACFO and the community it represented would maintain their support for all measures that would improve the linguistic management of Canada and Ontario. She urged him to stand by his commitment to including the promotion of linguistic duality in the next constitutional round and to make room for the ACFO in those negotiations.[121]

Despite all the brinkmanship, Mulroney's "roll of the dice" failed in a blaze of humiliating national publicity. Gary Filmon was either unable or unwilling to obtain the necessary unanimous approval from the members of the Manitoba legislature to alter the order of business without the normal two days' notice in order to bring the Meech Lake Accord to a vote. One solitary NDP member, Elijah Harper, a Cree from the Red Sucker Band, backed by the Manitoba Federation of Indians and the Assembly of First Nations led by Ovide Mercredi, refused for nearly two weeks to give his consent. When Filmon informed Wells late on the evening of 21 June that the Manitoba legislature would adjourn the following day at 12:30 PM without taking a vote, the Accord was to all intents and purposes dead. After close consultations with his Cabinet and caucus, Wells decided that it was counterproductive to put the Accord to a vote in the House of Assembly, where it would be soundly defeated for a second time, rubbing salt into the wounds of Bourassa, the Quebec government, and all francophones who had supported it over three tumultuous years. Senator Lowell Murray's desperate attempt to manipulate Wells into holding the vote on the grounds that the Supreme Court would extend the deadline for Manitoba also failed. The sordid episode simply confirmed Wells's perception of Mulroney's political conduct as unprincipled and validated his tenacious opposition to the Accord.[122] In the final analysis, mastery of mega-constitutional politics had eluded the prime minister and his Quebec ally. But the dramatic demise of the Meech Lake Accord would not teach them any profound lessons; instead, it strengthened their resolve to roll the dice once again in a more comprehensive round of constitutional wrangling.

Given their longstanding ambivalence, several flip-flops, eventual unconditional acceptance, and unrealistic raised expectations, it was not surprising that the Fédération and most of its affiliates considered the failure of the Accord a grievous blow to their future development. "Je ressens une profonde tristesse," declared Rolande Soucie, "face à la non-ratification de l'Accord du Lac Meech. Les Québécoises et les Québécois interpréteront sûrement cet échec comme le rejet du Canada anglais, rejet plus répandu qu'on ne le croyait de la thèse des deux peuples fondateurs. Il faut envisager qu'il devra avoir lieu un nouvel aménagement politique et constitutionnel du pays."[123] Nevertheless, she urged the Franco-Ontarian community to continue the struggle for their rights, to pursue an open dialogue with Quebec's francophone majority, to develop solidarity with the other francophone communities, to enhance links with all cultural and ethnic groups throughout Canada, and, finally, to inject themselves into the political and constitutional renewal of their country.[124]

CONCLUSION

Canada's francophone organizations and their leaders made a herculean effort to influence both the content and the process of mega-constitutional negotiations at all stages of the Meech Lake Accord's formulation and ratification. Responding to its provincial affiliates, the Fédération pursued two objectives. The first was to achieve constitutional recognition of the collective rights of Canada's two founding nations, French Canada and English Canada, equal in status, rights, and privileges, and present in all regions of the country. Most francophone minority community leaders came to believe that the constitutional entrenchment of their conception of a pan-Canadian cultural and linguistic duality could be complemented, even enhanced, by the entrenchment of the territorial Quebec/Canada view of duality held by Québécois neo-nationalists and the Bourassa government. Some francophone leaders and many of their constituents, however, were sceptical that these competing visions were in fact complementary. The Fédération's second aim was to obtain amendments to s. 23 of the Charter so that all francophone minority communities could achieve full school governance, which it hoped would serve as a model for similar governance over other important areas, beginning with health and social services.

Why did the Fédération and the provincial organizations fail to achieve their two objectives? Their biggest obstacle was the deep divide between themselves and the neo-nationalist majority, represented by Bourassa's government, over the competing – some would argue mutually exclusive – concepts of duality. From the territorial perspective, Quebec City was the capital of the Québécois nation and Ottawa was the capital of English Canada. This viewpoint left francophone and Acadian minorities with little choice but to turn to Ottawa. Entrenching this conception of duality began with the distinct society clause, which would enable Quebec to obtain, via the courts, powers over a range of jurisdictions not available to the other provinces. In due course, an asymmetrical federation would emerge reinforcing Quebec's distinctiveness. This vision of the nation was the basis for the Bourassa government's deepseated opposition to any clause giving Parliament and the federal government a constitutional obligation to both preserve and promote Quebec's English language minority community. Bourassa and his supporters saw the distinct society clause as referring to the francophone majority of Quebec; it did not include an obligation to promote the development of the English-speaking community. As for the other nine provinces, they were reluctant to be burdened with a similar obligation towards their French language minority communities. Nor was Bourassa interested in pressing them to take on this burden, for fear of setting a precedent for Quebec.

The second factor was that, over time, it became obvious that no Quebec government would ever accept an amendment to s. 23 making explicit the right of the official language communities to school governance. Bourassa's government, like that of his predecessor, was contemplating the replacement of Quebec's historic dual-denominational school system with a system based on two languages and designed and administered by an already powerful, interventionist Ministry of Education. A constitutional right to governance for Quebec's English language minority community was unacceptable for both political and ideological reasons. This standpoint was put in stark relief when Quebec sided with Alberta in *Mahé*. The alliance, which should have been expected but was not, explains why the ACFA rejected the Meech Lake Accord despite the repeated attempts by the Fédération and the ACFO to convince it to come on side.

Another reason for the failure of the francophone groups was the divisiveness within the communities themselves. Established in 1975, the Fédération lacked sufficient time to build consensus on crucial constitutional issues and devise the best strategies for reaching it goals. Much the same was true for its provincial affiliates. The imbroglio over the Meech Lake Accord demonstrated that mega-constitutional politics could make or break the Fédération. In theory, it shared with the Mulroney government the vision of Canada as a bicultural, bilingual nation-state made manifest in the comprehensive revision of the Official Languages Act in 1988. In practice, however, Mulroney could not push for a more comprehensive and explicit constitutional recognition of this pan-Canadian cultural and linguistic duality for fear of destroying the fragile consensus over the Accord. Thus, francophone organizations could not count on the Canadian government, their natural ally since the 1960s, to help them achieve their two main constitutional objectives.

Still, thanks in large measure to their determination, the federal and provincial governments were forced to make concessions looking ahead to a second round of constitutional negotiations. Moreover, Ottawa was obliged to pressure the recalcitrant provinces with offers of additional funds to get them to sign minority language education and cultural development agreements. Western francophone organizations took the opportunity to educate their constituencies about their constitutional rights and to gain public support in their battles with their respective governments.

Nevertheless, in the end Canada's francophone minority communities paid a heavy price for their internal divisions. Had the Fédération's leaders – in the central office, in the ACFO and the SAANB – held steady in their original rejection of the Accord despite Bourassa's overtures in October 1987, the premier might well have accepted a minimal amendment supporting federal promotion of the official language minority communities. Once Fontaine, Thériault, Doucet, and Soucie caved in, however, Bourassa realized that eventually all the holdouts would come on side. With the Fédération's solidarity shattered, it became virtually impossible for its leaders to convince Ottawa and a sufficient number of provinces to accept any amendments whatsoever. On the other hand, having failed to compromise on this and other aspects of the Accord, Mulroney and Bourassa ensured its demise. Consequently, the various players soon found themselves enmeshed in another, far more comprehensive and controversial, round of mega-constitutional politics. It was euphemistically dubbed the "Canada Round" to distinguish it from the Quebec and provincial rounds, both of which had gone down in flames.

7

The Canada Round:
A Clash of Nationalisms

Nous ne voulons pas une nouvelle nuit des longs couteaux. Nous voulons un rôle de promotion de la dualité linguistique par le gouvernement fédéral et nous y tenons.[1]

The failure of the Meech Lake Accord did not bring an end to destabilizing mega-constitutional politics. Within weeks, Canadians from coast to coast once again found themselves drawn into a powerful vortex of political intrigue surrounding Quebec's future in the federation. This second, more comprehensive round of constitutional negotiations – dubbed the Canada Round by the Mulroney government – severely exacerbated the conflict of competing nationalisms: western Canadian, pan-Canadian, Québécois, and aboriginal. It also gravely undermined national unity, contributed to the defeat of both the Mulroney and Bourassa governments, and provided the ideological fuel for a second, nearly successful, Quebec referendum on secession in 1995. Willing to gamble with political careers and Canada's territorial integrity alike, the Mulroney-Bourassa alliance was determined to make the Accord, in one form or another, part of the Constitution. If this meant accommodating the national aboriginal organizations, especially Chief Ovide Mercredi's highly nationalistic Assembly of First Nations, which had been ultimately responsible for the downfall of the deal, then so be it. What was not clear was whether the pair were willing to give consideration to the constitutional aspirations of other communities, especially the francophone minorites, who were dealt with so cavalierly throughout the Meech Lake debacle.

The Canada Round forced francophone leaders to continue their political and judicial campaigns for rights under s. 23 for a further two years. Their organizations worked hard, with considerable success, to avoid the internal dis-sension experienced earlier. They were determined to have their conception of pan-Canadian duality, anglophone and francophone, entrenched in a renewed Constitution.

At the outset, the Fédération's leaders attempted to rebuild their rapport with Robert Bourassa, hoping to make him more responsive to their constitutional needs and hopes. They repeatedly asked him to fulfill his responsibilities towards their communities through a series of new partnership arrangements. But Bourassa was unfortunately caught in a web of his own making. It became all too evident that Québécois nationalists and separatists cared little about any form of partnership; they sought two only goals. Nationalists of all political persuasions wanted a new territorially-based constitutional partnership between Canada and Quebec, a decentralized Quebec/Canada federation. Separatists promoted the secession of Quebec from the federation, by unilateral declaration if necessary, with some form of state-to-state economic partnership to follow.

Francophone leaders soon realized that the Bourassa government had no real intention of accommodating them. With the support of its provincial affiliates, the Fédération developed both policies and strategies towards reasonable, clear constitutional objectives. Moreover, it once again sought representation at the negotiating table when discussions concerned the francophone minority communities. Pushed by its western affiliates, the Fédération aligned itself in an informal coalition with the aboriginal organizations, national and provincial, to gain access to inside information and thereby enhance the bargaining power of all groups directly affected by the Charter and other nongovernmental participants.

Despite its best efforts, however, dissension resurfaced within the Fédération. As previously, it was pressured by the militant western groups to apply a more aggressive strategy in pursuing its constitutional objectives. In fact, this forceful stance, coupled with their collaboration with other organizations, eventually produced modest results for the Fédération and its affiliates. The Charlottetown Consensus Report (or Charlottetown Accord) was the result of intensive and chaotic closed-door negotiations among Ottawa, all the provinces except Quebec (until the last month), and four national aboriginal organizations. The deal acquired its name from the final symbolic meeting held on 28 August at the birthplace of Confederation: Charlottetown, Prince Edward Island. It went some distance towards recognizing the collective rights of the official language minorities as well as the Fédération's pan-Canadian conception of linguistic and cultural duality. In the so-called "Canada clause" this vision coexisted ambiguously with the Quebec nationalists' territorially-based conception expressed in the distinct society clause. It was a tenuous relationship that francophone leaders, national and provincial, were willing to support because it was an improvement over the Meech Lake Accord. The compromise also appeared to satisfy the Bourassa government and, initially, a majority of francophone Quebecers. Furthermore, the new deal promised to end the interminable mega-constitutional battles.

To the considerable dismay of the Fédération and its affiliates, a majority of Canadians, including those in Quebec and the native communities, rejected the Charlottetown Consensus Report in a referendum held on 26 October 1992. Canadians across all regions and party affiliations felt uncomfortable with its comprehensiveness, complexities, ambiguities, and potential radicalism. After nearly a decade of mega-constitutional politics courtesy of the Mulroney-Bourassa alliance, virtually nothing had been accomplished and Canada's constitutional integrity was in jeopardy. Francophone leaders had to rely on the Constitution Act of 1867 and 1982 for the survival of their communities. At the same time, Canada's constitutional political culture had been democratized in ways that few experts had anticipated. No government, federal or provincial, would be able to propose fundamental constitutional reforms without involving Canadian citizens in both the negotiations and their ratification. Canadians were well on their way to becoming a sovereign people. Moreover, Canada's francophone minority communities carved out a secure place for themselves within Pierre Trudeau's visionary Constitution Act, 1982 and its luminous diamond, the Canadian Charter of Rights and Freedoms.

GRAPPLING WITH THE FAILURE OF THE MEECH LAKE ACCORD

On 23 June 1990, the day after the Meech Lake Accord's demise in Manitoba and the day before Quebec's national holiday, Premier Robert Bourassa declared in the National Assembly: "No matter what anyone says or does, Quebec has always been, now, and always will be a distinct society, free and capable of assuming its own destiny and development."[2] Henceforth, Quebec would not return to the constitutional negotiating table; it would deal directly with Ottawa in defending and promoting its interests. If the Canadian government made acceptable constitutional proposals to Quebec, Bourassa might just agree to bilateral discussions on a new status for the province in the federation, one that reflected the Canada/Quebec vision outlined in the Meech Lake Accord. Bourassa set out to enhance his bargaining power vis-à-vis Ottawa by harnessing the sharp rise in support for secession among francophones. Determined to control and manipulate his caucus and party militants – some of whom were threatening to leave – he urged the Constitutional Committee of the Quebec Liberal Party, chaired by Jean Allaire, to get on with its work of analysing the province's constitutional options. On 4 September 1990, hoping to ride the wave of separatist sentiment, Bourassa had the National Assembly establish a Commission on the Political and Constitutional Future of Quebec to "examine and analyse the political and constitutional status of Quebec."[3] Including representatives from provincial and federal parties, nationalist organizations, labour centrals, and business groups, its mandate was to consult widely and make recommendations on the full range of options available to the Bourassa government, including, if necessary, independence.[4]

The new body became known as the Bélanger-Campeau Commission after its co-chairs, Michel Bélanger, federalist president of the Quebec-based National Bank, and Jean Campeau, secessionist chairman of the Caisse de Dépôt et Placement du Québec. Trying to outflank the leader of the Parti Québécois, Bourassa insisted that Lucien Bouchard, who had resigned from Mulroney's Cabinet over the Special Committee on the Companion Resolution, be a member. Moreover, believing it would increase Quebec's clout with Ottawa, the premier backed Bouchard's decision to create a secessionist party in Ottawa, the Bloc Québécois, a political home for disgruntled Quebec Conservative and Liberal Members of Parliament. Determined to obtain his Meech Lake Accord at any cost, an ailing Bourassa (he had skin cancer) played hardball by putting "a knife to the throat" of Canada.[5] Doing their best to back his strategy and tactics, Québécois politicians, academics, and journalists, together with a wide range of organizations and citizens' groups – many of whom submitted briefs and/or gave testimony to the Bélanger-Campeau Commission – stoked the fires of secessionism by fashioning a potentially destructive myth blaming English Canada for the defeat of the Accord.[6] All these developments pushed support for secession among francophone Quebecers to an all-time high of 64 per cent by November.[7]

The Fédération quickly learned how to manoeuvre in these turbulent waters. On 27 June, Fédération President Guy Matte wrote to Bourassa to commiserate with him over the demise of the Accord and to encourage him to continue his quest to entrench both conceptions of duality in a renewed federation: "Une société distincte, le Québec, se développant à l'intérieur d'un Canada dualiste avec la présence de communautés francophones partout à l'extérieur du Québec." Reminding him that much of the groundwork had been laid for important constitutional reforms, Matte noted that the Fédération was eager to participate in the work of the Bélanger-Campeau Commission which – he was certain – would have profound repercussions for Canada and the francophone minority communities. He requested a meeting with the premier to discuss these matters as well as the "principes de base du remaniement des relations entre tous les partenaires francophones du Canada."[8] In the interim, the premier set out to reassure the Fédération by thanking Matte for his organization's support for the Accord despite the dissension it created amongst the francophone communities. While Quebec would most assuredly defends its interests, the importance "de travailler et de soutenir les communautés francophones vivant à l'extérieur du Québec" would always be kept in mind. The Bélanger-Campeau Commission would take into account those communities' needs and the important contribution that Quebec could make to their expansion and development. His government remained sensitive to maintaining true solidarity among all Canadian francophones. He welcomed the Fédération's participation in the commission's proceedings and encouraged it to work with the appropriate authorities in the Canadian Intergovernmental Relations Secretariat to find concrete ways of consolidating "la francophonie canadienne." Once these developments were well underway, he would meet with representatives from the group to discuss the results.[9]

The Fédération's constitutional advisor, convinced that the Canadian federation was about to undergo a fundamental restructuring in the wake of the Accord's downfall, recommended that the organization develop comprehensive constitutional proposals placing it at the centre of the debate. It was crucial for francophone leaders to be fully aware of the constitutional policies of all the participants, governmental and non-governmental. Further, it was especially important to monitor the two bodies created by Bourassa: the Constitutional Committee of the Quebec Liberal Party and the Bélanger-Campeau Commission. The first of these was dominated by militant neo-nationalist Liberals who were pushing for special constitutional status for Quebec, while the latter was quickly coming under the strong influence of Jacques Parizeau's Parti Québécois and his secessionist forces within and outside of the National Assembly. Bourassa was clearly anxious to move quickly – the Commission had six months to produce its report and the government set 26 October 1992 as the latest possible date for a referendum on Quebec's future – so that negotiations could produce an agreement before his ally Brian Mulroney was thrown out of office by an angry and frustrated electorate.

While Bourassa believed he had the political capacity – if not the constitutional right – to secede from the federation, that was not his objective. He was attempting to create a "rapport de force" vis-à-vis Ottawa and the other nine provinces in order to achieve his Quebec/Canada model of confederation. The western premiers would have to jettison their concept of the equality of provinces and begin thinking in terms of Canada as a conglomeration of regions, as proposed by the Pépin-Robarts Task Force on National Unity in 1979 and the Quebec Liberal Party's *Beige Paper* on the Constitution in 1980. Such deep structural changes in the respective roles of the federal and provincial governments would be quite devastating for the francophone communities. Their leaders had to educate all Quebecers, living in "le foyer de la francophonie," to recognize their natural allies, the francophone and Acadian minorities. It was crucial that, as a distinct society, francophone Quebecers not pursue their own constitutional objectives single-mindedly. As their governments were fond of repeating and as past experience confirmed, it was up to the citizens of Quebec to determine their own future. Given the deep ideological gulf and the distrust between the political and intellectual classes of francophone Quebec and the francophone minority communities, it was imperative for the leaders of the latter to focus on influencing developments in Ottawa and in their respective provinces.[10]

It was also imperative to keep abreast of political developments in Quebec. In late August 1990 the Fédération's new Bureau de direction held a planning session on the restructuring of the Canadian federation. On the basis of the wide-ranging discussions, Director General Aurèle Thériault then prepared policy directives for the presidents' meeting to be held in Caraquet, New Brunswick in November. The directives outlined were based on four assumptions:

- Quebecers would opt for some modernized version of sovereignty-association rather than independence.
- The constitutional status quo was dead and no attempt should be made to revive it.
- There was no single English Canada. Many divergent, conflicting voices – Ottawa's, the premiers', and those of organizations based on region, gender, class, and ethnicity – would be involved in the debate.
- The status of the French language and the role of governments, especially Ottawa, in supporting language rights would undergo significant changes.

It was crucial for the Fédération to promote a positive message about the successes, strengths, and vitality of the pan-Canadian francophone communities. "À peu près tout pouvant être remis en question, les négotiations à venir prendront l'allure d'un rapport de force entre les différents noyaux de la société."[11] The challenge – and it was enormous – was to make sure that the pan-Canadian francophone communities, a fundamental dimension of Canada's specificity, were among the big winners in the protracted constitutional debate.

To this end, it was suggested that the Fédération should present a brief to the Bélanger-Campeau Commission to convince the Bourassa government that collaboration was imperative if the francophone minority communities were to survive in North America, no matter what new relationship Quebec obtained with Canada. Quebec must be persuaded not to do anything that would hinder the francophone communities in the course of fulfilling its role in the promotion of French. The Fédération must insist on having representatives on all the federal and provincial committees and task forces, since it was clear that the Canada/Quebec vision of Canada was alive and well. Alliances must be made wherever necessary, but only with the full support and cooperation of the provincial associations. In short, the Fédération must be pro-active and seek an honourable place for everyone in a redefined Canada. Its goal was to obtain a service infrastructure network that would enable semi-autonomous pan-Canadian francophone communities to conduct their lives in French.[12] Most importantly, the Fédération's message must be positive: "Il est peût-être temps de changer notre message et de promouvoir notre richesse collective en donnant un message positif des succès, des forces et de la vitalité de la communauté francophone hors Québec."[13] Henceforth, francophone leaders would portray their communities as fundamental entities of Canada's distinct identity.

The Fédération and two of its affiliates presented briefs to the commission in November and December 1990. The Fédération's brief, *Un Nouveau départ, en partenariat*, like those of the ACFO and the ACFA,[14] addressed many of the myths about the francophone minority communities – one million people, or 20 per cent of Quebec's francophone population. Contrary to popular belief, francophone and Acadian communities were not assimilated, nor did they constitute an unacceptable burden on Quebec. The Fédération concluded its brief history lesson with a resounding declaration that "Les francophones hors Québec sont une réalité historique du Canada qui remonte à plus de trois siècles. Nous ne sommes pas, comme certains le prétendent, une fiction politique créée pour ralentir l'épanouissement de la collecti-vité québécoise ... La francophonie, c'est le Québec et c'est aussi nous."[15]

With the Quiet Revolution, the longstanding institutional, ideological, and personal links between Quebec's francophone society and the francophone minority communities had begun to dissolve rapidly. Those communities, starting with the Acadians under Premier Louis Joseph Robichaud, were forced to restructure their relationships with their respective provincial governments and to rely on the federal government for support. Ottawa's chief contributions were the Official Languages Act and s. 23 of the Charter, two important developments that the Québécois nationalists mistrusted and rejected. The Meech Lake Accord highlighted the tension between Quebec francophone society with a powerful state at its disposal, and the francophone minority communities beholden to their respective provincial majorities.[16] The constitutional status quo was dead; a new beginning based on new partnerships was the only way to break the deadlock. In an increasingly globalizing world, the provinces required a more flexible economic arrangement with Ottawa, one based on an asymmetrical model of federalism rather than the unrealistic principle of the equality of provinces. For their part, the francophone minorities had to become more assertive towards and less dependent upon governments, federal and provincial. It was imperative for all their communities to develop close institutional links with Quebec, based on political, economic, social, and cultural partnerships.[17] A strong Quebec would without a doubt be a great asset for the minority communities because it would legitimize the French fact throughout Canada. However, the Fédération was convinced that Quebec had to recognize that, in turn, the development of the francophone communities would guarantee Quebec a more dynamic future. "En fait, chacune d'entre elles ont contribué à faire du fait français une réalité qui, depuis quelques siècles, est une *réalité d'Amérique*."[18]

The ACFA reiterated many of the points made by the Fédération. It began by addressing the troublesome misunderstanding that its opposition to the Meech Lake Accord had created in Quebec. It wanted to make clear that it had been rooted in genuine self-interest and its predicament vis-à-vis a recalcitrant provincial government, rather than any fundamental opposition to Quebec's constitutional objectives, which it supported.[19] The only way to bridge the gulf was to develop a new partnership between the two evolving sets of francophone communities. In return for their support for Quebec's constitutional aspirations, the francophone minorities and their organizations expected a true partnership based on mutual self-interest with Quebec francophones at all levels, including the government and political elites.[20] For example, in the field of education, it was imperative for the Quebec government to make a clear political statement "en faveur du droit pour les francophones de gérer et de contrôler leur institutions d'enseignements du niveau primaire et secondaire *par le biais de commissions scolaires autonomes.*"[21]

For the Fédération to plead with militant neo-nationalists and secessionists to expand their inward-looking territorial conception of the francophone nation and find concrete ways to fulfill Quebec's historical and moral responsibilities towards the francophone diaspora was a waste of time. At the end of January 1991, the Constitutional Committee of the Quebec Liberal Party released its report, *A Quebec Free to Choose* (known as the Allaire Report after its chair), calling for a radical political disengagement of Quebec from Canada with renewed economic ties: that is, sovereignty-association, a concept normally linked with the Parti Québécois. If the rest of Canada agreed with the report's recommendation of a transfer of powers to Quebec in twenty-two areas, then a referendum would be held in the fall of 1992 to ratify the new arrangement.[22] The Bélanger-Campeau Report, made public on 27 March 1991, proclaimed that "Quebecers are aware that they form a distinct national collectivity: the language of the majority of Quebecers and their culture, which are in a minority situation in Canada, are unique across the continent." Since Quebecers "have always expressed the need to be masters of their own destiny" it was imperative that they choose their constitutional future with "serenity." [23] The report mentioned the francophone minority communities, but only to highlight their constant legal battles and declare that "For reasons related to its own linguistic and constitutional position, it is not possible for Québec to take up the cause of French-speaking groups in all their legal undertakings."[24] It did not allude to the invitation for a comprehensive partnership between francophones in Quebec and the rest of Canada. Unable to reach a consensus on what Quebec's constitutional future might be, the commissioners recommended that the National Assembly adopt a two-track approach whereby the province would determine that future. The first entailed passing a bill authorizing a referendum on secession no later than 26 October 1992. The second called for the creation by legislation of a special parliamentary commission "to assess any offer of a new partnership of constitutional nature made by the Government of Canada."[25] Reinforcing his "knife-to-the-throat" strategy, Bourassa authorized this two-track approach in Bill 150, enacted by the National Assembly in May 1991.[26] Disappointed and worried, Guy Matte commented sarcastically "qu'avant de se proclamer le foyer de la francophonie en Amérique du Nord, le Québec devrait d'abord croire en celle-ci. Le rapport Bélanger-Campeau n'est pas la plus évidente démonstration de cette croyance."[27]

DESIGNING A NEW CONSTITUTIONAL FRAMEWORK
AND STRATEGY

Canada now faced the most serious challenge to its political integrity since Confederation. How would the Fédération help address the crisis? At a meeting in Caraquet, New Brunswick, the presidents established the Comité aviseur sur l'avenir du Canada to guide the organization in its decision-making on federal and provincial constitutional initiatives. The Comité de stratégies constitutionnelles, as it came to be called, included representatives from five provinces and the Fédération itself. At its first meeting on 14 December 1990, it expressed scepticism towards Brian Mulroney's constitutional initiatives. On 1 November 1990 the prime minister had created the Citizens' Forum on Canada's Future, chaired by Keith Spicer, then chairman of the Canadian Radio-television and Telecommunications Commission. The Citizens' Forum became a populist sounding board for English-speaking Canadians, especially in the west, who were angry with the Mulroney government's obsession with the Constitution and its inability to deal with the health, social, and economic issues facing the nation.[28] On 17 December Mulroney created a Special Joint Committee of the Senate and the House of Commons on the Process for Amending the Constitution of Canada, co-chaired by Senator Gérald Beaudoin, a former University of Ottawa law professor, and MP Jim Edwards. Its mandate was to recommend ways of circumventing the three-year term for amendments requiring unanimity – a requirement that Mulroney found rather vexing since it had enabled some premiers to defeat the Accord – and to propose ways of giving Quebec a constitutional veto.[29]

The Comité de strategies constitutionnelles objected to the Citizens' Forum on the grounds that it had no francophone minority representative and would merely foment opposition to constitutional reform, which is precisely what happened. Keith Spicer placed most of the blame for the constitutional crisis on the Mulroney government. Using the words of an angry citizen, the Forum's report concluded: "No hyperbole or political hedge can screen any member of any legislature who thwarts the will of the people on this matter. The voters are watching and waiting."[30] Handed an impossible task, the Beaudoin-Edwards Committee simply covered old ground and bought time for the Mulroney government. Nevertheless, the Comité felt that the Fédération should participate in both bodies and monitor their proceedings carefully. According to the Comité, the role of the Fédération was to provide general direction by disseminating a discourse that could be adapted to specific regions of the country. It should stress three themes: increased social and economic autonomy – self-government – for the francophone communities; the achievement of equality between the francophone and anglophone communities in order to consolidate official linguistic duality; and reinforcement of the idea that francophones comprised one of the three principal nations of Canadian society, alongside the aboriginal and anglophone nations.[31] Francophone leaders were willing to recognize the aboriginal nations, something the Quebec government and nationalists were not yet ready to do.

Committed to recognizing the reality of Canadian pluralism in its actions and approaches, the Fédération set out to establish a stronger bargaining position by developing links with the aboriginal organizations. The ACFA had already taken this initiative; now it was up to the Fédération to find common ground with the Assembly of First Nations. On the level of principles, the Bureau de direction proposed that the Fédération could recognize the first nations' right of self-determination, as well as the right to define the form of self-government best suited to their needs. The Fédération realized that establishing a working relationship with the AFN was a delicate undertaking, since there was little trust between the francophone and first nations leaders. Still, the attempt was worth making, since it was one way that the Fédération's commitment to the principles of pluralism and tolerance could be translated into positive action.[32]

At their meeting in late February 1991, the presidents – with the exception of the SAANB's president, who abstained – endorsed a resolution outlining in rather general terms the organization's constitutional position, which was predicated on its recognition of three pluralistic national communities and on its commitment to maintaining a united Canada. Any restructuring of the federal system had to take into account nine elements: Senate reform based on regional equality and the representation of different social groups; a redistribution of powers; the status of Quebec in the federation; the recognition of aboriginal self-government; the continuance of linguistic duality; regional development; a stronger economic union; the status of Yukon and the Northwest Territories; and greater autonomy for the pan-Canadian francophone community. The Fédération favoured the creation of a Constituent Assembly as the best means of achieving the renewal of the federation.[33] It would include representatives from the provincial and federal governments as well as from the various groups affected by the Charter. Any constitutional deal would require ratification by Parliament and the legislatures. At a press conference on 7 March, it made its constitutional policy

public, prompting many questions from the media. In May, the
Bureau de direction held three meetings – in Edmonton, Memram-
cook, NB, and Ottawa – to explain the policy to the Fédération's
membership. In addition, President Guy Matte attended several
public symposia and forums across the country, explaining his organization's position.

On March 18, ACFA President France Levasseur-Ouimet gave testimony before the Beaudoin-Edwards Committee. Declaring that
most Canadians believed the die were already cast, she denounced
the top-down, executive-driven renewal process. There had been
rumours circulating throughout western Canada that the premiers
wanted to use the upcoming Canada Round to gain full control over
language and cultural matters so the provinces could escape their
responsibility under s. 23. When neither Premier Don Getty nor
Prime Minister Brian Mulroney would give assurances that s. 23 was
not negotiable, the ACFA went on the attack. Its recommendations
were based on the idea that Canada should be perceived as comprised of three nations, anglophone, francophone, and aboriginal.
Like the Fédération, the ACFA recommended that a Constituent
Assembly be established to devise proposals addressing the full
range of issues. A two-thirds majority would be required on everything except language and cultural issues, over which aboriginals
and francophones would exercise a veto. It also urged that constitutional changes should be ratified by a reformed Senate rather than
the legislative assemblies or by referendum and that the notwithstanding clause and the three-year time limit on amendments
should be abolished.[34]

A month later, Guy Matte presented the Fédération's constitutional policy to the Beaudoin-Edwards Committee. He focused on
establishing a Constituent Assembly as the best method for democ-
ratizing the constitutional debate and the ratification process. To
those who proposed a referendum as the ultimate means of ratification, Matte replied that it was too inflexible and divisive. The committee did not respond favourably to the idea of a Constituent
Assembly, however, and subjected the Fédération representatives to a
tough cross-examination. Some argued that since Gil Rémillard had
spoken against it on behalf of the Quebec government, it was dead
in the water. This viewpoint was more than a little ironic, remarked
André Ouellet, given that Quebec had just heard from its own
version of the Constituent Assembly, namely the Bélanger-Campeau
Commission, of which he was a member and which had been
hijacked by the separatists. Its rather biased and vague report was
signed by Premier Bourassa, who then stated that his government

was not really bound by its recommendations.[35] The Fédération was not surprised, therefore, when the Beaudoin-Edwards Committee rejected the concept of a Constituent Assembly.[36] But it was pleased with several of the committee's central recommendations, including the maintenance of the unanimity clause for amending ss. 16–20 and 23 of the Constitution Act, 1982, replacing the 7/50 formula with one based on four regions, and granting the aboriginal organizations a central place at the bargaining table. Nevertheless, President Raymond Bisson expressed strong disappointment that, instead of having a Constituent Assembly come up with constitutional reform proposals, the First Ministers would undertake this crucial task behind closed doors.[37]

On 21 April, Guy Matte wrote to various ministers, including Joe Clark, Benoît Bouchard, and Jean Charest, explaining the Fédération's desire to participate actively in the process of constitutional reform. Minister of Intergovernmental Affairs Joe Clark met with the Fédération's president and staff members on 20 June 1991, the day after the House of Commons had authorized a Special Joint Committee on a Renewed Canada. Clark told them that it would study the government's constitutional proposals, due out in September, and that it could adopt special mechanisms to facilitate the participation of individuals and groups. He did not, however, agree to the Fédération's request to have representatives participating directly in the Special Joint Committee's proceedings when it was studying matters of language, culture, and communications. The last two subjects were of concern to the group because Clark had indicated that they, unlike language, were up for negotiation, since Quebec was interested in acquiring more authority in both areas. In a follow-up letter, Bisson thanked Clark for the meeting and reiterated the request for direct participation in the committee on matters deemed important to the francophone communities.[38] There was no reply from the minister. The Fédération and its affiliates were left on the outside looking in. Not much had changed since the closed-door negotiations that produced the ill-fated Meech Lake Accord.

ON THE OUTSIDE LOOKING IN

In late September 1991, a frazzled Mulroney government released its tentative and deliberately vague constitutional document, *Shaping Canada's Future Together*. It incorporated the five conditions of the Meech Lake Accord, elements of the Companion Resolution, and additional matters: the omnibus Canada clause, amendments to the Charter to guarantee property rights, aboriginal self-government,

Senate reform, the Supreme Court of Canada, the economic union, and the division of powers. If the government had its way, its proposals would produce a far more decentralized federation – except on economic matters – than the asymmetrical model outlined by Quebec in the Accord.[39] The proposals were referred to the Special Joint Committee of the Senate and the House of Commons on a Renewed Canada, chaired initially by Senator Claude Castonguay and Manitoba MP Dorothy Dobbie. The committee's proceedings got off to a disastrous start. Its hearings were abruptly adjourned in early November when no-one showed up at a public meeting in Manitoba. Before the end of the year, the disgruntled Castonguay resigned and was replaced by a more experienced constitutionalist, Gérald Beaudoin, who got the show back on the road by agreeing to the NDP's demand for five regional conferences on the government's constitutional proposals.[40]

Francophone leaders monitoring this circus from the sidelines were furious at having been locked out. On 16 September 1991, ACFA President France Levasseur-Ouimet sent Brian Mulroney a tough but diplomatic letter, following up on her 12 July letter to Joe Clark, stating that the francophone communities could not rely on either Quebec or Ottawa to defend their interests adequately. It was imperative that the francophone organizations be represented in the renewal process at some level. The following day, Clark replied that the ACFA would have an opportunity to participate by making submissions to the Special Joint Committee formed to study Ottawa's constitutional reform package. Mulroney repeated this unsatisfactory nostrum in his own reply of 1 November.[41]

The ACFA asked three constitutional experts – Michel Bastarache, Mary Moreau of the Edmonton law firm Rand Moreau, and University of Saskatchewan law professor Howard McConnell – to comment on the proposals in *Shaping Canada's Future Together*. Reminding the ACFA of its difficulties with Meech Lake, Bastarache noted that the new version of the distinct society/linguistic duality clause – which was now part of the Canada clause – applied only to the Charter, not, as in the Accord, to the entire Constitution. Its effect would therefore be felt only in relation to the interpretation or the application of s. 1, the reasonable limits clause. "Le fait de référer à des valeurs reconnues," he concluded, "va créer une validation à priori des restrictions et limiter, probablement, l'importance de la preuve requise pour justifier la restriction à un droit fondamental quelconque."[42] Bastarache questioned the use of the wording "the preservation of the existence of French-speaking Canadians" because "preservation" implied the maintenance of the status quo, while "French-speaking Canadians" avoided the recognition of collectivities. He believed that s. 27, on multiculturalism, would trump the distinct society/linguistic duality subclauses. What did the terms "protect and promote" mean when they referred to Quebec's sociological majority, and why was the definition of Quebec's distinct society left open-ended? The Canada clause's "recognition of the responsibility of governments to preserve Canada's two linguistic majorities and minorities" constituted a diminution of the Meech formula and while it applied to the entire Constitution "ne semble pas suffisant pour créer un empêchement de nuire aux communautés de langue officielle." The concept of linguistic duality in the overarching Canada clause and in the distinct society/linguistic duality subclauses had to subsume the promotion of linguistic and cultural communities by using such words as "le maintien et le développement des communautés de langues officielles en situation minoritaire."[43]

In her comprehensive analysis of Ottawa's proposals, subtitled "Le renouvellement de la fédération ou sa mise à l'enchère?", Mary Moreau concurred with Bastarache's critique of the new version of the distinct society/linguistic duality clause as well as with his suggestions for improving it. In her view, the francophone minority communities would find the proposals unsatisfactory and unacceptable because "ce sont des garanties d'un *statu quo* vaguement défini dans un document assymétrique que d'un côté respecte la notion de dualité linguistique et de l'autre, compromet les possibilités d'acheminement vers l'égalité des deux communautés linguistiques nationales." Going further than Bastarache, Moreau contended that the distinct society clause would allow Quebec to defend its laws on commercial signage without recourse to s. 33. More menacingly for the francophone communities, the distinct society/linguistic duality subclauses, as worded, would allow Quebec to trump ss. 16–23 of the Charter, on linguistic and educational rights for the official minorities. "La collision des intérêts du Québec et ceux des minorités francophones hors Québec est inévitable dans les prochaines négociations," she concluded. In short, the package threatened the francophone communities because it reflected a vision of political, economic, and social enclaves united in a highly decentralized federation.[44] Howard McConnell agreed with Moreau about the possible negative impact of the distinct society clause on s. 23 of the Charter.[45]

ACFA Director General Georges Arès was alarmed at Moreau's critical analysis because it meant that the francophone minorities faced an even tougher battle for recognition than they had encountered during the Meech Lake debacle. When federal politicians and senior civil servants immediately set out to discredit her interpretation of the distinct society clause, he asked Michel Bastarache for further detailed comments. Arès was a member of the Fédération's constitutional committee and wanted to be fully prepared for the meeting on the proposals scheduled for late November.[46] In the interim, Minister of Constitutional Affairs Joe Clark, following his speech to the sixty-fifth AGM of the ACFA on 2 November, was presented with a jar of pickles by Georges Arès, along with a stinging rebuke: "It seems that you want to put us in a pickle jar and put us on a shelf to accumulate dust until we gradually disappear." According to Arès, Ottawa's proposals posed a grave danger because they entailed "no promotion, no development of our community."[47] What particularly irked francophone leaders was that Canada's francophone communities were perceived as mere folkloric remnants of a once glorious past that deserved little more attention than museum artifacts.

The ACFA's new president, Denis Tardif, likewise went on the offensive. He fired off letters to Jean Chrétien, leader of the Liberal Party, Jean-Robert Gauthier, Liberal MP for Ottawa-Vanier and a strong supporter of the official language communities, and Premier Don Getty, explaining his organization's strong reservations about the constitutional package.[48] With its tough talk and direct action, the ACFA had put the Fédération on notice that it expected an aggressive approach to the Canada Round. Furthermore, it would continue to lobby vigorously while establishing a working relationship with the AFN and the Native Council of Canada.[49]

It was in this context that the presidents had analysed and debated the federal proposals at their October meeting. Following their directives, the Fédération prepared an extensive brief for the Beaudoin-Dobbie Committee. The presidents were frustrated that the Mulroney government's constitutional agenda excluded the concerns of the francophone communities, a development they believed threatened their existing rights. President Raymond Bisson issued a lengthy press release calling on the prime minister and the premiers to explain and promote the constitutional principles and objectives of the francophone communities. He warned Mulroney not to sacrifice the francophone and Acadian communities on the altar of constitutional negotiations. "Nous ne voulons pas une nouvelle nuit des longs couteaux. Nous voulons un rôle de promotion de la dualité linguistique par le gouvernement fédéral et nous y tenons."[50] When Clark announced the five public constitutional conferences, which the NDP had suggested, in mid-November, Bisson wrote to him requesting a sixth one because none of the five would be addressing the specific issues that mattered most to the Fédération. He reminded Clark that the prime minister had promised, during the dying days of the Meech Lake

Accord, that the constitutional concerns of the francophone and Acadian communities would be central to the next round of negotiations. The Fédération had a legitimate right to representation at the negotiating table, considering that many of its hard-earned rights were being endangered by the wholesale restructuring of the federation.[51]

By the time the Fédération was called to give testimony before the Beaudoin-Dobbie Committee on 17 December, Bisson was in a belligerent frame of mind, commenting that his organization was "royally fed-up." He virtually ignored the excellent brief prepared for the committee, which provided a lucid, comprehensive, yet supportive analysis of each of the government's proposals. Indeed, the document was a *tour de force* displaying the Fédération's tremendous knowledge of mega-constitutional issues and complex bargaining.[52] Bisson decided instead that it was time to play verbal hardball. "We understand the federal government's message as follows," he declared. "Out with those who are willing to co-operate! Mr. Mulroney and Mr. Clark, are you finally going to give your one million francophone allies a role in this process? ... Should we hold our conference, without the federal government? What are you waiting for, Mr. Mulroney and Mr. Clark, to give us our legitimate, equitable role, that will enable us to continue building a new Canada?"[53]

The Fédération considered the proposed s. 25.1(1)(b) of the distinct society/linguistic duality subclauses "regressive and worrisome." It stated: "The Charter shall be interpreted in a manner consistent with (b) the preservation of the existence of French-speaking Canadians, primarily located in Quebec but also present throughout Canada, and English-speaking Canadians, primarily located outside Quebec but also present in Quebec."[54] The Fédération saw it as a humiliating step backward inasmuch as it offered far less than the enlightened 1988 revision to the Official Languages Act. Using words drawn from that statute, the Fédération suggested amending the clause to read: "This Charter shall be interpreted in a manner consistent with (b) maintenance of Canada's two official languages and with the linguistic and cultural enhancement and development of official language communities living as minorities." It was also imperative that any reference in the Canada clause to the recognition of the two official language communities, before being inserted as s. 2 of the Constitution Act, 1867, use the words "enhancement" and "development" rather than "preservation." Bisson mentioned two additional essential points: the francophone communities must be guaranteed representation in an elected Senate, and the federal government must not relinquish its jurisdictional and spending powers in areas integral to its responsibilities to the official language minorities.[55] The one element missing from Bisson's testimony and mentioned only in passing in the brief was a clause, similar to the one proposed for Quebec, calling on the federal and provincial governments – in addition to Parliament and the legislatures – to preserve and promote the francophone minority communities. Failure to mention this asymmetrical approach to the responsibilities of both governments and legislatures – whether due to calculation or to oversight – would come back to haunt the Fédération.

The tough talk had considerable impact. Joe Clark offered to meet with twenty delegates from the Fédération and its affiliates for a two-hour meeting on 14 January 1992. Bisson's initial response was to flatly reject the offer, but the presidents then met with Clark to lobby directly for a separate conference. In lieu of a conference, they were offered a paltry one-day colloquium with seven Cabinet ministers to be held on 6 February 1992, the day before the Toronto conference *Identity, Rights, and Values,* dealing with the distinct society/linguistic duality subclauses, the Canada clause, and the Charter.[56] Still, it was the breakthrough that the Fédération, and its western affiliates in particular, had worked so long to obtain. Having a colloquium dedicated to their concerns and being present at the full conference gave francophone leaders the opportunity to make alliances and influence the deliberations. While the delegates accepted the linguistic duality clause as proposed by the government, they noted that "there were strong statements calling for the expansion of the clause to include both the preservation *and promotion* of minority language rights.[57]

Greater gains were made at both meetings than expected, despite the fact that AFN leader Ovide Mercredi and numerous aboriginal delegates monopolized the initial discussions with their demands for distinct society status for their communities. Thanks to the successful lobbying of the francophone representatives, some 240 delegates left convinced that the federal and provincial governments had the obligation of contributing to the enhancement and development of the official language communities rather than simply monitoring their preservation. Rolande Soucie and Georges Arès were elated but were also well aware that much remained to be done. The lobbying had to continue at the final conference in Vancouver to convince the Beaudoin-Dobbie Committee to address the francophone groups' constitutional demands in its final report. Soucie and Arès planned to use that report to persuade at least seven premiers to buy into their conception of a pan-Canadian linguistic and cultural duality.[58]

The lobbying efforts at the concluding Vancouver conference paid dividends as well; at long last, a consensus emerged that a new

Constitution had to embrace both conceptions of duality, a Quebec/Canada duality via the distinct society clause and a pan-Canadian linguistic duality via "an obligation on governments [not just legislatures] to support the linguistic and cultural development and growth of the official language communities living in a minority situation."[59] Bisson would have preferred the term "enhancement" along with a guarantee of francophone representation in a reformed Senate. Nevertheless, it was a good start. Given that linguistic duality had become central to the discussions, Bisson asked Joe Clark to make room for a representative of the Fédération in the federal delegation at the next First Ministers conference.[60] However, as we shall see, the negotiating process became far more convoluted than Bisson could have imagined.

The ACFA's representatives appeared before the Beaudoin-Dobbie Committee at the end of January, just days after Premier Don Getty had made rather dismissive remarks about linguistic duality and cultural pluralism.[61] President Denis Tardif restated, as diplomatically as possible, the two central messages outlined in his organization's hard-hitting brief. First, Alberta's premier was determined to use constitutional renewal to rid the province of its responsibilities under s. 23 of the Charter, and Ottawa's proposed wording of the distinct society and Canada clauses would give him and other premiers the opportunity to ask the Supreme Court to reconsider its decision in *Mahé*. Second, the transfer of powers to Alberta in areas critical to the official language communities was nothing short of disastrous. "Plus qu'un abandon complet par le fédéral de notre communauté, certain y verraient une trahison. Si c'est l'effet désiré, qu'on le dise clairement dans les propositions constitutionnelles!"[62] The direct message ruffled the feathers not only of the politicians but also of the Fédération. Tardif thanked the latter for its excellent work on the constitutional front, its firmly stated policies, and its determination. He encouraged it to continue to lobby aggressively for the rights and needs of the francophone communities, since their organizations were on the verge of gaining a legitimate role in the national unity debate and the renewal of the Constitution.[63] The Fédération president did not know whether to take this as a compliment or as incitement to become more forceful.

The Beaudoin-Dobbie Committee's report, released on 28 February 1992, went only part-way to satisfying the Fédération and its western affiliates. For s. (1)(b) of the distinct society/linguistic duality sub-clauses, the report recommended the words "vitality and development"; however, for the Canada clause it proposed the rather vague phrasing "a profound commitment to the vitality and development of official language minority communities," rather than specifying a responsibility on the part of the federal and provincial governments to both "preserve and promote" as it recommended for the Quebec government and legislature. On Senate reform, the report recommended the double majority principle for matters related to language and culture but did not propose guaranteed representation for the official language minority communities, though it did for the aboriginal communities.[64] While progress had been made, Bisson made it clear that the Fédération would be vigilant, to make sure that these important, if modest, recommendations were incorporated into the federal government's revised constitutional package, due out in April. He reiterated the organization's intention of acquiring an official seat at the First Ministers' conference. Its representatives then met with the Atlantic premiers, who assured them of support for the Beaudoin-Dobbie recommendations on linguistic duality.[65] The SAANB, however, while admitting that the report was a good start to sorting out the constitutional impasse, was disappointed that the committee had not understood the need to entrench New Brunswick's Bill 88 in the Constitution, along with a clause committing the province to promoting the equality of its two official language communities.[66]

MONITORING THE MULTILATERAL NEGOTIATIONS

Once the Beaudoin-Dobbie Committee had completed its work, Prime Minister Brian Mulroney grudgingly authorized Minister of Constitutional Affairs Joe Clark to chair multilateral negotiations involving the premiers of all provinces except Quebec and representatives of the four national aboriginal organizations: the AFN, the Native Council of Canada, the Inuit Tapirisat of Canada, and the Métis National Council. Since Ottawa had no clear constitutional position of its own, the debate was quickly dominated by the premiers, who introduced new elements, and by the aboriginal leaders, who lobbied successfully for what was later characterized as a comprehensive aboriginal constitution within the Canadian Constitution.[67]

The Fédération was incensed, and Raymond Bisson called a press conference to castigate the Mulroney government for demonstrating a lack of respect for the francophone communities. Ottawa obstinately continued to refuse to consider constitutional proposals dealing with linguistic duality, and denied the Fédération's request to have a representative at the First Ministers' conference. Adding insult to injury, the government had just announced the cancellation of the Court Challenges Program, which provided financial assistance for court challenges under the Charter. Seeing the latter as an attempt to silence francophone groups, Bisson fired off a letter to Mulroney expressing the Fédération's grievances with the government's policies and actions – or lack thereof – vis-à-vis the linguistic minorities. He reminded the prime minister that he had promised Franco-Manitobans on 29 March 1984 that his government would "ensure that French language minority rights and English language minority rights remain on our national agenda with a commitment to redeem the pledge on the basis of generosity and equality." Bisson concluded with a request for a meeting, since the prime minister had not met formally with the Fédération since 1984.[68]

Stung to the quick, the government went on the offensive. Minister of Health and Welfare Benoît Bouchard declared to a Canadian Press reporter that: "The francophones outside Quebec, unlike the aboriginals, will not be at the negotiating table. The Italians are a million strong and they have not demanded anything." Flabbergasted, Bisson denounced Bouchard for making such an incongruous comparison, given that francophones constituted one of Canada's two official language communities, and reminded him that the Fédération had never asked to be represented at the bargaining table except as part of the federal delegation.[69] Secretary of State Robert de Cotret replied to Bisson in a manner that cast doubt on the government's commitment to working for the enhancement of the francophone communities. Outlining the legislative and funding measures that had been enacted since 1984, he warned that budgetary constraints required cuts in funding to all programs and agencies. The government had done everything possible to help the Fédération attain its constitutional objectives; it would remain sensitive to them and do everything within reason to defend the interests of the francophone minorities throughout the constitutional renewal process.[70]

Blocked by Ottawa, the francophone organizations turned to some of the premiers. While on a tour between 4 and 7 May, Robert Bourassa and Gil Rémillard met with each of the four western associations, as well as with Raymond Bisson during their stopover in Manitoba. The meetings went reasonably well. Though he refused to play his hand, the wily Bourassa did agree that the Fédération's demand for "une clause d'épanouissement et de développement de la dualité linguistique" was legitimate and stated that he would support one if his legal advisors assured him it would not diminish the distinct society clause.[71] Ontario Premier Bob Rae was highly supportive of the Fédération's constitutional aspirations and promised to ask his two NDP colleagues in British Columbia and Saskatchewan for their support.[72] Subsequently, on 11 May, the Fédération discussed its constitutional concerns with Mike Harcourt and Roy Romanow, both of whom offered their backing, as did the national leader of the NDP, Audrey McLaughlin, on 13 May.

The following day, Bisson appeared before the Quebec National Assembly's Commission d'études sur toute offre d'un nouveau partenariat de nature constitutionnelle. He reiterated the urgent need for a new partnership, one based on true solidarity and reinforced by mutual self-interest, between Franco-Quebec society and the francophone and Acadian communities. The former was quite capable of playing a much greater role in the development of the latter, which – contrary to Québécois nationalist propaganda – were profoundly rooted in Canadian society and were not about to disappear. The Quebec government could begin building this partnership by supporting the Fédération's wording for the Canada clause: "l'épanouissement et le développement, linguistiques et culturels, des communautés de langue officielle vivant en situation minoritaire." Contrary to the exaggerated claims made by some nationalists, he went on, this clause was not a blatant attempt to bilingualize Quebec, to undermine Bills 101 and 178, thereby changing the linguistic face of the province. In return, the Fédération would push for an asymmetrical conception of federalism that would give Quebec all the constitutional tools necessary to preserve and promote its distinct society, while the federal government would retain all the powers and resources needed for the enhancement of the francophone and Acadian communities. This win-win approach was the only way to bridge the ever-widening political and constitutional gulf that had grown since the Quiet Revolution between French Quebec and the francophone and Acadian communities.[73]

The ACFA Promotes Asymmetrical Federalism

On 20 May, as the time approached for critical decision-making, members of the Fédération's Comité de stratégies constitutionnelles met in Montreal, where various provincial ministers responsible for constitutional matters were trying to iron out their differences. It was clear that the group had to closely monitor the discussions, which were to resume in Toronto the following week.[74] On 8 June, the ACFA jumped in by offering Premier Bourassa an asymmetrical approach to the treatment of the official language minorities; in return for his backing a clause giving the federal government responsibility for the development of the francophone communities, the ACFA would lobby an apparently receptive Alliance Québec to accept a clause requiring the Quebec government merely to protect its anglophone minority. "Comme vous le savez," replied Bourassa, "notre gouvernement a à coeur la situation de nos compatriotes des autres provinces, et les liens traditionnels qui les unissent aux Québécois constituent une réalité historique." He agreed that an asymmetrical approach to the language issue was an important contribution to the impasse.[75] The ACFA's proposal made the somewhat naive and dubious assumption that the Alliance had the support of the anglophone and allophone communities.

It was at this juncture that Georges Arès indicated that the ACFA was about to launch an advertising campaign in the Quebec media to pressure Bourassa into remembering and supporting the francophone communities. Michel Hébert of *Le Droit* quoted Arès as saying: "On n'a pas assez crié ... On n'a pas autant d'argent que les Cris [de Grande Baleine], mais on fera une tournée qui rappellera au Québécois comment les francophones sont traités."[76] Some interpreted his statement as a warning that the ACFA intended to launch the same kind of combative campaign against the province as the Crees of northern Quebec. ACFA President Denis Tardif had to reassure both his executive and the public that the quote was not accurate and that the group's intention was not to make political war on Quebec but simply to inform Franco-Quebecers of the francophone communities' situation and urgent constitutional needs.[77] Responding on behalf of the Fédération, Ray-mond Bisson stated that it had no intention of confronting Quebec on the constitutional question because that would be contrary to its policy of seeking a new partnership with the province irrespective of the outcome of negotiations. Moreover, he found Arès's comments regrettable.[78]

The ebullient Arès found no reason to withdraw his remarks. Despite the tensions, the ACFA continued its aggressive campaign to sell asymmetrical federalism to Bourassa and other premiers. The brilliant ad, "D'un Bourassa à l'autre: Henri Bourassa et Robert Bourassa," ran in a number of Quebec's French language newspapers on 10 June 1992. It called on Robert Bourassa not to contribute to the encirclement of Quebec by abandoning the francophone communities, and pointed out that, in a special edition of *Le Devoir* on 13 June 1992, he had cited a speech by Henri Bourassa to the effect that "la province de Québec a non seulement le droit mais le devoir rigoureux d'assurer la conservation des groupes français des autres provinces ... " Citing the entire quote was essential, since Henri Bourassa had gone on to say, "parce que leur survivance est la garantie de sa propre existence. Ne l'oublions pas: si, dans une pensée de lâche égoïsme ou dans la torpeur d'une apathie imbécile, nous laissons périr les uns après les autres les groupes français de la Confédération, rejetons épars du vieux tronc, nous ne tarderons pas à être attaqués sur notre propre terrain. Nous subirons la peine des lâches et des égoïstes." Indeed, as

the ACFA reminded Robert Bourassa, in the same speech Henri
Bourassa had referred not only to the rigorous need to conserve the
French language but "d'en favoriser l'expansion dans toutes les partis
de la Confédération." According to the *Dictionnaire Petit Robert,* "expansion" meant "development" and "enhancement." Like his predecessor,
Robert Bourassa could be a real champion of the francophone communities if he supported a Canada clause that would allow them to feel
at home throughout the land.

Following the slap on the wrist by the Fédération's president, the
ACFA decided that its representatives would attend the Conseil
national des présidents et des présidentes and the annual General
Assembly slated for late June as observers only, rather than active participants. In a letter to all the francophone associations Denis Tardif
expressed his group's disillusionment and impatience with the
Fédération's lack of strong political leadership on the constitutional
question. Despite a recent resolution by the Conseil, the Fédération
remained hesitant about forging an alliance with the national aboriginal organizations that would enable it to gain access to the negotiating process. Further, it rejected the ACFA's offer to Bourassa of an
asymmetrical solution to the language issue, then publicly defended
the anglophones of Quebec rather than its own francophone communities.[79] Disgusted, Georges Arès resigned from the Comité de
stratégies constitutionnelles and stated that since the publication of
the Beaudoin-Dobbie Report the Fédération had forgotten and/or
abandoned the constitutional principles set out for itself and member
associations by the Conseil. He wondered why the Fédération had
integrated itself with the New Brunswick government delegation
during the Toronto conference, thereby undermining its ability to
lobby for those principles and losing sight of the setbacks suffered by
the francophone organizations. "J'ai la nette impression," declared
Arès, "que depuis un certain temps la FCFA nous présente la position
du gouvernement du Québec plutôt que des communautés qu'elle se
doit de bien représenter."[80]

From this point onward, the ACFA acted as if it was leading the battle
for francophone minority community rights. Solidarity in the francophone organizations had, once again, broken down over the issue of
federal promotion of the linguistic minorities. By 12 June, negotiations had reached gridlock over Senate reform. In the interim, Parliament had passed Bill C-81, which enabled Ottawa to hold a Canada-
wide referendum on a constitutional deal. The Mulroney government
had initially opposed a referendum, then was forced to change its
policy. Both Alberta and British Columbia required a referendum to
ratify ·constitutional amendments. Jean Chrétien, after consulting

Pierre Trudeau, informed Mulroney that the Liberal Party's support for a constitutional package was conditional on holding a national referendum. Angry Conservative MPs from Quebec characterized the referendum legislation as interference in their province's affairs. Joe Clark convinced the prime minister to authorize him to convene the premiers – except Bourassa, who refused to attend – to a special First Ministers' meeting between 29 June and 7 July to try to achieve consensus on the Senate. The ACFA took this as another opportunity to lobby the premiers with both private and open letters explaining the need for an asymmetrical solution to the official language minority issue. Its proposed version of the Canada clause read as follows: "La législature et le gouvernement du Québec ont le rôle de protéger l'existence linguistique et culturel de la collectivité minoritaire anglaise au Québec" and "Le Parlement et le gouvernement du Canada ont le rôle d'assurer l'èpanouissement et le développement linguistique et culturel des collectivités minoritaires francophones partout au Canada."[81]

The ACFA's efforts finally paid off. During a week-long meeting in the Pearson Building in Ottawa, the western and eastern premiers coerced Ontario Premier Bob Rae and Joe Clark into a deal on Senate reform based on the principle of provincial equality but with reduced powers, in return for increased representation in the House of Commons for Ontario, British Columbia, Quebec, and Alberta. The Pearson Accord of 7 July 1992 also proposed a Canada clause stating that "les Canadiens *et leurs gouvernements* sont fermement engagés à assurer l'épanouissement et le développement des communautés de langues officielles." The question facing both the ACFA and Brian Mulroney was whether Bourassa would accept the Pearson Accord and join Ottawa and the other nine premiers in ratifying it. On 9 and 10 July, Denis Tardif wrote to Bourassa reminding him that he had told Georges Arès in June 1987 that it would never be possible to get all the premiers to agree to a promotion clause for their francophone minorities. "C'est à vous de décider, M. Bourassa, si nous allons finalement obtenir cet élément essentiel à notre survie en Alberta. S'il est vrai que le Québec ne doit pas être perdant, il ne faudrait pas non plus que la communauté francophone de l'Alberta soit perdante dans le débat sur le renouvellement du Canada." Tardif added that he was ready to meet with the premier to work out a slightly amended asymmetrical version of the new Canada clause that would address Quebec's concerns and to discuss the serious problems associated with the proposed Senate reforms.[82] When the Fédération got wind of these manoeuvres, its Director General Marc Godbout reminded Arès that it was the national organization's responsibility to negotiate with the government of Quebec.[83]

BOURASSA BOARDS THE CONSTITUTIONAL EXPRESS
TO CHARLOTTETOWN

The pressure on Bourassa to reject the Pearson Accord from the Québécois nationalist and secessionist political and intellectual classes, backed by most of the French language media, was overwhelming.[84] *Le Devoir's* Lise Bissonette, the doyenne of this movement, castigated virtually every element of the Accord: "C'est une duperie de comparer cet accord à celui de Meech." She regarded its institutional revolution involving the highly centralizing Triple E Senate as a catastrophe because it guaranteed the political decline of Quebec via its encirclement by the anglophone majority in Ottawa and the other nine provinces. Bissonnette believed that the political and ideological gulf between Quebec and the rest of Canada was too wide and deep to overcome. In short, the Bourassa government should pursue the logic of Bill 150 and hold a referendum on secession, as the Bélanger-Campeau Commission had recommended.[85] However, Brian Mulroney had convinced his friend and political ally Bourassa not to go down this road, since it would put him in the separatist camp in the referendum. Backed into a dilemma of his own making, Bourassa agreed to meet with the other premiers on two occasions, 4 and 10 August; then, strongarmed once again by the prime minister and fearful of losing a referendum on secession, he agreed to a full-scale constitutional conference in the Pearson Building beginning on 18 August.

By mid-July, the Fédération learned that Bourassa had agreed to board the constitutional express on condition that certain critical amendments were made to the Pearson Accord, one of which pertained to the official language minorities. He would accept a commitment (the French term was *engagement*) by governments towards their official language minority communities, but only if Quebec received – as it did in the Meech Accord – an ironclad non-derogation clause protecting "the powers, rights or privileges of the Parliament of Canada or the Government of Canada, or the legislatures or governments of the provinces."[86] Bourassa and Rémillard, backed by their legal advisors, were concerned that the federal government would use its enhanced constitutional responsibilities vis-à-vis Quebec's anglophone minority to impose official bilingualism on the province.

Fédération Director General Marc Godbout reminded Georges Arès that a non-derogation clause would effectively nullify Ottawa's commitment to promote the official language minority communities. He also informed Arès and his counterparts in the other provincial associations that there would be a presidents' telephone conference to discuss these developments and to provide informal guidelines for the

Fédération. The next formal meeting of the Conseil national des présidents et des présidentes would only occur once the First Ministers had produced a final document.[87] But the ACFA wanted to keep the pressure on the prime minister and the premiers throughout the negotiations. Tardif and Arès rejected the Fédération's "wait and see" strategy; they insisted on an immediate formal meeting of the Conseil and refused to give the necessary unanimous consent required for a telephone conference. Godbout thereupon polled the members to see whether they would consent to a meeting in Ottawa without the required twenty-one-day notice.[88]

In the interim, Arès sought advice from Michel Bastarache on the Pearson Accord and the ACFA's decision to push for an asymmetrical approach. Bastarache was rather blunt. He told Arès he did not believe most premiers would buy into the "whereas" wording proposed by the ACFA, since it was far too complicated for the courts to interpret and moreover violated the principle of equality of treatment for the official language minorities. He advised the ACFA to put all its lobbying efforts into obtaining the deletion of the non-derogation clause pertaining to the powers, rights, or privileges of all federal, provincial, and aboriginal governments. "Je crois," Bastarache wrote, "que c'est de la mesquinerie pour le Québec d'insister sur son inclusion et que celui-ci cédera sur ce point si quelques provinces insistent pour l'abroger." Bourassa, rather than accepting the ACFA's proposal for asymmetry, decided to protect the prerogatives of the Quebec government by insisting upon a non-derogation clause preventing any use of the Canada clause to alter the roles of governments and legislatures as set out in the existing Constitution.[89]

Arès decided to use his contact on the Native Council of Canada, Bob Graves, to push for the amendments deemed necessary by the ACFA. Thanking Graves for keeping him informed about all the developments in the constitutional negotiations, Arès told him that the government's proposed s. 25.(1)(b) could be eliminated only if a revised Canada clause stated that the Constitution, including the Charter, should be interpreted in a manner consistent with certain fundamental characteristics. Moreover, the non-derogation clause as proposed was totally unacceptable and must not be reinserted. It was imperative that "affirmative action" language be reinstated in s. 2(1)(d), dealing with the roles of governments. "Only French of the two official languages is threatened in·Canada. 2(1)(c) and 2(2) provided for the protection and promotion of the French language only in Quebec. What is missing is a similar affirmative clause for the French language outside Quebec. Surely if the French language needs protection and promotion anywhere in this country it is in provinces such as Alberta, British Columbia, etc." Arès asked Graves to lobby the other delegates as forcefully as possible on these matters.[90] At the same time, Denis Tardif sent a letter to Robert Bourassa, with copies to the other premiers and Joe Clark, outlining the ACFA's suggestions on Senate reform. Bourassa had made it clear in a press conference on June 9 that the Triple E Senate proposals in the Pearson Accord were unacceptable because of the "limited number of francophone Senators"; the problem could be resolved quite easily by the addition of one French-speaking senator per province. The francophone presence would thereby be consoli-dated and united throughout Canada rather than being identified strictly with Quebec. Francophones would constitute 24 per cent of the reformed Senate – the same as in the existing body – while Franco-Albertans' historic and traditional right to representation in the Senate would be restored.[91]

The ACFA did not reap an immediate reward for its intensive lobby-ing. On 16 July 1992, Joe Clark released the *Final Status Report of the Multilateral Meetings on the Constitution*. All further negotiations were now in the hands of Prime Minister Mulroney and the premiers. The *Final Status Report*'s extremely vague wording for the linguistic duality clause – the Charter must be interpreted in a manner consistent with "the vitality and development of the language and culture of French-speaking and English-speaking minority communities throughout Canada"[92] – was a great disappointment to francophone leaders. The next day, a furious Raymond Bisson denounced Premier Bourassa for rejecting the strong linguistic duality provisions outlined in the Pearson Accord and for insisting on a non-derogation clause as con-ditions for taking part in the negotiations.[93] One week later, Tardif and Arès travelled to Montreal to unveil the ACFA's preferred version of the Canada clause as well as its Senate reform proposal. They hoped to put additional pressure on Quebec through the media to accept the asym-metrical approach to the official minorities and stop insisting on a non-derogation clause, now referred to as the "safeguard clause for governments."[94]

Prior to their Montreal trip, the ACFA leaders became aware of a new version of the Canada clause's sections on the distinct society and lin-guistic duality and the asymmetrical approach, concocted by senior federal civil servants. Once again Arès sought and received the speedy advice of Michel Bastarache and Mary Moreau. They opined that the non-derogation clause was as important as the other two sections. Fur-thermore, it was not Bourassa but Clyde Wells and other premiers who had insisted on its reinsertion. However, it was ill-conceived and in practice was incompatible with an interpretive clause, since the term "derogate" was normally applied in the context of substantive rights rather than when rights were being qualified or interpreted. Further, the clause rendered meaningless all of s. 2(1), which enumerated some of the fundamental characteristics of Canada. "À notre point de vue," counselled Bastarache and Moreau, "rien ne permet de croire que la loi constitutionnelle n'affecte pas l'exercise des pouvoires, privilèges et droits des législatures et gouvernements. Pour que la loi et les rôles qu'elle impartit aient un sens, il faut que la clause de sauvegarde soit interprétée de manière à ne pas éliminer tout effet des caractéristique reconnues. Si nous avons raison, il se peut que la protection de la dualité ajoute aux droits actuels des minorités linguistiques en rendant inconstitutionnel l'exercise de pouvoirs dans le but ou avec l'effet de favoriser l'assimilation linguistique."[95]

When the Fédération became aware of the latest changes to the Canada clause – several premiers had insisted on the reinsertion of a non-derogation clause – Marc Godbout changed his organization's target and upbraided the federal government for adding insult to injury by failing to live up to its responsibilities towards the linguistic minority communities.[96] Through its contacts on the Native Council of Canada, the ACFA acquired a confirmed copy of the Composite Canada Clause of 22 July 1992. It concluded that the most recent version of s. 2(1)(d) was a major setback, because it stated that "Canadians ... are committed to the vitality and development of official language minority communities throughout Canada *and the role of their governments to protect the linguistic rights of those communities is affirmed* (emphasis added)." The reference to governments in the first part of s. 2(1)(d) had been dropped and the term "promote" had been replaced with "protect" in the second part. Tardif pleaded with Frank McKenna, as a recognized champion of the minority communities, to do everything in his power to convince his colleagues to come up with an acceptable version; the premier assured Tardif that he understood his concerns and would strive to conciliate all points of view on the Canada clause.[97]

As the prime minister and the premiers moved cautiously towards a formal constitutional conference at their meeting of 4 August, the ACFA sought more detailed counsel from Michel Bastarache and Mary Moreau. Bastarache informed Tardif and Arès on 5 August that New Brunswick, Ontario, and Newfoundland had not accepted the latest draft text proposed by Ottawa and Quebec; it also appeared that the Pearson Accord's proposals on the Senate had lost the backing of some of the seven initially supportive provinces. He felt the situation provided an opportunity for Ontario and New Brunswick and advised that discussion of the Canada clause should be put off until Senate reform and aboriginal rights had been resolved. If a deal was achieved on these two difficult issues, Bastarache doubted that Quebec would reject a reasonable compromise on linguistic duality. The solution to Quebec's dilemma resided in the affirmation that the values recognized in the Canada clause were concurrent "et que de ce fait, le rôle des gouvernements en matière de dualité doit, dans le cas du Québec, s'intérpréter 'dans le contexte' de la société distincte." He reiterated that the non-derogation clause was not essential to Quebec if the province was not obligated to promote the development of its linguistic minority. Finally, in his view the Triple E Senate proposal would not serve the interests of the francophone communities, inasmuch as the double majority vote required for language and cultural matters granted Quebec senators – the majority of whom were bound to be strong nationalists – a veto over all federal legislation in these areas.[98] Moreau, responding somewhat later but at greater length, arrived at the same conclusions as her colleague. She decried Quebec's determination to redefine Canada along territorial lines, and feared that the pan-Canadian vision of duality was in serious danger if significant amendments were not made to the latest version of the Canada clause.[99]

Tardif went on the offensive again, hoping to influence the outcome of the constitutional conference slated to begin on 18 August. First, he asked President Ron George to make Georges Arès part of the Native Council of Canada's formal delegation. He also asked Premier Don Getty to allow members of the ACFA to be included as official observers in the Alberta delegation, but received no response.[100] Bisson asked the presidents to stand by for a conference call once a date had been set for the conference and new developments occurred. However, the western associations, except the SFM, found his plan unacceptable because they were eager to remain on the offensive. Following their joint meeting in Edmonton on 13 August, Tardif called on Bisson to convene a press conference of all the presidents in Ottawa for the opening day of the constitutional meetings. Although he believed the move to be premature since he was not aware of any recent changes to the draft document, Bisson agreed but indicated that the Fédération would not defray any of the associated costs.[101]

The Fédération found that its lobbying of the Mulroney government had paid off; it was informed on 14 August that it could send representatives as part of the federal delegation. One of the four seats at the table would be made available to its president when matters pertaining to the linguistic minority communities were under discussion. Liberal Jean Chrétien, leader of the Official Opposition, wrote to Brian Mulroney pointing out that the role of the prime minister was to be more than just "a rubber stamp for the provinces" and that "a constitution is for people not governments." He also restated his party's constitutional principles, which included the recognition of linguistic duality and the affirmation of the "role of all governments and legislatures in enhancing the vitality and development of the official language minority communities." Finally, Chrétien reminded Mulroney that he wanted all Canadians to exercise their ultimate sovereignty over their Constitution by approving any agreement in a national referendum.[102] As noted earlier, a national referendum was fast becoming an imperative, since some of the western provinces required a referendum to ratify changes to the Constitution. The Mulroney-Bourassa alliance was increasingly being backed into a political corner.

THE PEOPLE VERSUS THE POLITICIANS:
AN EMPHATIC "NO" TO THE CANADA ROUND

All the dedication and hard work of the Fédération and its affiliates, especially the ACFA, produced only modest gains for the francophone communities in the Charlottetown Consensus Report. The comprehensive and complex document, agreed to at a highly symbolic conference held in Charlottetown on 28 August 1992 by anxious and disgruntled First Ministers after a difficult negotiating process, remained vague and far from complete, reflecting Canada's regional, linguistic, ethnocultural, and gender faultlines. It referred to some twenty-five political accords required to settle highly contentious outstanding issues with the provinces and aboriginal organizations.

The Consensus Report opened with an omnibus Canada clause incorporating both the territorial and pan-Canadian visions of duality, both circumscribed by other fundamental characteristics: democracy and the rule of law, recognition of aboriginal self-governance, gender equality, racial and ethnic equality, and the equality of the provinces. It next set out far-reaching, controversial reforms to national institutions. Canadians would elect sixty-two senators: six for each province, one for each territory, and a number to be negotiated of aboriginal representatives, exercising varying degrees of authority over four categories of legislation. The House of Commons would be increased to 337 seats, with a guarantee that Quebec would be assigned in perpetuity no fewer than 25 per cent of the seats. The existing Supreme Court – composed of nine members, three of whom had to be members of the civil law bar – was to be entrenched as Canada's general court of appeal. Ottawa would appoint judges on the basis of lists from the provinces and territories. Acknowledging an inherent right of self-governance, the Constitution would recognize aboriginal governments as one of three orders of government in Canada, with authority over their languages, cultures, economies, institutions, traditions, lands, waters, and environment. Finally, the Consensus Report proposed amendments to improve the social and economic union and placed conditions on Ottawa's spending power in areas of provincial jurisdiction.[103]

With virtually no sense of celebration, Raymond Bisson informed the member associations of the three elements in the Consensus Report dealing directly with the concerns of the minority communities. The francophone associations had obtained a clause whereby "Canadians *and their governments* are committed to the vitality and the development of official language minority communities throughout Canada." Unfortunately, the non-derogation clause – expanded to include aboriginal governments – which had the potential for undermining any effective enhancement of those communities, remained. On the crucial matter of Senate reform, there was only a political rather than a constitutional guarantee for the election of francophone senators; however, as a sop, the double majority rule would be based on all of them, not just those from Quebec. Regarding the transfer and delegation of powers to the provinces, Bisson commented that it was difficult to evaluate the effects without the legal text of the document. He also informed the presidents of a conference call slated for 26 August to discuss the Fédération's response to the Consensus Report and to coordinate strategy.[104]

Likewise, there was little enthusiasm in the Edmonton offices of the ACFA. In a letter of 26 August, Denis Tardif thanked Bourassa, Mulroney, and Clark for their work on the constitutional question and acknowledged that the Consensus Report constituted some progress for the Franco-Albertan community despite the retention of the non-derogation clause. He also made note of the discrepancy between the French and English versions of the clause pertaining to the approach taken by governments. The French wording was "*l'attachement* des Canadiens et de leurs gouvernements" while the English was "Canadians and their governments are *committed to.*" The difference was important because the appropriate translation of "commitment" was "engagement," a word Tardif deemed "beaucoup plus proactif et [que] lie les parties en cause alors que le terme 'attachement' fait réference davantage à un concept plus sentimental." "Attachement" was unacceptable and Tardif encouraged Bourassa, Mulroney, and Clark to use the appropriate term, "engagement," in the final version of the document.[105]

Clark, writing on behalf of the government, chose to respond only on 16 October. He stated that "engagement" was used in several sections of the Canada clause and was specifically not chosen for the section on linguistic duality; "attachement" was correct and in conformity with proper French usage in an abstract or ideal context. The government was confident that the courts would not find any substantial difference between the French and English versions of the Canada clause.[106] Ironically, Quebec had insisted on the use of "attachement" because it would denote an asymmetry between the province's treatment of its anglophone minority and the treatment by the English-speaking provinces of their francophone minority communities. Quebec could use the French version before the courts while the francophone associations could resort to the English version, since both had equal standing in law. Clark refused to acknowledge this ploy.

Michel Bastarache, like the francophone organizations, felt that the Charlottetown Consensus Report fell far short of what was expected. Nevertheless, the clause on the official language minorities did constitute some improvement on the existing situation. The francophone organizations would have to work hard to make sure that the courts not only gave a narrow reading to the safeguard clause but also infused the word "attachement" with some significance. Bastarache's contacts had informed him that Quebec was willing to compromise on the safeguard clause but the premiers of Alberta and Manitoba had remained intransigent, demanding a return to the text of 7 July, which included the provision. Under the political circumstances, Bastarache was certain that the ACFA had obtained the maximum possible and congratulated Georges Arès on the determination and intelligence he had displayed for the francophone cause.[107]

In a formal opinion rendered for the Fédération on 4 September, before the final draft of the Charlottetown Consensus Report was released, Bastarache refined and amplified both his legal and political analyses. Having checked all the dictionaries, English, French, and French-English, he concluded that the only appropriate French translation for the English word "commitment" was "engagement." Indeed, in s. 36 of the Charter, those were the two words used in the respective languages. Yet, given the confusion, he was certain that the courts would rely on the context of the section to ascertain the intent of the framers. "Ma conclusion est assez simple. La traduction est défectueuse, mais elle ne risque pas trop fortement de détourner la Cour Suprême de l'objet fondamental visé parce que l'attachement décrit doit figurer avec le rôle des gouvernements, qui ne peut s'interpréter que de façon active."[108] On the non-derogation clause, he argued that it was ambiguous because it inappropriately used the term "derogate" rather than stating clearly that the Canada clause did not create any *new* powers, rights, or privileges for legislatures and governments.

As Bastarache saw it, the premiers were divided into two camps. Wells, Rae, and McKenna wanted to limit "l'effet créateur de droits de la Clause Canada." Bourassa, Filmon, and Getty, on the other hand, wanted to eliminate any possible impact of the Canada clause on the existing powers of the provinces, rendering it a symbolic political statement with no judicial clout. He considered the first camp to be correct, since the interpretive clause, by definition, had to have a judicial resonance. But, since the term "role" was new in constitutional law, it was difficult to predict the extent of the legal obligations that would flow from it. In short, the Canada clause would not affect the extent of the powers, rights, or privileges of legislatures and governments, but it would influence their exercise. It constituted some progress over the existing situation because it would improve the francophone communities' chances of obtaining governance over their schools under s. 23 of the Charter. He advised the Fédération to accept the modest constitutional gains and not join the emerging "NO" campaign groups in their opposition to the deal. It was better to begin asking governments how they intended to fulfill their new "role" with respect to their official language minority communities.[109]

When Bastarache received his French copy of the Charlottetown Consensus Report and realized that there was no "role of governments and legislatures clause" pertaining to the official language minority communities, he was devastated. He sent Mary Moreau a copy of the formal opinion he had submitted to the Fédération, along with the appropriate pages of the report, making the cryptic comment that everything was changed thereby rendering his former opinion inconsequential.[110] Nevertheless, despite their disillusionment both Bastarache and Moreau remained reluctant supporters of the Consensus Report. Moreau stated as much in a letter to Arès.[111] Bastarache, meanwhile, expressed his views to a New Brunswick senator, Jean-Marie Simard, who had solicited his opinion. The document was quite imperfect, but still a considerable improvement over the draft text of 22 July. Its recognition of the minorities as "communities" introduced the concept of collective rights for interpreting ss. 16 to 23 of the Charter. Its use of the terms "vitality" and "development" rather than "protection" implied a duty to act, while the term "governments" conveyed the notion of public services. The three basic weakness of the Canada clause were the absence of a direct reference to the "role" of governments, as was the case for Quebec respecting the distinct society clause; the retention of the troublesome non-derogation clause; and the incorrect translation of "commitment" with the term "attachement." On the matter of the Senate, the double majority was defined as francophone/anglo-phone rather than Quebec/Canada. But the lack of a guarantee for francophone seats outside Quebec would give Quebec senators a *de facto* veto over all language and cultural legislation pertaining to the francophone communities – a very worrisome matter that needed to be addressed politically as soon as possible.[112]

After Bastarache had offered all this advice, the presidents were called to a special meeting in Ottawa on 12–13 September to formalize their decision on the Charlottetown Consensus Report and to discuss the role of their respective organizations in the national referendum slated for 26 October. The Conseil national des présidents et des présidentes approved the deal, which its members saw as recognizing "le rôle des gouvernements d'assurer le développement et l'épanouissement de la dualité linguistique canadienne." The presidents also agreed that they would continue to lobby the federal government to see to it that the words "committed to" were properly translated by "engagement" rather than the existing "attachement." Further, the Fédération would pressure all governments to guarantee franco-phones and Acadians representation in the elected Senate. Finally, the Conseil authorized the Fédération and its affiliates to register with Elections Canada as part of the "YES" campaign in the referendum.[113]

The Fédération's leaders were reluctant even to admit that they were joining the soon-to-be largely dysfunctional "YES" campaign team led by the detested Prime Minister Brian Mulroney. In fact, there was little that the Fédération or its member organizations could do to per-suade voters to support the Charlottetown Consensus Report, which like the Meech Lake Accord had been put together behind closed doors, albeit in a somewhat modified form of executive federalism. Moreover, any campaigning by the francophone minority community leadership was perceived by voters, especially in western Canada, as self-serving interest group politics. Consequently, francophone leaders played a rather limited role in the campaign. As early as the end of September, it was obvious to most astute observers that the complex, ambiguous, and far-from-complete Consensus Report was headed for a humiliating defeat in the referendum. When Pierre Trudeau inter-vened in the campaign with his article of late September in *Maclean's* and *l'Actualité* denouncing "Quebec's Blackmail," followed up with his devastatingly accurate critique of the Consensus Report on 1 October at the now-famous Maison Egg Roll, a Chinese restaurant in working-class St-Henri in Montreal, a "NO" victory was a foregone conclusion. For a second time, the retired Trudeau waded into mega-constitutional politics to protect his legacy, the Canadian Charter of Rights and Freedoms, by asking "Who Speaks for Canada?" The question was rhetorical. After 1982, a majority of Canadians had come to believe that on constitutional matters they were a sovereign people – they, not governments, had the final say over their Constitution.[114]

On 26 October, nearly 55 per cent of the electorate voted "NO." The Consensus Report was rejected by six provinces – including Quebec – and one territory, as well as by a majority of the Status Indian band chiefs and members who chose to exercise their franchise. The Quebec-centred asymmetrical federalism constitutional agenda of the Bourassa government could not be reconciled with the far more comprehensive decentralizing constitutional agenda of the nine other premiers and the aboriginal leaders who had negotiated the multilateral and Pearson accords under Joe Clark's supervision. As noted earlier, a set of deceivingly radical clauses in the Consensus Report granted Canada's aboriginal leaders a comprehensive constitution within the Canadian Constitution.[115] The recognition of aboriginal citizenship and a third order of government – theoretically more powerful than provincial governments – would ultimately encourage First Nations peoples to reject a shared Canadian citizenship. The deal made the distinct society clause, circumscribed by the omnibus Canada clause, look insignificant by comparison.[116] It was, as AFN Chief Ovide Mercredi freely admitted, a dramatic "historical arrangement." It was guaranteed to humiliate and anger francophone Quebecers, who had watched their pleas for the recognition of their province as a distinct society categorically rejected by AFN leaders during Meech Lake and whittled down in the Canada Round.

Both Brian Mulroney and Robert Bourassa paid a heavy political price for refusing to participate in the negotiating process, choosing instead to sit on the sidelines hoping that Joe Clark's multilateral process would fail and give them the opportunity to cut a bilateral Ottawa/Quebec deal. Once Bourassa's senior constitutional advisor, André Tremblay, and his Deputy Minister of Intergovernmental Affairs, Diane Whilhelmy, had admitted publicly – by accident rather than by design – that Quebec was getting far less than in the Meech Lake Accord, the Consensus Report's overwhelming defeat there was a foregone conclusion. Indeed, 57 per cent of the Quebec electorate rejected it – not far off the 62 per cent of Manitobans and 68 per cent of British Columbians. The citizens of all four western provinces, fully aware that they would not get their prized Triple E Senate while Quebec would be guaranteed 25 per cent of the seats in the House of Commons in perpetuity, were only too eager to humiliate their respective premiers and the prime minister by rejecting the Charlottetown Consensus Report. Ontarians, always fearful of an economic and political backlash from their neighbours in Quebec, hedged their bets, voting 50 per cent both for and against what most considered a badly flawed deal, inasmuch as it saw Premier Bob Rae accepting an equal Senate and thereby diminishing Ontario's historic clout in the federation to appease the Maritime and western provinces.[117]

In the end, the Charlottetown deal, a series of highly questionable compromises, satisfied neither the premiers and aboriginal leaders who had negotiated it nor its critics from across the political spectrum. Prime Minister Mulroney and Premier Bourassa, who had been mere bystanders until the final stages in August, suffered the full brunt of the electorate's political wrath, first in the referendum, then in federal and provincial elections. Mulroney's Quebec/western Canada political alliance, which had kept him in office since 1984, was shattered, leaving in its wake two highly sectional political movements, Preston Manning's ultra-conservative Reform Party and Lucien Bouchard's secessionist Bloc Québécois.

CONCLUSION

The road to Charlottetown was a bittersweet experience for Canada's francophone minority community leaders. Having experienced considerable frustration and disappointment as "outsiders" during the closed-door mega-constitutional negotiations surrounding the Meech Lake Accord, they were determined on a formal role in the Canada Round. Their primary objective was to make sure that Bourassa's quest for a Quebec/Canada constitutional structure did not undo their efforts towards constitutional recognition for the cultural and linguistic duality that would protect the minority communities. They proceeded on the assumption that their continued support for Bourassa's constitutional objectives, as laid out in the Meech Lake Accord, would be rewarded by his acceptance of their constitutional goals. The francophone leadership believed that these two conceptions of duality were complementary and could function successfully in an asymmetrical federation. This perception was no doubt driven by a combination of wishful thinking, naiveté, and a realization that there was little room to manoeuvre. Francophone minority organizations wielded minimal influence, and that only if they acted in concert. As this study has amply demonstrated, they lacked the decisive political power capable of dissuading the Mulroney government from backing – at virtually any cost – the constitutional agenda of the prime minister's political ally, Robert Bourassa. They failed to recognized that, once entrenched in the Canadian Constitution, the Quebec/Canada territorial duality would inevitably trump the politically and institutionally far weaker pan-Canadian conception of equal francophone and anglophone communities.

The francophone leaders faced a gargantuan challenge. The orchestrated explosion of Québécois nationalist and separatist outrage in the wake of the demise of the Meech Lake Accord left Bourassa and Mulroney high and dry. Initially, the pair decided to fuel, then, they hoped, harness the impassioned sentiment to pressure the premiers, Canada's political and economic leaders, and a majority of Canadians to support the Meech Lake provisions within an expanded set of constitutional proposals. They should have foreseen two developments, but did not. First, Québécois nationalism and separatism could not be turned on or off at will. Once Mulroney gave credence to the nationalist and separatist assertion that English Canada alone was responsible for the defeat of the Meech Lake Accord, the integrity of the federation was put in jeopardy. Second, quick to promote their respective interests, the premiers and aboriginal leaders jumped at the opportunity to devise constitutional proposals that ran parallel to, and on many crucial points contradicted, Quebec's objectives. When Mulroney and Bourassa belatedly entered the negotiating process in early August 1992 it was too late to achieve convergence between the two sets of constitutional demands.

Pushed by the ACFA, a divided and reluctant Fédération forged clearer constitutional policies, objectives, and strategies. The ACFA believed it necessary to deal directly with Bourassa, who was considered sympathetic to the francophone cause. Like many others, they failed to realize that his decision not to participate in the negotiations until the rest of Canada made an acceptable constitutional proposal to Quebec severely weakened Bourassa's bargaining position. Both the sovereignty-association Allaire Report and the secessionist Bélanger-Campeau Commission Report rejected cultural and linguistic duality. Bourassa clearly had no choice but to pursue his government's constitutional vision. The Fédération and its affiliates were therefore compelled to plead with Mulroney, some of the premiers, and sympathetic non-governmental organizations to advance their objectives. They monitored all and participated in many of the constitutional committees and task forces. Despite their efforts, the Beaudoin-Dobbie Committee Report recommended only that the federal and provincial governments express "a profound commitment to the vitality and development of official language minority communities" rather than advancing the much stronger constitutional obligation to preserve and promote those communities.

In the negotiations chaired by Joe Clark that resulted in the Charlottetown Consensus Report, the Fédération and its affiliates found themselves once again monitoring from the sidelines. In despair, the ACFA turned to Bourassa in an attempt to embarrass him and Mulroney into strengthening the cultural and linguistic duality provisions of the proposed Canada clause. Once Bourassa agreed to join the other premiers and the prime minister at the negotiating table, the concerns of the francophone minority community leaders took a back seat to the rival constitutional agendas of the provinces and Quebec. Desperate to achieve a constitutional deal, Mulroney did not dare to risk driving Bourassa away by insisting that Ottawa and the provinces take on a constitutional obligation to preserve and promote their respective official language minorities.

The future of Canada's official language minorities was sacrificed on the altar of Québécois nationalism, expansive provincial rights, and Ottawa's perceived need to head off a clash with Canada's highly nationalistic and politicized aboriginal communities. Given these powerful forces arrayed against them, it is quite remarkable that the Fédération and its affiliates obtained even minor gains in the unwieldy and incomplete Consensus Report. Even more remarkably, francophone leaders managed to protect the gains made in the Charter from the western premiers and Quebec, all of them intent on weakening Ottawa's role in official bilingualism and on gutting s. 23 education rights for the official language minorities. Had they failed to defend those rights and their liberal interpretation by the Supreme Court, it is highly unlikely that the francophone minority communities would have obtained any form of school governance from their respective provinces. A decade of hard work would have gone to waste.

It was not surprising that francophone leaders joined the YES campaign forces with little enthusiasm. Realizing that most Canadians remained sceptical about the Charlottetown Consensus Report, they were not overly disappointed when a sizeable majority, especially in Quebec and western Canada, rejected it in a referendum.

Canada's francophone organizations accomplished two laudable aims in the course of the rounds of constitutional negotiations. First, they played an important part in educating Canadians about the Constitution, helping to democratize our political culture. Second, they used the Canada Round to solidify, even enhance, their symbolic and real political spaces within the Canadian federation. The traditional Catholic French Canada laid to rest in the late 1960s was replaced by a regenerated pan-Canadian national entity comprised of Canada's francophone minority communities and supported by the provincial and national organizations and the federal and provincial governments. During any future round of mega-constitutional politics, those communities from coast to coast will have the experience and confidence to play important roles in framing the questions, invigorating the constitutional debate, and influencing the outcome.

8

The Past is Prologue

Canada's francophone and Acadian minority communities celebrated the *fin-du-siècle* by achieving – after more than a century of struggles – school governance for their children. How does one explain this remarkable reversal of fortune? We have seen throughout this study that their success was due to a propitious conjuncture of character and circumstance, played out in an intertwined manner over four difficult yet promising decades. A new generation of visionary francophone leaders – rising like a phoenix from the ashes of the traditional Catholic French Canada – developed modern provincial organizations, buttressed by a national Fédération, in order to rebuild their communities, in the process redefining their provincial and national identities and spaces within an evolving Canadian federation.

Our analysis has looked at how and why francophone leaders – spurred on by their internal crises, Québécois neo-nationalists' rejection of a pan-Canadian French Canada, the Royal Commission on Bilingualism and Biculturalism, the 1969 Official Languages Act, and the election of the Parti Québécois in 1976 – achieved two momentous goals in the Constitution Act, 1982. The Canadian Charter of Rights and Freedoms recognized English and French as the official languages of Canada and New Brunswick and mandated minority language educational rights under s. 23, opening the door to school governance by and for francophones. Did they possess the determination and the political skills to achieve school governance – the key to the institutional, social, cultural, and linguistic regeneration of their communities? Our close examination of their numerous campaigns proves conclusively that, indeed, Ontario, Alberta, and Manitoba francophone leaders did acquire and fine-tune the necessary political and judicial skills. Driven by their deep-rooted instinct for cultural and linguistic survival, francophone leaders used their political skills to overcome the deep-seated internal, provincial, and national cleavages undermining their communities' sense of solidarity. By redefining them as modern francophone communities equal in constitutional status, rights, and privileges to Canada's anglophone communities, francophone parent groups, backed by their provincial and national organizations, were able to undertake several judicial challenges leading to the watershed Supreme Court ruling in *Mahé* in 1990 and the Manitoba reference case decision in 1993, which granted them full school governance under s. 23.

There is overwhelming evidence that without the Charter and the Supreme Court justices' determination to give minority language education rights a broad, liberal, purposeful, and remedial interpretation, Canada's francophone communities would not have been able to overturn more than a century of discrimination. John T. Saywell, Canada's pre-eminent constitutional historian, concludes his seminal study on judicial power and the shaping of Canadian federalism by stating, "The *judicial lawmakers*, not John A. Macdonald or Sir Francis Reilly, are the real authors of Canadian constitutional law ... the law of the constitution is what the judicial lawmakers have said it is, and will be what they say it may be."[1] Indeed, the prominent, constructive, and at times imaginative role of Canada's Supreme Court justices in the interpretation of rights under s. 23 is not a departure from past practice. Rather, it is a continuation of their activist role, applied not to the resolution of power disputes between the federal and provincial governments but to the empowerment of citizens vis-à-vis the state. University of Toronto law professor Lorraine Weinrib makes a convincing case that an activist Supreme Court is essential to the proper functioning of our Constitution, the Charter, and parliamentary democracy.[2]

Using these judicial victories as a springboard, and backed by ongoing political and financial support from Ottawa, francophone organizations in Alberta, Manitoba, and Ontario successfully applied their micro-constitutional negotiating skills to obtain school governance. When some aspects of governance remained unresolved, determined francophone parents and community leaders appealed yet again to the courts to increase their political bargaining powers.[3] The remaining provincial and territorial governments were pressured into creating francophone school plans with varying degrees of governance. As in Alberta, Ontario, and Manitoba, negotiations were painfully slow, requiring patience, determination, and, ultimately, financial incentives from Ottawa before school governance could become a reality.[4] Some of the resulting plans, deemed inadequate, have been challenged in the courts by francophone parents, with the result that in 2000 the Supreme Court was required in *Arsenault-*

Cameron v. *the Government of Prince Edward Island* to confirm and clarify for a third time the precise nature and scope of rights under s. 23. French-speaking parents in Summerside, Prince Edward Island thereby won their demand for a local francophone school.[5]

We have also found in this study incontrovertible evidence that the Charter has democratized Canada's deferential political culture and its elitist, executive-controlled constitutional amending procedures. It has done so by fostering groups of Canadians – such as the official language minority and aboriginal organizations – who have assiduously advocated for improvements to their Charter rights and, when need be, marshaled a forceful defence of them. When several premiers decided to use the mega-constitutional negotiations in 1986–92 to restrict the scope of education rights under s. 23 by giving precedence to a Quebec/Canada conception of duality, francophone and Acadian organizations contributed to the demise of the Meech Lake Accord in June 1990, then obtained the recognition of an enhanced pan-Canadian vision of linguistic and cultural duality in the Charlottetown Consensus Report of 1992. However, in an innovative demonstration of constitutional democracy at work, Canadians decisively rejected the Charlottetown deal in Canada's first referendum on constitutional reforms. Ironically, Charter federalists learned – much to their dismay – that a majoritarian form of constitutional democracy could trump their conception of constitutionally entrenched minority community rights.

If the past is prologue, what does the future portend for Canada's francophone minority communities? At first glance, their survivability and vitality are being sapped by a steady decline in their population with respect to the Canadian total: a 34.4 per cent increase compared to a 115.8 per cent increase between 1951 and 1996. The proportion of Canadians with French as their mother tongue (outside Quebec) declined in the same period from 7.25 per cent to 4.5 per cent. The situation of the francophone minorities, excluding the Acadians, is even more precarious than these overall statistics indicate as a result of lower fertility rates, rising exogamy leading to a loss in intergenerational transmission of language and culture, ongoing urbanization, rapid aging, and ever-advancing bilingualism.[6]

Several scholars have concluded that school governance, while long overdue and essential, must not be seen as the only institution capable of guaranteeing the vitality of Canada's francophone communities. Now that schools and school boards under their own governance are a reality in all provinces and territories, francophones have embarked on a new, perhaps more challenging, stage of their struggle for survival and effective equality. Francophone leaders have recently been scrutinizing the full remedial potential of ss. 23 and 24 of the Charter, with an eye to developing systemic recovery mechanisms for linguistically assimilated francophone students that will guarantee effective equality in educational opportunities and conditions.[7] Pierre Foucher and other constitutional specialists maintain that such equality will be attained primarily through the courts, which, under s. 24, can and must mandate a special fund to ensure that francophone schools have all the resources necessary to offer French-speaking children access to an educational experience equal to that available to English-speaking children. In short, effective redress of past discrimination towards the francophone and Acadian minority communities requires different and special treatment if true equality in education is to be achieved.[8]

While sharing the same vision, Angéline Martel takes a different viewpoint. Thanks to the power and legitimacy conferred on them by s. 23, the francophone minority and Acadian communities – no longer victims – have taken on a new identity as affirmative agents by overcoming the domination of the majority. She concurs that there is a very strong remedial component to s. 23 that is immune to the notwithstanding clause, and she understands the socioeconomic and political conditions driving frustrated francophone and Acadian leaders and parents to pursue monetary redress through the courts under s. 24. On the other hand, she cautions that a confrontational approach risks turning francophones and Acadians into victims once again and recommends more constructive and affirmative approaches. Effective recovery and recuperation, rather than mere financial compensation for past violation of rights, must begin at the community level – that is, from the ground up rather than being imposed from above by the Supreme Court.[9] Ways and means must be found to convince a significantly higher proportion of eligible minority children – only 54 per cent of whom are now enrolled in francophone schools across Canada – to choose those schools for their education. Martel posits that this end can be achieved by designing, building, and administering schools that function as dynamic cultural and social community centres capable of attracting eligible parents and children who need to learn or relearn the French tongue while being immersed in the French culture required to sustain and nourish the language.[10]

Other scholars, such as Rodrique Landry, Director General of the Institut canadien de recherche sur les minorités linguistiques, and Serge Rousselle, Dean of Law at the University of Moncton, make a convincing argument for combining the legal, institutional, and community approaches in a concerted ten-year campaign. They contend that the Supreme Court can be convinced – on the basis of the need to attain real as opposed to formal equality – to extend the reach of

s. 23 beyond primary and secondary schools to kindergarten and post-secondary education in order to give the francophone minority and Acadian communities governance over a network of educational institutions and community social centres providing life-long learning. More controversially, they argue that s. 16(1) of the Charter ("English and French are the official languages of Canada and have equality of status and equal rights and privileges as to their use in all institutions of the Parliament and government of Canada.") and s. 16(3) of the Charter ("Nothing in this Charter limits the authority of Parliament or a legislature to advance the equality of status or use of English and French."), the reinforced Official Languages Act, 1988, and the proven remedial nature of s. 23 together impose a fiduciary obligation on the federal government towards those communities.[11] Having established the constitutional and quasi-constitutional obligations of the federal government, Landry and Rousselle call for a new plan of action entailing "global" participatory governance over all educational, social, and cultural institutions by the various stakeholders: francophone and Acadian parents, community organizations and their leaders, school boards, and the provincial and federal governments. At its heart they postulate five principles:

- full remediation of maternal language education to achieve real equality
- an enhanced role for school boards based on the concept of subsidiarity, that is, global planning with local implementation
- a global partnership of all the stakeholders exercising a "power of collaboration"
- an integrated leadership involving the federal government, the courts, and the communities functioning in a system of horizontal governance
- an imputability, individual and collective, of the partners among themselves and towards the beneficiaries of the plan of action, the francophone and Acadian communities

Landry and Rousselle realize that their proposal is innovative and leads in the direction of unknown and unexplored spaces, but they are convinced that it is imperative to go beyond s. 23 of the Charter in order to guarantee the vitality of the francophone minority and Acadian communities well into the new century.[12]

Clearly, the winning of school governance was never an end in itself. From the outset, francophone minority communities, organizations, and leaders envisaged linguistically homogeneous schools and school boards as the agents most necessary for ensuring their cultural survival, obtaining a greater degree of equality of treatment from their majority societies, and redefining themselves as provincial collectivities capable of playing a small but effective role on the national scene. Over four decades, francophone leaders used the instruments of micro- and mega-constitutional politics to modernize their provincial organizations, reformulate their provincial identities, and achieve school governance. All these developments enabled the francophone minority and Acadian communities to redefine their identity and create a Franco-Canadian citizenship based on equality with and respect from the majority. Given the tremendous obstacles they encountered along the way, this is truly a remarkable and propitious achievement.

Notes

INTRODUCTION

1 For an overview, consult Martel, *Official Language Minority Education Rights in Canada.*

2 Foucher, *Constitutional Language Rights of Official Language Minorities in Canada* ; Magnet, *Official Language Rights of Canada;* Martel and Villeneuve, "Droit constitutionnel et rapports de pouvoir," 25–63.

3 The most comprehensive descriptive analysis of the four decades of transformation and subsequent rupture of French Canada as a pan-Canadian entity into Canada's francophone minority communities is found in Thériault, ed., *Francophonies minoritaires au Canada.*

4 Frenette, *Brève histoire des Canadiens français;* Gervais, "Aux origines de l'identité franco-ontarienne," 132–42; and the excellent collection of essays in Louder and Waddell, eds., *French America.*

5 Juteau and Séguin-Kimpton, "La collectivité franco-ontarienne," 265.

6 Harvey, "Le Québec et le Canada français," 49–64.

7 Behiels, *Prelude to Quebec's Quiet Revolution.*

8 McRoberts, *Quebec: Social Change and Political Crisis,* 128–72.

9 Martel, "'Hors Québec, point de salut!," 130–1.

10 The most comprehensive and clearsighted analyses of this rupture can be found in Martel's *Le deuil d'un pays imaginé,* 171–8 and in Gervais, "Aux origines de l'identité franco-ontarienne," 129–32.

11 Thériault, "Les États généraux ...," 265. For critics of this interpretation consult Cardinal, "Le Canada Français à la lumière des États Généraux," 213–32.

12 Martel, *Le deuil d'un pays imaginé,* 148–62.

13 The concepts of socioeconomic transformation and identity rupture and renewal as interpretative tools for explaining the multiple socioeconomic, cultural, linguistic, and cultural crises faced by Canada's francophone

minority communities in the 1960s and 1970s were first applied to the
French Canadian community of Ontario by a sociologist: Juteau-Lee,
"Français d'Amérique ... ," 21–43; Juteau-Lee, "Ontarois and Québécois
as Distinct Collectivities," 53–68.

14 Bernard, *De Québécois à Ontarois*; Carrièrre, "La métamorphose de la communauté franco-ontarienne, 1960–1985," 306–18.

15 Thériault, ed., *Francophonies minoritaires au Canada*, 14–15.

16 The Acadian minority community, which constitutes over one-third of
the population of New Brunswick, was not selected for this study since its
socioeconomic, political, and constitutional situation is far superior to
that of the other francophone minority communities in Canada. Furthermore, there are numerous studies that analyse its modernization and the
role played by the Société des Acadiens et Acadiennes du Nouveau
Brunswick in its renewal. Consult Daigle, ed., *Acadia of the Maritimes* and
Thériault, *L'identité à l'épreuve de la modernité*.

17 Aunger, "Dispersed Minorities and Segmental Autonomy," 191–215.

CHAPTER ONE

1 Juteau and Séguin-Kimpton, "La collectivité franco-ontarienne," 265,
287–92.

2 Clark, "The Position of the French-Speaking Population," 62–85;
Bernard, *De Québécois à Ontarois*, 33–57.

3 The geographic dispersal and mobility factors affecting this socioeco-
nomic transformation are dealt by various authors in Louder and
Waddell, eds., *French America*; Arsenault, "Aires géographiques en
Acadie"; Gilbert,"Les espaces de la francophonie ontarienne"; and
Viaud, "La géographie du peuplement francophone de l'Ouest."

4 Banting, *The Welfare State and Canadian Federalism.*

5 Owram, *Born at the Right Time.*

6 Major dimensions of this upheaval are examined in Gervais, "L'histoire
de l'Ontario français"; in Thériault, dir. *Francophonies minoritaires au
Canada*, 153–59; Allaire, "Le rapport à l'*autre*"; and Carrièrre, "La métamorphose de la communauté franco-ontarienne, 1960–1985."

7 For an insider's account of the pleading by francophone minority leaders
consult Laurendeau, *The Diary of André Laurendeau*. As editor-in-chief of
Le Devoir, Laurendeau had visited many of their communities in the mid-
1950s and was depressingly aware of the assimilation pressures they were
experiencing. Also Horton, *André Laurendeau*, 216.

8 Canada, Royal Commission on Bilingualism and Biculturalism, *Report*,
General Introduction. Book I, 121.

9 Ibid., 123.

10   Canada, Royal Commission on Bilingualism and Biculturalism. *Report, Book II: Education.*

11   Gilbert, "Les espaces de la francophonie ontarienne," Tableau I, 60. For a detailed study see her *Espaces franco-ontariens* and Bernard, *Le Choc des nombres.*

12   Gervais, "Le Règlement XVII," 123–92.

13   Choquette, *Language and Religion.*

14   Boulay, *Du privé au public,* 59.

15   Guindon, "Pour lever les contradictions structurelles de l'ACFO," 35–41; ACFO, *Un plan de développement pour la communauté franco-ontarienne.*

16   Lafrenière, "Des luttes au consensus 1965–1982," 106–12.

17   Comité législatif de l'ACFÉO, "Présentation d'un projet de restructuration de l'ACFÉO, 1969," CRCCF, Fonds ACFO, C2/290/2.

18   Choquette, *L'Ontario français historique,* 205–7, 212–18.

19   Bureau, *Mêlez-vous de vos affaires.*

20   Viaud, "La géographie du peuplement francophone de l'Ouest," 86–8; Allaire, "Le rapport à l'*autre*," Carte IV, 176.

21   Allaire, "Le rapport à l'*autre*, 86–8; Tableau II, 177; Tableau III, 182. A very detailed study can be found in Bernard, *Le Choc des nombres.*

22   Allaire, "Le rapport à l'*autre*," 166–70; Silver, "French Canada and the Prairie Frontier," 36.

23   Blay, *L'Article 23,* 26–40.

24   Ibid., 41–72; SFM, *Le Manitoba français,* 1–6.

25   Huel, *Gestae Dei Per Francos,* 46–50.

26   Hébert and Vaillancourt, "French Canadians in Manitoba," 175–90.

27   Ibid., 179–80.

28   Ibid., 175–7, 181.

29   Blay, *L'Article 23,* 77–81.

30   AÉCFM, "Exposé des Franco-manitobains à Monsieur le Premier Ministre du Canada, le 17 octobre 1968," SHSB, SFM, 89/113/36, 3.

31   Ibid., 5–9.

32   Blay, *L'Article 23,* 82–6, quote at 83.

33   Allaire, "La construction d'une culture française dans l'Ouest canadien," 343–60.

34   Lalonde, "The French Canadians of the West," 100–16.

35   Allaire, "Le rapport à l'*autre*," Tableau II, 177.

36   Allaire, "Pour la survivance," 67–70.

37   Ibid., 73–8.

38   Ibid., 73–83. On the emerging debate about Alberta's bilingual schools consult Silla, ed., *École bilingue ou unilingue pour les Franco-Albertains?*

39   Hautecoeur, *L'Acadie du discours,* 92–194.

40   Roy, "Démographie et démolinguistique en Acadie, 1871–1991,"

141–206. See also Johnson and McKee-Allain, "La société et l'identité de l'Acadie contemporaine," 209–16.

41 Stanley, *Louis Robichaud,* 139–62; Doucet, *Le discours confisqué,* 23–46.

42 Hautecoeur, op. cit., 196–245.

43 Doucet, op. cit., 47–62.

44 Ibid., 90–1.

45 In the wake of Quebec's Quiet Revolution of the 1960s and, in particular, the emergence of the separatist Parti Québécois in 1968, Acadians experienced their own wave of neo-nationalism and separatism. Some of the new middle-class Acadian graduates of the University of Moncton – radicalized by their education, by events in Quebec and on the international scene, and by their desire to improve the treatment, conditions, and opportunities of the Acadian people – founded the Parti acadien in 1972. It survived barely a decade, torn apart by struggles between moderate reformers and extreme socialists and by the impracticality of its political project, the creation of a separate Acadian province. Competing for the support of increasingly radicalized Acadian youth, the SAANB's leaders felt compelled to advocate neo-nationalist political and constitutional objectives that often alienated them from their constituents and the provincial government. Cf. Doucet, Ouellet and Seguin, "L'espace politique et la vie politique en Acadie," 355–9.

46 Trudeau, *Federalism and the French Canadians;* Trudeau, "The Values of a Just Society," 357–85.

47 *Official Languages Act, 1968–69;* The Task Force on Canadian Unity, *Coming to Terms. The Words of the Debate,* 91–2.

48 PMO, *Federalism for the Future.*

49 Trudeau, *The Constitution and the People of Canada,* 20–2.

50 Ibid., 54, 56, 58.

51 Ibid., 58.

52 Stevens and Saywell, *Canadian Annual Review 1970,* 188–91.

53 Stevens and Saywell, *Canadian Annual Review 1971,* 41–64. For the Canadian Constitutional Charter, 1971, see 52–5.

54 Johnson, *A Canadian Myth,* 147.

55 ACFA, "Testimony to the Special Joint Committee of the Senate and of the House of Commons on the Constitution of Canada," *Minutes of Proceedings and Evidence,* session 3, issue 85; Association culturelle franco-canadienne de la Saskatchewan, ibid., session 3, issue 11; SFM, ibid., session 2, issue 11.

56 Canada, The Special Joint Committee of the Senate and of the House of Commons on the Constitution of Canada, *Final Report,* 23–4.

57 Ibid., 22.

58 Ibid., 24.

59 Ibid., 22.

60 Quebec, *Rapport de la Commission d'enquête sur la situation de la langue française et sur les droits linguistiques au Québec.*

61 Plourde, *La politique linguistique du Québec,* 9–19.

62 Pal, *Interests of State*; Cardinal, "La vie politique et les francophones hors Québec," 325–42.

63 Henceforth, the Fédération des communautés francophones et acadiennes du Canada will be referred to as the Fédération in the text, while the notes will refer either to the FFHQ or the FCFA, depending on the source.

64 FFHQ, *D'est en ouest* ... , 1–16; "Etre au Canada ou ne pas être au Québec ... ; FCFA, *Une francophonie à découvrir,* 1–4.

65 *Official Language Minority Schooling in Canada,* 7–8.

66 Interview with Senator Roméo LeBlanc, January 1992.

67 In response to a question from J. Boucher, Federal Undersecretary of State, as to the impact of federal aid for bilingualism on Quebec's education system, Quebec Deputy Minister of Education M. Yves Martin replied, "Pour le Québec, il s'agit là d'une aide inconditionelle, versée directement au fonds de revenu consolidé." Consult Francois Lebrun, Dossier: Bilinguisme en éducation au niveau pré-universitaire, Procès-verbal du réunion Québec-Ottawa sur le bilinguisme, 27 août 1973, Archives Nationales du Québec, Fonds E42 Ministère des affaires inter-gouvernementales 1993–08–002, Boîte 21. I wish to thank Matthew Hayday for this reference.

68 For an excellent analysis of the program as it applied to Ontario consult Hayday, "Confusion and Conflicting Agendas," 50–79.

69 Gaudet to Trudeau, 29 September 1976, Fonds FCFA, C84/52/7.

70 FFHQ, *Les héritiers de Lord Durham,* Vol. 1, 11. Emphasis in original.

71 Ibid., 49–55.

72 Ibid., 74.

73 Ibid., 61–74.

74 Ibid., 103–15 and 68–9. For confirmation of the Fédération's severe critique of the Bilingualism in Education Program, consult Hayday, op. cit., 50–79.

75 Gaudet to Trudeau, 13 and 25 April 1977 and Trudeau to Gaudet, 27 May 1977, CRCCF, Fonds FFHQ, C84/52/7.

76 "Document préparatoire de la réunion avec le premier ministre Trudeau le 31 mai 1977" and "Rencontre avec le premier ministre Trudeau, le 31 mai 1977," CRCCF, Fonds FFHQ, C84/52/8.

77 Gauthier to Trudeau, 18 May 1977, CRCCF, Fonds FFHQ, C84/52/7.

78 Interview with Hubert Gauthier and Paul Comeau on CBF, 1 June 1977," CRCCF, Fonds FFHQ, C84/52/8.

79 Gauthier to Tellier, 20 May 1977 and Gauthier, "Document suite à la rencontre avec le premier ministre P.E. Trudeau, n.d.," CRCCF, Fonds FFHQ, C84/52/8.

80 Roberts to Gaudet, 3 June 1977, CRCCF, Fonds FFHQ, C84/53/8.
81 Trudeau, "Preface," *A National Understanding*, 12. Emphasis added.
82 Ibid., Chapters 4, 5, and 6.
83 Ibid., 68.
84 Ibid.
85 Ibid., 69.
86 Ibid., 71.
87 Ibid., 78.
88 Gaudet to Tellier, 9 June 1977, CRCCF, Fonds FFHQ, C84/52/20.
89 Tellier to Gaudet, 15 June 1977, CRCCF, Fonds FFHQ, C84/52/20.
90 Gauthier to Tellier, 20 June 1977, CRCCF, Fonds FFHQ, C84/52/20.
91 Tellier to Gaudet, 30 June 1977, CRCCF, Fonds FFHQ, C84/52/20.
92 Gaudet to Trudeau, 5 July 1977 and Trudeau to Gaudet, 2 August
    1977, CRCCF, Fonds FFHQ, C84/52/7.
93 Gaudet to Trudeau, 29 July 1977 and Gauthier to Tellier, 29 July 1977,"
    CRCCF, Fonds FFHQ, C84/52/20.
94 Tellier to Gaudet, 11 August 1977, CRCCF, Fonds FFHQ, C84/52/20.
95 Trudeau to Gaudet, 3 October 1977, CRCCF, Fonds FFHQ, C84/52/7.
96 Government of Canada, "Cabinet Document no. 462–77RD: Politique
    du gouvernement relativement aux minorités de langue officielle, 17
    octobre 1977," CRCCF, Fonds FFHQ, C84/52/8.
97 Gauthier to Robertson, 28 October 1977 and Robertson to Gauthier, 4
    November 1977," CRCCF, Fonds FFHQ, C84/52/20.
98 Gaudet to all deputies and ministers of the House of Commons, 22
    November 1977 and Rochon to Gaudet, 14 December 1977, CRCCF,
    Fonds FFHQ, C84/52/7.
99 Moncion to Gaudet, 1 February 1978, CRCCF, Fonds FFHQ, C84/52/20.
100 "Mémoire présenté par la Société franco-manitobaine, l'Association cul-
    turelle franco-canadienne et l'Association canadienne-française de l'Al-
    berta aux ministres: Marc Lalonde, Roméo LeBlanc, Jean-Jacques Blais,
    John Roberts, le 11 mars 1978," SHSB, Fonds SFM, 89/108/08.
101 Gaudet to Trudeau, 20 February 1978, CRCCF, Fonds FFHQ, C84/52/7.
102 Trudeau to Gaudet, 23 March 1978, CRCCF, Fonds FFHQ, C84/52/7.
103 Gaudet to Trudeau, 13 June 1978, CRCCF, Fonds FFHQ, C84/52/7.
104 Trudeau to Comeau, 12 July 1978, CRCCF, Fonds FFHQ, C84/52/7.
105 Trudeau to Cyr, 20 April 1979. Trudeau, "Réponses au questionnaire
    de la FFHQ qui demandait au governement libéral de clarifier sa posi-
    tion sur les questions suivantes, le 20 avril 1979," CRCCF, Fonds FFHQ,
    C84/52/8, p.3.
106 Ibid., 5–6.
107 Cyr to Jarvis, 27 August 1979; "Rencontre entre la FFHQ et le Ministre
    de la Justice, le 21 août 1979"; Cyr to Flynn, 27 August 1979, CRCCF,
    Fonds FFHQ, C84/53/5.

108 Cyr to Trudeau, 19 February 1980, CRCCF, Fonds FFHQ, C84/52/7.

109 Plourde, *La politique linguistique du Québec*, 31–44. For the ideological principles underlying Bill 101, consult Laurin, *La politique québécoise de la langue française.*

110 Lévesque, "Statement Concerning Reciprocal Agreements in Education," 18th Annual Premiers Conference, St. Andrews, NB, 18–19 August 1977. Canadian Intergovernmental Conference Secretariat, Document: 850–8/012, 1–7, quotes at 2 & 4.

111 "Cooperation between Quebec and other Provinces in the Field of Education," 18th Annual Premiers' Conference, CICS, Document: 850–8/013, 23–8, for expenditures see Schedules I and II.

112 "An Agreement to Promote Access to Schooling for Certain Categories of Persons from Outside Quebec," 18th Annual Premiers' Conference, CICS, Document: 850–8/014, 1–4.

113 Blakeney, "News Release," 18 August 1977, 18th Annual Premiers' Conference, CICS, Document: 850–8/022.

114 Durocher, "Quebec," 144–5.

115 "Conference Statement on Language," 18th Annual Premiers' Conference, CICS, Document: 850–8/027.

116 Ibid.

117 Council of Ministers of Education, Canada, *The State of Minority Language Education in the Ten Provinces of Canada*, 1–2.

118 Ibid., 10.

119 Foucher, *Constitutional Language Rights of Official Language Minorities in Canada*, 3. He continues: "It will be noted that the emphasis has since (1977) shifted. We have moved from freedom of choice in language of instruction to the protection of minority rights, which is quite a different matter. Freedom of choice implies uncontrolled access by the majority to the schools of the minority. In practice ... such freedom of choice results in bilingual schools, which lead to the assimilation of minority language pupils." (3–4)

120 "Communiqué of the Conference," Premiers' Conference, Montreal, February 23, 1978, CICS, Document: 850–9/007.

121 Task Force on Canadian Unity, *A Future Together*, 121–2. For the rationale behind their recommendations, see 51–3.

122 Trudeau, *A Time for Action*, 20.

123 Ibid., 6, 9, 22.

124 House of Commons, Bill C-60, Third session, Thirtieth Parliament, 26–27 Elizabeth II, 1977–78, First reading, 20 June, 1978.

125 Trudeau, *A Time for Action*, 25.

126 "Constitutional Reform: The Position of the Provinces, Communiqué #2, 10 August 1978," 19th Annual Premiers' Conference, Regina/Waskesiu, 9–12 August 1978, CICS, Document: 850–10/012, 1–2.

127 Ibid., 6.

128 Davis, "A Restatement of Ontario's Views on Canada and the Constitu-
     tion," 19th Annual Premiers' Conference, CICS, Document:
     850–10/010, 6 and Hatfield, "Statement," 19th Annual Premiers' Con-
     ference, CICS, Document: 850–10/013, 11.

129 Durocher, "Quebec," 140; Trudeau, "Who Speaks for Canada?, 67–8.

130 Fletcher and Wallace, "The Federal Perspective," 88–90.

131 FFHQ, *Pour ne plus être ... sans pays*, 81.

132 Ibid., i-x, quote at ix.

133 Ibid., 3–7.

134 For an explicit statement of these two dualities, see Bastarache, "Les
     nationalistes en devenir," 71–98.

135 FFHQ, *Pour ne plus être ... sans pays*, 85–6 and chapter 1.

136 Ibid., 19–26.

137 Ibid., 86–7 and 37–48. The committee even suggested that those
     provinces that lacked the resources to fulfill their linguistic obligations
     be granted the right to delegate legislative powers in this field to
     Ottawa.

138 Ibid., 53–4.

139 Ibid., 55–60, quote at 56.

140 Ibid., 60–3, 87–9.

141 Ibid., 64–8, 89–90.

142 Ibid., 71–4, 90–1.

143 Ibid., 78.

144 Ibid., 77–80, 91–2.

CHAPTER TWO

1 Gold, "*La revendication de nos droits*, 106–28.

2 Morin, "Le Québec et les minorités francophones," Talk given to the
   SFM, 14 April 1977, SHSB, Fonds SFM, 89/110/17, 1–16, quote at 4.

3 Bisson, "Les Francophones Hors Québec Face au Référendum,
   Document de réflexion No. 1, le 3 janvier 1980," SHSB, Fonds SFM,
   89/131/04.

4 Teffaine to Cyr, 14 December 1979, SHSB, Fonds SFM, 89/131/05.

5 ACFC, "Communiqué, le 14 février 1980," SHSB, Fonds SFM, 89/102/01.

6 SFM, Executive Committee, "Procès-verbal de la réunion du 28 février
   1980" and "Procès-verbal de la réunion du 26 mars 1980," SHSB, Fonds
   SFM, 89/102/01.

7 Proteau, "Conférence de Presse, le 1 avril 1980," SHSB, Fonds SFM,
   89/131/05.

8 Bocquel, "La SFM appuie le OUI," *La Liberté*, 3 April 1980; Russell, "The
   controversial 'yes'," *The Winnipeg Free Press*, 7 April 1980, 9.

9 Turenne, "Lettre au rédacteur de *La Liberté*, le 3 avril 1980," SHSB, Fonds SFM, 89/131/04.

10 Hill, "Manitoba's 40,000 francophones divided," *The Ottawa Citizen*, 15 May 1980, 7.

11 Proteau to the members, 21 April 1980, SHSB, Fonds SFM, 89/131/05.

12 ACFA, "Communiqué – News Release, le 22 mars 1980," SHSB, Fonds SFM, 89/108/10.

13 Nogue, "Résumé de la réunion d'une délégation de l'ACFA, le lundi 5 mai courant, avec M. Dick Johnston," 7 May 1980, PAA, Fonds ACFA, no. 89.391 (10/236).

14 Lalonde, "Communiqué – News Release, le 6 mai 1980," PAA, Fonds ACFA, no. 89.391 (10/236).

15 Johnston to Lalonde, 14 May 1980, SHSB, Fonds SFM, 89/140/07.

16 Lalonde to Johnston, 17 June 1980, SHSB, Fonds SFM, 89/140/07.

17 FFHQ, "Suite au Référendum. Compte rendu de la réunion avec les représentants des Associations-membres tenue à Winnipeg, le 14 mai 1980," SHSB, Fonds SFM, 89/131/04.

18 Comeau to Trudeau, 13 May 1980, CRCCF, Fonds FFHQ, C84/52/7.

19 Lévesque to Comeau, 6 June 1980, SHSB, Fonds SFM, 89/131/05.

20 Radwanski, *Trudeau*.

21 Conklin, "Constitutional Ideology, Language Rights and Political Disunity in Canada," 39–65.

22 Cited in Bell and Wallace, "The Federal Perspective," 56.

23 Ibid., 58–74.

24 Trudeau, *Statement by the Prime Minister on the Government's Constitutional Resolution, October 2, 1980*, 8.

25 Ibid., 3.

26 Canada, *The Canadian Constitution, 1980*.

27 Bell and Wallace, "The Federal Perspective," 77–8.

28 Chrétien, *Notes for a Speech*, 6 October 1980, 5–6, 22.

29 Ibid., 16–17.

30 Ibid., 19.

31 Canada, *The Canadian Constitution, 1980*, 22.

32 Chrétien, *Notes for a Speech*, 6 October 1980, 18.

33 Canada, *The Canadian Constitution, 1980*, 20–2.

34 Chrétien, *Notes for a Speech*, 6 October 1980, 18.

35 FFHQ, *Pour ne plus être ... sans pays*, 19–20. Emphasis added.

36 Cyr to Trudeau, 19 February 1980, CRCCF, Fonds FFHQ, C84/52/7.

37 Fox to Comeau, 1 May 1980, CRCCF, Fonds FFHQ, C84/53/30.

38 Comeau to Trudeau, 13 May 1980, CRCCF, Fonds FFHQ, C84/52/7.

39 Télégrammes: Comeau to Trudeau, 21 May et le 5 June 1980; Jeannine Séguin to Trudeau, 18 June 1980; Séguin to Trudeau, 26 June 1980, CRCCF, Fonds FFHQ, C84/52/7.

40 Proteau to Lyon, 2 June 1980, SHSB, Fonds SFM, 89/140/19.

41 Bisson, "Reformes constitutionnelles. Droit linguistiques, Document de réflexion no. 3, le 27 juin 1980," SHSB, Fonds SFM, 89/140/07, 1–10.

42 "Compte-rendu d'une réunion des agents politiques de l'ouest, le 30 juin 1980," SHSB, Fonds SFM, 89/140/07.

43 Cyr to Premiers Davis, Peckford, Blakeney, and Hatfield, 10 July 1980, CRCCF, Fonds FFHQ, C84/41/9. Cyr to Lyon, 10 July 1980, SHSB, Fonds SFM, 89/140/10.

44 Déquier to Cyr, 14 July 1980 and Proteau to Lyon, 20 August 1980, SHSB, Fonds SFM, 89/140/10.

45 Manitoba, "Provincial Powers in Constitution Stressed," News Service, 22 August 1980, SHSB, Fonds SFM, 89/140/10.

46 Lyon to Proteau, 2 October 1980, SHSB, Fonds SFM, 89/128/22.

47 Séguin to Trudeau, 10 July 1980, CRCCF, Fonds FFHQ, C84/52/7. A similar letter was sent to Premiers Davis, Peckford, Blakeney, and Hatfield asking them what entrenchment of linguistic rights would mean in concrete terms for their francophone minorities: CRCCF, Fonds FFHQ, C84/41/9.

48 Hurley to Cyr, 18 November 1980, CRCCF, Fonds FFHQ, C84/53/27.

49 FFHQ, "Mécanisme de participation aux négociations constitutionnelles, document présenté à l'Assemblée générale, 1980," CRCCF, Fonds FFHQ, C84/37/9.

50 Canada, Special Joint Committee, *Minutes of Proceedings and Evidence* 2 (7 November 1980): 26–30, 40–44. They referred to Privy Council documents no. 800–14058 and no. 814–085.

51 Romanow, Whyte and Leeson, *Canada Notwithstanding*, 44–5, 76.

52 Canada, Special Joint Committee, *Minutes of Proceedings and Evidence* 2 (7 November 1980): 43.

53 Ibid., 3 (12 November 1980): 17.

54 FFHQ, "Mémoire de la Fédération des Francophones hors Québec présenté au Comité mixte spécial sur la Constitution du Canada, Ottawa, le 26 novembre 1980." CRCCF, Fonds FFHQ, C84/37/10.

55 Canada, Special Joint Committee, *Minutes of Proceedings and Evidence* 13 (26 November 1980), 27.

56 Ibid., 28–30.

57 Ibid., 43–4. Mackasey taunted Senator Tremblay, saying that if his "political party [Conservative] is ready, at this time, to move an extension of 133 to the whole country, I would be ready to vote for such a motion." (Ibid., 51)

58 Canada, Special Joint Committee, *Minutes of Proceedings and Evidence* 8 (19 November 1980), 31, 36, 43.

59 FFHQ, "Mémoire de la FFHQ presenté au Comité mixte spécial ... " CRCCF, Fonds FFHQ, C84/37/10, 10.

60 Canada, Special Joint Committee, *Minutes of Proceedings and Evidence*, 13 (26 November 1980), 29–30, quote at 30.

61 Ibid., 8 (19 November 1980), 32–3.

62 Ibid., 12 (25 November 1980), 9–10.

63 Ibid., 10 (21 November 1980), 26–7.

64 Ibid., (21 November 1980), 31, 40–1.

65 L'Association des juristes d'expression française de l'Ontario, "Propos sur un projet de réforme constitutionnelle soumis au comité spécial mixte du Sénat et de la Chambre du communes, le 2 février, 1981," CRCCF, Fonds FFHQ, C84/88/10, 1, 15.

66 ACFA, "Mémoire présenté au Comité mixte spécial sur le renouvellement constitutionnel, le 6 janvier 1981," SHSB, Fonds SFM, 89/108/10.

67 Ibid.

68 "Yves Saint-Denis, président général de l'ACFO à l'honorable Jean Chrétien, Ministre de la Justice, le 2 novembre 1981," CRCCF, Fonds ACFO, C11–6/34/13.

69 Canada, Special Joint Committee, *Minutes of Proceedings and Evidence* 6 (17 November 1980), 10–12.

70 Ibid., 13–15, 19, 26.

71 Yalden, "Statement to the Special Joint Committee of the Senate and of the House of Commons on the Constitution of Canada, 12 December 1980," CRCCF, Fonds FFHQ, C84/88/10.

72 Cyr to Trudeau, 25 November 1980, and Trudeau to Cyr, 18 December 1980, CRCCF, Fonds FFHQ, C84/52/7.

73 Chrétien, "Statement to the Special Joint Committee on the Constitution, 12 January 1981," CRCCF, Fonds FFHQ, C84/53/5, 3. For the text of Chrétien's Consolidated Resolution, including these amendments, tabled on 13 February 1981 with subsequent amendments by the House on 23 April 1981, consult Appendix B of McWhinney, *Canada and the Constitution 1979–1982*, 149–64.

74 Ibid., 10–12.

75 Ibid., 13.

76 "Réactions au projet de la loi consitutionnelle de 1981 présenté par la Société franco-manitobaine à Monsieur Robert Bockstael, Député de Saint-Boniface, le 24 janvier 1981"; Proteau to Bockstael, 3 February 1981; Proteau to Chrétien, 2 February 1981; Michelle Grimard for Prime Minister Trudeau to Proteau, 5 March 1981, SHSB, Fonds SFM, 89/140/10 and /12.

77 FFHQ, "Communiqué de presse, le 14 janvier 1980: Les amendements Chrétien constituent un net recul pour les francophones hors Québec," CRCCF, Fonds FFHQ, C84/37/12.

78 "Extraits du procès-verbal de l'Assemblée générale tenue à Montréal, les 14 et 15 février 1981," CRCCF, Fonds FFHQ, C84/37/12.

79 Association des juristes d'expression française de l'Ontario, "Propos sur un projet de réforme constitutionnelle, 2 février 1981," CRCCF, Fonds FFHQ, C84/88/10, quote at 15.

80 "Manifeste de la FFHQ portant adresse au Sénat et à la Chambre des Communes du Canada, le 26 février 1981," CRCCF, Fonds FFHQ, C84/37/12.

81 "Declaration de M. Florant Bilodeau sur le projet de la loi constitution-nelle de 1981, le 26 février 1981," CRCCF, Fonds FFHQ, C84/37/12.

82 Séguin to Trudeau and Bennett, 28 October 1981, CRCCF, Fonds FFHQ, C84/52/7.

83 For a copy of the second version of s. 23, consult Foucher, "Les droits scolaires des acadiens et la charte," 100.

84 Canada, Department of Justice, *A Consolidation of The Constitution Acts 1867 to 1982*, 63–4.

85 Ibid., French version, 65.

86 Sheppard and Valpy, *The National Deal*, 298–302.

87 Ibid., 64.

88 Smiley, "A Dangerous Deed," 74.

89 Ibid., 66, 70.

90 Hogg, *Constitutional Law of Canada*, 820. Quebec passed a law in 1982 requiring the consent of the legislature and not just the government, as allowed by s. 59.

91 Apps, "Minority Language Education Rights," 55.

92 SFM, "Note: résultats du mémoire de la société franco-manitobaine au comité spécial mixte sur la constitution, le 11 février 1982," SHSB, Fonds SFM, 89/140/12.

CHAPTER THREE

1 *Mahé* v. *Alberta* [1990] 1 S.C.R. 350 [hereafter *Mahé*].

2 Juteau and Séguin-Kimpton, "La collectivité franco-ontarienne, 265–70.

3 Carrièrre, "La métamorphose de la communauté franco-ontarienne," 306–18.

4 Sigurdson, "Left- and Right-Wing Charterphobia in Canada," 96.

5 Mandel, *The Charter of Rights*, ix-x, 308.

6 *Quebec Association of Protestant School Boards* v. *Quebec A.G.* (1982), C.S. 673 aff'd (1983), (C.A.), aff'd [1984] 2 S.C.R. 66.

7 Mandel, op. cit., 102–11.

8 Ibid., 125.

9 Ibid., 127.

10 Manfredi, *Judicial Power and the Charter*, 9.

11 Russell, *Constitutional Odyssey*.

12 Manfredi, "Litigation and Institutional Design: The Charter of Rights

and Freedoms and Micro-Constitutional Politics," paper presented at the 1993 Annual Meeting, Canadian Political Science Association, Carleton University, 6 June 1993, 1. For recent views on this debate, consult Howe and Russell, eds. *Judicial Power and Canadian Democracy* and James, Ableson and Lutsztig, eds., *The Myth of the Sacred.*

13 "Manifeste de la Fédération des Francophones Hors Québec portant adresse au Sénat et à la Chambre des Communes du Canada, le 26 février 1981," CRCCF, Fonds FFHQ, C84/37/12.

14 Séguin, "Les Francophones hors Québec face à la Constitution, n.d.," CRCCF, Fonds FFHQ, C84/37/12.

15 Trudeau to Séguin, 8 March 1982, CRCCF, Fonds FFHQ, C84/52/7.

16 FFHQ, *A la recherche du milliard ...* (Ottawa: FFHQ, 1981). FFHQ, "Communiqué, le 19 février: La FFHQ veut une révision en profondeur des programmes de langage officielles dans l'enseignement," CRCCF, Fonds FFHQ, C84–9/6/25.

17 FFHQ, Press release, n.d.: "La FFHQ dénonce l'indifférence de CMEC face aux besoins des francophones hors Québec"; FFHQ, "Document d'information présenté par la FFHQ au Conseil des Ministres de l'Éducation du Canada en vue de la rencontre du 4 décembre 1981 à Toronto," CRCCF, Fonds FFHQ, C84–9/6/25.

18 FFHQ, Press release, 22 October 1982, "Les droits constitutionnels des Francophones hors Québec," CRCCF, Fonds FFHQ, C84/37/11.

19 Cloutier to Crane, Gowling & Henderson, 7 December 1982, CRCCF, Fonds ACFO, C2–52/6/C3639.

20 Séguin to Trudeau, 10 November 1981, CRCCF, Fonds FFHQ, C84/21/10; FFHQ, Press release, 22 October 1982: "Demandes des Francophone hors Québec à faire inscrire à l'ordre du jour d'une prochaine conférence fédérale-provinciale sur la constitution," CRCCF, Fonds FFHQ, C84/37/11.

21 FFHQ, Press releases, 11 March 1983 and 7 March 1984, " A quant une conférence sur les droits linguistiques des Francophones hors Québec" and "Les premiers ministres provinciaux continueront-ils à saboter l'unité nationale?," CRCCF, Fonds FFHQ, C84–12/8/17.

22 FFHQ, "Projet national d'information sur le droit à l'éducation en langue française au Canada – Phase II, Présenté au Secrétariat d'État le 14 septembre 1983," CRCCF, Fonds FFHQ, C84/91/7.

23 "Entrevue avec Serge Joyal, le 8 octobre 1982, Post CFTM," CRCCF, Fonds FFHQ, C84/91/7, 2–7.

24 Consult Gérin, *D'un obstacle à l'autre.*

25 Ibid.

26 For the origins of the legislation, consult Ontario, Ministerial Committee on French Language Secondary Schools, *Report of the Committee on French Language Schools in Ontario*, 1–87. The Bériault Report, named after its chair Roland Bériault, who was a member of the Educational Policy and

Development Council of the Ontario Department of Education, was very influential. The creation of consultative committees was in part a compromise to offset the fact that the amalgamation of smaller school boards and districts put Franco-Ontarians in a minority situation on the larger boards.

27 Symons, "Ontario's Quiet Revolution," 185.

28 Boulay, *Du privé au public*, 1–79.

29 ACFO, "Procès-verbal de la 3e réunion du Comité d'orientation et de recherche en éducation tenue à la maison franco-ontarienne, le 22 novembre 1969," CRCCF, Fonds ACFO, C2/400/13.

30 Bordeleau, *Les écoles secondaires de langue française en Ontario*, 59.

31 Symons, "Ontario's Quiet Revolution," 187; Symons, *Commission ministérielle sur l'éducation secondaire en langue française*, 1–79.

32 Bordeleau, op. cit., 48–9.

33 Sylvestre, *Penetang: l'école de la résistance* and Bureau, *Mêlez-vous de vos affaires*, 30–4.

34 Gérin, op. cit.

35 Lévesque, *Pourquoi un conseil scolaire de langue française pour la région d'Ottawa-Carleton?*, 1–38.

36 Gérin, op. cit., 32–5.

37 Mayo, *Rapport de la Commission d'étude pour le remaniement d'Ottawa-Carleton*, 1–147. He also recommended full funding for Catholic schools together with an equitable sharing of all business, commercial, and industrial taxes in the region.

38 Gérin, op. cit., 38–48. Archibishop Plourde's concerns were no doubt lessened somewhat by the legal opinion provided to the Comité by Peter W. Hogg, a professor of constitutional law at Osgoode Hall, York University: Hogg, "Consultation Juridique. Constitutionalité d'un Conseil scolaire de langue française pour la région d'Ottawa-Carleton, le 28 août 1978," CRCCF, Fonds AFCSO, C11–6/54/13.

39 "Résolutions adoptées au 28e congrès générale de l'ACFO à Cornwall, les 26 et 27 août 1977," CRCCF, Fonds ACFO, C2/388/11.

40 AFCSO, "XXXIIe congrès annuel 1976; Suites données aux résolutions, voeux et recommandations du dernier congrès," CRCCF, Fonds AFCSO, C11–6/20/2.

41 AFCSO, "Procès-verbal du XXXIVe congrès annuel 1978," CRCCF, Fonds AFCSO, C11–6/21/4.

42 AFCSO, "Brief on French Language Education in Ontario presented to the Hon. Bette Stephenson, Minister of Education, 1 February 1979," CRCCF, Fonds AFCSO, C11–6/59/41.

43 Ontario, Ministry of Education, *Déclaration du gouvernement sur le remaniement des administrations locales dans la municipalité d'Ottawa-Carleton*, 8–25.

44 Paris to Stephenson, 31 May 1979, with attachment "Réponse de l'ACFO au Livre vert sur l'éducation," CRCCF, Fonds ACFO, C2/594/12.

45 AFCSO, "Réaction de l'AFCSO au Livre vert sur l'éducation du Ministère de l'éducation, le 6 juillet 1979," CRCCF, Fonds AFCSO, C11–6/59/18. On the CCLF, see Gérin, op. cit., 68–9.

46 "La création du Conseil francophone de planification scolaire d'Ottawa-Carleton, notes historiques: 1978–1980," CRCCF, Fonds du Conseil francophone de planification scolaire d'Ottawa-Carleton (CFPSOC), C95/1/1.

47 Ontario, Ministry of Education, *Décision prise par le gouvernement en ce qui concern l'éducation dans la municipalité d'Ottawa-Carleton.*

48 "La création du Conseil francophone de planification scolaire ... ," CRCCF, Fonds CFPSOC, C95/1/1; "Premier Davis à Claudette Boyer, Présidente, CCLF, Conseil scolaire d'Ottawa, le 19 mai 1981," CRCCF, Fonds AFCSO, C11–6/17/4.

49 CFPSOC, "Mémoire présenté au Comité mixte spécial sur la constitution du Canada, le 30 décembre 1980," CRCCF, Fonds ACFO, C2/604/13.

50 AFCSO, "Survol historique du dossier de la gestion scolaire. Démarches entreprises par AFCSO depuis 1978 à nos jours, préparé le 3 octobre 1984," CRCCF, Fonds ACFO, C2/35/6/2. See Annex 2 – Résolutions des congrès de 1981–1983–1984 au sujet de la gestion scolaire; "Discours d'Onésisme Tremblay, président du CÉFO, au congrès de la FAPI, 14 novembre 1981," ibid., C2/517/5.

51 Morin to Lucien Bradet, 21 October 1981, CRCCF, Fonds AFCSO, C11–6/34/13.

52 AFCSO, *La gestion scolaire pour les francophones par les francophones.* (Ottawa: AFCSO, December 1981), 1–22. CRCCF, Fonds AFCSO, C11–6/16/12.

53 AFCSO, "Message à tous nos membres, le 11 février, 1982," CRCCF, Fonds AFCSO, C11–6/17/2.

54 Ontario, Ministry of Education, *Report of the Joint Committee on the Governance of French Language Elementary and Secondary Schools*, Introductory letter to Premier Davis and Appendix A.

55 "Notes suite à la rencontre du Comité conjoint sur la gestion scolaire avec les organismes reliés à l'éducation, tenue le 12 mars 1982"; Bradet to Lalonde, 30 March 1982, CRCCF, Fonds AFCSO, C11–6/51/1.

56 Ontario, Ministry of Education, *Report of the Joint Committee on the Governance of French Language Elementary and Secondary Schools*, 1–29.

57 Ibid.; Appendix A for the position of the francophone minority members' report.

58 ACFO, Telegram to Davis, 30 April 1982 and "Press release, 17 May 1982; Conseil francophone de planification, Press release, 8 May 1982; Lalonde to Davis, 10 May 1982; CCLF, Conseil Scolaire de Toronto, to Davis, 11 May 1982, CRCCF, Fonds AFCSO, C11–6/16/15 & 17/2.

59 AFCSO, "Communiqué de presse re: Rapport du comité mixte, le 19 mai 1982"; ACFO, "Yves Saint-Denis à l'Honorable William Davis, le 14 mai 1982"; Conseil francophone de planification, Press release, 19 May 1982; AEFO,"Serge Plouffe à Monsieur William Davis, le 8 juin 1982; "L'AEFO réclame des changements dès janvier 1983, Communiqué, le 8 juin 1982," CRCCF, Fonds AFCSO, C11–6/17/2

60 Aubé to Stephenson, 16 June 1982, CRCCF, Fonds AFCSO, C11–6/8/5. The AEFO did not sign the letter.

61 AFCSO, Press Release, 21 July 1982: "Davis Tangoes on Governance of French Language Schools," CRCCF, Fonds ACFSO, C11–6/17/2.

62 Gérin, op. cit., 84–5. The report did prompt support from the Ottawa Board of Education for an Ottawa-Carleton Catholic/francophone board, but only on the condition that the OBE not be amalgamated with the Carleton public board. Cf. "Jane Dobell, Chairman of the Ottawa Board of Education to Bette Stephenson, Minister of Education, 24 June 1982," CRCCF, Fonds ACFO, C2/498/3.

63 AFCSO, "Rapport de la rencontre avec le Premier Ministre tenue le 2 septembre 1982, à Queen's Park," CRCCF, Fonds ACFSO, C11–6/16/15; Davis to Aubé, 3 September 1982, C11–6/23/4.

64 Aubé to Davis, 15 September 1982; Davis to Aubé, 7 October 1982, CRCCF, Fonds AFCSO, C11–6/58/4.

65 Cloutier to Crane, Gowling & Henderson, 7 December 1982, CRCCF, Fonds ACFO, C2–52/6C3639.

66 ACFO, "Compte-rendu de la conférence téléphonique des membres du Comité d'éducation, 9 décembre 1982," CRCCF, Fonds ACFO, C2/496/8. Soucie, *L'enseignements en Français en Ontario: revue des problèmes courants.* (Travail préparé pour l'ACFO et l'AEFO dans le cadre de leur dossier éducation: poursuite judiciaire, décembre 1982), 1–24, quote at 20. Also Rolande (Soucie) Faucher's curriculum vitae, dated January 2003, sent to the author.

67 Ontario, Ministry of Education, *Une proposition en réponse au Rapport du Comité mixte sur la gestion des écoles élémentaires et secondaires de langue française*, 1–19.

68 "Entente entre l'AFCSO et l'OSSTA sur la gestion des écoles de langue minoritaire au sein du système ontarien des écoles séparées catholiques, le 19 décembre," CRCCF, Fonds AFCSO, C11–6/9/10, 1–14; AFCSO, *L'Infoscolaire* (Novembre 1984), Fonds ACFO, c2–35/6/2.

69 ACFO, "Réaction à la proposition en réponse au Rapport du comité mixte sur la gestion des écoles élémentaires et secondaires de langue française, juillet 1983," CRCCF, Fonds ACFSO, C11–6/8/6.

70 AFCSO, "Réaction à une proposition en réponse au Rapport du Comité mixte sur la gestion des écoles élémentaires et secondaires de langue française, Ottawa, le 29 septembre 1983," CRCCF, Fonds AFCSO, C11–6/2/1.

71 Ontario, Minority Language Governance Study Committee, *Final Report*, 1–24. Found in CRCCF, Fonds AFCSO, C11–6/2/1.

72 AFCSO, "Survol historique du dossier de la gestion scolaire. Démarches entreprises par AFCSO depuis 1978 à nos jours, préparé le 3 octobre 1984," CRCCF, Fonds ACFO, C2/35/6/2.

73 Cloutier to Joyal, 13 October 1982 and Séguin to Joyal, 26 October 1982, CRCCF, Fonds FFHQ, C84/91/4.

74 Cloutier to Crane, Gowling & Henderson, 7 December 1982, CRCCF, Fonds ACFO, C2–52/6/C3639.

75 Richard M. Nolan to Jean Bernard Lafontaine, 25 October 1983, CRCCF, Fonds FFHQ, C84/91/7.

76 Department of the Secretary of State, *The Court Challenges Program*, CRCCF, Fonds FFHQ, C84/91/7; "Compte-rendu d'une réunion tenue le 9 janvier 1986," ibid., C84–12/8/14.

77 Foucher, "L'Article 23 de la Charte. Orientations et perspectives," 11–12.

78 Magnet, "Minority-Language Educational Rights," 214–16 and Magnet, "Les écoles et la Constitution," 145–55. Initially, Magnet was very pessimistic about the nature and extent of s. 23 rights. See his "Language Rights: Myth and Reality," 261–70.

79 Foucher, "L'Article 23 de la Charte. Orientations et perspectives," 13.

80 Magnet, "Minority-Language Educational Rights," 195–216.

81 Ibid., 206.

82 Ibid., 209–11, quote at 210. Magnet failed to point out that Quebec's educational system was legally confessional and not linguistic. French- and English-speaking public school advocates did not have full autonomy over their own school systems but had representatives on La Commission des écoles catholiques de Montréal.

83 Ibid., 204–9.

84 Ibid., 211.

85 Foucher, "Les droits scolaires des Acadiens et la Charte," 111, 113–14.

86 Case cited in Foucher, "L'article 23 de la Charte: un compromis audacieux," 220.

87 Foucher, "L'interprétation des droits linguistiques constitutionnels par la Cour suprême du Canada," 386–8, quote at 411.

88 Foucher, "L'article 23 de la Charte: un compromis audacieux," 225–9.

89 Ibid., 229. Foucher was drawing on the extensive work of Daniel Proulx, who argued that the courts were very reluctant to alter the power relationship between governments and the people, since s. 23 involved social rather than fundamental rights. See Proulx, "La précarité des droits linguistiques scolaires," 335–70.

90 Foucher, "L'article 23 de la Charte: un compromis audacieux," 230–1.

91 "Compte-rendu de la conférence téléphonique des membres du Comité

d'éducation de l'ACFO, tenue le 9 décembre 1982," CRCCF, Fonds ACFO, C2/496/8.

92 Cloutier to Crane, 7 December 1982, CRCCF, Fonds ACFO, C2–52/6/ C3639.

93 "Procès-verbal de la rencontre de concertation tenue samedi, le 5 février à l'Hotel Voyageur à North Bay," CRCCF, Fonds ACFO, C2–46/1/14.

94 Crane to Cavarzan, 20 April 1983, CRCCF, Fonds ACFO, C2/498/3.

95 Crane to Lévesque, 12 May 1983, CRCCF, Fonds ACFO, C2/498/3.

96 ACFO, Press release, 25 May 1983, "Franco-Ontarians want their right to manage and control their schools to be recognized by the government of Ontario." CRCCF, Fonds ACFO, C2–46/1/14. Copies of the formal statement of claim can be located in this same file.

97 Cloutier to Stephenson, 25 May 1983, CRCCF, Fonds ACFO, C2/498/3.

98 Archie Campbell, Deputy Attorney General, to W.G.C. Howland, Chief Justice of Ontario, 9 August 1983, CRCCF, Fonds ACFO, C2/498/3.

99 Crane to Cloutier, 1 September 1983, CRCCF, Fonds ACFO, C2/498/3.

100 Cloutier, letter, 19 November 1983, CRCCF, Fonds ACFO, C2/498/3.

101 "Exposé des faits et des questions de droits des intervenants: l'Association canadienne-française de l'Ontario, l'Association des enseignants franco-Ontariens, Augustin Desroches, Gilberte Brisson, Yolande Bélanger et Aldéric Godin," CRCCF, Fonds ACFO, C2–46/1/14, 10.

102 Ibid., 5–10.

103 Ibid., 10–16; quote at 16.

104 Ibid., 16.

105 Ibid., 18–26; Ontario, Order in Council, o.c. 2154/83, Honorable R. Roy McMurtry, Attorney General, 4 August 1983," CRCCF, Fonds ACFO, C2/498/3.

106 Ibid., 39–47.

107 Ibid., 46–7.

108 Ibid., 26–39; quote at 36.

109 FFHQ, Press release, 27 October 1983, "La FFHQ demande à intervenir devant la cour d'Appel de l'Ontario"; Letourneau to Joyal, 2 November 1983; Joyal to Letourneau, 29 November 1983, CRCCF, Fonds FFHQ, C84–12/8/20 and C84/91/5.

110 Soucie, "Sommaire des présentations sur la question des droits des francophones en matière d'éducation," CRCCF, Fonds ACFO, C2–46/1/14.

111 Gauthier to Cloutier, 13 February 1984, CRCCF, Fonds ACFO, C2/498/3.

112 Brad Smith had interpreted s. 23 as follows: "contrôle et direction francophones si nécessaires, mais pas nécessairement direction francophone." See "Douglas Frith, le député de Sudbury, à Monsieur André Cloutier, le 5 mars 1984," CRCCF, Fonds ACFO, C2/498/3.

113 Letourneau to MacGuigan, 20 January 1984, CRCCF, Fonds FFHQ, C84/53/5.

114 Letourneau to Trudeau, 25 January 1984 and Letourneau to Trudeau, 8 February 1984, CRCCF, Fonds FFHQ, C84–12/8/20.

115 Broadbent to Cloutier, 4 April 1984, CRCCF, Fonds ACFO, C2/498/3.

116 Tassé to Letourneau, 13 April 1984, CRCCF, Fonds FFHQ, C84/53/5; MacGuigan to Cloutier, 24 April 1984," CRCCF, Fonds ACFO, C2–46/1/14.

117 Justice Canada, Intervention of the Federal Attorney General in the Supreme Court of Ontario, Court of Appeal, in the matter of minority language educational rights, additional submissions, 30 March 1984, CRCCF, Fonds ACFO, C2–46/1/14.

118 Trudeau to Letourneau, 7 May 1984, CRCCF, Fonds FFHQ, C84–12/8/20.

119 Trudeau to Davis, 23 May 1984, CRCCF, Fonds ACFO, C2/52/6/C3639.

120 Davis to Trudeau, 12 June 1984," CRCCF, Fonds ACFO, C2/52/6/C3639.

121 *Reference re Education Act of Ontario and Minority Language Education Rights* (1984) 47 O.R. (2nd) 1 at 17 (C.A.)

122 Ibid., 17–27.

123 Ibid., 28–33.

124 Ibid., 44–51; quote at 51.

125 Ibid., 51–6.

126 Ibid., 33–44; quote at 43.

127 Ibid., 57.

128 Cloutier to Matte, 6 June 1984, CRCCF, Fonds ACFO, C2–46/1/14.

129 *Toronto Star*, 8 November 1984. In CRCCF, Fonds AFCSO, C11–6/9/10.

130 AFCSO, "Procès-verbal de la réunion du Comité provisoire de la gestion scolaire, le 21 octobre 1984," CRCCF, Fonds AFCSO, C11–6/9/10.

131 AFCSO, "A Brief to the Social Development Committee of the Legislative Assembly of Ontario, 6 November 1984," CRCCF, Fonds AFCSO, C11–6/9/10, 1–2.

132 ACFO, "Position relative au projet de loi 160, 15, 16 et 17 février 1985," CRCCF, Fonds ACFO, C2–35/7/5.

133 Rouleau, "Discours sur le 'projet de loi 160' sur la gestion scolaire, le 13 avril au congrès annuel de l'AFCSO," CRCCF, Fonds AFCSO, C11–6/24/12, quote at 11.

134 "Position relative au projet de loi 28, le 1 mai 1985," CRCCF, Fonds ACFO, C2–35/7/5.

135 Gérin, op. cit., 100.

136 "Procès-verbal, réunion des organismes Franco-ontariens impliqués en éducation (AFCSO, ACFO, AEFO, ASFO, FAPI, CÉFO, FESFO), le 10 juillet 1985"; "Procès-verbal, réunion de concertation des organismes Franco-ontariens impliqués en éducation, le 23 juillet 1985," CRCCF, Fonds ACFO, C2–35/7/10.

137 AFCSO, "Mémoire au Comité de développement social de l'Assemblée législative de l'Ontario sujet du projet de loi 30," CRCCF, Fonds AFCSO, C11–6/9/10.

138 Foucher, "Projet de loi concernant un Conseil scolaire de langue française en Ontario. Rapport Final présenté à l'AFCSO, le 17 octobre 1985," CRCCF, Fonds AFCSO, C11–6/9/10.

139 Gérin, op. cit., 104–5.

140 Conway, "Statement to the Legislature on French Language Governance, 12 December 1985," CRCCF, Fonds AFCSO, C11–6/24/12.

141 Loi modifiant la Loi sur l'éducation et la Loi sur la municipalité de la communauté urbaine de Toronto. Lois de l'Ontario de 1986, Chapitre 29 (projet de loi 75), publié par le ministère du Procureur général, Imprimeur de la Reine pour l'Ontario, 10 juillet 1986.

142 AFCSO, Press release, 13 December 1985: "L'AFCSO se réjouit," CRCCF, Fonds AFCSO, c11–6/9/10.

143 "Compte-rendu de l'AFCSO. Réunion des organismes Franco-Ontariens impliqués en éducation, le 20 janvier 1986," CRCCF, Fonds AFCSO, C11–6/50/4.

144 Bastarache, "Notes en vue de la rencontre des conseillers scolaires francophones, le 27 janvier 1986," CRCCF, Fonds AFCSO, C11–6/24/12.

145 Plouffe, "Mémoire relatif au projet de loi 75, mars 1986," CRCCF, Fonds ACFO, C2–35/7/6.

146 AFCSO, "Mémoire au Comité permanent des affaires gouvernementales de l'Ontario au sujet du projet de loi 75, le 2 avril 1986," CRCCF, Fonds ACFSO, C11–6/56/10; AFCSO, Région No. 1, "Mémoire relatif à la gestion scolaire présenté au Comité, le 16 mars 1986," CRCCF, Fonds ACFO, C2–35/7/6.

147 Gérin, op. cit., 105–8.

148 Ontario, Ministry of Education, Comité d'étude pour l'éducation en langue française d'Ottawa-Carleton, *Rapport*, 14–15.

149 Ibid., 42.

150 Ontario, Ministry of Municipal Affairs, *Formulaire de recensement 1988*.

151 Projet de loi 109 (chapitre 47, Lois de l'Ontario de 1988), loi portant sur le création d'un conseil scolaire de langue française pour la municipalité régionale d'Ottawa-Carleton (Toronto: Queen's Printer for Ontario, 29 June 1988).

152 Gérin, op. cit., 126–30.

153 Ibid., 135–50.

154 CEFCUT, *Rapport du comité de travail établi pour faciliter la mise en oeuvre du Conseil des écoles françaises de la communauté urbaine de Toronto* (Toronto: CEFCUT, 23 February 1988).

155 Canada, Commissioner of Official Languages, *Annual Report 1990*, 238.

156 Rouleau, "Projet de recherche et d'analyse de la situation de la gestion scolaire de langue française (loi 75)," prepared for the AFCSO, September 1988, Toronto, CRCCF, Fonds AFCSO, C11–6/54/14; Gratton, "La gestion de l'éducation en langue française, janvier 1989," CRCCF, Fonds AFCSO, C11–7/12/7.

157 AFCSO, Comité de travail ministériel sur la gestion scolaire en langue française, "Rapport, janvier 1990," CRCCF, Fonds AFCSO, C11–7/12/7.

158 Ginette Gratton to Susan Hanna, 22 September 1989," CRCCF, Fonds AFCSO, C11–7/1/31.

159 Les associations provinciales franco-ontariennes oeuvrant en éducation, Press conference, 10 January 1990: "L'engagement du gouvernement libéral de l'Ontario à l'égard des droits des francophones en matière scolaire: existe-t-il?" CRCCF, Fonds FFHQ, C84/19/3/2; Ladouceur, "La gestion scolaire en Ontario: un bilan. Présentée le 3 mars 1990 dans le cadre de la Conférence nationale organisée par le Programme de contestation judiciaire," CRCCF, Fonds AFCSO, C11–7/16/8.

160 *Mahé* v. *Alberta* [1990] 1 S.C.R. at 344–5.

161 Peterson to Ronald Marion, 20 April 1990, CRCCF, Fonds AFCSO, C11–7/12/8.

162 Ontario, French Language Education Governance Advisory Group, *Mandate*, 3 December 1990, CRCCF, Fonds AFCSO, C11–7/11/17.

163 Cousineau to Gandolfo, 3 December 1990, CRCCF, Fonds AFCSO, C11–7/11/17.

164 AFCSO, "Mémoire présenté devant le Groupe de travail sur la gestion scolaire présidé par Madame Tréva Cousineau, Toronto, février 1991," CRCCF, Fonds AFCSO, C11–7/11/17.

165 Ontario, *Rapport du groupe consultatif sur la gestion de l'éducation en langue française.*

166 Ibid., 4–8.

167 Ibid., 94–101.

168 "Réaction de l'Association française des Conseils scolaires de l'Ontario au rapport du Groupe consultatif sur la gestion de l'éducation en langue française, novembre 1991," CRCCF, Fonds AFCSO, C11–7/11/17; quote at 25.

169 Gérin, op. cit., 158–62.

170 Ontario, Rapport de la Commission royale sur l'éducation, *Pour l'amour d'apprendre*, abridged version, recommendations 120 and 121.

171 Ontario, *Rapport final du Groupe d'étude sur la réduction du nombre de conseils scolaires en Ontario* (Toronto: Government of Ontario, February 1996).

172 The eight Catholic school boards are Grandes-Rivières in Timmins, Franco-Nord in North Bay, Nouvel-Ontario in Sudbury, Auréoles Boréales in Thunder Bay, Sud-Ouest in London, Centre-Sud in

Toronto, Est-Ontarien in L'Orignal, and Centre-Est in Ottawa. The four public boards are Nord-Est in North Bay, Grand-Nord in Sudbury, Centre Sud-Ouest in Toronto, and Ottawa. Canada, Commissioner of Official Languages, *Annual Report 1998*, 97.

173   Gérin, op. cit., 169–74.

174   Canada, Commissioner of Official Languages, *Annual Report 1998*, 97.

175   Cited in Canada, Commissioner of Official Languages, *Annual Report 1997*, 103.

176   Canada, Commissioner of Official Languages, ibid.

177   Trudeau to Davis, 23 May 1984 and Davis to Trudeau, 12 June 1984, CRCCF, Fonds ACFO, C2–52/6/C3639.

CHAPTER FOUR

1   Mahé, "Quinze années en sisyphes de la politique linguistique," 115.

2   Allaire, "Pour la survivance," 80–2.

3   ACFA, "Rapport Annuel de 1981," *Le Franco*, Novembre 1981.

4   Allaire, op. cit., 83–4.

5   Dubé, "Une étude de cas portant sur la genèse … ," 706.

6   Dubé, "Les conditions d'émergence du cas Bugnet," 190–1.

7   Ibid., 192–3; Martel, "Processus initié par la promulgation de l'article 23," 391.

8   Martel, "Processus initié par la promulgation de l'article 23," 390–1. Georges Bugnet was a pioneer Franco-Albertan writer, school trustee, and horticulture specialist who settled in the province in 1904.

9   Silla, ed., *École bilingue ou unilingue pour les Franco-Albertains?* For an overview of this social science literature with an extensive bibliography, consult Landry and Allard, "Choix de la langue d'enseignement," 480–500 and "L'éducation dans la francophonie minoritaire," 403–33.

10   Mahé, "Quinze années en sisyphes de la politique linguistique," 114.

11   Martel, "Processus initié par la promulgation de l'article 23," 395–401; Dubé, "Les conditions d'émergence du cas Bugnet," 194–8 and "Une étude de cas portant sur la genèse … ," 708.

12   Mahé, "Quinze années en sisyphes de la politique linguistique," 117.

13   ACFA, "Rapport Annuel," *Le Franco*, 16 February 1983.

14   Dubé, "Presentation: Procès-verbal de l'assemblée générale annuelle de l'ACFA, le 5 mars 1983," in *Le Franco*, 15 February 1984.

15   Julien, "The Evolution of Francophone Schools," 717–20 and "Les Franco-Albertains et la gestion de leurs écoles," 124–5. Editorial, "École française, oui; École Bugnet, non," *Le Franco*, 19 January 1983.

16   Goyette, "La décision de fermature est la responsabilité de l'école Bugnet," *Le Franco*, 10 October 1984.

17   Martel, "Processus initié par la promulgation de l'article 23," 402.

18 Goyette, "Lettre du président de l'ACFA," *Le Franco*, 9 November 1983; "Statement," *Edmonton Journal*, 16 July 1984.

19 Julien, "The Quest for All-French Schools in Alberta," 28–9. For an overview of these events, see Lavertu, "Quand la débâcle se fait attendre," *Le Droit*, 13 February 1985.

20 ACFA, "L'école française en Alberta. Position de l'ACFA, le 7 juin," PAA, Fonds ACFA, 90.580 (9/238).

21 ACFA, "Procès-verbal, réunion du comité provincial de l'éducation, le 5 novembre 1983"; "Procès-verbal, réunion du comité provincial de l'éducation, le 21 janvier 1984"; and Lemire, "Aux membres du comité provincial de l'éducation, le 10 janvier 1984," PAA, Fonds ACFA, 89.391 (3/81).

22 ACFA, "Énonce de principes, le 10 janvier 1984," PAA, Fonds ACFA, 90.580 (9/238).

23 ACFA, "Communiqué, le 8 mars 1984: L'ACFA rencontre de nouveau le ministre de l'Éducation," PAA, Fonds ACFA, 90.580 (9/238).

24 ACFA, "Communiqué, le 15 juin 1984: L'éducation en français en Alberta: le droit n'est pas encore acquis," PAA, Fonds ACFA, 90.580 (9/238).

25 "Paul A. Poirier, directeur général de l'ACFA, aux membres de la délégation, le 5 juillet 1984," PAA, Fonds ACFA, 90.580 (9/238).

26 Goyette to King, 9 October 1984, PAA, Fonds ACFA, 90.580 (9/238).

27 Goyette to King, 31 October 1984, PAA, Fonds ACFA, 90.580 (9/238), 1–5.

28 Ibid., 5.

29 Ibid., 6–9.

30 Goyette to King, 8 November 1984, PAA, Fonds ACFA, 90.580 (9/238), 1–5.

31 King to Board Chairmen, 19 November 1984, PAA, Fonds ACFA, 90.580 (9/237).

32 ACFA, "Communiqué: un tout petit pas dans la direction ... , le 26 novembre 1984," PAA, Fonds ACFA, 90.580 (9/238).

33 King to Goyette, 28 November 1984, PAA, Fonds ACFA, 90.580 (9/238), 1–3.

34 "Demarches entreprises depuis 15 mois par l'ACFA provinciale en vue de la revendication du droit à l'éducation en français, le 29 novembre, 1984," PAA, Fonds ACFA, 90.580 (9/238).

35 Poirier, "Recommandations de la délégation à l'exécutif de l'ACFA, le 30 novembre 1984," PAA, Fonds ACFA, 90.580 (9/238).

36 Poirier, "Revendication du droit à l'éducation en français. Plan d'action de l'ACFA, le 4 décembre 1984 (adopté à la réunion du Conseil Général du 1er décembre 1984)," PAA, Fonds ACJC, 90.580 (9/238).

37 Desrochers to Lougheed, 24 October 1984 and Lougheed to Desrochers, 22 January 1985, PAA, Fonds ACFA, 90.580 (9/237).

38 "Summary of Proceedings. Meeting with l'Association canadienne-française de l'Alberta, 21 February 1985," PAA, Fonds ACFA, 90.580 (9/237).

39 Laberge to King, 4 March 1985, PAA, Fonds ACFA, 90.580 (9/237).

40 Laberge to King, 19 June 1985, PAA, Fonds ACFA, 90.580 (9/237).

41 Association Georges-et-Julia-Bugnet, Press release, 13 March 1990: "Historical Summary of the Bugnet Court Case," CRCCF, Fonds FFHQ, C84–19/5/5, 1–2; Dubé, "Une étude de cas portant sur la génèse ... ," 708–11.

42 Martel, "Processus initié par la promulgation de l'article 23," 385–7, 396–8.

43 *Mahé* v. *R. in Right of Alta* [1985] 39 Alta. L.R. (2nd), 215 (Q.B.) at 224–6. Cited hereafter as *Mahé* v. *R.* [1985] 39 Alta. L.R. (2nd)

44 *Mahé* v. *R.* [1985] 39 Alta. L.R. (2nd), 232.

45 *Mahé* v. *R.* [1985] 39 Alta. L.R. (2nd), 243.

46 *Mahé* v. *R.* [1985] 39 Alta. L.R. (2nd), 242–3.

47 Laberge to King, 24 June 1985, PAA, Fonds ACFA, 90.580 (9/237).

48 Alberta Education, "News Release # 16," 31 July 1985, PAA, Fonds ACFA, 90.580 (9/237).

49 King to Laberge, 3 September 1985, PAA, Fonds ACFA, 90.580 (9/237).

50 Laberge to King, 30 October 1985, PAA, Fonds ACFA, 90.580 (9/237).

51 Association Georges-et-Julia Bugnet, "Historical Summary of the Bugnet Court Case," 3.

52 Factum of the Appellants in *Mahé et al.* v. *The Queen in Right of Alberta* [1988] 42 D.L.R. (4th), 514 (C.A.), at 5–10, 32–9, and 39–43 of factum. Cited hereafter as *Mahé* v. *Alberta* [1988] 42 D.L.R. (4th), 514 (C.A.) See also the factums of the intervenors, the ACFA and the FFHQ, both prepared by Michel Bastarache, which advanced essentially the same arguments.

53 Factum of the Respondents in *Mahé* v. *Alberta* [1988] 42 D.L.R. (4th), 514 (C.A.), 1–16.

54 *Mahé* v. *Alberta* [1988] 42 D.L.R. (4th), 514 (C.A.), 518.

55 Ibid., 534–5.

56 Ibid., 536–42.

57 Ibid., 542–50.

58 Ibid., 552.

59 Poirier to Tremblay, 20 December 1985 and 17 January 1986; Laberge to Tremblay, 17 January 1986, PAA, Fonds ACFA, 92.31 (6/150).

60 Association Georges-et-Julia Bugnet, "Historical Summary of the Bugnet Court Case," 3.

61 "Compte rendu de la rencontre des associations, comités, sociétés des parents pour l'éducation francophone, le 18 janvier 1986," PAA, Fonds ACFA, 92.379 (1/14).

62 Ad Hoc Committee, "Procès verbal de la première rencontre, le 5 avril 1986"; Procès verbal de la deuxième rencontre, le 9 juin 1986," PAA, Fonds ACFA, 92.379 (1/14).

63 "Entente entre l'Association canadienne-française de l'Alberta et la Fédération des parents francophones d'Alberta en éducation, le 23 mai 1987," Fonds ACFA, 5800.1; "Documents d'appui. Entente ACFA/FPFA, mai 1987," Fonds ACFA, 5800.87.

64 Le Blanc, "Note de service à Monsieur Fortier sur la mise en oeuvre de l'article 23 – perspective albertaine, le 8 juillet 1988," Fonds ACJC, 908.90.

65 Desjarlais, *C'est maintenant, l'heure de l'école franco-albertaine*, 1–12.

66 Ibid., 12–17.

67 Ibid., 34–47; quote at 35.

68 Ibid., 18–33.

69 ACFA, Press releases: "Le Rapport Desjarlais, n.d."; "Mahé à Giguère, le 21 novembre 1988," and "C'est maintenant, l'heure de l'école franco-albertaine," *Smokey River Express*, 25 October 1989, Fonds ACFA, 908 and 908.1.

70 ACFA, FPFA, and FJA, "Lettre ouverte à la Commission scolaire de Saint-Paul, le 24 juillet 1989"; "Lettre à Monsieur Jim Dinning, le 25 juillet 1989"; Dinning to Arès, 1 September 1989; and Société des parents pour l'éducation francophone (St-Paul et région) to County of St. Paul #19 Board of Education, 28 December 1989, Fonds ACFA, 5916.

71 Comité consultatif sur la gestion des écoles franco-albertaines, "Mandat des experts conseils, le 16 décembre 1989," Fonds ACFA 909.3.

72 Comité consultatif sur la gestion des écoles franco-albertaines, "Procès-verbal, le 28 octobre 1989"; "Procès verbal, le 10 novembre 1989"; "Procès-verbal, les 15 et 16 décembre 1989"; "Mandat, le 2 novembre 1989," Fonds ACFA, 908.1 and 908.2.

73 Rémillard, Unofficial English language text of speech to the Mont-Gabriel Conference, Rebuilding the Relationship: Quebec and its Con-federation Partners, 9 May 1986, 104.

74 Correspondence between the author and Georges Arès, 14 September 1994.

75 "Compte rendu de la première réunion du Comité des affaires juridiques/constitutionnelles de la F.F.H.Q., le 7 mai 1986," CRCCF, Fonds FFHQ, C93/37/13.

76 Correspondence between the author and Georges Arès, 14 September 1994.

77 Arès, "The Accord Abandons Canada's Battered and Defenceless Minori-ties," 219–24.

78 Arès to Thériault, 16 October 1987 and Thériault to Arès, 21 October 1987, CRCCF, Fonds FFHQ, C 84–19/5/4.

79 Ryan to Matte, 16 March 1989, CRCCF, Fonds FFHQ, C84–19/5/4.

80 Correspondence between the author and George Arès, 14 September 1994.

81 Bastarache to Thériault, 23 March 1989, CRCCF, Fonds FFHQ, C84–19/5/4.

82 Bastarache to Samson, 5 May 1989, CRCCF, Fonds FFHQ, C84–19/5/4. For Bastarache's critical analysis of central and accessory issues before the Supreme Court in *Mahé*, consult his "L'article 23 de la Charte canadienne des droits et libertés," 35–46.

83 Bastarache to Thériault, 10 May 1989, CRCCF, Fonds FFHQ, C84–19/5/4.

84 Matte to Bourassa, Ryan, and Rémillard, 11 May 1989, CRCCF, Fonds FFHQ, C84–21/3/14; Matte to the presidents, 17 May 1989, ibid., C84–19/5/4. Matte reminded the affiliates that the FFHQ's presidents had passed a resolution at their March meeting giving the organization the authority to publicly censure the Quebec government if it adopted an unfavourable position on the *Mahé* case.

85 FFHQ, Press release, 1 June 1989: "La F.F.H.Q. est déçue mais invite au dialogue," CRCCF, Fonds FFHQ, C84–19/5/4.

86 "Compte-rendu de la rencontre FFHQ/Gouvernement du Québec re: Mémoire du Procureur du Québec dans la Cause *Mahé c. la Reine*, le 2 juin 1989," CRCCF, Fonds FFHQ, C84–19/5/4.

87 Matte to the presidents, 5 June 1989, CRCCF, Fonds FFHQ, C84–19/5/4. President Rolande Soucie wrote a strongly worded letter of reprimand to Bourassa, Rémillard, and Ryan on 8 June 1989; see CRCCF, Fonds FFHQ, C84–19/5/4.

88 Correspondence between the author and Georges Arès, 14 September 1994 and 10 September 1996.

89 ACFA, Press release: "Le gouvernement du Québec veut-il la disparition des Franco-Albertains?" CRCCF, Fonds FFHQ, C84–19/5/4.

90 Fontaine, "L'ACFA en colère contre Bourassa," *La Presse*, 1 June 1989.

91 Lessard, "Les Franco-Albertains accusent Bourassa de les avoir vendus contre un appui au Lac Meech," *La Presse*, 6 June 1989, B8; Dansereau, "Georges Arès outré pas une telle position," *Le Soleil*, 6 June 1989.

92 Comeau, "Le cri des Franco-Albertains," *Le Devoir*, 9 June 1989; Bissonnette, "Quebec fails to help franco-Albertans on schools issue," *The Globe and Mail*, 10 June 1989; Adam, "Le Québec contre les Franco-Albertains," *La Presse*, 13 June 1989. The Conseil was responding to pressure from the ACFA, which had asked it to intervene in the dispute. Correspondence between the author and Georges Arès, September 14, 1994.

93 Dubé to Arès, 7 June 1989, CRCCF, Fonds FFHQ, C84–19/5/4; Proulx, "Au tour de la FFHQ de dénoncer Québec," *Le Devoir*, 7 June 1989. The Association Bugnet tried unsuccessfully to convince Bastarache that the Quebec government's submission to the Supreme Court supported the ACFA's position rather than that of the Alberta government. Caught on

the defensive, Dubé allowed his letter to find its way into print. Correspondence between the author and Georges Arès, 14 September 1994.

94 *Mahé* v. *Alberta* [1990] 1 S.C.R. 342 at 351. The other intervenors were the ACFO, the AEFO, the Commissioner of Official Languages, the Quebec Association of Protestant School Boards, Alliance Québec, and the Attorney Generals of Canada and New Brunswick. The respondent, the province of Alberta, was supported in different respects by the Attorney Generals of Saskatchewan and Quebec, the Alberta School Trustees' Association, and the Edmonton Roman Catholic Separate School District no. 7.

95 Arès to Thériault, 16 October 1987 and Thériault to Arès, 21 October 1987, CRCCF, Fonds FFHQ, C 84–19/5/4.

96 Factum of the Appellants, in *Mahé* v. *Alberta* [1990], 1–9; Mémoire de l'Association canadienne-française de l'Alberta in *Mahé* v. *Alberta* [1990], 3–4.

97 Mémoire de l'Association canadienne-française de l'Alberta" in *Mahé* v. *Alberta* [1990], 6.

98 Factum of the Appellants, in *Mahé* v. *Alberta* [1990], 16–17; Mémoire de l'Association canadienne-française de l'Alberta" in *Mahé* v. *Alberta*, [1990], 5–11.

99 Factum of the Appellants, in *Mahé* v. *Alberta* [1990], 17–22; Mémoire de l'Association canadienne-française de l'Alberta in *Mahé* v. *Alberta* [1990], 14–16.

100 Factum of the Respondent in *Mahé* v. *Alberta* [1990], 1–4.

101 Factum of the Respondent in *Mahé* v. *Alberta* [1990], 9–13.

102 "Factum of the Appellants in *Mahé* v. *Alberta* [1990], 23 and 25; Mémoire de l'Association canadienne-française de l'Alberta in *Mahé* v. *Alberta* [1990], 13–14, 16–18. Bastarache advised Bugnet before the Supreme Court hearing to downplay the argument based on s.15 because he felt it would not be accepted. Correspondence between the author and Georges Arès, 14 September 1994.

103 Factum of the Respondent in *Mahé* v. *Alberta* [1990],14–27; quotes at 14, 19, and 25.

104 Factum of the Appellants in *Mahé* v. *Alberta* [1990], 28–33. The ACFA was of the opinion that Regulation 490/82 embodied an important social objective but pointed to evidence that the knowledge of English was not a problem in Edmonton's only francophone elementary school. Mémoire de l'Association canadienne-française de l'Alberta in *Mahé* v. *Alberta* [1990], 20.

105 Factum of the Respondent in *Mahé* v. *Alberta* [1990], 32–5; quote at 34.

106 Factum of the Appellants in *Mahé* v. *Alberta* [1990], 35, 33–36.

107 Factum of the Appellants in *Mahé* v. *Alberta* [1990], 37–40. They also requested the full costs of their action.

108 Factum of the Respondent in *Mahé* v. *Alberta* [1990], 36–43; quotes at 36 and 43.

109 *Mahé* v. *Alberta* [1990], 361.

110 Ibid., 362, 365.

111 Ibid., 365–7.

112 Ibid., 369–370.

113 Ibid., 373–9; quote at 380.

114 Ibid., 382.

115 Ibid., 384–6; quote at 385.

116 The number of 242 students had been established during the initial trial. By the time of the Supreme Court hearings there were over 500 students enrolled in the school, but this fact was not considered by Justice Dickson. Correspondence between the author and Georges Arès, 14 September 1994.

117 *Mahé* v. *Alberta* [1990], 388–9.

118 Ibid., 389–97; quote at 393.

119 ACFA, Press release, 26 March 1990: "Le cas Mahé-Bugnet: un pas en avant, mais de quelle ampleur?," Fonds ACFA, Arès files; also cited in Levasseur-Ouimet, "Paroles et gestes d'une communauté," 24. Correspondence between the author and Georges Arès, 14 September 1995.

120 FFHQ, Press release, 15 March 1990: "L'Article 23 doit être modifié croit la F.F.H.Q.," CRCCF, Fonds FFHQ, C84–19/5/5. Matte had the support of Pierre Foucher, who was an expert on s. 23. See Foucher, "Après Mahé ... Analyse des démarches accomplies," 6–7.

121 CNPF, Press release: "L'avenir de la minorité francophone entre les mains des provinces?," CRCCF, Fonds FFHQ, C84–19/3/2.

122 Dumaine, "L'Affaire Mahé de l'Alberta: Analyse du jugement, le 25 avril 1990," CRCCF, Fonds FFHQ, C84–19/5/5, 1–7; Thériault and Dumaine, "L'ère post-Mahé: un véritable test pour la Constitution canadienne," 40–2.

123 Matte, "La décision Mahé: interprétation et incidences," Talk given at the University of Ottawa, 11 May 1990, CRCCF, Fonds FFHQ, C84–19/5/5, 1–15, quotes at 6 and 13.

124 Dubé, "Une étude de cas portant sur la génèse ... ," 711–12.

125 Ibid., 712–13.

126 Dubé, "L'école de la minorité et le jugement *Mahé*," 33.

127 Arès, "Notes of a meeting with J. Dinning and R. Bossetti, 27 March 1990," Fonds ACFA, Arès files.

128 Lamoureux and Tardif, *Consultations portant sur la gestion des écoles franco-albertaines*.

129 Comité consultatif sur la gestion des écoles franco-albertaines, "Procès-verbal, le 31 mars 1990"; "Procès-verbal, le 25 avril 1990," Fonds ACFA, 909.1.

130 Lamoureux and Tardif, *Minority Language Rights in Education.*

131 Lamoureux and Tardif, *An Educational System for Franco-Albertans.*

132 Ibid., 11.

133 Ibid., 36–45, 56–61.

134 Ibid., 68–70; quote at 70.

135 Levasseur-Ouimet to Getty, 26 March 1990; Getty to Levasseur-Ouimet, 30 April 1990, Fonds ACFA, 410.6.

136 Dinning to Richard, St Paul School District, 1 June 1990; Dinning to Lindberg, County of St Paul, 1 June 1990, Fonds ACFA, 5916.

137 Dinning to Levasseur-Ouimet, 13 August 1990, Fonds ACFA, 909.7.

138 Foucher, "Evaluation du document de travail de la province de l'Alberta en réaction au jugement de la Cour suprême du Canada dans l'affaire *Mahé*, Mai 1990," Fonds ACFA, Arès files.

139 Alberta Teachers' Association, Press release, 8 May 1990: "L'ATA se prononce sur les droits de la minorité franco-albertaine à gérer ses écoles"; Savage to Dinning, 1 October 1990, Fonds ACFA, 909.3; Alberta School Trustees Association, Press release, 30 May 1990: "Francophone Regional Boards Recommended," CRCCF, Fonds FFHQ, C84/19/3/2.

140 ACFA, Press release, 6 September 1990: "L'ACFA demande la formation d'une 'comité de travail' sur la gestion scolaire"; FPFA, Press release, 6 September 1990: "The government of Alberta must act on the recommendations of the Lamoureux-Tardif report," Fonds ACFA, 909.6.

141 Levasseur-Ouimet to Dinning, 12 October 1990; and Dinning to Levasseur-Ouimet, 19 November 1990, Fonds ACFA, 909.7.

142 Bastarache to Charbonneau, 27 January 1991; Bastarache to Beaubien, 28 January 1991, Fonds ACFA, Arès files.

143 Gallant to Giguère, 25 January 1991; FFHQ, "Commentaires concernant le document de base des discussions sur la gestion des écoles françaises en Alberta, le 28 janvier 1991," Fonds ACFA, 909.8.

144 Dinning to Levasseur-Ouimet, 1 January 1990, with Department of Education Ministerial Order # 1/91 attached; Alberta Education, Education News, "Working Group – French Education in Alberta, 4 February 1991," Fonds ACFA, 909.8.

145 Giguère to regional offices of the ACFA, 5 February 1991, Fonds ACFA, 909.8.

146 Conseil régional d'éducation française de Rivière-la-Paix and ACFA Régionale de Lethbridge to Walter Paszkowski, 20 February 1991, Fonds ACFA, Arès files.

147 Levasseur-Ouimet to Weiner, 11 February 1991, Fonds ACFA, 909.8.

148 Note from Giguère to Levasseur-Ouimet and Roy, 15 February 1991, Fonds ACFA, 909.8.

149 Alberta Education, "Proposed francophone Regional School Board for

the Smoky River/Spirit River/Peace River Region, March 1991";
Hyman, ATA, "Another Proposal for the Governance of francophone
Education," Fonds ACFA, Arès files.

150 Notes from Giguère to Levasseur-Ouimet and Roy, 8 and 14 March
1991; Note from Tardif to Levasseur-Ouimet and Roy, 14 March 1991,
Fonds ACFA, 909.8.

151 Giguère to Levasseur-Ouimet, Roy, and Desrochers, 19 March 1991,
Fonds ACFA, 909.8.

152 Alberta Education, French Language Working Group, Minutes of 22
and 27 March and 12 April 1991 meetings, Fonds ACFA, 909.8.

153 Alberta Education, Press Release and Backgrounder, 24 June 1991:
"Summary of the Report of the French Language Working Group,"
Fonds ACFA, 909.8.

154 Levasseur-Ouimet and Roy to Getty, 18 June 1991; Desrochers to Getty,
17 June 1991; ATA, Press release, 24 June 1991: "Association speaks out
against government inaction," Fonds ACFA, 909.8.

155 ACFA, Press release, 18 June 1991: Veuillez reconsidérer la décision du
gouvernement de l'Alberta monsieur Getty!" Fonds ACFA, 909.8.

156 Kubish, "Parents Talk of Court Fight," *Edmonton Sunday Sun*, 23 June
1991, 28; ACFA, Press release, 24 June 1991: "Sans droits reconnus, sans
appui, sans recours, devrons-nous nous rendre jusqu'à l'ONU," Fonds
ACFA, Arès files.

157 Levasseur-Ouimet to Mulroney and Clark, 26 June 1991, Fonds ACFA,
909.8; Tardif to Minister Responsible for Constitutional Affairs, 23
December 1991, Fonds ACFA, 2155.45.

158 Dinning to Levasseur-Ouimet and Roy, 27 June 1991; Dinning to
Desrochers, 15 July 1991, Fonds ACFA, 909.8.

159 Correspondence with Georges Arès and Denis Tardif, September 1996.

160 Cymbol to Tardif, 8 July 1992 and Tardif to Cymbol, 22 July 1992,
Fonds ACFA, 909.8.

161 Bastarache to Charbonneau, 13 July 1992, Fonds ACFA, 909.10.

162 Tardif to Getty, 14 September 1992; Tardif to N. Betowski, Minister of
Health, 15 September 1992; Tardif to Dinning, 15 September 1992;
Getty to Tardif, 15 September 1992; Tardif to Mulroney and McKenna,
14 September 1992, Fonds ACFA, 2155.4.3R.

163 Brault, "Ralph Klein et la gestion scolaire," *Le Franco*, 11 December
1992, 3.

164 Tardif to Klein, 14 December 1992 and Klein to Tardif, 1 February
1993, Fonds ACFA, 909.10.

165 Education Alberta, Francophone Implementation Committee, Minutes
of Meetings, 19 January, 3 March, and 20 April 1993, Fonds ACFA,
909.10.

166 Julien, "The Quest for All-French Schools in Alberta," 34–6.

167 Ibid., 37–9; Julien, "The Evolution of francophone Schools," 725–6, 733. Commissioner of Official Languages, *Annual Report 1991*, 124–5. Commissioner of Official Languages, *Annual Report 1992*, 105–6.

168 Maurais, "Les Franco-Albertains s'adresseront à leur tour à l'ONU," *Le Devoir*, 21 May 1993. Bastarache to Charbonneau, 23 March 1993, Fonds ACFA, 909.10.

169 Correspondence between the author and Georges Arès, 10 September 1996. See also Turp to Beaubien, 22 June 1993, Fonds ACFA, Arès files.

170 Correspondence between the author and Georges Arès, 10 September 1996.

171 ACFA and FPFA, "Procès-verbaux des réunions, les 14 et 25 juin, les 12 et 15 juillet 1993"; Turp to Beaubien and Arès, 18 July 1993, Fonds ACFA, Arès files. The ACFA had not authorized a second legal opinion from Turp and Foucher solicited by the FPFA. As a result, the ACFA refused to share in these additional legal costs: Arès to Beaubien, 16 March 1994, Fonds ACFA, Arès files.

172 Tardif to Klein, 30 June 1993 and Klein to Tardif, 29 July 1993, Fonds ACFA, 909.10.

173 La communauté francophone de l'Alberta à l'honorable R. Klein, le 27 août 1993," Fonds ACFA, 909.10; Panzeri, "Francophones await legislation promise," *The Edmonton Journal*, 31 August 1993, A5.

174 Coalition pour l'éducation française (Rivière-la-paix), *Implementation of francophone Governance in the Region of Rivière-la-paix*. Brief presented to the Honourable Halvar Jonson, Minister of Education, 15 September 1993. Fonds ACFA, 909.10.

175 Denis to Klein, 22 November 1993 and Klein to Denis, 22 December 1993, Fonds ACFA, 909.10.94.

176 Alberta, Alberta Education, *Guide de mise en oeuvre de la gestion scolaire francophone*. The guide has a map of the francophone education regions in Alberta as at 1994.

177 Aunger, "Dispersed Minorities and Segmental Autonomy"; refer to 207 for a detailed table.

178 ACFA and FPFA, Press release, 2 February 1994: "Les élections scolaires francophones sont déclenchées!" Comité de mise en oeuvre de la gestion scolaire, "Compte rendu de la réunion du 7 février 1994"; "Arès, directeur général, aux enseignantes des écoles francophones, le 4 février 1994," Fonds ACFA, 909.10.

179 FPFA, "Édition spéciale," *Le Chaînon*, March 1994, 1–31.

180 Alberta, Alberta Education, *Financement des autorités régionales et des conseils de coordination*.

181 Alberta, Alberta Education, *Guide de mise en oeuvre de la gestion scolaire francophone*, 48; Commissioner of Official Languages, *Annual Report 1993*, 117–18.

182 Commissioner of Official Languages, *Annual Report 1994*, 83–4; Commissioner of Official Languages, *Annual Report 1995*, 71–2.

183 Correspondence between the author and Georges Arès, 14 September 1995.

CHAPTER FIVE

1 Re *Manitoba Public Schools Act Reference* [1993] 1 S.C.R. 866.

2 For an excellent account of this epic battle see Blay, *L'Article 23*; the legal cases involved are analysed in Magnet, *Official Languages of Canada*, 102–9.

3 Allaire, "Le rapport à l'*autre*, 166–72.

4 Consult Hébert, "The Manitoba French-Language Crisis, 1983–84."

5 Blay, *L'Article 23*, 34–5; Hebert, "The Manitoba French-Language Crisis, 1983–84," 24–6.

6 Blay, *L'Article 23*, 42–7.

7 Cited in ibid., 83.

8 Ibid., 84–6.

9 FPCP, Pamphlet outlining its structure and mandate (Saint-Boniface, 1980), SHSB, Fonds SFM, 89/143/31. The FPCP was a member of the Commission nationale des parents francophones, which had its headquarters in Winnipeg.

10 Piché to Lyon, 22 June 1979, SHSB, Fonds SFM, 89/128/22.

11 FPCP, "Brief presented to: The Standing committee on Education measures, 22 October 1979"; SFM, "Presentation to the Intercessional Committee of the Legislative Assembly of Manitoba for Revision of the Public Schools Act," SHSB, Fonds SFM, 89/128/02.

12 Lyon to Proteau, 21 September 1981, SHSB, Fonds SFM, 89/128/22.

13 "Summary of main points to be discussed at a meeting between Société franco-manitobaine and other representatives of the Francophone community and the Government of Manitoba, 29 September 1981," SHSB, Fonds SFM, 89/128/22.

14 SFM, Comité éxécutif, "Procès-verbal de la réunion des 12 et 13 avril 1980 à l'Hôtel Birchwood de Winnipeg," SHSB, Fonds SFM, 89/102/01.

15 Correspondence between the author and Raymond Hébert, 9 December 1996.

16 Proteau to Pawley, 22 January 1982, SHSB, Fonds SFM, 89/128/19.

17 FPCP, "Mise en situation, le 2 novembre 1984," document attached to a letter from Michèle Lagimodière-Gagnon to Gilberte Proteau, 1 November 1984, SHSB, Fonds SFM, 89/136/22, 1–3.

18 Ibid., 3–4; Comité directeur du dossier structures scolaires, "Communiqué aux présidents des comités de parents, le 30 novembre 1983," SHSB, Fonds SFM, 89/111/20.

19 Lagimodière-Gagnon to Proteau, 1 November 1984, SHSB, Fonds SFM, 89/136/22.

20 Correspondence between the author and Raymond Théberge, 18 September 1997.

21 Lagimodière-Gagnon to Proteau, 1 November 1984, SHSB, Fonds SFM, 89/136/22

22 Proteau to Lagimodière-Gagnon, 6 November 1984, SHSB, Fonds SFM, 89/136/22.

23 "Proposition adopté lors de la réunion du conseil d'administation de la SFM le 12 novembre 1985," SHSB, Fonds SFM, 89/138/10.

24 "Propositions concernant 'l'éducation' faites et adoptées lors de l'assem-blée annuelle de la Société franco-manitobaine le 2 mars 1985," SHSB, Fonds SFM, 89/138/09. The FPCP agreed to the broader composition of the Comité directeur.

25 Comité directeur, "Vers l'accès, l'égalité et la gestion, memoir presénté à Madame le Ministre de l'Education, Maureen Hemphill, le 21 mars 1985," SHSB, Fonds SFM, 89/138/10.

26 Ibid. ; "Notes sommaires. Rencontre avec la Ministre de l'éducation, le 21 mars 1985," SHSB, Fonds SFM, 89/138/10.

27 Comité directeur to Hemphill, 22 April 1985, SHSB, Fonds SFM, 89/138/10.

28 Hemphill to Sabourin, 15 October 1985, SHSB, Fonds SFM, 89/138/10.

29 Blanchette to Hemphill, 17 October 1985, SHSB, Fonds SFM, 89/138/10.

30 Sabourin to Hemphill, 4 November 1985, SHSB, Fonds SFM, 89/138/10.

31 Hemphill to Sabourin, 25 November 1985 and Sabourin to Hemphill, 18 December 1985, SHSB, Fonds SFM, 89/138/10.

32 Blanchette to Storie, 5 June 1986 and Storie to Blanchette, 27 June 1986, SHSB, Fonds SFM, 89/145/07.

33 Comité directeur, *Rapport Annuel, le 31 janvier 1986*," SHSB, Fonds SFM, 89/135/09, 4.

34 "Propositions concernant 'l'éducation' faites et adoptées lors de l'assem-blée annuelle de la Société franco-manitobaine le 2 mars 1985," SHSB, Fonds SFM, 89/138/09, 2.

35 Roy to the FPCP, 14 March 1985, SHSB, Fonds SFM, 89/138/09.

36 Bastarache to Lagimodière-Gagnon, 8 July 1985, SHSB, Fonds SFM, 89/138/10.

37 SFM, "Stratégies proposées en vue d'une réponse de la Ministre de l'édu-cation sur le document 'Vers l'accès, l'égalité et la gestion ...', le 2 octobre 1985," SHSB, Fonds SFM, 89/138/10.

38 Bastarache to the FPCP, 12 December 1985, SHSB, Fonds SFM, 89/138/10.

39 "Lettre ouverte de Réal Sabourin, le 23 décembre 1985," SHSB, Fonds SFM, 89/138/10.

40 Comité directeur, "Document de travail sur les positions du CDSS, le 20 juin 1986," SHSB, Fonds SFM, 89/145/07.

41 FPCP, "Conference de presse par Gilbert Savard, le 9 septembre 1986," SHSB, Fonds SFM, 89/143/31.

42 Bastarache to Fontaine, 8 December 1986, SHSB, Fonds SFM, 89/145/07.

43 Sabourin to Savard, 2 December 1986, SHSB, Fonds SFM, 89/143/31.

44 Savard to Sabourin, 9 December 1986, SHSB, Fonds SFM, 89/143/31.

45 Sabourin to Savard, 12 January 1987, SHSB, Fonds SFM, 89/143/31.

46 Bastarache to Fontaine, 24 February 1987, SHSB, Fonds SFM, 89/145/07.

47 "Démarche politique en éducation, le 24 mars 1987," SHSB, Fonds SFM, 89/145/11.

48 Blanchette to Pawley, 23 September 1987, SHSB, Fonds SFM, 89/145/07.

49 Comité directeur, *Rapport Annuel, le 31 janvier 1986*, 5.

50 Frechette to Blanchette, 7 January 1988, SHSB, Fonds SFM, 89/143/31.

51 Blanchette to Fréchette, 17 February 1988, SHSB, Fonds SFM, 89/143/31.

52 Piché to MacLeod, Court Challenges Program, 2 May 1988; MacLeod to Piché, 17 May 1988; Bastarache to MacLeod, 20 May 1988; Weiler to Bastarache, 29 June 1988; Blanchette to Weiler, 14 November 1988; Ruff to Blanchette, 23 December 1988, SHSB, Fonds SFM, 89/151/15.

53 Reference re *Public Schools Act* (Man.) 67 D.L.R. (4th) 493.

54 Ibid., 511.

55 Ibid., 512 and 500.

56 Ibid., 516 and 515.

57 Ibid., 519–21, 541, 557, and 563.

58 Ibid., 521–2 and 529.

59 Ibid., 522–9, quote at 524.

60 Ibid., O'Sullivan, 532 and 537–8.

61 Ibid., 553–63, quote at 560–1.

62 Ibid., 527–8 and 561–2.

63 CAP, *La gestion des écoles: un modèle a suivre* (Comité directeur, January 1988), 14, 30, and Annexe D; Molgat to Sabourin, 6 January 1986, SHSB, Fonds SFM, 89/137/27.

64 For its report the CAP drew upon the work of Paul R. Ruest, who had just been granted a Ph.D. from the Faculty of Education at the University of Manitoba in April 1987 for his dissertation, "Les attentes éducatives de la population franco-manitobaine." Ruest was in fact a member of the CAP.

65 CAP, *La gestion des écoles*, 17–18.

66 Ibid., 20–5.

67 Ibid., 30–4; quote at 31.

68 Ibid., 36–41.

69 Ibid., 42–51.

70 Gagnon to Filmon, March 1990, Bureau de la SFM, dossier gestion scolaire.

71 "Mémoire concernant la mise en oeuvre de la gestion scolaire présenté par la délégation de la collectivité franco-manitobaine au premier ministre du Manitoba, le 30 mai 1990," Bureau de la SFM, dossier gestion scolaire.

72 Manitoba, Press release, 2 August 1990: "Task Force to Study Governance of Franco-Manitoban School." Also Manitoba Task Force on Francophone Schools Governance, *Report*, Appendix 4 (Winnipeg: Manitoba Education and Training, May 1991), 47.

73 Manitoba, Press release, 6 November 1990: "Task Force to Study French School Governance," 48.

74 Gallant, "Notes," Conférence fédérale/provinciale sur l'enseignement en langue minoritaire officielle, Ottawa, 22 October 1990. Bureau de la SFM, dossier gestion scolaire.

75 "Simone Robinson, coordinatrice – CDSS aux membres, le 7 novembre 1990," Bureau de la SFM, dossier gestion scolaire.

76 Manitoba Task Force on Francophone Schools Governance, *Report*, 7.

77 Ibid., 9–15; quote at 14.

78 Ibid., 17–23.

79 Ibid., 25–8.

80 Ibid., 29–31.

81 FPCP, *Gestion Scolaire. Pour un juste retour de l'histoire ... Les parents se prononcent*, 1–51.

82 Manitoba, Press release, 27 June 1991: "Présentation du Rapport du Groupe de Travail sur la gestion des écoles franco-manitobaines," Bureau de la SFM, dossier gestion scolaire.

83 FPCP, Press release, 27 June 1991: "Le gouvernement manitobain devra respecter les recommandations de son groupe de travail," Bureau de la SFM, dossier gestion scolaire.

84 Bisson to Gallant, 5 July 1991, Bureau de la SFM, dossier gestion scolaire.

85 Carstairs to Bisson, 12 July 1991, Bureau de la SFM, dossier gestion scolaire.

86 FPCP, "Réflexions sur le communiqué de la Ministre Vodrey du 26 mars et du 22 septembre," Bureau de la SFM, dossier gestion scolaire, 4. The author of this document was Gérard Lécuyer.

87 Manitoba, Press release, 26 March 1992: "Francophone Governance Implementation Plans," Bureau de la SFM, dossier gestion scolaire.

88 FPCP, Press release, 26 March 1992: "Des propositions anti-constitutionnelles"; et FCFA, Press release, 27 March 1992: "Gestion scolaire francophone au Manitoba," Bureau de la SFM, dossier gestion scolaire.

89 FPCP, "Réflexions sur le communiqué de la Ministre Vodrey du 26 mars et du 22 septembre," Bureau de la SFM, dossier gestion scolaire, 2–3.

90 FPCP, Press release, 26 March 1992: "Des propositions anti-constitution-nelles;" Bureau de la SFM, dossier gestion scolaire.

91 Savard to Filmon, 30 March 1992; Savard to Vodrey, 14 April 1992, Bureau de la SFM, dossier gestion scolaire.

92 FPCP, "Notes pour la réunion avec le premier Ministre le 5 mai 1992," Bureau de la SFM, dossier gestion scolaire.

93 Savard *et al.* to Filmon, 12 May 1992, Bureau de la SFM, dossier gestion scolaire.

94 Savard to Filmon, 8 June 1992, Bureau de la SFM, dossier gestion scolaire.

95 FPCP, "Réflexions sur le communiqué de la Ministre Vodrey du 26 mars et du 22 septembre," Bureau de la SFM, dossier gestion scolaire, 10.

96 Ibid., 6.

97 SFM and FPCP, "Nous ne pourrons faire partie du comité d'appui," Bureau de la SFM, dossier gestion scolaire.

98 SFM and FPCP, "Dates et événements historiques importants reliés au domaine de l'éducation et d'intérêt pour les parents," Bureau de la SFM, dossier gestion scolaire.

99 Manitoba, Press release, 22 September 1993: "Francophone School Governance Team Chairperson Announced," Bureau de la SFM, dossier gestion scolaire.

100 Carlyle to Druwé, 22 September 1992; Carlyle to Savard, 22 September 1992, Bureau de la SFM, dossier gestion scolaire.

101 FPCP, "Réflexions sur le communiqué de la Ministre Vodrey du 26 mars et du 22 septembre," Bureau de la SFM, dossier gestion scolaire, 9–10. The government had responded quickly to the decision of the Manitoba Court of Queen's Bench of 13 August 1992 that s. 84 of the Public Schools Act, pertaining to religious exercises, violated ss. 15 and 2 of the Charter; it issued directives to school boards to comply even before the offending section had been deleted by the legislature.

102 Ibid., 10.

103 Ibid., 12.

104 "Réunion des membres des conseils d'aministration de FPCP-SFM-EFM-CEFM-CJP-ADEFM, le 7 octobre 1992," Bureau de la SFM, dossier gestion scolaire.

105 Presidents to Vodrey, 9 October 1992, Bureau de la SFM, dossier gestion scolaire.

106 Factum of the appellant (FPCP) in Reference re *Public Schools Act* (Man.), 7–9.

107 Factum of the Commission nationale des parents francophones, inter-venor, in Reference re *Public Schools Act* (Man.), 2–4. Bastarache was

also the lawyer for the SFM, so he got two opportunities to present arguments to the court.

108 Factum of the appellant (FPCP) in Reference re *Public Schools Act* (Man.), 5.

109 Factum of the Commission nationale des parents francophones, intervenor, in Reference re *Public Schools Act* (Man.), 13.

110 Factum of the respondent, The Attorney General of Manitoba, in Reference re *Public Schools Act* (Man.), 32–7; quote at 34.

111 Factum of the appellant (FPCP) in Reference re *Public Schools Act* (Man.), 5 and 11–16; Factum of the SFM in Reference re *Public Schools Act* (Man.), 6–7 and 18–19.

112 Factum of the respondent, The Attorney General of Manitoba, in Reference re *Public Schools Act* (Man.), 32–8; quote at 38.

113 Ibid., 38–41. See also Factum of the respondent, The Attorney General of Manitoba, in Reference re *Public Schools Act* (Man.), 5–14.

114 Factum of the appellant (FPCP) in Reference re *Public Schools Act* (Man.), at 16–29; Factum of the SFM in Reference re *Public Schools Act* (Man.), 7–8 and 19–20.

115 Factum of the appellant (FPCP) in Reference re *Public Schools Act* (Man.), 29–40.

116 Factum of the SFM in Reference re *Public Schools Act* (Man.), 20.

117 Factum of the Commission nationale des parents francophones, intervenor, in Reference re *Public Schools Act* (Man.), 11–13.

118 Factum of the respondent, The Attorney General of Manitoba, in Reference re *Public Schools Act* (Man.), 42.

119 Ibid., 42–8; quotes at 43 and 44.

120 Ibid., 48–50.

121 Reply of the respondent, The Attorney General of Manitoba, in Reference re *Public Schools Act* (Man.), 21.

122 Acker, "A Judgment for all seasons," 22–4. Acker acted as counsel for the Commissioner of Official Languages in the case.

123 Re *Manitoba Public Schools Act Reference* [1993] 1 S.C.R. 839.

124 Ibid., 848.

125 Ibid., 850–2, quote at 852.

126 Ibid., 852–6; quotes at 853 and 855.

127 Ibid., 856–9; quotes at 857 and 859.

128 Ibid., 860–3; quote at 863.

129 Bastarache to Charbonneau, 6 March 1993, Bureau de la SFM, dossier gestion scolaire, 1.

130 Ibid., 1–2.

131 Ibid., 3–4.

132 Ducharme, *Status Report: Minority-Language Education Rights*, 24.

133 Commissioner of Official Languages, *Annual Report 1993*, 121.

134 Ducharme, op. cit., 25.

135 Commissioner of Official Languages, *Annual Report 1994*, 86. Just over 1,000 Franco-Manitoban children continued to attend schools offering French as a first language that were administered by majority language boards.

136 Ibid.; Ducharme, op. cit., 27.

137 Tétrault, "Mots du président aux finissant(e)s et aux parents"; Bisson, "Une nouvelle génération," *Nouvelles-gestion, le Bulletin d'information de la DSFM* I, no. 7 (June 1995): 3–4.

138 Commissioner of Official Languages, *Annual Report 1995*, 75.

139 Commissioner of Official Languages, *Annual Report 1998*, 101–2.

CHAPTER SIX

1 FFHQ, "Mémoire présenté au premier ministre du Québec Monsieur Robert Bourassa, le 22 janvier 1990," CRCCF, Fonds FFHQ, C84–18/1/6, 3–22; quote at 21.

2 For an excellent critique of the centralization thesis, consult Kelly, "Reconciling Rights and Freedoms during Review of the Charter of Rights and Freedoms," 321–55.

3 Doucet, *Le discours confisqué*, 127–220.

4 Drummond, "Parliament and Politics," 10–19.

5 Gagnon, "Le Quebec et les Tories," *L'Actualité* 8, no. 4 (April 1983): 72–9; Lesage, "Le rêve de Brian Mulroney," *L'Actualité* 8, no. 4 (June 1983): 38–44.

6 Aubin, "La bataille du Québec," *L'Actualité* 9, no. 4 (April 1984), 68–74; MacDonald, *Mulroney*, 288–90; quote at 289.

7 Goar, "The Conservatives' mandate for change," *Maclean's* 97, no. 38 (17 September 1984): 12–20.

8 Behiels, "The Meech Lake Accord and the Process of Political Realignment in Canada, 1979–90," 399–410.

9 Rémillard, " A quelles conditions le Québec peut-il signer la Loi constitutionnelle de 1982?," 209–22.

10 Leslie, "Quebec and the Constitutional Impasse," 67.

11 Rémillard, Unofficial English-language text of speech to the Mont-Gabriel Conference, Rebuilding the Relationship: Quebec and its Confederation Partners, 9 May 1986, 99.

12 Ibid., 103–4.

13 Ibid., 104.

14 Leslie, "Quebec and the Constitutional Impasse," 91–2; Bouchard, "Allocution du secrétaire d'état au colloque de Mont-Gabriel, le 9 mai 1986," CRCCF, Fonds FFHQ, C84/37/13, 7–8.

15 Wallace, "Ottawa and the provinces," 72–6.

16 Coyne, *A Deal Undone*, 1–18.
17 Ibid., 99–117.
18 FFHQ, "Orientation politique de la Fédération des Francophones Hors Québec, Ottawa, Mars 1987," CRCCF, Fonds FFHQ, C84–14/24/7, 6.
19 Fraser, *René Lévesque and the Parti Québécois in Power*, xiii-xxix.
20 Bastarache to Marcoux, 11 March 1985, CRCCF, Fonds FFHQ, C84–21/3/15.
21 "Rapport du Président au Conseil d'Administration, le 15 mars 1986," CRCCF, Fonds FFHQ, C84–14/24/3.
22 "Johanne Kemp à Gilles Leblanc, 26 février 1986, sur la formation du comité juridique de la FFHQ"; "Compte rendu de la première réunion du comité des affaires juridiques/constitutionnelles de la FFHQ," CRCCF, Fonds FFHQ, C84–14/24/3 and C84/37/13.
23 "Pierre Foucher à Gilles Leblanc, le 1er juin 1986, avec son rapport des délibérations du collogue sur le Québec et ses partenaires dans la confédération," CRCCF, Fonds FFHQ, C84/37/13, 1–12.
24 Sabourin to Rémillard, 9 July 1986; Foucher to Gagné, 16 October 1986, SHSB, Fonds SFM, 89/146/26 & 27.
25 ACFA, "Mémoire addréssé à l'honorable Gil Rémillard en vue d'une rencontre avec une délégation de l'ACFA, août 1986," PAA, Fonds ACFA, 92.379 (4/102), 5.
26 Ibid.; Correspondence between the author and Georges Arès, 21 May 1997.
27 "Négotiations constitutionnelles. Ottawa/Québec/les provinces, août 1986," CRCCF, Fonds FFHQ, C84–21/3/15.
28 "Procès-verbal de l'Assemblée du Conseil National des Présidents, tenue les 8 et 9 novembre 1986, Montréal," CRCCF, Fonds FFHQ, C84–14/24/7.
29 FFHQ, "Les francophones à l'extérieur du Québec et les négotiations constitutionnelles. Un document de réflexion et d'action ... avril 1987," CRCCF, Fonds FFHQ, C84–14/24/6, 3. The bilingual/bicultural concept of duality had been analysed thoroughly and lucidly by one of the committee members. Cf. Bastarache, "Dualisme et égalité dans la Constitution nouvelle."
30 FFHQ, "Le spécificité du Québec et les francophones à l'extérieur du Québec, avril 1987," CRCCF, Fonds FFHQ, C84–14/24/6, 2–5, quote at 4.
31 FFHQ, "Les quatres autres propositions du Québec et les francophones à l'extérieur du Québec, avril 1987," CRCCF, Fonds FFHQ, C84–14/24/6, 3–4.
32 Ibid., 8–9.
33 Ibid., 10–12.
34 FFHQ, "Les droits linguistiques de la Charte et les francophones à l'extérieur du Québec, avril 1987," CRCCF, Fonds FFHQ, C84–14/24/6, 4.
35 Ibid., 10.

36 Correspondence between the author and Georges Arès, 21 May 1997.

37 Schwartz, *Fathoming Meech Lake*, 232. For the French text of the clause, see 237.

38 FFHQ, "Conférence de presse/communiqué, le 26 mai 1987" and "Communique de presse, le 3 juin 1987," CRCCF, Fonds FFHQ.

39 Meeting of First Ministers on the Constitution, "1987 Constitutional Accord, 3 June 1987," in Behiels, ed., *The Meech Lake Primer*, 541.

40 FFHQ, "Statement to the Special Committee of the Senate and of the House of Commons on the 1987 Constitutional Accord," *Minutes of Proceedings and Evidence* 3 (5 August 1987): 6 and 21.

41 Ibid., 15; quote at 19.

42 Article reprinted in Johnson, ed., *With a Bang, Not a Whimper*, 9.

43 Coyne, *A Deal Undone*, 103.

44 Correspondence between the author and Georges Arès, 21 May 1997.

45 FFHQ, "Statement to the Special Joint Committee of the Senate and of the House of Commons on the 1987 Constitutional Accord," *Minutes of Proceedings and Evidence* 3 (5 August 1987): 7–8, 11–13.

46 Ibid., 9–10, 17–18.

47 Special Joint Committee of the Senate and the House of Commons, *Report*, in *Minutes of Proceedings and Evidence of the Special Joint Committee of the Senate and of the House of Commons* 17 (9 September 1987): 147–54.

48 Ibid., 49–50.

49 Correspondence between the author and Georges Arès, 21 May 1997.

50 Doucet, *Le discours confisqué*, 127–60.

51 Fontaine to Mulroney, 2 October 1987 and Mulroney to Fontaine, 12 January 1988, CRCCF, Fonds FFHQ, C84–13/1/7.

52 FFHQ, "Communiqué de presse, le 28 septembre 1987"; FFHQ and SAANB, "Communiqué de presse, le 12 novembre 1987," CRCCF, Fonds FFHQ, C84–13/1/7.

53 Correspondence between the author and Georges Arès, 21 May 1997.

54 "Procès-verbal de l'Assemblée du Conseil national des présidents, tenue les 20 et 21 novembre 1987, Hôtel Four Seasons, Edmonton," CRCCF, Fonds FFHQ, C84–13/1/7.

55 "Procès-verbal de la Conférence téléphonique de l'Assemblée extraordinaire du Conseil National des Présidents, tenue le 2 février 1988," CRCCF, Fonds FFHQ, C84–13/1/8.

56 Arès, "The Accord Abandons Canada's Battered and Defenceless Minorities," 221.

57 Ibid., 223.

58 Bastarache, "Statement," *Proceedings of the Senate Submissions Group on the Meech Lake Constitutional Accord* 5 (18 March 1988): 24–32.

59 Fontaine to Mulroney, 2 March 1988, CRCCF, Fonds FFHQ, C84–21/3/12.

60 Mulroney to Fontaine, 30 March 1988, CRCCF, Fonds FFHQ, C84–21/3/12.

61 Comité ad hoc de stratégie de la FFHQ, "Rapport Confidentiel, Québec, le 26 mars 1988" CRCCF, Fonds FFHQ, C84–14/1/9; "Procès-verbal de l'Assemblée du Conseil National des Présidents, tenue les 26 et 27 mars 1988, Québec," ibid., C84–14/24/7. Arès, a member of the Ad Hoc Committee, had proposed that the Fédération and its affiliates boycott the Sommet de la Francophonie in Quebec City and take out advertisements asking French President Mitterand to defend the rights of the francophone minority communities since Mulroney would not. The idea was rejected and the francophone leaders, except Arès and one other, participated in the summit. Correspondence between the author and Georges Arès, 21 May 1997.

62 Christian, "L'affaire Piquette."

63 ACFA, Press release, 11 April 1988: "L'ACFA n'est plus intéressée à rencontrer m. Bourassa," CRCCF, Fonds ACFO, C2–48/11/16.4.1.

64 Arès to Mulroney, 10 May 1988, CRCCF, Fonds ACFO, C2–48/11/16.4.1.

65 Mulroney to Soucie, 16 June 1988 and Soucie to Mulroney, 16 June 1988, CRCCF, Fonds ACFO, C2–48/11/16.4.1.

66 Gilbert to Mulroney, 29 June 1988, CRCCF, Fonds ACFO, C2–48/11/16.4.1.

67 Arès to Mulroney, 11 July 1988, PAA, Fonds ACFA, 92.379 (9/226).

68 Arès to Mckenna, 6 July 1988, PAA, Fonds ACFA, 92.379 (9/226).

69 ACFA, Press release, 23 August 1988: "L'ACFA demande au gouvernement fédéral de devenir un véritable partenaire dans le développement complet de la francophonie Albertaine," CRCCF, Fonds ACFO, C2–48/11/16.4.1.

70 Correspondence between the author and Georges Arès, 21 May 1997.

71 ACFA, Press release: "Les Franco-Albertains feront-ils les frais de la politique de reconciliation nationale et de l'Accord du Lac Meech?" CRCCF, Fonds ACFO, C2–52/10/16.4.1.

72 Mulroney to Levasseur-Ouimet, 16 January 1990, CRCCF, Fonds FFHQ, C84–21/3/13.

73 Bastarache, "Notes concernant l'impact de l'entente du Lac Meech sur les minorités linguistiques provinciales, le 10 juin 1988, avec lettre à René Piché de la SFM," SHSB, Fonds SFM, 89/147/10.

74 Bastarache, "L'impact de l'entente du Lac Meech sur les minorités linguistiques provinciales, le 13 décembre 1988, au Collège Universitaire de Saint-Boniface," SHSB, Fonds SFM, 89/151/17.

75 SFM, Bulletin, "Lac Meech et les francophones hors Québec, juin 1988 résisé en janvier 1989," SHSB, Fonds SFM, 89/151/17.

76 Robinson, "Weiner denies bid to buy support for Meech," *The Gazette*, 17 March 1989.

77 Taillefer to Clément, 21 March 1989; Blanchette to Clément, 28 March 1989, SHSB, Fonds SFM, 89/115/16.

78 SFM, "Projet de mémoire présenté au Comité de l'Assemblée Législative du Manitoba chargé d'étudier l'Accord Constitutionnel du Lac Meech, avril 1989," Bureau de la SFM, 1–27.

79 Mulroney to Devine, 8 April 1988, CRCCF, Fonds FFHQ, C84–13/1/31.

80 "Procès-verbal de l'Assemblée du Conseil national des présidents et des présidentes, tenue le 24 juin 1988, Ottawa," CRCCF, Fonds FFHQ, C84–13/1/10.

81 Correspondence and telephone interview between the author and Rolande (Soucie) Faucher, May 2002.

82 "Yvon Fontaine au Bureau de direction, le 7 décembre 1988"; "Rapport du Président, M. Yvon Fontaine dans le cadre du Conseil national des Présidents, le 9 décembre 1988," CRCCF, Fonds FFHQ, C84–16/3/1.

83 "Procès-verbal de la réunion du conseil national des présidents et des présidentes, les 9, 10, et 11 décembre 1988," CRCCF, Fonds FFHQ, C84–14/1/11.

84 "Suivi au procès-verbal de la réunion du Conseil national des présidents et des présidentes, tenue les 8, 9 et 10 décembre 1988"; "Procès-verbal de la réunion du Conseil national des présidents et des présidentes, tenue les 3, 4, et 5 mars 1989 à Toronto," CRCCF, Fonds FFHQ, C84–14/1/12.

85 Doucet to Murray, 27 January 1989 and Murray to Doucet, 30 January 1989, CRCCF, Fonds FFHQ, C84–13/1/31.

86 "Procès-verbal de la réunion du Conseil national des présidents et des présidentes, tenue les 3, 4, et 5 mars 1989 à Toronto," CRCCF, Fonds FFHQ, C84–14/1/12.

87 FFHQ, "La FFHQ et le dossier des négotiations constitutionnelles. Propositions de libéllés constitutionnels, Septembre 1989," CRCCF, Fonds FFHQ, C84–21/3/12, 2.

88 Ibid., 3–8.

89 Fontaine to Thériault, 10 October 1989, CRCCF, Fonds FFHQ, C84–21/3/12. Fontaine's recommendations were not included in the final draft, which was sent out to the presidents in time for their February 1990 meeting: CRCCF, Fonds FFHQ, C84–18/1/6.

90 "Procès-verbal de la réunion du Conseil national des présidentes et des présidents, tenue les 17, 18 et 19 novembre 1989, Résolution no. 033." CRCCF, Fonds FFHQ, C84–18/1/6.

91 FFHQ, "Mémoire présenté au premier ministre du Québec Monsieur Robert Bourassa, le 22 janvier 1990," CRCCF, Fonds FFHQ, C84–18/1/6, 3–22; quote at 21.

92 Comité des revendications politiques, "Concernant l'Accord du Lac Meech soumis au conseil d'administration de la SFM, le 6 février 1990," Bureau de la SFM, Dossier Lac Meech.

93 SFM, Press release, 12 February 1990: "La position de la Société franco-

manitobaine concernant l'Accord du Lac Meech," CRCCF, Fonds FFHQ, C84–21/3/13.

94 Matte, "Rapport du Président," in "Procès-verbal de la réunion du Conseil national des présidentes et des présidents, tenue les 16, 17 et 18 février 1990," CRCCF, Fonds FFHQ, C84–18/1/6, pp. 7.1–7.2.

95 Tison, "Les francophones hors Québec appuient l'Accord du la Meech," *La Presse*, 18 February 1990.

96 Correspondence to the author from Rolande Faucher, May 2002; telephone interview with Rolande Faucher, 5 June 2002.

97 "Procès-verbal de la réunion du Conseil national des présidentes et des présidents, tenue les 16, 17 et 18 février 1990, Résolution 009," CRCCF, Fonds FFHQ, C84–18/1/12, 17–18.

98 Cohen, *A Deal Undone*, 224–8.

99 Correspondence between the author and Georges Arès, 21 May 1997.

100 FFHQ, "Testimony before the Special Committee of the House of Commons to study The Proposed Companion Resolution to the Meech Lake Accord," *Minutes of Proceedings and Evidence* 4 (11 April 1990); SAANB, ibid., 2 (9 April 1990): 4–15; SFM, ibid., 10 (23 April 1990): 58–77; ACFO, ibid., 19 (3 May 1990): 95–109.

101 SFM, ibid., 10 (23 April 1990): 62, 75. Consult SFM, *Mémoire concernant la résolution d'accompagnement proposée par le Gouvernement du Nouveau-Brunswick présenté au Comité Parlementaire lors des audiences publiques tenues à Winnipeg, le 23 avril 1990* (Winnipeg: Bureau de la SFM, Meech Lake files).

102 FFHQ, ibid., 12,17–18, 23–24; for Yvon Fontaine's excellent testimony, consult ibid., 2 (9 April 1990): 32–53. Edgar Gallant, also a former federal bureaucrat specializing in federal/provincial relations and constitutional renewal, wrote a letter to Jean Charest in which he effectively demolished the arguments of Gordon Robertson against the need for a promotion clause: Gallant to Charest, 20 April 1990, CRCCF, Fonds FFHQ, C84–16/3/5.

103 SAANB, ibid., 4–8.

104 ACFO, ibid., 103–4. See also ACFO, "Présentation au Comité spécial de la Chambre des Communes sur le projet de résolution d'accompagnement à l'Accord du Lac Meech présenté par le gouvernement du Nouveau-Brunswick, mai 1990," CRCCF, Fonds FFHQ, C84–19/5/8.

105 Lessard, "Les minorités: après Meech, dit Québec," *La Presse*, 9 May 1990.

106 FFHQ, "Testimony before the Special Committee of the House of Commons to study The Proposed Companion Resolution to the Meech Lake Accord," *Minutes of Proceedings and Evidence* 4 (11 April 1990): 5–26, quote at 8.

107 Canada, House of Commons, *Report of the Special Committee to Study the*

Proposed Companion Resolution to the Meech Lake Accord, in *Minutes of Proceedings and Evidence* 21 (8–15 May 1990): 7.

108 Ibid., 5.

109 Cohen, op. cit., 218–21; Robertson, *Memoirs of a very civil servant*, 343–5.

110 Cohen, op. cit., 228.

111 Ibid., 231–2.

112 Coyne, *Roll of the Dice*.

113 Ibid., 134.

114 Cohen, op. cit., 252–5; Coyne, op. cit., 134.

115 FFHQ, "À Chacun son Meech? Est-ce que les médias attisent les tensions entre francophones et anglophones?" CRCCF, Fonds FFHQ, C84–19/5/8.

116 Thériault, "Mémoire de la FFHQ présenté au Comité constitutionnel du Parti libéral du Québec concernant les négotiations constitutionnelles, le 12 juin 1990," CRCCF, Fonds FFHQ, C84–21/3/13.

117 SFM, "Réunion spéciale de représentants de divers organismes franco-manitobaines, le 13 juin 1990," Bureau de la SFM, Meech Lake files.

118 Association des juristes d'expression française du Manitoba, "Mémoire concernant l'entente conclue entre les premiers ministres du Canada au sujet de la ratification de l'Accord du Lac Meech, juin 1990," Bureau de la SFM, Meech Lake files.

119 SFM, "Position à l'égard de la ratification de l'Accord du Lac Meech par la Législature manitobaine, le 20 juin 1990," Bureau de la SFM, Meech Lake files.

120 Bisson to Filmon, Doer, Carstairs, and Wells, 21 June 1990, Bureau de la SFM, Meech Lake files.

121 Soucie to Peterson, 11 June 1990, CRCCF, Fonds FFHQ, C84–19/5/8.

122 Coyne, op. cit., 143–4.

123 ACFO, Press release, 25 June 1990: "L'Après-Meech et les francophones de l'Ontario," CRCCF, Fonds FFHQ, C84–19/5/8.

124 Soucie, "Lettre à la communauté Franco-ontarienne, le 25 juin 1990," CRCCF, Fonds FFHQ, C84–19/5/8.

CHAPTER SEVEN

1 FCFA, Press release, 28 October 1991: "Réforme constitutionnelle," Bureau de l'ACFA, dossier 2155.4.3.

2 MacDonald, *From Bourassa to Bourassa*, 321.

3 An Act To Establish the Commission on the Political and Constitutional Future of Quebec (Bill 90), s. 2.

4 Johnson, *A Canadian Myth: Quebec*, 260–1.

5 MacDonald, *From Bourassa to Bourassa*, 322–3. The expression "a knife to the throat" was first used by renowned Laval University political scientist Léon Dion during his testimony before the Bélanger-Campeau Commission.

6 Nemni, "Canada in Crisis and the Destructive Power of Myth," 222–39.

7 McRoberts, *Quebec: Social Change and Political Crisis*, 449.

8 Matte to Bourassa, 27 June 1990, CRCCF, Fonds FFHQ, C84–24/1/6.

9 Bourassa to Matte, 25 July 1990, CRCCF, Fonds FFHQ, C84–24/1/6.

10 FFHQ, "La restructuration de la fédération canadienne. Rapport d'étape, Ottawa, le 7 août 1990," CRCCF, Fonds ACFO, C2–52/6/c-3639, 1–10.

11 FFHQ, "Session de planification du Bureau de Direction, du 21 au 23 août 1990. Sommaire des discussions. Ottawa, le 11 septembre 1990," CRCCF, Fonds FFHQ, C84–24/1/6, 1–2, 8.

12 Ibid., 4–7.

13 Ibid., 10.

14 ACFO, "Notre place aujourd'hui ... pour demain. Mémoire présenté à la Commission sur l'avenir politique et constitutionnelle du Québec," Novembre 1990; ACFA, "Pour un véritable partenariat francophone. Mémoire présenté à la Commission sur l'avenir politique et constitutionnel du Québec," Novembre 1990.

15 FFHQ, *Un Nouveau départ, en partenariat*, 7.

16 Ibid., 8–11.

17 Ibid., 12–21.

18 Ibid., 22.

19 ACFA, "Pour un véritable partenariat francophone," 4.

20 Ibid., 12–25.

21 Ibid., 19.

22 Quebec Liberal Party, *A Quebec Free to Choose*.

23 Quebec, *Report of the Commission on the Political and Constitutional Future of Quebec*, 15.

24 Ibid., 70.

25 Ibid., 79–82.

26 An Act Respecting the Process for Determining the Political and Constitutional Furture of Quebec, s. 1.

27 "Rapport du Président au Conseil national des présidents et présidentes, 13–14 juin 1991, Ottawa," CRCCF, Fonds FFHQ, C84–18/1/7.

28 Citizens' Forum, *Report to the People and Government of Canada*.

29 Russell, *Constitutional Odyssey*, 163–64.

30 Citizens' Forum, *Report to the People and Government of Canada*, 137.

31 Dumaine, "Rencontre du comité aviseur de la Fédération des Francophones Hors Québec sur l'avenir du Canada. Tenue à Ottawa le 14 décembre, Première rencontre," CRCCF, Fonds FFHQ, C84–24/1/6.

32 Conseil national des présidents et des présidentes, briefing book, "Mise à jour du Dossier Constitutionnel. Processus d'élaboration d'un discours sur l'avenir du Canada, le 28 janvier 1991"; "Rapport d'étape sur le dossier autochtones," CRCCF, Fonds FFHQ, C84–24/1/6.

33 "Procès-verbal de la réunion du Conseil national des présidents et des

présidentes de la FFHQ, tenue les 21, 22 et 23 février 1991," CRCCF, Fonds FFHQ, C84–18/1/7.

34 ACFA, "Testimony to the Special Joint Committee of the Senate and the House of Commons on the Process for Amending the Constitution of Canada," *Minutes of Proceedings and Evidence* 10 (18 March 1991): 79–90.

35 FFHQ, "Testimony to the Special Joint Committee of the Senate and the House of Commons on the Process for Amending the Constitution of Canada," *Minutes of Proceedings and Evidence* 23 (18 April 1991: 86–106). For the testimony of the ACFO, which provided further details, see ibid., 26 (24 April 1991): 57–85.

36 Canada, Special Joint Committee of the Senate and the House of Commons, *The Process for Amending the Constitution of Canada. The Report*, Ch. V, Constituent Assemblies, 43–51.

37 FFHQ, Press release, 20 June 1991: "Rapport de la Commission Beaudoin-Edwards," CRCCF, Fonds FFHQ, C84–18/1/7.

38 "Rencontre entre Joseph Clark, Ministre des Affaires constitutionnelles et la FCFA du Canada tenue le 20 juin 1991, Compte rendu, Ottawa, le 28 juin 1991"; Bisson to Clark, 28 June 1991, Bureau de l'ACFA, dossier 2155.9.

39 Canada, *Shaping Canada's Future Together. Proposals.*

40 Russell, *Constitutional Odyssey*, 170–6.

41 Levasseur-Ouimet to Mulroney, 16 September 1991; Clark to Levasseur-Ouimet, 17 September 1991; Mulroney to Levasseur-Ouimet, 1 November 1991, Bureau de l'ACFA, dossier 2155.4.5.

42 Bastarache, "Quelques réflexions concernant la clause relative à la société distincte, préparer pour et envoyer à l'ACFA, le 18 octobre 1991," Bureau de l'ACFA, dossier 2155.4.1, 2

43 Ibid., 3–8.

44 Moreau, "Les propositions constitutionnelles de 1991. Le renouvelle-ment de la fédération ou sa mise à l'enchère?", 21 October 1991, 1–24, quotes at 5 and 12; Moreau to Arès, 30 October 1991; "L'impact des propositions constitutionnelles sur l'interprétation de l'article 23 de la Charte, le 5 novembre 1991," Bureau de l'ACFA, dossier 2155.9.2.

45 McConnell, "Analysis of the 1991 Constitutional Proposals as They Affect Western and Northern Francophones," Bureau de l'ACFA, dossier 2155.9.2, 1–8.

46 Arès to Bastarache, 8 November 1991, Bureau de l'ACFA, dossier 2155.4.5.

47 Danylchuk and Aikenhead, "Clark put in a real pickle by Franco-Albertan leader," *The Edmonton Journal*, 3 November 1991, A4.

48 Tardif to Chrétien, 12 November 1991; Tardif to Gauthier, 14 November 1991; Tardif to Getty, 26 November 1991, Bureau de l'ACFA, dossier 2155.4.5.

49 Tardif to Mercredi, 15 January 1992; Tardif to Chief Ron George, 14
   April 1992, Bureau de l'ACFA, dossiers 2155.92 and 2155.4.3.

50 FFHQ, Press release, 28 October 1991: "Réforme constitutionnelle,"
   Bureau de l'ACFA, dossier 2155.4.3.

51 FCFA, Press release, 14 November 1991: "Processus de consultation constitutionnelle," Bureau de l'ACFA, dossier 2155.4.3.

52 FCFA, *Bâtir ensemble l'avenir du Canada*, 1–67.

53 FCFA, "Testimony to the Special Joint Committee of the Senate and of the
   House of Commons on a Renewed Canada," *Minutes of Proceedings and
   Evidence* 31 (17 December 1991): 19; Press release, 17 December 1991:
   "Comparution devant le comité Beaudoin-Dobbie," Bureau de l'ACFA,
   dossier 2155.4.3.

54 Canada, *Shaping Canada's Future Together*, 14.

55 Ibid., 16–19; quote at 17. For the government's version of s. 25, see ibid.,
   14.

56 FCFA, "Colloque sur les communautés de langue officielle"; Clark to
   Tardif, 27 January 1992, Bureau de l'ACFA, dossiers 2155.4.3 and 2155.4.5.

57 Canada, *Renewal of Canada Conferences*, "Identity, Rights & Values. Conference Report," 9.

58 FCFA, Press release, 8 February 1992: "Les francophones canadiens
   gagnent la première manche à Toronto," Bureau de l'ACFA, dossier
   2155.4.3.

59 Canada, *Renewal of Canada Conferences*, "Concluding Conference Report,"
   7–8.

60 FCFA, Press release, 16 February 1992: "Conférence constitutionnelle de
   Vancouver," Bureau de l'ACFA, dossier 2155.4.3.

61 Editorial, "Getty's bilingual reveries," *The Edmonton Journal*, 10 January
   1992, A10.

62 ACFA, "Mémoire au Comité mixte spécial sur le renouvellement du
   Canada, Janvier 1992," Bureau de l'ACFA, dossier 2153.3; quote at 11.
   ACFA, "Testimony to the Special Joint Committee of the Senate and of
   the House of Commons on a Renewed Canada," *Minutes of Proceedings
   and Evidence* 50 (22 January 1992): 32–43.

63 Tardif to Bisson, 27 January 1992, Bureau de l'ACFA, dossier 2155.4.3.

64 The Report of the Special Joint Committee of the Senate and of the
   House of Commons on a Renewed Canada, *A Renewed Canada*, in *Minutes
   of Proceedings and Evidence* 66 (28 February 1992): 24–6, 33, 57.

65 FCFA, Press releases, 2 March 1992: "General Satisfaction with the Beaudoin-Dobbie report" and "Meeting with representatives of the Fédération
   du Canada"; SFM, Press release, 9 March 1992: "Le rapport Beaudoin/
   Dobbie constitue une base," Bureau de l'ACFA, dossier 2155.4.3.

66 SAANB, "Testimony to the Special Joint Committee of the Senate and of
   the House of Commons on a Renewed Canada, *Minutes of Proceedings and*

Evidence 43 (15 January 1992): 22–4; Press release, 3 March 1992: Le Rapport Beaudoin-Dobbie," Bureau de l'ACFA, dossier 2155.4.3. For a complete analysis of the SAANB's role in the Charlottetown Round, consult Doucet, *Le discours confisqué.*

67 Russell, *Constitutional Odyssey,* 193–208; Cairns, "The Charlottetown Accord," 25–63.

68 FCFA, Press release, 16 March 1992: "Constitutional and Linguistic Affairs"; Bisson to Mulroney, 16 March 1992, Bureau de l'ACFA, dossier 2155.4.3.

69 Bisson to Bouchard, 19 March 1992, Bureau de l'ACFA, dossier 2155.4.3.

70 de Cotret to Bisson, 30 March 1992, Bureau de l'ACFA, dossier 2155.4.3.

71 Godbout, "Mise à jours dans le dossier constitutionnel, le 25 mai 1992"; La Fédération des Franco-Colombines, Press release, 5 May 1992: "M. Bourassa se dit incapable de se prononcer et faveur de la clause de développement et d'épanouissement," Bureau de l'ACFA, dossier 2155.4.3.

72 Bisson, Note, 18 March 1992: "Rencontre avec Bourassa"; Note, 15 April 1992: "Rencontre avec Rae," Bureau de l'ACFA, dossier 2155.4.3.

73 Bisson, "Allocution du président de la Fédération devant la Commission d'études sur toute offre d'un nouveau partenariat de nature constitution-nelle, le 14 mai 1992, à Quebec"; FCFA, Press release, 14 May 1992: "Comparution devant le Commission d'étude," Bureau de l'ACFA, dossier 2155.4.3.

74 Godbout, "Mise à jours dans le dossier constitutionnel, le 25 mai 1992," Bureau de l'ACFA, dossier 2155.4.3.

75 Tardif to Bourassa, 8 June 1992 and Bourassa to Tardif, 14 July 1992, Bureau de l'ACFA, dossier 2155.4.3.

76 Hébert, "Les francophones hors Québec vont imiter les Cris," *Le Droit,* 9 June 1992, 20.

77 "Lyne Lemieux aux membres de l'exécutif de l'ACFA, le 9 juin 1992," Bureau de l'ACFA, dossier 2155.4.3.

78 FCFA, Press release, 10 June 1992: "La Fédération n'entend pas faire campagne contre le Québec," Bureau de l'ACFA, dossier 2155.4.3.

79 "Denis Tardif aux associations membres de la Fédération du Canada, le 17 juin 1992," Bureau de l'ACFA, dossier 2155.4.3.

80 Arès to Bisson, 17 June 1992, Bureau de l'ACFA, 2155.4.3.

81 Tardif to McKenna, 2 July 1992; "Open Letter to the Premiers of Canada," *The Globe and Mail,* 3 July 1992.

82 Tardif to Bourassa, 9 and 10 July 1992, Bureau de l'ACFA, dossier 2155.4.2R.

83 Godbout to Arès, 13 July 1992, Bureau de l'ACFA, dossier 2155.4.3.

84 For an excellent overview of the rise and fall of the Charlottetown

Accord consult Campbell and Pal, *The Real Worlds of Canadian Politics*, 142, 210.

85 Bissonnette, "L'encerclement du Québec – I et II," *Le Devoir*, 10 and 11 July 1992; "L'écart," *Le Devoir*, 13 July 1992.

86 Russell, *Constitutional Odyssey*, Appendix: "Consensus Report on the Constitution, Charlottetown, August 28, 1992," 240.

87 Godbout to Arès, 13 July 1992, Bureau de l'ACFA, dossier 2155.4.3.

88 Godbout, "Aux présidents et présidentes, Prochain réunion du CNPP et dossier constitutionnel, le 14 juillet"; Tardif to Bisson, 17 July 1992, Bureau de l'ACFA, dossier 2155.4.3.

89 ACFA, "Memo à Michel Bastarache au sujet de la section 2(1)(d) de la clause Canada, juillet 1992"; Bastarache to Arès, 13 July 1992, Bureau de l'ACFA, dossier 2155.4.3.

90 Arès to Graves, 17 July 1992, Bureau de l'ACFA, dossier 2155.4.3.R.

91 Tardif to Bourassa, copying Clark and Getty, 17 July 1992, Bureau de l'ACFA, dossier 2155.4.3.

92 Canada, CCMC, *Final Status Report of the Multilateral Meetings on the Constitution*, 16 July 1992 (Ottawa), 1.

93 FCFA, Press release, 17 July 1992: "Les magouilleurs à l'oeuvre," Bureau de l'ACFA, dossier 2155.4.3.

94 ACFA, Press release, 24 July 1992: "L'ACFA propose des éléments de solution à la question épineuse de la dualité linguistique," Bureau de l'ACFA, dossier 2155.4.3; Picard, "Franco-Albertans unveil Senate plan," *The Globe and Mail*, 25 July 1992, A3; Rubin, "Franco-Albertans beg Quebec not to abandon unity quest," *The Gazette*, 25 July 1992, A6; Paré, "Les Franco-Albertains proposent à Bourassa une alliance sur le Sénat," *Le Devoir*, 25 July 1992, A2.

95 ACFA, "Distinct Society and Linguistic Duality. Another Formula, 22 July 1992"; Bastarache and Moreau to Arès, 23 July 1992; Denison to Bastarache, 22 July 1992; Moreau to Arès, 27 July 1992, Bureau de l'ACFA, dossier 2154.4.3.B.

96 Cornellier, "Le fédéral ajoute l'insulte à l'injure," *Le Journal de Montréal*, 25 July 1992, 20.

97 Tardif to McKenna, 30 July 1992; "Composite Canada Clause, 29 July 1992"; McKenna to Tardif, 11 August 1992," Bureau de l'ACFA, dossier 2155.4.3.

98 Bastarache to Arès, 5 August 1992, Bureau de l'ACFA, dossier 2155.4.3.B.

99 Moreau to Arès, 17 August 1992, Bureau de l'ACFA, dossier 2155.4.3.

100 Tardif to George, 12 August 1992; George to Tardif, 19 August 1992; Tardif to Getty, 12 August 1992, Bureau de l'ACFA, dossier 2155.4.3.

101 "Raymond Bisson aux membres du réseau de la Fédération du Canada, le 14 août 1992," Bureau de l'ACFA, dossier 2155.4.3.

102 "Yvon Samson, L'Agent de liaison, aux Membres du réseau de la Fédération, le 17 août 1992"; Chrétien to Mulroney, 17 August 1992, Bureau de l'ACFA, dossier 2155.4.3.

103 *Consensus Report of the Constitution,* Charlottetown, 28 August 1992, in Russell, *Constitutional Odyssey,* 237–63. Cf. "Draft Legal Text of Charlottetown Accord, October 9, 1992," prepared by the officials representing all the First Ministers and aboriginal and territorial leaders. In author's archives.

104 "Raymond Bisson au Bureau de direction, présidentes et présidents, directrices et directeurs généraux, le 24 août 1992," Bureau de l'ACFA, dossier 2155.4.3.

105 Tardif to Bourassa, 26 August 1992; Tardif to Mulroney, 26 August 1992; Tardif to Clark, 26 August 1992, Bureau de l'ACFA, dossier 2155.4.3.

106 Clark to Tardif, 16 October 1992, Bureau de l'ACFA, dossier 2157B.

107 Bastarache to Arès, 2 September 1992, Bureau de l'ACFA, dossier 2155.4.3.

108 Bastarache to Godbout, 4 September 1992, Bureau de l'ACFA, dossier 2155.4.3.

109 Ibid., 2–3.

110 Bastarache to Moreau, 8 September 1992, Bureau de l'ACFA, dossier 2155.4.3.

111 Moreau to Arès, 11 September 1992, Bureau de l'ACFA, dossier 2155.4.3.

112 Bastarache to Simard, 10 September 1992, Bureau de l'ACFA, dossier 2155.4.3.

113 FCFA, Press release, 14 September 1992: "Reconnaissance de la dualité linguistique. La Fédération du Canada donne son appui à l'entente de Charlottetown," Bureau de l'ACFA, dossier 2155.4.3R.

114 Behiels, "Who Speaks for Canada?," 345–9.

115 Cairns, "Aboriginal Canadians, Citizenship, and the Constitution," 246–9.

116 Cairns, *Citizens Plus,* 70–1, 81–3.

117 Campbell and Pal, *The Real Worlds of Canadian Politics,* 172–87.

CHAPTER EIGHT

1 Saywell, *The Lawmakers,* 308–9. His emphasis.

2 Weinrib, "The Activist Constitution," 80–6.

3 Commissioner of Official Languages, *Annual Report, 1998,* 81–113.

4 For an overview of the developments in all provinces and territories, consult Canada, Office of the Commissioner of Official Languages, *School Governance: The Implementation of Section 23 of the Charter.*

5 *Arsenault-Cameron* v. *the Government of Prince Edward Island* [2000] 1 S.C.R. 1. The Supreme Court reminded provincial governments that language and culture are linked and that francophone children have a right to education in every part of their province. The purpose of s. 23 is remedial and true linguistic equality may, given specific circumstances, require different treatment in order to ensure that the standard of education for the official language minorities is equivalent to that received by the official language majority.

6 Martel, *Rights, Schools and Communities in Minority Contexts, 1986–2002,* 20–21, 51–52, 59; Landry and Rousselle, *Éducation et droits collectives: Au delà de l'article 23 de la Charte,* 37–77.

7 Consult Léger, ed., *"De violations à réparations": Symposium national sur la réparation constitutionnelle (selon les articles 23 et 24 de la Charte canadienne des droits et libertés).*

8 Foucher, "Le potentiel réparateur des articles 23 et 24 de la Charte," 29–86. The first study on s. 24 was done by Gibson, "Enforcement of the Canadian Charter of Rights and Freedoms (s. 24)." He concluded that while s. 24 might be given a rather narrow interpretation by the courts, "it does not exhaust the legal remedies available to those whose rights under the Canadian Charter of Rights and Freedoms are violated." (526–7)

9 Martel, "L'Article 23 de la *Charte canadienne* (1982) est-il réparateur?", 205–21.

10 Martel, *Rights, Schools and Communities in Minority Contexts, 1986–2002.*

11 Landry and Rousselle, *Éducation et droits collectives: Au delà de l'article 23 de la Charte,* 139–173.

12 Ibid., 175–183.

Bibliography

PRIMARY SOURCES

Manuscripts

Archives de la Faculté Saint-Jean, University of Alberta
   Fonds Bugnet
Archives de Saint-Boniface, Manitoba
   Fonds de la Société franco-manitobaine
Association canadienne-française de l'Alberta, central office records
Association canadienne-française de l'Ontario, central office records
Centre de recherche en civilisation canadienne-française (CRCCF)
   Fonds de la Fédération des Francophones Hors Québec (FFHQ)
   Fonds de la Fédération des communautés francophones et acadiennes du
   Canada (FCFA)
   Fonds de l'Association canadienne-française de l'Ontario (ACFO)
   Fonds de l'Association canadienne d'éducation de la langue française
   (ACELF)
   Fonds de l'Association française des Conseils scolaires de l'Ontario
   (AFCSO)
   Fonds des l'Association des enseignants franco-ontariens (AEFO)
Provincial Archives of Alberta (PAA)
   Fonds de l'Association canadienne-française de l'Alberta (ACFA)
Société franco-manitobaine (SFM), central office records

Jurisprudence

Arsenault-Cameron v. the Government of Prince Edward Island [2000] 1 S.C.R.
Attorney-General of Quebec v. Quebec Association of Protestant School Boards [1984]
   2 S.C.R. 66
Jacques Marchand v. The Simcoe County Board of Education (1986) 29 D.L.R.

(4th) 596 (Ontario Supreme Court); 44 D.L.R. (4th) 171 (Ontario
Supreme Court)

Mahé v. *Alberta* [1990] 1 S.C.R. 342; 68 D.L.R. (4th) 69 (Supreme Court of
Canada)

Mahé v. *R. in Right of Alberta* [1985] 39 Alta. L.R. (2d) 215 (Alberta Court of
Queen's Bench)

Mahé et al. v. *The Queen in Right of Alberta* [1988] 42 D.L.R. (4th) 514 (Alberta
Court of Appeal)

Mercure v. *A.G. Saskatchewan* [1988] 1 S.C.R. 234

Protestant School Board of Greater Montreal v. *Quebec Minister of Education* (1978)
83 D.L.R. (3rd) 645 (C.S.)

Quebec v. Ford et al. [1988] 2 S.C.R. 712

Quebec Association of Protestant School Boards v. *Attorney General of Quebec* [1982]
C.S. 673, 140 D.L.R. (3rd) 19 (Quebec Superior Court); confirmed [1983]
C.A. 77 (Quebec Court of Appeal); confirmed [1984] 2 S.C.R. 66, 10 D.L.R.
(4th) 321 (Supreme Court of Canada)

Quebec Association of Protestant School Boards v. *Attorney General of Quebec* [1989]
(Supreme Court of Canada)

Reference re Education Act of Ontario and Minority Language Education Rights
(1984) 10 D.L.R. (4th) 491(Ontario Court of Appeal) (1984) 47 O.R.
(2nd) 1

Reference re *Manitoba Language Rights* [1992] 1 S.C.R. 212

Reference re *Public Schools Act* (Man.) 67 D.L.R. (4th) 488

Re *Manitoba Public Schools Act Reference* [1993] 1 S.C.R. 839

Société des Acadiens du N.B. Inc. v. *Assn. of Parents for Fairness in Education,
Grand Falls Dist. 50 Branch* (1986) 27 D.L.R. (4th); [1986] 1 S.C.R. 549; 69
N.B.R. (2d) 27

Trustees of the Roman Catholic Separate Schools for Ottawa v. *Mackell* [1917] A.C.
62 (Privy Council Judicial Committee)

Interviews and Correspondence

Georges Arès   Denis Tardif
Raymond Hébert   Rhéal E. Teffaine
Rolande Soucie Faucher

SECONDARY SOURCES

Acker, Stephen B. "A Judgment for all seasons." *Language and Society* 43
(Summer 1993): 22–4.

An Act To Establish the Commission on the Political and Constitutional
Future of Quebec (Bill 90).

Alberta, Alberta Education. *Financement des autorités régionales et des conseils de coordination.* Edmonton: Alberta Education, School Business Administration Services, 1995.

– *Guide de mise en oeuvre de la gestion scolaire francophone.* Edmonton: Alberta Education, School Business Administration Services, 4 mars 1994.

Alberta, Department of Education. *French Education in Alberta: Discussion Paper.* Edmonton: Department of Education, 23 April 1990.

– *Language Education Policy for Alberta.* Edmonton: Department of Education, 1988.

– *Management and Control of French Education in Alberta.* Edmonton: Department of Education, November 1990.

Allaire, Gratien. "La construction d'une culture française dans l'Ouest canadien: la diversité originelle." In Gérard Bouchard, ed. *La construction d'une culture: le Québec et l'Amérique française.* Sainte-Foy: Les Presses de l'Université Laval, 1993.

– "De l'Église à l'État: le financement des organismes francophones de l'Ouest, 1945–1970." In Jean Lafontant, ed. *L'État et les Minorités.* Saint Boniface: Éditions du Blé et les Presses de l'Université Saint-Boniface, 1993.

– "Pour la survivance: l'Association canadienne-française de l'Alberta." In Monique Bournot-Trites, William Bruneau and Robert Roy, eds. *Les outils de la francophonie.* Vancouver: Centre d'études franco-canadiennes de l'Ouest, 1988.

– "Le rapport à l'*autre*: l'évolution de la francophonie de l'Ouest." In Joseph Yvon Thériault, ed. *Francophonies minoritaires au Canada: l'état des lieux.* Moncton: Les Éditions d'Acadie, 1999.

– and Laurence Fedigan. "D'une génération à l'autre: le changement linguistique en Alberta." In André Fauchon, ed. *Langue et communication.* Saint Boniface: Centre d'études franco-canadiennes de l'Ouest, 1990.

Apps, Eric. "Minority Language Education Rights." *University of Toronto Faculty of Law Review* 43, no. 2 (1985): 45–71.

Arès, Georges. "The Accord Abandons Canada's Battered and Defenceless Minorities." In Michael D. Behiels, ed. *The Meech Lake Primer: Conflicting Views of the 1987 Constitutional Accord.* Ottawa: University of Ottawa Press, 1989.

Arsenault, P. *L'Enchassement des droits de la minorité canadienne-française dans la Constitution du Canada.* Moncton: Les Éditions de l'Université de Moncton, 1982.

Arsenault, Samuel P. "Aires géographiques en Acadie," in Joseph Yvon Thériault, ed. *Francophonies minoritaires au Canada: l'état des lieux.* Moncton: Les Éditions d'Acadie, 1999.

Association canadienne d'éducation de la langue française. "Compte rendu d'une réunion de comité de la constitution canadienne." Québec: ACÉLF, 1983.

Association canadienne-française de l'Alberta. "Pour une véritable partenariat francophone. Mémoire de l'ACFA présenté à la Commission sur l'avenir politique et constitutionnel du Québec." Edmonton: ACFA, 1990.

Association canadienne-française de l'Ontario. "Notre place aujourd'hui ... Pour demain." Mémoire de l'ACFO présenté à La Commission sur l'avenir politique et constitutionnel du Québec. Novembre 1990. Ottawa: ACFO, 1990.

– *Un plan de développement pour la communauté franco-ontarienne.* Ottawa: ACFO, 1983.

– and Conseil des Minorités du Québec. "Testimony before the Special Joint Committee of the Senate and House of Commons on the Constitution of Canada." *Minutes of Proceedings and Evidence* 8 (19 November 1980): 30–53.

Association culturelle franco-canadienne de la Saskatchewan. "Brief to and Testimony before the Special Joint Committee of the Senate and House of Commons on the Constitution of Canada." *Minutes of Proceedings and Evidence* 12 (25 November 1980): 7–26.

Aunger, Edmund A. "The Decline of a French-speaking Enclave: A Case Study of Social Contact and Language Shift in Alberta." *Canadian Ethnic Studies* 25 (1993): 65–83.

– "Dispersed Minorities and Segmented Autonomy: French-Language School Boards in Canada." *Nationalism and Ethnic Politics* 2, no. 2 (Summer 1996): 191–215.

– "Language and Law in the Province of Alberta." In Paul Pupier and José Woehrling, eds. *Language and Law.* Montreal: Wilson & Lafleur, 1989.

– "The Mystery of the French Language Ordinances: An Investigation into Official Bilingualism and the Canadian North-West, 1870 to 1895." *Canadian Journal of Law and Society* 13 (1998): 89–124.

Banting, Keith. *The Welfare State and Canadian Federalism.* Rev. ed. Montreal and Kingston: McGill-Queen's University Press, 1997.

Bastarache, Michel. "L'article 23 de la Charte canadienne des droits et libertés: les enjeux actuels et futurs." In Claude Deblois and Alain Prujiner, eds. *Les écoles françaises hors Québec: rétrospective et prospective.* Québec: Les Cahiers du Laboratoire de recherche en administration et politique scolaires, Faculté de droit, Université de Laval, 1991.

– *Les droits linguistiques au Canada.* Cowansville: Les Éditions Yves Blais, 1986.

– "Les droits linguistiques dans le domaine scolaire: guide d'interprétation de l'article 23 de la Charte canadienne des droits et libertés." *Égalité – revue acadienne d'analyse politique* 19 (1986): 147–69.

– "Dualisme et égalité dans la Constitution nouvelle." *Revue de l'Université de Moncton* 13, no. 3 (September 1980).

– *Language Rights in Canada.* Montreal: Yves Blais, 1987.

– "The Linguistic and Cultural Rights of Acadians from 1713 to the Present." In Jean Daigle, ed. *Acadia of the Maritimes. Thematic Studies from the Beginning to the Present.* Moncton: Chaire d'études acadiennes, Université de Moncton, 1995.

– "Les nationalistes en devenir: Acadie, Québec." *Egalité – revue acadienne d'analyse politique* 6 (1982): 71–98.

Bayefsky, A.F. and M. Eberts, eds. *Equality Rights and the Canadian Charter of Rights and Freedoms.* Toronto: University of Toronto Press, 1984.

Beaudoin, Gérald. "Les droits des minorités: mythe ou réalité? La protection constitutionnelle des minorités." *Les Cahiers de Droit* 27, no. 1 (March 1986): 31–52.

– "Les obligations crées par l'article 23 de la Charte canadienne des droits et libertés." Mimeo text prepared for the 15–16 April 1988 colloquium, Montreal, 1988.

– "La question de l'établissement d'un conseil scolaire homogène francophone en Ontario. Un commentaire succinct." *Revue Général de Droit* 18 (1987): 481–94.

Behiels, Michael D. "Canada's Francophone Minority Communities and Micro-constitutional Politics of Section 23 of the Charter of Rights and Freedoms." In Sylvie Léger, ed. *Les droits linguistiques au Canada: collusions ou collisions?/ Linguistic Rights in Canada: Collusions or Collisions?* Ottawa: Centre Canadien des droits linguistiques, 1995.

– "The Meech Lake Accord and the Process of Political Realignment in Canada, 1979–90." In C.H.W. Remie and J.-M Lacroix, eds. *Canada on the Threshold of the 21st Century. European Reflections upon the Future of Canada.* Amsterdam and Philadelphia: John Benjamins Publishing Co., 1991.

– *Prelude to Quebec's Quiet Revolution. Liberalism versus Neo-nationalism, 1945–1960.* Montreal & Kingston: McGill-Queen's University Press, 1985.

– "Who Speaks for Canada? Trudeau and the Constitutional Crisis." In Andrew Cohen and J. L. Granatstein, eds. *Trudeau's Shadow. The Life and Legacy of Pierre Elliott Trudeau.* Toronto: Random House of Canada, 1998.

– ed. *The Meech Lake Primer. Conflicting Views of the 1987 Constitutional Accord.* Ottawa: University of Ottawa Press, 1989.

Belaboba, E.P. and Eric Gertner, eds. *The New Constitution and the Charter of Rights.* Toronto: Butterworths, 1983.

Bélanger, Réal-A., ed. *L'adhésion du Québec à l'Accord du Lac Meech.* Montréal: Les Éditions Thémis, 1988.

Bell, David V.J. and Donald C. Wallace. "The Federal Perspective." In *Canadian Annual Review, 1980.* Toronto: University of Toronto Press, 1982.

Bernard, Bernard. *Le Choc des nombres: dossier statistique sur la francophonie canadienne, 1951–1986.* Ottawa: Fédération des jeunes Canadiens français, 1990.

Bernard, Roger. *De Québécois à Ontarois.* 2nd ed. Ottawa: Les Éditions du Nordir, 1996.

Bilodeau, R. "La langue, l'éducation et les minorités: avant et depuis la Charte canadienne des droits et libertés." *Manitoba Law Journal* 13 (1983): 371–88.

Blay, Jacqueline. *L'Article 23. Les péripéties législatives et juridiques du fait français au Manitoba, 1870–1986.* Winnipeg: Les Éditions du Blé, 1987.

Bonin, Daniel, ed. *Towards Reconciliation? The Language Issue in Canada in the 1990s*. Proceedings of a conference jointly organized with the Faculty of Law of the University of Moncton. Kingston: Institute of Intergovernmental Relations and Queen's University, 1992.

Bordeleau, Jean-Louis. *Les écoles secondaires de langue française en Ontario: dix ans après*. Toronto: Ministère de l'éducation, 1980.

Boudreau, Françoise. "La francophonie ontarienne au passé, au présent et au futur: un bilan sociologique." In Jacques Cotnam, Yves Frenette and Agnès Whitfield, eds. *La francophonie ontarienne et perspectives de recherche*. Hearst: Le Nordir, 1995.

Boulay, Gérard. *Du privé au public: les écoles secondaires franco-ontariennes à la fin des années soixante*. Sudbury: University of Sudbury, Société historique du Nouvel-Ontario, 1987.

Bourhis, Richard Y. "Introduction and Overview of Language Events in Canada." *International Journal of Sociology of Language* 105/106 (1994): 5–36.

Braën, A. "Les Droits scolaires des minorités de langue officielle du Canada et l'interprétation judiciaire." *Revue générale de droit* 19, no. 2 (1988): 311–37.

– "Language Rights." In Michel Bastarache, ed. *Language Rights in Canada*. Montreal: Yves Blais, 1987.

Brent, Audry S. "The Right to Religious Education and the Constitutional Status of Denominational Schools." *Saskatchewan Law Review* 40, no. 2 (1975–76): 239–67.

Bureau, Brigitte. *Mêlez-vous de vos affaires. 20 ans de luttes franco-ontariennes*. Ottawa: L'Association canadienne-française de l'Ontario, 1989.

Cadrin, Gilles. "L'affirmation des minorités francophones depuis la Révolution tranquille." In Gratien Allaire, Paul Dubé and Gamila Morcos, eds. *Après dix ans ... : bilan et prospective*. Edmonton: Institut de recherche de la Faculté Saint-Jean, 1992.

Cairns, Alan C. "Aboriginal Canadians, Citizenship, and the Constitution." In Douglas E. Williams, ed. *Reconfigurations: Canadian Citizenship and Constitutional Change. Selected Essays by Alan C. Cairns*. Toronto: McClelland and Stewart, 1995.

– "The Charlottetown Accord: Multinational Canada v. Federalism." In Curtis Cook, ed. *Constitutional Predicament. Canada after the Referendum of 1992*. Montreal and Kingston: McGill-Queen's University Press, 1994.

– *Citizens Plus: Aboriginal Peoples and the Canadian State*. Vancouver: UBC Press, 2000.

Campbell, Robert M. and Leslie A. Pal. *The Real Worlds of Canadian Politics. Cases in Process and Policy*. 3rd ed. Peterborough: Broadview Press, 1994.

Canada. *The Canadian Constitution, 1980. Proposed Resolution for Joint Address to Her Majesty the Queen Respecting the Constitution of Canada*. Ottawa: Publications Canada, 1980.

Canada. *The Constitution and the People of Canada*. White paper presented to the second meeting of the Constitutional Conference, 10–12 February 1969. Ottawa: Queen's Printer, 1969.

Canada. *A National Understanding. The Official Languages of Canada. Statement of the Government of Canada on the official languages policy.* Ottawa: Minister of Supply and Services, 1977.

Canada. *Shaping Canada's Future Together. Proposals.* Ottawa: Minister of Supply and Services, 1991.

Canada, Commissioner of Official Languages. *Annual Reports.* Ottawa: Minister of Supply and Services, 1986 to 2000–2001.

Canada, Continuing Committee of Ministers on the Constitution. *Final Status Report of the Multilateral Meetings on the Constitution, July 16, 1992.* Ottawa: Government of Canada, 1992.

Canada, Department of Justice. *The Constitution Acts 1867 to 1982: A Consolidation.* Ottawa: Supply and Services Canada, 1989.

Canada, The House of Commons. *Bill C-60.* Third session, Thirtieth Parliament, 26–27 Elizabeth II, 1977–78, First reading, 20 June 1978.

Canada, Office of the Commissioner of Official Languages. *School Governance: The Implementation of Section 23 of the Charter.* Ottawa: Minister of Public Works and Government Services Canada, 1998.

Canada, Royal Commission on Bilingualism and Biculturalism. *Report, General Introduction. Book I: The Official Languages.* Ottawa: Queen's Printer, 1967.

– *Report, Book II: Education.* Ottawa: Queen's Printer, 1968.

Canada, Special Joint Committee of the Senate and of the House of Commons. *Minutes of Proceedings and Evidence.* Issues no. 2, 3, 6, 8, 10, 12, and 13 (November 1980). Ottawa: Queen's Printer, 1980.

Canada, Special Joint Committee of the Senate and of the House of Commons on the Constitution of Canada. *Constitution of Canada. Final Report.* Ottawa: Queen's Printer, 1972.

Canada, Special Joint Committee of the Senate and of the House of Commons on the 1987 Constitutional Accord. *Minutes of Proceedings and Evidence.* No. 3 (August 1987); No. 17 (September 1987). Ottawa: Queen's Printer, 1987.

– *The Process for Amending the Constitution of Canada. The Report.* Ottawa: Queen's Printer, 20 June 1991.

Canada, The Task Force on Canadian Unity. *A Future Together. Observations and Recommendations.* Ottawa: Minister of Supply and Services, 1979.

– *Coming to Terms. The Words of the Debate.* Ottawa: Minister of Supply and Services, 1979.

Cardinal, Linda. "Le Canada Français à la lumière des États Généraux: critique de la thèse de la rupture." In Marcel Martel and Robert Choquette, eds. *Les États généraux du Canada français, trente ans après.* Ottawa: Centre de recherche en civilisation canadienne-française de l'Université d'Ottawa, 1998.

– "La vie politique et les francophones hors Québec," In Joseph Yvon Thériault, ed. *Francophonies minoritaires au Canada. L'état des lieux.* Moncton: Les Éditions d'Acadie, 1999.

Carrière. Fernan. "La métamorphose de la communauté franco-ontarienne, 1960–1985." In Cornelius Jaenen, ed. *Les Franco-Ontariens.* Ottawa: University of Ottawa Press, 1993.

Castonguay, Charles. "Why Hide the Facts? The Federalist Approach to the Language Crisis in Canada." *Canadian Public Policy* 5, no. 1 (Winter/hiver 1979): 4–15.

Choquette, Robert. *Language and Religion: A History of English-French Conflict in Ontario.* Ottawa: University of Ottawa Press, 1975.

– "La sécularisation dans la diaspora canadienne." In Brigitte Caulier, ed. *Religion, sécularisation, modernité. Les expériences francophones en Amérique du Nord.* Sainte Foy: Les Presses de l'Université Laval, 1996.

Chrétien, Jean. "Brief to and Testimony before the Special Joint Committee of the Senate and House of Commons on the Constitution of Canada." *Minutes of Proceedings and Evidence* 2 (7 November 1980): 20–50; and 3 (12 November 1980): 11–87.

– *Notes for a speech.* House of Commons, 6 October 1980. Ottawa: Office of the Prime Minister, 1980.

Christian, Timothy. "L'affaire Piquette." In David Schneiderman, ed. *Language and the State.* Cowansville: Éditions Yvon Blais, 1991.

– "The Limits to Section 23." Paper prepared for the 15–16 April 1988 colloquium, Montreal, 1988.

Churchill, Stacy. *Official Languages in Canada: Changing the Language Landscape.* Ottawa: Canadian Heritage, 1998.

– Norman Frenette and Saeed Quazi. *Éducation et besoins des Franco-Ontariens: Le diagnostic d'un système d'éducation.* Vol. 1: *Problèmes de l'ensemble du système: l'élémentaire et le secondaire.* Vol. 2: *Le postsecondaire et rapport technique.* Toronto: Conseil de l'éducation franco-ontarienne, Ministère de l'éducation, 1985.

Citizens' Forum on Canada's Future. *Report to the People and Government of Canada.* Ottawa: Ministry of Supply and Services Canada, 1991.

Clark, S.D. "The Position of the French-Speaking Population in the Northern Industrial Community." In Richard J. Ossenberg, ed. *Canadian Society: Pluralism, Change and Conflict.* Scarborough: Prentice-Hall Canada, 1971.

Cohen, Andrew. *A Deal Undone. The Making and Breaking of the Meech Lake Accord.* Vancouver/Toronto: Douglas & McIntyre, 1990.

Conklin, W.C. "Constitutional Ideology, Language Rights and Political Disunity in Canada." *University of New Brunswick Law Journal* 28 (1979): 39–65.

Cook, Curtis, ed. *Constitutional Predicament. Canada after the Referendum of 1992.* Montreal and Kingston: McGill-Queen's University Press, 1994.

Council of Ministers of Education. *The State of Minority Language Education in the Ten Provinces of Canada.* Toronto: Council of Ministers of Education, January 1978.

Council of Quebec Minorities. "Brief to and Testimony before the Special Joint Committee of the Senate and the House of Commons on the Constitution of Canada." *Minutes of Proceedings and Evidence* 8 (19 November 1980): 30–53.

Coyne, Deborah. *Roll of the Dice. Working with Clyde Wells during the Meech Lake Negotiations.* Toronto: Lorimer, 1992.

Daigle, Jean, ed. *L'Acadie de Maritimes: études thématiques, des débuts à nos jours.* Moncton: Université de Moncton, Chaire d'études acadiennes, 1993.

d'Anglejan, Alison. "Language Planning in Quebec: An Historical Overview and Future Trends." In Richard Y. Bourhis, ed. *Conflict and Language Planning in Quebec.* Cleverdon, England: Multilingual Matters Ltd., 1984.

Deschênes, Jules. *Ainsi parlèrent les tribunaux: conflits linguistiques au Canada 1968–1980.* 2 vols. Montréal: Wilson et Lafleur Ltée, 1980 and 1985.

Desjarlais, Lionel. *C'est maintenant, l'heure de l'école franco-albertaine. Une étude du régime d'application en Alberta de l'Article 23 de la Charte canadienne des droits et libertés* (version abrégée). Edmonton: ACFA, 1989.

Doucet, Michel. *Le discours confisqué.* Moncton: Les Éditions d'Acadie, 1995.

Doucet, Philip, Roger Ouellet and Marie-Thérèse Seguin, "L'espace politique et la vie politique en Acadie." In Joseph Yvon Thériault, ed. *Francophonies minoritaires au Canada. L'état des lieux.* Moncton: Les Éditions d'Acadie, 1995.

Drummond, Robert J. "Parliament and Politics." In *Canadian Annual Review 1984.* Toronto: University of Toronto Press, 1987.

Dubé, Paul. "L'arrêt Mahé et l'avenir du français et des minorités francophones dans l'Ouest canadien." *Cahiers franco-canadiens de l'Ouest* 2, no. 2 (1990): 137–49.

– "Les conditions d'émergence du cas Bugnet et ses implications pour l'avenir des minorités francophones." In J. Lafontant and R. Théberge, eds. *Demain, la francophonie en milieu minoritaire.* Saint-Boniface: Centre de recherche du Collège de Saint-Boniface, 1987.

– "L'école de la minorité et le jugement *Mahé*: le jugement de l'avenir." *Éducation et francophonies* 19, no. 1 (April 1991): 28–33.

– "Une étude de cas portant sur la genèse et les résultats de la judicalisation des droits scolaires: le cas Bugnet en Alberta." *La revue canadienne des langues vivantes/The Canadian Modern Languages Review* 49, no. 4 (June/juin 1993): 704–15.

– "Je est un autre ... et l'autre est moi. Essai sur l'identité franco-ontarienne." In Jocelyn Létourneau and Roger Bernard, eds. *La question identitaire au Canada francophone. Récits, parcours, enjeux, hors-lieux.* Sainte-Foy: Les Presses de l'Université Laval, 1994.

– "La judicalisation des revendications scolaires en tant que réappropriation de l'espace réel et symbolique." In Jean-Guy Quenneville, ed. *A la mesure du Pays* ... Muenster, SK: St Peter's Press, 1991.

– "La Québéphobie. Essai sur les rapports entre l'establishment francophone et le Québec." In Gratien Allaire, Paul Dubé and Gamila Morcos, eds. *Après*

dix ans ... Bilan et prospective. Edmonton: Centre d'études franco-canadiennes de l'Ouest, 1992.

Ducharme, Jean-Charles. *Status Report: Minority-Language Education Rights. The
Implementation of the Canadian Charter of Rights and Freedoms*. Ottawa: Canadian Heritage, 1996.

Dumaine, François. *Section 23 of the Charter and Education for Francophone Communities. The 90's Decade Consolidation Period*. Ottawa: FFHQ, 1990.

Dupras, Daniel and David Johansen. "Minority Language Education Rights:
Section 23 of the Charter." Ottawa: Library of Parliament, Research Branch,
Current Issue Review, 89–6E, 24 May 1989, Reviewed 14 March 1991.

Durocher, René. "Quebec." In *Canadian Annual Review 1977*, 144–5. Toronto:
University of Toronto Press, 1979.

– "Quebec," In *Canadian Annual Review, 1978*. Toronto: University of Toronto
Press, 1980.

Falardeau, Philippe. *Hier, la francophonie. Fenêtre historique sur le dynamisme des
communautés francophones*. Dans le cadre du projet Dessein 2000: pour un
espace francophone. Ottawa: FFHQ, 1991.

Fédération de communautés francophones et acadiennes du Canada. *Bâtir
ensemble l'avenir du Canada. Les communautés francophones et acadiennes et le
projet de réforme du fédéralisme canadien*. Ottawa: FCFA, 17 December 1991.

Fédération des Francophones Hors Québec. "Débloquer l'impasse. La néces-
sité d'une assemblée constituante." Mémoire présenté par la FFHQ devant le
Comité mixte spécial sur le procédure de modification de la Constitution.
Ottawa, 18 April 1991.

– *Dessein 2000: pour un espace francophone. Rapport Préliminaire*. Ottawa: FFHQ,
May 1991.

– *La FFHQ et le dossier de l'Accord Constitutionnel du Lac Meech*. Ottawa: FFHQ,
1989.

– *Les Francophones à l'extérieur du Québec et les negotiations constitutionnels*.
Ottawa: FFHQ, April 1987.

– *The Heirs of Lord Durham*. Ottawa: Burns and MacEachern Ltd., 1978.

– *Les héritiers de Lord Durham. Vol. 1*. Ottawa: FFHQ, 1977.

– *Un nouveau départ, en partenariat. Mémoire présenté par la FFHQ devant le Commission sur l'avenir politique et constitutionnel du Québec*. Ottawa: FFHQ, December 1990.

– *Pour ne plus être ... sans pays. Une nouvelle association pour les deux peuples fondateurs*. Ottawa: FFHQ, 1979.

– "Testimony before the Special Joint Committee of the Senate and House of
Commons on the Constitution of Canada." *Minutes of Proceedings and Evidence* 13 (26 November 1980): 26–52.

Fédération nationale des femmes canadiennes-françaises. "An analysis of the
federal proposals Shaping Canada's Future Together." Ottawa: FNFCF, 1992.

Fettes, Mark. "Is the Language Tide Turning in Canada? A Quiet Revolution

is Sweeping Canada. Almost Most of the Country Knows Little About It."
Cultural Survival Quarterly (Summer 1993).

Fletcher F.J. and D.C. Wallace, "The Federal Perspective." *Canadian Annual Review, 1979.* Toronto: University of Toronto Press, 1981.

Fontaine, Yvon. "La politique linguistique au Canada: l'impasse?" In Ronald L. Watts and Douglas M. Brown, eds. *Canada: The State of the Federation 1989.* Kingston: Institute of Intergovernmental Affairs and Queen's University, 1989.

– "Réforme de Sénat et Francophones hors Québec." Rapport soumis à la FFHQ, June 1990.

Formation permanente du Barreau du Québec. *Développements récents en droit scolaire: Textes des conférences du colloque du 18 mars 1994.* Cowansville: Éditions Yvon Blais, 1994.

Foucher, Pierre. "L'Acadie du Nouveau-Brunswick et la Constitution." *Revue de l'Université de Moncton* 28, no. 1 (1994): 11–45.

– "L'Accord du lac Meech et les francophones hors Québec." In *Canadian Human Rights Yearbook/Annuaire des droits de la personne, 1988.* Ottawa: University of Ottawa Press, 1989.

– "Après Mahé ... Analyse des démarches accomplies et à accomplir dans le dossier de l'éducation minoritaire au Canada." *Education et francophonie* 19, no. 1 (April 1991): 6–9.

– "L'article 23 de la Charte: un compromis audacieux." *La Revue Juridique Thémis* 23 (1989): 220–32.

– "L'article 23 de la Charte: orientations et perspectives. Opinion soumise à la Fédération des Francophones Hors Québec, Avril 1985." CRCCF, Fonds FFHQ, C84–21/3/15, 1–15.

– *Constitutional Language Rights of Official Language Minorities in Canada.* Ottawa: Supply and Services Canada, 1985.

– "Les droits scolaires des Acadiens et la Charte." *University of New Brunswick Law Journal* 33 (1984): 97–153.

– "Éducation en français au Canada: l'état du dossier juridique." *Education et Francophonie* 17, no. 3 (December 1989): 5–7.

– "L'évolution des droits scolaires des minorités linguistiques francophones au Canada." In Claude Deblois and Alain Prujiner, eds. *Les écoles françaises hors Québec: rétrospective et prospective.* Quebec: Les Cahiers du Laboratoire de recherche en administration et politique scolaires, Faculté de droit, Université de Laval, 1991.

– "Fédéralisme et droits des minorités: tension ou complémentarité." In Jean Lafontant *et al.*, eds. *L'État et les minorités.* Saint-Boniface: Les Éditions du Blé et Les Presses universitaires de Saint-Boniface, 1993.

– "L'interprétation des droits linguistiques constitutionnels par la Cour suprême du Canada." *Ottawa Law Review/Revue de droit d'Ottawa* 19, no. 2 (1987): 381–411.

- "Language Rights and Education." In Michel Bastarache, ed. *Language Rights in Canada.* Montreal: Yves Blais, 1987.
- "Le potentiel réparateur des articles 23 et 24 de la *Charte.* In Sylvie Léger, ed. *"De violations à réparations."* *Symposium national sur la réparation constitutionnelle (selon les articles 23 et 24 de la Charte canadienne des droits et libertés).* Ottawa: Canadian Centre for Linguistic Rights, 1997.
- "Le rôle d'une intervention judiciaire dans une stratégie de revendication politique." *Égalité* 17 (1986): 65–78.
- "Six Ans après: L'article 23 de la Charte et les tribunaux. Synthèse des jugements au 15 mars 1988 et de l'état du dossier." March 1988 study prepared for Angéline Martel. *Official Language Minority Education Rights in Canada: From Instruction to Management.* Ottawa: Office of the Commissioner of Official Languages, January 1991.

Fraser, Graham. *René Lévesque and the Parti Québécois in Power.* 2nd ed. Montreal and Kingston: McGill-Queen's University Press, 2001.

Frenette, Yves. *Brève histoire des Canadiens français.* Montréal: Boréal, 1998.

Gallant, Edgar. "Le contexte post-Mahé: un moment critique pour l'avenir des francophones." *Éducation et francophonie* 19, no. 1 (April 1991): 46–8.

Gaudreau, Guy, ed. *Bâtir sur le ROC. De l'ACFÉO à l'ACFO du Grand Sudbury (1910–1987).* Sudbury: La Société historique du Nouvel-Ontario, 1994.

Gérin, Odile. *D'un obstacle à l'autre: vers le Conseil scolaire de langue française.* Vanier, ON: Les Éditions Interligne, 1998.

Gervais, Gaétan. "Aux origines de l'identité franco-ontarienne." In *Cahiers Charlevoix 1, études franco-ontariennes.* Sudbury: Société Charlevoix et Prise de parole, 1995.
- "Le Règlement XVII (1912–1927)." *Revue du Nouvel-Ontario* 18 (1996): 123–92.

Gibson, D. "Enforcement of the Canadian Charter of Rights and Freedoms (s. 24)." In Gérald A. Beaudoin and Walter S. Tarnopolsky, eds. *The Canadian Charter of Rights and Freedoms: Commentary.* Toronto: Carswell, 1982.

Gilbert, Anne. "Les espaces de la francophonie ontarienne." In Joseph Yvon Thériault, ed. *Francophonies minoritaires au Canada: l'état des lieux.* Moncton: Les Éditions d'Acadie, 1999.
- *Espaces franco-ontariens.* Ottawa: Le Nordir, 1999.

Gold, Gerald L. *"La revendication de nos droits:* The Quebec Referendum and Francophone Minorities in Canada." *Ethnic & Racial Studies* 7, no. 1 (January 1984): 106–28.

Government of Canada. *Renewal of Canada Conferences: Compendium of Reports.* Ottawa: Constitutional Conferences Secretariat, March 1992.

Gray, Andrew and Eleni Yiannakis. "Language, Culture and Interpretation: An Interview with Mr. Justice Michel Bastarache." *University of Toronto Faculty of Law Review* 58, no. 1 (2000): 78–83.

Guindon, R. "Pour lever les contradictions structurelles de l'ACFO," *Revue du Nouvel-Ontario* 2 (1979): 35–41.

Harvey, Fernand. "Le Québec et le Canada français: histoire d'un déchirure." In Simon Langlois, ed. *Identité et cultures nationales. L'Amérique française en mutation.* Sainte-Foy: Les Presses de l'Université Laval, 1995.

Hautecoeur, Jean-Paul. *L'Acadie du discours. Pour une sociologie de la culture acadienne.* Quebec: Les Presses de l'Université Laval, 1975.

Hayday, Matthew. "Confusing and Conflicting Agendas: Federalism, Official Languages and the Development of the Bilingualism in Education Program in Ontario, 1970–1983." *Journal of Canadian Studies/Revue d'études canadiennes* 36, no. 1 (Spring 2001): 50–79.

Heaton, G. "Strength in Numbers: The Supreme Court rules that Edmonton Francophones should control their own schools." *Alberta (Western) Report* 17, no. 15 (26 March 1990): 38, 40.

Hébert, Raymond. "Essai sur l'identité franco-manitobaine." In Jocelyn Létourneau and Roger Bernard, eds. *La question identitaire au Canada francophone. Récits, parcours, enjeux, hors-lieux.* Sainte-Foy: Les Presses de l'Université Laval, 1994.

– "Historique de la législation scolaire au Manitoba." *Revue de l'ACÉLF* 6, no. 2 (1976)

– *The Manitoba French-Language Crisis, 1983–84: Origins and Early Legislative Debates.* Ph.D. Dissertation. Winnipeg: University of Manitoba, 1991.

– and Jean-Guy Vaillancourt. "French Canadians in Manitoba: Elites and Ideologies." In Jean Leonard Elliott, ed. *Immigrant Groups.* Scarborough: Prentice Hall, 1971.

Heller, Monica. *Crossroads: Language, Education and Ethnicity in French Ontario.* Berlin: Mouton de Gruyter, 1994.

– Normand Labrie, Denis Wilson and Sylvie Roy. *Les conseils d'école et l'évolution de l'éducation franco-ontarienne.* Toronto: Centre de recherches en éducation franco-ontarienne, 1997.

Hogg, Peter. *Canada Act, 1982 Annotated.* Toronto: Carswell, 1982.

– *Constitutional Law of Canada.* 2nd ed., Toronto: Carswell, 1985.

Horton, Donald J. *André Laurendeau. French-Canadian Nationalist, 1912–1968.* Toronto: University of Toronto Press, 1992.

Howe, Paul and Peter Russell, eds. *Judicial Power and Canadian Democracy.* Montreal and Kingston: McGill-Queen's University Press, 2001.

Huel, Raymond J.A. "*Gestae Dei Per Francos:* The French Canadian Experience in Western Canada." In Benjamin G. Smillie, ed. *Visions of the New Jerusalem (Religious Settlements on the Prairies).* Edmonton: NeWest Press, 1983.

Huppé, L. "Société des acadiens c. Association of Parents." *Canadian Bar Association* 67 (1988): 128–41.

Hutchison, Brian. "French Education Rights go North: 600 Catholic taxpayers fail to block francophone classes." *Alberta (Western) Report* 16, no. 30 (10 July 1989): 27.

Institute of Intergovernmental Relations. *The Response to Quebec: The Other Provinces and the Constitutional Debate.* Kingston: Queen's University Press, 1980.

James, Patrick, Donald E. Ableson and Michael Lutsztig, eds. *The Myth of the Sacred. The Charter, the Courts, and the Politics of the Constitution in Canada.* Montreal and Kingston: McGill-Queen's University Press, 2001.

Johnson, Donald, ed. *With a Bang, Not a Whimper. Pierre Trudeau Speaks Out.* Toronto: Stoddart, 1988.

Johnson, Marc and Isabelle McKee-Allain. "La société et l'identité de l'Acadie contemporaine." In Joseph Yvon Thériault, ed. *Francophonies minoritaires au Canada: l'état des lieux.* Moncton: Les Éditions d'Acadie, 1999.

Johnson, William. *A Canadian Myth. Quebec, Between Canada and the Illusion of Utopia.* Montreal: Robert Davies Publishing, 1994.

Julien, Richard. "The Evolution of Francophone Schools: The Case of Alberta (1982–1993)." *The Canadian Modern Languages Review/La revue canadienne des langues vivantes* 49, no. 4 (June/juin 1993): 716–33.

– "Les Franco-Albertains et la gestion de leurs écoles." *Cahiers franco-canadiens de l'Ouest* 7, no. 1 (1995): 119–54.

– *The French School in Alberta: An Analysis of an Historical and Constitutional Question.* 2 vols. Ph.D. Dissertation. Edmonton: University of Alberta, 1991.

– "The Legal Recognition of All-French Schools in Saskatchewan: A Long and Often Difficult Odyssey!" *Canadian Ethnic Studies* 27, no. 2 (1995): 101–4.

– "The Quest for All-French Schools in Alberta: A Quixotic Struggle?" *Canadian Ethnic Studies* 25, no. 1 (1993): 25–49.

Juteau, Danielle. "Ontarois and Québécois as Distinct Collectivities." In Dean R. Louder and Eric Waddell, eds. *French America. Mobility, Identity, and Minority Experience Across the Continent.* Baton Rouge and London: Louisiana State University Press, 1983.

– and Lise Séguin-Kimpton. "La collectivité franco-ontarienne: structuration d'un espace symbolique et politique." In Cornelius Jaenen, ed. *Les Franco-Ontariens.* Ottawa: University of Ottawa Press, 1993.

Juteau-Lee, Danielle. "Français d'Amérique, Canadiens, Canadiens-français, Franco-Ontariens, Ontarois: Qui sommes-nous?" *Pluriel-Débats* 24 (1980): 21–43.

– and Jean Lapointe. "From French Canadians to Franco-Ontarians and Ontarois: New Boundaries, New Identities." In Jean L. Elliot, ed. *Two Nations, Many Cultures; Ethnic Groups in Canada.* 2nd ed. Scarborough: Prentice-Hall, 1983.

Kaihla, P. "Controlling the Schools: A landmark ruling for francophone rights." *Macleans* 103, no. 13 (26 March 1990): 25–6.

Kelly, James B. "Reconciling Rights and Federalism during Review of the Charter of Rights and Freedoms: The Supreme Court of Canada and the Centralization Thesis, 1982–1999." *Canadian Journal of Political Science* 34, no. 2 (June/juin 2001): 321–55.

Kerr, R.W. "The Future of Language Rights under Canada's Constitutional Options." In S. Beck and I. Bernier, eds. *Canada and the New Constitution: The Unfinished Agenda.* Vol. 1. Montreal: L'institut de recherche politique, 1983.

Kovacs, Peter. "La protection des langues des minorités ou la nouvelle approche de la protection des minorités?" *Revue générale de droit international public* 97 (1993): 411–18.

Labrie, Normand and Gilles Forlot, eds. *L'enjeu de la langue en Ontario français.* Sudbury: Prise de Parole, 1999.

La Forest, G.V. "Brief to and Testimony before the Special Joint Committee of the Senate and House of Commons on the Constitution of Canada." *Minutes of Proceedings and Evidence* 34 (8 January 1981): 6–31, 34–7, 40–55.

– "The Canadian Charter of Rights and Freedoms: An Overview." *The Canadian Bar Review* LXI, no. 1 (March 1983): 19–29.

Lafrenière, Julie. "Des luttes au consensus 1965–1982." In Guy Gaudreau, ed. *Bâtir sur le ROC. De l'ACFÉO à l'ACFO du Grand Sudbury (1910–1987).* Sudbury: La Société historique du Nouvel-Ontario, 1994.

Lalonde, André. "The French Canadians of the West: Hope, Tragedy, Uncertainty." In Dean R. Louder and Eric Waddell, eds. *French America. Mobility, Identity, and Minority Experience Across the Continent.* Baton Rouge and London: Louisiana State University Press, 1983.

Lalonde, Gisèle and Kipp Berchmans. *Rapport du comité mixte sur la gestion des écoles élémentaires et secondaires de langue française.* Toronto: Government of Ontario, April 1982.

Lamoureux, P.A. and Denis Tardif. *Consultations portant sur la gestion des écoles franco-albertaines.* Edmonton: ACFA and FPFA, February 1990.

– *An Educational System for Franco-Albertans. A Study on the Management and Control of Francophone Education in Alberta.* Edmonton: ACFA and FPFA, June 1990.

– *Minority Language Rights in Education: Sequel to the Supreme Court of Canada Judgement, March 15, 1990.* Edmonton: ACFA and FPFA, 10 April 1990.

Landry, Rodrique and Réal Allard. "Choix de la langue d'enseignement: une analyse chez des parents francophones en milieu bilingue soustractif." *The Modern Language Review/La Revue canadienne des langues vivantes* 41, no. 3 (1985): 480–500.

– "L'éducation dans la francophonie minoritaire." In Joseph Yvon Thériault, ed. *Francophonies minoritaires au Canada: l'état des lieux.* Moncton: Les Éditions d'Acadie, 1999.

Landry, Rodrique and Serge Rousselle. *Éducation et droits collectives. Au delà de l'article 23 de la Charte.* Moncton: Les Éditions de la Francophonie, 2003.

Lange, D.J. "Constitutional jurisprudence, Politics and Minority Language Education Rights." *Manitoba Law Journal* 11 (1980): 33–57.

Laurendeau, André. *The Diary of André Laurendeau: Written During the Royal Commission on Bilingualism and Biculturalism, 1964–1967.* Toronto: Lorimer, 1991.

Laurin, Camille. *La politique québécoise de la langue française.* Quebec: Editeur officiel, 1977.

Le Blanc, Jean-Claude. "Minority Language Education after the Supreme Court Decision." *Language & Society* 32 (Fall 1990): 31–5.

Leslie, Peter M. "Les droits des minorités ethniques et nationales: l'aspect politique et collectif." *Les Cahiers de Droit* 27 (1986): 156–88.
– "Quebec and the Constitutional Impasse." In Peter M. Leslie, ed. *Canada:
   The State of the Federation, 1986.* Kingston: Queen's University and the Institute of Intergovernmental Relations, 1986.
Levasseur-Ouimet, France. "Paroles et gestes d'une communauté." *Éducation et
   francophonie* 19, no. 1 (April 1991): 22–7.
Lévesque, Gérard. *Pourquoi un conseil scolaire de langue française pour la région
   d'Ottawa-Carleton?* Ottawa: Association française des Conseils scolaires de
   l'Ontario, 1977.
Louder, Dean and Eric Waddell. *Du continent perdu à l'archipel retrouvé: le Québec
   et l'Amérique française.* Quebec: Les Presses de l'Université Laval, 1983.
MacDonald, L. Ian. *From Bourassa to Bourassa. Wilderness to Restoration.* 2nd ed.
   Montreal and Kingston: McGill-Queen's University Press, 2002.
– *Mulroney. The Making of the Prime Minister.* Toronto: McClelland and Stewart,
   1985.
MacDonald, M.C. *Legal Rights in the Canadian Charter of Rights and Freedoms.*
   Toronto: Carswell, 1989.
Magnet, Joseph Eliot. "The Charter's Official Language Provisions: The Impli-
   cations of Entrenched Bilingualism." *Supreme Court Law Review* 4 (1982):
   163–216.
– "Collective Rights, Cultural Autonomy and the Canadian State." *McGill Law
   Journal* 32, no. 1 (1986): 170–86.
– *Constitutional Law of Canada.* Vol. 2. Cowansville: Les Éditions Yvon Blais,
   1989.
– "Les écoles et la Constitution." *Les Cahiers de Droit* 24, no. 1 (March 1983):
   145–55.
– "The Future of Official Language Minorities." *Les Cahiers de Droit* 27 (1986):
   189–202.
– "Language Rights: Myth and Reality." *Revue générale de droit* 12, no. 1 (1981):
   261–70.
– "Minority-Language Educational Rights." In E.P. Belaboba and Eric Gertner,
   eds. *The New Constitution and the Charter of Rights.* Toronto: Butterworths, 1983.
– *Official Languages of Canada. Perspectives from Law, Policy and the Future.* Cow-
   ansville: Les Éditions Yvon Blais, 1995.
Mahé, Jean-Claude. "Quinze années en sisyphes de la politique linguisque." In
   Sylvie Léger, ed. *"De violations à réparations." Symposium national sur la répara-
   tion constitutionnelle (selon les articles 23 et 24 de la Charte canadienne des droits
   et libertés).* Ottawa: Canadian Centre for Linguistic Rights, 1997.
Mandel, Michael. *The Charter of Rights and the Legalization of Politics in Canada.*
   Toronto: Wall & Thompson, 1989.
Manfredi, C.P. *Judicial Power and the Charter, Canada and the Paradox of Liberal
   Constitutionalism.* Toronto: McClelland & Stewart, 1993.

Manitoba, Groupe de Travail sur la gestion des écoles franco-manitobaines. *Rapport.* Manitoba: Government of Manitoba, 27 June 1991.

Manitoba, Manitoba Task Force on Francophone Schools Governance, *Report.* Winnipeg: Manitoba Education and Training, May 1991.

Martel, Angéline. "L'Article 23 de la *Charte canadienne* (1982) est-il réparateur? Éclairages idéologiques et statistiques." In Sylvie Léger, ed. *"De violations à réparations." Symposium national sur la réparation constitutionnelle (selon les articles 23 et 24 de la Charte canadienne des droits et libertés).* Ottawa: Canadian Centre for Linguistic Rights, 1997.

– "Competition idéologique et les droits scolaires francophones en milieu minoritaire au Canada." *Revue canadienne des langues vivantes/Canadian Modern Languages Review* 49, no. 4 (1993): 734–59.

– *Official Language Minority Education Rights in Canada: From Instruction to Management.* Ottawa: Office of the Commissioner of Official Languages, January 1991.

– "Processus initié par la promulgation de l'article 23 de la Charte canadienne des droits et libertés: les revendications scolaires de la minorité de langue officielle française." In David Schneiderman, ed. *Language and the State: The Law and Politics of Identity.* Edmonton: Centre for Constitutional Studies, University of Alberta, 1991.

– *Rights, Schools and Communities in Minority Contexts, 1986–2002: Toward the Development of French Through Education: An Analysis.* Ottawa: Office of the Commissioner of Official Languages, Minister of Public Works and Government Services, 2001.

– and Daniel Villeneuve. "Droit constitutionnel et rapports de pouvoir: Les droits scolaires des francophones minoritaires du Canada avant 1960." *Canadian Journal of Law and Society/Revue canadienne de droit et société* 10, no. 1 (1995): 25–63.

– "Trois sources de polysémie inhérentes à l'Article 93 de la Loi Constitutionnelle de 1867: Hiatus entre projets éducatifs des francophones minoritaires et droits constitutionnels." In Sylvie Léger, ed. *Les droits linguistiques au Canada: collusions ou collisions?/ Linguistic Rights in Canada: Collusions or Collisions?* Ottawa: Centre Canadien des droits linguistiques, 1995.

Martel, Marcel. *Le deuil d'un pays imaginé: Rêves, luttes et déroute du Canada français. Les rapports entre le Québec et la francophonie canadienne (1867–1975).* Ottawa: University of Ottawa Press, 1997.

– *French Canada: An account of its creation and break-up, 1850–1967.* Ottawa: The Canadian Historical Association, Canada's Ethnic Group Series, Booklet no. 24, 1998.

– "'Hors Québec, point de salut." In Michael D. Behiels and Marcel Martel, eds. *Nation, Ideas, Identities: Essays in Honour of Ramsay Cook.* Toronto: Oxford University Press, 2000.

Matte, Guy. "La décision Mahé: interprétation et incidences." Talk given at the

University of Ottawa by the president of the FFHQ, 11 May 1990. Ottawa: FFHQ, 1990.

Mayo, Henry B. *Rapport de la Commission d'étude pour le remaniement d'Ottawa-Carleton.* Toronto: Government of Ontario, October 1976.

McRoberts, Kenneth. *Quebec: Social Change and Political Crisis.* 3rd ed. Toronto: Oxford University Press, 1993.

McWhinney, Edward. *Canada and the Constitution, 1979–82: Patriation and the Charter of Rights and Freedoms.* Toronto: University of Toronto Press, 1982.

– "The Canadian Charter of Rights and Freedoms: The Lessons of Comparative Jurisprudence." *Canadian Bar Review* 61 (1983): 55–68.

– *Quebec and the Constitution, 1960–78.* Toronto: University of Toronto Press, 1979.

Migneault, Gaétan. "Vers une théorie générale de l'article 23: le critère du nombre suffisant." *Revue de la Common law en français* 2, no. 2 (1999): 257–300.

Monahan, P. *Politics and the Constitution: The Charter, Federalism and the Supreme Court of Canada.* Toronto: Carswell, 1987.

Monnin, Alfred. "L'égalité juridique des langues et l'enseignement: les écoles françaises hors-Québec." *Les Cahiers de Droit* 24, no. 1 (March 1983): 157–67.

Munro, Kenneth. "Teaching in the French Language in Alberta: An Historical Perspective." *Prairie Forum* 12, no. 1 (1987): 12–31.

Munroe, David. "The organization and administration of education in Canada." Ottawa: Ministry of the Secretary of State, 1974.

Nemeth, Mary and Brian Bergman. "Francophone Parents across the West Sue for French Schools." *Alberta Report* 13 (9 June 1986): 38.

Nemni, Max. "Canada in Crisis and the Destructive Power of Myth." *Queen's Quarterly* 99, no. 1 (Spring 1992): 222–39.

Nicholls, Glenn and Guy L. Roy. *A Report of Major Developments in French-language Education in Manitoba from 1970 to 1987.* Winnipeg: Department of Education, 18 July 1988.

Ontario. *Rapport de la Commission royale sur l'éducation. Pour l'amour d'apprendre.* Toronto: Queen's Printer for Ontario, December 1994.

Ontario. *Rapport final du Groupe d'étude sur la réduction du nombre de conseils scolaires en Ontario.* Toronto: Government of Ontario, February 1996.

Ontario. *Rapport du groupe consultatif sur la gestion de l'éducation en langue française.* Toronto: Government of Ontario, September 1991.

Ontario, Ministerial Committee on French-language Secondary Schools. *Report of the Committee on French Language Schools in Ontario.* Toronto: Ministry of Education, 1968.

Ontario, Ministry of Education. *Décision prise par le gouvernement en ce qui concerne l'éducation dans la municipalité d'Ottawa-Carleton.* Toronto: Ministry of Education, 28 December 1979.

– *Déclaration du gouvernment sur le remaniement des administrations locales dans la municipalité d'Ottawa-Carleton.* Livre Vert. Toronto: Ministry of Education, 28 February 1979.

- *Une proposition en réponse au Rapport du Comité mixte sur la gestion des écoles élémentaires et secondaires de langue française.* Toronto: Ministry of Education, 23 March 1983.

- *Report of the Joint Committee on the Governance of French Language Elementary and Secondary Schools.* Toronto: Ministry of Education, April 1982.

- Comité d'études pour l'éducation en langue française d'Ottawa-Carleton. *Rapport.* Toronto: Ministry of Education, December 1986.

Ontario, Ministry of Municipal Affairs. *Formulaire de recensement 1988.* Toronto: Ministry of Municipal Affairs, 1988.

Ontario, Minority Language Governance Study Committee. *Final Report of the Minority Language Governance Study Committee to the Government of Ontario.* Toronto: Ministry of Education, February 1984.

Otis, Ghislain. "La réparation pécuniaire pour la mise en oeuvre tardive ou défectueuse des droits linguistiques scolaires des minorités francophones." In Sylvie Léger, ed. *"De violations à réparations." Symposium national sur la réparation constitutionnelle (selon les articles 23 et 24 de la Charte canadienne des droits et libertés).* Ottawa: Canadian Centre for Linguistic Rights, 1997.

Pal, Leslie. *Interests of State.* Montreal and Kingston: McGill-Queen's University Press, 1993.

Pelletier, Benoît. "La Cour suprême du Canada fait preuve d'angélisme." *La CLEF* 10, no. 1 (June 1993): 13–16.

Plourde, Michel. *La politique linguistique du Québec, 1977–1987.* Quebec: Institut Québécois de recherche sur la culture, 1988.

Pollard, B.G. "Minority Language Rights in Four Provinces." In Peter Leslie, ed. *Canada: The State of the Federation 1985.* Kingston: Institute of Intergovernmental Relations and Queen's University, 1985.

Premiers. *18th Annual Premiers' Conference,* St Andrews, NB, 18–19 August 1977. NP: Canadian Intergovernmental Conference Secretariat, 1977.

Premiers. *19th Annual Premiers' Conference,* Regina/Waskesiu, SK, 9–12 August 1978. NP: Canadian Intergovernmental Conference Secretariat, 1978.

Premiers. *Premiers' Conference,* Montreal, 23 February 1978. NP: Canadian Intergovernmental Conference Secretariat, 1978.

Prime Minister's Office. *Federalism for the Future: A Statement of Policy by the Government of Canada.* Ottawa: Queen's Printer, 1968.

Protestant School Board of Greater Montreal. "Testimony before the Special Joint Committee of the Senate and House of Commons on the Constitution of Canada." *Minutes of Proceedings and Evidence* 11 (24 November 1980): 6–26.

Proulx, J.P. "Le Choc des Chartes: histoire des régimes juridiques québécois et canadiens en matière de la langue d'enseignement." *La Revue Juridique Thémis* 23, no. 1 (1989): 67–172.

- "Les normes périjuridiques dans l'idéologie québécoise et canadienne en matière de langue d'enseignement." *Revue générale de droit* 19, no. 1 (1988): 209–23.
- "La précarité des droits linguistiques scolaires ou les singulières difficultés de mises en oeuvres de l'article 23 de la Charte canadienne des droits et libertés." *Revue générale de droit* 14 (1983): 335–70.

Quebec. *Rapport de la Commission d'enquête sur la situation de la langue française et sur les droits linguistiques au Québec.* Vol. 1. *La langue du travail.* Vol. 2. *Les droits linguistiques.* Quebec: Gouvernement du Québec, 1972.

Quebec. *Report of the Commission on the Political and Constitutional Future of Quebec.* Quebec: Bibliothèque nationale du Québec, March 1991.

Quebec Liberal Party, Constitutional Committee. *A Quebec Free to Choose.* Quebec: Quebec Liberal Party, 1991.

Radwanski, George. *Trudeau.* Toronto, Macmillan of Canada, 1979.

Réaume, P. and L. Green. "Education and Linguistic Security in the Charter." *McGill Law Journal* 34 (1989): 777–816.

Rémillard, Gil. "Brief to and Testimony before the Special Joint Committee of the Senate and House of Commons on the Constitution of Canada." *Minutes of Proceedings and Evidence* 34 (1980): 4–25 and 28–49.

- "A quelles conditions le Québec peut-il signer la Loi constitutionnelle de 1982?" I, II, & III. *Le Devoir,* 26–28 February 1985. English version in Michael D. Behiels, ed. *Quebec Since 1945. Selected Readings.* Toronto: Copp Clark, 1987.
- "Unofficial English-language text of speech 'Rebuilding the Relationship: Quebec and its Confederation Partners,' Mont-Gabriel Conference, 9 May 1986." Appendix to Peter M. Leslie, "Quebec and the Constitutional Issue." In Peter M. Leslie, ed. *Canada: The State and the Federation 1986.* Kingston: Queen's University and the Institute of Intergovernmental Relations, 1986.

Riddell, A. "A la recherche du temps perdu: La Cour Suprême et l'interprétation des droits linguistic constitutionnels dans les années 80." *Les Cahiers de Droit* 29 (1988): 829–55.

Robertson, Gordon. *Memoirs of a very civil servant. Mackenzie King to Pierre Trudeau.* Toronto: University of Toronto Press, 2000.

Romanow, Roy, John Whyte and Howard Leeson. *Canada Nothwithstanding. The Making of the Constitution 1976–82.* Toronto: Carswell/Methuen, 1984.

Roy, Muriel. "Démographie et démolinguistique en Acadie, 1871–1991." In Jean Daigle, ed. *L'Acadie de Maritimes: études thématiques, des débuts à nos jours.* Moncton: Université de Moncton, Chaire d'études acadiennes, 1993.

Russell, Peter. *Constitutional Odyssey. Can Canadians be a Sovereign People?* 2nd rev. ed. Toronto: University of Toronto Press, 1993.

- "The Political Purposes of the Canadian Charter of Rights and Freedoms." *Canadian Bar Review* 61 (1983): 30–54.
- Rainer Knopff and Ted Morton, eds. *Federalism and the Charter. Leading Constitutional Decisions.* New edition. Ottawa: Carleton University Press, 1989.

Ryan, Claude. "La politique linguistique dans l'Ouest Canadien: problèmes et perspectives. Texte reconstitué d'une intervention faite le 12 mai 1984 au Colloque sur les langues officielles tenu à Edmonton sous les auspices du Commissaire aux langues officielles du Canada." PAA, no. 89.391 (13/306).

Sarra-Bournet, Michel and Lucien-Pierre Bouchard. "Au-delà de la rupture politique entre les francophonies canadienne et québécoise." In Marcel Martel and Robert Choquette, eds. Les États généraux du Canada français, trente ans après. Ottawa: Centre de recherche en civilisation canadienne-française de l'Université d'Ottawa, 1998.

Saywell, John T. The Lawmakers. Judicial Power and the Shaping of Canadian Federalism. Toronto: The Osgoode Society for Canadian Legal History and University of Toronto Press, 2002.

Schwartz, Brian. Fathoming Meech Lake. Winnipeg: Legal Research Institute of the University of Manitoba, 1987.

– "The Other Section 23." Manitoba Law Journal 15 (1986): 347–57.

Sheppard, Robert and Michael Valpy. The National Deal. The Fight for a Canadian Constitution. Toronto: Fleet Books, 1982.

Sigurdson, R. "Left- and Right-Wing Charterphobia in Canada: A Critique of the Critics." International Journal of Canadian Studies/Revue internationale d'études canadiennes 7–8 (Spring-Fall/1993): 95–115.

Silla, Ousmane, ed. École bilingue ou unilingue pour les Franco-Albertains? Edmonton: Collège universitaire Saint-Jean, 1974.

Silver, A.I. "French Canada and the Prairie Frontier." Canadian Historical Review 50, 1 (1969).

Smiley, Donald. "A Dangerous Deed: The Constitution Act, 1982." In Keith Banting and Richard Simeon, eds. And No One Cheered. Federalism, Democracy and The Constitution Act. Toronto: Methuen, 1983.

Smith, Donald. "A History of French-Speaking Albertans." In Howard Palmer and Tamara Palmer, eds. Peoples of Alberta: Portraits of Cultural Diversity. Saskatoon: Western Producer Prairie Books, 1985.

Société franco-manitobaine. "Brief to and Testimony before the Special Joint Committee of the Senate and House of Commons on the Constitution of Canada." Minutes of Proceedings and Evidence 10 (21 November 1980): 20–45.

– Le Manitoba français: une francophonie au coeur de l'Amérique. Saint-Boniface: Société franco-manitobaine, 1995.

Soucie, Rolande. "L'enseignement en Français en Ontario: revue des problèmes courants (Travail préparé pour l'ACFO et l'AEFO dans le cadre de leur dossier éducation: poursuite judiciaire." Ottawa: ACFO and AEFO, December 1982.

– "Section 23 of the Charter: Provincial Implementation." Current Issue Review. Ottawa: Library of Parliament, Research Branch, 15 December 1986, Reviewed 15 April 1988.

Stanley, Della M.M. *Louis Robichaud: A Decade of Power.* Halifax: Nimbus Publishing, 1984.

Stebbins, R.A. *The French Enigma: Survival and Development in Canada's Francophone Societies.* Calgary: Detselig Enterprises, 2000.

Stevens, Paul and John Saywell, eds. *Canadian Annual Review of Politics and Public Affairs, 1970.* Toronto: University of Toronto Press, 1971.

– *Canadian Annual Review of Politics and Public Affairs, 1971.* Toronto: University of Toronto Press, 1972.

Sylvestre, Paul-François. *Penetang: l'école de la résistance.* Sudbury: Prise de Parole, 1980.

Symons, T.H.B. *Commission ministérielle sur l'éducation secondaire en langue française.* Toronto: Ministry of Education, February 1972.

– "Ontario's Quiet Revolution. A Study of Change in the Position of the Franco-Ontarian Community." In R.-M. Burns, ed. *One Country or Two?* Montreal and Kingston: McGill-Queen's University Press, 1971.

Tardif, Claudette. "L'identité socio-culturelle des élèves francophones en milieu minoritaire: un portrait d'assimilation." In Claude Deblois and Alain Prujiner, eds. *Les écoles françaises hors Québec: rétrospective et prospective.* Quebec: Les Cahiers du Laboratoire de recherche en administration et politique scolaires, Faculté de droit, Université de Laval, 1991.

Tetley, William. "Language and Education Rights in Quebec and Canada (a legislative history and personal political diary)." In Paul Davenport and Richard H. Leach, eds. *Reshaping Confederation. The 1982 Reform of the Canadian Constitution.* Durham, NC: Duke University Press, 1984.

Thériault, Aurèle. "Pour un espace francophone: Obsèques du réflexe minoritaire." *L'action nationale* 80, no. 10 (1990): 1451–9.

– and François Dumaine. "L'ère post-Mahé: un véritable test pour la constitution canadienne." *Éducation et francophonies* 19, no. 1 (April 1991): 40–2.

Thériault, Joseph Yvon. "Les États généraux et la fin du Canada français." In Marcel Martel et Robert Choquette, eds. *Les États généraux du Canada français, trente ans après.* Ottawa: Centre de recherche en civilisation canadienne-française de l'Université d'Ottawa, 1998.

– *L'identité à l'épreuve de la modernité: écrits politiques sur l'Acadie et les francophonies canadiennes minoritaires.* Moncton: Les Éditions d'Acadie, 1995.

– ed. *Francophonies minoritaires au Canada: l'état des lieux.* Moncton: Les Éditions d'Acadie, 1999.

Trakman, Leon E. "Group Rights: A Canadian Perspective." *Journal of International Law and Politics* 24 (1992): 1579–1650.

Trudeau, Pierre Elliott. *The Constitution and the People of Canada. An Approach to the Objectives of Confederation, the Rights of People and the Institutions of Government.* Ottawa: The Queen's Printer, 1969.

– *Federalism and the French Canadians.* Toronto: Macmillan, 1968.

– *A National Understanding. The Official Languages of Canada. A Statement of the*

Government of Canada on the official languages policy. Ottawa: Ministry of Supply and Services, 1977.

– *Statement by the Prime Minister on the Government's Constitutional Resolution, October 2, 1980.* Ottawa: Ministry of Supply and Services, 1980.

– *A Time for Action. Toward the Renewal of the Canadian Federation.* Ottawa: Ministry of Supply and Services, 1978.

– "The Values of a Just Society." In Thomas S. Axeworthy and Pierre Elliott Trudeau, eds. *Towards a Just Society.* Toronto: Viking, 1990.

– "Who Speaks for Canada?: Defining and Sustaining a National Vision." In Michael D. Behiels, ed. *The Meech Lake Primer. Conflicting Views of the 1987 Constitutional Accord.* Ottawa: University of Ottawa Press, 1989.

Trudel, Pierre. "Journée de mise au point sur l'article 23 de la Charte des droits et libertés tenu à Montréal le 16 avril 1988. Transcriptions des discussions et des discours."

Viaud, Gilles. "La géographie du peuplement francophone de l'Ouest." In Joseph Yvon Thériault, ed. *Francophonies minoritaires au Canada: l'état des lieux.* Moncton: Les Éditions d'Acadie, 1999.

Wallace, Donald C. "Ottawa and the provinces." *Canadian Annual Review 1986.* Toronto: University of Toronto Press, 1990.

Weiler, P. and R.M. Elliot. *Litigating the Values of a Nation: The Canadian Charter of Rights and Freedoms.* Toronto: Carswell, 1986.

Weinrib, Lorraine Eisenstat. "The Activist Constitution." In Paul Howe and Peter H. Russell, eds. *Judicial Power and Canadian Democracy.* Montreal and Kingston: McGill-Queen's University Press, 2001.

Woehrling, José. "Minority Cultural and Linguistic Rights and Equalities in the Charter of Rights and Freedoms." *McGill Law Journal* 31 (1985): 50–92.

Yalden, M.F. "Perspective de l'égalité juridique des langues au Canada." *Les Cahiers de Droit* 24 (1983): 169–76.

– "Testimony Before the Special Joint Committee of the Senate and House of Commons on the Constitution of Canada." *Minutes of Proceedings and Evidence* 6 (17 November 1980):10–46.

Index